Optical Network Control

Architecture, Protocols, and Standards

Greg Bernstein
Bala Rajagopalan
Debanjan Saha

Addison-Wesley

Boston • San Francisco • New York • Toronto • Montreal
London • Munich • Paris • Madrid
Cape Town • Sydney • Tokyo • Singapore • Mexico City

The publisher offers discounts on this book when ordered in quantity for bulk purchases and special sales. For more information, please contact:

U.S. Corporate and Government Sales
(800) 382-3419
corpsales@pearsontechgroup.com

For sales outside of the U.S., please contact:

International Sales
(317) 581-3793
international@pearsontechgroup.com

Visit Addison-Wesley on the Web: www.awprofessional.com

A CIP catalog record for this book can be obtained from the Library of Congress.

ISBN: 0-20-175301-4
Text printed on recycled paper
1 2 3 4 5 6 7 8 9 10
First printing, Junc 2003

Optical Network Control

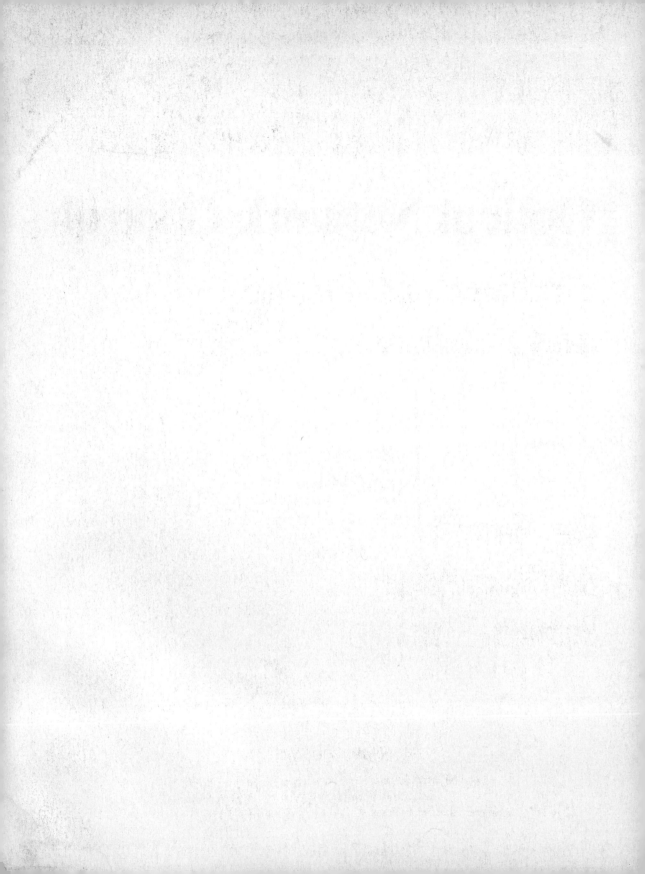

CONTENTS

PREFACE

Optical networks were initially designed and deployed to provide high-capacity transport for carrying telephone calls. Today they are used to transport not only voice traffic, but also data traffic, including Internet traffic. In fact, it is the Internet that has driven the rapid and unprecedented growth of optical networks in the past several years. New technologies, such as Dense Wavelength Division Multiplexing (DWDM) and intelligent optical switches, have been the other catalysts of growth. Although this rapid growth of optical networks has ushered in a new era in high-speed communication, it has also created a new problem. Managing a large and dynamic optical network is a difficult task, and the existing network management infrastructure is inadequately tooled to handle it.

Service providers manage their optical backbones using Element Management Systems (EMSs) provided by the equipment vendors and Network Management Systems (NMSs) that are often built in-house. Both EMSs and NMSs use proprietary technologies and often need tedious manual interventions. Due to the proprietary nature of the management systems, it is difficult to quickly and cost-effectively integrate new technologies into the existing infrastructure. The intrinsically manual nature of the management systems increases the cost and the turnaround time of provisioning new services. It also increases the risk of inadvertent mistakes. The growing complexity of optical networks is making these problems even worse.

In order to better understand the complexity of the problem we are dealing with, let us consider a representative continental optical network shown in Figure 1-4 in Chapter 1. As shown in the figure, the network consists of multiple subnetworks at different levels of the network hierarchy. A number of network elements playing different roles, potentially manufactured by different vendors, and managed by vendor proprietary EMSs and NMSs add to the complexity of the network. Now consider the routine task of provisioning a connection between two offices of an enterprise located in City A and City B. The provisioning process in today's networks involves a number of steps, many of which requiring manual intervention:

> *First, the path has to be planned.* This requires information on available resources in different subnetworks from City A to City B. Today, this process is mostly manual. The work order is broken up into multiple sub-tasks and assigned to different planning teams. The end-to-end path is planned in a piece-wise manner from City A to City B.

The connection now has to be provisioned over the planned path. Different provisioning teams responsible for different parts of the network execute this process. This requires configuring the network elements and the associated network management systems in the connection path from City A to City B.

The next phase is testing. It is now the job of the testing team to verify that the end-to-end service is actually working and all the databases (inventory, billing, etc.) are properly updated so that the service can actually be turned on and handed over to the customer.

The provisioning process described above has been intentionally simplified for the purpose of presentation. It gives an idea, however, as to why the typical turnaround time for provisioning optical services is several weeks to months. It also explains why even after a precipitous drop in network equipment prices, the cost of running a network is still very high. Note that service provisioning is only one aspect of network control and management. The other components of network management are equally cumbersome and inefficient. In fact, 80 percent of the cost of running a network comes from the cost of managing it. The bottom line is that in order to harness the benefits of technological breakthroughs, such as DWDM and intelligent optical switches, there needs to be a better way of controlling and managing the networks. Specifically, a gradual migration from an antiquated, semimanual network management infrastructure to one that is more intelligent and automatic has to occur.

To be fair, it should be noted that the control infrastructure seen in today's optical networks is there for a reason. The last generation of optical networking equipment was kept "dumb" for technology reliability and for time to market reasons. Also, static voice transport did not require the "on-demand" service expected by dynamic data networks and applications. Today there is both the need and the means to develop an intelligent control plane for optical networks. It was this observation that spurred vendors to create optical control planes for their equipment. The standards development organizations, such as the Internet Engineering Task Force (IETF), the Optical Interworking Forum (OIF), and the International Telecommunication Union (ITU), were quick to follow. This confluence of interest and influence has led to development of control architectures, protocols, and standards at an unprecedented speed.

Now that we have made a case for the technical desirability of the optical control plane, does it make business sense? In today's difficult telecom environment are service providers willing to make the investment to deploy a dynamic control plane? While no one has a definitive answer to this question, a strong case can be made for the value of the optical control plane from the point of view of "return on investment." Most of the cost of running a network today comes from operating expenses (opex). Due to the growing size and complexity of the network, this cost is actually increasing both in absolute and relative terms. In fact, many experts predict that even if service providers freeze their capital expenditure (capex), the ever-growing opex coupled with a decreasing revenue stream will seriously erode their profitability. The only way service providers can come out of this vicious cycle is by reducing their opex through better automation. Deployment of the optical control plane can help in this process. So, although it is an investment that service providers have to make, there seems to be a good reason to make that investment.

Notwithstanding these arguments, it is clear that the optical control plane is not going to be widely deployed overnight. Like any new technology, the adoption of the optical control plane will be gradual and in phases. This evolutionary process is probably a good idea both from technology and business standpoints. The control plane is still a fairly new and an evolving concept and hence gradual deployment will mitigate the risks associated with deploying a new technology. From the business standpoint, a phased deployment, with an objective to maximize the "bang for the buck" is a likely strategy.

In this regard, a number of service providers have started deploying intelligent optical networks and the associated optical control plane. Most of these early deployments, however, use vendor-proprietary protocols and software. Slowly but surely these proprietary technologies will evolve to become standards compliant. Evidence of this can be seen from the trials and prototype deployments of control plane standards developed by the IETF and the OIF. This process is likely to accelerate as service providers feel more pressure to upgrade their operations and management infrastructure to control the runaway operational cost.

The optical control plane has the potential to be the next most important development in optical networks. Consequently, it is an important topic with which service providers, vendors, and the business community dealing with transport network should be familiar. We have been intimately associated with optical control plane right from its genesis, not only as technologists but also as practitioners involved in the development and the deployment of this technology. In this book we share our firsthand experience in developing the architecture, protocols, products and standards for intelligent optical control plane. The book has been organized as follows. In the first few chapters, we review the existing optical networking technology, architecture, and standards. Our focus is on Synchronous Optical Network (SONET) and Synchronous Digital Hierarchy (SDH), which are the predominant technologies in this area. We then introduce the modern optical control plane and describe its components in detail. Next, we address the interaction between the optical control plane and the existing network management systems. We conclude with a discussion of control plane interworking, including the state of the standards and deployment.

O N E

Technology Overview

1.1 Introduction

Modern optical transport networks consist primarily of optical switches interconnected using Dense Wavelength Division Multiplexing (DWDM) transmission systems. In this chapter, we review the basic characteristics of optical transmission and switching systems. Specifically, we describe the working principles that guide the generation and reception of optical signals and its transmission through the optical fiber. We also review the technological foundation behind optical switching, an important element of modern optical transport networks. The discussion in this chapter highlights the physical properties of optical networks, many of which may appear as constraints in the control plane.

1.2 Optical Transmission Systems

1.2.1 Overview

The first step in the development of fiber optic transmission over meaningful distances was to find light sources that were sufficiently powerful and narrow. The light-emitting diode (LED) and the laser diode proved capable of meeting these requirements. Lasers went through several generations in the 1960s, culminating with the semiconductor lasers that are most widely used in fiber optics today.

The next step was to overcome the loss of signal strength, or *attenuation*, seen in glass. In 1970, Corning produced the first communication-grade fibers. With attenuation less than 20 decibels per kilometer (dB/km), this purified glass fiber exceeded the threshold for making fiber optics a viable technology.

Innovation at first proceeded slowly, as the telephone companies—the main users of the technology—were rather cautious. AT&T first standardized transmission at DS3 speed (45 Mbps) for *multimode* fibers. Soon thereafter, *single-mode* fibers were shown to be capable of transmission rates ten times that of the older type, as well as to support spans of up to 32 km (20 miles). In the early 1980s, MCI, followed by Sprint, adopted single-mode fibers for its long-distance network in the United States.

Further developments in fiber optics were closely tied to the use of the specific regions on the optical spectrum where optical attenuation is low. These regions, called *windows*, lie between areas of high absorption. The earliest systems were developed to operate around 850 nm, the first window in silica-based optical fiber. A second window (S band), at 1310 nm, soon proved to be superior because of its lower attenuation, followed by a third window (C band) at 1550 nm with an even lower optical loss. Today, a fourth window (L band) near 1625 nm, is under development and early deployment.

Transmission of light in optical fiber presents several challenges that must be dealt with. These fall into the following three broad categories [Agrawal97]:

1. Attenuation—decay of signal strength, or loss of light power, as the signal propagates through the fiber.
2. Chromatic dispersion—spreading of light pulses as they travel down the fiber.
3. Nonlinear effects—cumulative effects from the interaction of light with the material through which it travels, resulting in changes in the lightwave and interactions between light waves.

These are described in more detail below.

1.2.2 Attenuation

Attenuation in optical fiber is caused by intrinsic factors, primarily scattering and absorption, and by extrinsic factors, including stress from the manufacturing process, the environment, and physical bending. The most common form of scattering, *Rayleigh scattering*, is caused by small variations in the density of glass as it cools. These variations are smaller than the wavelengths used and therefore act as scattering objects. Scattering affects short wavelengths more than long wavelengths and limits the use of wavelengths below 800 nm.

Attenuation due to absorption is caused by a combination of factors, including the intrinsic properties of the material itself, the impurities in the glass, and any atomic defects in the glass. These impurities absorb the optical energy, causing the light to become dimmer. While Rayleigh scattering is important at shorter wavelengths, intrinsic absorption is an issue at longer wavelengths and increases dramatically above 1700 nm. Absorption due to water peaks introduced in the fiber manufacturing process, however, is being eliminated in some new fiber types.

The primary factors affecting attenuation in optical fibers are the length of the fiber and the wavelength of the light. Attenuation in fiber is compensated primarily through the use of optical amplifiers.

1.2.3 Dispersion

Dispersion is the spreading of light pulses as they travel down optical fiber. Dispersion results in distortion of the signal, which limits the bandwidth of the fiber. Two general types of dispersion affect DWDM systems. One of these effects, *chromatic dispersion*, is linear, while the other, *Polarization Mode Dispersion (PMD)*, is nonlinear.

Chromatic dispersion occurs because different wavelengths propagate at different speeds. In single-mode fiber, chromatic dispersion has two components, *material* dispersion and *waveguide* dispersion. Material dispersion occurs when wavelengths travel at different speeds through the material. A light source, no matter how narrow, emits several wavelengths within a range. When these wavelengths travel through a medium, each individual wavelength arrives at the far end at a different time. The second component of chromatic dispersion, waveguide dispersion, occurs because of the different refractive indices of the *core* and the *cladding* of fiber (see section 1.2.5). Although chromatic dispersion is generally not an issue at speeds below 2.5 Gbps, it does increase with higher bit rates.

Most single-mode fibers support two perpendicular polarization modes, vertical and horizontal. Because these polarization states are not maintained, there occurs an interaction between the pulses that results is a smearing of the signal. PMD is generally not a problem at transmission rates below 10 Gbps.

1.2.4 Nonlinear Effects

In addition to PMD, there are other nonlinear effects. Because nonlinear effects tend to manifest themselves when optical power is very high, they become important in DWDM (see section 1.2.9). Linear effects such as attenuation and dispersion can be compensated, but nonlinear effects accumulate. They are the fundamental limiting mechanisms to the amount of data that can be transmitted in optical fiber. The most important types of nonlinear effects are *stimulated Brillouin scattering*, *stimulated Raman scattering*, *self-phase modulation*, and *four-wave mixing* [Agrawal97]. In DWDM, four-wave mixing is the most critical of these types. Four-wave mixing is caused by the nonlinear nature of the *refractive index* (see the next section) of the optical fiber. Nonlinear interactions among different DWDM channels create sidebands that can cause interchannel interference. Three frequencies interact to produce a fourth frequency, resulting in cross talk and signal-to-noise level degradation. Four-wave mixing cannot be filtered out, either optically or electrically, and increases with the length of the fiber. It also limits the channel capacity of a DWDM system.

1.2.5 Optical Fiber

The main requirement on optical fibers is to guide light waves with a minimum of attenuation (loss of signal). Optical fibers are composed of fine threads of glass in layers, called the core and cladding, in which light can be transmitted at about two-thirds its speed in vacuum. Although admittedly an oversimplification, the transmission of light in optical fiber is commonly explained using the principle of *total internal reflection*. With this phenomenon, 100 percent of light that strikes a surface is reflected. By contrast, a mirror reflects about 90 percent of the light that strikes it.

Light is either reflected (it bounces back) or refracted (its angle is altered while passing through a different medium) depending on the angle of incidence (the angle at which light strikes the interface between an optically denser and optically thinner material). Total internal reflection happens when the following conditions are met:

1. Beams pass from a material of higher density to a material of lower density. The difference between the optical density of a given material and a vacuum is the material's refractive index.
2. The incident angle is less than the *critical* angle. The critical angle is the angle of incidence at which light stops being refracted and is instead totally reflected.

An optical fiber consists of two different types of very pure and solid glass (silica): the core and the cladding. These are mixed with specific elements, called *dopants*, to adjust their refractive indices. The difference between the refractive indices of the two materials causes most of the transmitted light to bounce off the cladding and stay within the core. The critical angle requirement is met by controlling the angle at which the light is injected into the fiber (see Figure 1–1). Two or more layers of protective coating around the cladding ensure that the glass can be handled without damage.

There are two general categories of optical fiber in use today, multimode and single-mode. Multimode, the first type of fiber to be commercialized, has a larger core than single-mode fiber. It gets its name from the fact that numerous *modes*, or light rays, can be simultaneously carried by it. The second general type of fiber, single-mode, has a much smaller core that allows only one mode of light at a time through the core. As a result, the fidelity of the signal is better retained over longer distances. This characteristic results in higher bandwidth capacity than achievable using multimode fibers. Due to its large information-carrying capacity and low intrinsic loss, single-mode fibers are preferred for longer distances and higher bandwidth applications, including DWDM.

Designs of single-mode fiber have evolved over several decades. The three principle types are:

1. Non-dispersion-shifted fiber
2. Dispersion-shifted fiber
3. Non-zero dispersion-shifted fiber

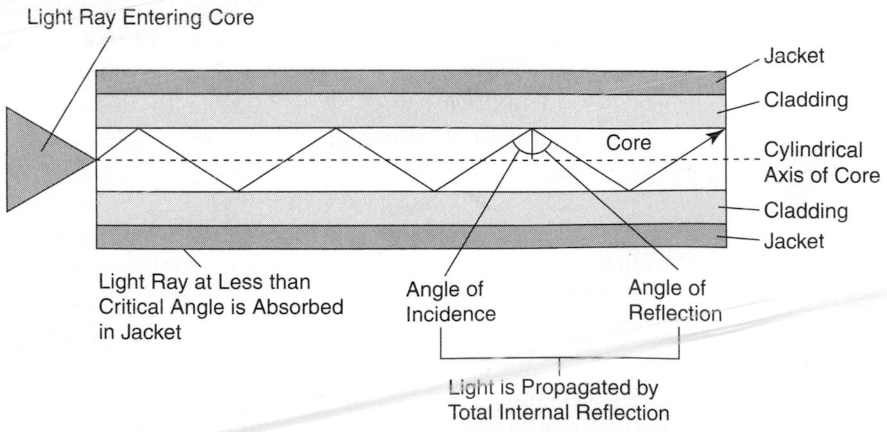

Figure 1–1 *Propagation of Light through a Fiber Optic Cable*

As discussed earlier, there are four windows within the optical spectrum that have been exploited for fiber transmission. The first window, near 850 nm, was used almost exclusively for short-range, multimode applications. Non-dispersion-shifted fibers, commonly called standard single-mode (SM) fibers, were designed for use in the second window, near 1310 nm. To optimize the fiber's performance in this window, the fiber was designed so that chromatic dispersion would be close to zero near the 1310-nm wavelength.

The third window, or C band, has much lower attenuation. However, its dispersion characteristics are severely limiting. To alleviate this problem, manufacturers came up with the dispersion-shifted fiber design, which moved the zero-dispersion point to the 1550-nm region. Although this solution meant that the lowest optical attenuation and the zero-dispersion points coincided in the 1550-nm window, it turned out that there were destructive nonlinearities in optical fiber near the zero-dispersion point for which there was no effective compensation. Because of this limitation, these fibers are not suitable for DWDM applications.

The third type, non-zero dispersion-shifted fiber, is designed specifically to meet the needs of DWDM applications. The aim of this design is to make the dispersion low in the 1550-nm region, but not zero. This strategy effectively introduces a controlled amount of dispersion, which counters nonlinear effects such as four-wave mixing that can hinder the performance of DWDM systems [Dutton99].

1.2.6 Optical Transmitter and Receivers

Light emitters and light detectors are active devices at opposite ends of an optical transmission system. Light emitters, are transmit-side devices that convert electrical signals to light pulses. This conversion is accomplished by externally modulating a continuous wave of light based on the input signal, or by using a device that can generate modulated light directly. Light detectors perform the opposite function of light emitters. They are receive-side opto-electronic devices that convert light pulses into electrical signals.

The light source used in the design of a system is an important consideration because it can be one of the most costly elements. Its characteristics are often a strong limiting factor in the final performance of the optical link. Light-emitting devices used in optical transmission must be compact, monochromatic, stable, and long lasting. Two general types of light-emitting devices are used in optical transmission: light-emitting diodes (LEDs) and laser diodes or semiconductor lasers. LEDs are relatively slow devices, suitable for use at speeds of less than 1 Gbps; they exhibit a relatively wide spectrum width, and they transmit light in a relatively wide cone. These inexpensive devices are often used in multimode fiber communications. Semiconductor lasers, on the other hand, have performance characteristics better suited to single-mode fiber applications.

Requirements for lasers include precise wavelength, narrow spectrum width, sufficient power, and control of *chirp* (the change in frequency of a signal over time). Semiconductor lasers satisfy nicely the first three requirements. Chirp, however, can be affected by the means used to modulate the signal. In directly modulated lasers, the modulation of the light to represent the digital data is done internally. With external modulation, the modulation is done by an external device. When semiconductor lasers are directly modulated, chirp can become a limiting factor at high bit rates (above 10 Gbps). External modulation, on the other hand, helps to limit chirp.

Two types of semiconductor lasers are widely used: monolithic *Fabry-Perot* lasers and *Distributed Feedback* (DFB) lasers. The latter type is particularly well suited for DWDM applications for several reasons: it emits a nearly monochromatic light, it is capable of high speeds, it has a favorable signal-to-noise ratio, and it has superior linearity property. DFB lasers also have center frequencies in the region around 1310 nm, and from 1520 to 1565 nm. There are many other types and subtypes of lasers. Narrow spectrum tunable lasers are available, but their tuning range is limited to approximately 100–200 GHz. Wider spectrum tunable lasers, which will be important in dynamically switched optical networks, are under development.

On the receive end, it is necessary to recover the signals transmitted on different wavelengths over the fiber. This is done using a device called the *photodetector*. Two types of photodetectors are widely deployed, the *Positive-Intrinsic-Negative* (PIN) photodiode and the *Avalanche Photodiode* (APD). PIN photodiodes work on principles similar to, but in the reverse of, LEDs. That is, light is absorbed rather than emitted, and photons are converted to electrons in a 1:1 relationship. APDs are similar devices to PIN photodiodes, but provide gain through an amplification process: One photon acting on the device releases many electrons. PIN photodiodes have many advantages, including low cost and reliability, but APDs have higher reception sensitivity and accuracy. APDs, however, are more expensive than PIN photodiodes. They may also have very high current requirements and they are temperature sensitive.

1.2.7 Regenerators, Repeaters, and Optical Amplifiers

Optical signals undergo degradation when traversing optical links due to dispersion, loss, cross talk, and nonlinearity associated with fiber and optical components. Regenerators are devices consisting of both electronic and optical components to provide "3R" regeneration—Reamplification, Reshaping and Retiming. Retiming and reshaping detect the digital signal that is distorted and noisy, and re-create it as a clean signal (see Figure 1–2). In practice, signals can travel for up to 120 km (74 miles) between amplifiers. At longer distances of 600 to 1000 km (372 to 620 miles), the signal must be regener-

"3R" Retime, Reshape and Reamplify the signal–by knowing a lot about the signal, re-create it (e.g. SONET)

"2R" Reshape and Reamplify the signal–ignore timing but, for example, restore pulse shape by finding zero crossings (supports "translucent" digital transport)

"1R" Amplify the signal–restore signal amplitude and also amplify any accumulated noise or signal distortions (supports fully transparent transport including "analog" signals)

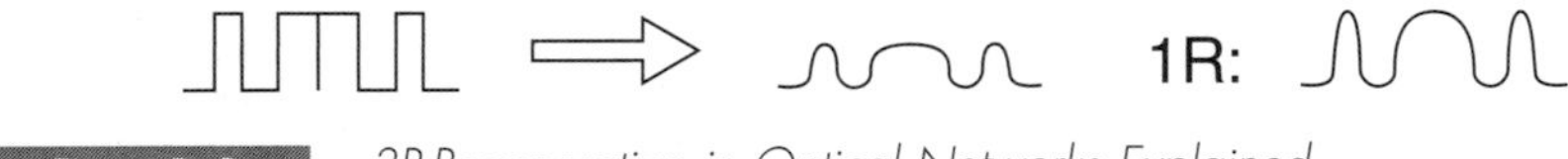

Figure 1–2 *3R-Regeneration in Optical Networks Explained*

ated. This is because an optical amplifier merely amplifies the signals and does not perform the other 3R functions (reshape and retime). Recent advances in transmission technology have increased the distance that can be traversed without amplification and 3R regeneration. It should be noted that amplifiers are purely optical devices whereas regenerators require optical-to-electrical (O/E) conversion and electrical-to-optical (E/O) conversion.

Before the arrival of optical amplifiers (OAs), every signal transmitted had to be individually regenerated or amplified using repeaters. The OA has made it possible to amplify all the wavelengths at once and without optical-electrical-optical (OEO) conversion. Besides being used on optical links, optical amplifiers can also be used to boost signal power after multiplexing or before demultiplexing, both of which can introduce loss in the system. The *Erbium-Doped Fiber Amplifier* (EDFA) is the most commonly deployed OA.

Erbium is a rare-earth element that, when excited, emits light around 1.54 micrometers—the low-loss wavelength for optical fibers used in DWDM.

A weak signal enters the erbium-doped fiber, into which light at 980 nm or 1480 nm is injected using a pump laser. This injected light stimulates the erbium atoms to release their stored energy as additional 1550-nm light. As this process continues down the fiber, the signal grows stronger. The spontaneous emissions in the EDFA also add noise to the signal; this determines the noise figure of an EDFA.

The key performance parameters of optical amplifiers are gain, gain flatness, noise level, and output power. The target parameters when selecting an EDFA, however, are low noise and flat gain. Gain should be flat because all signals must be amplified uniformly. Although the signal gain provided by the EDFA technology is inherently wavelength-dependent, it can be corrected with gain flattening filters. Such filters are often built into modern EDFAs. Low noise is a requirement because noise, along with the signal, is amplified. Because this effect is cumulative and cannot be filtered out, the signal-to-noise ratio is an ultimate limiting factor in the number of amplifiers that can be concatenated. This limits the length of a single fiber link.

1.2.8 Characterizing Optical Signals and Performance

The basic measure of digital signal transmission performance is a probabilistic quantity known as the Bit Error Rate (BER). Given a large sample of received bits, the BER gives the percentage of those received in error. The following basic phenomena affect the bit error rate of a signal:

1. Noise, and in particular, noise per bit.
2. Intersymbol interference, that is, the signal interfering with itself.
3. Interchannel interference, that is, other channels interfering with the signal.
4. Nonlinear effects (see [Ramaswamy+02] for a discussion).

Analysis of 1–4 for general communication systems is highly dependent on the modulation method used and the type of detection employed. In optical systems, the modulation method most frequently used is *On-Off-Keying* (OOK). As its name suggests, it is just like turning on and off the light (albeit very rapidly) according to the bits being sent (that is, "on" if a bit is 1 and "off" if the bit is 0). BER of the OOK modulated signal increases with the increasing bit rate of the signal.

Intersymbol interference takes place when a signal interferes with itself. This can happen in a couple of ways. First, if the channel the signal passes through is bandwidth-limited, then the nice square edges on the signal can get "rounded" so that the various individual bits actually interfere with each other. This *band limiting* may take place at the transmitter, receiver, or within the channel. Within the fiber, dispersion occurs when the different wavelengths that compose the signal travel at different velocities down the fiber.

Interchannel interference occurs when signals based on different wavelengths interfere with each other, that is, their individual spectrums overlap. Hence, the channel spacing in a Wavelength Division Multiplexing (WDM) system must be wide enough to prevent the signal spectrums from overlapping. For a system with 100 GHz spacing carrying OC-48 signals (2.5Gbps bit rate), this is not a problem. As we shrink the spacing down to 12.5 GHz for OC-192 signals, it is more challenging to prevent interchannel interference.

Thus, both the wavelength of an optical signal and its bandwidth affect interference. Moreover, the BER is dependent on the signal modulation method and the bit rate. Thus, impairments such as line noise, loss, dispersion, and nonlinear effects must be taken into consideration when selecting a route to achieve the required performance criteria.

1.2.9 DWDM Systems

WDM [Green92, Agrawal97, Saleh+91] is an analog multiplexing technique where the original signals are "frequency shifted" to occupy different portions of the frequency spectrum of the transmission media. For example, commercial broadcast radio stations take a base audio signal (typically with a frequency between 20 and 20,000 Hz), use this to modulate a higher frequency *carrier* signal, and then broadcast this new signal into free space. This signal does not interfere with other signals if there is sufficient "spacing" between the carriers of the different radio stations. The required spacing is a function of both the spectral characteristics, spectrum, of the original signal and the modulation method.

In optical networking, the transmission medium is an optical fiber rather than free space. The signals of interest, rather than being analog audio content, are typically digital signals of various types. The carrier, rather than being an electromagnetic signal in the KHz or MHz range, is an electromagnetic signal with a frequency around 193 THz, that is, 1.93×10^{14} Hz! And like the radio case, there are a variety of different modulation methods that can be used to apply the digital signal to this carrier for transmission. As we go from radio to optical signals, the technologies change completely, for example, from electronic oscillators to lasers for generating the carrier signal.

The commercial U.S. AM radio broadcasts have carrier frequencies in the range of 560–1600 KHz with a spacing of 10 KHz, that is, signals may exist at 560 KHz, 570 KHz, 580 KHz, and so on. The spectral content of the audio signal is restricted to be between approximately 100–5000 Hz. Early WDM began in the late 1980s using the two widely spaced wavelengths in the 1310 nm and 1550 nm (or 850 nm and 1310 nm) regions, sometimes called *wideband* WDM. The early 1990s saw a second generation of WDM, sometimes called *narrowband* WDM, in which two to eight channels were used. These channels were spaced at an interval of about 400 GHz in the 1550 nm window. By the mid-1990s, *dense* WDM (DWDM) systems were emerging with sixteen to forty channels and spacing from 100 to 200 GHz. By the late 1990s, DWDM systems had evolved to the point where they were capable of sixty-four to 160 parallel channels, densely packed at 50 or even 25 GHz intervals.

In the WDM case, there has been some initial standardization of frequencies and spacing. In particular, ITU-T has specified the frequencies in terms of offsets from the reference frequency of 193.1 THz [ITU-T98c]. The standard offsets are 200 GHz, 100 GHz, and 50 GHz. It should be noted that there are deployed WDM systems operating with grid spacing as narrow as 25 GHz and even narrower spacing is in the works. The ITU-T specification [ITU-T98c] does not preclude these systems.

Unfortunately, even with a standard set of frequencies, WDM systems from different vendors currently do not interoperate. To understand why this is so, consider a WDM system as shown in Figure 1–3. The current trend in the long haul market place has three aspects: (1) longer distances between regenerators, (2) denser spacing between channels, and (3) higher data rates carried per channel. These trends push the capabilities of the fiber and the systems so that linear and nonlinear effects rather than just signal attenuation must be compensated for or otherwise taken into consideration. Vendors use proprietary techniques to address these issues leading to lack of interoperability. Please refer to [Ramaswamy+02] for more information on transmission impairments in optical networks.

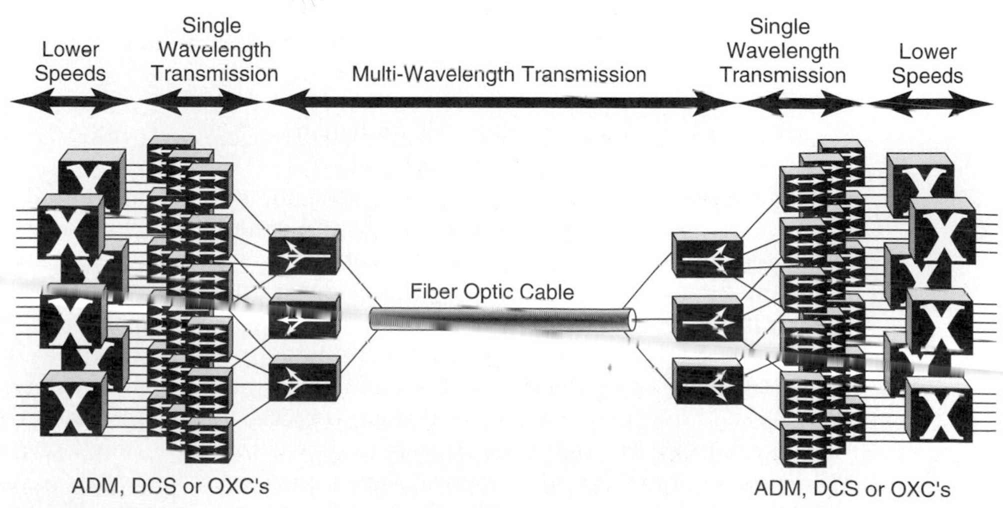

Figure 1–3 *A Point-to-Point WDM System (Courtesy Ciena Corporation)*

At its core, DWDM involves a small number of physical-layer functions. A typical DWDM system performs the following main functions:

- *Generating the signal:* The source, a solid-state laser, must provide stable light within a specific, narrow bandwidth that carries the digital data, modulated as an analog signal.
- *Combining the signals:* Modern DWDM systems employ multiplexers to combine the signals. There is some inherent loss associated with multiplexing and demultiplexing. This loss is dependent on the number of channels but can be mitigated with optical amplifiers, which boost all the wavelengths at once without electrical conversion.
- *Transmitting the signals:* The effects of cross talk and optical signal degradation or loss must be dealt with in fiber optic transmission. These effects can be minimized by controlling channel spacing, wavelength tolerance, and laser power levels. The signal may need to be optically amplified over a transmission link.
- *Separating the received signals:* At the receiving end, the multiplexed signals must be separated out. Although this task would appear to be simply the opposite of combining the signals, it is actually more difficult.
- *Receiving the signals:* The de-multiplexed signal is received by a photodetector.

In addition to these functions, a DWDM system must also be equipped with client-side interfaces to receive the input signal. This function is performed by *transponders*. Interfaces to the optical fiber that links DWDM systems are on the other side.

1.3 Multiplexing, Grooming, and Switching

Transmission systems alone are not enough to build an optical network. Optical signals need to be multiplexed and demultiplexed at the end points. They also need to be *groomed* and *switched* at intermediate nodes. Grooming is the function of dropping a lower rate signal from one rate speed signal and adding it to another. Switching allows a signal received on one input port and channel to be transmitted on a different output port and channel.

Based on the switch fabric technology, optical switches can be broadly classified into two categories—opaque (or OEO) and transparent (or OOO) [Mouftah+98, Hinton93]. Opaque optical switches, also called *optical cross-connects* or *OXCs*, convert optical signals received at the input to electric signal, switch the electrical signals using an electronic switching fabric, and finally convert the electrical signal back to optical signal at the output. The name OEO captures the operational principle of the switch in the sense that it converts the incoming optical signal into electrical signal and then converts it back to optical signal. Transparent switches, also called *photonic cross-connects* or *PXCs*, on the other hand, do not perform this optical to electrical translation; they switch the incoming optical signal from the input port to the output port in the optical form (hence, OOO). Optically transparent switches operate over a range of wavelengths called the passband. For any given steady state, optical transparency allows a device to function independent of the type (e.g., analog, digital), format (e.g., SCM, SONET, GbE), or rate (e.g., 155 Mbps, 10 Gbps, 10 GHz) of the information on the optical signal being conveyed.

One of the problems with the OEO switches is that they need to perform multiple opto-electrical translations that can be both complex and expensive. On the positive side, as a by-product of opto-electrical translation, the optical signal undergoes regeneration and wavelength translation comes for free. OOO switches on the other hand, do not perform opto-electrical translation. As a result, they have the potential of being cheaper. OOO switches, however, are incapable of signal regeneration and wavelength translation. They also lack some of the performance monitoring and fault management capabilities that OEO switches offer. In the following we discuss different types of OEO and OOO switching elements.

1.3.1 Digital Cross-Connects and Add/Drop Multiplexers

Digital cross-connects, although not purely optical elements, play an important role in today's optical networks [Ramaswamy+02, Stern+99, Mukherjee97]. They can operate on either optical or electrical signals. Their switching fabric, however, is purely electrical.

Digital cross-connects are used for sub-wavelength level grooming and switching, that is, they work on time division multiplexed signals that may be carried as a wavelength in a WDM signal. Depending on switching granularity, they can be categorized as *wideband*, *broadband*, or *ultraband* cross-connects. Wideband cross-connects switch signals at the granularity of 1.5Mbps (DS1) while broadband cross-connects operate at 50 Mbps (STS-1) granularity. Ultraband is the latest addition to the digital cross-connect family. This type of cross-connect operates on optical signals and uses a 2.5Gbps (STS-48) electrical switching fabric. It is similar in functionality to an optical wavelength switch except that it is an OEO switch as opposed to an OOO switch. Advances in integrated circuit technology have allowed the creation of "ultra high" capacity broadband cross-connects with raw switching capacity similar to that of Ultraband cross-connects but with 50 Mbps switching granularity.

Digital cross-connects are typically located in Telco Central Offices, as shown in Figure 1–4. Wideband cross-connects are used for grooming, multiplexing, and interconnecting traffic between access and collector rings. Broadband cross-connects are used for the same function, but typically in metro-core and wide-area rings. The ultraband cross-connects are primarily concerned with interconnecting DWDM systems in wide area mesh and ring structured optical transport networks.

Today's optical networks also use add-drop multiplexers (ADM) quite extensively. ADMs are typically arranged in a ring topology connecting multiple service provider PoPs (points-of-presence). As the name suggests, they are used to add/drop traffic at a PoP to/from the ring. ADM rings operate at different speeds, and traffic can be added/dropped at different granularities. For example, metro-access rings typically operate at 150 Mbps (OC-3) and 622 Mbps (OC-12), and ADMs in these rings can add/drop traffic at 1.5 Mbps (DS1) or higher granularity. Interoffice metro rings and wide-area rings operate at 2.5Gbps (OC-48) and 10 Gbps (OC-192) speeds and typically traffic is added/dropped at 50Mbps (DS3) or higher speeds.

Standards currently exist that specify the exact characteristics and structure of various signals that digital cross-connects and ADMs operate on (see

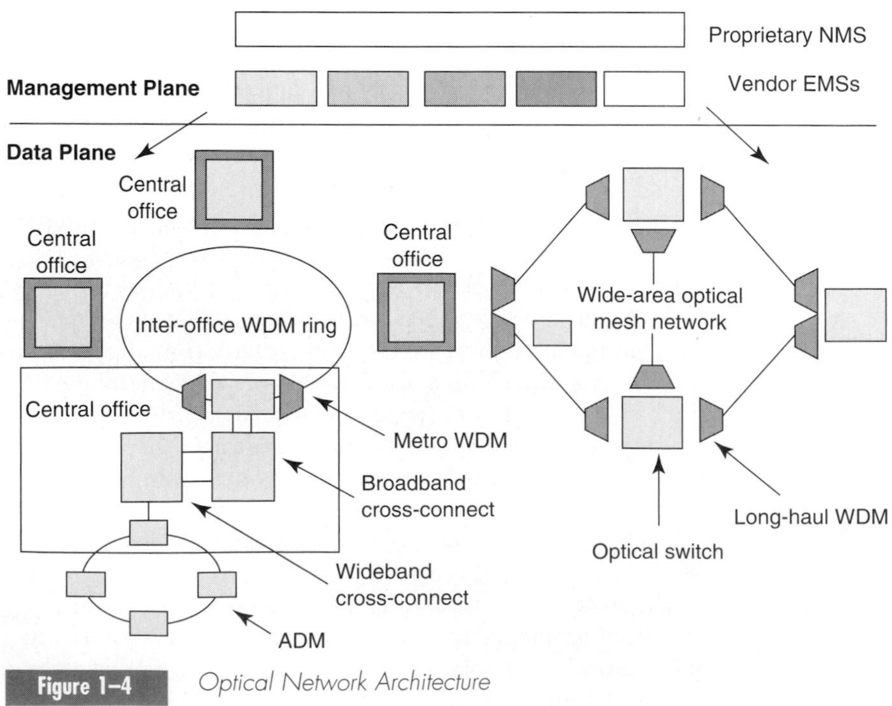

Figure 1–4 *Optical Network Architecture*

Chapters 2 and 3). This is in sharp contrast to the OOO case where few standards yet exist and intervendor interoperability is very uncommon.

1.3.2 OOO Switch Fabrics

Research, development, and commercialization of OOO (photonic) switches encompasses a variety of switching technologies, including opto-mechanical, electro-optic, acousto-optic, thermal, micro-mechanical, liquid crystal, and semiconductor switch technologies [Mouftah+98, Hinton93]. The performance characteristics and hence possible application of photonic switches may depend on the technology used. It is difficult to predict breakthroughs, but should they occur, they may well revolutionize switching in telecommunications networks. Some technologies utilized in commercially available photonic switches are described in this section.

In order to appreciate the relative merits and shortcomings of different switching technologies, it is important to understand the different metrics used to characterize the performance of a photonic switch fabric. With an *ideal* photonic switch, all the optical power applied at any input port can be completely transferred to any output port, that is, the switch has zero *insertion loss*. Also, the optical power does not leak from any input port to any other input port or any undesired output port, that is, it has infinite *directivity* and zero cross talk. In addition, switch connections can be reconfigured instantaneously, that is, the *switching time* is zero, and any new connection can be made without rearranging existing connections, that is, the switch is *non-blocking*. Unfortunately, no switch is ideal.

In practice, the following characteristics of photonic switch elements and fabrics affect their performance:

- Switching speed: The switching speed of photonic switches ranges from sub-nanosecond to hundreds of milliseconds. Depending on the application, any of these can be acceptable, but some applications require higher speed than others.
- Switching efficiency: In an ideal switch, all the power is transferred from a given input port to the desired output port, and no power is transferred to any other port, in either forward or backward direction. How a switch performs these functions is measured using four primary metrics: insertion loss, cross talk, return, and directivity. Insertion loss is the power lost due to the presence of the switching device: the ratio of output power to input power. The cross talk of a switch is defined in terms of worst case power transfer from the input port into an unintended output port. The return of a switch is defined in terms of power transferred from the input port back into the same fiber. The directivity of a switch is defined in terms of the power transferred from the input port to a different input port.

Insertion loss and cross talk should be as low as possible. Return loss and directivity should be as high as possible, indicating very little reflection back into the input.

- Wavelength dependence: Ideally, the performance of a photonic switch should be independent of the specific wavelength being switched. In practice, certain types of switches, such as opto-mechanical switches, are nearly wavelength independent. Waveguide based switches, on the other hand, are frequently optimized for narrower wavelength region. All the properties of the photonic switch must meet optical specifications across the wavelength range over which the switch is intended to be used. The main wavelength bands of interest for optical communication are those centered on the fiber loss minima at 1310 nm and 1550 nm.
- Polarization dependence: Switches need to have low polarization dependent loss (PDL), low polarization mode dispersion (PMD), and low polarization dependence in switching efficiency. If the signal passes through many switches, PDL can accumulate and lead to large variations in power levels. PMD is a problem primarily at high data rates. PMD in switches can be corrected, since it is a constant, unlike time-varying PMD in optical fiber. Polarization dependent switching efficiency can be problem if it leads to unacceptable cross talk for one of the polarizations.

In the following we discuss different switching technologies. Specifically, we describe the basic principle of switching under different technologies and discuss the intrinsic performance limitations and possible reliability concerns.

1.3.2.1 OPTO-MECHANICAL

This broad category of optical switching technology can be identified based on the use of motion to realize optical switching. They typically have very low loss, and extremely low cross talk. Switching speed of these switches vary from tens of milliseconds to hundreds of milliseconds. Opto-mechanical switches are the most commonly used optical switches today. This broad category can be further divided based on implementation specifics.

There are two types of opto-mechanical switches: moving fiber type and moving deflector type. Moving fiber technology uses direct moving fiber-to-fiber, or collimator-to-collimator alignment to reconfigure optical connections.[1] Moving deflector technology uses a moving mirror or prism that moves in and out of the optical path of fixed collimators to reconfigure optical connections.

[1]A collimator is a device to which a fiber is attached. The collimator then outputs a fixed beam of limited cross-section.

Fiber or deflector motion may be created with a relay, a solenoid, or a stepper motor.

The most popular opto-mechanical switches are based on Micro-Electro-Mechanical Systems (MEMS). A MEMS is a small device that has both electrical and mechanical components. It is fabricated using the tools of the semiconductor manufacturing industry: thin film deposition, photolithography, and selective etching. Frequently, MEMS devices involve the use of semiconductor materials, such as silicon wafers, as well. MEMS devices offer the possibility of reducing the size, cost, and switching time of optical switches, and the ability to manufacture large arrays and complex networks of switching elements.

The switching element in a MEMS optical switch can be a moving fiber, or a moving optical component such as a mirror, lens, prism, or waveguide. The actuation principle for moving the switching element is typically electromagnetism, electrostatic attraction, or thermal expansion. One of the most popular forms of MEMS switches is based on arrays of tiny tilting mirrors, which are either two-dimensional (2D) or three-dimensional (3D). In a typical 2D array, the mirrors simply flap up and down in the optical equivalent of a crossbar switch. When they are down, light beams pass over them. When they are up, they deflect the beam to a different output port. With 3D arrays (see Figure 1–5), the mirrors can be tilted in any direction. The arrays are typically arranged in pairs, facing each other and at an angle of 90 degrees to each

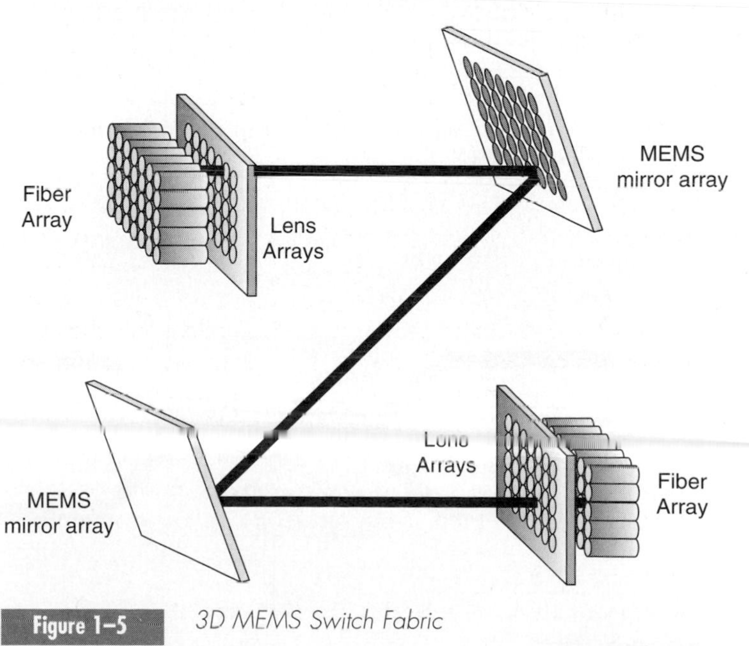

Figure 1–5 *3D MEMS Switch Fabric*

other. Incoming light is directed onto a mirror in the first array that deflects it onto a predetermined mirror in the second array. This in turn deflects the light to the predetermined output port. The position of the mirrors has to be controlled very precisely, for example, to millionths of degrees.

1.3.2.2 ELECTRO-OPTIC SWITCHES

Electro-optic switches are based on directional couplers. A 2 × 2 coupler consists of two input ports and two output ports, as shown in Figure 1–6. It takes a fraction of the power, α, from input 1 and places it on output 1. The remaining power, 1-α, is placed on output 2. Similarly, a fraction, 1-α of the power from input 2 is distributed to output 1 and the remaining power to output 2. A 2 × 2 coupler can be used as a 2 × 2 switch by changing the coupling ratio α. In electro-optic switches, the coupling ratio is changed by changing the refractive index of the material in the coupling region. One commonly used material for this purpose is lithium niobate ($LiNbO_3$). Switching is performed by applying the appropriate voltage to the electrodes. Electro-optic switches tend to be fast with switching times in the nanosecond range. Since the electro-optic effect is sensitive to *polarization,* electro-optic switches are inherently polarization sensitive, and tend to have relatively high loss.

1.3.2.3 ACOUSTO-OPTIC SWITCHES

In an acousto-optic device, a light beam interacts with traveling acoustic waves in a transparent material such as glass. Acoustic waves are generated with a transducer that converts electromagnetic signals into mechanical vibrations. The spatially periodic density variations in the material, corresponding to compressions and rarefactions of the traveling acoustic wave, are accompanied by corresponding changes in the medium's index of refraction. These

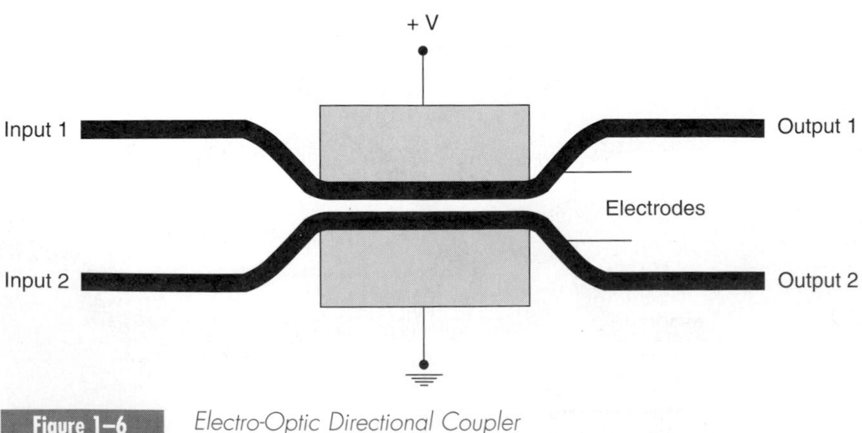

Figure 1–6 *Electro-Optic Directional Coupler*

periodic refractive index variations diffract light. Sufficiently powerful acoustic waves can diffract most of the incident light and therefore deflect it from its incident direction, thus creating an optical switching device. Acousto-optic switches are wavelength dependent and are more suitable for wavelength selective switches.

1.3.2.4 THERMO-OPTIC SWITCHES

These switches are based on *Mach-Zehnder interferometers* [Green92, Ramaswamy+02]. A Mach Zehnder interferometer is constructed out of two directional couplers interconnected through two paths of differing lengths as shown in Figure 1–7. By varying the refractive index in one arm of the interferometer, the relative phase difference between two arms can be changed, resulting in switching an input signal from one input port to another. These switches are called thermo-optic switches because the change in the refractive index is thermally induced. Thermo-optic switches suffer from poor cross talk performance and are relatively slow in terms of switching speed.

1.3.2.5 MAGNETO-OPTIC SWITCHES

The magneto-optic effect refers to a phenomenon in which an electromagnetic wave interacts with a magnetic field. The Faraday effect is an important magneto-optic effect whereby the plane of polarization of an optical signal is rotated under the influence of a magnetic field. Magneto-optic switches use Faraday effect to switch optical signal. These switches are typically characterized with low loss and slow switching speed. They are somewhat wavelength dependent.

1.3.2.6 LIQUID CRYSTAL OPTICAL SWITCHES

A liquid crystal is a phase between solid and liquid. Liquid crystal-based optical switches also utilize polarization diversity and polarization rotation to achieve optical switching. Switches of this type are typically quite wavelength

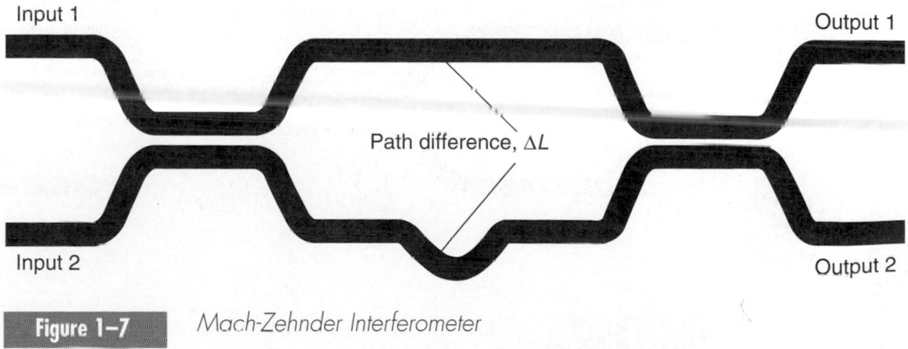

Figure 1–7 *Mach-Zehnder Interferometer*

dependent, since the amount of polarization rotation depends on wavelength. Liquid crystal polarization rotation is also intrinsically temperature dependent. Switching speed is relatively slow, usually between 10–30 ms range, since the switching mechanism requires reorientation of rather large molecules.

1.4 Summary

In this chapter, we gave an overview of the key elements of modern optical networking. Although the theoretical underpinnings are rather specialized [Ramaswamy+02], it is useful to have a high-level understanding of the technology to appreciate the networking and control plane concepts that follow in later chapters. Our review in this chapter is by no means exhaustive. Readers may refer to [Ramaswamy+02, Stern+99, Mukherjee97] for in-depth treatment of optical network architecture. For a thorough treatment of optical transmission systems including DWDM, please refer to [Agrawal97, Green92]. For a detailed discussion on optical switching, please refer to [Mouftah+98, Hinton93].

T W O

SONET and SDH Basics

2.1 Introduction

SONET and SDH define technologies for carrying multiple digital signals of different capacities in a flexible manner. Most of the deployed optical networks are based on SONET and SDH standards. Consequently, a basic understanding of SONET and SDH is a prerequisite for understanding the optical control plane issues discussed in later chapters.

The basis for signal transport under SONET and SDH is a technique called *Time Division Multiplexing* (TDM). *Multiplexing* in general refers to the process of combining individual signals for transmission. The term *de-multiplexing* is used to denote the process of separating individual signals from a multiplexed stream. While there are many techniques for doing these, TDM is commonly used in telecommunication networks. This chapter begins with an introduction to TDM. Following this, the basic features of SONET and SDH are described. The next chapter deals with more advanced features of SONET and SDH.

2.2 Time Division Multiplexing (TDM)

TDM is a digital technology under which individual signals (i.e., a stream of binary digits or *bits*) are interleaved in time to produce the multiplexed, composite signal. Under TDM, recurring *time-slots* or *channels* are created such that each channel carries the bits from an individual signal. The total transmission bandwidth is split among the time-slots, with each component channel getting some fixed percentage of the total signal bandwidth. This total signal includes not only the payload bits for various component channels but also bits for performing overhead functions. TDM signals have a *frame* structure that repeats at regular intervals.

TDM has a long history in telecommunication networks. Prior to the advent of TDM, telephone calls were handled in the analog domain. Long distance calls were routed over twisted pair, coaxial cable, or analog microwave between switching offices. In early 1960s AT&T began installing *DS-1 T-carrier* services between long distance switching centers. Under this service, there were channel banks, which took 24 analog telephone lines, converted them to digital signals (called *DS-0*), time-division multiplexed them into a DS-1 signal, and then transmitted them over copper wire. At the other end, the DS-1 signal was de-multiplexed into the constituent DS-0 signals, which were then converted back into analog. T-carrier reduced the number of copper circuits required between switching centers and improved the quality of the telephone calls by reducing noise and cross talk. As the traffic volume grew, the number of T-carrier circuits between switching centers increased. In order to cope with the demand, higher speed T-carriers were introduced. In the late 1970s, optical communications became feasible, enabling high-speed and high-fidelity digital communication. One of the first commercial fiber circuits was installed in Chicago in 1977 and operated at 45 Mbps (DS-3 rate).

The frame structures of the DS-1 [ANSI95b] and the European *E1* [ITU-T98a] signals are shown in Figure 2–1. The DS-1 signal consists of 24 payload channels plus overhead. The basic frame of each of these signals repeats every

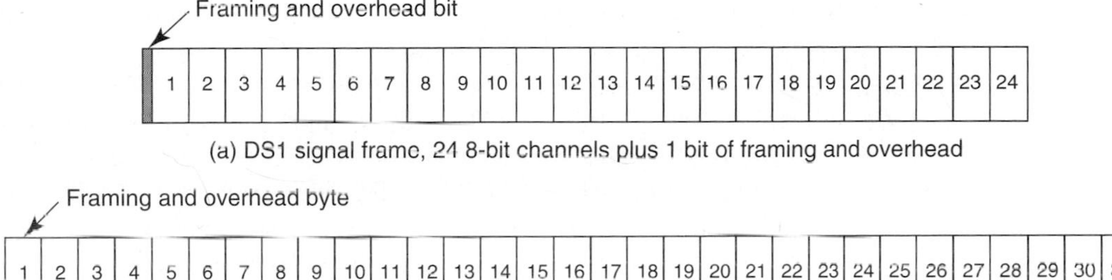

Figure 2–1 *Basic Frame Structures for the DS-1 and E1 TDM Signals*

125 μs, that is, 8000 times per second. With 8 bits carried in each channel, this gives rise to a basic data rate of 64 Kbps for each channel. The requirement for this data rate stems from the need to sample the analog telephony signal 8000 times per second and encoding each sample in 8 bits.

A DS-1 frame contains 24 channels, each consisting of 8 bits, plus 1 framing/overhead bit, leading to a total of 193 bits. Since the frame repeats every 125 μs (or 8000 times a second), the total bit rate of the DS-1 signal is 1.544 Mbps. Similarly, the total bit rate of the E1 signal is 2.048 Mbps (32 channels of 8 bits, repeating every 125 μs).

In a TDM frame, each channel within the frame gets a fixed amount of bandwidth that is not shared with any other channel. It is, however, necessary to determine the start of a TDM frame to de-multiplex the channels within.

With DS-1 signals, the start of frame can be identified by a particular pattern of framing/overhead bits occurring in a consecutive series of frames. A DS-1 *superframe* consists of 12 regular frames as shown in Figure 2–2 [ANSI95b]. The twelve-bit pattern, 100011011100, occurring in the superframe is used to delimit DS-1 frames. In addition to enabling this function, the superframe structure allows the subdivision of the bits in a channel into lower rate channels.

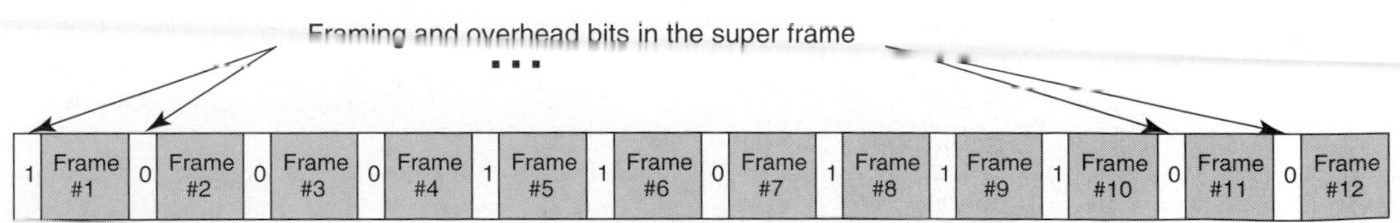

Figure 2–2 *The DS-1 Superframe Structure*

In DS-1 networking, a technique called "robbed bit" signaling is used to convey signaling for each of the 24 channels within a DS-1 signal. Under this technique, the least significant bit of each channel (i.e., bit 8) in frames 6 and 12 of the superframe are used to convey signaling for that channel. The bit rate of this signaling channel can be computed as follows. A single bit out of a channel corresponds to a bit rate of 8000 bps (since the frame containing the channel occurs 8000 times per second). Because the signaling bit is present in only two out of twelve frames, this rate is reduced by 1/6, that is, 8000/6 = 1333.3 bps. Note that robbed bit signaling prevents the use of this bit for carrying user data. Hence, only 7 of the 8 bits are usually used for data services, leading to a 56 Kbps service over each channel.

While the DS-1 superframe allows signaling for the payload channels, there is no provision for conveying information between the end points to aid in managing the signal. This was addressed with the DS-1 *extended superframe* (ESF) format [ANSI95b]. The ESF is 24 regular frames long. Of the 24 overhead bits, 6 are used for frame alignment, another 6 are used for error monitoring, and the remaining 12 are used to form a 4 Kbps data link between the sender and receiver.

With the E1 signal, the first octet (byte) in the frame contains overhead bits. A *multiframe* consisting of 16 frames is used with the base E1 signal.

2.3 Getting to Know the SONET and SDH Signals

North American standardization of SONET started in the mid 1980s with international standardization of SDH starting soon thereafter. The following are the essential features of SONET [ANSI95a] and SDH [ITU-T00a]:

- A base TDM frame structure along with a similarly structured set of progressively larger frames (for faster signals).
- A limited variety of "payload envelopes" (SONET) or "virtual containers" (SDH) of fixed capacity (bandwidth) that are synchronously multiplexed into the base signal (or multiples of the base signal).
- A flexible byte interleaving synchronous multiplexing method for placing the payload envelopes (or virtual containers) into the base signal such that short-term rate variations are accommodated and latency is minimized.

An ever-increasing set of standardized payload mappings indicate how payloads as diverse as DS-3 and IP packets are mapped into the payload envelopes or virtual containers. These features are described in detail in this and in the next chapter.

2.3.1 The Base SONET and SDH Signals

Let us start looking at SONET/SDH signals from their most concrete aspect, that is, the basic signal types for which optical interfaces exist. We can then examine the structure of these signals until complete familiarity with their constituent parts is achieved. The basic physical SONET signal is known as an *Optical Carrier–level 1* (OC-1) signal [ANSI95a]. This is an optical signal with a bit rate of 51.840 Mbps and a host of physical parameters defined by national and international standards. For the purposes of this book, the frame structure, rather than the physical layer signal itself, is more relevant.

SONET uses the terminology *Synchronous Transport Signal—level 1* (STS-1) to denote the logical signal contained within the optical signal, that is, the recurring TDM frame structure. Because the TDM frame structure in SONET/SDH is much longer compared with those of the DS-1 and the E1 signals, a compact "row and column" representation is used when describing SONET/SDH signals. Figure 2–3 shows the representation of the SONET STS-1 signal, which has 90 columns and 9 rows of bytes. The basic frame repeats every 125 μs and the transmission order relative to this representation is from left to

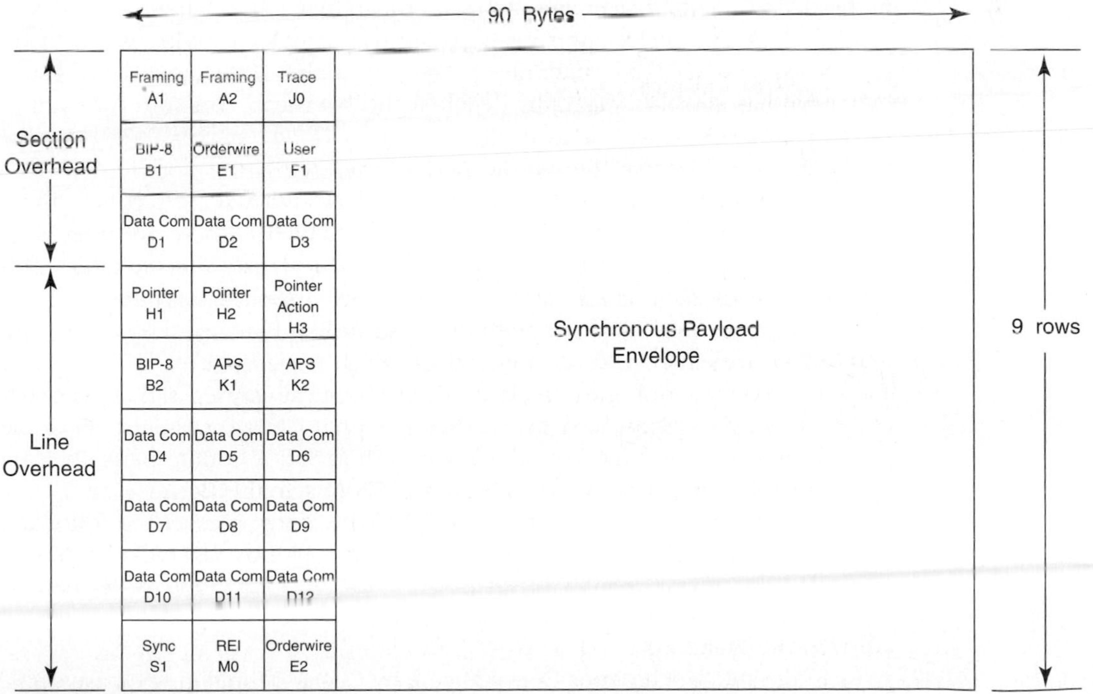

Figure 2–3 *Format of a SONET STS-1 Frame*

right, and top to bottom. That is, the bytes in the first row are transmitted first, from left to right, followed by the bytes in the second row, and so forth. The SONET frame contains both *overhead* bytes and a *Synchronous Payload Envelope* (SPE) that carries the payload. The purpose of the overhead bytes is described in section 2.4.

Let us now compute the bit rate of a SONET STS-1 signal. The STS-1 frame consists of 810 bytes (90 columns times 9 rows). With 8000 frames per second and 8 bits in each byte, the total bit rate is 51.84 Mbps. The bit rate of the SPE portion can be computed as follows. Given that 3 columns of the frame are dedicated to section and line overhead, there are 87 columns and 9 rows used for the SPE in each frame. This gives 783 bytes per frame, and with 8000 frames per second and 8 bits/byte, the bit rate of the SPE is 50.112 Mbps. Thus, the line and section overhead shown in Figure 2–3 add approximately 3.33 percent overhead.

The basic structure of the higher rate SONET signals, the STS-3, -12, -48, -192 and -768 is very similar to the STS-1 structure to permit easy multiplexing of the constituent signals. In fact, these higher rate SONET signals are obtained by byte-interleaving *N* STS-1 signals. Figure 2–4 shows the basic structure of an STS-*N* signal. The overhead and the payload envelope capacity of this signal are *N* times the size of the corresponding fields of the STS-1 signal. These are, however, *N* distinct signals. Also, there are slight differences in the definition and placement of the overhead bytes. It is actually the SONET SPEs that are completely preserved during the byte interleaving when lower rate SONET signals are multiplexed into a higher rate signal. Reference [ANSI95a] has separate diagrams detailing the overhead structure for each of the STS-1, STS-3, STS-12, STS-48, STS-192, and STS-768 signals.

Figure 2–5 shows the overhead (line and section) associated with an STS-3 signal. Here, the framing pattern bytes (A1 and A2) are repeated three times (once for each STS-1 interleaved signal). Similarly, there are three separate sets of pointer bytes (H1–H3) that are used to locate the "floating" SPEs associated with each STS-1. Some overhead bytes such as section trace (J0) need not be repeated and hence the corresponding bytes of the second and third STS-1 are either reserved for growth or left undefined.

The bit rates of the standard SONET optical carrier signals, that is, OC-3, OC-12, OC-48, and OC-192, can be computed as follows. First, since the optical carriers are just the optical version of their STS-*N* counterparts, their bit rates are the same as the corresponding STS-*N* signals. Because an STS-*N* frame is obtained by byte interleaving *N* STS-1 frames, we get the following signal bit rates: (a) OC-3 (3 × 51.84 Mbps) = 155.52 Mbps, (b) OC-12 = 622.08 Mbps, (c) OC-48 = 2.48832 Gbps, (d) OC-192 = 9.95328 Gbps. Note that the rates (c) and (d) are typically rounded up and referred to as 2.5 Gbps and 10 Gbps in the literature.

Under the Synchronous Digital Hierarchy (SDH) definition, the base signal is known as a *Synchronous Transport Module* (STM). SDH does not differentiate between the optical and electrical signals as SONET does with its OC-*N*/STS-*N*

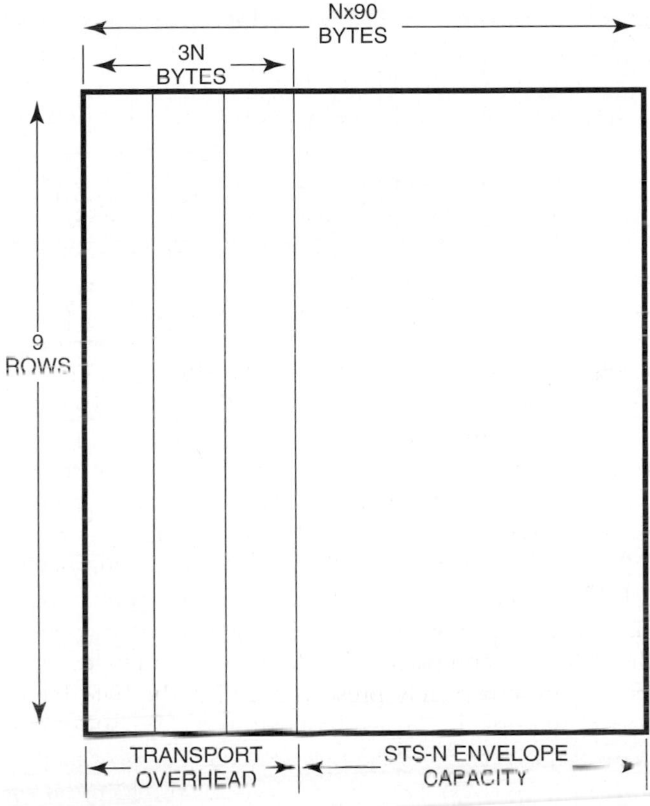

Figure 2–4 The STS-N Frame Structure (from [ANSI95a])

terminology. The frame structure of the STM-*N* signal is shown in Figure 2–6. The STM-*N* frame is very similar in structure to the STS-*N* frame except that it is three times larger. For example, an STM-1 signal is very similar to an STS-3 signal.

2.3.2 Payload Envelopes and Virtual Containers

Instead of just laying a user's signal into the payload of and STS-*N* or STM-*N* signal, the user's signal first gets placed into a payload envelope. This is called the SPE in SONET or a Virtual Container (VC) in SDH. Earlier, we saw the entire SPE as part of a SONET frame. The structure of an STS-1 SPE itself is shown in Figure 2–7. This is also referred to as an STS-1 *path layer* signal, and it is very similar to an SDH VC-3.

To aid in multiplexing multiple STS-1 SPEs into an STS-*N*, the STS-1 SPE signal "floats" within the payload bytes of the STS-1 frame. The starting

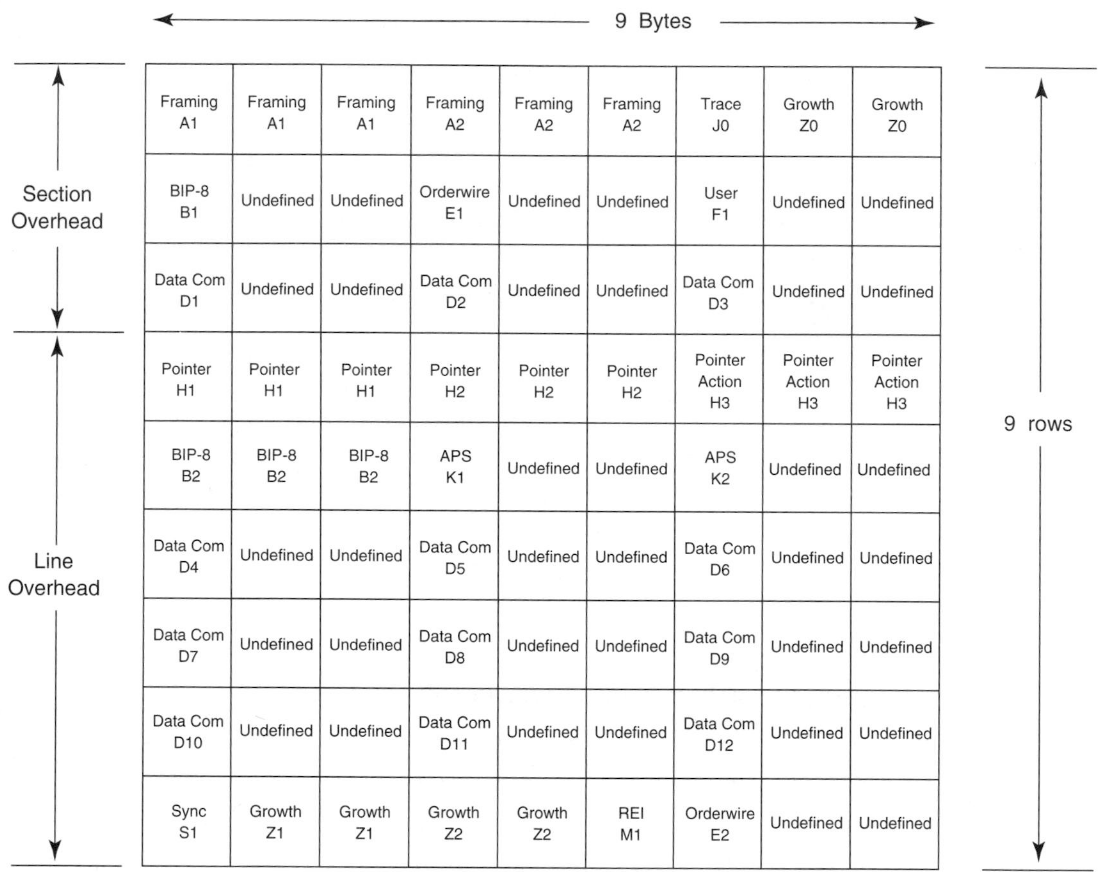

Framing A1	Framing A1	Framing A1	Framing A2	Framing A2	Framing A2	Trace J0	Growth Z0	Growth Z0
BIP-8 B1	Undefined	Undefined	Orderwire E1	Undefined	Undefined	User F1	Undefined	Undefined
Data Com D1	Undefined	Undefined	Data Com D2	Undefined	Undefined	Data Com D3	Undefined	Undefined
Pointer H1	Pointer H1	Pointer H1	Pointer H2	Pointer H2	Pointer H2	Pointer Action H3	Pointer Action H3	Pointer Action H3
BIP-8 B2	BIP-8 B2	BIP-8 B2	APS K1	Undefined	Undefined	APS K2	Undefined	Undefined
Data Com D4	Undefined	Undefined	Data Com D5	Undefined	Undefined	Data Com D6	Undefined	Undefined
Data Com D7	Undefined	Undefined	Data Com D8	Undefined	Undefined	Data Com D9	Undefined	Undefined
Data Com D10	Undefined	Undefined	Data Com D11	Undefined	Undefined	Data Com D12	Undefined	Undefined
Sync S1	Growth Z1	Growth Z1	Growth Z2	Growth Z2	REI M1	Orderwire E2	Undefined	Undefined

Figure 2–5 *Overhead Bytes in an STS-3 Frame*

point of the STS-1 SPE is indicated by the line overhead pointer bytes, H1 and H2. In particular, if we consider the H1 and H2 bytes together as a 16-bit word, then bits 7–16 are used as a 10 bit offset into the STS-1 envelope starting after the H3 overhead byte. Since the size of the envelope capacity is $9 \times 87 = 783$, the valid range for this offset is between 0 and 782, not counting the transport overhead locations. Figure 2–8 shows how the offset is counted within the STS-1 frame. For example, in an STS-1, a pointer value of 0 indicates that the SPE starts at the byte location immediately following the H3 (pointer action) byte, and an offset of 174 ($= 2 \times 87$) indicates that the STS SPE starts immediately after the D6 byte, that is, two rows down.

As seen in Figure 2–7, the SONET STS-1 SPE (SDH VC-3) has one column of bytes dedicated to overhead. It turns out that all SONET SPEs and SDH

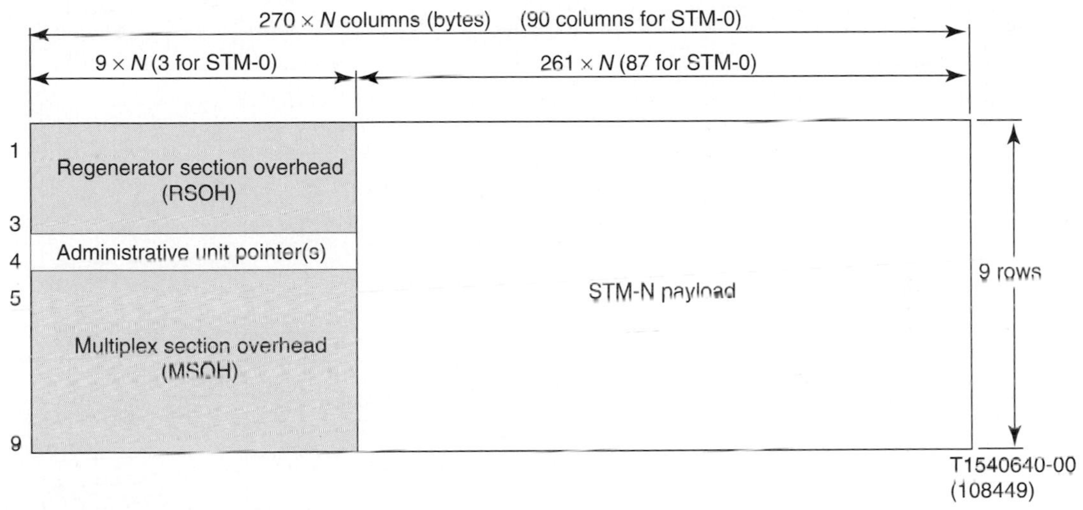

Figure 2–6 *Frame Structure of an STM-N (from [ITU-T00a])*

VCs have a reasonable amount of overhead. This overhead and the flexible multiplexing of these signals allow the easy switching, adding, and dropping of the signals.

We can compute the signal rate of a single byte of overhead or payload within an STS-1 signal as follows. Since each byte has 8 bits, and since the STS-1 frame occurs 8000 times per second, the signal rate corresponding to each byte is 8000 × 8 = 64 Kbps. The bit rate available for the STS-1 payload is 49.536 Mbps (87 columns – 1 column path overhead) × (9 bytes/column) × (8 bits/byte) × (8000 frame/sec) = 49.536 Mbps).

2.3.2.1 LARGER PAYLOAD ENVELOPES (VIRTUAL CONTAINERS)

While 49.536 Mbps payload capacity for a SONET STS-1 SPE is a good chunk of bandwidth, SONET would have not lived long without a natural way to create larger synchronous payload envelopes. The mechanism for doing this is called *contiguous concatenation*. An STS-*Nc* signal is constructed by concatenating the envelope capacities of *N* STS-1 signals to carry an STS-*Nc* SPE. These are also known as *super-rate* signals in SONET.

Note that this is just a fancy way of saying that *N* STS-1 payloads are glued together to form a larger payload. This "gluing" operation is supported via the use of pointer bytes H1-H3. In particular, the pointer bytes of the first STS-1 of the STS-*Nc* signal are used to locate the entire STS-*Nc* SPE. The pointer bytes of the remaining STS-1s are set to a special "concatenation indication."

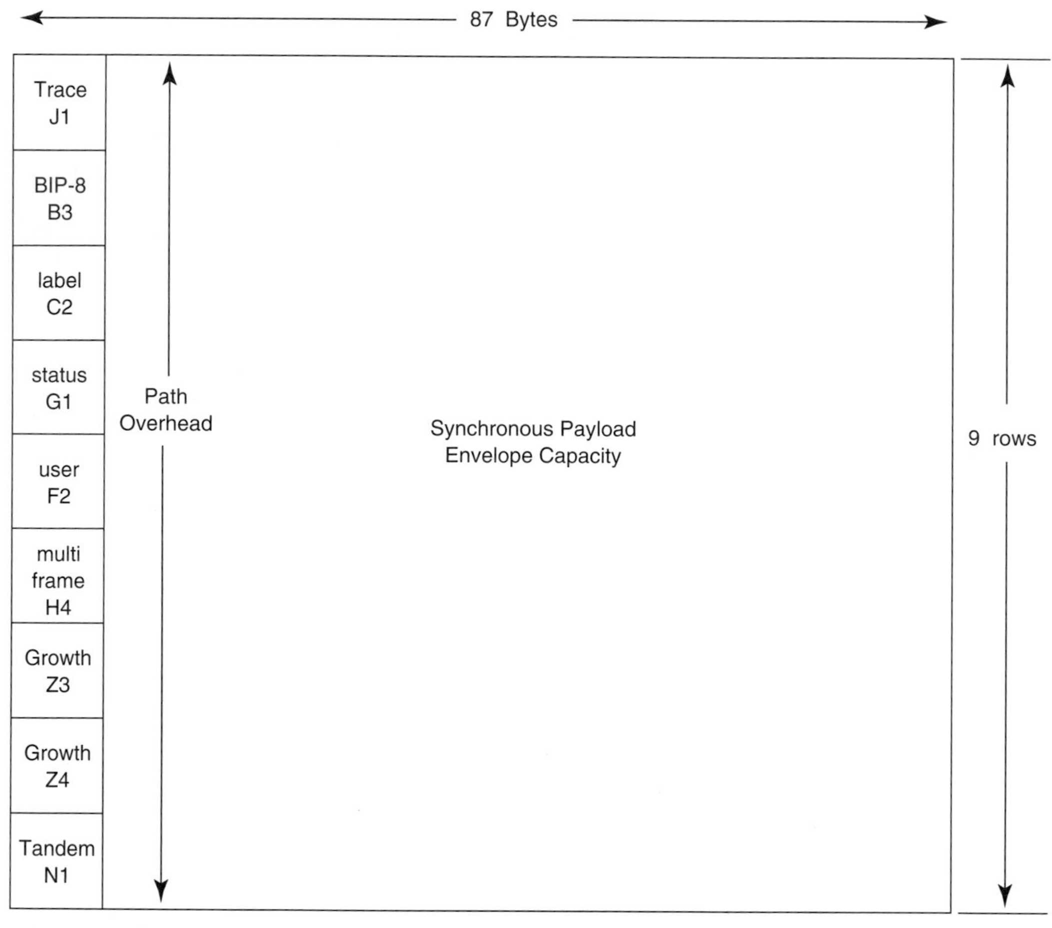

Figure 2–7 *SONET STS-1 Synchronous Payload Envelope (SONET Path Signal)*

For compatibility with SDH and to minimize overhead, an STS-3c SPE only includes one set of path overhead bytes, as shown in Figure 2–9. In SDH, this signal is known as VC-4. The *N* in STS-*Nc* signals is restricted to 3*X* where *X* = 1, 4, 16, 64, resulting in STS-3c, STS-12c, STS-48c, and STS-192c SPEs. In order to minimize the overhead, an STS-12c SPE is built by gluing together STS-3c SPEs, rather than STS-1 SPEs. In SDH, VC-4s are concatenated and the notation VC-4-Xc is used, where *X* = 4, 16, or 64. SDH does not support contiguous concatenation of VC-3s. Different types of concatenation are described in the next chapter.

The payload capacity of an STS-3c SPE can be calculated as follows. There are 260 usable columns (3 × 87 columns in the SPE, less 1 overhead

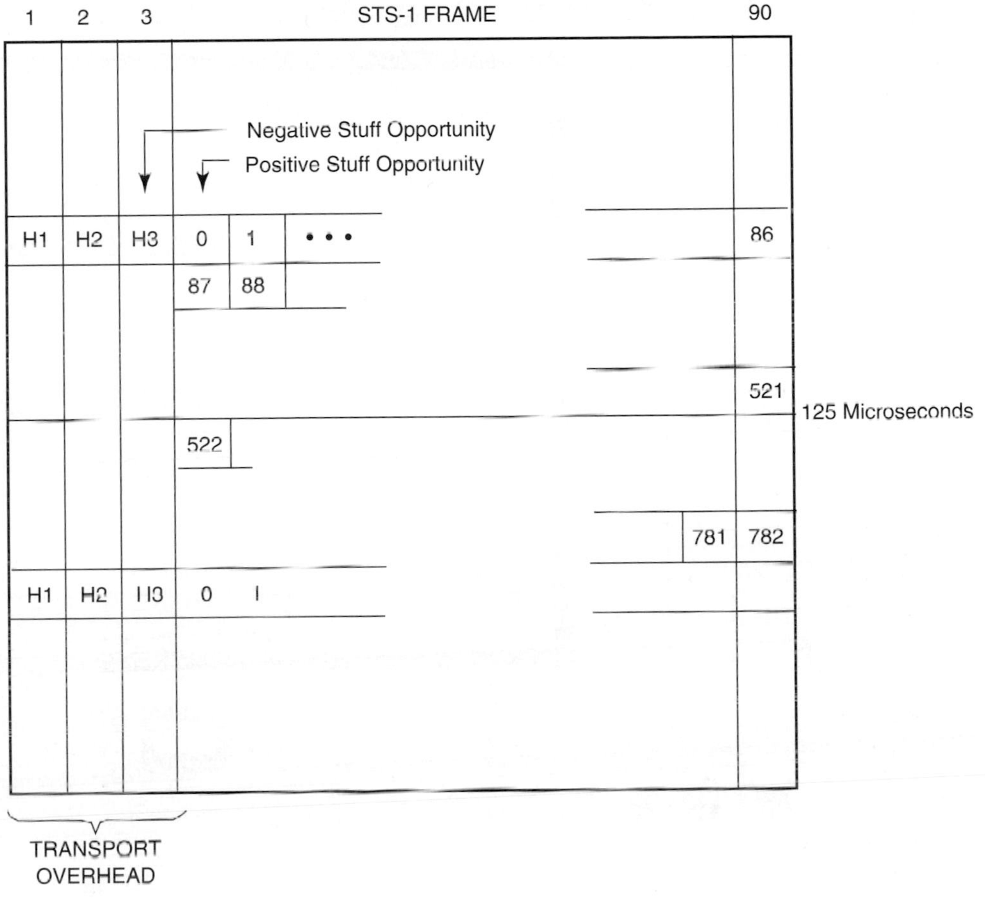

Figure 2–8 *Pointer Offset Counting Used to Locate the STS-1 SPE within an STS-1 Frame (from [ANSI95a])*

column). With 9 bytes per column, 8 bits per byte and at the rate of 8000 frames per second, the net capacity is 149.76 Mbps.

2.3.2.2 SMALLER PAYLOAD ENVELOPES (CONTAINERS)

To efficiently handle payloads smaller than the STS-1 SPE, SONET introduces a new set of SPEs called *Virtual Tributaries* (VTs). In SDH, these are known as *Lower-Order Virtual Containers* (LOVCs). Figures 2–10 through 2–12 depict the essential frame structure of SONET VT1.5 (SDH VC-11), VT2 (SDH VC-12), VT3 (no SDH equivalent), and VT6 (SDH VC-2) signals.

Since each byte in the VT structure provides 64 Kbps for transport (payload or overhead), the bit rates of VT1.5, VT2, VT3, and VT6 SPEs are as

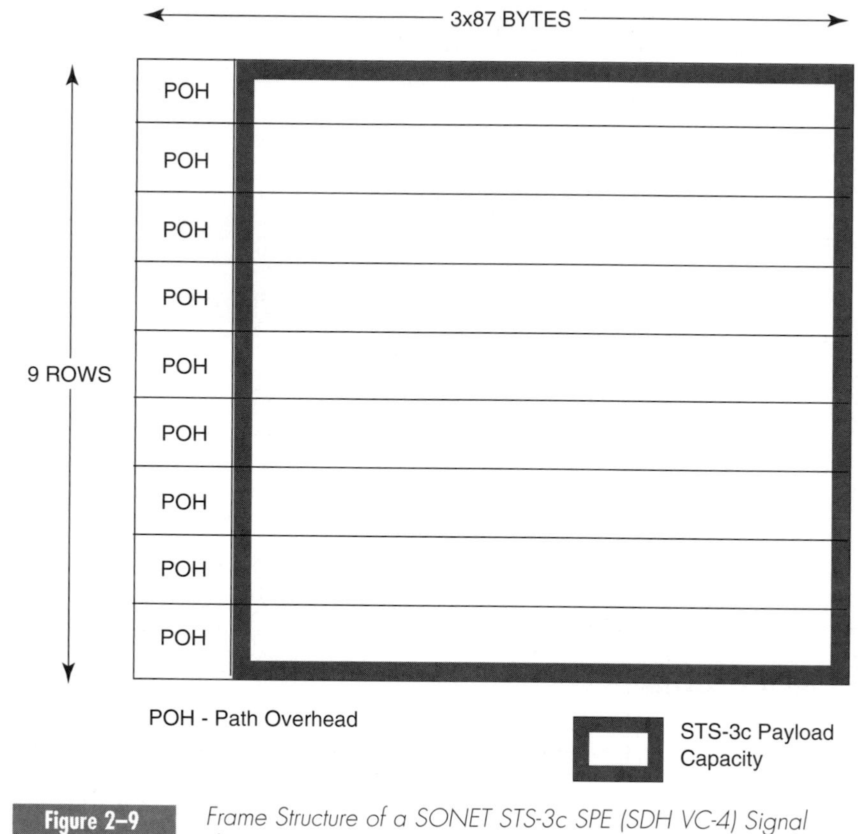

Figure 2–9 *Frame Structure of a SONET STS-3c SPE (SDH VC-4) Signal (from [ANSI95a])*

follows: VT1.5: 27 × 64 Kbps = 1.728 Mbps, VT2: 36 × 64 Kbps = 2.304 Mbps, VT3: 54 × 64 Kbps = 3.456 Mbps, and VT6: 108 × 64 Kbps = 6.912 Mbps.

The first byte of each of these SONET VTs (SDH lower-order VCs) is allocated to a pointer, which is used to locate the beginning of the VT-level SPE. This SPE includes one byte of overhead. Note that the pointer byte is a separate byte from the overhead byte of the SPE (as shown in Figures 2–10 through 2–12).

It can be verified that the SONET VT1.5 (SDH VC-11) and VT2 (SDH VC-12) signals can efficiently accommodate the T1 and E1 signals, respectively. Recall that a T1 frame consists of 24 bytes for payload and 1 bit for framing and overhead. The VT1.5 structure consists of 27 bytes, of which 2 are used for overhead purposes. This leaves 25 bytes for carrying the T1 signal. Note that both the SONET and the T1 frames repeat every 125 μs. Thus, not surprisingly, we have a near perfect fit! For the E1 signal, we have a 32-byte frame repeating every 125 μs. The VT2 structure has 36 bytes, of which 2 are used for overhead purposes. This leaves 34 bytes to accommodate the E1 signal.

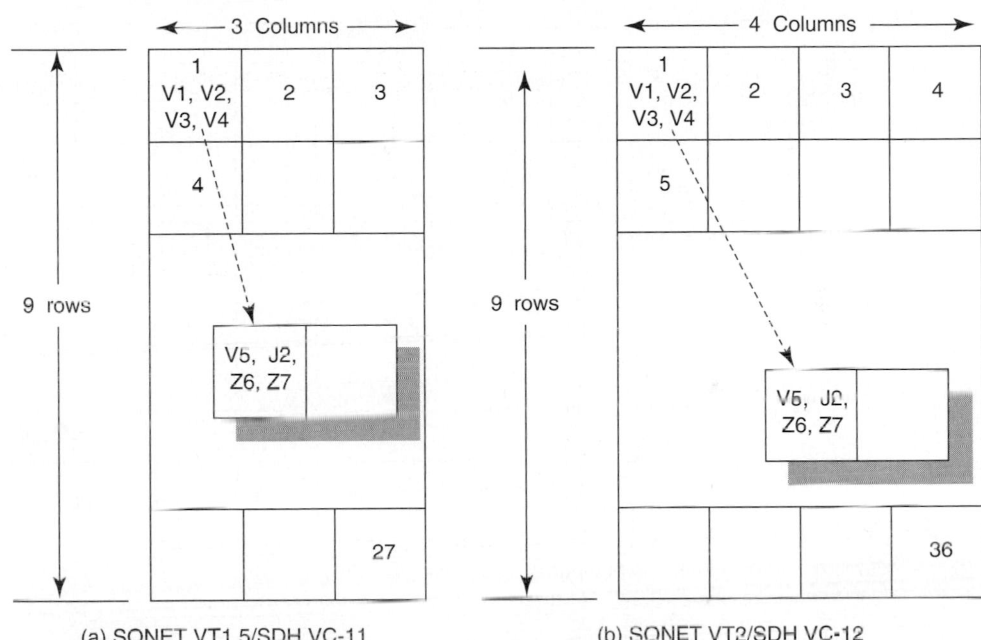

Figure 2–10 *SONET Virtual Tributaries/SDH Virtual Containers*

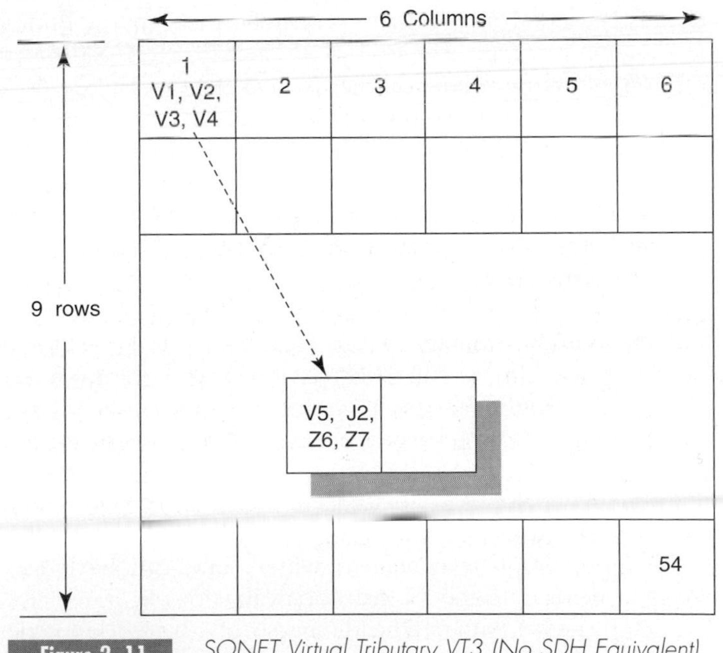

Figure 2–11 *SONET Virtual Tributary VT3 (No SDH Equivalent)*

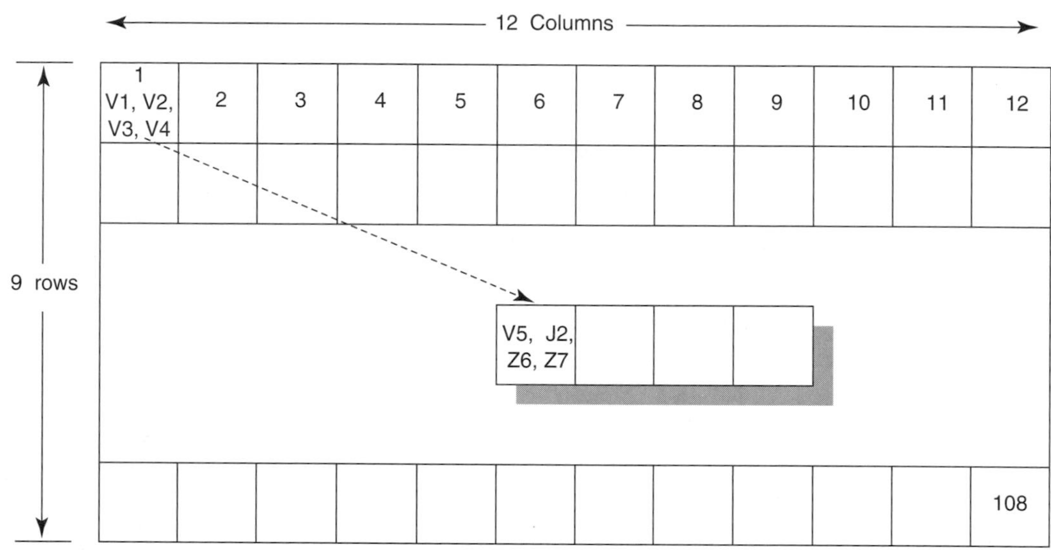

Figure 2–12 *SONET Virtual Tributary VT6 / SDH Virtual Container VC-2*

To realize pointer and maintenance functions efficiently for these lower rate signals, a multiframe structure analogous to those used with E1 and T1 signals is used. This multiframe consists of four normal frames, and therefore its duration is 500 μs. The H4 byte in the STS-1 SPE path overhead keeps track of the multiframe sequence, that is, counts from 1 to 4.

This bit of extra complexity is needed to reduce the amount of overhead in these lower rate signals. Hence, in the figures, the payload pointer bytes, V1–V4, share a single byte of overhead and so do the VT path overhead bytes V5, J2, Z6, and Z7. Note the similarity to the STS-1 structure in which fixed pointer bytes (V1-V4) point to the beginning of a floating payload.

To summarize,

- Virtual tributary (VT) is a structure designed for the transport and switching of sub-STS-1 payloads. The pointer bytes V1, V2, V3, and V4 (in the 500 μs superframe) are part of the VT signal. (This is analogous to the pointer bytes in the line overhead pointing to the start of the path SPE.)
- A VT SPE is a 500 μs frame structure carried within a VT. It is composed of VT path overhead (POH) and bandwidth for payload. The envelope is contained within, and can have any alignment with respect to the VT envelope capacity.
- The VT path overhead consists of 4 bytes, denoted as V5, J2, Z6, and Z7. These bytes are used for control communication between the

origination and the termination point of the VT SPE. These four bytes are part of the VT SPE, and they are separate from the VT pointer.

2.3.3 Synchronous Multiplexing

2.3.3.1 THE SONET MULTIPLEX HIERARCHY

The overall SONET multiplexing hierarchy is shown in Figure 2–13. The Virtual Tributaries, VT1.5, VT2, VT3, and VT6, are not just dropped into an STS-1 SPE. There are some specific structuring and interleaving rules that must be obeyed. The first is that VTs of similar types are grouped together into a common size "block" known as a *VT group* (VTG). The size of a VTG is the least common multiple of the size of all the VTs, that is, 12 columns by 9 rows (see Figures 2–10–2–12). Hence, a VTG can accommodate 4 VT1.5, 3 VT2, 2 VT3, or 1 VT6, but VT types cannot be mixed within a VTG. In addition, the columns of the VTs that form a VT group are interleaved and the VTGs within an STS SPE are themselves column-interleaved. The net effect of all this interleaving, once again, is to minimize the need for buffering when multiplexing fixed bit rate channels together. The interleaving and placement rules are precisely defined in [ANSI95a] and are not described here further.

We can verify that seven VTGs can be transported within an STS-1 SPE as follows. The STS-1 SPE, shown in Figure 2–7, consists of 9 rows by 87 columns of bytes. One of these columns is devoted to STS-1 path overhead, leaving 86 columns by 9 rows of envelope capacity. Since VTGs are 12 columns wide, we see that seven VTGs (requiring 84 columns) can be accommodated. The remaining 2 columns are referred to as *fixed stuff* and are placed at column positions 30 and 59 within the STS-1 SPE.

Note the restrictions on the usage of the VTG. As soon as, say, one VT1.5 is placed in a VTG, that VTG can only carry VT1.5s. In addition, once an STS-1 SPE is used to transport VTs then the entire STS-1 SPE is structured in

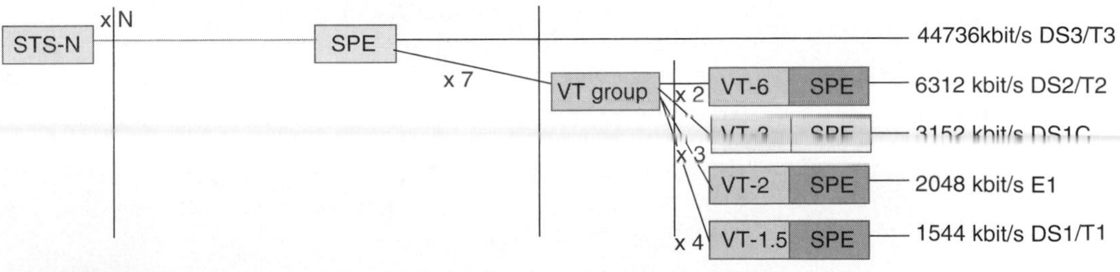

Figure 2–13 *SONET Multiplexing Hierarchy (Not Including Concatenated Signals)*

terms of VTGs. Such restrictions have an impact on the efficiency and the complexity of algorithms used for computing connection paths in a SONET network (see Chapter 11).

Due to the convenience of multiplexing and switching within the SONET signal hierarchy, interfaces (signals) have been defined specifically for the transport of VT-1.5 and VTG structures [ANSI96a]. A corresponding set of interfaces for the TU-12 and TUG-2 structures (see below), albeit a bit more general, has also been defined for SDH [ITU-T99a].

2.3.3.2 THE SDH MULTIPLEX HIERARCHY

Figure 2–14 depicts the SDH multiplex hierarchy. Table 2–1 lists the correspondence between SONET and SDH terminology. In the following, the SDH structure is described with a little more detail than what is apparent from Figure 2–14 or Table 2–1.

From Table 2–1, we see that SDH virtual containers VC-3 and VC-4 are equivalent to SONET STS-1 and STS-3c path signals, respectively. The SONET line layer pointers aid the multiplexing of SONET paths. In SDH, the higher-order virtual containers (VC-3 and VC-4) are grouped with their pointers into what are called *administrative units* (AU-3 and AU-4).

The situation is similar with the lower-order SDH virtual containers, VC-11, VC-12, and VC-2, which are equivalent to the SONET VT1.5, VT2, and

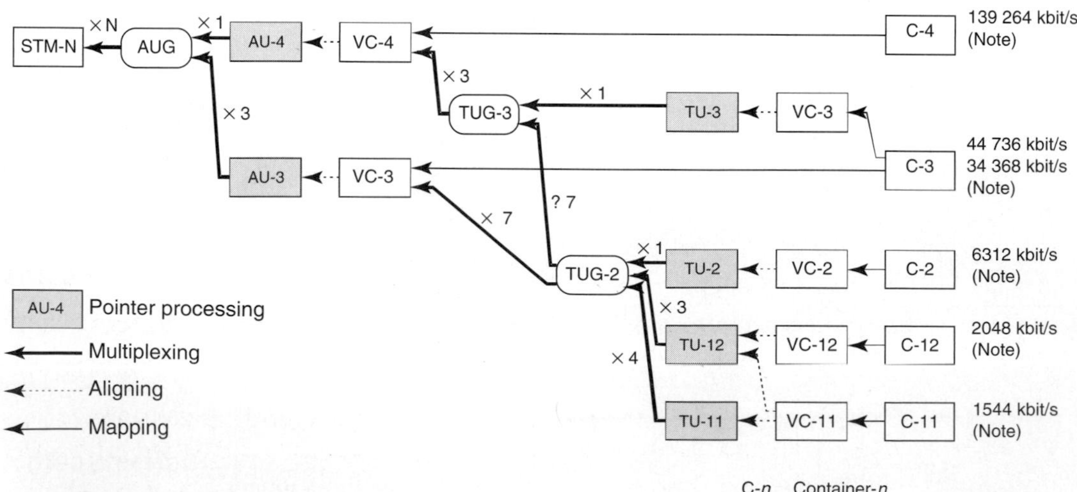

Figure 2–14 *SDH Multiplexing Hierarchy (Not Including Concatenated Signals, From [ITU-T00a])*

Table 2–1 *Correspondence between SONET and SDH Terminology*

SONET	SDH
Synchronous Transport Signal 3N (STS-3N)	Synchronous Transport Module N (STM-*N*)
SONET Section	Regenerator Section (RS)
SONET Line	Multiplex Section (MS)
STS Group (not really a SONET term)	Administrative Unit Group (AUG)
STS Channel (not really a SONET term)	Administrative Unit 3 (AU-3)
STS-3c Channel (not really a SONET term)	Administrative Unit 4 (AU-4)
STS-1 Path (i.e., STS SPE but without the fixed stuff in columns)	Virtual Container 3 (VC-3)
STS-3c Path (i.e., STS-3c SPE)	Virtual Container 4 (VC-4)
No SONET equivalent	Tributary Unit Group 3 (TUG-3)
No SONET equivalent	Tributary Unit 3 (TU-3)
VT Group	Tributary Unit Group 2 (TUG-2)
VT-1.5 Channel (not really a SOET term)	Tributary Unit 11 (TU-11)
VT-2 Channel (not really a SONET term)	Tributary Unit 12 (TU-12)
VT-3 Channel (not really a SONET term)	No SDH equivalent
VT-6 Channel (not really a SONET term)	Tributary Unit 2 (TU-2)
VT-1.5 Path	Virtual Container 11 (VC-11)
VT-2 Path	Virtual Container 12 (VC-12)
VT-3 Path	No SDH equivalent
VT-6 Path	Virtual Container 2 (VC-2)
VT1.5 payload capacity	Container 11 (C-11)
VT2 payload capacity	Container 12 (C-12)
VT3 payload capacity	No SDH equivalent
VT6 payload capacity	Container 2 (C-2)
STS-1 payload capacity	Container 3 (C-3)
STS-3c payload capacity	Container 4 (C-4)
STS-*N*c SPE N>3	VC-4-Xc (X=N/3)

VT6 path signals. In SONET, the VT pointers (V1–V4) were not considered part of the VT path nor were they part of the STS-1 SPE or VTG structure. SDH gives the association between the lower-order VCs and their pointers a nice name, *Tributary Unit* (TU). Specifically, TU-11, TU-12, and TU-2 are defined. There is no signal in SDH corresponding to the SONET VT3 path signal.

The *Tributary Unit Group-2* (TUG-2) is equivalent to the SONET Virtual Tributary Group (VTG), and it has the same multiplexing properties, that is, it contains one type of lower-order tributary unit. One interesting and important difference between SDH and SONET is that SDH allows direct multiplexing of lower-order VCs into a VC-4 (the equivalent of an STS-3c path signal). This is done via the TUG-3 structure for which there is no SONET equivalent. In addition, VC-3s can be mapped into an STM-1 in two different ways, either via AU-3s (just like SONET) or via TU-3 into a VC-4 (which has no SONET equivalent). Thus, some type of gateway equipment is required for SONET/SDH interworking, that is, the VC-3s are compatible but would need to be removed from the VC-4 and packaged via AU-3.

2.3.3.3 BYTE INTERLEAVING AND FREQUENCY COMPENSATION

As described in section 2.3.1, an STS-*N* signal consists of a set of *N* byte-interleaved STS-1 signals with some differences in the transport overhead usage. The older DS-3 signals were bit-interleaved, and thus one may wonder about the rationale for byte interleaving. Byte interleaving in fact has two advantages. First, it minimizes the buffer sizes needed when multiplexing signals together. Second, it minimizes the latency, that is, the absolute delay, of the signal as it runs through multiplexers and switches. This is because byte interleaving allows more parallelism in the processing of the signals in switches and multiplexers, that is, eight times faster as opposed to a serial bit interleaving approach.

So far we have not addressed the question of exactly what is meant by the term *synchronous* in SONET and SDH. Synchronous means that all network elements use essentially the same clock, that is, they are "synchronized." In particular this applies to the signals generated by a network element, that is, all signals generated by equipment in the network use a clock that is derived from a *primary reference source* (PRS). The PRS is an extremely accurate timing reference with a minimum long-term accuracy (percentage deviation) of $\pm 1 \times 10^{-11}$. This is also known as a *Stratum* 1 source. This does not mean that every piece of network equipment has a clock that is this accurate, but only that the local clock can be synchronized to a Stratum 1 source via a timing distribution system. Table 2–2 lists the various stratum levels of the clocks used in SONET [ANSI99a]. It should be noted that there are a number of other criteria used to specify the quality of a clock in addition to accuracy and holdover stability [ANSI96b, ANSI99a].

Two methods are used to distribute timing in a SONET network: Building Integrated Timing Supply (BITS) or line timing. BITS timing is distributed within a central office using either T1 or E1 signals. With line timing, a SONET (SDH) OC-*N* signal is used as a timing reference. Note that the holdover requirements for different stratum levels ensure clock accuracy even

Table 2–2 *SONET Clock Accuracy Levels*

Stratum Level	Minimum Long Term Accuracy	Holdover Stability
Stratum 1	$\pm 1 \times 10^{-11}$	Not Applicable
Stratum 2	$\pm 1.6 \times 10^{-8}$	1×10^{-10} per day in the first 24 hours of holdover
Stratum 3E	$\pm 4.6 \times 10^{-6}$	1×10^{-8} per day in the first 24 hours of holdover
Stratum 3	$\pm 4.6 \times 10^{-6}$	≤255 DS-1 slips in the 1st 24 hours of holdover
Stratum 4	$\pm 3.2 \times 10^{-5}$	None required

with short-term interruptions in the availability of a timing reference. The main driver for the need for accurate clocks in SONET/SDH comes from the need to carry existing *Plesiochronous Digital Hierarchy* (PDH) signals such as DS-1s, DS3s, E1s, E3s, and so on. Although PRS clocks are typically very expensive, reasonably priced systems that derive PRS quality reference from signals emitted by the Global Positioning System (GPS) are readily available.

Although the clocks in all the network elements are all synchronized to a Stratum 1 reference, this does not remove the variations between clocks. In fact, even Stratum 1 clocks can differ from each other. SONET and SDH handle these (small) differences via the pointer bytes H1–H3. We saw previously how 10 bits out of the H1 and H2 bytes were used to point to the beginning of a STS-1 SPE. Consider an STS-1 signal being multiplexed onto an STS-*N* signal. Suppose that the STS-1 SPE had been generated with a slightly slower clock than the one used to generate the STS-*N* signal. Then, there would come a time when there would not be data from the STS-1 SPE available for insertion in the appropriate place in the STS-*N* frame. SONET and SDH handle this situation in a nicely controlled manner. Prior to reaching the condition of data exhaustion, a "positive" pointer adjustment would be performed. That is, a dummy byte is inserted in the position that the STS-1 frame would normally have begun, and the corresponding pointer value is increased by one. Such an operation is shown in Figure 2–15. On the other hand, if the STS-1 SPE was generated faster, then there could be an overflow of a byte at some point in time. Once again, SONET and SDH cover this situation in a very nice way. Specifically, the H3 byte is used to accommodate this "extra byte" so that no data are lost. This is known as a "negative" pointer adjustment and "negative" stuff opportunity and is shown in Figure 2–16. The details of both these operations are described in reference [ANSI95a].

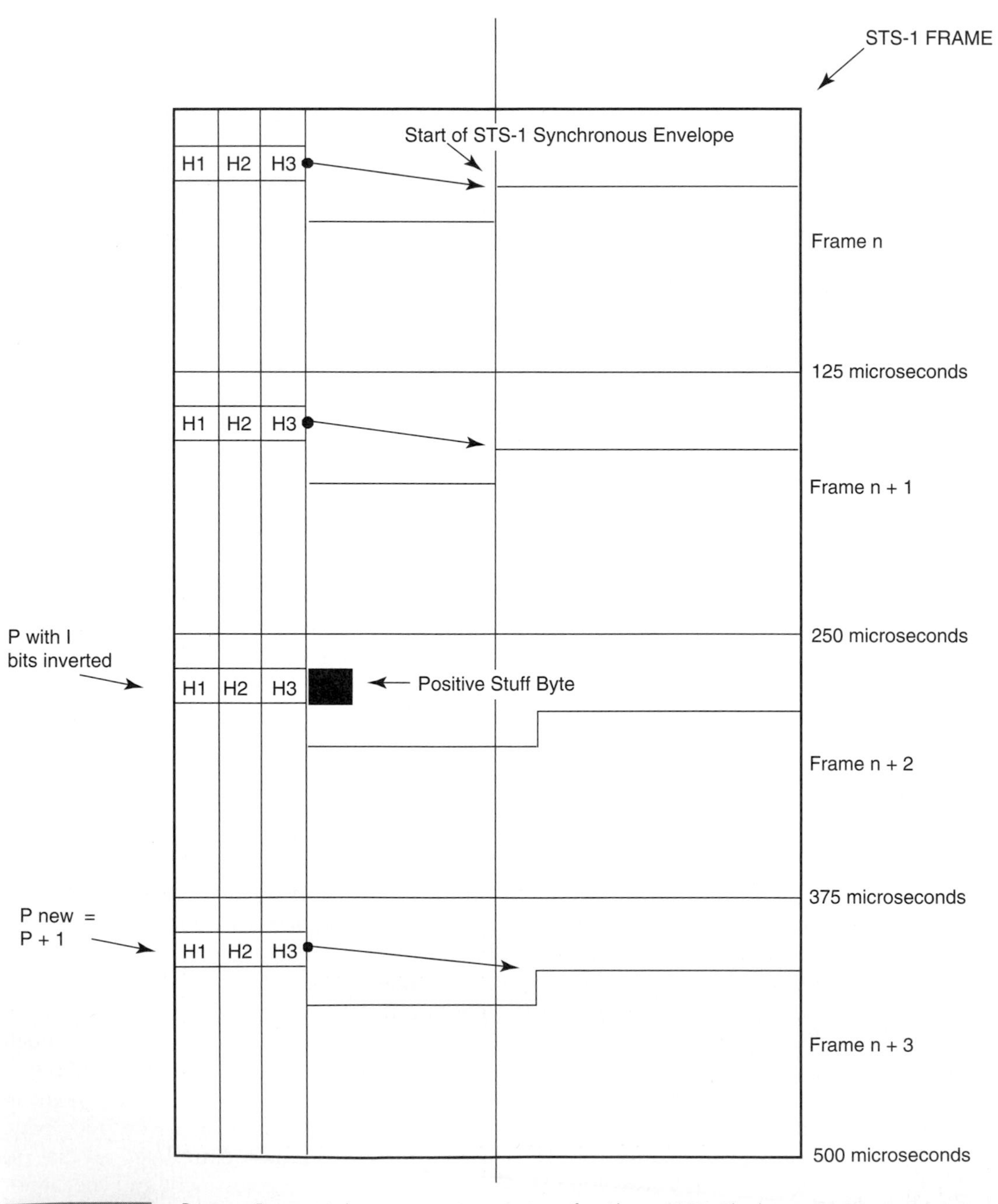

Figure 2–15 *Positive Pointer Adjustment to Compensate for Slower SPE Clock*

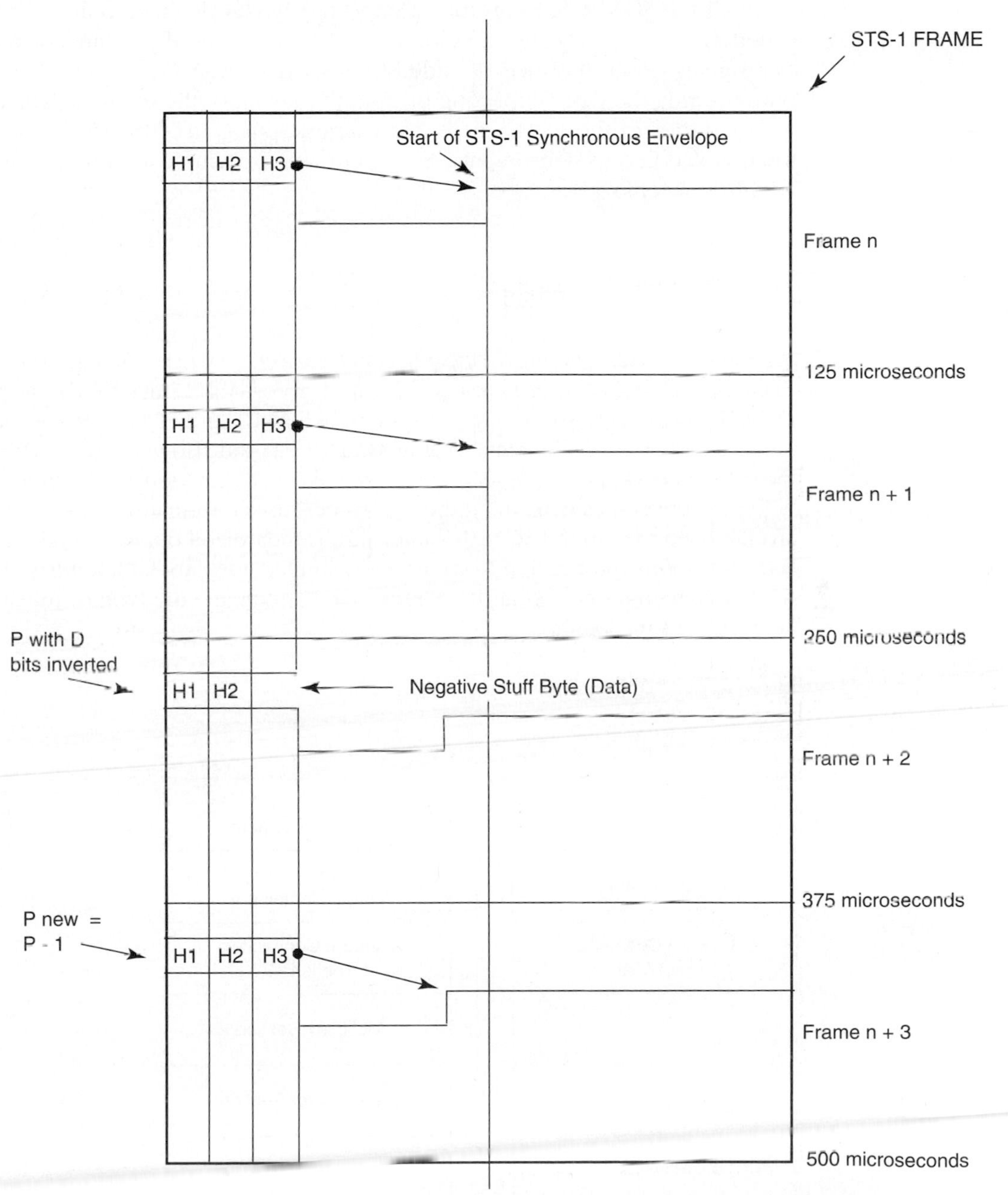

Figure 2–16 *Negative Pointer Adjustment to Compensate for Faster SPE Clock*

All the SONET SPEs, at the STS and the VT levels, have pointers associated with them. The same holds for SDH VCs. This allows any of these "subsignals" to be dropped or added to a SONET OC-*N* (SDH STM-M) without requiring the de-multiplexing or re-multiplexing of the entire signal. This is in contrast to the PDH where, for example, an entire DS-3 must be demultiplexed into its constituent DS-1s and then re-multiplexed for any signal addition or removal.

2.4 SONET/SDH Layering

Analogous to the layering models seen in packet networks [Stallings03], the TDM optical networks can also be layered according to the functions performed. Figure 2–17 shows layer diagrams of SONET and SDH, with the overhead usage and functionality illustrated. The VT path (lower-order VC) and the STS path (higher-order VC) level signals were previously described as being the envelopes containing the end-to-end user information. The physical layer is used to map the SONET frames into standardized optical signals. Each layer transports information from the layer immediately above it *transparently*, that is, without changing the content while adding some type of transport networking functionality.

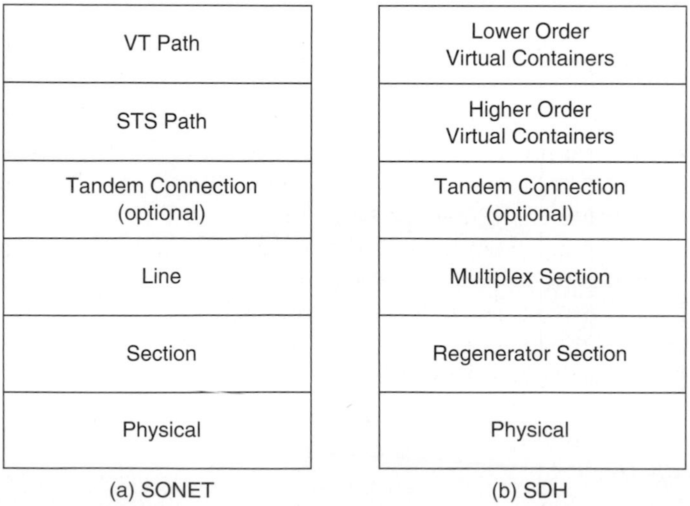

(a) SONET	(b) SDH
VT Path	Lower Order Virtual Containers
STS Path	Higher Order Virtual Containers
Tandem Connection (optional)	Tandem Connection (optional)
Line	Multiplex Section
Section	Regenerator Section
Physical	Physical

Figure 2–17 *SONET/SDH Layers*

2.4.1 The SONET Section (SDH Regenerator Section) Layer

Optical signals need to be regenerated after they have traversed a certain distance, which depends on a number of physical factors. This process can be applied to the signal amplitude (regenerate the signal), the signal's shape (reshaping), and timing (retiming). This is sometimes called *3R* regeneration, and this happens at the physical layer. The SONET section layer is concerned with framing (A1 and A2 bytes) and scrambling. Since both these functions are key to re-timing, the section layer is closely coupled to the physical layer. The section layer, however, adds significant functionality to these basic regenerator functions in the form of error monitoring (B1 byte), a data communications channel (D1-D3 bytes), a signal trace (J0 byte), a user channel (F1 byte), and a local order-wire (E1) (see Figure 2–5).

These functions were incorporated into SONET to support regenerator equipment. Thus, the SDH terminology for this is *regenerator section* layer. As an example, suppose there is a long-haul fiber optic link, which requires the use of 3R regenerators. Then, the SONET section layer allows the performance (*Bit Error Rate*—BER) to be monitored on the segments between successive regenerators; the data communication channel permits communications with regenerator equipment for control and management purposes (see Chapter 6); the section trace (J0) feature aids in neighbor discovery and port connectivity verification (see Chapter 6); and the local order-wire can be used to furnish basic telephony communications at regenerator equipment sites. Equipment that terminates SONET section layer overhead is called *Section Terminating Equipment* (STE).

2.4.1.1 SCRAMBLING

Given an STS-*N* (or the corresponding SDH STM signal), all the A1, A2, J0/Z0 bytes are transported without modification. All the other bytes, both payload and overhead, are subject to "scrambling." The framing bytes are sent without being scrambled so that the beginning of the frame can be easily delimited. Scrambling the rest of the frame prevents the unintentional introduction of the framing pattern of *N* A1s and A2s anywhere else into the frame (which could lead to the receiver becoming misaligned). Misalignment is called a *Loss of Frame* (LOF) condition, and it results in the loss of all data within the SONET/SDH signal. Another reason for scrambling is to maintain an adequate number of bit transitions. This enables clock recovery at the receiver. Inability to recover the signal timing at the receiver is one cause of the *Loss of Signal* (LOS) condition, which results in all the data in the signal being lost.

At SONET rates, scrambling is done in hardware with a simple circuit that (bit-wise) adds a pseudorandom bit sequence to all the bits in the frame (with the exceptions noted above). At the receiving end, the same pseudorandom sequence is (bit-wise) "subtracted" from the signal. The pseudorandom sequence has nice "randomness" properties, but it actually repeats (if it did not repeat, the transmitter's and the receiver's scramblers cannot be synchronized). These types of sequences and the circuits to produce them are typically studied in texts on spread-spectrum communication [Holmes82, Sklar88]. In SONET/SDH, the scrambler's bit sequence repeats every 127 bits and is restarted at the beginning of every frame.

We can determine the number of payload bytes that pass until the scrambler sequence repeats. This is in fact 16 bytes ($\lceil 127 \text{ bits} / 8 \text{ bits per byte} \rceil = 16$). Is it possible to inject a false framing pattern in a VT structured STS-1? Due to the byte interleaving of VTGs and VTs in an STS-1, this would only be possible with synchronized coordination across multiple VTs and VTGs. Thus, this is highly unlikely. Is it possible to inject (willfully and maliciously) a false framing pattern in an STS-*N*c carrying a data payload? Unfortunately, in early versions of Packet over SONET, this was possible. We will see how this problem was addressed in the next chapter.

One method of generating a pseudorandom bit sequence is by using a sequence of shift registers and binary adders (XOR gates). Such a circuit to generate the section layer scrambling sequence is shown in Figure 2–18. The bits (the D flip-flops shown) are reset to 1 at the beginning of the SONET/SDH frame. With every clock tick they are shifted right one position. Assuming the input data stream is all zeros, 256 bits of the output stream are:

11111110000001000001100001010001111001000101100111010100111110
10000111000100100110110101101111011000110100101110111001100101
01011111110000001000001100001010001111001000101100111010100111
11010000111000100100110110101101111011000110100101110111001100
10101011.

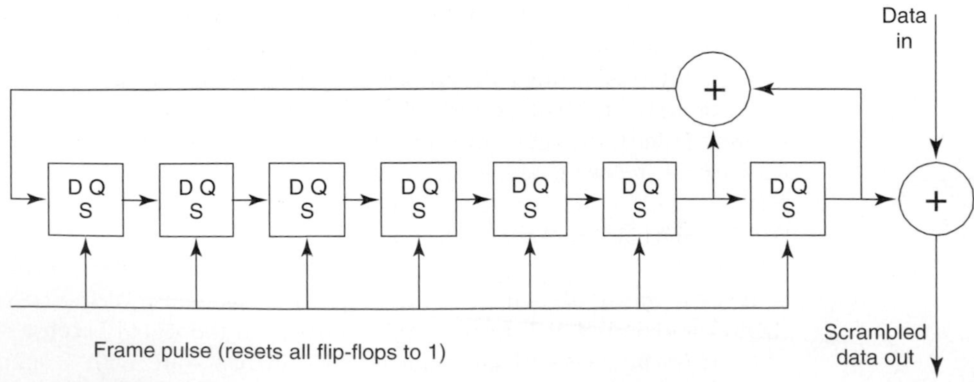

Figure 2–18 *SONET Section Scrambler Circuit (Clock Lines Not Shown)*

It can be verified that this sequence is 127 bits long, and it repeats (beginning with 1111111).

2.4.2 The SONET Line (SDH Multiplex Section) Layer

The SONET *line (SDH multiplex section)* layer provides error monitoring (B2 byte) capability, a data communications channel (bytes D4-D12) with thrice the capacity of the section layer DCC, and an order-wire (E2 byte) capability (see Figure 2–5). The main purpose of the SONET line layer, however, is to provide multiplexing and synchronization support for STS path signals (SDH VC-3s and VC-4s). The pointer bytes (H1, H2, and H3) in the line overhead specify the location of the STS path signals within the payload and allow frequency compensation. Note that with concatenation, all the STS path signals contained within an STS-*N* do not need to be of the same size. For example, an STS-192 (OC-192) signal can support STS-1, STS-3c, STS-12c, and STS-48c paths all at the same time (depending on time slot availability). Because multiplexing is the key purpose of the SONET line layer, SDH chose to give this layer a bit more descriptive name, that is, the *multiplex section layer.*

In addition to the above essential capabilities, the line layer adds support for remote error indication (M0 byte), synchronization status messaging (S1 byte), and line automatic protection switching (APS) via the K1 and K2 bytes. Error monitoring, remote error indications, and alarms are discussed in the next chapter. Synchronization in SONET/SDH networks was covered in section 2.3.3.3, and APS is covered in Chapter 4.

2.4.3 The Tandem Connection Layer

The tandem connection layer is a very thin optional sublayer that allows the network, as opposed to the Path Termination Equipment (PTE), to monitor the health of one or more STS path signals, including concatenated signals [ANSI94a]. The N1 byte of the STS SPE (Figure 2–7) is allocated for this purpose. Four bits in this byte are used for error monitoring and the others are used to form a 32 Kbps path *data channel.* Although they share the same byte, the path data channel can be used independent of the bits being used for error monitoring.

2.4.4 The SONET Path (SDH Higher-Order Virtual Container) Layer

The SONET path layer is responsible for mapping payloads into a format convenient for multiplexing at the line layer. To this end, it provides some of the basic functionality of signal trace (J1 byte), error monitoring (B3) byte, and a user channel.

Since various signals can be mapped into a path layer payload, a byte of overhead is dedicated to the *path signal label* (byte C2). Table 2–3 gives a list of currently defined mappings.

Note that two of the most important protocols are not listed in Table 2–3: IP and Ethernet. As we will see in the next chapter, there do exist IP over SONET standards, and emerging standards for Ethernet and a number of other data communications protocols over SONET and SDH. The extended use of the signal label in these cases can ease interoperability and debugging, and could permit automatic configuration of PTE capable of processing multiple data protocols.

The frame structure of the STS-1 path signal was shown in Figure 2–7. In addition to error monitoring via the B3 byte, the path layer provides a mechanism for the terminating PTE to report the path termination status and performance (error rates) to the originating PTE. The *path status* byte G1 is used for this purpose.

When VT signals are multiplexed into an STS path signal, two bits from the *multiframe indicator* byte H4 are used to count from 0 to 3 repeatedly for each 125 μs SONET frame. This 500 μs repeating structure is the superframe discussed earlier. When the multiframe indicator is used in combination with VT pointers or overhead, it turns the one allocated byte of VT pointer per frame into 4 bytes of VT pointer per superframe.

2.4.5 The VT Path Layer

Before we discuss the VT path layer, we have to examine the VT pointer bytes V1 through V4. These occur as the first byte of the VT structures, as shown in Figures 2–10–2–12. The VT structures repeat four times within the superframe. Of these bytes, only V1–V3 are actually used. Also, all but 2 bits of the combined V1 and V2 bytes are dedicated to pointer values and operations, and the remaining 2 bits indicate the size of the VT.

How does the SONET VT processing hardware locate VTs within an STS SPE if the seven VTGs that comprise that SPE contain different types of VTs? In other words, how does the hardware know where the pointer bytes are located when the VT1.5, VT2, VT3, and VT6 all use a different number of columns? Recall that all VTGs are the same size regardless of the VTx flavor that they carry and that each VTG only contains only one type of VTx. Recall also that the VTxs within a VTG are column interleaved, that is, the first column of each of the VTxs within a VTG comes first, then the respective second columns, and so on. On top of this, all seven of the VTGs within the STS SPE are also column interleaved. This means that the first column from each of the VTGs occur sequentially within the STS SPE (after the path overhead column). The first byte contains the pointer bytes V1-V4, which also include the information on the size of the VT. Thus, the size of the VTxs within all the VTGs are known as soon as the first 7 bytes (following the first path overhead

Table 2–3 *Payload Types Specified by the Signal Label Byte C2*

Code (in hex)	Payload Type
0x00	Unequipped (i.e., no path originating equipment)
0x01	Equipped, nonspecific (this can always be used)
0x02	Floating VT mode
0x04	Asynchronous mapping for DS3
0x12	Asynchronous mapping for 139.264Mbps
0x13	Mapping for ATM
0x14	Mapping for DQDB
0x15	Mapping for FDDI
0x16	PPP mapping with x^43+1 scrambling, RFC2615 [Malis+99]
0xCF	PPP mapping without scrambling, RFC1619 [Simpson94]

byte) are received. From this information, the pointer bytes for the rest of the VTxs can be located within each of the VTGs.

Of the four VT path overhead bytes, V5, J2, Z6, and Z7, only V5, J2, and 3 bits of Z7 have been specified so far. The eight bits constituting the V5 byte are used to provide the following functions: error performance monitoring (2 bits), a VT path remote error indication (1 bit), a path signal label (3 bits), and a path remote defect indication (1 bit, plus 3 bits from Z7).

2.4.6 Transparency

The layered model shown in Figure 2–17 is accompanied by the notion of *transparent* transport. That is, a lower layer treats the signal of the layer immediately above it as payload, and transports it without modification. In addition, different optical network elements may operate in different layers. A network element is said to be Section-, Line-, Tandem-, Connection-, or Path-terminating if it receives and processes the signal and the overhead at that layer, all layers below, and none above it (Figure 2–19). For example, the term Section Terminating Equipment (STE) denotes a network element that terminates and processes the physical and section layers of a SONET signal, but does not modify the line or path layers in any way. We have similar definitions for Line Terminating Equipment (LTE), Tandem Connection Terminating Equipment (TCTE), and Path Terminating Equipment (PTE). A PTE could be an STS PTE, a VT PTE or both, depending on the signals terminated.

Let us consider the following optical networking equipment and determine the SONET layer in which they operate: (a) a WDM system with OC-192 short reach interfaces, (b) an IP router with OC-48 or any OC-*N* interface,

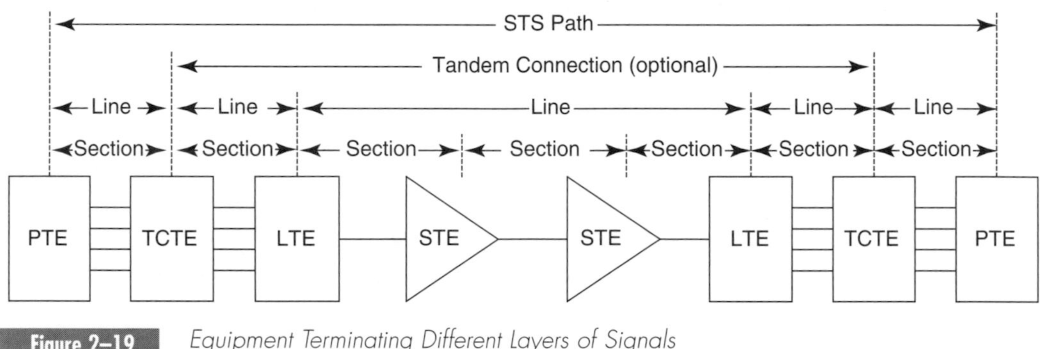

Figure 2–19 *Equipment Terminating Different Layers of Signals*

(c) an STS-level digital cross connect (called OXC, see Chapter 1), and (d) a T1 multiplexer with an OC-3 up link.

A WDM system with a SONET short reach interface on it will at least be terminating and regenerating the signal at the physical layer. It could provide section overhead functionality, if desired. However, since WDM systems came into existence after section level regenerators and there was a desire not to interfere with section layer communication and monitoring, most WDM systems do not perform STE functions.

An IP router with a SONET OC-*N* interface must be a PTE, since one of its functions is to pack IP packets into SONET STS paths. Note that many routers use a concatenated path signal of the same size as the SONET line, for example, an STS-48c path signal carried by an OC-48 optical signal. One might be tempted to say that in this case that the router uses the whole optical wavelength and hence requires a "lambda" (an entire wavelength) from the optical network. But this is not true! The router only requires that the path layer signal be transported transparently. The service it receives from the optical network does not change if the STS-48c path is later multiplexed with other STS-48c paths onto an OC-192 for efficient transport across the optical network.

An STS level OXC is a SONET path switch that can switch STS-1 and STS-*N*c path signals but not VT level signals. In addition, such a switch does not alter the STS path signals in anyway. Note that this does not mean a switch of this type is not allowed to monitor path overhead, if it has the capability to do so. The act of switching STS paths from one SONET line to another requires de-multiplexing and re-multiplexing of STS paths onto SONET lines. Hence, the switch must terminate the SONET line overhead. In particular, it will have to rewrite the pointer bytes on egress. This cross-connect is a thus a SONET LTE.

A T1 multiplexer, by definition, has to take T1 (DS-1) signals and map them into VT1.5 paths, which then get packed into a VTG. The VTG is in turn packed into an STS-1 SPE, which is then carried in an OC-*N*. Hence, this equipment is a VT PTE. Note that it is also an STS PTE.

The SONET and SDH overhead bytes support different types of fault, performance and maintenance functionality. This does not mean, however, that all of this functionality must be implemented, present, and/or used in every deployment. Guidance on this comes from the standards with the notions of *drop-side* and *line-side* interfaces. A drop-side interface is an interface used for an intraoffice link. A line-side interface is one that is used for an interoffice link (i.e., between network elements). As an extreme example, consider the line order-wire capability (byte E2) for voice telephony communications between two LTEs. This capability is not meant for use over a drop side interface, for instance, to let two people within the same office communicate. The ANSI SONET standard [ANSI95a], in some cases, seems to rule out too much functionality on drop-side interfaces. For example, the section trace (J0), section DCC (D1-D3), and line DCC (D4-D12) are considered not applicable on the drop side. All these are methods provided by SONET for *in-fiber* communications between neighboring NEs, and they are essential for implementing neighbor discovery and port connectivity verification (see Chapter 6). Prohibiting these on the drop side may not have mattered when relatively few fibers were found in a central office. But with hundreds or thousands of fibers expected to terminate on new generation equipment, these capabilities become very important even on the drop side.

We continue our discussion of SONET and SDH in the next chapter, where we describe some of the more advanced features and recent additions to SONET/SDH for handling data traffic efficiently.

T H R E E

SONET and SDH: Advanced Topics

3.1 Introduction

In the previous chapter, we described TDM and how it has been utilized in SONET and SDH standards. We noted that when SONET and SDH were developed, they were optimized for carrying voice traffic. At that time no one anticipated the tremendous growth in data traffic that would arise due to the Internet phenomenon. Today, the volume of data traffic has surpassed voice traffic in most networks, and it is still growing at a steady pace. In order to handle data traffic efficiently, a number of new features have been added to SONET and SDH.

In this chapter, we review some of the advanced features of SONET and SDH. Specifically, we describe the different ways of concatenating SONET and SDH signals, and different techniques for mapping packet data onto SONET and SDH connections. We also address transparency services for carrier's carrier applications, as well as fault management and performance monitoring capabilities. The subject matter covered in this chapter will be used as a reference when we discuss optical control plane issues in later chapters. A rigorous understanding of this material, however, is not a prerequisite for dealing with the control plane topics.

3.2 All about Concatenation

Three types of concatenation schemes are possible under SONET and SDH. These are:

- Standard contiguous concatenation
- Arbitrary contiguous concatenation
- Virtual concatenation

These concatenation schemes are described in detail next.

3.2.1 Standard Contiguous Concatenation in SONET and SDH

SONET and SDH networks support *contiguous concatenation* whereby a few standardized "concatenated" signals are defined, and each concatenated signal is transported as a single entity across the network [ANSI95a, ITU-T00a]. This was described briefly in the previous chapter.

The concatenated signals are obtained by "gluing" together the payloads of the constituent signals, and they come in fixed sizes. In SONET, these are called STS-*N*c Synchronous Payload Envelopes (SPEs), where $N = 3X$ and X is restricted to the values 1, 4, 16, 64, or 256. In SDH, these are called VC-4 (equivalent to STS-3c SPE), and VC-4-*X*c where *X* is restricted to 1, 4, 16, 64, or 256.

The multiplexing procedures for SONET (SDH) introduce additional constraints on the location of component STS-1 SPEs (VC-4s) that comprise the STS-*N*c SPE (VC-4-*X*c). The rules for the placement of standard concatenated signals are [ANSI95a]:

1. Concatenation of three STS-1s within an STS-3c: The bytes from concatenated STS-1s shall be contiguous at the STS-3 level but shall not be contiguous when interleaved to higher-level signals. When STS-3c signals are multiplexed to a higher rate, each STS-3c shall be wholly contained within an STS-3 (i.e., occur only on tributary input boundaries 1–3, 4–6, 7–9, etc.). This rule does not apply to SDH.
2. Concatenation of STS-1s within an STS-*N*c ($N = 3X$, where $X = 1$, 4, 16, 64, or 256). Such concatenation shall treat STS-*N*c signals as a single entity. The bytes from concatenated STS-1s shall be contiguous at the STS-*N* level, but shall not be contiguous when multiplexed on to higher-level signals. This also applies to SDH, where the SDH term for an STS-*N*c is an AU-4-*X*c where $X = N/3$.
3. When the STS-*N*c signals are multiplexed to a higher rate, these signals shall be wholly contained within STS-M boundaries, where M could be 3, 12, 48, 192, or 768, and its value must be the closest to, but greater than or equal to *N* (e.g., if $N = 12$, then the STS-12c must occur only on boundaries 1–12, 13–24, 25–36, etc.). In addition to being contained within STS-*M* boundaries, all STS-*N*c signals must begin on STS-3 boundaries.

The primary purpose of these rules is to ease the development burden for hardware designers, but they can seriously affect the bandwidth efficiency of SONET/SDH links.

In Figure 3–1(a), an STM-16 (OC-48) signal is represented as a set of 16 time slots, each of which can contain a VC-4 (STS-3c SPE). Let us examine the

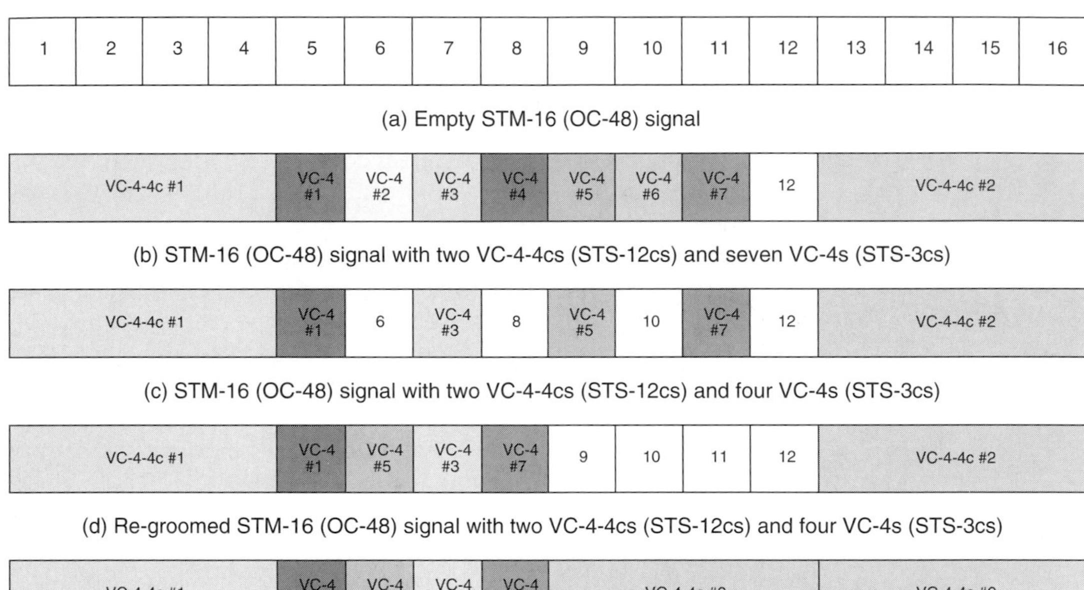

Figure 3–1 *Timeslot Constraints and Regrooming with Contiguous (Standard) Concatenation*

placement of VC-4 and VC-4-4c (STS-3*c* and STS-12c SPE) signals into this structure, in line with the rules above. In particular a VC-4-4c (STS-12c SPE) must start on boundaries of 4. Figure 3–1(b) depicts how the STM-16 has been filled with two VC-4-4c (STS-12c) and seven VC-4 signals. In Figure 3–1(c), three of the VC-4s have been removed, that is, are no longer in use. Due to the placement restrictions, however, a VC 4-4c cannot be accommodated in this space. In Figure 3–1(d), the STM-16 has been "regroomed," that is, VC-4 #5 and VC-4 #7 have been moved to new timeslots. Figure 3–1(e) shows how the third VC-4-4c is accommodated.

3.2.2 Arbitrary Concatenation

In the above example, a "regrooming" operation was performed to make room for a signal that could not be accommodated with the standard contiguous concatenation rules. The problem with regrooming is that it is service impacting, that is, service is lost while the regrooming operation is in progress. Because service impacts are extremely undesirable, regrooming is not frequently done, and the bandwidth is not utilized efficiently.

To get around these restrictions, some manufacturers of *framers*, that is, the hardware that processes the SDH multiplex section layer (SONET line layer), offer a capability known as "flexible" or arbitrary concatenation. With this capability, there are no restrictions on the size of an STS-*N*c (VC-4-*X*c) or the starting time slot used by the concatenated signal. Also, there are no constraints on adjacencies of the STS-1 (VC-4-*X*c) time slots used to carry it, that is, the signals can use any combination of available time slots. Figure 3–2 depicts how the sequence of signals carried over the STM-16 of Figure 3–1 can be accommodated without any regrooming, when the arbitrary concatenation capability is available.

3.2.3 Virtual Concatenation

As we saw earlier, arbitrary concatenation overcomes the bandwidth inefficiencies of standard contiguous concatenation by removing the restrictions on the number of components and their placement within a larger concatenated signal. Standard and arbitrary contiguous concatenation are services offered by the network, that is, the network equipment must support these capabilities. The ITU-T and the ANSI T1 committee have standardized an alternative, called *virtual concatenation*. With virtual concatenation, SONET and SDH PTEs can "glue" together the VCs or SPEs of separately transported fundamental signals. This is in contrast to requiring the network to carry signals as a single concatenated unit.

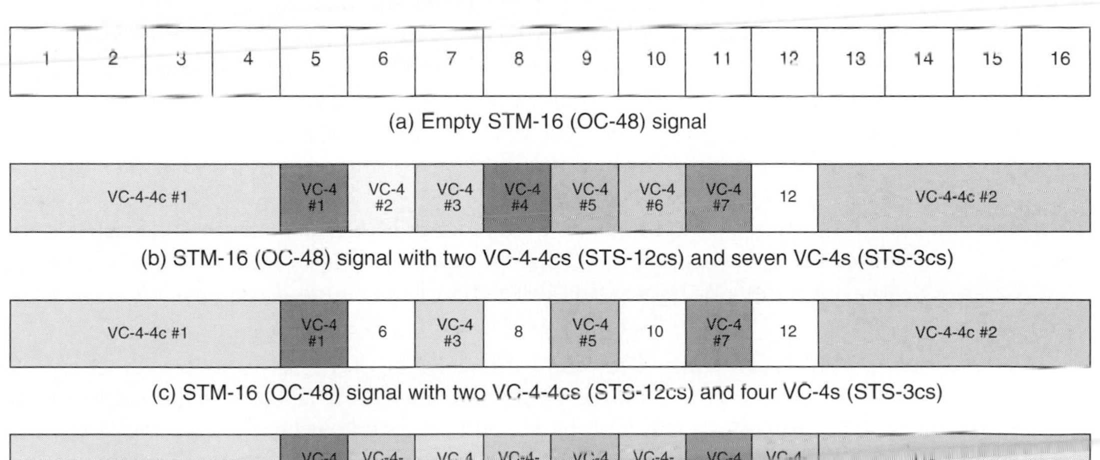

(a) Empty STM-16 (OC-48) signal

(b) STM-16 (OC-48) signal with two VC-4-4cs (STS-12cs) and seven VC-4s (STS-3cs)

(c) STM-16 (OC-48) signal with two VC-4-4cs (STS-12cs) and four VC-4s (STS-3cs)

(d) STM-16 (OC-48) signal with two VC-4-4cs (STS-12cs) and four VC-4s (STS-3cs) with arbitrary concatenation being used on VC-4-4c #3 to avoid regrooming

Figure 3–2 *Timeslot Usage with Arbitrary Concatenation*

3.2.3.1 HIGHER-ORDER VIRTUAL CONCATENATION (HOVC)

HOVC is realized under SONET and SDH by the PTEs, which combine either multiple STS-1/STS-3c SPEs (SONET), or VC-3/VC-4 (SDH). Recall that the VC-3 and STS-1 SPE signals are nearly identical except that a VC-3 does not contain the fixed stuff bytes found in columns 30 and 59 of an STS-1 SPE. A SONET STS-3c SPE is equivalent to a SDH VC-4.

These component signals, VC-3s or VC-4s (STS-1 SPEs or STS-3c SPEs), are transported separately through the network to an end system and must be reassembled. Since these signals can take different paths through the network, they may experience different propagation delays. In addition to this fixed differential delay between the component signals, there can also be a variable delay component that arises due to the different types of equipment processing the signals and the dynamics of the fiber itself. Note that heating and cooling effects can affect the propagation speed of light in a fiber, leading to actual measurable differences in propagation delay.

The process of mapping a concatenated container signal, that is, the raw data to be transported, into a virtually concatenated signal is shown in Figure 3–3. Specifically, at the transmitting side, the payload gets packed in *X* VC-4s just as if these were going to be contiguously concatenated. Now the question is, How do we identify the component signals and line them up appropriately given that delays for the components could be different?

The method used to align the components is based on the multiframe techniques described in Chapter 2. A jumbo (very long) multiframe is created by overloading the multiframe byte H4 in the path overhead. Bits 5–8 of the H4 byte are incremented in each 125μs frame to produce a multiframe consisting of 16 frames. In this case, bits 5–8 of H4 are known as the multiframe indicator 1 (MFI1). This multiframe will form the first stage of a two-stage multiframe. In particular, bits 1–4 of the H4 byte are used in a way that depends on the position in the first stage of the multiframe. This is shown in Table 3–1.

Within the 16-frame first stage multiframe, a second stage multiframe indicator (MFI2) is defined utilizing bits 1–4 of H4 in frames 0 and 1, giving a total of 8 bits per frame. It is instructive to examine the following:

1. How long in terms of the number of 125μs frames is the complete HOVC multiframe structure? Answer: The base frame (MFI1) is 16 frames long, and the second stage is $2^8 = 256$ frames long. Since this is a two-stage process, the lengths multiply giving a multiframe that is $16 \times 256 = 4096$ frames long.
2. What is the longest differential delay, that is, delay between components that can be compensated? Answer: The differential delay must be within the duration of the overall multiframe structure, that is, 125μS × 4096 = 512mS, that is, a little over half a second.

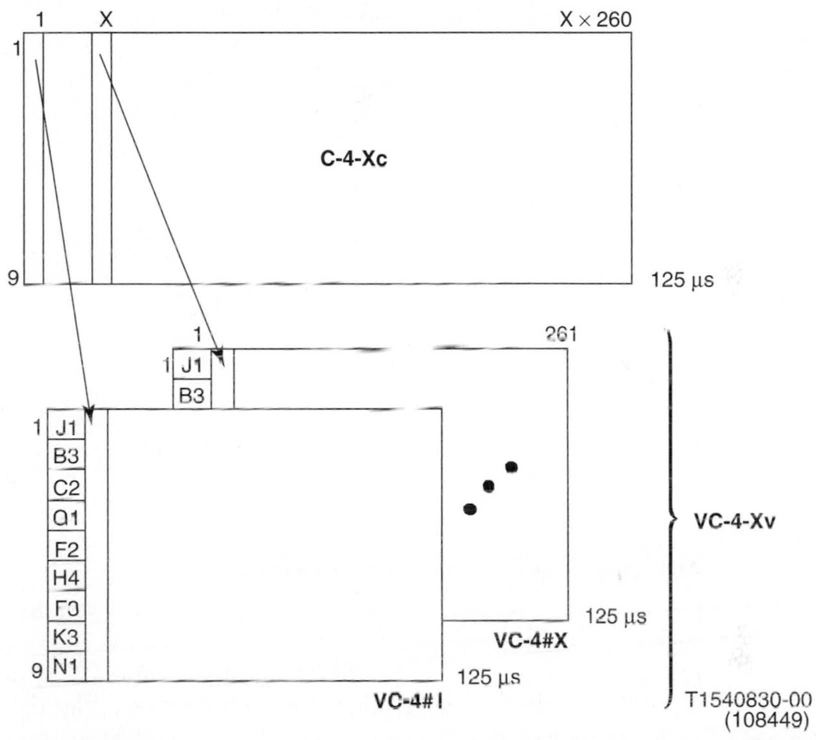

Figure 3–3 *Mapping a Higher Rate Payload in a Virtually Concatenated Signal (from [ITU-T00a])*

3. Suppose that an STS-1-2v is set up for carrying Ethernet traffic between San Francisco and New York such that one STS-1 goes via a satellite link and the other via conventional terrestrial fiber. Will this work? Answer: Assuming that a geo-synchronous satellite is used, then the satellite's altitude would be about 35775 km. Given that the

Table 3–1 *Use of Bits 1–4 in H4 Byte for First Stage Multiframe Indication (MFI1)*

Multi-Frame Indicator 1 (MFI1)	Meaning of Bits 1–4 in H4
0	2nd multiframe indicator MFI2 MSB (bits 1–4)
1	2nd multiframe indicator MFI2 LSB (bits 5–8)
2–13	Reserved (0000)
14	Sequence indicator SQ MSB (bits 1–4)
15	Sequence indicator SQ LSB (bits 5–8)

speed of light is 2.99792×10^8 m/sec, this leads to a round trip delay of about 239 ms. If the delay for the fiber route is 20 ms, then the differential delay is 209 ms, which is within the virtual concatenation range. Also, since the average circumference of the earth is only 40,000 km, this frame length should be adequate for the longest fiber routes.

Now, the receiver must be able to distinguish the different components of a virtually concatenated signal. This is accomplished as follows. In frames 14 and 15 of the first stage multiframe, bits 1–4 of H4 are used to give a sequence indicator (SQ). This is used to indicate the components (and not the position in the multiframe). Due to this 8-bit sequence indicator, up to 256 components can be accommodated in HOVC. Note that it is the receiver's job to compensate for the differential delay and to put the pieces back together in the proper order. The details of how this is done are dependent on the specific implementation.

3.2.3.2 LOWER-ORDER VIRTUAL CONCATENATION (LOVC)

The virtual concatenation of lower-order signals such as VT1.5s (VC-11), VT2 (VC-12), and so on are based on the same principles as described earlier. That is, a sequence number is needed to label the various components that make up the virtually concatenated signal, and a large multiframe structure is required for differential delay compensation. In the lower-order case, however, there are fewer overhead bits and bytes to spare so the implementation may seem a bit complex. Let us therefore start with the capabilities obtained.

LOVC Capabilities and Limitations • Table 3–2 lists the LOVC signals for SONET/SDH, the signals they can be contained in and the limits on the number of components that can be concatenated. The last two columns are really the most interesting since they show the range of capacities and the incremental steps of bandwidth.

LOVC Implementation • Let us first examine how the differential delay compensating multiframe is put together. This is done in three stages. Recall that the SONET VT overhead (lower-order SDH VC overhead) is defined in a 500 μs multiframe, as indicated in the path layer multiframe indicator H4. This makes available the four VT overhead bytes V5, J2, Z6, and Z7, from one SONET/SDH frame byte. Since a number of bits in these bytes are used for other purposes, an additional second stage of multiframe structure is used to define extended VT signal labels.

This works as follows (note that SDH calls the Z7 byte as K4 but uses it the same way): First of all, the V5 byte indicates if the extended signal label is being used. Bits 5 through 7 of V5 provide a VT signal label. The signal

Table 3–2 *Standardized LOVC Combinations and Limits*

Signal SONET/SDH	Carried in SONET/SDH	*X*	Capacity (kbit/s)	In steps of (kbit/s)
VT1.5-*X*v SPE/VC-11-Xv	STS-1/VC-3	1 to 28	1600 to 44800	1600
VT2-*X*v SPE/VC-12-Xv	STS-1/VC-3	1 to 21	2176 to 45696	2176
VT3-*X*v SPE	STS-1	1 to 14	3328 to 46592	3328
VT6-*X*v SPE/VC-2-Xv	STS-1/VC-3	1 to 7	6784 to 47448	6784
VT1.5/VC-11-*X*v	STS-3c	1 to 64	1600 to 102400	1600
VT2/VC-12-*X*v	STS-3c	1 to 63	2176 to 137088	2176
VT3-*X*v SPE	STS-3c	1 to 42	3328 to 139776	3328
VT6-*X*v SPE/VC-2-Xv	STS 3c	1 to 21	6784 to 142464	6784
VT1.5/VC-11-*X*v	unspecified	1 to 64	1600 to 102400	1600
VT2/VC-12-*X*v	unspecified	1 to 64	2176 to 139264	2176
VT3-*X*v SPE	unspecified	1 to 64	3328 to 212992	3328
VT6-*X*v SPE	unspecified	1 to 64	6784 to 434176	6784

Note: *X* is limited to 64 due the sequence indicator having 6 bits.

label value of 101 indicates that a VT mapping is given by the extended signal label in the Z7 byte. If this is the case, then a 1-bit frame alignment signal "0111 1111 110" is sent in bit 1 of Z7, called the extended signal label bit. The length of this second stage VT level multiframe (which is inside the 500 μs VT multiframe) is 32 frames. The extended signal label is contained in bits 12–19 of the multiframe. Multiframe position 20 contains "0." The remaining 12 bits are reserved for future standardization.

Bit 2 of the Z7 byte is used to convey the third stage of the multistage multiframe in the form of a serial string of 32 bits (over 32 four-frame multiframes and defined by the extended signal label). This is shown in Figure 3–4. This string is repeated every 16 ms (32 bits × 500 μs/bit) or every 128 frames.

Bit number

1–5	6–11	12	13	14	15	16	17	18	19	20	21	22	23	24	25	26	27	28	29	30	31	32
Frame count	Sequence indicator	R	R	R	R	R	R	R	R	R	R	R	R	R	R	R	R	R	R	R	R	R

R = Reserved

Figure 3–4 *Third Stage of LOVC Multiframe Defined by Bit 2 of the Z7 Byte over the 32 Frame Second Stage Multiframe*

The third stage string consists of the following fields: The third stage virtual concatenation frame count is contained in bits 1 to 5. The LOVC sequence indicator is contained in bits 6 to 11. The remaining 21 bits are reserved for future standardization.

Let us now consider a concrete example. Suppose that there are three stages of multiframes with the last stage having 5 bits dedicated to frame counting. What is the longest differential delay that can be compensated and in what increments? The first stage was given by the H4 byte and is of length 4, resulting in 4×125 µs = 500 µs. The second stage was given by the extended signal label (bit 1 of Z7) and it is of length 32. Since this is inside the first stage, the lengths multiply, resulting in 32×500 µs = 16 ms. The third stage, which is within the 32-bit Z7 string, has a length of $2^5 = 32$ and is contained inside the second stage. Hence, the lengths multiply, resulting in 32×16 ms = 512 ms. This is the same compensation we showed with HOVC. Since the sequence indicator of the third stage is used to line up the components, the delay compensation is in 16 ms increments.

3.3 Link Capacity Adjustment Scheme

Virtual concatenation allows the flexibility of creating SONET/SDH pipes of different sizes. The Link Capacity Adjustment Scheme or LCAS [ITU-T01a] is a relatively new addition to the SONET/SDH standard. It is designed to increase or decrease the capacity of a Virtually Concatenated Group (VCG) in a hitless fashion. This capability is particularly useful in environments where dynamic adjustment of capacity is important. The LCAS mechanism can also *automatically* decrease the capacity if a member in a VCG experiences a failure in the network, and increase the capacity when the fault is repaired. Although autonomous addition after a failure is repaired is hitless, removal of a member due to path layer failures is not hitless. Note that a "member" here refers to a VC (SDH) or an SPE (SONET). In the descriptions below, we use the term member to denote a VC.

Note that virtual concatenation can be used without LCAS, but LCAS requires virtual concatenation. LCAS is resident in the H4 byte of the path overhead, the same byte as virtual concatenation. The H4 bytes from a 16-frame sequence make up a message for both virtual concatenation and LCAS. Virtual concatenation uses 4 of the 16 bytes for its MFI and sequence numbers. LCAS uses 7 others for its purposes, leaving 5 reserved for future development. While virtual concatenation is a simple labeling of individual STS-1s within a channel, LCAS is a two-way handshake protocol. Status messages are continuously exchanged and consequent actions taken.

From the perspective of dynamic provisioning enabled by LCAS, each VCG can be characterized by two parameters:

- X_{MAX}, which indicates the maximum size of the VCG and it is usually dictated by hardware and/or standardization limits
- X_{PROV}, which indicates the number of provisioned members in the VCG

With each completed ADD command, X_{PROV} increases by 1, and with each completed REMOVE command X_{PROV} decreases by 1. The relationship $0 \leq X_{PROV} \leq X_{MAX}$ always holds. The operation of LCAS is unidirectional. This means that in order to bidirectionally add or remove members to or from a VCG, the LCAS procedure has to be repeated twice, once in each direction. These actions are independent of each other, and they are not required to be synchronized.

The protocols behind LCAS are relatively simple. For each member in the VCG (total of X_{MAX}), there is a state machine at the transmitter and a state machine at the receiver. The state machine at the transmitter can be in one of the following five states:

1. IDLE: This member is not provisioned to participate in the VCG.
2. NORM: This member is provisioned to participate in the VCG and has a good path to the receiver.
3. DNU: This member is provisioned to participate in the VCG and has a failed path to the receiver.
4. ADD: This member is in the process of being added to the VCG.
5. REMOVE: This member is in the process of being deleted from the VCG.

The state machine at the receiver can be in one of the following three states:

1. IDLE: This member is not provisioned to participate in the VCG.
2. OK: The incoming signal for this member experiences no failure condition. Or, the receiver has received and acknowledged a request for addition of this member.
3. FAIL: The incoming signal for this member experiences some failure condition, or an incoming request for removal of a member has been received and acknowledged.

The transmitter and the receiver communicate using control packets to ensure smooth transition from one state to another. The control packets consist of X_{MAX} control words, one for each member of the VCG. The following control words are sent from source to the receiver in order to carry out dynamic provisioning functions. Each word is associated with a specific member (i.e., VC) in the VCG.

- F_{ADD}: Add this member to the group.
- F_{DNU}: Delete this member from the group.
- F_{IDLE}: Indicate that this VC is currently not a member of the group.
- F_{EOS}: Indicate that this member has the highest sequence number in the group (EOS denotes End of Sequence).
- F_{NORM}: Indicate that this member is normal part of the group and does not have the highest sequence number.

The following control words are sent from the receiver to the transmitter. Each word is associated with a specific VC in the VCG.

- R_{FAIL} and R_{OK}: These messages capture the status of all the VCG members at the receiver. The status of all the members is returned to the transmitter in the control packets of each member. The transmitter can, for example, read the information from member No. 1 and, if that is unavailable, the same information from member No. 2, and so on. As long as no return bandwidth is available, the transmitter uses the last received valid status.
- R_{RS_ACK}: This is a bit used to acknowledge the detection of renumbering of the sequence or a change in the number of VCG members. This acknowledgment is used to synchronize the transmitter and the receiver.

The following is a typical sequence for adding a member to the group. Multiple members can be added simultaneously for fast resizing.

1. The network management system orders the source to add a new member (e.g., a VC) to the existing VCG.
2. The source node starts sending F_{ADD} control commands in the selected member. The destination notices the F_{ADD} command and returns an R_{OK} in the link status for the new member.
3. The source sees the R_{OK}, assigns the member a sequence number that is one higher than the number currently in use.
4. At a frame boundary, the source includes the VC in the byte interleaving and sets the control command to F_{EOS}, indicating that this VC is in use and it is the last in the sequence.
5. The VC that previously was "EOS " now becomes "NORM" (normal) as it is no longer the one with the highest sequence number.

The following is a typical sequence for deleting the VC with the highest sequence number (EOS) from a VCG:

1. The network management system orders the source to delete a member from the existing VCG.
2. The source node starts sending F_{IDLE} control commands in the selected VC. It also sets the member with the next highest sequence number as the EOS and sends F_{EOS} in the corresponding control word.
3. The destination notices the F_{IDLE} command and immediately drops the channel from the reassembly process. It also responds with R_{FAIL} and inverts the R_{RS_ACK} bit.

In this example, the deleted member has the highest sequence number. If this is not the case, then the other members with sequence numbers between the newly deleted member and the highest sequence number are renumbered.

LCAS and virtual concatenation add tremendous amount of flexibility to SONET and SDH. Although SONET and SDH were originally designed to transport voice traffic, advent of these new mechanisms has made it perfectly suitable for carrying more dynamic and bursty data traffic. In the next section, we discuss mechanisms for mapping packet payloads into SONET and SDH SPEs.

3.4 Payload Mappings

So far, the multiplexing structure of SONET and SDH has been described in detail. To get useful work out of these different sized containers, a payload mapping is needed, that is, a systematic method for inserting and removing the payload from a SONET/SDH container. Although it is preferable to use standardized mappings for interoperability, a variety of proprietary mappings may exist for various purposes.

In this regard, one of the most important payloads carried over SONET/SDH is IP. Much of the bandwidth explosion that set the wheels in motion for this book came from the growth in IP services. Hence, our focus is mainly on IP in the rest of this chapter. Figure 3–5 shows different ways of mapping IP packets into SONET/SDH frames. In the following, we discuss some of these mechanisms.

3.4.1 IP over ATM over SONET

The “Classical IP over ATM” solution supports robust transmission of IP packets over SONET/SDH using ATM encapsulation. Under this solution, each IP packet is encapsulated into an ATM Adaptation Layer Type 5 (AAL5) frame using multiprotocol LLC/SNAP encapsulation [Perez+95]. The resulting AAL5 Protocol Data Unit (PDU) is segmented into 48-byte payloads for ATM cells. ATM cells are then mapped into a SONET/SDH frame.

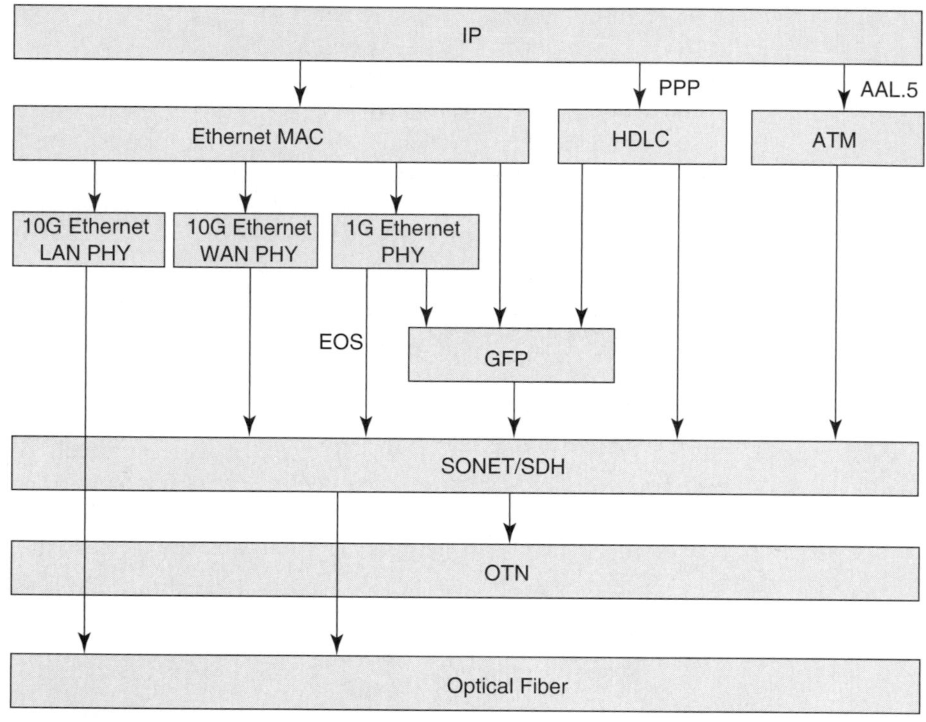

Figure 3–5 *Different Alternatives for Carrying IP Packets over SONET*

One of the problems with IP-over-ATM transport is that the protocol stack may introduce a bandwidth overhead as high as 18 percent to 25 percent. This is in addition to the approximately 4 percent overhead needed for SONET. On the positive side, ATM permits sophisticated traffic engineering, flexible routing, and better partitioning of the SONET/SDH bandwidth. Despite the arguments on the pros and cons of the method, IP-over-ATM encapsulation continues to be one of the main mechanisms for transporting IP over SONET/SDH transport networks.

3.4.2 Packet over SONET/SDH

ATM encapsulation of IP packets for transport over SONET/SDH can be quite inefficient from the perspective of bandwidth utilization. Packet over SONET/SDH (or POS) addresses this problem by eliminating the ATM encapsulation, and using the Point-to-Point Protocol (PPP) defined by the IETF [Simpson94]. PPP provides a general mechanism for dealing with point-to-point links and includes a method for mapping user data, a

Link Control Protocol (LCP), and assorted Network Control Protocols (NCPs). Under POS, PPP encapsulated IP packets are framed using high-Level Data Link Control (HDLC) protocol and mapped into the SONET SPE or SDH VC [Malis+99]. The main function of HDLC is to provide framing, that is, delineation of the PPP encapsulated IP packets across the synchronous transport link. Standardized mappings for IP into SONET using PPP/HDLC have been defined in IETF RFC 2615 [Malis+99] and ITU-T Recommendation G.707 [ITU-T00a].

Elimination of the ATM layer under POS results in more efficient bandwidth utilization. However, it also eliminates the flexibility of link bandwidth management offered by ATM. POS is most popular in backbone links between core IP routers running at 2.5 Gbps and 10 Gbps speeds. IP over ATM is still popular in lower-speed access networks, where bandwidth management is essential.

During the initial deployment of POS, it was noticed that the insertion of packets containing certain bit patterns could lead to the generation of the Loss of Frame (LOF) condition. The problem was attributed to the relatively short period of the SONET section (SDH regenerator section) scrambler, which is only 127 bits and synchronized to the beginning of the frame. In order to alleviate the problem, an additional scrambling operation is performed on the HDLC frames before they are placed into the SONET/SDH SPEs. This procedure is depicted in Figure 3–6.

3.4.3 Generic Framing Procedure (GFP)

GFP [ITU-T01b] was initially proposed as a solution for transporting data directly over dark fibers and WDM links. But due to the huge installed base of SONET/SDH networks, GFP soon found applications in SONET/SDH networks. The basic appeal of GFP is that it provides a flexible encapsulation framework for both block-coded [Gorsche+02] and packet oriented [Bonenfant+02] data streams. It has the potential of replacing a plethora of

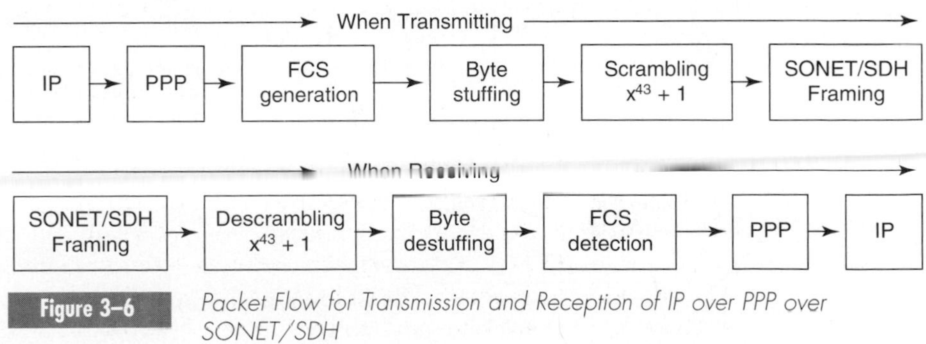

Figure 3–6 *Packet Flow for Transmission and Reception of IP over PPP over SONET/SDH*

proprietary framing procedures for carrying data over existing SONET/SDH and emerging WDM/OTN transport.

GFP supports all the basic functions of a framing procedure including frame delineation, frame/client multiplexing, and client data mapping [ITU-T01b]. GFP uses a frame delineation mechanism similar to ATM, but generalizes it for both fixed and variable size packets. As a result, under GFP, it is not necessary to search for special control characters in the client data stream as required in 8B/10B encoding,[1] or for frame delineators as with HDLC framing. GFP allows flexible multiplexing whereby data emanating from multiple clients or multiple client sessions can be sent over the same link in a point-to-point or ring configuration. GFP supports transport of both packet-oriented (e.g., Ethernet, IP, etc.) and character-oriented (e.g., Fiber Channel) data. Since GFP supports the encapsulation and transport of variable-length user PDUs, it does not need complex segmentation/reassembly functions or frame padding to fill unused payload space. These careful design choices have substantially reduced the complexity of GFP hardware, making it particularly suitable for high-speed transmissions.

In the following section, we briefly discuss the GFP frame structure and basic GFP functions.

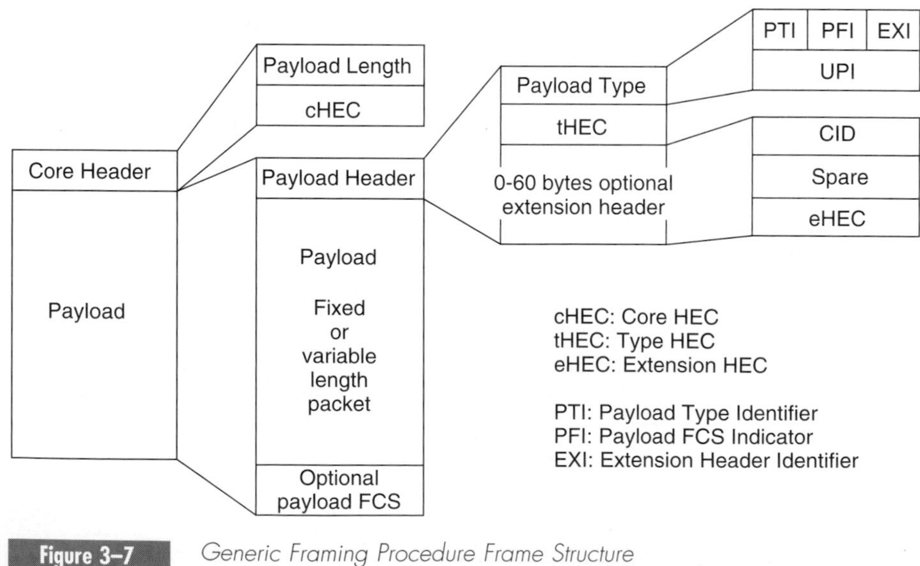

Figure 3–7 *Generic Framing Procedure Frame Structure*

[1]An encoding scheme that converts an 8-bit byte into one or two possible 10-bit characters; used for balancing 1s and 0s in high-speed transports.

3.4.3.1 GFP FRAME STRUCTURE

A GFP frame consists of a core header and a payload area, as shown in Figure 3–7. The GFP core header is intended to support GFP-specific data link management functions. The core header also allows GFP frame delineation independent of the content of the payload. The GFP core header is 4 bytes long and consists of two fields:

PAYLOAD LENGTH INDICATOR (PLI) FIELD • A 2-byte field indicating the size of the GFP payload area in bytes.

CORE HEADER ERROR CORRECTION (cHEC) FIELD • A 2-octet field containing a cyclic redundancy check (CRC) sequence that protects the integrity of the core header.

The payload area is of variable length (0–65,535 octets) and carries client data such as client PDUs, client management information, and so on. Structurally, the payload area consists of a payload header and a payload information field, and an optional payload Frame Check Sequence (FCS) field. The FCS information is used to detect the corruption of the payload.

PAYLOAD HEADER • The variable length payload header consists of a payload type field and a type Header Error Correction (tHEC) field that protects the integrity of the payload type field. Optionally, the payload header may include an extension header. The payload type field consists of the following subfields:

- Payload Type Identifier (PTI): This subfield identifies the type of frame. Two values are currently defined: user data frames and client management frames.
- Payload FCS Indicator (PFI): This subfield indicates the presence or absence of the payload FCS field.
- Extension Header Identifier (EXI): This subfield identifies the type of extension header in the GFP frame. Extension headers facilitate the adoption of GFP for different client-specific protocols and networks. Three kinds of extension headers are currently defined: a null extension header, a linear extension header for point-to-point networks, and a ring extension header for ring networks.
- User Payload Identifier (UPI): This subfield identifies the type of payload in the GFP frame. The UPI is set according to the transported client signal type. Currently defined UPI values include Ethernet, PPP (including IP and MPLS), Fiber Channel [Benner01], FICON [Benner01], ESCON [Benner01], and Gigabit Ethernet. Mappings for 10/100 Mb/s Ethernet and digital video broadcast, among others, are under consideration.

Payload Information Field • This field contains the client data. There are two modes of client signal payload adaptation defined for GFP: frame-mapped GFP (GFP-F) applicable to most packet data types, and transparent-mapped GFP (GFP-T) applicable to 8B/10B coded signals. Frame-mapped GFP payloads consist of variable length packets. In this mode, client frame is mapped in its entirety into one GFP frame. Examples of such client signals include Gigabit Ethernet and IP/PPP. With transparent-mapped GFP, a number of client data characters, mapped into efficient block codes, are carried within a GFP frame.

3.4.3.2 GFP Functions

The GFP frame structure was designed to support the basic functions provided by GFP, namely, frame delineation, client/frame multiplexing, header/payload scrambling, and client payload mapping. In the following, we discuss each of these functions.

Frame Delineation • The GFP transmitter and receiver operate asynchronously. The transmitter inserts GFP frames on the physical link according to the bit/byte alignment requirements of the specific physical interface (e.g., SONET/SDH, OTN, or dark fiber). The GFP receiver is responsible for identifying the correct GFP frame boundary at the time of link initialization, and after link failures or loss of frame events. The receiver "hunts" for the start of the GFP frame using the last received four octets of data. The receiver first computes the cHEC value based on these four octets. If the computed cHEC matches the value in the (presumed) cHEC field of the received data, the receiver tentatively assumes that it has identified the frame boundary. Otherwise, it shifts forward by 1 bit and checks again. After a candidate GFP frame has been identified, the receiver waits for the next candidate GFP frame based on the PLI field value. If a certain number of consecutive GFP frames are detected, the receiver transitions into a regular operational state. In this state, the receiver examines the PLI field, validates the incoming cHEC field, and extracts the framed PDU.

Client/Frame Multiplexing • GFP supports both frame and client multiplexing. Frames from multiple GFP processes, such as idle frames, client data frames, and client management frames, can be multiplexed on the same link. Client data frames get priority over management frames. Idle frames are inserted when neither data nor management frames are available for transmission.

GFP supports client-multiplexing capabilities via the GFP linear and ring extension headers. For example, linear extension headers (see Figure 3–7) contain an 8-bit channel ID (CID) field that can be used to multiplex data from up to 256 client sessions on a point-to-point link. An 8-bit spare field is available for future use. Various proposals for ring extension headers are currently being considered for sharing GFP payload across multiple clients in a ring environment.

HEADER/PAYLOAD SCRAMBLING • Under GFP, both the core header and the payload area are scrambled. Core header scrambling ensures that an adequate number of 0-1 transitions occur during idle data conditions (thus allowing the receiver to stay synchronized with the transmitter). Scrambling of the GFP payload area ensures correct operation even when the payload information is coincidentally the same as the scrambling word (or its inverse) from frame-synchronous scramblers such as those used in the SONET line layer (SDH RS layer).

CLIENT PAYLOAD MAPPING • As mentioned earlier, GFP supports two types of client payload mapping: frame-mapped and transparent-mapped. Frame mapping of native client payloads into GFP is intended to facilitate packet-level handling of incoming PDUs. Examples of such client signals include IEEE 802.3 Ethernet MAC frames, PPP/IP packets, or any HDLC framed PDU. Here, the transmitter encapsulates an entire frame of the client data into a GFP frame. Frame multiplexing is supported with frame-mapped GFP. Frame-mapped GFP uses the basic frame structure of a GFP client frame, including the required payload header.

Transparent mapping is intended to facilitate the transport of 8B/10B block-coded client data streams with low transmission latency. Transparent mapping is particularly applicable to Fiber Channel, ESCON, FICON, and Gigabit Ethernet. Instead of buffering an entire client frame and then encapsulating it into a GFP frame, the individual characters of the client data stream are extracted, and a fixed number of them are mapped into periodic fixed-length GFP frames. The mapping occurs regardless of whether the client character is a data or control character, which thus preserves the client 8B/10B control codes. Frame multiplexing is not precluded with transparent GFP. The transparent GFP client frame uses the same structure as the frame-mapped GFP, including the required payload header.

3.4.4 Ethernet over SONET/SDH

As shown in Figure 3–5, there are different ways of carrying Ethernet frames over SONET/SDH, OTN, and optical fiber. Ethernet MAC frames can be encapsulated in GFP frames and carried over SONET/SDH. Also shown in the figure are the different physical layer encoding schemes, including Gigabit Ethernet physical layer, and 10Gigabit Ethernet physical (PHY) layer optimized for LAN and WAN. Gigabit Ethernet physical layer is 8B/10B coded data stream, and it can be encapsulated into GFP frames and carried over SONET/SDH. 10-Gigabit Ethernet WAN PHY is SONET/SDH encoded, and hence it can be directly mapped into STS-192/STM-16 frames.

3.5 SONET/SDH Transparency Services

SONET and SDH have the following notions of transparency built-in, as described in Chapter 2:

1. Path transparency, as provided by the SONET line and SDH multiplex section layers. This was the original intent of SONET and SDH, that is, transport of path layer signals transparently between PTEs.
2. SONET line and SDH multiplex section transparency, as provided by the SONET section and SDH regenerator section layers, respectively.
3. SONET section and SDH regenerator section transparency, as provided by the physical layer.

Of these, only (1) was considered a "user service" within SONET and SDH. There are reasons now to consider (2) and (3) as services, in addition to newer transparency services.

Figure 3–8 shows a typical scenario where transparency services may be desired. Here, two SONET networks (labeled "Domain 1") are separated by an intervening optical transport network of some type (labeled "Domain 2"). For instance, Domain 1 could consist of two metro networks under a single administration, separated by a core network (Domain 2) under a different administration. The two disjoint parts of Domain 1 are interconnected by provisioning a "link" between network elements NE1 and NE2, as shown. The characteristics of this link depend on the type of transparency desired. In general, transparency allows NE1 and NE2 to use the functionality provided by SONET overhead bytes in various layers. For instance, section transparency allows the signal from NE1 to NE2 to pass through Domain 2 without *any* overhead information being modified in transit. An all-optical network or a

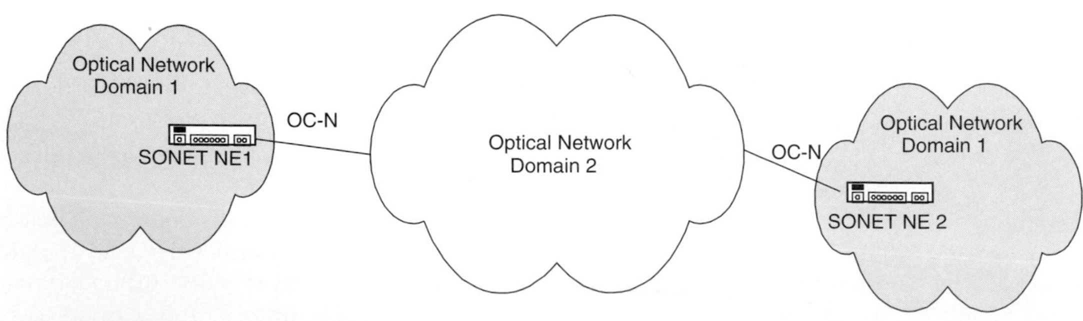

Figure 3–8 *Networking Scenario Used to Define SONET/SDH Transparency Services*

network with transparent regenerators can provide section layer transparency. This service is equivalent to having a dedicated wavelength (lambda) between NE1 and NE2. Thus, the service is often referred to as a *lambda service*, even if the signal is electrically regenerated within the network. Section transparency allows NE1 and NE2 to terminate the section layer and use the section (and higher layer) overhead bytes for their own purposes.

If the OC-*N* to be transported between NE1 and NE2 is the same size (in terms of capacity) as those used within the optical network, then the section transparency service is a reasonable approach. If the optical network, however, deals with signals much larger than these OC-*N* signals, then there is the potential for inefficient resource utilization. For example, suppose the optical network is composed of DWDM links and switches that can effectively deal with OC-192 signals. A "lambda" in this network could indeed accommodate an OC-12 signal, but only 1/16th of the capacity of that lambda will be used. In such a case, the OC-12 signal has to be multiplexed in some way into an OC-192 signal. But SONET (SDH) multiplexing takes place at the line (multiplex section) layer. Hence, there is no standard way to convey the OC-12 overhead when multiplexing the constituent path signals into an OC-192 signal. This means that section and line overhead bytes presented by NE1 will be modified within Domain 2. How then to transfer the overhead bytes transparently across Domain 2? Before we examine the methods for accomplishing this, it is instructive to look at the functionality provided by overhead bytes and what it means to support transparency.

Tables 3–3 and 3–4 list the overhead bytes available at different layers, the functionality provided and when the bytes are updated (refer to Figures 2–4 and 2–5).

Table 3–3 *SONET Section (SDH Regenerator Section) Overhead Bytes and Functionality*

Overhead Bytes	Comments
A1 and A2 (Framing)	These are repeated in all STS-1 signals within an OC-*N*. No impact on transparency.
J0 (Trace)	Only conveyed in the 1st STS-1, and covers entire frame. J0 bytes in signals 2–N are reserved for growth, i.e., Z0. Used to identify entire section layer signal.
B1 (Section BIP-8)	Only conveyed in the 1st STS-1, and covers entire frame. B1 bytes in signals 2–N are undefined. B1 byte must be updated if section, line or path layer content changes.
E1 (Orderwire) F1 (User)	Only conveyed in the 1st STS-1, and covers for entire frame. E1 and F1 in signals 2–N are undefined.
D1-D3 (Section DCC)	Only conveyed in the 1st STS-1, and covers the entire frame. D1-D3 bytes in signals 2–N are undefined.

Table 3–4 *SONET Line (SDH Multiplex Section) Overhead Bytes and Functionality*

Overhead Bytes	Comments
H1, H2, H3 (Pointer bytes)	These are repeated in all STS-1s within an STS-*N*.
B2 (Line BIP-8)	This is used for all STS-1s within an STS-*N*. Must be updated if line or path layer content changes. Used to determine signal degrade conditions.
K1, K2 (APS bytes)	Only conveyed in the 1st STS-1 signal, and covers entire line. This space in signals 2 – *N* are undefined. This is the line APS functionality.
D4-D12 (Line DCC)	Only conveyed in the 1st STS-1 for the entire line. D4–D12 bytes in signals 2 – *N* are undefined.
S1 (Synchronization byte)	Only conveyed in the 1st STS-1, and carries the synchronization status message for the entire line. S1 bytes in STS-1 signals 2 – *N* are reserved for growth (Z1 byte). Note that if a remultiplexing operation were to take place, this byte cannot be carried through.
M0, M1, (Line, Remote Error indication)	M0 or M1 is conveyed in the *Nth* STS of the STS-*N* signal. If $N > 1$, this byte is called M1. If $N = 1$, this byte is called M0. When $N > 1$, the corresponding bytes in signals 1 to $N - 1$ are reserved for growth (Z2 byte).
E2 (Line order wire)	Only conveyed in the 1st STS-1, and covers the entire line. The E2 bytes in signals 2 – *N* are undefined.

With standard SONET/SDH path layer multiplexing, the H1–H3 (pointer) bytes must be modified when the clocks are different for the streams to be multiplexed. The B2 byte must be updated when any of the line layer bytes are changed. Also related to timing is the S1 byte, which reports on the synchronization status of the line. This byte has to be regenerated if multiplexing is performed. Thus, it is not possible to preserve all the overhead bytes when the signal from NE1 is multiplexed with other signals within Domain 2. The additional procedures that must be performed to achieve transparency are discussed next.

3.5.1 Methods for Overhead Transparency

We can group the transport overhead bytes into five categories as follows:

1. Framing bytes A1 and A2, which are always terminated and regenerated

2. Pointer bytes H1, H2 and H3, which must be adjusted for multiplexing, and the S1 byte
3. General overhead bytes: J0, E1, F1, D1-D3, K1, K2, D4-D12, M0/M1, E2
4. BIP-8 error monitoring bytes B1 and B2
5. An assortment of currently unused growth bytes

With regard to the network shown in Figure 3–8, the following are different strategies for transparently transporting the general overhead bytes:

- *Information forwarding:* The overhead bytes originating from NE1 are placed into the OC-*N* signal and remain unmodified in Domain 2.
- *Information tunneling:* Tunneling generally refers to the encapsulation of information to be transported at the ingress of a network in some manner and restoring it at the egress. With respect to Figure 3–8, the overhead bytes originating from NE1 are placed in unused overhead byte locations of the signal transported within Domain 2. These overhead bytes are restored before the signal is delivered to NE2.

As an example of forwarding and tunneling, consider Figure 3–9, which depicts four STS-12 signals being multiplexed into an STS-48 signal within Domain 2. Suppose that the J0 byte of each of these four signals has to be transported transparently. Referring to Table 3–1, it can be noted that

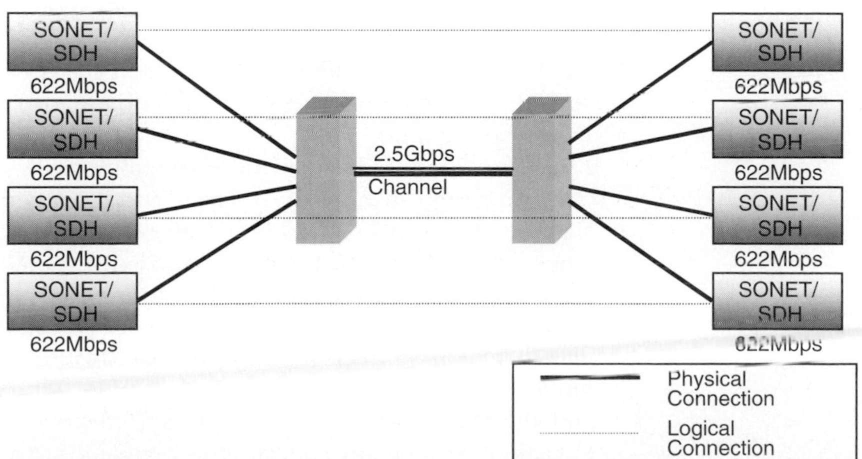

Figure 3–9 *Transparency Example to Illustrate Forwarding and Tunneling*

the J0 space in signals 2–4 of the STS-48 are reserved, that is, no specific purpose for these bytes is defined within Domain 2. Thus, referring to the structure of the multiplexed overhead information shown in Figure 2–5, the J0 bytes from the second, third, and fourth STS-12 signals can be *forwarded* unmodified through the intermediate network. This is not true for the J0 byte of the first STS-12, however, since the intermediate network uses the J0 byte in the first STS-1 to cover the entire STS-48 signal (Table 3–1). Hence, the J0 byte of the first STS-12 has to be *tunneled* by placing it in some unused overhead byte in the STS-48 signal at the ingress and recovering it at the egress.

Now, consider the error monitoring bytes, B1 and B2. Their usage is described in detail in section 3.6. Briefly, taking SONET as an example, B1 and B2 bytes contain the parity codes for the section and line portion of the frame, respectively. A node receiving these bytes in a frame uses them to detect errors in the appropriate portions of the frame. According to the SONET specification, B1 and B2 are terminated and regenerated by each STE or LTE, respectively. With regard to the network of Figure 3–8, the following options may be considered for their transport across Domain 2:

- *Error regeneration*: B1 and B2 are simply regenerated at every network hop.
- *Error forwarding*: As before, the B1 and B2 bytes are regenerated at each hop. But instead of simply sending these regenerated bytes in the transmitted frame (as in the previous case), the bytes are XOR'd (i.e., bit wise summed) with the corresponding bytes received. With this process, the B1 or B2 bytes will accumulate all the errors (at the appropriate layer) for the transparently transported signal. The only drawback of this method is that the error counts within Domain 2 would appear artificially high, and to sort out the true error counts, correlation of the errors reported along the transparent signal's path would be required.
- *Error tunneling*: In this case, the incoming parity bytes (B1 and/or B2) are carried in unused overhead locations within the transport signal in Domain 2. In addition, at each network hop where the bytes are required to be regenerated, the tunneled parity bytes are regenerated and then XOR'd (bit wise binary summation) with the error result that was obtained (by comparing the difference between the received and calculated BIP-8s). In this way, the tunneled parity bytes are kept up to date with respect to errors, and the standard SONET/SDH B1 and B2 bytes are used within Domain 2 without any special error correlation/compensation being performed.

3.5.2 Transparency Service Packages

We have so far looked at the mechanisms for providing transparent transport. From the perspective of a network operator, a more important issue is the determination of the types of transparency *services* that may be offered. A transparency service package defines which overhead functionality will be transparently carried across the network offering the service. As an example, let us consider the network shown in Figure 3–9 again. The following is a list of individual services that could be offered by Domain 2. These may be grouped in various combinations to create different transparency service packages:

1. J0 transparency: Allows signal identification across Domain 2.
2. Section DCC (D1–D3) transparency: Allows STE to STE data communication across Domain 2.
3. B2 and M0/M1 transparency: Allows line layer error monitoring and indication across Domain 2.
4. K1 and K2 byte transparency: Allow line layer APS across Domain 2. This service will most likely be used with (3) so that signal degrade conditions can be accurately detected and acted upon.
5. Line DCC (D4-D12) transparency: Allows LTE to LTE data communication across Domain 2.
6. E2 transparency. Allows LTE to LTE order wire communication across Domain 2.
7. Miscellaneous section overhead transparency, that is, E1 and F1.

Whether overhead/error forwarding or tunneling is used is an internal decision made by the domain offering the transparency service, based on equipment capabilities and overhead usage. Note that to make use of equipment capable of transparent services, a service provider must know the overhead usage, termination, and forwarding capabilities of equipment used in the network. For example, the latest release of G.707 [ITU-T00a] allows the use of some of the unused overhead bytes for physical layer forward error correction (FEC). Hence, a link utilizing such a "feature" would have additional restrictions on which bytes could be used for forwarding or tunneling.

3.6 When Things Go Wrong

One of the most important aspects built into optical transport systems is their "self-diagnosis" capability. That is, the ability to detect a problem (i.e., observe a symptom), localize the problem (i.e., find where it originated), and discover the root cause of the problem. In fact, SONET and SDH include many mechanisms to almost immediately classify the root cause of problem. This is done by monitoring the signal integrity between peers at a given layer, and also when transferring a signal from a client (higher) layer into a server (lower) layer (Figure 2–17).

In the following, we first consider the various causes of transport problems. Next, we examine how problems are localized and how signal quality is monitored. Finally, we review the methods and terminology for characterizing problems and their duration.

3.6.1 Transport Problems and Their Detection

Signal monitoring functionality includes the following: continuity supervision, connectivity supervision, and signal quality supervision. These are described next.

3.6.1.1 CONTINUITY SUPERVISION

A fundamental issue in telecommunication is ascertaining whether a signal being transmitted is successfully received. Lack of continuity at the optical or electrical layers in SONET/SDH is indicated by the *Loss of Signal* (LOS) condition. This may arise from either the failure of a transmitter (e.g., laser, line card, etc.) or break in the line (e.g., fiber cut, WDM failure, etc.). The exact criteria for when the LOS condition is declared and when it is cleared are described in reference [ITU-T00b]. For optical SDH signals, a typical criterion is the detection of no transitions on the incoming signal (before unscrambling) for time T, where $2.3\ \mu s \leq T \leq 100\ \mu s$. An LOS defect is cleared if there are signal transitions within 125 μs. When dealing with other layers, the loss of continuity is discovered using a maintenance signal known as the *Alarm Indication Signal* (AIS). AIS indicates that there is a failure further upstream in the lower layer signal. This is described further in section 3.6.2.1.

3.6.1.2 CONNECTIVITY SUPERVISION

Connectivity supervision deals with the determination of whether a SONET/SDH connection at a certain layer has been established between the intended pair of peers. This is particularly of interest if there has been an outage and some type of protection or restoration action has been taken. A *trail trace identifier* is used for connection supervision. Specifically,

- The J0 byte is used in the SONET section (SDH regenerator section) layer. The section trace string is 16 bytes long (carried in successive J0 bytes) as per recommendation G.707 [ITU-T00a].
- The J1 byte is used in the SONET/SDH higher-order path layer (e.g., SONET STS-1 and above). The higher-order path trace string could be 16 or 64 bytes long as per recommendation G.707 [ITU-T00a].

- The J2 byte is used in the SONET/SDH lower-order path layer (e.g., SONET VT signals). The lower-order path trace string is 16 bytes long as per recommendation G.707 [ITU-T00a].

For details of trail trace identifiers used for tandem connection monitoring (TCM), see recommendations G.707 [ITU-T00a] and G.806 [ITU-T00c]. The usage of this string is typically controlled from the management system. Specifically, a trace string is configured in the equipment at the originating end. An "expected string" is configured at the receiving end. The transmitter keeps sending the trace string in the appropriate overhead byte. If the receiver does not receive the expected string, it raises an alarm, and further troubleshooting is initiated.

3.6.1.3 SIGNAL QUALITY SUPERVISION

Signal quality supervision determines whether a received signal contains too many errors and whether the trend in errors is getting worse. In SONET and SDH, parity bits called Bit Interleaved Parity (BIP) are added to the signal in various layers. This allows the receiving end, known as the *near-end*, to obtain error statistics as described in section 3.6.3. To give a complete view of the quality of the signal in both directions of a bidirectional line, the number of detected errors at the *far end* (transmitting end) may be sent back to the near-end via a *Remote Error Indicator* (REI) signal.

The following bits and bytes are used for near-end signal quality monitoring under SONET and SDH:

- SONET section (SDH regenerator section) layer: The B1 byte is used to implement a BIP-8 error detecting code that covers the previous frame.
- SONET line (SDH multiplex section) layer: In the case of SDH STM-*N* signals, a BIP $N \times 24$ composed of the 3 STM-1 B2 bytes is used. In the case of SONET STS-*N*, a BIP $N \times 8$ composed of the *N* B2 bytes is used. These cover the entire contents of the frame excluding the regenerator section overhead.
- SONET path (SDH HOVC) layer: The B3 byte is used to implement a BIP-8 code covering all the bits in the previous VC-3, VC-4, and VC-4-Xc.
- SONET VT path (SDH LOVC) layer. Bits 1 and 2 of the V5 byte are used to implement a BIP-2 code covering all the bits in the previous VC-1/2.

SONET/SDH provides the following mechanisms for carrying the REI information. For precise usage, see either T1.105 [ANSI-95a] or G.707 [ITU-T00a].

- Multiplex section layer REI: For STM-*N* (N = 0, 1, 4, 16), 1 byte (M1) is allocated for use as Multiplex Section REI. For STM-*N* (N = 64 and 256), 2 bytes (M0, M1) are allocated for use as a multiplex section REI. Note that this is in line with the most recent version of G.707 [ITU-T00a].
- Path layer REI: For STS (VC-3/4) path status, the first 4 bits of the G1 path overhead are used to return the count of errors detected via the path BIP-8, B3. Bit 3 of V5 is the VT Path (VC-1/2) REI that is sent back to the originating VT PTE, if one or more errors were detected by the BIP-2.

3.6.1.4 ALIGNMENT MONITORING

When receiving a time division multiplexed (TDM) signal, whether it is electrical or optical, a critically important stage of processing is to find the start of the TDM frame and to maintain frame alignment. In addition, when signals are multiplexed together under SONET/SDH, the pointer mechanism needs to be monitored.

Frame Alignment and Loss of Frame (LOF) • The start of an STM-*N* (OC-3N) frame is found by searching for the A1 and A2 bytes contained in the STM-*N* (OC-3*N*) signal. Recall that the A1 and A2 bytes form a particular pattern and that the rest of the frame is scrambled. This framing pattern is continuously monitored against the assumed start of the frame. Generally, the receiver has 625 μs to detect an out-of-frame (OOF) condition. If the OOF state exits for 3 ms or more then a *loss of frame* (LOF) state will be declared. To exit the LOF state, the start of the frame must be found and remain valid for 3 ms.

Loss of Multiframe • SDH LOVCs and SONET VTs use the multiframe structure described earlier. The 500 μs multiframe start phase is recovered by performing multiframe alignment on bits 7 and 8 of byte H4. Out-of-multiframe (OOM) is assumed once when an error is detected in the H4 bit 7 and 8 sequence. Multiframe alignment is considered recovered when an error-free H4 sequence is found in four consecutive VC-*n* (VT) frames.

Pointer Processing and Loss of Pointer (LOP) • Pointer processing in SONET/SDH is used in both the HOVC (STS path) and LOVC (VT path) layers. This processing is important in aligning payload signals (SDH VC or SONET paths) into their containing signals (STM-*N*/OC-3N). Without correct pointer processing, essentially one per payload signal, the payload signal is essentially "lost." Hence, pointer values are closely monitored as part of pointer processing [ITU-T00a, ITU-T00b]. A *loss of pointer* state is declared under severe error conditions.

3.6.2 Problem Localization and Signal Maintenance

Once a problem has been detected, its exact location has to be identified for the purposes of debugging and repair. SONET/SDH provides sophisticated mechanisms to this in the form of Alarm Indication Signals (AIS) and the Remote Defect Indication (RDI). These are described below.

3.6.2.1 ALARM INDICATION SIGNALS

Suppose that there is a major problem with the signal received by an intermediate point in a SONET network. In this case, a special Alarm Indication Signal is transmitted in lieu of the normal signal to maintain transmission continuity. An AIS indicates to the receiving equipment that there is a transmission interruption located at, or upstream, of the equipment originating the AIS. Note that if the AIS is followed upstream starting from the receiver, it will lead to the location of the error. In other words, the AIS signal is an important aid in fault localization. It is also used to deliver news of defects or faults across layers.

A SONET STE will originate an *Alarm Indication Signal-Line* (AIS-L) (MS AIS in SDH) upon detection of an LOS or LOF defect. There are two variants of the AIS-L signal. The simplest is a valid section overhead followed by "all ones" pattern in the rest of the frame bytes (before scrambling). To detect AIS-L, it is sufficient to look at bits 6, 7, and 8 of the K2 byte and check for the "111" pattern. A second function of the AIS-L is to provide a signal suitable for normal clock recovery at downstream STEs and LTEs. See [ANSI95a] for the details of the application, removal, and detection of AIS-L.

A SONET LTE will generate an *Alarm Indication signal-Path* (AIS-P) upon detection of an LOS, LOF, AIS-L, or LOP-P defect. AIS-P (*AU AIS* in SDH) is specified as "all ones" in the STS SPE as well as the H1, H2, and H3 bytes. STS pointer processors detect AIS-P as "111 . . ." in bytes H1 and H2 in three consecutive frames.

A SONET STS PTE will generate an *Alarm Indication signal-VT* (AIS-V) for VTs of the affected STS path upon detection of an LOS, LOF, AIS-L, LOP-P, AIS-P, or LOP-V defect. The AIS-V signal is specified as "all ones" in the entire VT, including the V1-V4 bytes. VT pointer processors detect AIS-V as "111 . . ." in bytes V1 and V2 in three consecutive VT superframes.

The SDH AIS signals for its various layers are nearly identical as those of SONET in definition and use as shown in Table 3–5.

3.6.2.2 REMOTE DEFECT INDICATION

Through the AIS mechanism, SONET allows the downstream entities to be informed about problems upstream in a timely fashion (in the order of milliseconds). The AIS signal is good for triggering downstream protection or restoration actions. For quick recovery from faults, it is also important to let

Table 3–5 *SDH AIS Signals by Layer*

Layer	Type	AIS Overhead	AIS Activation Pattern	AIS Deactivation Pattern
MSn	MS-AIS	K2, bits 6 to 8	"111"	≠ "111"
VC-3/4	AU-AIS	H1, H2	See Annex A/G.783 [ITU-T00b]	
VC-3/4 TCM	IncAIS	N1, bits 1 to 4	"1110"	≠ "1110"
VC-11/12/2	TU-AIS	V1, V2	S11/12/2 (VC-11/12/2)	
VC-11/12/2	TU-AIS	V1, V2	See Annex A/G.783 [ITU-T00b]	
VC-11/12/2 TCM	IncAIS	N2, bit 4	"1"	"0"

the upstream node know that there is a reception problem downstream. The *Remote Defect Indication (RDI)* signal is used for this purpose. The precise definition of RDI, as per [ANSI95a], is

> A signal transmitted at the first opportunity in the outgoing direction when a terminal detects specific defects in the incoming signal.

At the line level, the *RDI-L* code is returned to the transmitting LTE when the receiving LTE has detected an incoming line defect. RDI-L is generated within 100 ms by an LTE upon detection of an LOS, LOF, or AIS-L defect. RDI-L is indicated by a 110 code in bits 6,7,8 of the K2 byte (after unscrambling).

At the STS path level, the *RDI-P* code is returned to the transmitting PTE when the receiving PTE has detected an incoming STS path defect. There are three classes of defects that trigger RDI-P:

1. Payload defects: These generally indicate problems detected in adapting the payload being extracted from the STS path layer.
2. Server defects: These indicate problems in one of the layers responsible for transporting the STS path.
3. Connectivity defects: This only includes the trace identifier mismatch (TIM) or unequipped conditions.

Table 3–6 shows current use of the G1 byte for RDI-P purposes (consult [ANSI95a] for details).

The remote defect indication for the VT path layer, RDI-V, is similar to RDI-P. It is used to return an indication to the transmitting VT PTE that the receiving VT PTE has detected an incoming VT Path defect. There are three classes of defects that trigger RDI-V:

Table 3–6 *Remote Defect Indicator—Path (RDI-P) via the G1 Byte*

G1, bit 5	G1, bit 6	G1, bit 7	Meaning
0	1	0	Remote payload defect
0	1	1	No remote defect
1	0	1	Server defect
1	1	0	Remote connectivity defect

1. Payload defects: These generally indicate problems detected in adapting the payload being extracted from the VT path layer.
2. Server defects: These generally indicate problems in the server layers to the VT path layer.
3. Connectivity defects: These generally indicate that there is a connectivity problem within the VT path layer.

For more information, see [ANSI95a] for details. RDI-V uses the Z7 bytes (bits 6 and 7).

One thing to note about RDI signals is that they are "peer to peer" indications, that is, they stay within the layer that they are generated. The AIS and RDI signals form the "fast" notification mechanisms for protection and restoration, that is, these are the primary triggers. Examples of their usage are given in the next chapter. The RDI signals in various SDH layers are nearly identical to those of SONET and they are summarized in Table 3–7.

Table 3–7 *RDI Signals for Various SDH Layers*

Layer	Type	RDI/ODI Overhead	RDI/ODI Activation Pattern	RDI/ODI Deactivation Pattern
MSn	RDI	K2, bits 6 to 8	"110"	≠ "110"
S3D/4D (VC-3/4 TCM option 2)	RDI	N1, bit 8, frame 73	"1"	"0"
S11/12/2 (VC-11/12/2)	RDI	V5, bit 8	"1"	"0"
S11D/12D/2D (VC-11/12/2 TCM)	RDI	N2, bit 8, frame 73	"1"	"0"

3.6.3 Quality Monitoring

3.6.3.1 BLIPS AND BIPS

The bit error rates are typically extremely low in optical networks. For example, in 1995, the assumed worst-case bit error rate (BER) for SONET regenerator section engineering was 10^{-10}, or one error per 10 billion bits. Today, that would be considered quite high. Hence, for error detection in a SONET frame, we can assume very few bit errors per frame.

As an example, the number of bits in an STS-192 frame is 1,244,160 (9 rows × 90 columns per STS-1 x 8 bits/byte × 192 STS-1). With a BER of 10^{-10}, it can be expected that there will be one bit error in every 8038 frames. The probability of two errors in the same frame is fairly low. Since the bit rate of an STS-192 signal is 10 Gbps (or 10^{10} bits per second), a BER of 10^{-10} gives rise to one bit error every second on the average. This is why a BER of 10^{-10} is considered quite high today.

Figure 3–10 shows the general technique used in SONET and SDH for monitoring bit errors "in-service" over various portions of the signal. This method is known as the Bit Interleaved Parity 8 Bits, or BIP-8 for short. Although the name sounds complex, the idea and calculation are rather simple. In Figure 3–10, X1-X5 represents a set of bytes that are being checked for transmission errors. For every bit position in these bytes, a separate running tally of the *parity* (i.e., the number of 1s that occur) is kept track of. The corresponding bit position of the BIP-8 byte is set to "1" if the parity is currently odd and a zero if the parity is even. The BIP-8 byte is sent, typically in the following frame, to the destination. The destination recomputes the BIP-8 code based on the contents of the received frame and compares it with the BIP-8 received. If there are no bit errors, then these two codes should match. Figure 3–10(b) depicts the case where one of the bytes, X2, encounters a single bit error during transmission, that is, bit 2 changes from 1 to 0. In this case, the received BIP-8 and the recomputed BIP-8 differ by a single bit and, in fact, the number of differing bits can be used as an estimate of the number of bit errors.

Note that the BIP-8 technique works well under the assumption of low bit error rates. The study of general mechanisms for error detection and correction using redundant information bits is known as algebraic coding theory (see [Lin+83]).

BIP-8 is used for error monitoring in different SONET/SDH layers. At the SONET section layer, the B1 byte contains the BIP-8 calculated over all the bits of the previous STS-*N* frame (after scrambling). The computed BIP-8 is placed in the B1 byte of the first STS-1 (before scrambling). This byte is defined only for the first STS-1 of an STS-*N* signal. SDH uses this byte for the same purpose. Hence, the BIP-8 in this case is calculated over the entire SONET frame and covers a different number of bytes for different signals, for example, STS-12 vs. STS-192.

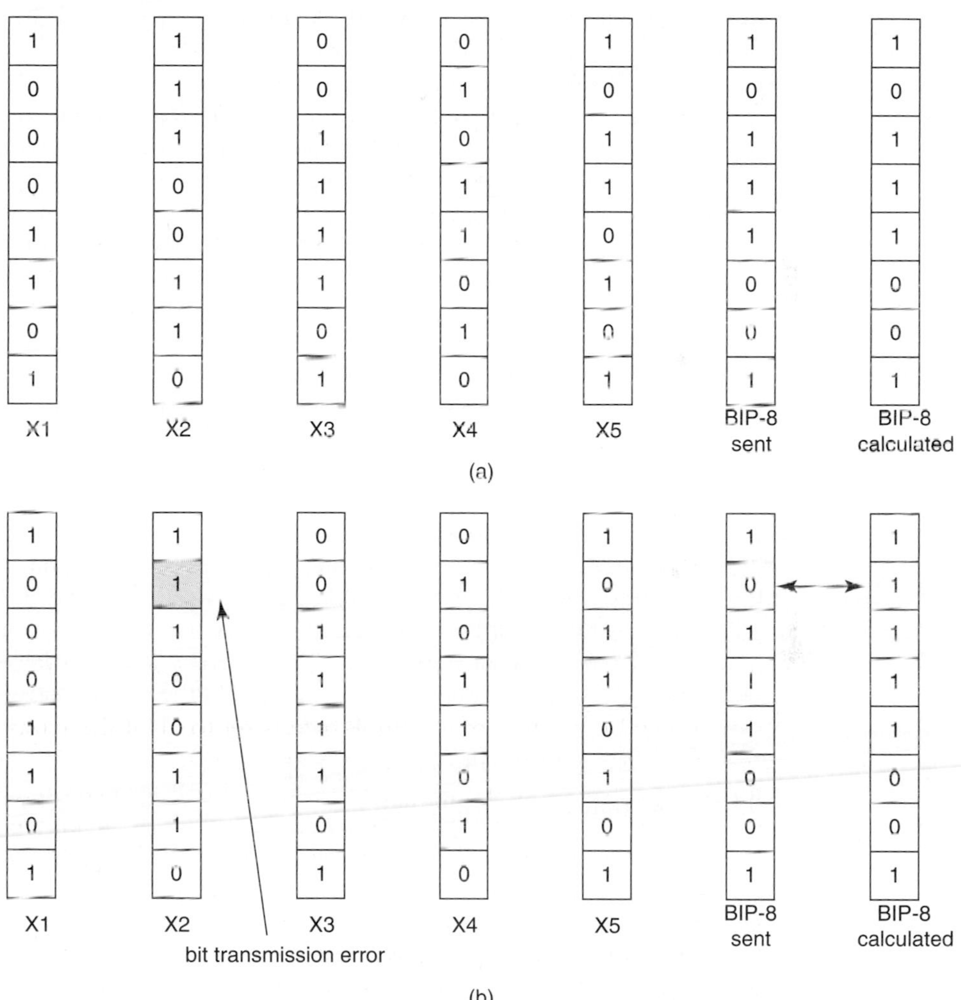

Figure 3–10 *Example of BIP-8 Calculation and Error Detection*

At the SONET line layer, BIP-8 is calculated over all the bits of the line overhead and the STS-1 SPE (before scrambling). The computed BIP-8 is placed in the B2 byte of the next STS-1 frame (before scrambling). This byte is separately computed for all the STS-1 signals within an STS-*N* signal. These *N* BIP-8 bytes are capable of detecting fairly high bit error rates, up to 10^{-3}. To see this, consider an STS-1 line signal (i.e., an STS-1 frame without section layer overhead). The number of bytes in this signal is 804 (9 rows × 90 columns – 6 section bytes). Each bit in the line BIP-8 code is used to cover 804 bits (which are in the corresponding bit position of the 804 bytes in the line signal). Since a BER of 10^{-3} means an average of one bit error every 1000 bits, there will be less than one bit error in 804 bits (on the average). This, the line BIP-8 code is sufficient for detecting these errors. Note, however, that BIP-8 (and any parity based error detection mechanism) may fail if there are multiple, simultaneous bit errors.

At the STS Path level, BIP-8 is calculated over all the bits of the previous STS SPE (before scrambling) and carried in the B3 path overhead byte. SDH uses this byte for the same purpose but excludes the fixed stuff bytes in the calculation. The path BIP-8, like the section BIP-8, covers a different number of bytes depending on the size of the STS path signal, that is, STS-3 vs. STS-12.

At the VT path level, 2 bits of the VT path level overhead byte V5 are used for carrying a BIP-2. The technique for this is illustrated in Figure 3–11. To save on overhead, the parity counts over all the odd and the even bit positions are combined and represented by the two bits of the BIP-2 code, respectively. Recall that the VT SPE is a multiframe spanning four SONET frames. The BIP-2 is calculated over all bytes in the previous VT SPE, including all overhead but the pointers (Figure 3–11).

Let us examine how effective the BIP-2 code is. The number of bits in the VT1.5 SPE is 832 ([(9 rows × 3 columns) – 1 pointer byte] × 8 bits/byte × 4 frames per SPE). Each bit of the BIP-2 code covers half the bits in the VT1.5 SPE, that is, 416 bits. Hence, BIP-2 can handle error rates of 1 in 500 bits (BER between 10^{-2} and 10^{-3}). Now, a VT6 is four times the size of the VT1.5. In this case, each parity bit covers 1664 bits, handling a BER slightly worse than 10^{-4}.

3.6.4 Remote Error Monitoring

The error monitoring capabilities provided by SONET and SDH enables the receiver to know the error count and compute the BER on the received signal at various layers. Based on this information, it is useful to let the sender learn about the quality of the signal received at the other end. The following mechanisms are used for this purpose.

The STS-1 line REI (M0 byte) is used by the receiver to return the number of errored bits detected at the line layer to the sender. The receiver arrives at this number by considering the difference between the received and the recomputed BIP-8 (B2) codes. In the case of an STS-*N* signal, the M1 byte is used for conveying the REI information. Clearly, up to 8 × *N* errors could be detected with STS-*N* BIP-8 codes (as each STS-1 is covered by its own BIP-8). But only a count of at most 255 can be reported in the single M1 byte. Thus, in signals of OC-48 and higher rates, the number 255 is returned when 255 or more errors are detected.

At the path layer, the receiver uses the first four bits of the G1 path overhead to return the number of errors detected (using the path BIP-8) to the sender. At the VT path layer, the receiver uses bit 3 of the V5 byte to indicate the detection of one or more errors to the sender.

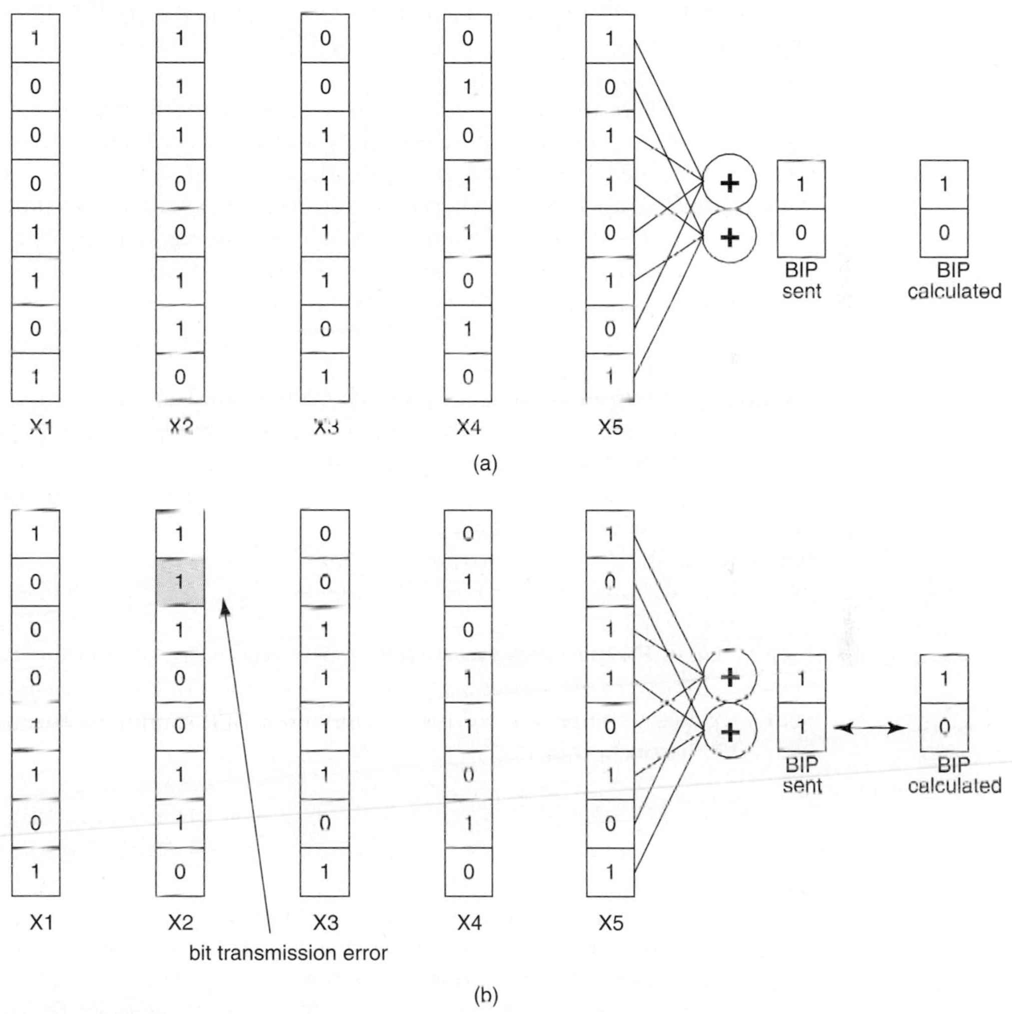

Figure 3–11 *BIP Calculation at the VT Path Level*

3.6.5 Performance Measures

When receiving word of a problem, one is inclined to ask some general questions such as: "How bad is it? "How long has it been this way?" and "Is it getting worse or better?" The following terminology is used in the transport world. An *anomaly* is a condition that gives the first hint of possible trouble. A *defect* is an affirmation that something has indeed gone wrong. A *failure* is a state where something has truly gone wrong. Whether an event notification or an alarm is sent to a management system under these conditions is a separate matter. Performance parameters in SONET and SDH are used to quantify these conditions.

A SONET or an SDH network element supports performance monitoring (PM) according to the layer of functionality it provides. A SONET network element accumulates PM data based on overhead bits at the Section, Line, STS Path, and VT Path layers. In addition, PM data are available at the SONET Physical layer using physical parameters. The following is a summary of different performance parameter defined in SONET. Similar performance parameters are also monitored and measured in SDH. For a detailed treatment on PM parameters on SONET refer to [Telcordia00].

PHYSICAL LAYER PERFORMANCE PARAMETERS • The physical layer performance measurement enables proactive monitoring of the physical devices to facilitate early indication of a problem before a failure occurs. Several physical parameters are measured, including laser bias current, optical power output by the transmitter, and optical power at the receiver. Another important physical layer parameter is the *Loss of Signal (LOS) second*, which is the count of 1-second intervals containing one or more LOS defects.

SECTION LAYER PERFORMANCE PARAMETERS • The following section layer performance parameters are defined in SONET. Note that all section layer performance parameters are defined for the near-end. There are no far-end parameters at the Section layer.

- *Code Violation* (*CV-S*): The CV-S parameter is a count of BIP errors detected at the section layer. Up to eight section BIP errors can be detected per STS-*N* frame.
- *Errored Second* (*ES-S*): The ES-S parameter is a count of the number of 1 second intervals during which at least one section layer BIP error was detected, or an SEF (see below) or LOS defect was present.
- *Errored Second Type A* (*ESA-S*) and *Type B* (*ESB-S*): ESA-S is the count of 1-second intervals containing one CV-S, and no SEF or LOS defects. ESB-S is the count of 1-second intervals containing more than one but less than *X* CV-S errors, and no SEF or LOS defects. Here, *X* is a user-defined number.
- *Severely Errored Second* (*SES-S*): The SES-S parameter is a count of 1-second intervals during which *K* or more Section layer BIP errors were detected, or an SEF or LOS defect was present. *K* depends on the line rate and can be set by the user.
- *Severely Errored Frame Second* (*SEFS-S*): The SEFS-S parameter is a count of 1-second intervals during which an SEF defect was present. An SEF defect is detected when the incoming signal has a minimum of four consecutive errored frame patterns. An SEF defect is expected

to be present when an LOS or LOF defect is present. But there may be situations when this is not the case, and the SEFS-S parameter is only incremented based on the presence of the SEF defect.

LINE LAYER PERFORMANCE PARAMETERS • At the SONET line layer, both near-end and far-end parameters are monitored and measured. Far-end line layer performance is conveyed back to the near-end LTE via the K2 byte (RDI-L) and the M0 or M1 byte (REI-L). Some of the important near-end performance parameters are defined below. The far-end parameters are defined in a similar fashion.

- *Code Violation (CV-L)*: The CV-L parameter is a count of BIP errors detected at the line layer. Up to 8*N* BIP errors can be detected per STS-*N* frame.
- *Errored Second (ES-L)*: The ES-L parameter is a count of 1-second intervals during which at least one line layer BIP error was detected or an AIS-L defect is present.
- *Errored Second Type A (ESA-L)* and *Type B (ESB-L)*: ESA-L is the count of 1-second intervals containing one CV-L error and no AIS-L defects. ESB-L is the count of 1-second intervals containing *X* or more CV-L errors, or one or more AIS-L defects. Here, *X* is a user-defined number.
- *Severely Errored Second (SES-L)*: The SES-L parameter is a count of 1-second intervals during which *K* or more line layer BIP errors were detected, or an AIS-L defect is present. *K* depends on the line rate and can be set by the user.
- *Unavailable Second (UAS-L)*: Count of 1-second intervals during which the SONET line is unavailable. The line is considered unavailable after the occurrence of 10 SES-Ls.
- *AIS Second (AISS-L)*: Count of 1-second intervals containing one or more AIS-L defects.

PATH LAYER PERFORMANCE PARAMETERS • Both STS path and VT path performance parameters are monitored at the path layer. Also, both near-end and far-end performance parameters are measured. Far-end STS path layer performance is conveyed back to the near-end STS PTE using bits 1 through 4 (REI-P) and 5 through 7 (RDI-P) of the G1 byte. Far-end VT path layer performance is conveyed back to the near-end VT PTE using bit 3 of the V5 byte (REI-V), and either bits 5 through 7 of the Z7 byte or bit 8 of the V5 byte (RDI-V). Some of the important near-end STS path performance parameters are defined below. The far-end parameters are defined in a similar fashion.

- *Code Violation (CV-P)*: Count of BIP-8 errors that are detected at the STS-path layer.

- *Errored Second (ES-P)*: Count of 1-second intervals containing one or more CV-P errors, one or more AIS-P, LOP-P, TIM-P, or UNEQ-P defects.
- *Errored Second Type A (ESA-P)* and *Type B (ESB-P)*: ESA-P is the count of 1-second intervals containing one CV-P error and no AIS-P, LOP-P, TIM-P, or UNEQ-P defects. ESB-P is the count of 1-second intervals containing more than one but less than *X* CV-P errors and no AIS-P, LOP-P, TIM-P, or UNEQ-P defects. Here, *X* is a user-defined number.
- *Severely Errored Second (SES-P)*: Count of 1-second intervals containing *X* or more CV-P errors, one or more AIS-P, LOP-P, TIM-P, or UNEQ-P defects. Here, *X* is a user-defined number.
- *Unavailable Second (UAS-P)*: Count of 1-second intervals during which the SONET STS-path is unavailable. A path is considered unavailable after the occurrence of 10 SESs.
- *Pointer Justification Counts*: To monitor the adaptation of the path payloads into the SONET line, the pointer positive and negative adjustment events are counted. The number of 1-second intervals during which a pointer adjustment event occurs is also kept track of.

3.7 Summary

SONET and SDH-based optical transport networks have been deployed extensively. It is therefore important to understand the fundamentals of these technologies before delving into the details of the control plane mechanisms. After all, the optical network control plane is a relatively recent development. Its primary application in the near term will be in SONET/SDH networks. In this context, it is vital to know about the low-level control mechanisms that already exist in SONET and SDH and how they help in building advanced control plane capabilities. The next chapter continues with a description of another key topic relevant to the control plane, that is, protection and restoration mechanisms in SONET and SDH networks. Following this, the subject of modern optical control plane is dealt with in earnest.

FOUR

Protection, Restoration, and Diversity in Optical Networks

4.1 Introduction

4.1.1 Overview

With a plethora of natural and man-made disasters that could affect telecommunication links and nodes, protection and restoration of telecommunication services is necessary not only to satisfy regulatory requirements and/or service level agreements (SLAs), but also to provide service differentiation. Before utilizing any particular form of protection or restoration, the time frame for the corrective action and the implications of failing to restore service within a particular time frame should be considered. In [Sosnosky94], Sosnosky reviewed the impact on public switched telephone network (PSTN) customers of progressively longer restoration times. This work is summarized in Figure 4–1.

Although this work reflects services common at the time of its publication, the service mix in today's networks is dramatically different. With the increase in volume and importance of IP traffic, a new set of threshold targets have to be considered. These include application timeouts based on lack of connectivity at the TCP layer and link failures and route removals detected by IP routing protocols. More important, the loss of revenue and other impacts to businesses could determine the tolerance to disruption in services.

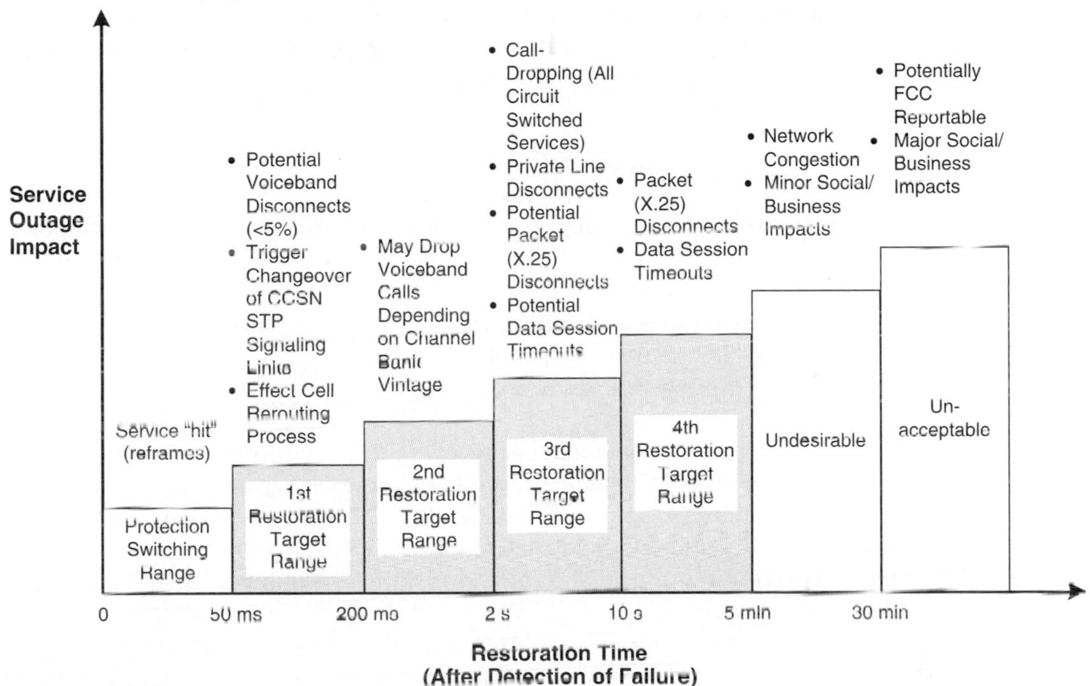

Figure 4–1 *Restoration Impact on PSTN Customers circa 1994 [Sosnosky94]*

4.1.2 Protection and Restoration Techniques and Trade-offs

The general idea behind protection and restoration techniques is to utilize redundant resources as backup when failures affect "primary" resources in use. The term *protection* is used to denote the paradigm whereby a dedicated backup resource is deployed to recover the services provided by a failed resource. In contrast, the term *restoration* is used to denote the paradigm whereby backup resources are not dedicated to specific primary resources, but a pool of resources is kept available for overall recovery purposes. Failure of a primary resource results in the allocation of a backup resource dynamically. This may result in significantly longer recovery times as compared with the protection case, but with possible improvements in network utilization. As we shall see in this chapter, there is in fact a continuum of techniques for recovery with specific advantages and disadvantages. Thus, the terms protection and restoration are used rather loosely in this chapter.

There are three fundamental qualities of any protection/restoration scheme: robustness, bandwidth efficiency, and recovery time. In addition, there are a number of practical aspects such as complexity, inter-vendor interoperability, and interoperability with control plane automation techniques, which have to be considered when evaluating protection and restoration schemes.

4.1.2.1 RELIABILITY/ROBUSTNESS

The main factors affecting the reliability and robustness of a restoration method are

- Failure types that are restorable
- Implementation complexity
- Distributed vs. centralized restoration

The types of failures that are recoverable range from single line failures to arbitrary network failures. The trade-off in considering schemes that handle limited failure scenarios and those that deal with more general failure is between flexibility and the increase in recovery time or in the variance of the recovery time (more general restoration methods will have larger variances in the time to recover).

The implementation complexity of a restoration scheme affects not only its ability to correctly perform its task when invoked, but also its ability to do no harm when not invoked. This condition is typically known as *imperfect fault coverage* or *imperfect fail-over.* If the probability of missing a fault or failing to restore is reasonably small (it does not have to be nearly as small as the failure probability for the connection or line), then the statistics for mean time to failure (for a connection) are still very good [Trivedi82]. If, on the other hand, the implementation complexity leads one astray from the protection maxim "do no harm," then the probability of this occurring directly impacts the overall connection reliability.

4.1.2.2 BANDWIDTH EFFICIENCY

The main factors affecting the bandwidth efficiency of a restoration method are

- Network structure
- Bandwidth granularity
- Distributed vs. centralized restoration
- Impact on existing connections

The restoration techniques and concepts are applicable to different layers in the communications hierarchy, for example, the optical layer, the electrical TDM hierarchy, or in virtual circuit packet switched technologies such as MPLS, Frame Relay, and ATM. In general, the coarser the granularity of restoration relative to the average span capacity, the fewer the circuits to be restored (repaired). There is, however, a trade-off between restoration granularity and bandwidth efficiency since fewer routing options may be available with coarser granularity, that is, it is more difficult to pack bigger circuits tightly than smaller ones in a given network.

It is clear that as the control of restoration is centralized, the vulnerability of restoration control increases and its robustness decreases. On the other hand, it is also true that distributed restoration cannot globally optimize the use of bandwidth over an entire network the way a centralized mechanism can. For instance, the global network optimization problem can be cast as a multicommodity flow problem, which is amenable to solution via linear programming techniques (see Chapter 11). Such techniques can be applied to those connections affected by a failure in the case of centralized control. Between distributed and centralized control, there is a spectrum of schemes that involve varying degrees of coordination.

Related to the centralized vs. distributed issue is whether one allows the disruption of some services, in order to restore some or all of the services affected by a failure. In other words, to restore the connections affected by the outage, other connections may need to be rerouted or preempted. In the case of centralized control, a global rerouting of connections in the network may be considered. In the case of distributed control, preemption mechanisms may be employed. Both approaches might result in a network running close to its capacity, but negatively impact a significant number of other connections not directly affected by the failure event. This also violates the "do no harm" principle.

4.1.2.3 RECOVERY TIME (SPEED AND DETERMINISM)

The main factors affecting the recovery time, speed and determinism are

- Network size and geographic extent
- Local versus end-to-end restoration
- Method used to find alternate routes
- Bandwidth reservation versus coordination time

There is nothing that a restoration algorithm can do to increase the speed of light. Hence, the geographic extent of the network sets a fundamental limit on how fast a restoration mechanism can react. As an example, the 4-fiber Bidirectional Line-Switched Ring (4F-BLSR) specification [ITU T95a] gives a recovery time performance, which scales with the physical dimensions of the ring. Another aspect that can affect the performance of a restoration algorithm is the size of the network in terms of the number of nodes and links.

The manner in which alternate paths are determined reflects a trade-off between robustness and recovery speed. Preconfiguration of alternate paths results in less path computation and set-up latency after a failure event.

Preconfigured paths, however, can only deal with a limited set of failure scenarios. Hence, preconfiguration is not as robust as computing alternate paths based on the current network information available after a failure event.

A trade-off exists between the amount of bandwidth reserved for restoration (and hence unavailable for other use) and the amount of time spent in adjudicating between connections that compete for that bandwidth. Bandwidth reservations are effective only in a limited number of failure scenarios. Additional coordination mechanisms can expand the failure scenarios that may be handled, but these increase the recovery time. Typical mechanisms used for coordination include priorities (which connection gets access to a bandwidth resource), preemption (can one connection disrupt another and under what circumstances), and crank-back (the ability to start the recovery procedure over and look for an alternate path). We will see examples of these in the protection mechanisms discussed in this chapter.

4.1.2.4 INTEROPERABILITY

There are three interoperability issues:

- Interoperability with other protection mechanisms
- Interoperability with automated provisioning, and
- Multivendor interoperability

4.2 Linear Protection

4.2.1 Introduction to Linear Protection

Linear protection is the simplest and perhaps the fastest of all the protection mechanisms. Figure 4–2 illustrates linear protection. In this figure, N (≥ 1) primary (or *working*) lines and M (≥ 1) backup (or *protection*) lines are shown. This is sometimes referred to as linear M:N protection. The lines shown can be SONET lines, WDM optical links, SDH paths, and so on. Additionally, the equipment shown on either end of the working and protection lines are those that terminate these signals in some form. There may be other equipment between these line termination equipment, but their operation will be essentially transparent and they do not participate in the linear protection mechanism. The basic idea behind linear protection is fairly simple: Should any of the N working lines fail, then the signal being transported over that line will be switched onto an available protection line. It seems like nothing could be simpler! There are, however, a few issues that need to be dealt with: (a) What is the benefit of linear protection? (b) What triggers the switchover to protection (called the "protection switch")? (c) If there are more working lines than protection lines, should

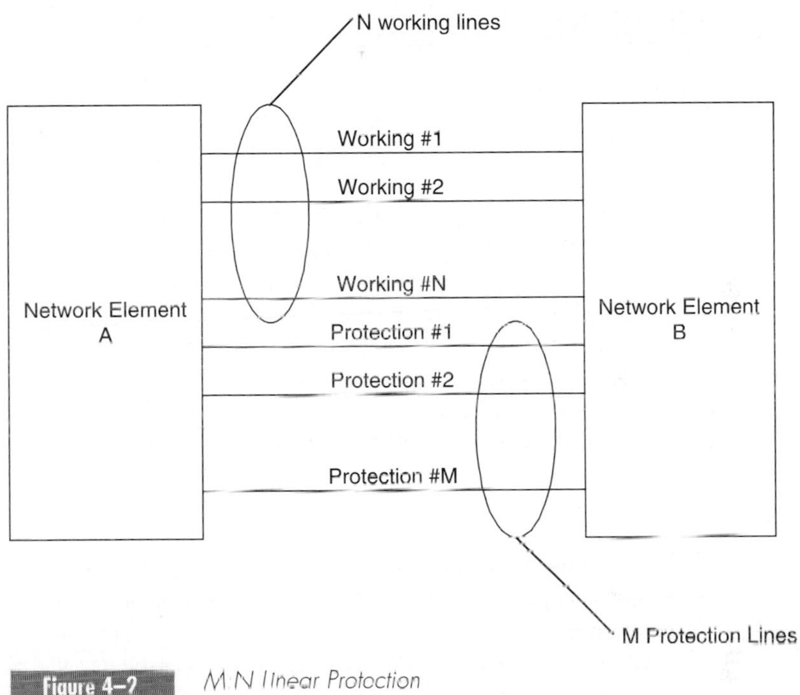

Figure 4–2 M:N Linear Protection

the traffic be *reverted* back to the original working line from the protection line once the working line is repaired? (d) If signals are bidirectional, then should protection be bidirectional or unidirectional? (e) How much coordination is involved between the two sides in implementing protection? and (f) Could idle protection line bandwidth be used for carrying working traffic?

4.2.1.1 BENEFIT OF LINEAR PROTECTION

To a provider of communications services, the *availability* of the service to customers is of prime concern since it tends to have associated legal and monetary consequences. Availability is a statistical quantity. Equation (1) gives the definition of availability in terms of *mean time before failure* (*MTBF*) and *mean time to repair* (*MTTR*), both of which are statistical quantities.

$$Availability = \frac{MTBF}{MTBF + MTTR} \quad (1)$$

Availability is typically expressed as a percentage, or in common jargon as "X nines." For example "five nines" is 99.999 percent, which implies that if the MTBF is one year than the MTTR must be less than 5.25 minutes.

Table 4–1 shows more examples of availability, MTBF and MTTR.

Table 4–1 *Example Availability, MTBF and MTTR*

Availability	MTBF	MTTR	MTBF	MTTR
99.999%	1 year	5.25 minutes	1 Month	25.9 seconds
99.9999%	1 year	31.5 seconds	1 Month	2.6 seconds

It is clear that the longer the time between failures and the quicker the time to repair, the higher the availability.

4.2.1.2 DETECTING THAT SOMETHING IS WRONG

MTTR also includes the time to detect the failure. This is significant since a correctable fault could go unnoticed until a phone call comes in from an unhappy customer. This, in effect, lengthens the MTTR unnecessarily. On the other hand, falsely reporting a fault violates the maxim of "do no harm" as it causes outages due to unnecessary protection switches. Hence, timely and accurate indication of fault conditions is an important aspect of any protection scheme. This is easier with some technologies than with others. For example, with SONET/SDH signals, loss of frame (LOF) or loss of pointer (LOP) can be detected very quickly and accurately. In addition, the extensive performance monitoring capabilities of SONET and SDH make it fairly easy to detect signal degrade or signal fail conditions that result in unacceptable signal quality (bit error rate). This is not the case in transparent (OOO) optical networks, where the main indicator of problems is a "loss of light" condition. Unfortunately, the presence of light does not necessarily indicate that the signal is in good shape.

4.2.1.3 TYPES OF LINEAR PROTECTION AND COMMUNICATION REQUIREMENTS

Figure 4–3 illustrates a very specialized form of linear protection known as 1+1 unidirectional protection. In this form of protection, the same signal (content) is sent on both the working and the protection lines. The receiver is responsible for selecting one of these signals, based on signal quality or fault information. No coordination is required between the sender and the receiver.

Figure 4–4 illustrates 1+1 protection for bidirectional links, that is, each "link" consists of receive and transmit fibers. In this case, the unidirectional 1+1 protection described earlier can still be applied. Specifically, the receiving node can select the signal from either the working or the protection lines. This could, however, result in one node receiving the signal from the working line while the other node receives the signal from the protection line. It may be required that both nodes receive the signal from the same line, working or

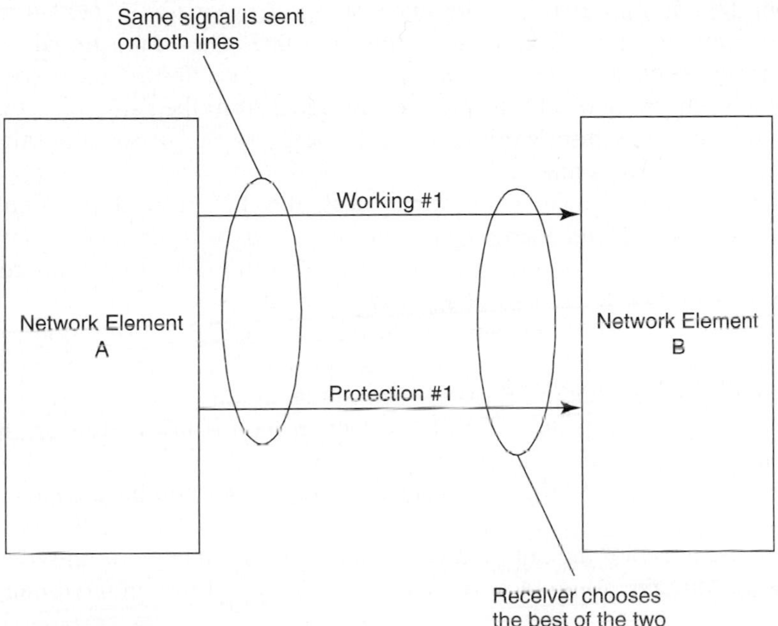

Figure 4–3 *Unidirectional 1+1 Protection*

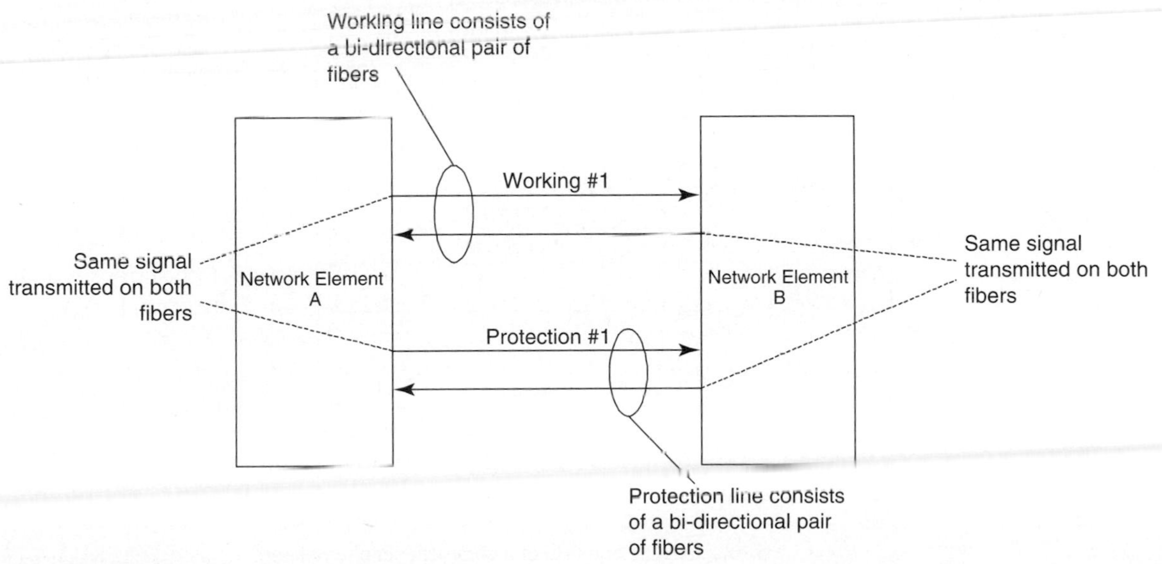

Figure 4–4 *Bidirectional 1+1 Protection*

protection. This is important, for instance, if servicing is to be performed on a fiber carrying the working or the protection line. The bidirectional 1+1 protection can be used in these cases. This type of protection requires coordination between the two sides to receive the signal from the same line, that is, if one side switches from working to protection (or vice versa), the other side should also do the same.

The next level of complexity comes with the 1:*N* protection scheme shown in Figure 4–5. Here, a single protection line is used to protect *N* working lines. When a failure occurs, the node detecting the failure must coordinate with the other node to determine which of the *N* working lines needs to be backed up by the protection line. As in the 1+1 case, the restoration can occur in unidirectional or bidirectional mode. Because the protection line is being shared among multiple working lines, the unidirectional mode can potentially restore more faults since the protection path is not tied up in the direction along which the working link is still functioning.

Finally, the general *M:N* case was shown in Figure 4–2. In this case, there are N working lines and M protection lines with $N > M$. Under *M:N* protection, the node detecting the failure must indicate to the other node the identity of the working line to protect, as well as the identity of the protection line to use.

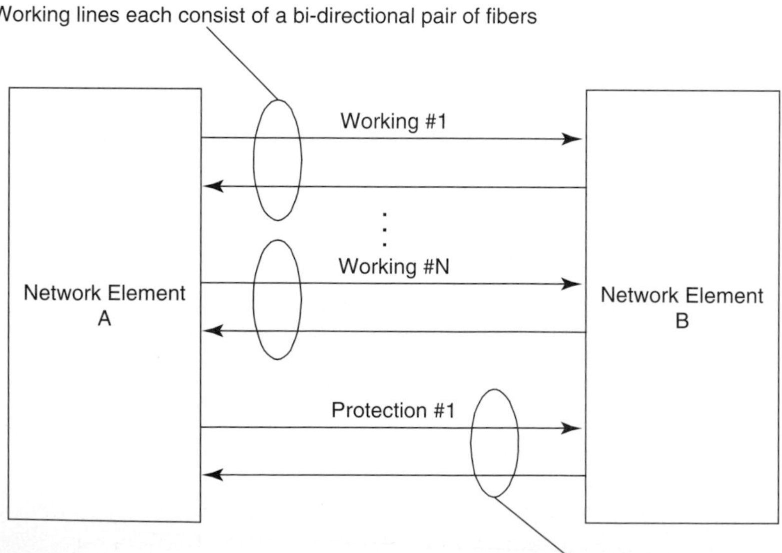

Figure 4–5 *Bidirectional 1:N Protection*

4.2.1.4 EXTRA TRAFFIC

Under 1+1 protection, the signal is concurrently sent on both the working and the protection lines. Under 1:*N* or *M:N* protection, however, the protection lines remain unused until a failure occurs. Thus, it seems reasonable to consider using the bandwidth on the protection line(s) for carrying lower priority traffic (called "extra traffic") that could be preempted. That is, the extra traffic would be dropped whenever the corresponding protection line is used to back up a working line after a failure event.

4.2.1.5 REVERSION

In the 1:*N* and *M:N* cases, what should be done after a protection switch? Well, a good idea would be to repair the fault in the working line. After that the signal may be *reverted* back to the repaired working line. This frees up the protection resources and also allows extra traffic to return to the protection link.

4.2.2 Theoretical Underpinning of Linear Protection

Although this section is not needed to understand the rest of this chapter, the subject is important as it deals with the quantitative benefits of protection and its limitations. Specifically, it will be shown that the benefits of *M:N* protection as compared with 1:*N* protection are not as significant as one might think. This is one of the reasons why interoperable standards for *M:N* linear protection do not yet exist.

The probabilistic quantities quoted here are based on "classic" assumptions of independence between the failure probabilities of the components of the protection group, that is, working and protection lines. It is assumed that the "lifetimes" of the lines involved are all exponentially distributed with the same mean λ, that is, each of the lines have an MTBF = 1/λ. The exponential nature of the probability distribution is actually quite a reasonable approximation as described in [Trivedi82].

As given in [Trivedi82], the MTBF for an *m-out-of-n* system with components having independent exponential lifetimes with mean λ is

$$MTBF_{m-out-n} = \sum_{i=m}^{n} \frac{1}{i\lambda} \qquad (2)$$

By an m-out-of-n system, we mean a system where m components out of n ($m <= n$) must be operational for the system to function. Since a 1:1 or 1+1 linear protection system can be viewed as a 1-out-of-2 system,

$$MTBF_{1:1,1+1} = \frac{1}{\lambda} + \frac{1}{2\lambda} \qquad (3)$$

Equation (3) shows that by adding a redundant line, the MTBF does not double but only increases by a half as compared with that of an unprotected line. If an additional redundant line is added to the 1:1 or 1+1 system, the MTBF only increases by a factor of $1/3\lambda$; hence we see that (1) gives us a "law of diminishing returns" in terms of the additional cost needed for each protection line. Another issue not reflected in (2) is that if a line fails (whether working or protect) it will be repaired. With a 1:*N* protection group, this is a significant effect since it frees the protection line once the failed line is repaired.

4.2.3 SONET/SDH Line Protection

SONET line (SDH Multiplex Section (MS) protection can be applied between two interconnected pieces of SONET line (SDH MS) equipment, and it is one of the most widely used forms of optical protection. In linear 1+1 switching, the same SONET line signal is sent (bridged) on two separate SONET links, and the receiving equipment selects which of the copies to use. In the linear 1:*N* case, *N* working lines share one protection line (which can also be used to carry extra traffic). Although linear protection is the simplest category of protection, the SONET/SDH protocols for this are somewhat complex due to the features supported.

SONET/SDH protection switching is automatically initiated under two general conditions: signal fail and signal degrade. Signal fail is a hard failure condition such as loss of signal, loss of frame or the occurrence of AIS-L (see Chapter 3). In addition, signal fail is also declared when the line BER exceeds a user-specified threshold in the range, 10^{-3} to 10^{-5}. The signal degrade condition, on the other hand, is a soft failure condition triggered when the line BER exceeds a user-specified threshold in the range, 10^{-5} to 10^{-9}. These threshold settings are associated with individual SONET lines (SDH Multiplex Sections).

4.2.4 SDH/SONET Linear 1:N Protection

4.2.4.1 INTRODUCTION

Linear 1:*N* protection allows up to fourteen working lines to be protected by one protection line. In addition, when not used for protection purposes a protection line can also be used to carry extra traffic [ANSI95c, ITU-T95a].

The user can assign a protection priority (high or low) for each working channel. This priority is used to determine which requests for protection take precedence in the APS protocol. In the case of a tie, the channel with the lowest APS channel number is given priority. Note that the APS channel number is a user-assigned protection attribute for the line and is distinct from other line identifiers (port numbers, etc.). It must be consistently set at each end of a SONET/SDH link.

4.2.4.2 GROUP CONFIGURATION

The configuration of a linear APS system first requires the configuration of a linear 1:*N* APS group. This starts with the creation of a new APS group and the selection of its attributes (Table 4–2). These include name, type (1:*N* or 1+1), reversion, and wait-to-restore period. The next step is to add the protection and working lines to this APS group.

The APS protocol requires the use of channel numbers for the working lines in an APS group. These are numbers between 1 and 14 assigned to the working lines independently of their port numbers. Note that the number 0 is reserved for the protection channel (sometimes referred to as the null channel), and 15 is reserved for describing extra data that can optionally be carried over the protection channel.

4.2.4.3 LINE PARAMETERS

Table 4–3 lists the parameters that can be set at the individual line level. Note that the user must necessarily specify those parameters without defaults.

In addition to the line level parameters, two key APS statistics are kept at the line level: Protection Switch Count (PSC) and Protection Switch Duration (PSD).

4.2.5 SONET/SDH K1/K2 Linear APS (LAPS) Protocol

The K1 and K2 bytes in the SONET line (SDH MS) overhead are used to control automatic protection switching (APS). Although most of the configuration of APS groups is done at the management layer, a few code points from the

Table 4–2 *APS Group Parameters*

Parameter	Description	Default
Name	The name of the group	N/A
Protection Group Type	= 1+1, 1:N	N/A
Protection Line	The protection line	N/A
Working Line	A list of the working lines	N/A
Directionality	Unidirectional (only in 1+1 case) or Bi-directional	N/A
Reversion	Nonrevertive or Revertive option. Default for 1:N is revertive, for 1+1 nonrevertive [Bellcore95]	See description
WTR Period	Wait-to-Restore period (for revertive switching only)	5 minutes

Table 4–3 *APS Line Parameters*

Parameter	Description	Default
Channel Number	= 0 – 14 (limited by the K1 bits 5-8, see for details)	N/A
APS Line Type	Working or Protect	N/A
Extra Traffic	Extra Traffic State, applies to protect line only	N/A
APS Line Priority	APS line priority: High or Low	Low
SF BER Exponent	BER threshold to cause switchover due to signal failure.	10-5
SD BER Exponent	BER threshold to cause switchover due to signal degrade	10-7

K1 byte (bits 5–8) are also used to inform the other side of the link about APS configuration (e.g., whether the APS group is configured for 1+1 or 1:*N* operation, unidirectional or bidirectional modes, etc.). Table 4–4 illustrates this. The K1 and K2 bytes of the protection channel are used in both directions as the signaling channel for the APS group. These bytes are considered valid if

Table 4–4 *K1 bits (1–4) Request Codes for LAPS*

Bits 1-4	Condition
1111	Lockout of protection
1110	Forced switch
1101	Signal fail—high priority (not used in 1+1)
1100	Signal fail—low priority
1011	Signal degrade—high priority (not used in 1+1)
1010	Signal degrade—low priority
1001	(Not used)
0110	Wait-to-restore (revertive only)
0101	(Not used)
0100	Exerciser
0010	Reverse request (bidirectional only)
0001	Do not revert (nonrevertive only)
0000	No request

they are identical in three successive frames. Since the frame time is 125 μs, this gives a worse case of 375 μs notification (signaling) latency, not including propagation delay.

4.2.5.1 UNIDIRECTIONAL CASE

The linear APS (LAPS) protocol is described by considering the unidirectional case first (Figure 4–6). As per standard APS terminology [ANSI95c], the transmitter of the signal is denoted as the *head end* and the receiver of the signal as the *tail end*. It is the tail end's duty is to request an APS switch based upon the detection of either signal fail, signal degrade, or an external command. When the tail end detects such a condition, it puts the appropriate command code (see Table 4–4) in bits 1–4 of the K1 byte being sent to the head end on the *protection line*. The tail end sends the channel number of the line requesting protection action in bits 5–8 of the K1 byte, as shown in Table 4–5. (Note that the command code is mostly informative in the unidirectional switching case, but it is important in the bidirectional, multiple failure case.)

When the head end receives the request from the tail end, it first bridges or switches the appropriate working line onto the protection line. It then writes the channel number of this working line in bits 1–4 of the K2 byte of the protection line, as shown in Table 4–6. At this point, the tail end selects the protection line as a substitute for the failed working line.

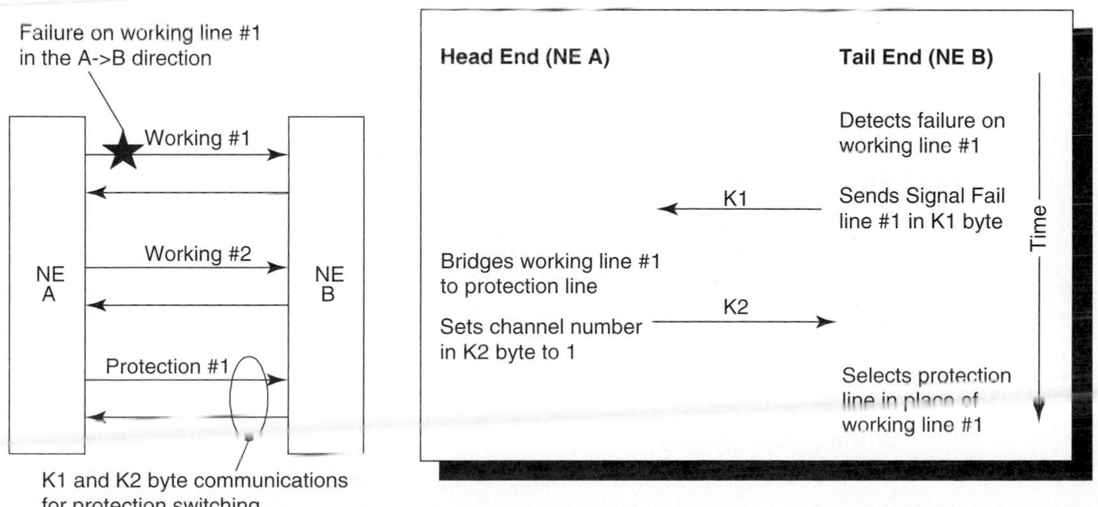

Figure 4–6 *1:N Unidirectional LAPS Switch-Over*

Table 4–5 *K1 (bits 5–8), Channel Numbers and Meaning*

Channel Number	Function
0	Protection channel requesting switch action. The protection channel will be supplied with a signal containing valid transport overhead for carriage of the APS bytes and line BIP-8.
1–14	Number of the working channel requesting switch action
15	Extra traffic is present on the protection channel (not valid for 1+1)

4.2.5.2 BIDIRECTIONAL CASE

In the unidirectional case, the tail end used the K1 byte to request a bridge from the head end and the head end indicated the completion of this request by writing the channel number into bits 1–4 of the K2 byte. In the bidirectional case, the head end is also responsible for initiating the second half of the bidirectional switch. It does this by putting the *reverse request code*, 0010, into bits 1–4 of the K1 byte and the channel number of the working line to be switched into bits 5–8 of the K1 byte. The tail end processes this switch request and puts the desired working line onto the protection line. It also places the channel number into bits 1–4 of the K2 byte sent on the protection line. At this point, the bidirectional APS switch has completed. This process is shown in Figure 4–7.
Now, in the unidirectional case the priorities of APS requests from different working lines within the same protection group could be evaluated based on local information only. In the bidirectional case, requests received from the far

Table 4–6 *K2 Bit Functions*

Bits	Function
1–4	These bits indicate the number of the channel that is bridged onto the protection line unless channel 0 is received on bits 5–8 of K1 (in this case, they will be set to 0000)
5	1 = Provisioned for 1:N mode
	0 = Provisioned for 1+1 mode
6–8	111 = AIS-L
	110 = RDI-L
	101 = Provisioned for bidirectional switching
	100 Provisioned for unidirectional switching
	000-011 reserved for future use

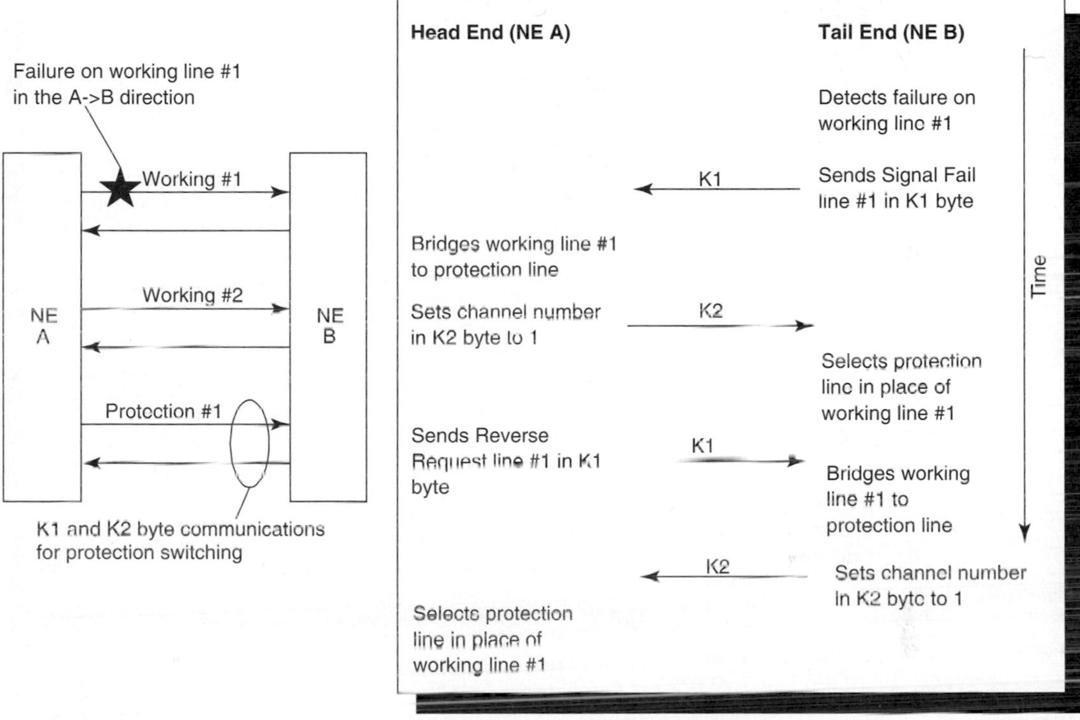

Figure 4–7 *Bidirectional 1:N LAPS with Message Sequence Chart*

end via the K1 byte also need to be evaluated. Figure 4–8 illustrates a bidirectional 1:2 protection group. In this example, working line #2 undergoes a signal degrade condition first, prompting a bidirectional protection switch. Note that Network Element (NE) A sends an indication to NE B via the K1 byte of this signal degrade condition on line #2. At a later time, working line #1 experiences a signal fail. This signal failure is detected directly at NE B. Since this is a higher priority request (i.e., the locally detected signal failure vs. the asserted signal degrade via the K1 byte), the signal on working line #1 will be switched onto the protection line. At the time of the failure on line #1, NE B compares the remote request being received on K1 from NE A to the local condition that it has detected.

4.2.5.3 REVERSION AND WAIT TO RESTORE

Since a single protection line protects many working lines, it is highly desirable to switch a signal back to the original working line once the fault condition that caused the switchover has been cleared. This process is called *rever-*

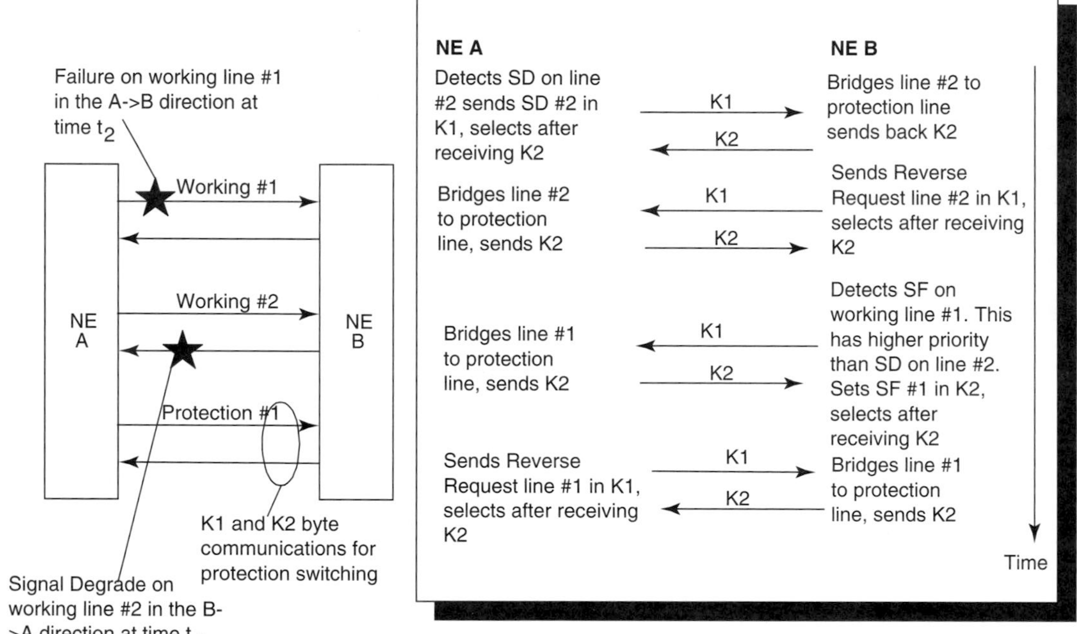

Figure 4–8 *Bidirectional 1:N Protection with Multiple Failures of Different Priorities*

sion. A potential issue with reversion is that a line can experience an intermittent failure, that is, one that comes and goes. When such a condition exists, the signal on that line would tend to be switched back and forth between the working and protection lines. Rapid protection switching and reversion can wreak havoc on the signal quality. Hence, instead of reverting the signal back to its working line immediately after the failure is cleared, the reversion is delayed for an interval of time. This time interval is known as the *Wait To Restore* (WTR) period. This is typically 5 minutes but can usually be set to other values (some service providers may want to wait till a non-peak traffic period to restore).

Now, what happens if there is a failure on another line during the WTR period? From Table 4–4, it can be seen that the WTR is also a command sent in the K1 byte to indicate that the protection line is in the WTR "mode." This command has a lower priority than either the signal fail or the signal degrade condition. Hence, another line experiencing a failure or degrade condition can be immediately switched onto the protection line during the WTR period.

4.2.6 APS Commands

The "external" APS commands are listed in Table 4–7 in order of their priority, with *protection lockout* having the highest precedence. Automatically generated "commands," for example, such as switching based on detection of signal fail, have lower priority than *forced* switch and higher priority than *manual* switch. Hence, a switch based on signal degrade or a signal fail conditions takes precedence over a manual switch request, but not a forced switch request.

4.2.7 Linear Subnetwork Connection Protection

Linear *M:N* protection, as discussed earlier, works on a link basis. A transport network, however, may consist of a number of switching layers as discussed in previous chapters. Figure 4–9 illustrates a SONET line (SDH MS) being carried over a network of transparent optical switches (or at least switches that appear transparent to the SONET line layer) denoted as PXCs (see Chapter 1). In this case, the connection between the SONET line equipment via the transparent optical network can be considered as a *subnetwork connection*. In such a situation, the individual subnetwork connections (SNCs) can be protected via a linear protection scheme implemented by the end systems that terminate that SNC.

When setting up the working and protection SNCs within a protection group, it is important to understand whether the SNCs are physically diverse across the subnetwork. For example, if it turns out that these connections traverse the same path within the subnetwork, then the probability of the protection SNC being available in the event of a problem with the

Table 4–7 *APS Commands*

Command	Description
Protection Lockout	Prevents the chosen working line from being switched to the protection line. If the protection line is chosen, this will lockout all protection switching requests.
Forced Switch	Forces a switch from either a working line—to the protection line or the protection line—to a working line without regard to the state of either line.
Manual Switch	Initiates a switch from either a working line—to the protection line or the protection line—to a working line, assuming the line being switched is not in the failed state. This command has lower priority than the previous two. Also, this command has lower priority than automatically initiated requests based on signal fail or degrade conditions.
Exercise	Exercises the APS protocol without causing a switchover.
Clear	Clears any of the above switching requests or protocol exercises.

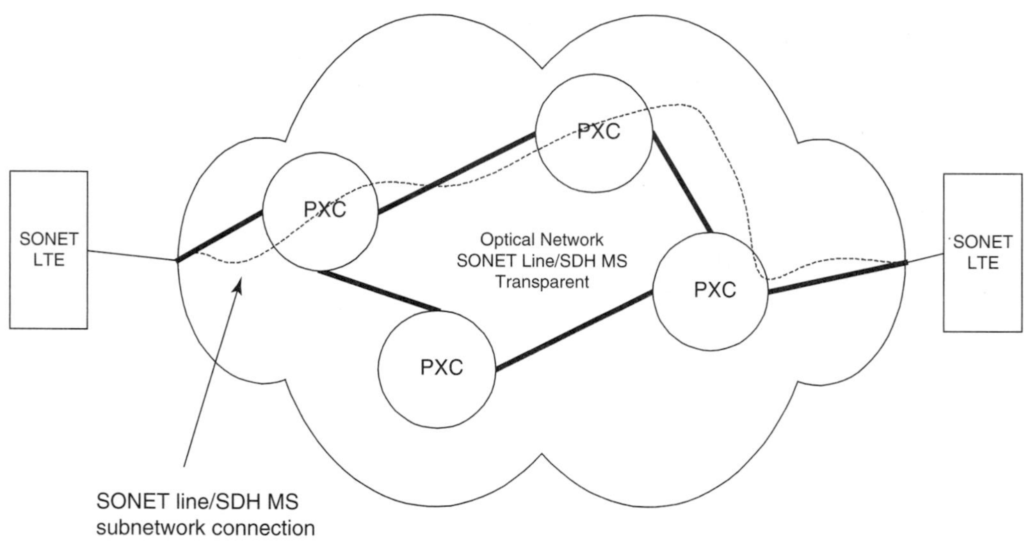

Figure 4–9 *Example of a SONET Line/SDH MS as a Subnetwork Connection across a Transparent Optical Network*

working SNC will be greatly reduced. In particular, in Figure 4–9, if the links within the subnetwork are single fiber WDM links, then two SNCs on the same path are actually on the same fiber and hence vulnerable to the same fiber cuts.

4.2.7.1 1+1 SUBNETWORK CONNECTION PROTECTION

The primary responsibility for implementing SNC protection rests with the end systems rather than the subnetwork elements. Since elaborate linear protection mechanisms are currently only defined for the SONET line (SDH MS) layer, most SNC protection is done via the unidirectional 1+1 approach discussed in section 4.2.1.3. It was seen previously, however, that 1+1 mechanisms are not bandwidth efficient when compared to 1:N methods. But if only a relatively few finer granularity SNCs require additional protection then a 1+1 SNC method may be appropriate.

As an example, consider a SONET OC-48 (2.5 Gbps) line containing a mix of different types of traffic. Suppose it is desired that a particular STS-1 SPE within this OC-48 be protected. For this, either 1:1 protection can be established at the SONET line level (with 2.5 Gbps of protection capacity ensured on all the links within the line level subnetwork), or a 1+1 protection group can be set up at the STS-1 SPE level. The latter would require an additional 51 Mbps of capacity within the subnetwork. Since the SONET STS path level supports good performance monitoring and fault management capabilities, implementation of the 1+1 SNC functionality is straightforward. Hence, instead of requiring another OC-48 line dedicated to protection purposes (2.5 Gbps) only an additional 51 Mbps of bandwidth needs to be found on an alternative link (this other link does not have to have the same overall capacity).

4.2.7.2 VIRTUAL 1:*N* SUBNETWORK CONNECTION PROTECTION

Linear SNC protection considered in the previous two sections requires minimal involvement from the subnetwork itself, that is, only the end systems were involved in restoration and the subnetwork only provided diverse

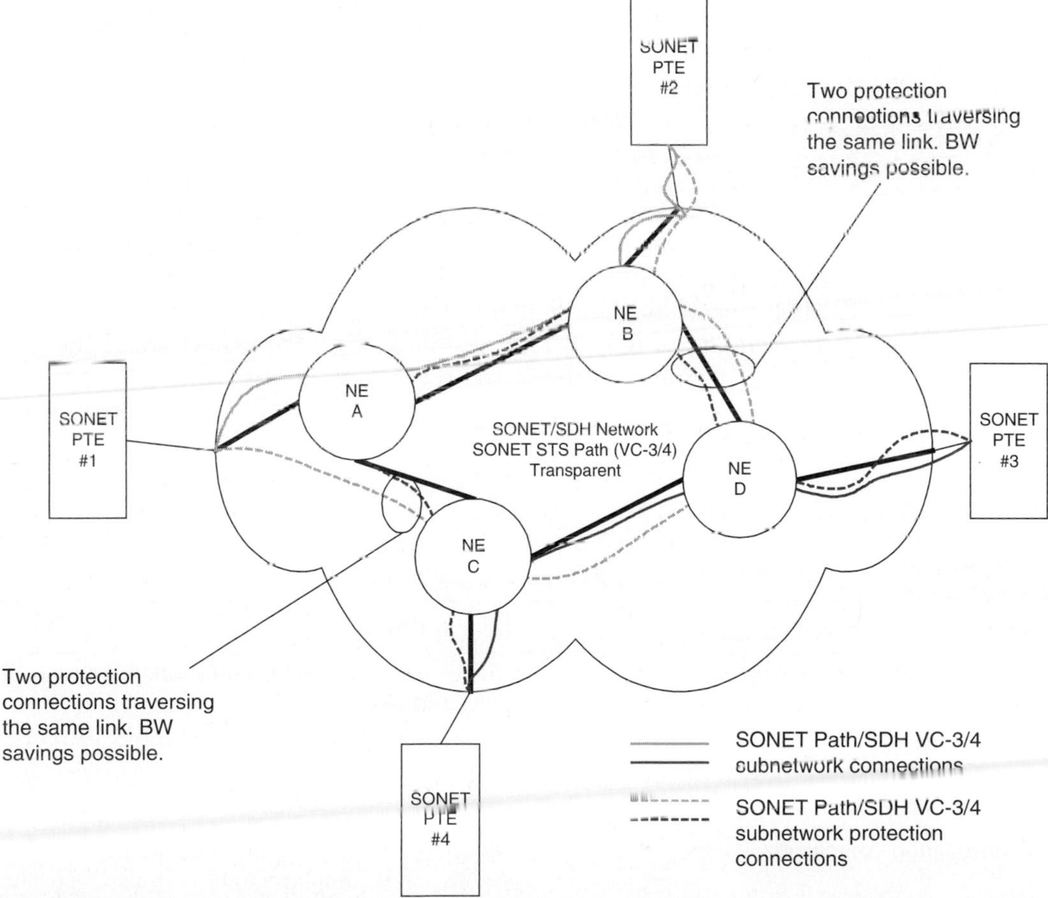

Figure 4–10 *Potential Bandwidth Savings with Linear SNC Protection (Virtual 1:N SNC)*

paths for working and protection SNCs. Figure 4–10 illustrates SNC level protection. Here, two SONET path level (SDH VC-3/4 level) SNCs are set up between two pairs of SONET path termination equipment (PTE). In addition, two diversely routed protection connections are set up between these pairs of PTE.

As seen from Figure 4–10, the two protection connections *could* share the capacity on the links between NE A and NE C, and between NE B and NE D. For the sharing to be implemented, the sub-network itself must now get involved, that is, the subnetwork must understand the difference between working and protection connections so that only protection connections are allowed to share bandwidth on a link. More elaborate mechanisms are possible to avoid the sharing of bandwidth among protection connections whose working connections are vulnerable to the same failures. For the subnetwork to respond to a failure or signal degrade condition, either it must be informed of such a condition by the end system(s) or it must perform some type of nonintrusive fault and/or performance monitoring of the SNC.

This type of protection generally works in a mesh subnetwork, and it is called "shared mesh protection." Recall that in section 1.2 it was emphasized that there are always trade-offs involved with various restoration techniques. The SNC protection scheme described above gives up robustness for bandwidth efficiency. Specifically, a connection cannot be restored if failures impact both the working and protection paths. This is analogous to 1:N line level protection in that the diversity of the working and protection paths determines the overall reliability. Table 4–8 summarizes the design choices concerning reliability and robustness of virtual 1:N SNC protection. Table 4–9 summarizes the bandwidth efficiency and restoration speed design choices.

Table 4–8 *Virtual 1:N SNC Protection: Reliability and Robustness Design Choices*

Factor	Design Choice
Failure types that are restorable	One or more failures that affect the original path only, and not the diverse reserved path
Distributed vs. Centralized restoration	Distributed
Interoperability with other protection schemes	Fully interoperable with line layer 1+1, 1:N, BLSR and source rerouted mesh
Implementation complexity	Set up of diverse path and reserved protection path slightly more complicated than regular connection establishment. Restoration behavior simpler than source reroute mesh restoration.

Table 4–9 *Virtual 1:N SNC Protection: Bandwidth Efficiency and Restoration Speed Design Choices*

Factor	Design Choice
Bandwidth granularity	Same as connection granularity
Impact on existing connections	None. If "extra traffic" option is used then this traffic will be preempted in the case of restoration
Local vs. End-to-End restoration	End-to-end restoration
Method(s) used to find alternative routes	Precalculated diverse route
Bandwidth reservation vs. coordination time	Protection bandwidth is reserved. No contention coordination is required.

4.3 Ring-Based Protection

4.3.1 Introduction/Background

Ring-based protection has been part of the transport network landscape for some time due to the wide deployment of ring network topologies. More recently, interest has arisen in ring-based protection independent of the underlying network topology. In this chapter, the theoretical underpinnings of ring-based protection are reviewed and a wide range of ring implementations and applications are studied. This includes access rings, shared protection transport rings, a variant of the shared protection ring suitable for transoceanic cable use, software defined rings, and a new ringlike protection mechanism known as *p-cycles*.

4.3.2 Theoretical Background on Rings

Suppose that there are a number of nodes that have to be interconnected. Given that their bandwidth requirements are similar, what is the advantage of a more complex ring topology compared with a simpler (linear) tree topology? The justification given here is a generalization of an example given in [Cahn98]. Certain simplifying assumptions are made in this description, but these do not affect the fundamental results. First, node failures are ignored. Second, it is assumed that all link failures are uncorrelated and that the probability of failure for a link is denoted by p (≤ 1). Taking a global view, the reliability of a network is defined to be the probability that the nodes remain "connected" by working links (i.e., it is possible to reach any node from any other). Given that N nodes are to be interconnected in a network topology, the fewest links are utilized when the topology is a tree. This topology would consist of N-1 links. The probability of failure of a network with a tree topology is the same as the probability that one or more links fail, or conversely, 1 minus the probability that no link fails. This is given by equation (4) below.

$$P_{tree}(failure) = 1 - (1 - p)^{n-1} \quad (4)$$

If a ring configuration, instead of the tree topology, is chosen, an additional link will be required for a total of N links. The reliability of the ring topology is the same as the probability that two or more links have failed, or conversely, it is 1 – (the probability that no links have failed + that one link has failed). This is given by equation (5) below.

$$P_{ring}(failure) = 1 - (1 - p)^n - np(1 - p)^{n-1} \quad (5)$$

Now, if $p << 1$, that is, the probability of link failure is small, then using some manipulations based on the binomial expansion of powers of sums and only keeping the dominant terms, the following approximations to the preceding probabilities are obtained:

$$P_{tree}(failure) \approx (n - 1)p \quad (6)$$

$$P_{ring}(failure) \approx \frac{n(n-1)}{2} p^2(1 - p)^{n-2} \quad (7)$$

Equations (6) and (7) confirm the intuitive notions concerning rings and tree (or linear) networks. In particular, rings have a better reliability, that is, the network failure probability decreases as the square of the link failure probability p rather than only at a linear rate for a tree network. Also, the reliability gets worse as the ring size (n) increases. This is because the larger the number of nodes n, the higher the probability that two links will be simultaneously out of service.

4.3.3 UPSRs (Unidirectional Path Switched Rings)

The simplest ring topology to implement is also the one most often used in access networks. A Unidirectional Path-Switched Ring (UPSR) is essentially a 1+1 unidirectional protection scheme incorporated in a ring network architecture. Figure 4–11 illustrates a SONET UPSR. There is a SONET bidirectional fiber transmission pair between each pair of nodes. These pairs form two different "counter-rotating" rings, that is, rings whose transmission directions are in opposite directions. When a node wishes to communicate with another node, it sends two copies of the signal in opposite directions around the ring, that is, on the two different counter-rotating transmission paths. Thus, one of these paths can be considered the working path and the other the protection path.

The "path" part of the UPSR comes from the fact that indications from the SONET STS-*Nc* path layer (VC-3/VC-4 in SDH) are used to select the better quality signal from the working and protection paths. The "unidirectional" part of a UPSR is a little less obvious since information is being sent along

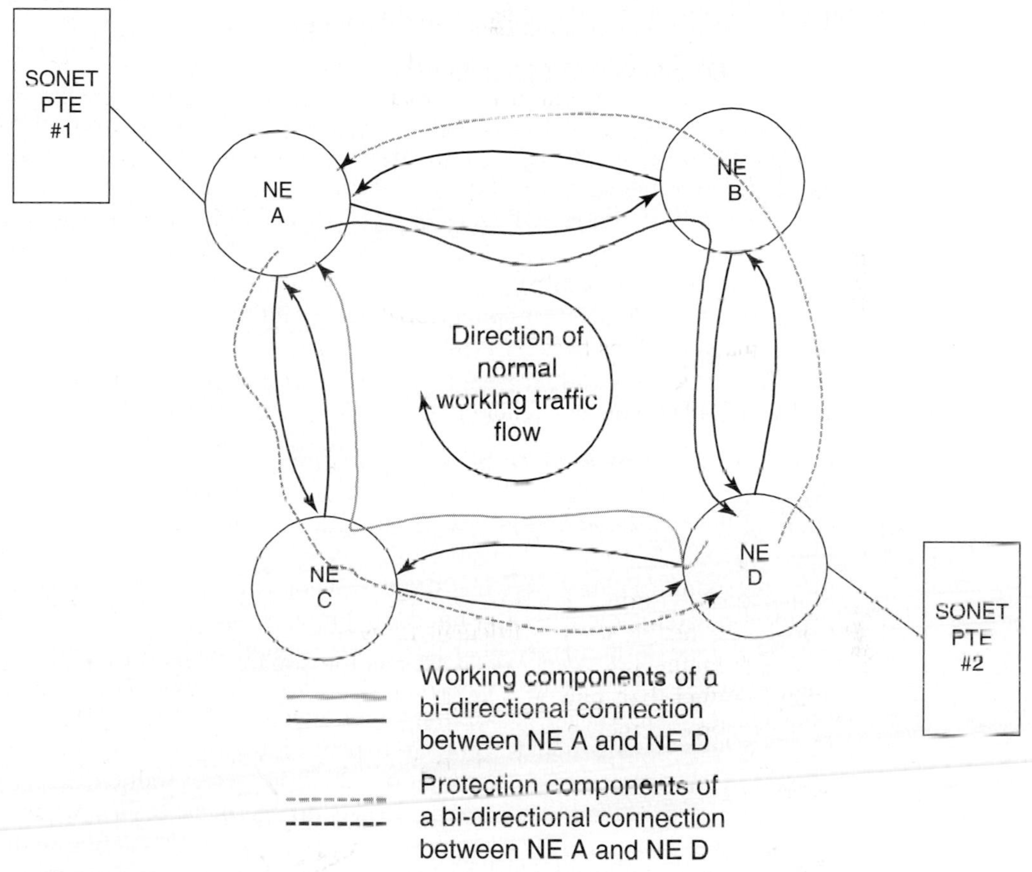

Figure 4–11 *UPSR Example*

both directions of the ring. Figure 4–11 shows a bidirectional path connection over the UPSR between nodes A and D. The working path from A to D is A-B-D, while the working path from D to A is D-C-A. Hence the two-way traffic between nodes travels only a single direction around the ring under normal circumstances. The advantage of this arrangement is that given a fiber cut anywhere on the ring only one direction of the connection has to be restored (via a very fast select operation).

Note that bidirectional communication between any two nodes requires bandwidth around the entire ring. This may be fine in access situations where all the traffic is heading between "access nodes" and a "head end," but it is extremely wasteful in more general networking applications.

4.3.4 BLSR–Bidirectional Line Switched Rings (MS Shared Protection Rings)

Bidirectional Line Switched Ring (BLSR) (called Multiplex Section Shared Protection Ring or MS SPRING in SDH) was developed to overcome the bandwidth inefficiency of UPSRs. In the following, we first consider the Two Fiber Bidirectional Line Switched Ring (2F-BLSR) and compare it with UPSR. We then consider Four Fiber BLSR (4F-BLSR). To understand the functionality and advantages of BLSR, service classes in ring networks will be examined, followed by an examination of the operation of BLSRs using K byte protocols.

4.3.4.1 TWO FIBER BLSRs

Figure 4–12 illustrates a 2F-BLSR, where time slots are allocated in each fiber for working and protection traffic. In particular, working traffic on channel m ($< N/2$) on one fiber is protected by channel $N/2+m$ on the other fiber.

As seen in Figure 4–12, half the bandwidth in a 2F-BLSR is reserved for protection. Here, there is a connection between nodes A and B and one between nodes A and D. Neither has a preassigned protection connection.

Figure 4–13 illustrates protection in a 2F-BLSR. Here, the link between nodes C and D has failed, disrupting the connection between nodes A and D. Both nodes C and D initiate protection procedures by redirecting traffic the other way around the ring. In addition, they both select traffic that previously came from the failed link from the protection channels. Nodes A and B simply allow the protection channel traffic to *pass through*. This is one of the reasons why both 2F-BLSRs and 4F-BLSRs are so fast, that is, only two nodes must perform active switching during ring protection. This is quite an advantage over more general mesh protection techniques.

Figure 4–14 illustrates an alternative failure scenario. Comparing this figure to Figure 4–13, it is seen that the same protection channels on the link from NE A to NE C and the link from NE B to NE D are used in both failure scenarios. This is why a BLSR is more bandwidth efficient than a UPSR. SDH therefore refers to BLSRs as shared protection rings.

Considering Figures 4–12 through 4–14, particularly the connection from node A to node D via node C, it can be seen that the time slots used on each link are the same for the connection. This restriction simplifies the amount of information that must be known on the ring to perform a ring switch. This, however, can also exacerbate the bandwidth fragmentation problem described in Chapter 3 (section 3.2.1). An alternative is to allow *time slot interchange* at the nodes in a ring, that is, each node can, if desired, map the connection to different channels.

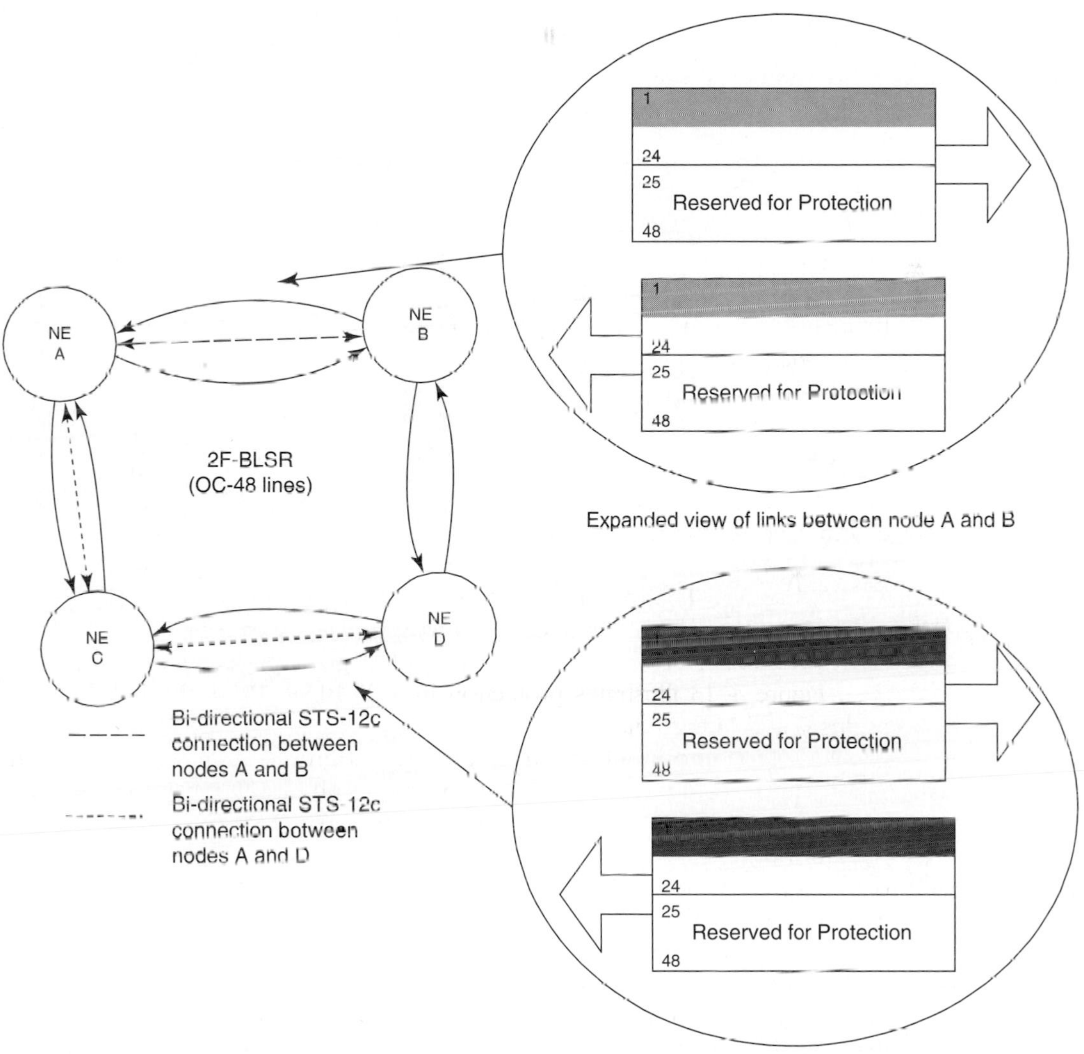

Figure 4–12 *2F-BLSR Network*

4.3.4.2 FOUR FIBER BLSRs

Four fiber BLSR (4F-BLSR) is used when more capacity is needed than what is available in a 2F-BLSR. Each link of a 4F-BLSR contains a dedicated pair of fibers for carrying working traffic and another dedicated pair for protection

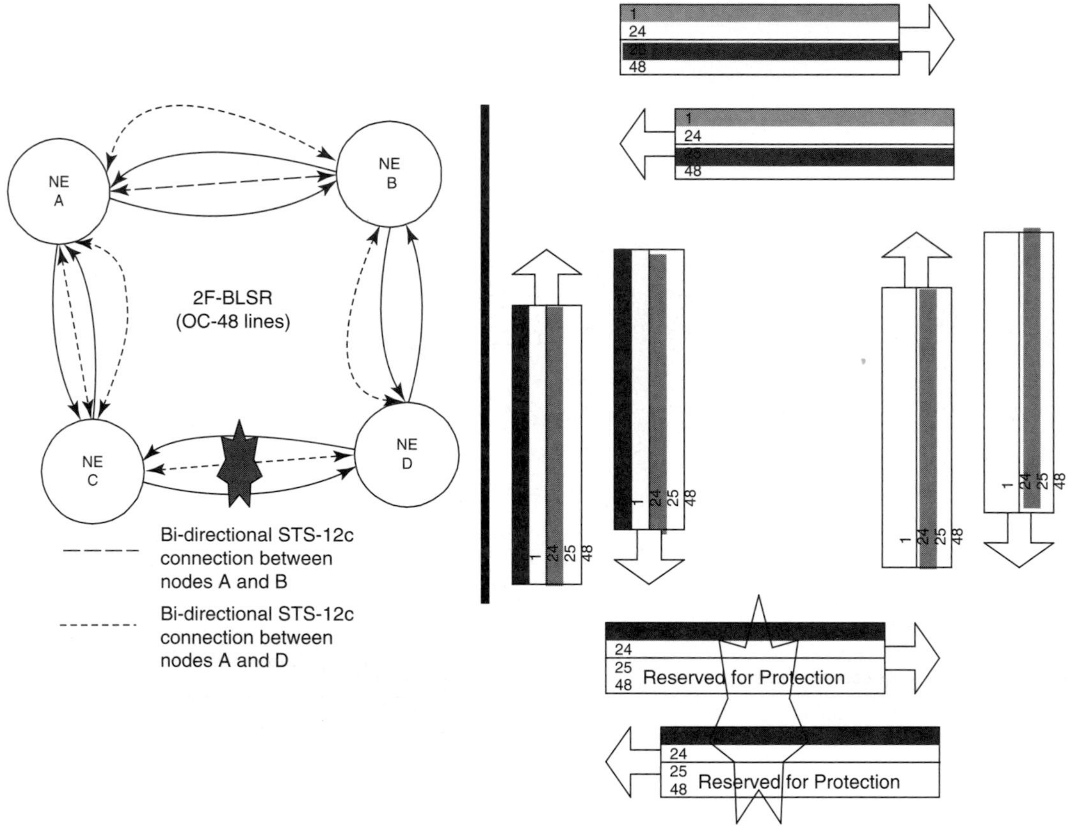

Figure 4–13 *Ring Protection in a 2F-BLSR Network*

traffic. Figure 4–15 illustrates the original UPSR network (Figure 4–11), upgraded to a 4F-BLSR. As in a 2F-BLSR, half of the bandwidth on this ring is reserved for protection purposes. A 4F-BLSR, however, has one additional advantage even over a 2F-BLSR due to the fact that both working and protection fiber links are present on each span between nodes on the ring. This is the ability to perform 1:1 span-based protection in addition to ring-based protection.

Figure 4–16 depicts the 4F-BLSR protocol for reacting to a break in the working fiber on a single span. Here, a fault has occurred on the working fiber pair between nodes C and D. Because the protection fiber pair is still operational, a simple span switch as in the bidirectional 1:1 linear case is used to restore the working line.

The reliability of UPSR and 2F-BLSR topologies are comparable to that of a protected linear network with the same connectivity. Comparing 4F-BLSR

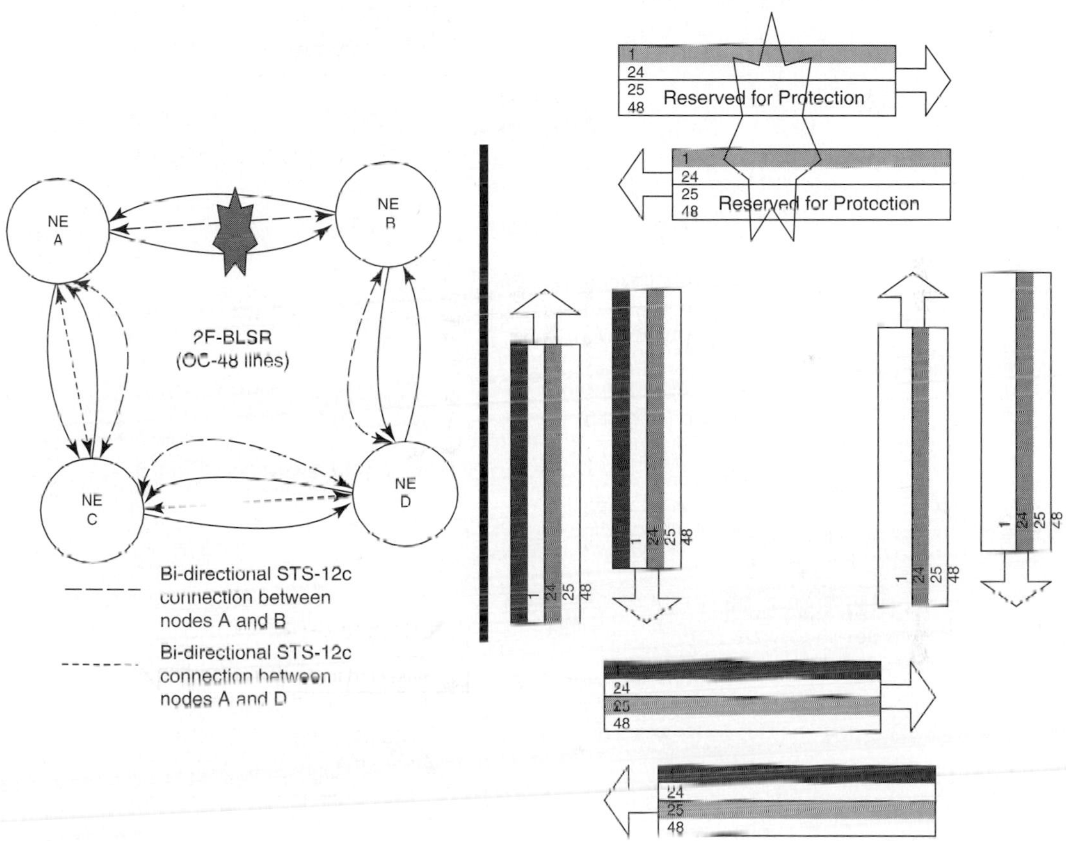

Figure 4–14 *Alternative 2F-BLSR Network Failure Scenario*

with a linear network where every span is protected via linear 1:1 protection, the failure probability p used in equations (3) and (4) (sections 4.2.2 and 4.3.2) is that of the entire 1:1 link failing (not just the working link). Hence, the theoretical reliability of a 4F-BLSR is the best of the structures investigated so far, and its bandwidth efficiency is similar to 1:1 and 2F-BLSR protection mechanisms.

If a span switch will not resolve the failure, a ring switch will be performed as shown in the example in Figure 4–17. Hence, one can think of a 4F-BLSR as actually offering two types of protection: (a) span protection (1:1), of which there can be multiple instances occurring on the ring at the same time, and (b) ring protection of which there can only be one instance on the ring.

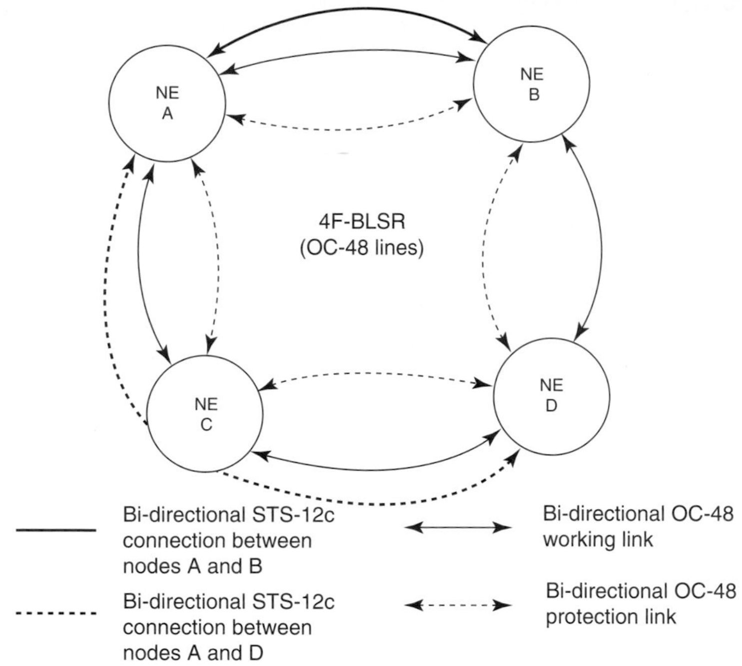

Figure 4–15 *A 4F-BLSR Network*

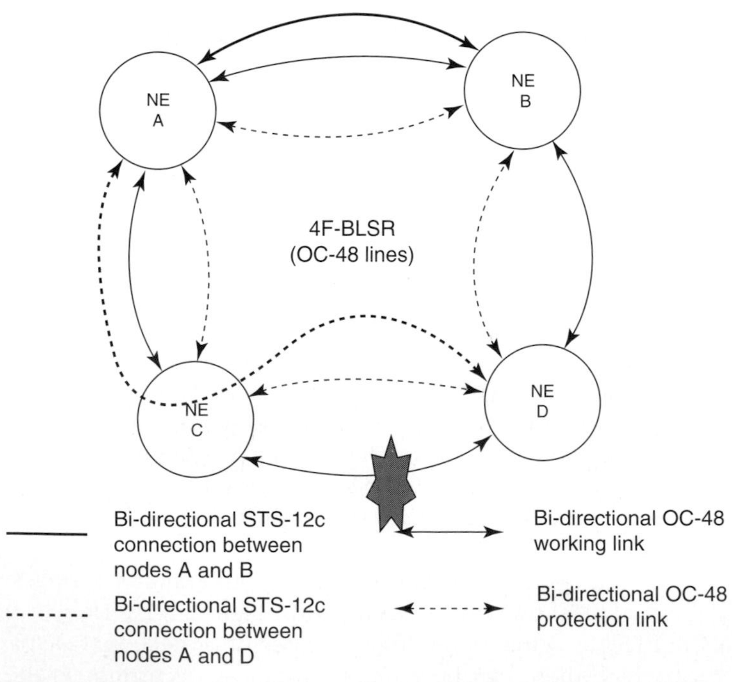

Figure 4–16 *Example of Span Protection within a 4F-BLSR Network*

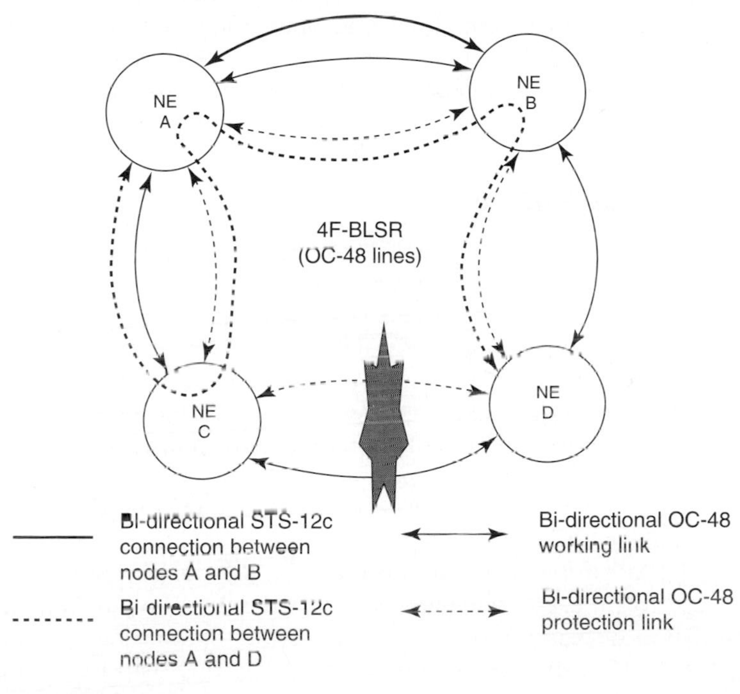

Figure 4–17 *Example of Ring Protection in a 4F-BLSR Network*

4.3.4.3 SERVICE CLASSES IN BLSRs (MS SPRINGs)

Two and four fiber BLSRs support three classes of service: (1) protected traffic, that is, "normal" ring traffic; (2) extra traffic, which uses the protection channels when they are not being used and is subject to preemption; and (3) *Non-preemptible Unprotected Traffic* (NUT). NUT is traffic that will not be restored in the case of a failure, that is, this traffic will not be "ring switched" (2/4-F BLSR) or "span switched" (4F-BLSR). The traffic, however, will also not be preempted to make way for other traffic. NUT results in bandwidth savings, since it can be carried in both working and protection time slots. Note that this works because the working traffic is unprotected, that is, will never be transferred to the corresponding protection channels. Also, any NUT on the protection channels cannot be preempted.

Besides the bandwidth savings, NUT is a handy service when the transport protocol layers above the SONET STS-*Nc* (SDH VC-3/4) have their own protection mechanism in operation and interactions between the protection mechanisms at various layers are to be avoided.

NUT does complicate ring operations. For example, ring switches are prevented for the NUT channels all the way around the ring (not just on a span). Hence, information on NUT connections must be distributed around the ring.

4.3.4.4 BLSR OPERATIONS

The virtues of 2F-BLSR over UPSR and those of 4F-BLSR over a 2F-BLSR have been extolled so far. The price paid for the increased efficiency and in the case of 4F-BLSR, the resiliency, is that of a significant increase in complexity. 2/4F-BLSRs are significantly more complicated to develop, implement, and operate than say a 1:N linear protected span. In fact, due to this complexity and due to the incomplete specification of the supporting information, 2/4F-BLSR equipment from different vendors do not typically interoperate. A high level overview of BLSR operations follows.

The most basic information needed concerning a ring (2/4F-BLSR) is the connectivity of the nodes within the ring. For the purposes of utilizing a K1/K2-byte based protection protocol, the number of nodes on a ring is limited to 16. Each node must be numbered, but the numbering, besides the limitation of being in the range 0 to 15, can be arbitrary. A *ring map* gives the ordering of the nodes around a ring. The ring map for Figure 4–15 would be {A, B, D, C}. It turns out that information concerning the connections active on the ring also needs to be distributed. It was seen that this is needed for NUT, but it is also needed to prevent misconnection of traffic in the case of certain types of failures. The process of preventing misconnection in rings is known as *squelching* [ITU-T95a]. The distribution of ring maps and connection information around a ring is not standardized as it is typically handled via a management system.

Each node in a BLSR can be in one of three main states: idle, switching, or pass-through. As mentioned earlier, one of the reasons that BLSRs can be so fast is that only two nodes need to be involved in any protection operation. The rest can be either *idle* (in the case of a span switch somewhere else on the ring) or in the pass-through state (in the case of a ring switch somewhere else on the ring).

K1/K2 byte usage is shown in Table 4–10 and Table 4–11. The bridge request codes of Table 4–10 are given in priority order. In addition, whether these codes are originated internally (int) or externally (ext) is indicated. Note that the destination and source nodes are specified in the K1/K2 bytes.

The precise operation of a BLSR is given in references [ANSI95c] and [ITU-T95a] using a fairly large and elaborate set of rules. The motivated reader is recommended to peruse these specifications for the exact details. To understand the basics of how BLSR works, we may consider the K1 and K2 byte as a "message." The K2 byte contains the source node ID and the K1 byte contains the destination node ID, and when a failure condition occurs, these

Table 4–10 *K1 Byte Usage [ITU-T95a]*

Bits	Bridge Request Code (Bits 1–4)	Ext/Int	Destination Node Identification (Bits 5–8)
1 2 3 4			
1 1 1 1	Lockout of Protection (Span) LP-S or Signal Fail (Protection)	Ext	
1 1 1 0	Forced Switch (Span) FS-S	Ext	
1 1 0 1	Forced Switch (Ring) FS-R	Ext	
1 1 0 0	Signal Fail (Span) SF-S	Int	
1 0 1 1	Signal Fail (Ring) SF-R	Int	The destination node ID is set to the ID of the node for which the K1 byte is destined. The destination node ID is always that of an adjacent node (except for default APS bytes).
1 0 1 0	Signal Degrade (Protection) SD-P	Int	
1 0 0 1	Signal Degrade (Span) SD-S	Int	
1 0 0 0	Signal Degrade (Ring) SD-R	Int	
0 1 1 1	Manual Switch (Span) MS-S	Ext	
0 1 1 0	Manual Switch (Ring) MS-R	Ext	
0 1 0 1	Wait-To-Restore WTR	Int	
0 1 0 0	Exerciser (Span) EXER-S	Ext	
0 0 1 1	Exerciser (Ring) EXER-R	Ext	
0 0 1 0	Reverse Request (Span) RR-S	Int	
0 0 0 1	Reverse Request (Ring) RR-R	Int	
0 0 0 0	No Request NR	Int	

Note: Reverse Request assumes the priority of the bridge request to which it is the response.

Table 4–11 *K2 Byte Usage [ITU-T95a]*

Source Node Identification (Bits 1–4)	Long/Short (Bit 5)	Status (Bits 6–8)
Source node ID is set to the node's own ID.	0 Short path code (S)	1 1 1 MS-AIS
	1 Long path code (L)	1 1 0 MS-RDI
		1 0 1 Reserved for future use
		1 0 0 Reserved for future use
		0 1 1 Extra Traffic on protection channels
		0 1 0 Bridged and Switched (Br&Sw)
		0 0 1 Bridged (Br)
		0 0 0 Idle

messages are sent from the node(s) detecting the failure to the node at the other side of the failure (known from the ring map). Hence, all the nodes in the ring know the identity of the affected link by observing these messages and knowing the ring map. Also there is a bit in the K2 byte indicating whether the message came along the long or the short path around the ring. A node involved in the switch sources these K bytes both ways around the ring. A node in "pass through" state essentially forwards these on with possible changes in some status bits (without changing the command).

4.3.5 Software-Defined BLSRs

It was seen that 4F-BLSR is extremely resilient, that is, given a probability of link failure of a 1:1 link, $p << 1$, the probability of connection disruption on a 4F-BLSR is on the order of p^2. On the other hand, ring network topologies are not the most flexible. Indeed, modern optical cross-connects can be used to construct general topology mesh networks. It therefore might be desirable to use ring-oriented protection schemes in a general mesh network to get the best of both worlds. Figure 4–18 illustrates a mesh network with two software-defined BLSRs protecting a subset of the links. Such "ring emulation" can provide enhanced reliability and increase the restoration speed for connections along certain routes.

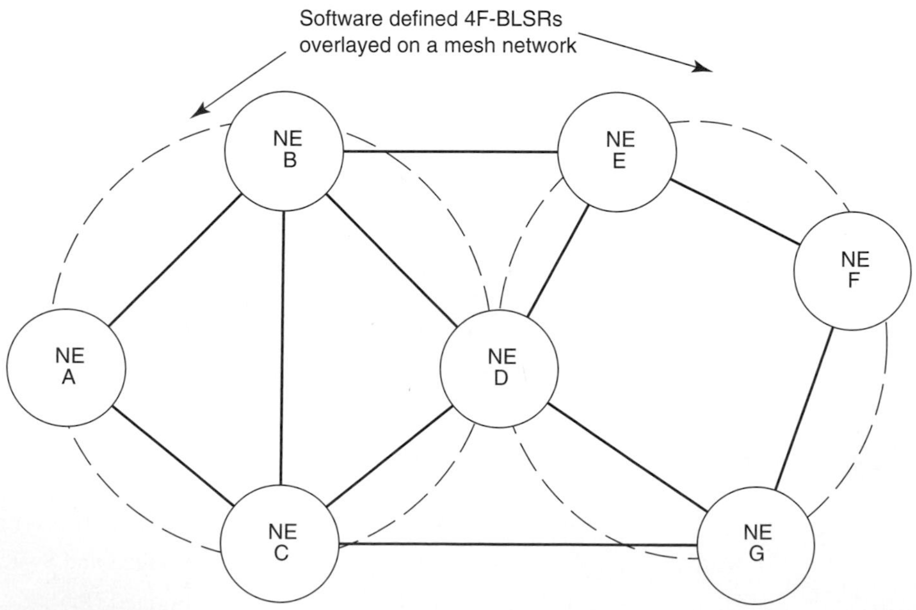

Figure 4–18 *Two Software-Defined 4F-BLSRs Overlaid on a Mesh Network*

4.3.6 Transoceanic Rings

It was stated earlier that BLSR protection is very fast and that part of that speed comes from involving only two nodes in the switching, that is, the two nodes adjacent to the fault. In some situations, this simplified protection action can present a problem. Consider the BLSR network shown in Figure 4–19. A portion of the ring, segments B-E and C-D, cross a large body of water (such as an ocean). A protected connection traversing nodes B-E-F of the ring is shown. Suppose a fault occurs on the ring between nodes E and F. This leads to a BLSR ring switch. With the ordinary BLSR ring switch, it is seen that the circuit, instead of having one transoceanic crossing, now has three! This leads to quite a bit of additional circuit delay and is usually considered unacceptable.

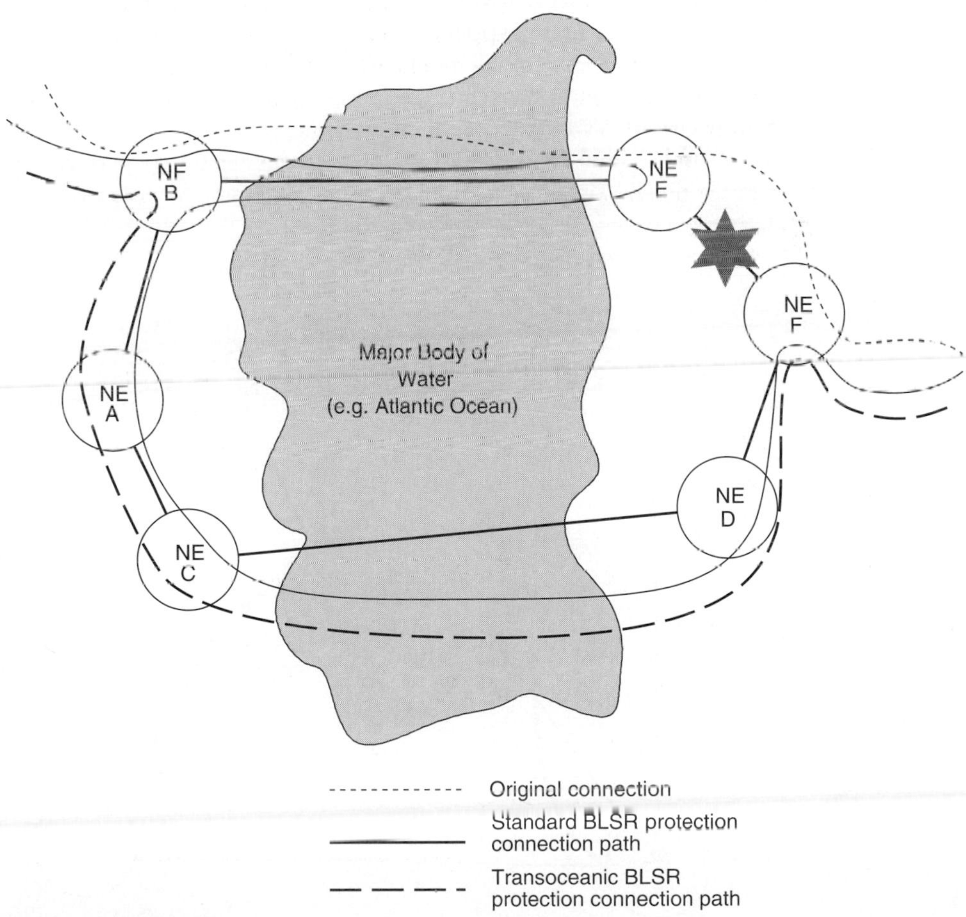

Figure 4–19 *Transoceanic BLSR Network Example*

The alternative is to route the circuit the other way around the ring, not at the point closest to the fault but at the point where the circuit enters and leaves the ring. This is the essence of the transoceanic variant of the 2/4F-BLSR specified in appendix A of reference [ITU-T95a].

Because more network elements get involved with the recovery of the same line fault now, the time to restore is longer. The target restoration time for a transoceanic ring is 300 mSec, approximately six times longer than that of an ordinary 2/4F-BLSR.

4.3.7 Protection Cycles

Continuing the extension of ring protection from the software-defined 4F-BLSR and the transoceanic ring, a ring-like protection mechanism called the *p-cycle* is arrived at [Grover+98]. Like the software-defined BLSR, a p-cycle is a ring-like entity that is applied in general mesh networks. Also, like the 2/4F-BLSR, only two network elements are involved in a protection switching operation. As with the transoceanic ring, the switching granularity is at the SONET path (SDH HOVC) level.

Unlike any of the ring mechanisms, however, a p-cycle can protect links that do not lie on the cycle. Figure 4–20 illustrates a network with a p-cycle defined over it. The cycle is the closed loop on the graph A-B-E-F-G-H-D-C-A.

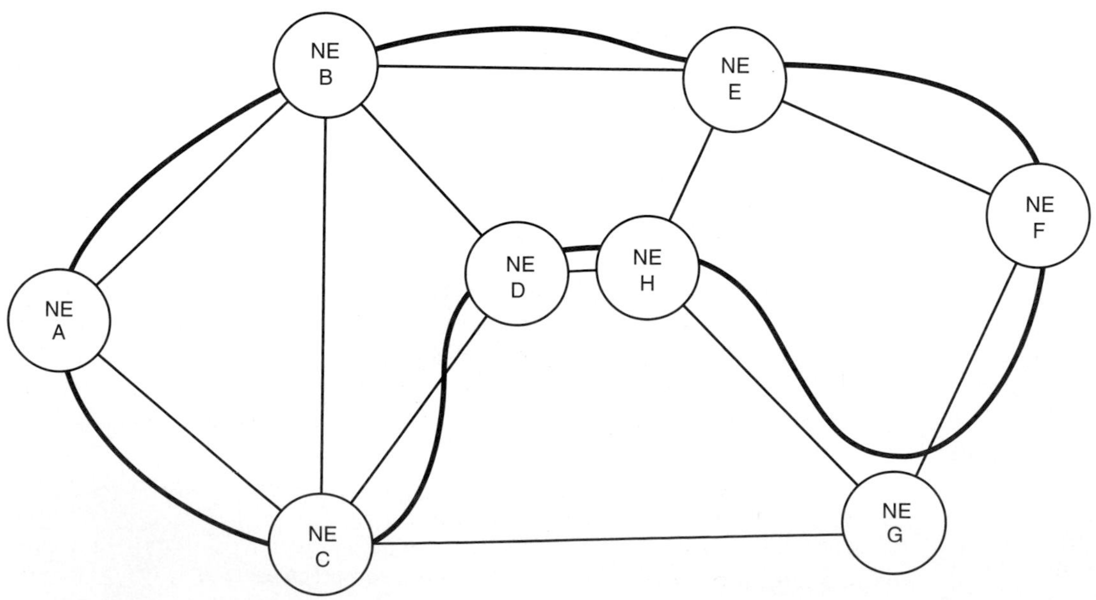

Figure 4–20 *Network Protected by a P-Cycle*

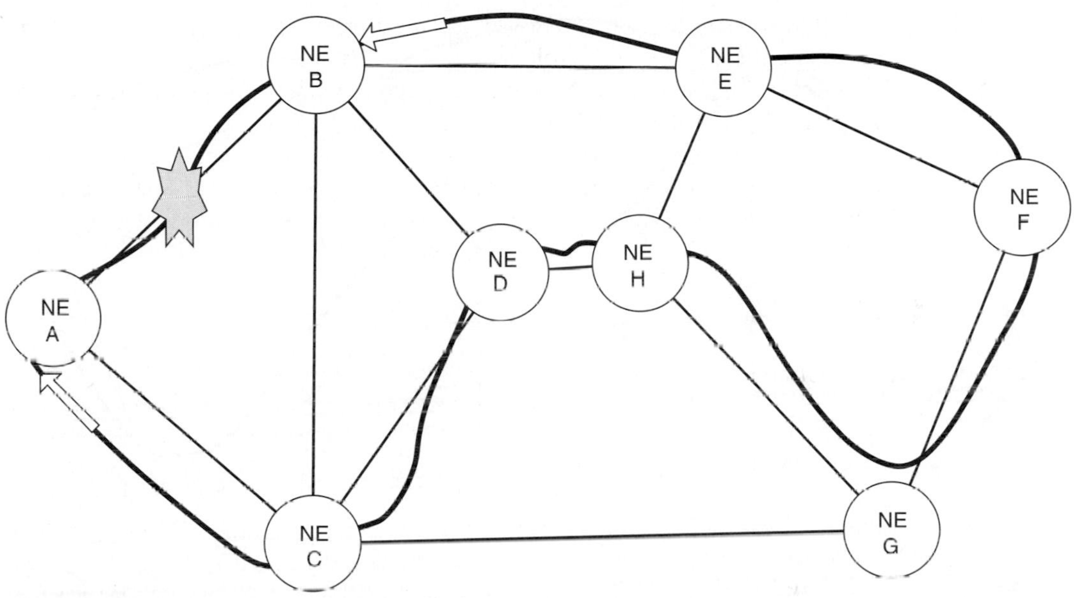

Figure 4–21 P-Cycle Protection a Link that Lies on the Cycle

Any link on the cycle is protected and an example of this "on cycle" protection is illustrated in Figure 4–21. Connections that used to take the link between nodes A and B will be rerouted over the portion of the p-cycle, B-E-F-G-H-D-C-A.

In addition, any link that "straddles" the cycle can also be protected as shown in Figure 4–22. Note how links straddling the cycle actually have two options for restoration. For example, two distinct portions of the cycle C-A-B and B-E-F-G-H-D-C can protect the link between nodes B and C.

P-cycles have been investigated for use at the WDM layer [Ellinas+00], SONET path layer [Grover+98], and even the IP layer [Stamatelakis+00]. P-cycles combine the advantages of mesh and ring configurations. With proper placement of connections and cycles over a mesh topology, they can achieve good bandwidth efficiency, that is, similar to that of general mesh. Because only two network elements are involved with a protection switch, their restoration time can approach that of BLSRs. Like a 2F-BLSR, the protection bandwidth is shared by all the links on the ring. In addition, all "straddling" links that are protected also share the p-cycle protection bandwidth. Hence, there is a limit to how large a p-cycle can be. Recall the protocol limit is 16 nodes for 2F-BLSR and 14 lines for 1:N SONET/SDH LAPS. It should be noted that no standardization efforts are yet underway for p-cycle based protection.

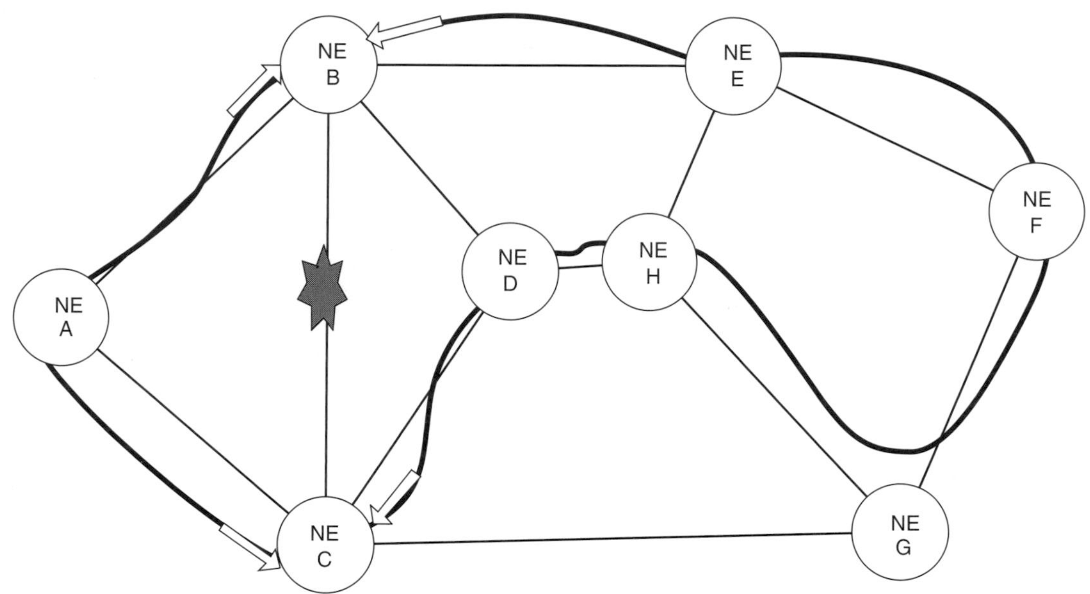

Figure 4–22 P-Cycle Protecting a Link that Straddles the Cycle

4.4 Mesh Restoration

The previous sections described two fundamental protection concepts, that is, linear protection and ring protection. In the course of this, it was seen that specific techniques were applicable to general mesh connected networks, that is, virtual 1:N SNC protection, software-defined BLSR, and p-cycles. In this section, mesh network based *restoration* is described. With mesh restoration, connections are not individually protected, but adequate bandwidth is provisioned in the network to reroute connections in the event of failures. This type of restoration is natural to consider in newer mesh networks with a distributed control plane. In the following, we first examine the potential bandwidth efficiency of in mesh restoration. Following this, an example of mesh restoration is presented.

4.4.1 Bandwidth Efficiency of Mesh Restoration

Mesh restoration techniques, or more properly restoration techniques applicable to mesh networks, are frequently touted as being bandwidth efficient especially with respect to rings. What is the basis for this claim? Is it always true? Is there a limit on how efficient a mesh restoration technique can be? In this section, we attempt to answer these questions.

First, the relevant terminology should be introduced. Specifically, a *span* between two network elements is defined as the fundamental failure unit. The

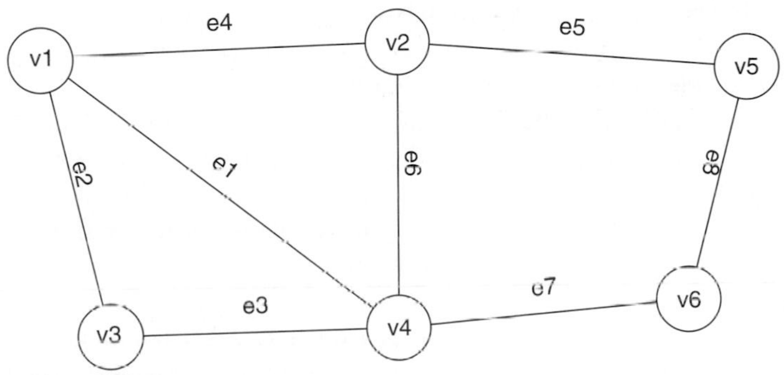

Figure 4–23 Graph Representation of a Communications Network

span may be composed of many "*links*." Note that the spans correspond to the units of "diversity" and the links correspond to the increments of bandwidth. For example, in SONET there could be a single OC-48 span and the "link" being the unit of bandwidth that we are protecting during a span failure (e.g., STS-1 channels).

Certain properties of the graph describing the communications network of interest must be considered. In such a graph, the switching systems are the vertices and the communication spans are the edges. This is shown in Figure 4–23.

The *degree*, *d*, of a vertex is defined as the number of edges incident on that vertex. For example, in the graph depicted in Figure 4–23, vertex *v4* has 4 incident edges and, hence, has a degree of 4, while vertex *v5* has a degree of 2. The degree of a graph, G, can be defined as being the average of the degree of all the vertices within the graph G. The degree of the graph shown in Figure 4–23 is 16/6 = 2.667.

To determine a lower bound on the amount of bandwidth required to support mesh restoration, the first step is to specify under which fault conditions connections are completely restorable. The most common criterion is known as "one line out" restorability. This indicates that recovery is possible from any sin-

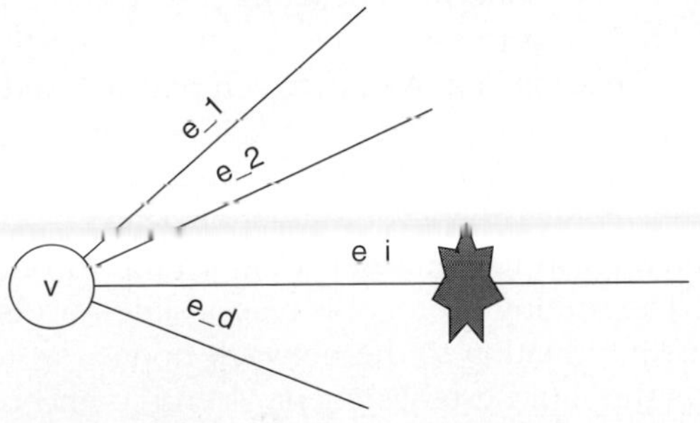

Figure 4–24 Vertex of Degree d with a Failure on One of the Spans

gle span failure. Considering what happens at a single vertex of degree *d*, as shown in Figure 4–24, a lower bound can be obtained. In particular, at this vertex, one of the *d* spans carrying traffic has had a failure. This implies that possibly all the other traffic coming and/or going to this vertex through this failed span must travel over the other spans entering the vertex. Hence, if this load is split among the other spans, then on average $1/(d-1)$ of extra bandwidth has to be reserved on each of these spans to allow for restoration. Now, extending this idea to the entire graph, a reasonable lower bound on required spare capacity for mesh restoration is $1/(d(g)-1)$ where $d(g)$ is the degree of the graph.

Considering SONET/SDH ring networks, the degree of each vertex is 2 and hence the degree of the graph representing the ring network is 2. The above bound indicates that a ring requires a protection bandwidth capacity equal to 100 percent of its working bandwidth. This is indeed the bandwidth that was set aside for protection in a 2/4F-BLSR. For the network of 4-23, a lower bound of 60 percent of its working bandwidth is required for protection, that is, this network does not have a good mesh structure. Hence, it is seen from this bound that mesh networks can require significantly less bandwidth to be set aside for protection. The amount required, however, is first dependent on the network topology and second on how the working and protection bandwidth is allocated across the network. Note that the bandwidth savings comes from sharing the unused (protection) capacity throughout the network and was made subject to the "one line out" assumption previously discussed.

4.4.2 End-to-End Source Rerouted Mesh Restoration

For the highest reliability, robustness, and bandwidth efficiency, a distributed, end-to-end (source) rerouted restoration scheme is difficult to beat. Such a method operates at the bandwidth granularity of the users' connections and therefore provides the highest bandwidth efficiency. End-to-end source rerouting can restore the maximum number of connections regardless of the type and extent of the network fault, that is, if there is a way to reestablish a connection within the bandwidth constraints of the network, the source rerouting technique will do it.

A simple example of connections being mesh-restored is illustrated in Figure 4–25 and Figure 4–26. In Figure 4–25, there are two connections, (A, C) and (A, E) that both traverse the same link, A-C, between nodes A and C. In Figure 4–26, the result of source re-route protection when link A-C fails is shown. Notice how the two connections can take different routes around the failure. This is the result of the fine granularity, connection-level restoration action.

Source rerouted mesh restoration is built on top of optical signaling and routing protocols. The routing protocol is responsible for distributing network topology and status information to the network nodes (switches). The signaling protocol allows the rapid establishment of end-to-end connections.

Table 4–12 reviews the characteristic of source rerouted mesh restoration in terms of the criteria discussed in section 4.1.2.

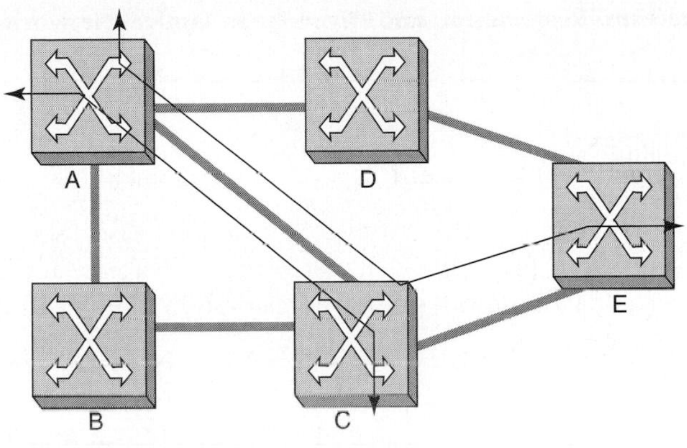

Figure 4–25 *Mesh Network with Two Connections*

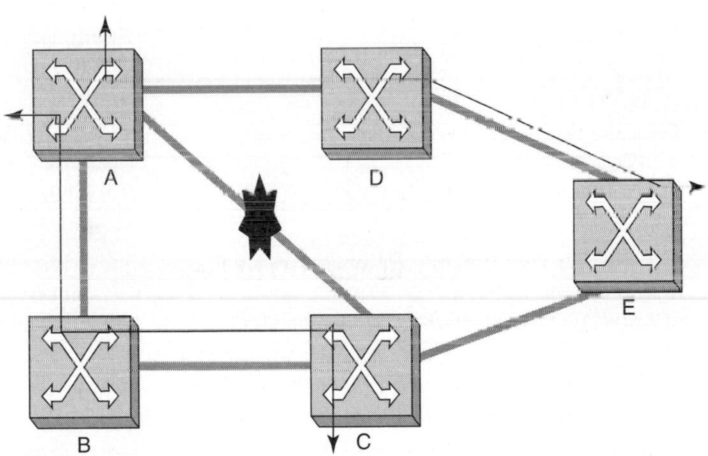

Figure 4–26 *Source Rerouted Mesh Restoration to Recover from a Fiber Cut*

Table 4–12 *Source Re-route Reliability and Robustness Design Choices*

Factor	Design Choice
Failure types that are restorable	Any restorable failure type, e.g., multiple lines, multiple nodes, network partitioning, etc.
Distributed vs. Centralized restoration	Completely distributed restoration for maximum robustness
Interoperability with other protection and automated provisioning	Interoperable with 1+1, 1:N and BLSR line protection schemes
Implementation complexity	Uses much of the infrastructure needed for rapid provisioning

4.5 Summary

Table 4–13 summarizes the survivability options discussed in this chapter. It can be seen from this table that network survivability techniques involve a multidimensional trade-off between restoration time, bandwidth efficiency, and failure robustness.

Table 4-13 *Properties of Protection/Restoration Methods*

Name	Restoration Time	Bandwidth Required	Failure Robustness
1+1 Linear (SDH/SONET)	Typically under 50 ms	$2x$	Only as good as the diversity of the alternative paths. Handles single failure.
1:N Linear (SDH/SONET)	Typically under 50 ms		Only as good as the diversity of the paths, Handles single failure.
Bi-directional Line Switched Ring (BLSR) Failures.	Typically under 100 ms	$2x$	Diversity built in, one line out, except in 4F case which can handle multiple span.
Source Re-route Mesh Restoration	Depends on the number of circuits, the number of hops, and propagation delay	Network design consideration (less than $2x$) As close as one can get to mesh limit	Can handle any recoverable situation, permits graceful degradation if desired.
Unidirectional Path Switched Ring (UPSR)	Typically under 50 ms	$2x$	Diversity built in, can handle certain node failures.
Path Level (SNC) 1:N	Depends on the number of circuits, the number of hops, and propagation delay	Less than $2x$, but above mesh limit. Dependent on sharing	The diversity of the paths determines robustness. Handles single failure.
P-cycle	Depends on propagation delay and the method for conveying protocol messages	Less than $2x$ but above mesh limit	Handles single failure.

FIVE

Modern Optical Network Control Plane

5.1 Introduction

The fundamental use of optical networks is to provide communication bandwidth from one geographic location to another. For instance, consider provisioning a link between two geographically separated IP routers. Such a link could be realized by establishing a SONET path layer connection between the routers through an optical network. This is shown in Figure 5–1, where the IP routers, R1 and R2, are designated as *clients* of the optical network. Figure 5–2 illustrates the details of the interconnections between O1 and O2 within the optical network, based on the discussion in the preceding chapters. Specifically, this figure shows OEO optical switching elements (called OXCs, see Chapter 1) and line systems that comprise the network. The establishment of a SONET path layer connection between the routers first requires the deter-

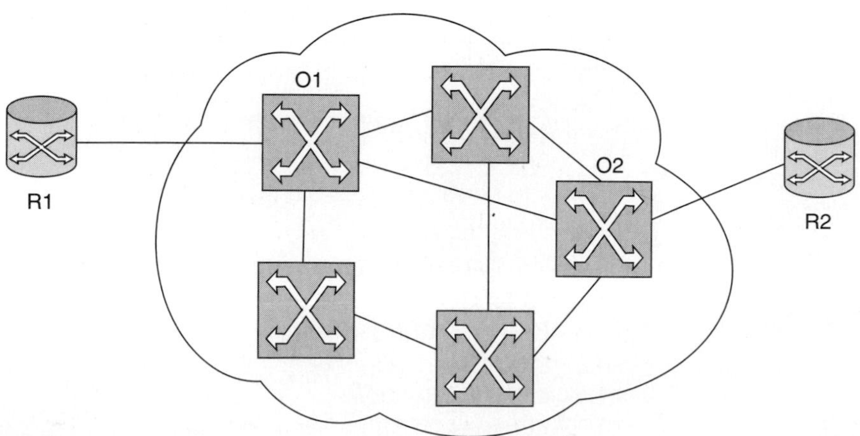

Figure 5–1 *IP Routers Connected to an Optical Network*

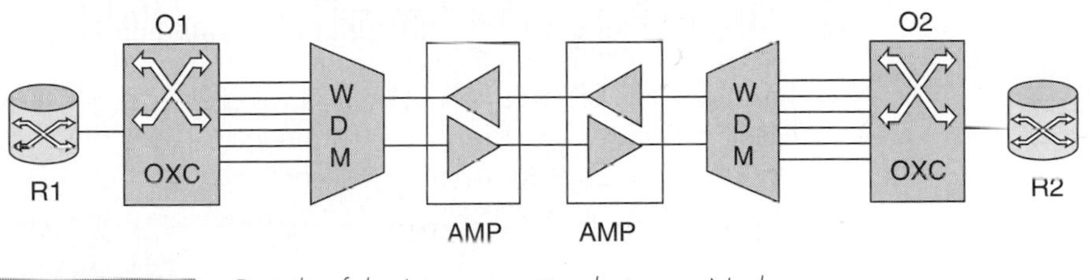

Figure 5–2 Details of the Interconnection between Nodes

mination of the connection route within the optical network. Then, a series of SONET line layer connection segments must be established between the switches (LTEs) en route, and the switches must be cross connected properly so that an end-to-end connection is realized. This, in essence, describes *connection provisioning* in an optical network.

A provisioned connection may be subject to automatic protection and/or restoration (referred to as "recovery"). As described in Chapter 4, the recovery mechanism may be applied at each hop (e.g., linear APS) and/or end-to-end (e.g., path-level restoration). When end-to-end restoration is used, a physically diverse alternate route within the optical network must be determined, and the connection must be activated along the alternate path after a failure occurs along the primary path.

Both provisioning and recovery capabilities require control intelligence in the optical network. Such control intelligence may be centralized, say in a management system, with a well-defined communication interface between the management system and the network elements. On the other hand, the control intelligence may be distributed among the network elements. Or, a combination of the above methods may be used. Thus, an optical network consists of a *transport* plane, a *control* plane, and a *management* plane. The transport plane refers to the logic and hardware required for the physical transfer of data in the network. The control plane refers to the infrastructure and distributed intelligence that controls the establishment and maintenance of connections in the network. This intelligence is typically realized in the form of various communication protocols. Such protocols can be broadly classified into *signaling*, *routing*, and *discovery* protocols. The details of such protocols are covered in later chapters. The management plane refers to the systems, interfaces, and protocols used to manage the network and its services. In the rest of this book, the focus is mainly on the control plane. This chapter describes the high level architecture of the modern optical network control plane, which has evolved from IP, ATM, and MPLS control architectures. This evolution is described in this chapter. The following chapters contain detailed descriptions of the optical network control mechanisms. An overall roadmap is provided in this chapter to the material that follows.

5.2 Control Plane Architecture and Functional Model

To describe the architecture of the control plane, it is useful to first consider the functional structure of an optical network. From both a control and transport point of view, an optical network consists of *layers* and *partitions*. Layering is inherent in SONET/SDH technology and optical transport. This layering was described in Chapter 2, where it was shown that SONET (for instance) has Path, Line, and Section layers. Figure 5–2 illustrates equipment that operate at different layers. For example, the WDM equipment shown in the figure terminates the section layer overhead, the OXCs shown are line and section terminating, and the routers terminate path, line, and section overheads. Layering implies a client-server abstraction whereby the layer below provides a specific service to the layer above while hiding the details of implementation of the service. For instance, Path-Terminating Equipment (PTE) at the edges of the optical network (e.g., the routers in Figure 5–1) receive path layer connectivity from the collection of equipment operating at lower layers (e.g., the optical network in Figure 5–1). The PTEs need not be aware of how switching and transmission happens at the line and section layers. Similarly, adjacent line terminating equipment (LTE, e.g., the OXCs in Figure 5–2) are connected to each other through section layer equipment without being aware of the precise operation of the section layer. Thus, when we refer to the "control plane," it is often associated with a specific layer. The focus in this book is on the control of the switching layer in optical networks. The mechanisms described in this book address both the control of OXCs (e.g., SONET/SDH cross-connects), and the control of PXCs that transparently switch wavelengths (see Chapter 1). Because of the similarities of the control issues in the optical switching layer to those in ATM, IP and MPLS networks, the control plane mechanisms developed for these networks can be adapted for use in optical networks. The rest of this chapter and the book are indeed devoted to describing these mechanisms.

Now, partitioning, as the name implies, is concerned with the division of a network into smaller parts for administrative, scalability, or other reasons. Two types of partitioning are possible. The first is *topological* partitioning whereby a large network is partitioned into multiple smaller networks (called *subnetworks*) for scalability reasons. The second is *control* partitioning whereby a large network is divided into multiple *control domains*, where each control domain defines specific control and/or management procedures for a part of the network. Both topological and control partitioning can be recursive, that is, a partition can itself be partitioned, and so on.

It is important to recognize the relationship between topological and control partitioning. Topological partitioning is typically used to improve the scalability of control procedures within a single control domain. Within a topological partition, homogeneous control procedures are implemented in all the subnetworks. An example of this is a large ATM network running the P-NNI protocols, whose topology is split into P-NNI peer groups (see section 5.6 and Chapter 7). Control partitioning, on the other hand, typically occurs when a network has to be partitioned on the basis of administrative or other criteria. For instance, a network may contain islands of equipment from different vendors with differing control and/or management procedures. In this case, the network may have to be partitioned into multiple control domains. Topological partitioning may be used within each control domain for scalability. Control plane procedures within a single control domain are referred to as *intradomain* procedures. These include signaling and routing procedures as described in Chapters 7–10. More challenging, however, are *interdomain* procedures for integrating individual, potentially disparate, control domains to build a unified, end-to-end control architecture. This is the subject of Chapter 12.

Both layering and partitioning, as well as the functional components and requirements of the control plane, have been formalized by ITU-T in a series of recommendations. In the following, a brief overview of the ITU-T models is given.

5.2.1 Network Model and Layering

ITU-T recommendation G.805 describes the "generic functional architecture of transport networks" [ITU-T00d]. This recommendation describes the architectural components, as well as the layering concepts, independent of the underlying networking technology. Figure 5–3 illustrates the functional model of the network as per G.805. This figure illustrates several architectural components. These can be broadly classified into:

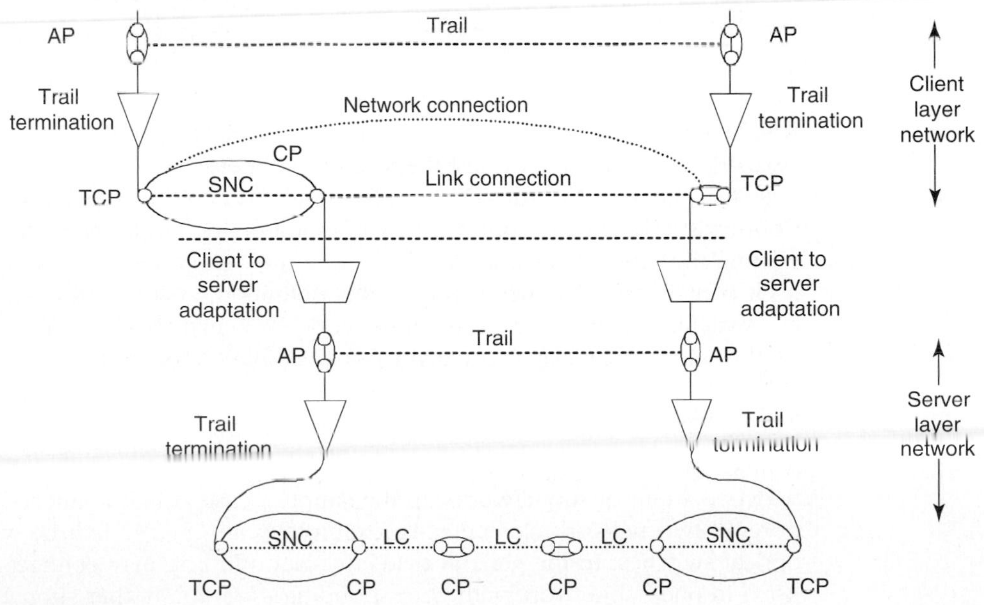

Figure 5–3 *Transport Network Functional Model per [ITU-T00d]*

- Topological components, which include access points (AP), layer networks, links and subnetworks.
- Transport entities, which include link connections (LC), subnetwork connections (SNC), network connections and trails.
- Transport processing functions, which include adaptation and trail termination.

These components are described below.

5.2.1.1 CLIENT AND SERVER LAYER NETWORKS

A layer network is defined by the set of capabilities available for transferring information specific to that layer (called *characteristic* information). For example, an IP network is a layer network, with IP packets being the characteristic information. A layer network could be a client or a server network in relation to another layer network. The connectivity between elements in a client layer network, and hence its topology, is established by utilizing connectivity provided by the server layer network. For instance, an IP network could be the client layer network utilizing connectivity services from an optical (server layer) network (Figure 5–1).

The client-server relationship may be applied recursively, that is, a server layer network may itself be a client layer for another server layer network. Figure 5–4 illustrates this in an SDH network. Here, the higher order path (HOP) layer network serves the lower order path (LOP) layer client, which in turn serves ATM and PDH clients. The client layer characteristic information is also illustrated.

5.2.1.2 SUBNETWORK

A subnetwork exists within a single layer network. It is defined by the set of network elements that are members of the subnetwork, and the set of ports that are available for transferring information specific to the layer network. Connectivity between subnetworks within a layer network occur by interconnecting the ports. The subnetwork definition is recursive: a subnetwork may itself contain other subnetworks. By this definition, a single network element (or switching matrix) can be a subnetwork. In Figure 5–3, the ellipses at the bottom of the figure denote (server layer) subnetworks.

5.2.1.3 LINK

A link represents the topological relationship and available transport capacity between a pair of subnetworks. In the simplest case, a link connects a pair of ports in two network elements. An example is an OC-192 link between two optical switches. In the general case, a compound link may connect multiple ports in one subnetwork with corresponding ports in another subnetwork.[1]

[1]Such a compound link is called a *traffic engineering link* or TE-link in MPLS, see Chapter 10.

Client layer	Server layer	Client characteristic information
VC-2 LOP	VC-3 or VC-4 HOP	VC-2 + frame offset
VC-3 LOP	VC-4 HOP	VC-3 + frame offset
VC-3 HOP	STM-N Multiplex section	VC-3 + frame offset
VC-4 HOP	STM-N Multiplex section	VC-4 + frame offset
STM-N Multiplex section	STM-N Regenerator section	STM-N rate, N = 1, 4, 16, 64

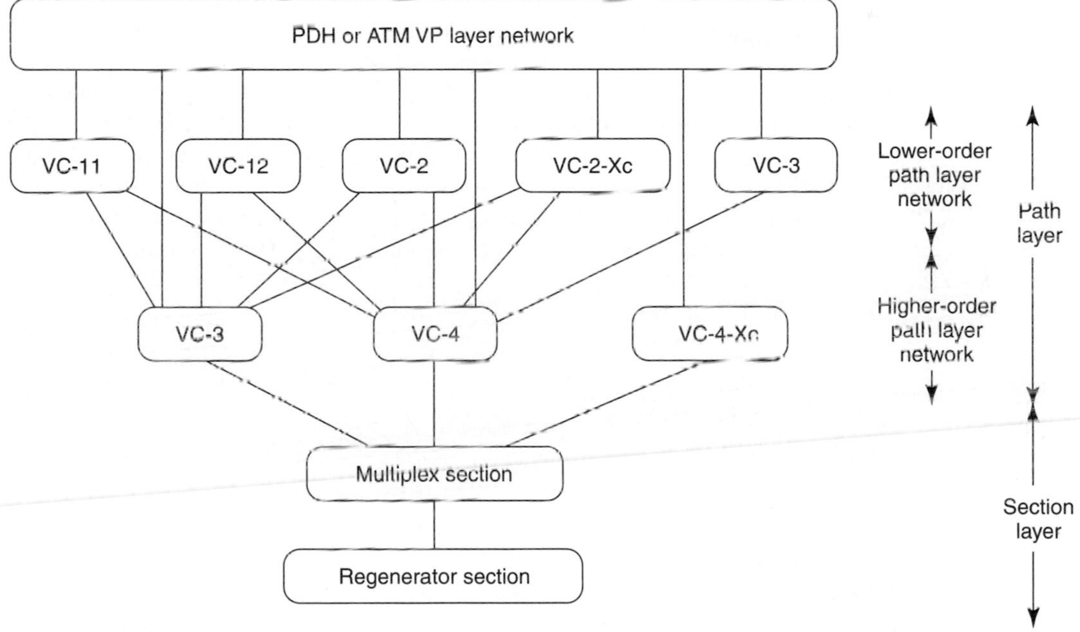

Figure 5–4 *Client and Server Layer Networks (from [ITU-T00d])*

5.2.1.4 LINK CONNECTION

A link connection (LC) transfers information transparently across a link without monitoring the integrity of the transfer. It is delimited by a port at each end. A link connection in the client layer represents a pair of adap-tation functions and a trail in the server layer. For example, considering Figure 5–2, an STS-48c path layer trail in the optical network will be con-sidered a link connection between the IP routers (in the IP client layer). A pair of associated unidirec-tional link connections provide bidirectional in-formation transfer between the corresponding end points. The source and sink reference points of the link connection are referred to as *Connection Points* (CP, see Figure 5–3).

5.2.1.5 SUBNETWORK CONNECTION

A subnetwork connection (SNC) transfers information transparently across a subnetwork without monitoring the integrity of the transfer. It is delimited by ports at the boundary of the subnetwork and represents the association between these ports. Consider now a subnetwork that may itself contain other smaller subnetworks. A connection in this subnetwork is constructed from a concatenation of connections *across* the included subnetworks, and link connections *between* the included subnetworks. From the control plane point of view, an SNC represents a part of the end-to-end connection that may be established independently within a subnetwork.

5.2.1.6 NETWORK CONNECTION

A network connection is an end-to-end connection across a layer network, delimited by Termination Connection Points (TCPs). It is formed by concatenating subnetwork connections and/or link connections. There is no explicit information to allow the integrity of the transferred information to be monitored. As an example, an STS-1 network connection would consist of concatenated STS-1 subnetwork and/or link connections spanning multiple switches.

5.2.1.7 TRAIL

A trail represents the transfer of monitored, adapted characteristic information of the client layer network between access points. For example, the optical network in Figure 5–2 may provide an STS-48c path layer trail between the two end clients (e.g., IP routers). A trail is delimited by a trail termination point at each end.

A trail in the server layer could be a link connection in the client layer. Continuing the earlier example, the STS-48c path layer trail provided by the optical network in Figure 5–1 will appear as a link connection in the IP layer between the two IP routers. If the client layer is itself a server layer for some other client layer, this definition continues.

From a control plane point of view, the request to create a trail from a client layer entity results in the creation of a trail in the server layer and the establishment of the appropriate adaptations in the end points of the trail. Thus, when we loosely say that an STS-48c (link) connection is established between two routers, it means that an STS-48c path layer trail is created in the optical network. Furthermore, an appropriate mapping of the IP payload and other path layer functions are established in the routers.

5.2.1.8 ADAPTATION FUNCTION

Adaptation refers to the process whereby characteristic information in the client layer is mapped onto a form suitable for transport over a trail in the server layer network and the recovery of the client layer information from the server layer trail. An *adaptation source* is the point where the client layer information is mapped on to the server layer trail, and the *adaptation sink* represents the point where the mapped information is recovered.

5.2.1.9 TRAIL TERMINATION FUNCTION

The trail termination function is defined by the following entities:

- *Trail termination source*: A transport processing function that accepts adapted characteristic information from a client layer network at its input, adds information to allow the trail to be monitored, and presents the characteristic information of the server layer network at its output. An example of a trail termination function at the source is the addition of BIP-8 code for performance monitoring of the trail, as described in Chapter 3.
- *Trail termination sink*: A transport processing function that accepts the characteristic information of the server layer network at its input, removes the information related to trail monitoring, and presents the remaining information at its output. An example of a trail termination function at the sink is the use of BIP-8 information added at the source to calculate the bit error rate of the trail.

The above concepts are illustrated using a practical example in Figure 5-5. Here, two routers interconnected via an optical network are shown. The optical switches have OC-192 links between them. The routers have OC-48 links to the optical switches. A link connection at the IP layer has to be established between the two routers. This link connection is realized as shown, over an STS-48c path layer trail. This trail in turn is realized over the underlying line and section layers as shown. Connections and trail shown are assumed to be bidirectional. Various access points (AP), trail termination points (TTP) and adaptation functions are shown.

5.2.2 Partitioning and Control Interfaces

Topological and control partitioning were described earlier. Figure 5–6 illustrates partitioning of a large network. In this figure, each large oval represents a control domain, which is topologically partitioned into multiple subnetworks as shown. The links shown are abstractions of actual physical links between network elements (see Chapter 12).

In addition to network partitioning, links may be aggregated or partitioned. In the definition of a link in section 5.2.1.3, a compound link was described as a collection of several simple links. The aggregation of simple links is called *link bundling*. A simple link in a bundle is also referred to as a *component link*. A bundled (compound) link may itself be a component link in another bundle. Thus, bundling could be recursive. The levels of bundling depend on how various link properties are represented in the control plane.

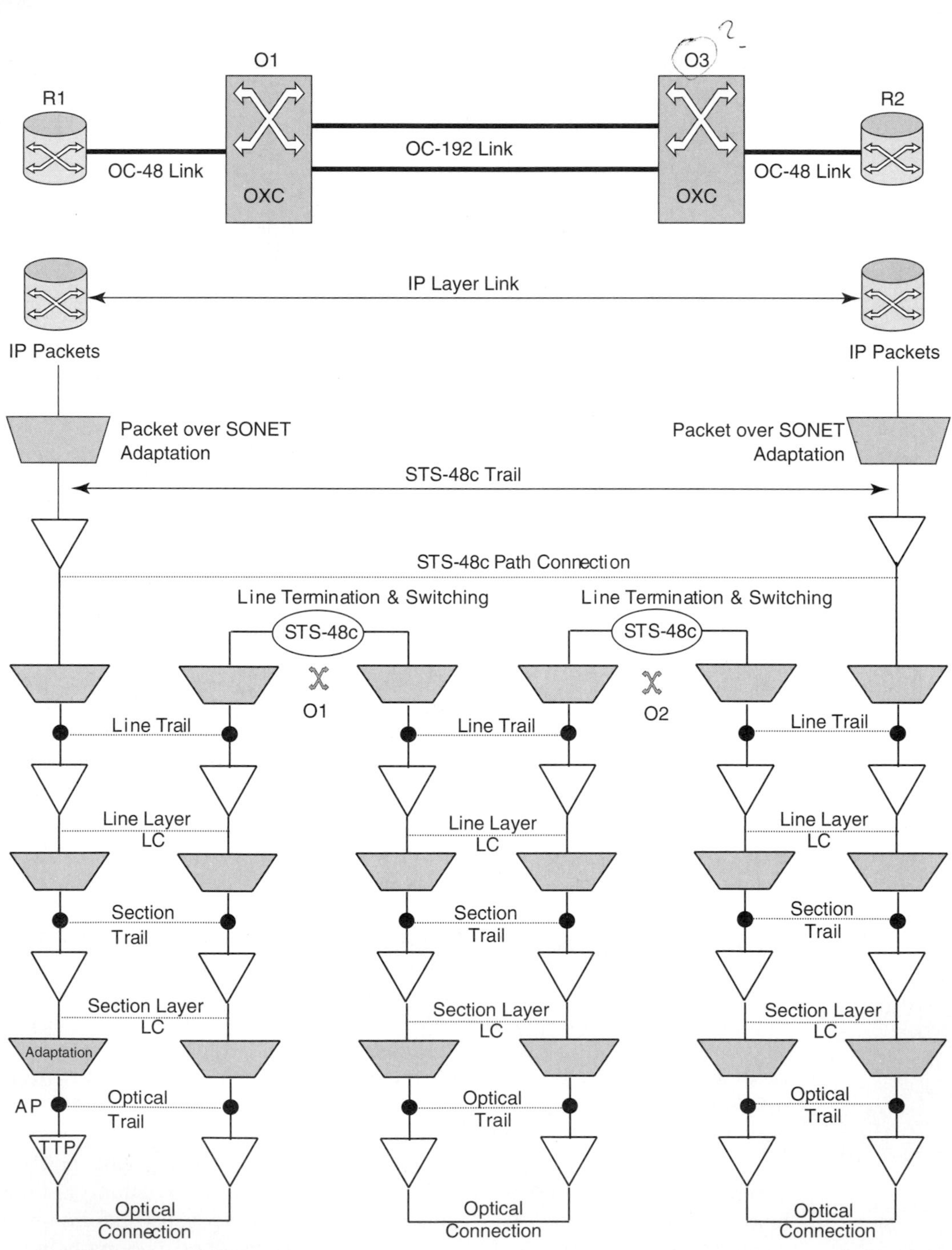

Figure 5–5 *Example of Mapping the Functional Model*

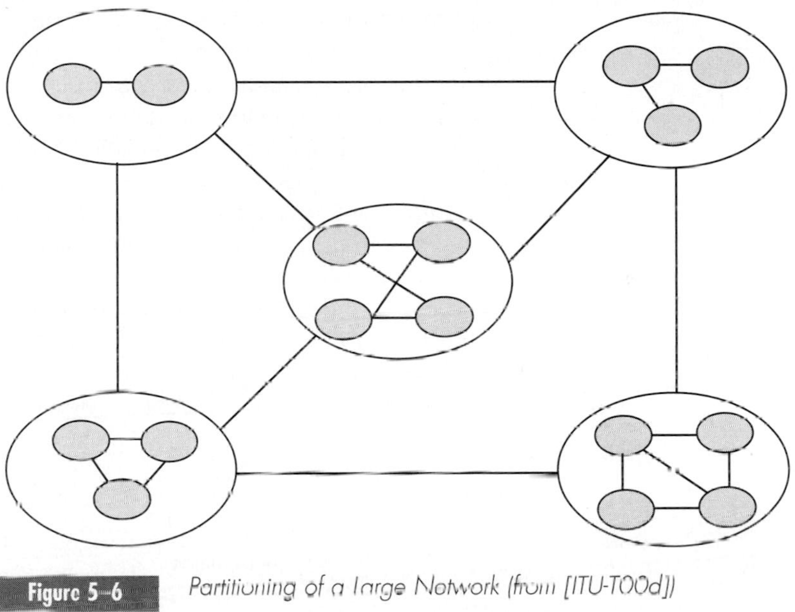

Figure 5–6 Partitioning of a Large Network (from [ITU-T00d])

Figure 5–7 illustrates a compound link and the constituent component links between two subnetworks. Link bundling is further described in Chapter 10.

From a control plane point of view, a partitioned network presents certain requirements. First, the control procedures within different control domains may not be the same. This could especially be the case in a multi-vendor network. A unified control plane spanning the entire network must therefore accommodate heterogeneous control domains. The ultimate goal, of course, is to be able to provision and maintain network connections across multiple control domains.

Second, the scope of the overall control plane must be carefully defined. The notion of a "standard" control plane is to facilitate interoperability

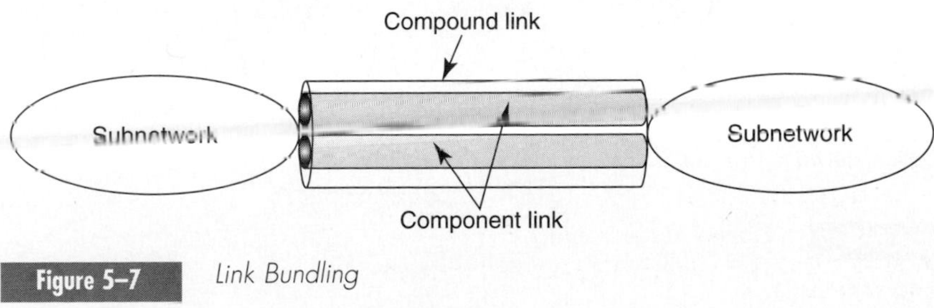

Figure 5–7 Link Bundling

between multivendor equipment. But at what points in the network that interoperable procedures are required must be determined.

Finally, the implementation of a control plane requires information transfer between entities that participate in the control process. Partitioning invariably results in the curtailment of the information flow across control domain and subnetwork boundaries. This is also referred to as *information abstraction*. The precise mechanics of information abstraction determine the characteristics of the control plane procedures, and hence must be determined carefully.

Figure 5–8 illustrates the commonly accepted view of control interfaces in a network. Two optical networks, administered by different service providers, are shown in this figure. Each optical network is partitioned into control domains as shown, and two client networks connecting to the optical network are shown. The control interfaces shown are:

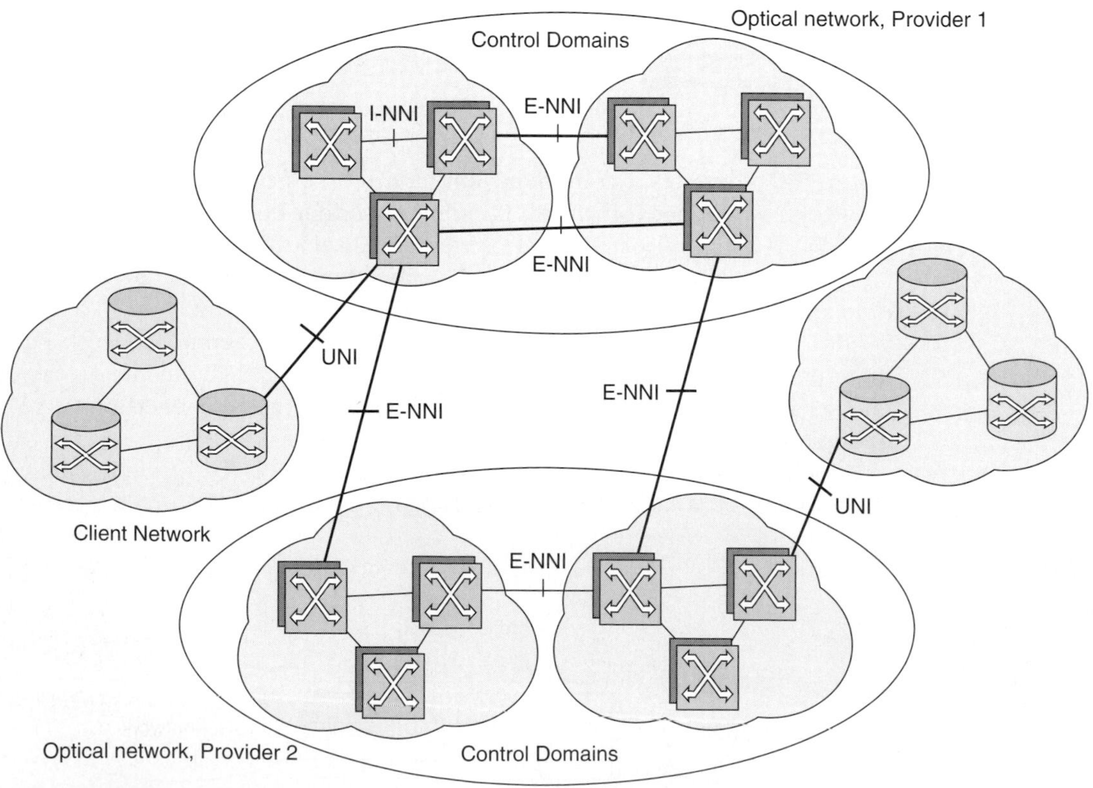

Figure 5–8 *Control Plane Interfaces*

- *The User-Network Interface (UNI):* This is the control interface between a node in the client network and a node in the optical network.
- *The Interior Network-Network Interface (I-NNI):* This is the control interface between two subnetworks (or nodes) within the same control domain.
- *The Exterior Network-Network (E-NNI):* This is the control interface between two nodes in different control domains. This definition does not distinguish between the case where the control domains are administered by the same service provider and the case where the control domains are administered by different service providers. As a result, such a distinction, where necessary, must be made explicitly.

The control interfaces in Figure 5–8 indicate the points where control plane interactions occur. An issue is whether the control plane functionality must be present in the network elements themselves. Typically, this is the case in IP networks, where the routing and the signaling protocols are implemented directly in the routers. In the case of optical networks, however, the control functionality can be distinct from the transport functionality. Indeed, the control plane functionality may be implemented outside of the network elements by a proxy agent. Figure 5–9 illustrates the generic control plane abstraction, where the control "agents" depicted can be either built into or physically separate from the network elements. In the latter case, a single control agent can represent multiple network elements. The (internal) interface between the network elements and control agents need not be standardized.

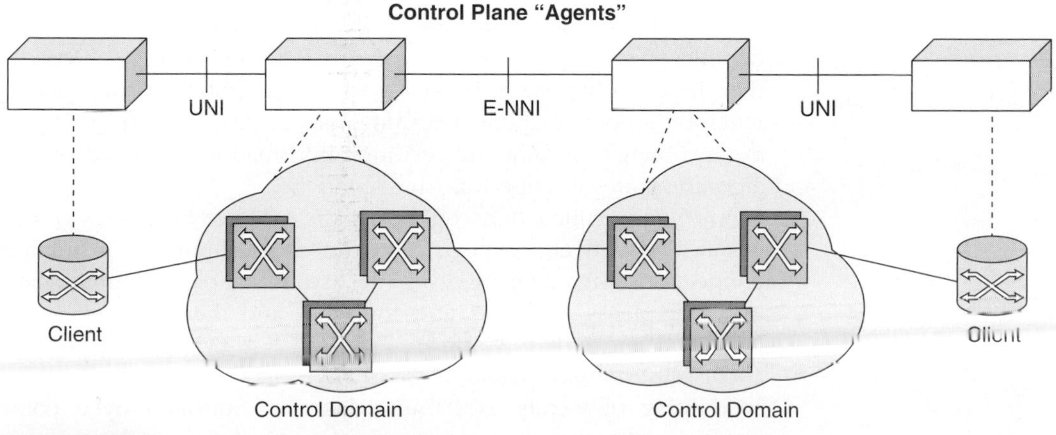

Figure 5–9 *Control Plane Abstraction*

Whether or not the control functionality is integrated with the network elements, a function that can only be executed over the transport links between the network elements is neighbor discovery. This is described next. Also, the connectivity shown in Figure 5–9 between the control agents defines the control plane *adjacency*. Two adjacent control plane agents, in reality, do not necessarily need direct physical connectivity. The only requirement is *reachability* between adjacent control agents. A data communication network (DCN), which in the simple case could be a direct physical link, provides this reachability.

5.2.3 Control Plane Functions

The main control plane functions are summarized below. They are covered in greater detail in the following chapters.

- *Neighbor discovery*: In simple terms, neighbor discovery is a function whereby a network element automatically determines the details of its connectivity to all its data plane neighbors. These details include the identity of the neighbors, the identity of the link terminations, and so on. Neighbor discovery applies to both the UNI and the NNI shown in Figure 5–8, and it is the subject of Chapter 6.
- *Routing*: Routing broadly covers two control aspects. The first is automatic topology and resource discovery. The second is path computation. The first capability allows each control agent to determine the data plane connectivity and resource availability in the entire network. This procedure typically relies on a mechanism to propagate link connectivity and resource information from one control agent to all others in the network. What information is propagated and how the information is represented at each control agent depend on the type of routing scheme. Various routing schemes are described in Chapters 9, 10, and 12. Path computation is a procedure whereby a control agent determines a path for a connection using the available topology and resource information. Path computation algorithms are described in Chapter 11.
- *Signaling*: Signaling denotes the syntax and the semantics of communication between control agents in establishing and maintaining connections. Signaling involves the use of standard communication protocols across the UNI and the NNI, and these procedures are described in Chapters 7 and 8.
- *Local resource management*: This refers to the representation and accounting of locally available resources controlled by a control agent. Concise resource representation is essential for the scalability of routing mechanisms. Local resource management aspects are covered in Chapter 10.

5.2.4 The Data Communications Network

The data communications network (DCN) refers to the communication infrastructure used for messaging between control agents in an optical network. The DCN may also be used to provide connectivity between the control agents and element or network management systems (see Chapter 13). Typically, control communication is packet oriented (e.g., using TCP/IP). Thus, the DCN is typically packet based (e.g., IP) over an underlying network technology (e.g., ATM). The DCN therefore provides network layer (OSI Layer 3 [Stallings03]) connectivity between control entities in an optical network. Under the partitioning paradigm shown in Figures 5–6 and 5–8, control communication may happen at several levels. For instance, communication is required between control entities in different control domains as well as control entities within the same control domain. The network infrastructure for interconnecting control agents across subnetworks could potentially be different than the one used within a subnetwork. The term DCN, however, will be used to refer to the overall network infrastructure for control communication.

The main issues with regard to the design of a DCN are:

- *Network layer protocol used:* Since the DCN provides network layer connectivity, a specific network layer protocol (and technology) must be selected. From a practical perspective, the choices today are IP version 4, IP version 6, or OSI Connection-Less Network Protocol (CLNP). A DCN may support more than one network layer (e.g., CLNP and IP) with built-in gateway functionality.
- *Network infrastructure:* The main choice with regard to the network infrastructure (upon which the DCN is built) is whether the network is associated with the optical data plane. With SONET or SDH data plane, certain overhead bytes can be used to realize packet communication between control elements. In this case, the DCN network infrastructure is said to be realized *in-fiber*. On the other hand, a separate network technology not associated with the optical data plane can be used to realize the DCN. For example, an external IP network can be used. In this case, the DCN is said to be realized *out-of-fiber*. As mentioned earlier, a DCN could comprise of different parts that are interconnected, for instance, an in-fiber part in one subnetwork and an out-of-fiber part external to that subnetwork.
- *Application requirements:* The DCN may support multiple applications, such as signaling, routing, and communication with management systems. These applications may pose certain requirements on the DCN, such as latency, packet loss, security, and so on. In general, the DCN must support low latency and low packet loss. In addition, the DCN must be secure and not be vulnerable to external interference.

ITU-T recommendation G.7712 [ITU-T01c] describes the general architectural aspects of the DCN. The specific details of in-fiber versus out-of-fiber realization of the DCN are discussed in Chapter 6. In the following, the control plane aspects in IP, MPLS, and ATM networks are briefly described.

5.3 Control Plane Aspects in IP Networks

Figure 5–10 illustrates a simple IP network. Here, the IP networking infrastructure consists of Local Area Networks (LANs; vertical and horizontal bars) interconnected by routers, whose task is to forward packets from a source end-system to a destination end-system. An end-system is typically a *host* attached to a LAN (routers can also be sources and destinations of IP packets, specifically those related to the control plane). An IP packet thus contains a source address and a destination address, among other information, as shown in Figure 5–11. Each router maintains a routing table (also called forwarding table) that lists the address of the next router (or end-system) corresponding to each known destination address. Thus, a router receiving an IP packet looks up its routing table, determines the next hop, and forwards the packet to that address. This way, a packet is forwarded hop by hop to its destination.

The above is a simple description of the transport plane of IP networks. The control plane that enables the forwarding of IP packets is more complex. Specifically, the control plane has the following components of interest to us:

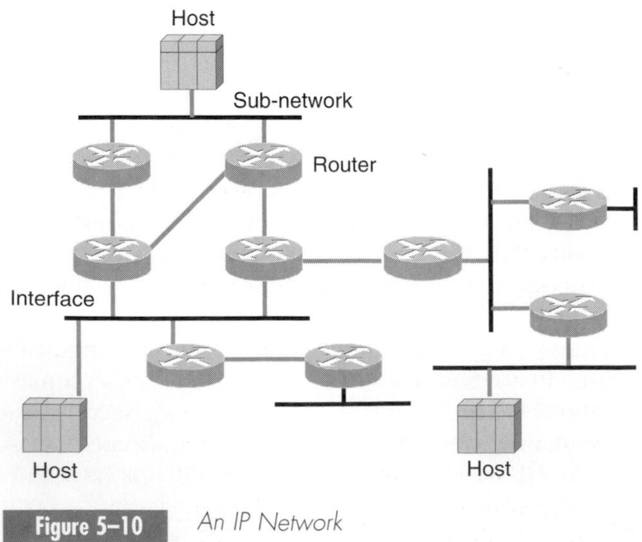

Figure 5–10 *An IP Network*

Vers	HLEN	TOS & Prec	Total Length	
Identification			Flags	Frag. Offset
TTL		Protocol	Header Checksum	
Source IP Address				
Destination IP Address				

IP Packet Header

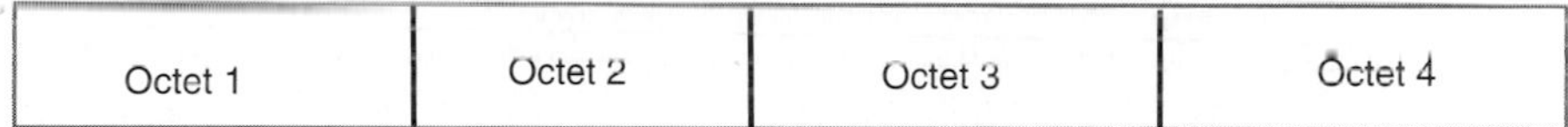

Written as *w.x.y.z*, where $255 \leq w,x,y,z \leq 0$

IP Address Format

Figure 5–11 *IP Header and Address*

1. Addressing: The manner in which routers and hosts are assigned unique addresses
2. Discovery: The manner in which routers discover neighboring routers
3. Routing: The manner in which the routing table is built at each router

Understanding these aspects of the IP network control plane is essential for developing an IP-centric control plane for optical networks.

5.3.1 Addressing

In IP networks, each network interface and/or node (router or host) must be assigned a unique IP address. The uniqueness is defined within the scope of the routing domain, for example, a private network or the entire Internet. Address assignment can be manual or automatic, for example, using the Dynamic Host Configuration Protocol (DHCP) [Alexander+97]. The former method is typically used to assign addresses to routers and their interfaces. The latter is used to assign addresses dynamically to hosts that may connect and disconnect from an IP network, for example, over a dial-up connection. Either way, the assignment of unique addresses allows a packet to be routed to the correct destination.

IP addresses, as shown in Figure 5–11, are 32 bits long. An IP address *prefix* is a string whose length is less than or equal to 32 bits. A prefix represents all IP addresses that have the same values in the corresponding bit positions. Figure 5–12 illustrates a 24-bit IP address prefix and the IP addresses rep-

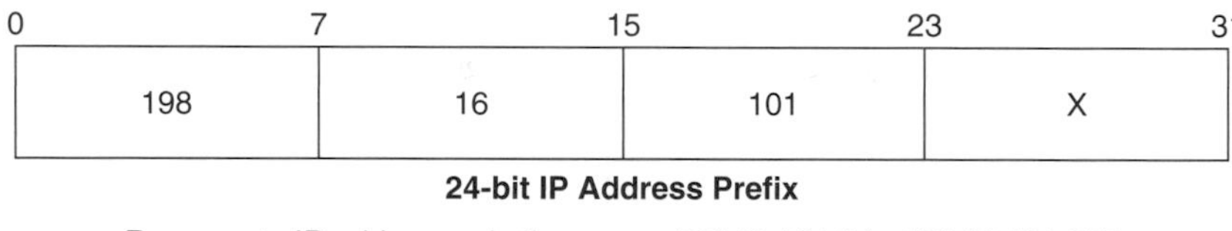

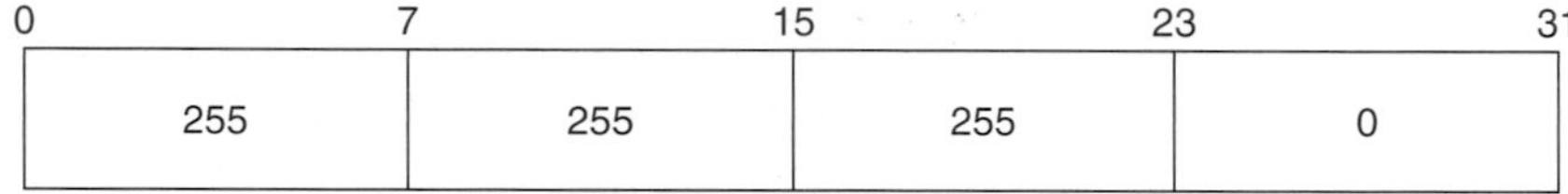

Figure 5–12 *IP Address Prefix and Mask*

resented by the prefix. Prefixes are used as shorthand to represent multiple IP addresses, especially in IP routing protocols. By using prefixes, the amount of information maintained and propagated by an IP routing protocol decreases thereby improving the scalability of routing. A prefix is typically represented as a 32-bit number and a *mask* that indicates which bits are "active" in the prefix. Figure 5–12 shows the representation of a prefix in this manner.

A given IP address could be included in more than one prefix. For example, considering Figure 5–12 again, the address 198.16.101.12 is included in the 24-bit prefix 198.16.101 shown. The same address is also included in the 16-bit prefix 198.16. When there are multiple prefixes including a given address, the *longest matching* prefix is the one with the most number of bits. In the current example, the 24-bit prefix is longer than the 16-bit prefix. An IP routing table may contain multiple prefixes that include a given destination address. In this case, the entry corresponding to the longest matching prefix is considered most specific. Thus, a router with multiple prefixes matching a given destination address will typically select the next hop corresponding to the longest matching prefix.

Finally, IP addresses can be classified into unicast or multicast. A multicast IP address is a logical address denoting more than one physical destination. An IP packet sent to a multicast address will be received by all the destination nodes. Support for multicast requires specialized routing procedures within the network [Tanenbaum02].

5.3.2 Discovery

A router must determine whether it has direct connectivity to other routers. This information is essential for building its routing table. The discovery of adjacent routers is typically a part of IP routing protocols. Under one realization, each router periodically sends a keep-alive message over each of its interfaces. This message contains the identity of the sender (e.g., its IP address), and it is addressed to a special "all routers" multicast IP address. A router receiving such a message becomes aware of the existence of the sending router in its neighborhood.

5.3.3 Routing

Each router in an IP network must know whether a given IP destination address is reachable, and if so, to which next hop the packet should be forwarded. This is essentially the information available in the routing table. The routing table could be built automatically using a distributing IP routing protocol, or by manual configuration. The details of IP routing protocols are described in Chapter 9. Here, we just note briefly the functions of an IP routing protocol and the different types of protocols.

- An IP routing protocol allows a router to determine directly reachable IP addresses, propagate this information to other routers in the network, and use this information, along with information received from other routers, to build its own routing table. The global Internet consists of a large set of interconnected, administratively independent IP networks. IP routing is therefore structured into *intradomain* and *interdomain* routing. An intradomain routing protocol is used within an independently administered network, also called an Autonomous System (AS). For historical reasons, such a protocol is also referred to as an Interior Gateway Protocol (IGP). Examples of IGP are the Routing Information Protocol (RIP) [Hedrick88] and the Open Shortest-Path First (OSPF) protocol [Moy98]. An interdomain routing protocol is used to route packets across different ASs. Historically, such a protocol has been referred to as an Exterior Gateway Protocol (EGP). An example of an EGP is the Border Gateway Protocol (BGP) [Rekhter+95]. It should be noted that although both IGPs and EGPs are used for building routing tables, the criteria used in these protocols for selecting routes and the manner in which routing information is propagated are different. One aspect that is considered important in EGPs is the aggregation of IP addresses propagated across ASs. Specifically, address assignment within an AS must be such that it must be possible to summarize the addresses with a few prefixes. If this is not the case, the routing tables in routers running EGPs tend to grow large, affecting the scalability of the EGP. IGPs and EGPs are further described in Chapter 9.

5.4 Control of MPLS Networks

5.4.1 MPLS Overview

MPLS is the acronym for Multi-Protocol Label Switching. To understand the rationale for MPLS, consider packet forwarding in an IP network. As an IP packet is forwarded from the source to the destination, each router en route makes an independent forwarding decision for that packet. That is, each router analyzes the packet header (in particular the destination IP address) and independently chooses a next hop for the packet. Choosing the next hop can therefore be thought of as the composition of two functions. The first function partitions the entire set of possible packets into a set of Forwarding Equivalence Classes (FECs). The second maps each FEC to a next hop. A FEC, for instance, can be a destination IP address indicating that all packets with that destination address belong to the same FEC and hence are forwarded to the same next hop. In general, any information in the IP packet header can be used to classify a packet as belonging to a specific FEC.

A *label* is a short, fixed length value used to denote a specific FEC. A label is assigned to a packet when it enters an MPLS network, based on the analysis of the header. The packet, when forwarded to its next hop, carries the label with it. At subsequent hops, there is no further analysis of the packet's IP header. Rather, the label is used as an index into a table that specifies the next hop and a new label. The old label is replaced with the new label, and the packet is forwarded to its next hop. In the MPLS forwarding paradigm, once a packet is assigned to a FEC, no further IP header analysis is done by subsequent routers; all forwarding is driven by the labels. Routers in an MPLS networks are thus called Label-Switching Routers (LSRs).

MPLS forwarding has certain advantages over conventional IP network packet forwarding. First, the forwarding process is simplified. In a conventional IP network, a router must match the destination IP address in a packet with prefixes in its routing table, and find the longest matching prefix. MPLS forwarding, on the other hand, requires only a fixed length label to be looked up. This performance aspect was one of the main motivations originally when MPLS was developed. Subsequently, with advancements in router hardware, this has become less of an issue. Second, a packet needs to be classified only once (when it enters an MPLS network). LSRs that process the packet subsequently need not perform classification functions, but merely switch the labels and forward the packet. This implies that interior LSRs in an MPLS network can potentially be simpler than ingress and egress LSRs. Third, in a traditional IP network, packets are typically routed based only on destination address. An MPLS network, on the other hand, allows multiple routes be preestablished for packets belonging to different FECs even if these packets enter and leave the network at the same ingress and egress LSRs, respectively. That is, packets entering the ingress LSR can be classified into different FECs based on administratively established criteria. These packets can then be assigned appropriate distinguishing labels and forwarded along different paths in the MPLS network. This property is the most valuable and it forms the basis for MPLS traffic engineering. Indeed, this has become one of the primary areas of focus for the usage of MPLS technology. Finally, an MPLS packet can carry a stack of labels rather than a single label. With this arrangement, interior LSRs can operate on the label at the top of the stack while the ingress and the egress LSRs can use other labels for classifying distinct packet streams. Label push and pop operations have been defined under MPLS to add or delete the top-level label to increase or decrease the stack depth. Among other benefits, label stacking allows the implementation of Virtual Private Networks (VPNs), which is an important application of the MPLS technology. MPLS features and usage are described in [Rosen+01].

Forwarding in an MPLS network is illustrated in Figure 5–13. Here, it is seen that the ingress LSR inserts an MPLS header over the IP header. This header contains the label, whose value is switched at each hop. The egress LSR strips this header off before sending the packet out of the MPLS network. Although this example shows IP packets being forwarded through an MPLS network, other network layer packets can be dealt with similarly (hence the name Multi Protocol).

5.4.2 Label Distribution

It was seen that LSRs rely on a forwarding table to map the incoming label and interface to an outgoing label and interface. Just as routing protocols are used in IP networks to populate IP routing tables, label distribution protocols are used in MPLS networks to build forwarding tables. In this context, an "upstream" LSR is an LSR that sends a packet with a given outgoing label to the next hop. A "downstream" LSR is the LSR that receives the packet. That is, a downstream LSR is farther away from the source of the packet than the upstream LSR. Under the MPLS architecture, the outgoing label values used by

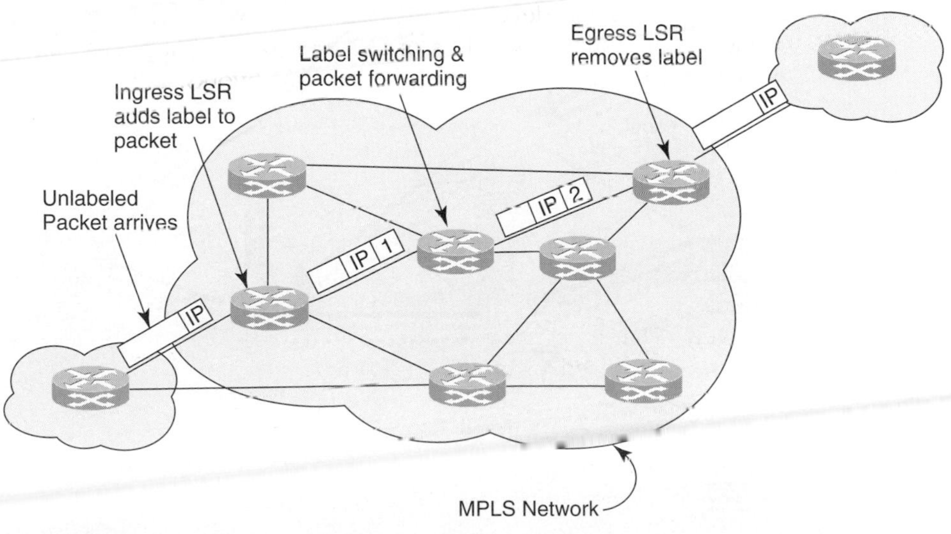

Figure 5–13 *MPLS Forwarding*

an LSR must be obtained from the corresponding downstream LSRs. Thus, labels are "downstream-assigned," and the bindings between FECs and label values are distributed in the "downstream-to-upstream" direction.

The MPLS architecture allows two different modes for label distribution. Under the first mode, an LSR may explicitly request a label binding for a FEC from the next hop (downstream) LSR for that FEC. This is known as "downstream-on-demand" label distribution. Under the second mode, an LSR may distribute bindings to neighboring LSRs that have not explicitly requested them. This is known as "unsolicited downstream" label distribution. In defining these modes, it has been implicitly assumed that all the LSRs have consistent knowledge about the different FECs used in the MPLS network. In the simplest case, a FEC is an IP destination address. In this case, each LSR in an MPLS network must assign a label value corresponding to each destination address and distribute this value to its neighbors. Figure 5–14 illustrates downstream-on-demand label distribution corresponding to an IP destination. In this example, an LSR (e.g., LSR G) assigns a label and sends it to the upstream requester (e.g., LSR D) only after receiving the corresponding allocation from the LSR that is the next hop towards the IP destination, that is, LSR I.

The MPLS architecture allows the possibility of different label distribution protocols being used in different networks. LDP (also standing for Label Distribution Protocol) is one such protocol. LDP allows different label distribution and retention modes, and it runs over TCP between neighboring LSRs.

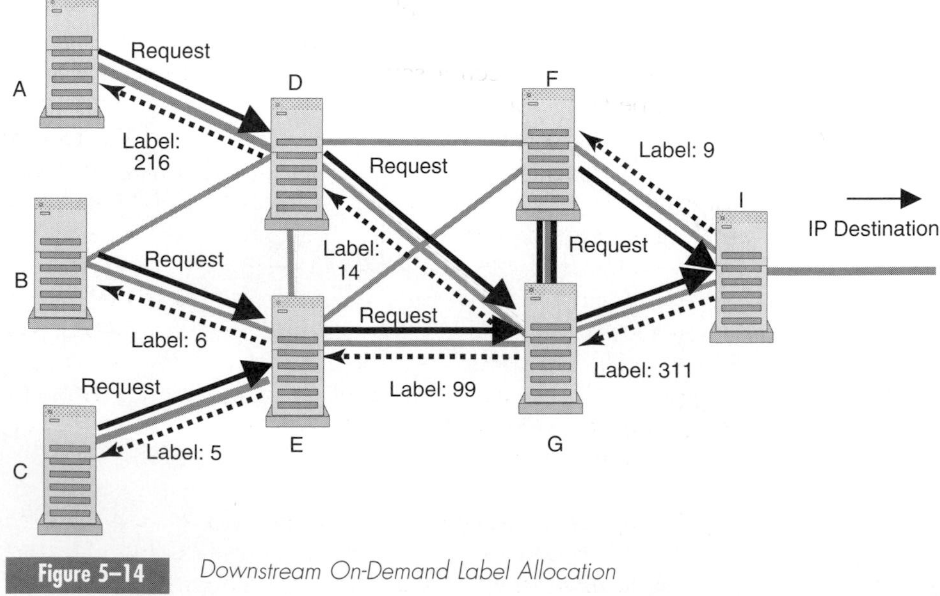

Figure 5–14 *Downstream On-Demand Label Allocation*

The LDP functionality and message set are described in [Andersson+01]. A notable feature of LDP is that it only allows the distribution of labels corresponding to different FECs but not the enforcement of specific routes for labeled packets. That is, an IP routing protocol is required to determine the upstream-downstream relationships between LSRs corresponding to different destinations (and the FECs based on destinations).

5.4.3 MPLS Traffic Engineering (MPLS-TE)

Traffic Engineering (TE) is concerned with performance optimization of operational networks. In general, it deals with the measurement, modeling, characterization, and control of traffic to achieve specific performance objectives. A major goal of traffic engineering is to facilitate efficient and reliable network operations while simultaneously optimizing network resource utilization and traffic performance [Awduche+99].

Traffic engineering is used to satisfy both traffic-oriented as well as resource-oriented performance objectives. Traffic-oriented performance objectives include minimization of packet loss, minimization of delay, maximization of throughput, and enforcement of service level agreements. Resource oriented performance objectives include the aspects pertaining to the optimization of resource utilization. For instance, it may be desirable to ensure that some network resources do not become strained while other resorces remain underutilized. Bandwidth is a crucial resource in contemporary networks. Therefore, a central function of TE is to efficiently manage bandwidth resources.

A valuable feature of MPLS is its applicability for traffic engineering. Specifically, the notion of explicitly routed Label-Switched Paths (LSPs) plays a central role in MPLS TE. Suppose certain guaranteed bandwidth is required for packet flow between a source and a destination. The source-destination pair can be treated as a unique FEC, and an LSP can be established from the source to the destination. This LSP can be assigned the required bandwidth on all links along the path. If the bandwidth allocated for different LSPs on a link is correctly accounted for, then each LSP gets the required quality of service (QoS). Furthermore, a network operator can route LSPs between the same source-destination pair along different paths in the network. This gives the network operator the ability to control traffic loads in different parts of the network, optimize resource usage, and to route traffic along paths that would satisfy the required QoS.

An LSP is defined by the label mappings in the ingress, the egress, and the intermediate LSRs in the path. To set up an LSP for TE purposes, the following actions are required:

1. Specification of the LSP attributes, for example, the required bandwidth, source and destination addresses, the information that characterizes the FEC that the LSP represents.

2. Determination of a feasible route for the LSP within the MPLS network. A feasible route is one in which the intermediate links and LSRs can accommodate the LSP attributes.
3. Establishment of appropriate label mappings in the ingress, the egress, and the intermediate LSRs along the route determined.

LDP, described earlier, is not sufficient for the establishment of explicitly routed LSPs. What we need instead are protocols that allow the specification of LSP attributes and the explicit route so that label mappings and QoS parameters can be established in the appropriate LSRs. Two such protocols are available. One is the Resource reServation Protocol with Traffic Engineering extensions (RSVP-TE), and the other is LDP with Constraint-based Routing extensions (CR-LDP). These are described in more detail in Chapter 7.

5.4.4 MPLS-TE Routing

IP routing protocols typically compute the shortest path to a destination based on static link cost metrics. TE routing, on the other hand, requires the computation of paths based on multiple *constraints*, such as bandwidth availability, latency, link costs, and so on. The MPLS-TE routing model is based on the distributed routing paradigm, where each node keeps track of the network topology, resource availability, and link and node characteristics. Using this information, each node can compute *explicit routes* for connections destined for other nodes, subject to different constraints. MPLS-TE routing protocols are extensions of a class of IP routing protocols, called *link state* protocols. These protocols allow each node to propagate local topology and resource information to all the other nodes in a network. Furthermore, these protocols support a two-level hierarchical routing approach for scalability. MPLS-TE routing is described in detail in Chapter 10.

5.4.5 Recovery in MPLS Networks

The term "recovery" is used to denote LSP protection and restoration operations under MPLS. The basic premise of recovery is that a (primary) LSP affected by a link or node failure can be replaced quickly by another (backup) LSP. Recovery is a notion that has been developed in the context of MPLS-TE. Specifically, MPLS-TE signaling protocols can be used to provision primary and backup LSPs, and to switch data from primary to backup LSPs after a failure event.

MPLS recovery mechanisms support both *local* as well as *end-to-end* recovery paradigms. Local recovery refers to the rerouting of data locally around a failed resource (node or link) using appropriate backup LSP segments. End-to-end recovery refers to the rerouting of data from the source node after a failure. MPLS recovery mechanisms are described in Chapter 8.

Some of the signaling mechanisms used in MPLS recovery can be reused in the optical context, but recovery in optical networks is more complex. These aspects are also described in Chapter 8.

5.5 Generalized MPLS (GMPLS)

5.5.1 GMPLS Overview

MPLS, as originally defined, applies to packet[2] networks. In essence, an MPLS LSR receives a packet from one interface, replaces the (incoming) label in the MPLS header by an outgoing label, and forwards the packet out of another interface. Thus, MPLS defines a virtual circuit capability. Now, consider a true circuit-switched network. Depending on the type of the network, the switching operations would differ:

1. Time-Division Multiplexing (TDM) networks: In these networks, a node switches data from time slots in an incoming interface to time slots in an outgoing interface. An example is a SONET network in which an LTE switches the path layer payload from one channelized interface to another as described in Chapter 3.
2. Port or fiber switching networks: In these networks, a node switches the data received over an incoming interface onto an outgoing interface. An example is a SONET network in which an LTE switches the path layer payload from one unchannelized interface to another. Another example is an all-optical network in which a PXC switches light from one interface to another.
3. Lambda switching networks: In these networks, the nodes switch wavelengths. An example is an optical network with PXCs, which operate at the granularity of an individual wavelength. Each PXC in such a network would be able to switch a wavelength received over an incoming interface to an outgoing interface (with or without wavelength conversion).

From these examples, one can see a correlation between the MPLS label switching operation and different circuit switching operations. Whereas the labels in MPLS networks are explicit, the "labels" are implicit in the other networks. Table 5–1 illustrates the "labels" in the three types of networks described above:

Table 5–1 *Different Types of "Labels"*

Network Type	"Label"
TDM	Time Slot
Port or Fiber Switching	Port Number
Lambda Switching	Wavelength

[2]We loosely use the term *packet* to mean either frames or cells (as in ATM).

Thus, in TDM networks, for instance, the switching of data from a time slot on an incoming interface to a time slot on an outgoing interface is similar to the act of MPLS label switching. The difference, of course, is that whereas MPLS labels are bound to packets, TDM switching applies to specific circuits as they traverse a switch. What this analogy leads to is the conclusion that the same control plane mechanisms used under MPLS for establishing label mappings in switches can be used for setting up cross-connect tables in circuit switched networks. This was first highlighted in a contribution to the IETF on *MPλS* (Multi-Protocol Lambda Switching) [Awduche+01a] in the context of lambda switching. Since then, it has been realized that the analogy applied to many different circuit switching networks, and the term Generalized MPLS (GMPLS) has been adopted to denote the generalization of the MPLS control plane to support multiple types of switched networks. The term "LSP" is used under GMPLS to denote different types of circuits such as a SONET/SDH connection, an optical light path, an MPLS LSP, and so on.

Under GMPLS, a suite of distributed control plane protocols is defined. These protocols cover three main functions:

- *Link management:* This deals with neighbor discovery, maintenance of signaling control channels, and so on.
- *Topology and resource discovery:* This deals with topology and resource information propagation within a GMPLS control domain. This function is also referred to as "GMPLS routing."
- *Signaling:* This deals with protocols for connection provisioning and restoration.

The protocols for topology and resource discovery and signaling are adapted from MPLS-TE routing and signaling protocols. Link management is a new function defined under GMPLS.

5.5.2 GMPLS Link Management

Unlike MPLS LSRs, the optical network nodes may have several tens or even hundreds of links to adjacent nodes. Neighbor discovery is a function that allows each network node to determine the identity of the neighboring nodes and the details of link connectivity to these nodes. This information is necessary for both topology discovery and signaling. Normally, in MPLS networks running IP routing protocols with TE extensions, such adjacencies will be discovered by the routing protocol. In networks with dense interconnections, it is inefficient to have the routing protocol run over multiple links between the same pair of nodes. Thus, GMPLS supports a separate link management function, which permits automatic neighbor discovery as a precursor to topology discovery. Link management is a function implemented between every pair of neighboring nodes, and supports the maintenance of the signaling control channels and the verification of configured parameters in addition to neighbor discovery. Link management is described in detail in Chapter 6.

5.5.3 GMPLS Routing

The MPLS-TE routing protocols have been extended to support topology and resource discovery under GMPLS. As with MPLS-TE routing, GMPLS routing permits the assignment of various attributes to links and the propagation of link connectivity and attributes (resource) information from one node to all others in a network. The attributes assigned to a link are specific to the underlying technology. To deal with dense interconnections, GMPLS routing allows multiple links between a pair of nodes to be bundled into a single TE link in topology descriptions. This is particularly useful in optical networks, where many tens of links may exist between neighboring nodes. GMPLS routing also incorporates the notion of Shared Risk Link Groups (SRLGs), used for indicating which physical facilities could be affected by a common failure event. GMPLS routing allows the partitioning of a large network into multiple, smaller areas. In this case, GMPLS routing extends the multiarea TE concepts used under MPLS-TE. As in MPLS-TE, the path computation algorithms themselves are not specified as part of GMPLS routing. GMPLS routing implementations are free to choose the path computation algorithms. GMPLS routing is described in detail in Chapter 10.

5.5.4 GMPLS Signaling

GMPLS signaling utilizes MPLS-TE signaling protocols (RSVP-TE and CR-LDP) with extensions for handling multiple switching technologies. The significant extensions are:

- *Generalized label:* The MPLS notion of label is generalized to include different label formats corresponding to packet and circuit-switched technologies (see Table 5–1).
- *Common end-to-end label:* This extension allows switches in a network to determine a common end-to-end "label." This feature is useful in all-optical networks without wavelength conversion, where the same wavelength (label) must be used end-to-end.
- *Bidirectionality:* GMPLS signaling extensions support the provisioning of both unidirectional and bidirectional connections. This is in contrast to MPLS-TE, which supports only unidirectional LSPs
- *Separation of control and data planes:* MPLS-TE signaling typically occurs over the same network node interfaces over which data flow. GMPLS signaling allows control and data interfaces to be distinct. Thus, a single control link between network elements can be used to control several data links between them. Furthermore, GMPLS sig-

naling is designed such that failures in the control plane do not affect data transport over previously established connections.

- *Control plane restart procedures:* These extensions allow network elements to recover their signaling control states after a node or link failure.

GMPLS signaling is described in detail in Chapter 7.

5.6 Control of ATM Networks: The P-NNI Protocols

In ATM networks, Virtual Circuits (VCs) provide connectivity between two ATM end points. An ATM VC is a logical circuit with associated bandwidth, delay, and other service parameters. The P-NNI protocols, described next, provide the routing and signaling capabilities required for establishing and deleting VCs. It is quite feasible to adapt these protocols for use in optical networks, and hence it is instructive to look into their details.

5.6.1 The P-NNI Hierarchy

Private Network-Network Interface (P-NNI) denotes both the interface between border switches in two ATM subnetworks as well as the interface between two switches within a network.[3] The ATM Forum P-NNI specification defines automated routing and signaling procedures across these interfaces to aid in connection provisioning [ATMF02].

Both P-NNI routing and signaling support a multilevel hierarchical network structure. The notion of a *peer group* is used under P-NNI to describe this hierarchical structure. At the lowest level, a peer group consists of a collection of individual nodes. Two or more such lowest level peer groups can be grouped to form the next higher level peer group and so on. Each peer group is distinguished by its *level* and its *identifier*. Figure 5–15 illustrates the hierarchical organization of a sample network. This network has 23 nodes interconnected as shown. Six first-level peer groups are formed, with identities A.1–A.4 and B.1–B.2. These peer groups are shown enclosed in dotted boxes. In each peer group, a node is elected as the *peer group leader*. The peer group leader can be any node in the peer group. In the figure, the peer group leaders are shown shaded. Each level of the hierarchy is identified with a "level" number. This is explained in the next section. Each node in the network has an associated identifier. For the moment, let us assume that the numbers 1–23 indicated in the figure are the node identifiers. The actual formats of the node and peer group identifiers are described in the next section.

[3] In essence, what this means is that the procedures defined for the network-network interface can also be used at the node-node interface. The term P-NNI is used to denote both these interfaces.

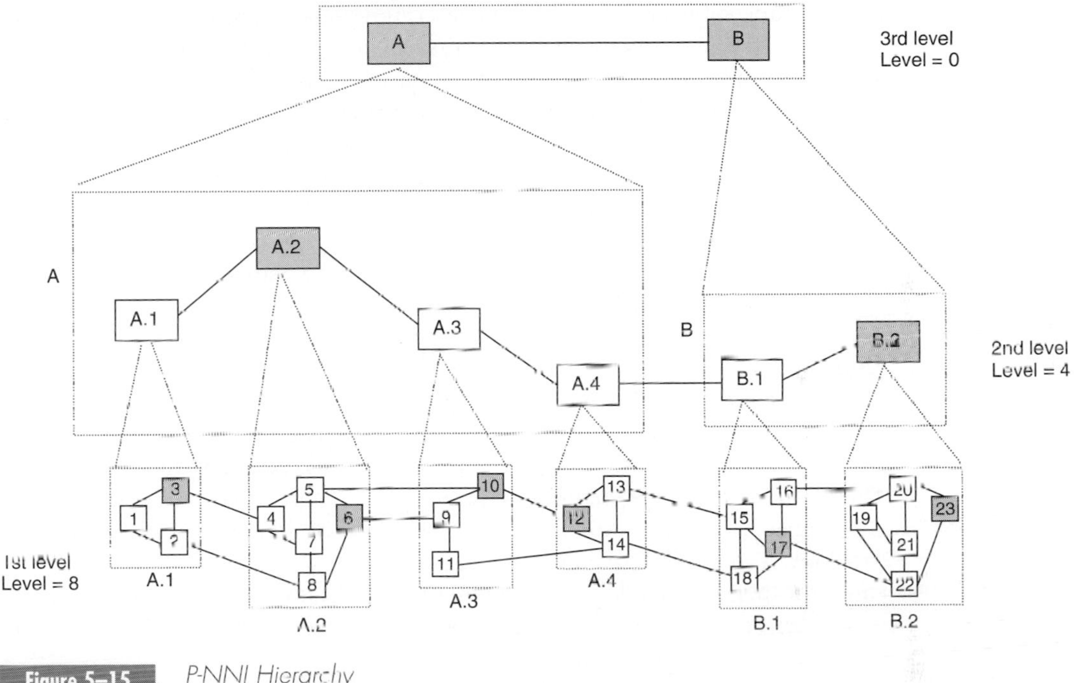

Figure 5–15 *P-NNI Hierarchy*

The connectivity between peer groups at the first level is defined by the physical links that interconnect border nodes. The second level peer group now consists of *logical nodes* (A.1–A.4, B.1–B.2) that represent the first level peer groups, along with logical links that capture the connectivity between the peer groups in the first level. Similarly, the third level peer group is formed containing two logical nodes, A and B, and a single logical link as shown.

Peer groups at various levels are formed through a combination of manual configuration and P-NNI routing intelligence. First, the network administrator must decide how to structure the network and assign the first level peer group identifier to each node. Taking the example of Figure 5–15, each of the 23 nodes is configured with its first level peer group identifier, that is, nodes 1–3 are configured with the identifier A.1, nodes 4–8 with A.2, and so on. Now, it can be seen that the second level peer group identifiers are a prefix of the first level identifier, that is, A is a prefix of A.1–A.4 and B is a prefix of B.1–B.2. This is not an accident. The peer group identifiers are structured in such a manner that two adjacent nodes in the network can determine the "lowest common" peer group to which they both belong. As an example, nodes 3 and 4 can compare their peer group identifiers and determine that they are both part of the next higher level peer group, A. Similarly, nodes 13 and 15 can determine that the lowest common peer group is the third level peer group. Thus, under P-NNI, the first level peer group identifier is configured in each node, and the rest of the structure is determined by the nodes themselves as part of P-NNI routing. This procedure is aided by the structure of the peer group identifier, as described in the next section.

The peer group leader in each peer group is responsible for importing and exporting information to/from the peer group to higher level peer groups. In essence, a peer group leader represents the logical node in the higher level peer group topology. The control plane adjacencies between logical nodes correspond to control channels between the corresponding peer group leaders. These control channels, called Routing Control Channels, are usually switched virtual circuits between peers, either adjacent physical nodes or logical nodes. As an example, consider Figure 5–15. Peer group leaders 3 and 6 represent logical nodes A.1 and A.2 in the higher level. There is a control channel between these nodes even though they are not physically adjacent in the topology. There is also a control channel between nodes 3 and 4 as they are adjacent.

Finally, P-NNI routing allows each node to build a "view" of the network topology. The procedures for this are rather involved, and the interested reader can refer to [ATMF02]. From a signaling point of view, it is important to know what the topology view at a node looks like. Considering node 1 in Figure 5–15, the view will contain:

- The complete topology of peer group A.1. This consists of a representation of all the nodes, links, and the associated parameters (e.g., link metrics, node attributes, etc.).
- The topology of interconnection between peer group A.1 and adjacent peer groups in the second level. This contains the logical nodes A.2–A.4, the interconnection between A.1 and A.2, and the logical links interconnecting A.2–A.4. As before, the topology information includes the relevant node and link parameters.
- The topology of interconnection at the third level. This consists of logical node B and the logical link between A.4 and B, along with the associated parameters.

Figure 5–16 illustrates this topology view.

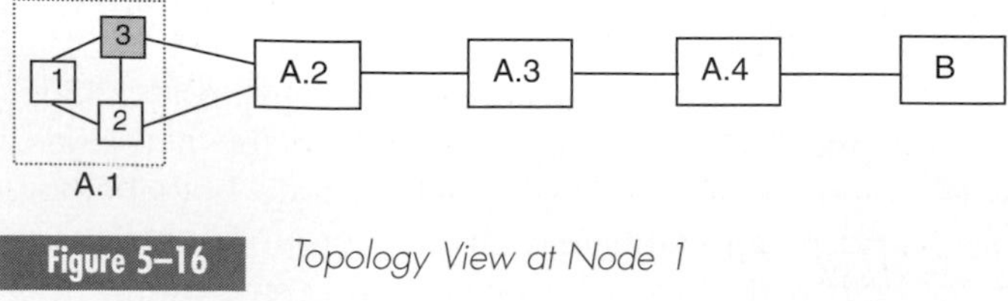

Figure 5–16 *Topology View at Node 1*

5.6.2 Addressing and Identification

Addressing and identification are two distinct concepts under P-NNI. Specifically, interfaces to end-systems (e.g., hosts) and other destinations of P-NNI signaling (e.g., node interfaces) have addresses. Nodes and peer groups have associated identifiers. Since P-NNI protocols are designed for ATM networks, the addressing supported is the ATM End-System Addresses, or AESA for short. The ATM Forum has defined four formats for AESA, all of them 20 bytes long [ATMF99]. The generic format of the AESA is shown in Figure 5–17a. From the point of view of P-NNI protocols, an AESA is taken simply to be a 20-byte (160-bit) number. Of this, the first 19 bytes (152 bits) are used for P-NNI routing and signaling, and the last byte (selector, SEL) is used for end-system selection at a destination node. Logical node identifiers, however, utilize the 6-byte End System Identifier (ESI) field of the AESA.

Now, a *prefix* of a given AESA is a string of bits whose length n is less than 160 bits and which matches exactly the first n bits of the AESA. Figure 5–17b illustrates an AESA and a prefix that matches in the first 10 bytes (the rest of the prefix are set to 0). Here, each byte of the AESA is represented by two hexadecimal digits. An ATM node can be assigned a 19-byte prefix, and the node can then generate up to 256 AESAs by assigning different values to the last byte. Such node-generated AESAs can be assigned to end-systems. One of them can also be taken by the node as its identifier. To be able to establish connections, nodes and end-systems must have an address (AESA) assigned.

Now, a prefix of length n bits ($n < 160$) is said to *summarize* all AESAs whose first n bits are the same as the prefix. Summarization is the key to the scalability of P-NNI routing. The hierarchical structure of the network must be such that it should be possible to summarize the address of all the end-systems (and nodes) reachable inside any peer group with a few prefixes.

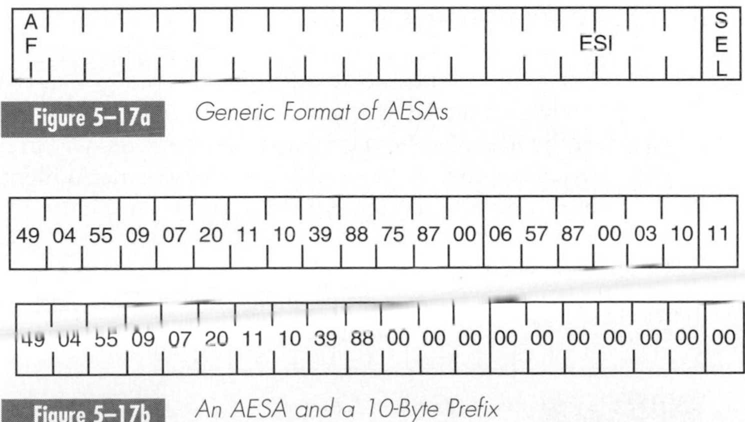

Figure 5–17a Generic Format of AESAs

Figure 5–17b An AESA and a 10-Byte Prefix

Each peer group is assigned an identifier. A peer group ID can be up to 13 bytes (104 bits) long. The format of the ID is shown in Figure 5–18. The *level* field shown indicates the length of the peer group ID in bits. When the level field contains a value n, the leftmost n bits of the identifier field contain the peer group ID. The rest of the bits (104 – n right most bits) are set to 0. A peer group ID with level = n is said to be a prefix of another peer group ID with level = m if $n < m$ and the corresponding identifier fields match exactly in the leftmost n positions. This is similar to the concept of AESA prefixes. Looking at Figure 5–15 again. If we assume that the peer group IDs shown represent two hexadecimal digits (each 4 bits long), the level of peer group A.1 is 8 (8 bits total) and the level of peer group A is 4. The top level is assigned the value 0.

A peer group whose identifier is a prefix of another peer group is said to be a parent of the latter. Thus, two adjacent nodes that are in peer groups at levels k and m, and whose identifiers match in the first n bits ($n < k, m$) can assume that they are part of a common parent peer group at level n. This can be illustrated using Figure 5–15. Considering nodes 3 and 4, their peer group identifiers are A.1 and A.2, respectively. Comparing the identifiers, they match in the first 4 bits (the hex digit "A"). Thus, the nodes are part of the same parent peer group "A" (whose level is 4). The peer group A, in fact, contains four logical nodes A.1–A.4 as shown in Figure 5–15. Similarly, considering nodes 13 and 15, their peer group IDs are A.4 and B.1, respectively. Thus, there is no match, and these nodes have a common parent peer group at the top-most level (i.e., level 0, the peer group containing A and B).

The P-NNI specification recommends that a peer group identifier be a prefix of the AESAs reachable within the peer group. There is, however, no requirement that there is a correlation between peer group identifiers and reachable addresses for the P-NNI procedures to work.

A node identifier is a 22-byte number with the following structure: a 1-bye level indicator followed by a 21-byte identifier field. The assignment of these values for physical and logical nodes is as follows:

- For physical nodes, the level indicator contains the level of the node's immediately enclosing peer group. The first (left most) byte of the identifier field contains the value 160 (A0 in hex). The next 20 bytes contain an AESA of the node. The node identifier corresponding to node 1 in Figure 5–15 is shown in Figure 5–19a.

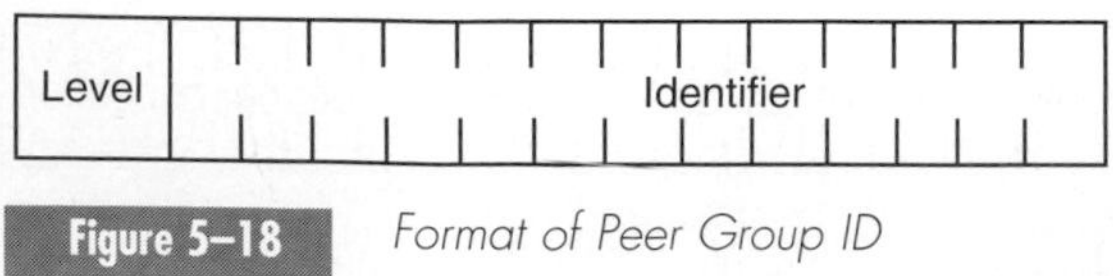

Figure 5–18 *Format of Peer Group ID*

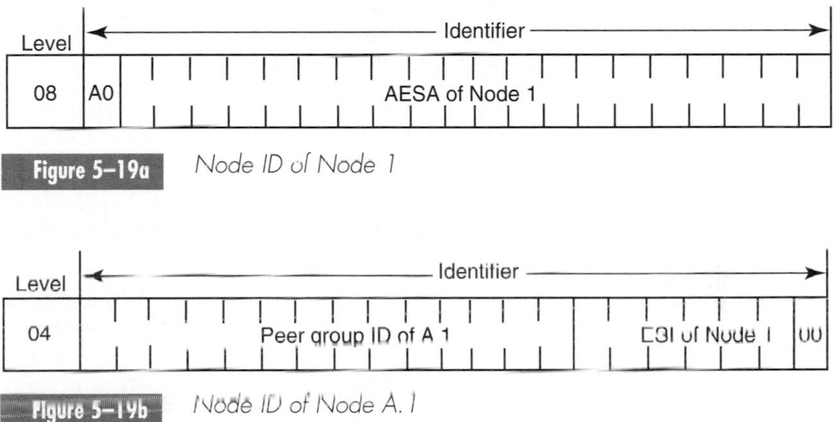

Figure 5–19a *Node ID of Node 1*

Figure 5–19b *Node ID of Node A.1*

- For logical nodes, the level indicator contains the level of the node's immediately enclosing peer group. The first (left most) 14 bytes of the identifier field contain the ID of the lower level peer group to which the corresponding physical node belongs (note that logical nodes are represented by peer group leaders of a lower level peer group). The next six bytes contain the ESI of the physical node. The last byte is set to 0. The node identifier corresponding to logical node A.1 in Figure 7–38 is shown in Figure 5–19b.

Finally, a port identifier is a 32-bit number locally assigned by a node to each of its ports. A link (logical or physical) is identified by the pair, <node ID, port ID>, where node ID is the identity of the node at either end of the link and port ID is the identifier assigned by the node to the port to which the link attaches.

P-NNI signaling and routing are described further in Chapters 7 and 9, respectively.

5.7 Summary

In this chapter, we described the formal architectural models for the optical control plane and gave an overview of its components. The control plane supports neighbor discovery, distributed routing, and signaling for connection provisioning and restoration. While the optical control plane protocols are predominantly IP and MPLS based, the ATM P-NNI protocols have also been adopted for optical network control. The following chapters describe these protocol components in detail.

SIX

Neighbor Discovery

6.1 Introduction

Neighbor discovery refers to procedures by which an optical Network Element (NE) automatically determines its connectivity to different types of adjacent elements (called *neighbors*). Neighbor discovery is perhaps the most useful control plane function. Its utility in a network is independent of whether other distributed control plane functions like routing and signaling are implemented. The connectivity information determined using neighbor discovery procedures is essential for connection routing and provisioning. Without neighbor discovery, the interconnection information must be manually configured in provisioning systems. In a network with many NEs, and with each NE having numerous ports, manual configuration of this information could be error-prone and inconvenient. Furthermore, keeping track of changes in the connectivity between NEs manually could become difficult. As we shall see in this chapter, neighbor discovery procedures also aid in detecting errors in physical wiring or connectivity between adjacent NEs.

It should be noted that while neighbor discovery procedures allow an NE to determine its local connectivity, how this information is disseminated and used depends on the nature of the provisioning system. With a centralized provisioning system, the local connectivity information would be collected by the central system from each NE for use in route computation. With a distributed control plane, the local connectivity information would be propagated by the routing protocol to form the topology map at each NE (see Chapter 10). In addition to its use in connection provisioning, the neighbor information could be used to verify that link parameters are configured in a consistent manner at both ends of a link. This is called *link property correlation*. With a centralized provisioning system, link property correlation can be done at the central system. With a distributed control plane, a protocol is required for neighboring nodes to exchange and compare configuration information pertaining to discovered links.

In the rest of this chapter, we examine neighbor discovery and link property correlation in detail. In the next section, we describe the different types of adjacencies and define the neighbor discovery function. In section 6.3, we look at the protocol requirements for neighbor discovery and link property correlation. The Link Management Protocol (LMP) developed by the IETF is discussed in section 6.4. This protocol aims to support neighbor discovery in both networks with OEO and OOO switching elements, and hence it is somewhat more complex than a protocol targeted solely for OEO elements. Finally, conclusions are discussed in section 6.5.

6.2 Types of Adjacencies and Discovery Procedures

ITU-T recommendation G.7714 [ITU-T02a] defines three types of adjacencies. These are described below.

6.2.1 Layer Adjacency

Consider Figure 6–1a, which illustrates a network segment with IP routers, OEO (e.g., SONET) optical cross connects (OXCs), WDM devices, and amplifiers. The figure depicts physical links between network elements, for example, between the OXCs and the WDM devices. The transmission system, consisting of the WDM devices and optical amplifiers, is referred to as the optical line system. Figure 6–1b depicts connectivity at various SONET layers— path, line, and section (see also Figure 5–5). Two network elements are said to be neighbors at a certain layer if each terminates the overhead information for that layer generated by the other, and all the intermediate network elements pass this information transparently. For example, the two OXCs shown in Figure 6–1a are neighbors at the line layer. The connectivity at each layer, as shown in Figure 6–1b, defines logical links at that layer as seen from the layer above. Thus, *layer adjacency* defines the associations between the two end

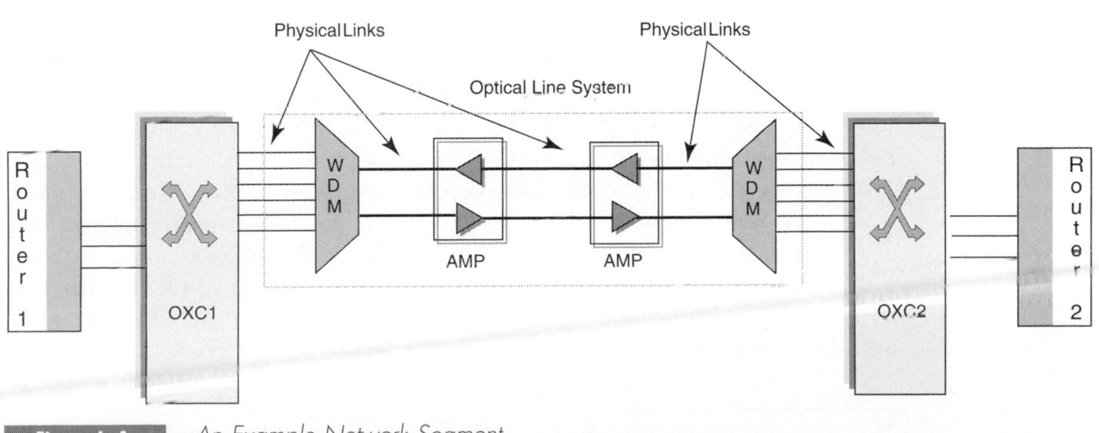

Figure 6–1a *An Example Network Segment*

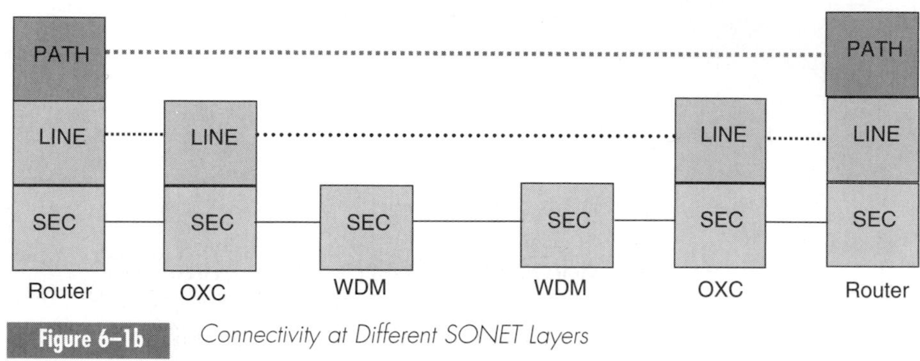

Figure 6–1b *Connectivity at Different SONET Layers*

points that terminate a logical link at a given layer. In reality, the association is defined by a mapping of the two end point identifiers. For instance, if the end points are identified by two numbers *i* and *j*, respectively, the adjacency is defined by recognizing that end point *i* on one side is related to end point *j* on the other side. This recognition is brought about by running the neighbor discovery procedures, and the resulting mapping between the end point identifiers is used in signaling and routing (see, e.g., Chapter 7).

In Figure 6–1a, there are six links between the two OXCs, all carried over the same fiber. Each of these links could in fact support multiple communication channels.[1] For instance, suppose each link is a channelized OC-48 link, capable of carrying 48 STS-1 connections. Each channel has to be recognized by an identifier at each end of the link. These identifiers, however, can be the same on both sides, since the channels have a fixed association to the link. For example, the first channel can be identified as channel 1, the second as channel 2, and so on, on each side. Thus, there is no need for an explicit discovery mechanism to detect channel associations within a logical link.

Let us now look at some other configurations and see how layer adjacency is defined. Figure 6–2a depicts two SONET STS-1 cross-connects interconnected through an intervening core network supporting only STS-48 services. Each STS-1 OXC has an OC-48 interface to the core network, and the network supports line-transparent STS-48 connections (see Chapter 3). Figure 6–2b shows such a connection between the two STS-1 OXCs. This connection, from the point of view of the two OXCs, looks like a channelized STS-48 link. Thus, there is a line layer adjacency between the two OXCs. Similarly, there is a section layer adjacency between each STS-1 OXC and an OXC in the core network. As before, there is a fixed association between the STS-1 channels and the STS-48 link that runs between the two STS-1 OXCs.

[1]In the terminology of Chapter 5, such a logical link is in fact a server layer trail supporting multiple client layer link connections. In the interest of simplicity, we choose to be informal in this section.

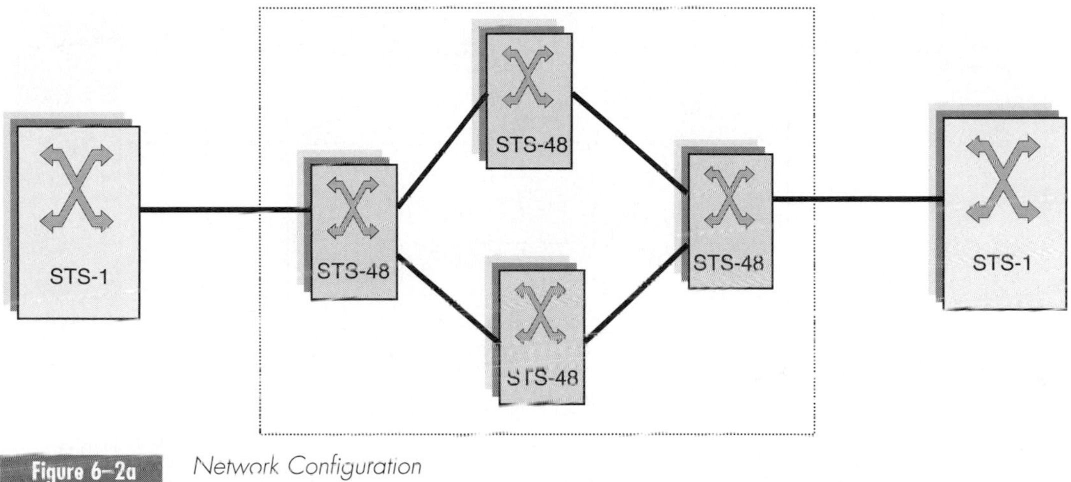

Figure 6–2a *Network Configuration*

Figure 6–3 depicts the connectivity at various layers of the network segment shown in Figure 6–1a, when Photonic Cross-Connects (PXCs) are used. A PXC cross-connects the optical signal from an incoming port to an outgoing port without converting it to the corresponding electrical signal. Hence, a PXC performs OOO switching (see Chapter 1), and it is transparent to the format of the signal. Despite the transparency, the connectivity between the PXCs still defines the optical network topology from the perspective of provisioning and restoration of path-layer connections. But at what layer are the PXCs adjacent? Figure 6–4 shows the anatomy of a PXC. It is seen that the PXC interfaces are connected to WDM transponders that determine the rate and other characteristics of the link between two PXCs. For instance, this could be an OC-192 link, although none of the SONET overheads are terminated by the PXCs. In this scenario, it might be appropriate to say that the PXCs are adjacent at the physical layer. In reality, the precise classification of this adjacency does not matter as much as the identification of the two end points of the link.

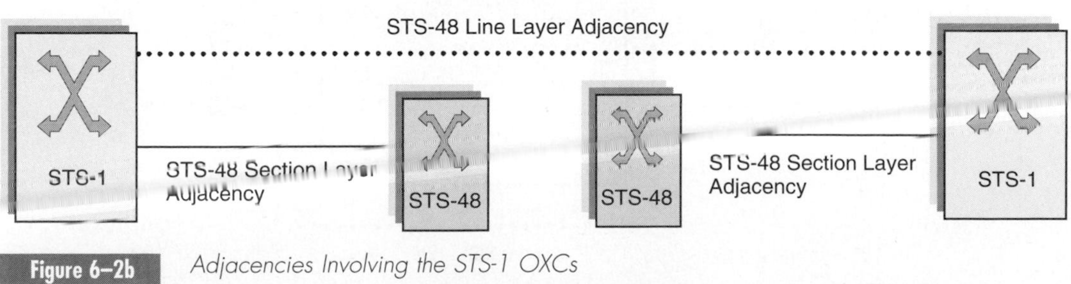

Figure 6–2b *Adjacencies Involving the STS-1 OXCs*

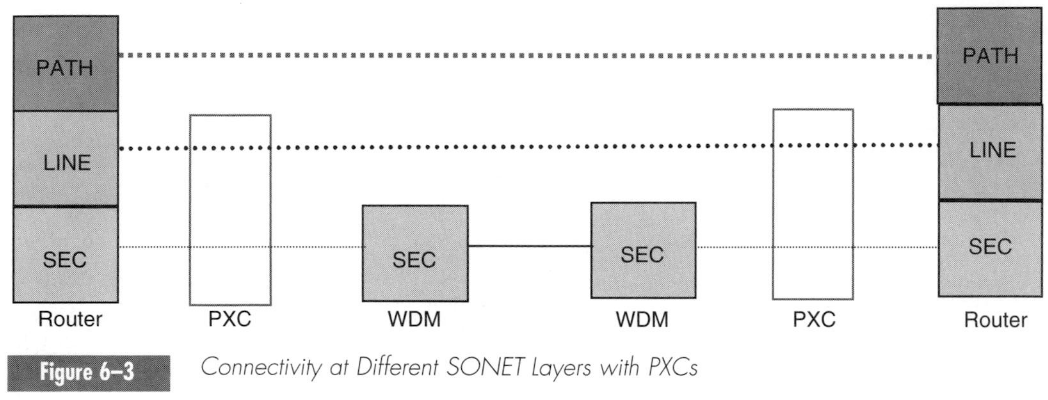

Figure 6–3 *Connectivity at Different SONET Layers with PXCs*

6.2.2 Physical Media Adjacency

Physical media adjacency, as the name implies, describes the adjacency between two network elements that have a direct physical connection. For example, considering Figure 6–1a, the OXCs have direct connections to WDM devices, that is, each OXC port is connected to a port in a WDM device. The association between the identities of the interconnected ports defines the physical adjacency.

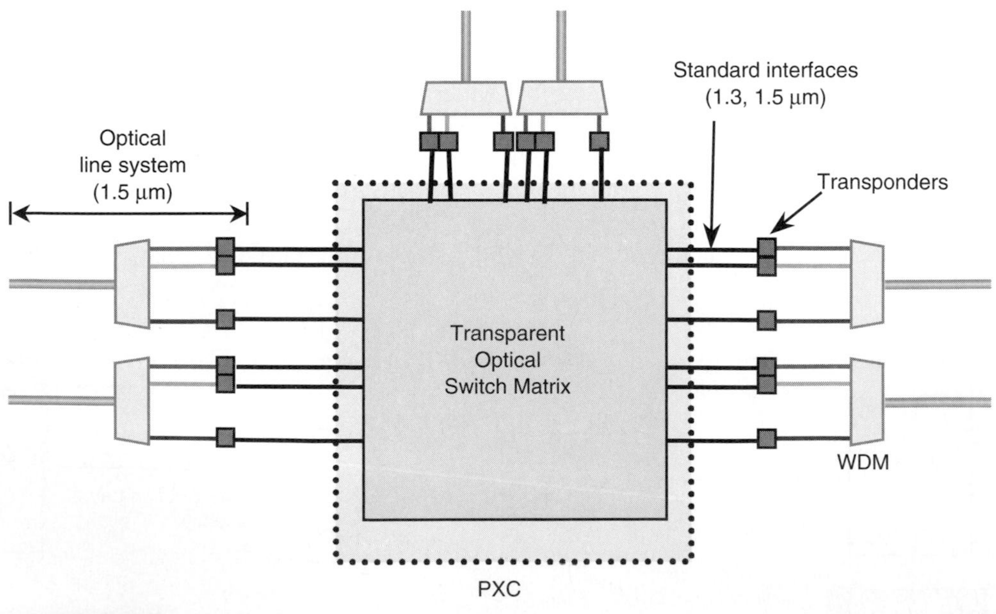

Figure 6–4 *Interface between a PXC and WDM Devices*

6.2.3 Control Adjacency

In a network that utilizes control communication between NEs, it is necessary for each NE to know all its control plane adjacencies. For instance, OXCs 1 and 2 in Figure 6–1a could be peers in the control plane if signaling were to be used for connection provisioning (see Chapter 7). An association of the higher layer protocol identifiers for the two control end points defines the control adjacency. For example, suppose the GMPLS RSVP-TE protocol (see Chapter 7) is used for signaling between the two OXCs. The control channel between the two NEs could be identified by the interface IP address at each end. Neighbor discovery procedures can aid in automatically discovering control plane adjacencies.

6.2.4 Neighbor Discovery Procedures

Now that we have defined three types of adjacencies, the questions are which of these types of discovery are needed in a given network and how is discovery done? To answer these questions, we have to look at the role of discovery in some detail. We briefly mentioned earlier that discovery is essential for route computation and signaling. Let us see why this is so.

Figure 6–5 depicts a scenario for provisioning connections in an optical network via a centralized provisioning system. Here, to provision a connection from port 1 in node A to port 2 in node D, it is necessary to determine the precise path in terms of all the intermediate nodes and ports. This implies that the central provisioning system must have a detailed representation of the network topology, including information about

- The identities of OXCs in the network
- The manner in which OXCs are connected, that is, the identities of nodes and interfaces at the two ends of each link
- The type of each link, for example, channelized OC-48
- The properties of each link as pertaining to connection routing. These properties include
  - Shared-risk link group information: An SRLG is a unique identifier associated with physical facilities (e.g., a fiber or a conduit) and denotes a common or "shared" level of risk with other members of its group. Each link can be associated with one or more SRLGs depending on the physical facilities it utilizes. The assignment of SRLGs to links allows the computation of physically diverse paths.
  - Link span distance (also called fiber miles): This information indicates the geographic distance (e.g., number of miles) spanned by the link.
  - Link cost (also called Traffic Engineering (TE) metric): A number that indicates the administrative cost assigned to the link.

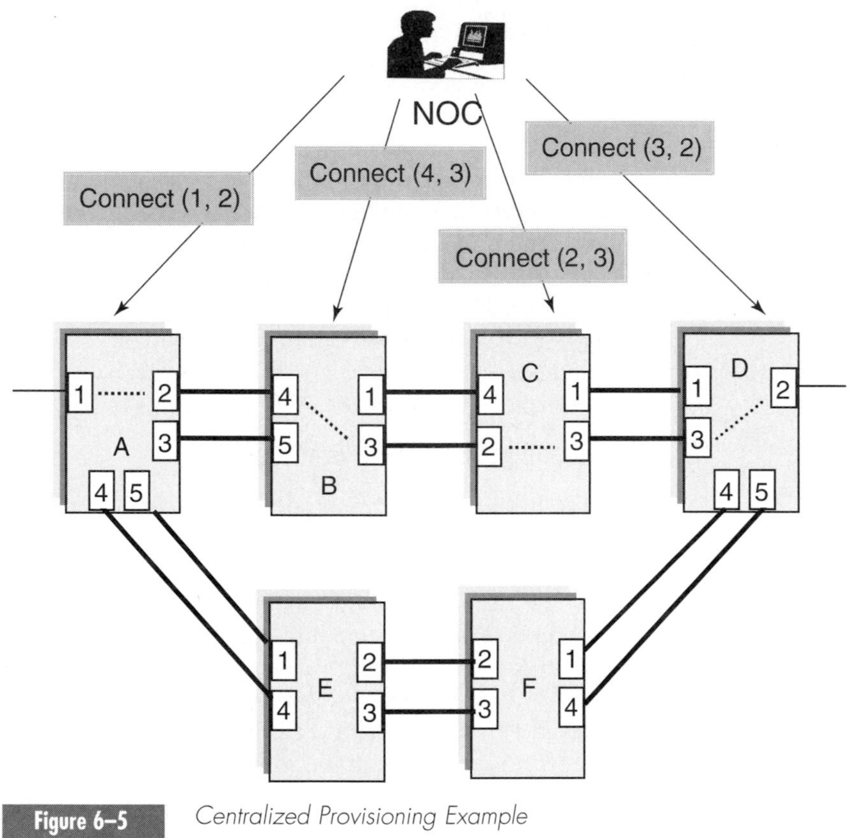

Figure 6–5 *Centralized Provisioning Example*

- Administrative color: This is usually a number that indicates an administrative grouping for the link. Links with similar color values are said to be in the same administrative class with respect to applicable policies.

Thus, it is necessary to gather many different items of information in the provisioning system. Furthermore, the information must be updated as changes occur in the network. Automated procedures that aid in this process by minimizing the amount of manual configuration would be quite useful. Suppose that each OXC could automatically discover the identity of the remote OXC and the identity of the remote interface to which each of its local interfaces is connected. Furthermore, suppose that any changes in this information can be detected automatically and quickly. Then the provisioning system can simply collect up-to-date connectivity information from the individual OXCs to form the network topology map. This procedure, for a two-node network, is shown in Figure 6–6. Here, each node periodically sends over each link its own identity and the identity of the interface. Each node also keeps track of the information received from its neighbor. The provisioning system collects the information from both nodes, performs the correlation, and obtains the accurate connectivity information.

The alternative to this procedure is to manually enter the connectivity information in the provisioning system. This could be a rather cumbersome task, considering the number of ports in new generation optical switches and the need to keep track of connectivity changes as they occur.

A side benefit of automatic link identification is the ability of OXCs to detect inconsistent wiring of bidirectional interfaces. Specifically, it is possible to automatically detect situations where the transmit side of interface *x* in OXC A is connected to the receive side of interface *y* in OXC B, but the receive side of interface *x* is not connected to the transmit side of interface *y*. This feature is very useful when OXCs with high port densities are interconnected. This is further described later in this chapter.

Instead of the centralized provisioning system shown in Figure 6–5, let us now consider the case where distributed IP-centric routing and signaling

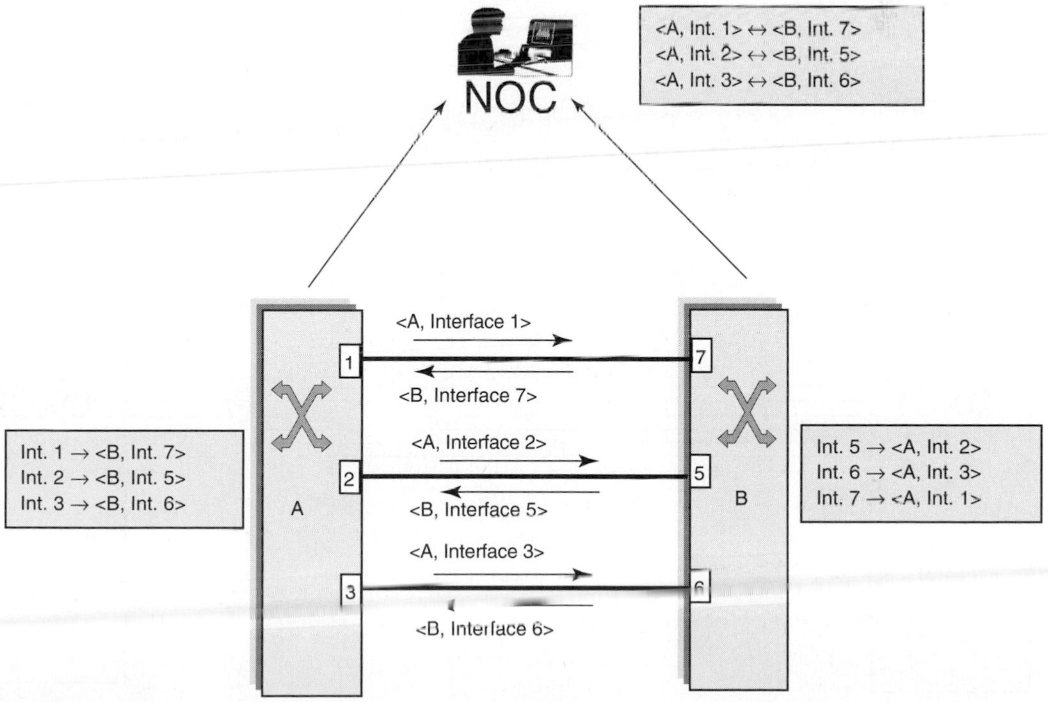

Figure 6–6 *Link Identification Exchange*

protocols are implemented in the network. Here, provisioning activities are decentralized, and each OXC must keep track of the topology and the link information that a centralized provisioning system would have normally maintained. Note that in the distributed system configuration, the topology information maintained by a node need not be as detailed as that maintained by a centralized provisioning system. Specifically, information about links between OXC may be aggregated or *bundled* so that connectivity information may be abstracted. This concept is illustrated in Figure 6–7, where nineteen links between a pair of OXCs are abstracted into four bundles based on link type and SRLG values. So, with link bundling, is there a need for detailed link identification as in the centralized provisioning case? Yes! This information is now needed during the signaling phase of connection provisioning. Figure 6–8 illustrates the provisioning of a connection under distributed control between an ingress and an egress port (i.e., port 1 of OXC A to port 2 of OXC D). The source OXC (A) computes an explicit route (ER) which specifies the sequence of OXCs from the ingress to the egress, along with an identification of the specific link bundle at each OXC. In this example, there is a single bundle between each node pair, denoted by B1. Each intermediate OXC is responsible for selecting a specific link within the bundle to route the connection, and signaling the choice to the next OXC in the explicit route. The figure depicts

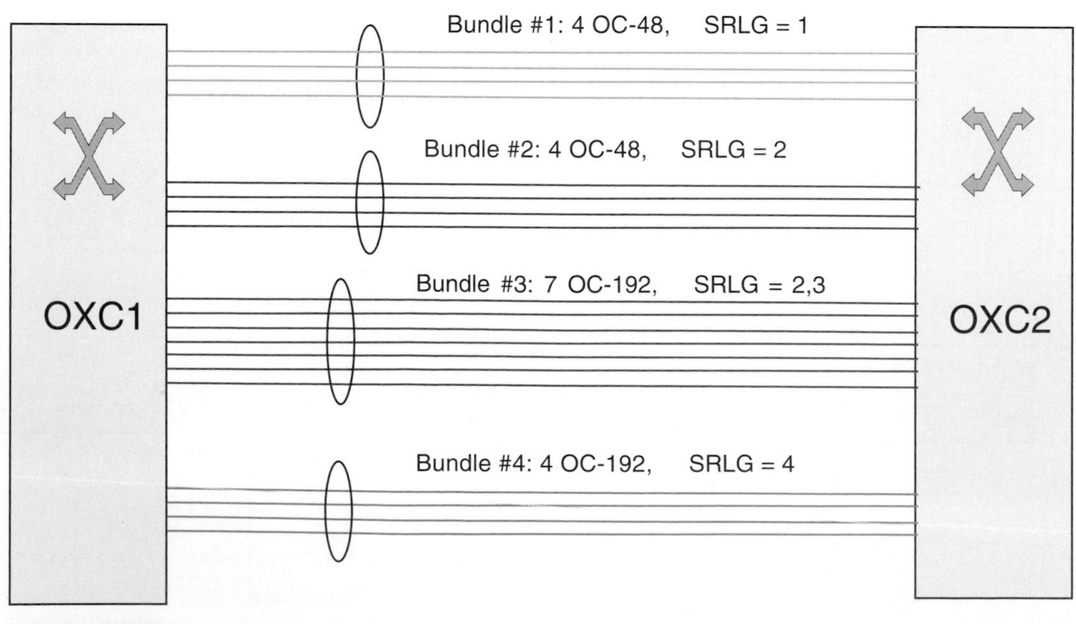

Figure 6–7 *Link Bundles*

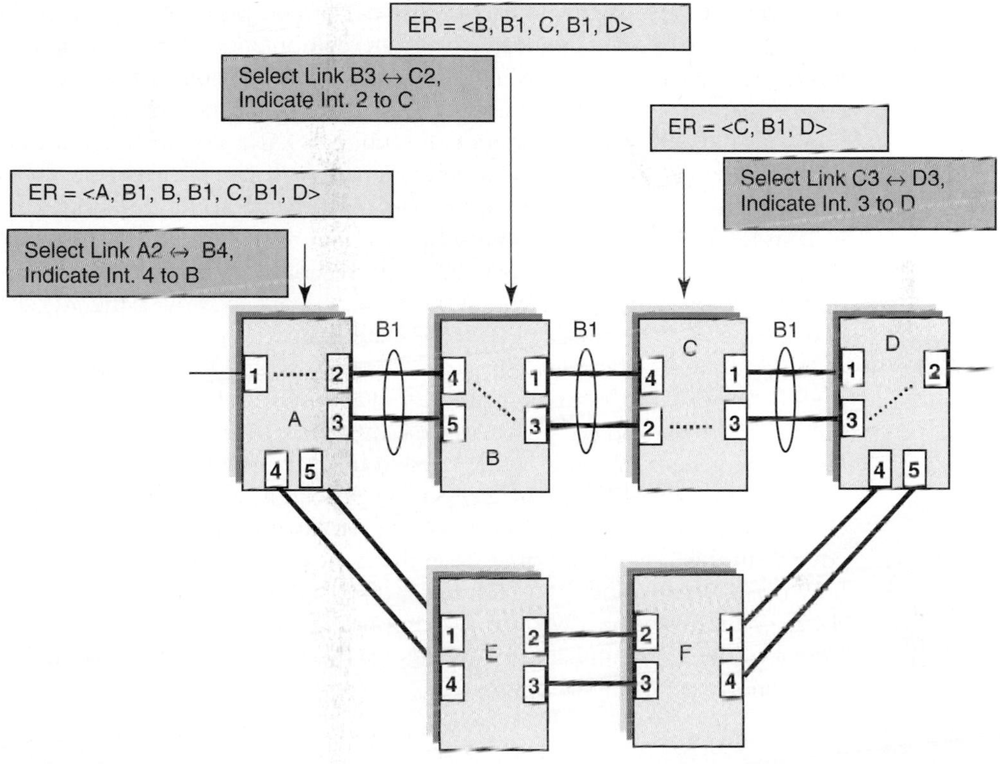

Figure 6–8 *Distributed Connection Provisioning*

the explicit route received by each intermediate OXC and the link selected by it. Since the link identifier could be different in the two ends, neighboring OXCs must agree on the identification of each topological link prior to signaling. The procedure depicted in Figure 6–6 could be used for this purpose. This would allow an OXC to know the identity of a link on the remote side and indicate it in signaling messages.

Those familiar with IP routing may wonder why the link identification procedure shown in Figure 6–6 is required if a distributed IP routing protocol (e.g., OSPF) with optical network extensions is running in each OXC. Such a protocol already incorporates an automatic adjacency discovery function. The reason for this is that even though an IP routing protocol might run in each OXC, there is no need to have a routing adjacency over each link. Indeed, as described in Chapter 10, the routing and signaling adjacencies in densely connected optical networks should be independent of the number of links between neighboring OXCs. To this end, it is desirable to create a separate procedure for the discovery of adjacencies and identification of links.

Thus, layer adjacency discovery is performed primarily over *topological links*, that is, links of significance to route computation. The specific layer in which adjacencies are determined depends on the scope of the routing procedures. For instance, in the network of Figure 6–1a, the line layer adjacency between the OXCs is important for routing SONET connections within the optical network. Outside of this network, the path layer adjacencies between the IP routers (which define the IP layer links) needs to be determined to aid in IP routing. Likewise, in the example of Figure 6–2, the line layer adjacencies between the STS-1 OXCs need to be discovered to route STS-1 connections in the outer network. Within the core network, however, the adjacencies between the STS-48 OXCs need to be determined.

In all these examples, physical adjacency was not a concern. It may be useful, however, to determine this for diagnostic and network management functions. As for control adjacency discovery, it is relevant only when control channels for signaling and routing need to be established between network elements. In other words, this is necessary only with a distributed control plane.

In the rest of this chapter, we focus on layer and control adjacency discovery. In this regard, the discussion that follows answers the question about how discovery is done. At a high level, discovering a layer adjacency requires some communication over the corresponding logical link. The content and format of this communication depends on the means available for such communication, as described next.

6.3 Protocol Mechanisms

The basic neighbor discovery protocol mechanism consists of periodic keep-alive or "Hello" message exchanges by neighboring NEs. These messages are sent over each logical link whose end point identifiers need to be associated. In SONET/SDH networks, logical links are bidirectional, that is, the transmit and the receive links are paired in an OXC and their end points are identified by a single identifier (e.g., a bidirectional port ID). With PXCs, there may or may not be an association between transmit and receive links. Hence, in the neighbor discovery procedures, the transmit and receive end points may be separately identified (e.g., a unidirectional port ID). The protocol, in its simplest form, can be described as follows for bidirectional links:

- Consider an NE attached to one or more links. Over each link, it periodically transmits a Hello message containing the link identifier at its end.
- Suppose the same NE receives a Hello message over a link. This message will contain the link identifier at the other end. The NE then transmits both the local and the remote link identifiers in the Hello messages it sends on that link.

Thus, the Hello messages received by an NE over a logical link will eventually contain the identification of both end points of a logical link.

This simple procedure is applicable in SONET/SDH networks where control communication can utilize the overhead bytes available on logical link (see Chapter 2). The various options for running the discovery protocol using the overhead bytes are described next. Where such communication is not possible, the procedure would be more complex. This is the case with PXCs. What could be done in this case is described later.

Now, control adjacency can be determined as part of the layer adjacency discovery procedure. Specifically, an NE can include the control channel end point identifier in the Hello messages if possible. Otherwise, control adjacency has to be manually configured.

6.3.1 Neighbor Discovery Using the J0 Byte

From the discussions in Chapter 2, it may be recalled that J0 is the trace byte in the section overhead, J1 is the trace byte in the path overhead, and J2 is the trace byte in the VT path overhead. As the name implies, these bytes can be used to insert a trace pattern at one end, which can be recovered at the other end of a section, path, or VT path. In fact, it is possible to introduce a 16-byte trace string by concatenating consecutive bytes received on the J0, J1, or J2 overhead as per ITU-T G.707 specification [ITU-T00a]. In this section, we focus on the usage of J0 bytes for neighbor discovery. The J1 and J2 bytes can be used for detecting path layer adjacencies in a similar manner.

J0-based neighbor discovery can be used between two section-terminating NEs.[2] As per our definition of layer adjacency, these NEs must be "section-layer adjacent." In Figure 6–1a, for instance, each OXC is section-layer adjacent to a WDM device. Similarly, the two WDM devices are adjacent. It is also possible to discover line layer and physical (regenerator) layer adjacencies using J0 bytes. For instance, we could potentially use the J0 bytes to discover the line layer adjacency between the two OXCs shown. *Multilayer discovery* is the name used for the procedure that utilizes J0 bytes to discover adjacencies at multiple layers. This is described later in this section.

Now, the J0 byte is normally used for doing section traces. To do neighbor discovery, the J0 byte is periodically "borrowed." Once the adjacency is determined, the byte is released for normal section trace functions. Because the J0 byte is used for a specific purpose, the format of its content is well defined, and hardware exists to read and write the byte in that format. Specifically, J0 bytes in sixteen consecutive frames are used for the regenerator section trace in SDH [ITU-T00a]. The first byte is a combination frame start marker and CRC-7 code. This leaves only 15 bytes available. In each of these bytes, the first bit (bit 0) is required to be set to 0. Hence this results in a

[2]The corresponding SDH terminology is "multiplex section" (see Chapter 2). In this section, we use just the SONET terminology for simplicity.

reduced 7-bit content for each byte. A further limitation on these available bytes is that they must conform to T.50 character set [ITU-T92a]. The format of the section trace string is illustrated in Figure 6–9.

Unfortunately, fifteen characters are not adequate to carry the information required in the Hello protocol described earlier. To see this, note that Hello messages must eventually carry both the local and the remote logical link identifiers. The link identifier in turn is typically expressed as the pair, {Node ID, Port ID}. Here, Node ID uniquely distinguishes an NE in a network, and Port ID is an identifier unique with respect to the given node. When IP is used for management system and/or control plane communications, Node ID can be taken to be an IP address assigned to the node. Thus, to encode the link identifier at each end point, we need:

- Node ID: 32-bit (or 4-byte) IP address. Each byte in this address can take a value from 0 to 255, and hence can be represented by two hexadecimal characters (from 00 to FF). Thus, eight T.50 characters are required to represent the Node ID.
- Port ID: Suppose we allocate 16 bits (2 bytes) for the Port ID. This would allow the existence of up to 2^{16} ports in a node. As before, the 2 bytes require four hexadecimal characters for representation.

Thus, the identifier for each end of a link requires twelve characters. It is thus impossible to fit the IDs of both end points of a link in the section trace string. So, how does neighbor discovery using the J0 bytes work? There are two ways of doing this. The first method requires an out-of-band control channel. Such a channel, for instance, could be an Ethernet link between two colocated NEs, or an IP link between two adjacent NEs implementing a distributed control plane. The second method does not have the out-of-band control channel requirement, but the neighbor discovery protocol is more complex in this case. Both these methods, and the multilayer neighbor discovery procedure, use a common J0 message format, shown in Figure 6–10. The usage of the type and flag fields in the message are described in the following sections.

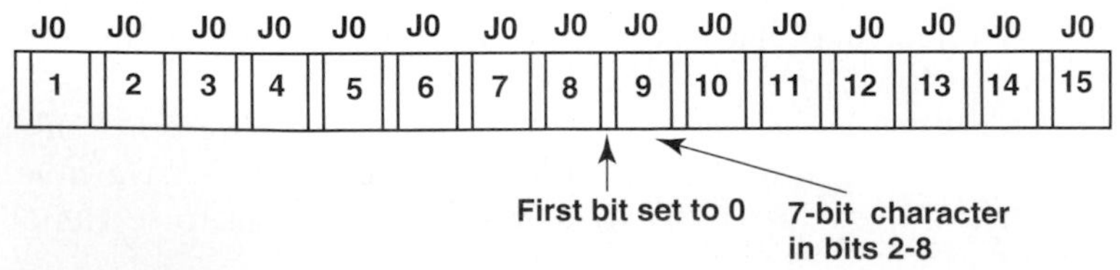

Figure 6–9 *J0 Section Trace String*

1	2	3	4	5	6	7	8	9	10	11	12	13	14	15
Type	Flag	Free	Node ID								Port ID			

Figure 6–10 *J0 Message Format*

6.3.1.1 J0-BASED DISCOVERY WITH AN OUT-OF-BAND CONTROL CHANNEL

Consider two NEs with multiple logical links between them, each defining a section-layer adjacency. It is assumed that an out-of-band control channel is configured between the two NEs. Both these NEs send and receive J0 discovery messages on each link. The following rules are used:

- Sending: The NE sets the Node ID field to the 8-byte hexadecimal representation of its IP address, and Port ID field to the 4-byte hexadecimal representation of the identifier of the port over which the message is sent. The other fields are not used.
- Receiving: The NE translates the hexadecimal values received in Node ID and Port ID fields to the IP address and port number, respectively, pertaining to the remote node. It then determines the control channel to use to contact the neighbor whose Node ID has been received. Over this control channel, the NE sends a message to its neighbor containing the following information:
  - The Node ID and Port ID received from the neighbor in the J0 message, and
  - Its own Node ID and the local ID of the port over which the J0 message was received.

Thus, both NEs can build a map of associations between the local and remote link identifiers. Note that in the procedure above, the sending NE must keep transmitting the J0 information continuously until it receives a response over the control channel (or a timeout occurs signaling the failure of the procedure).

Figure 6–11 shows an example of this procedure, where nodes A and B send their local information using the J0 string and the link identifier association using the control channel. Now, this procedure also allows each NE to detect errors in wiring. Specifically, for bidirectional logical links, this can detect the situation where the transmit and receive pair at one end are not connected to the same receive and transmit pair at the other end. This is illustrated in Figure 6–12, where an error has occurred in connecting Node A to

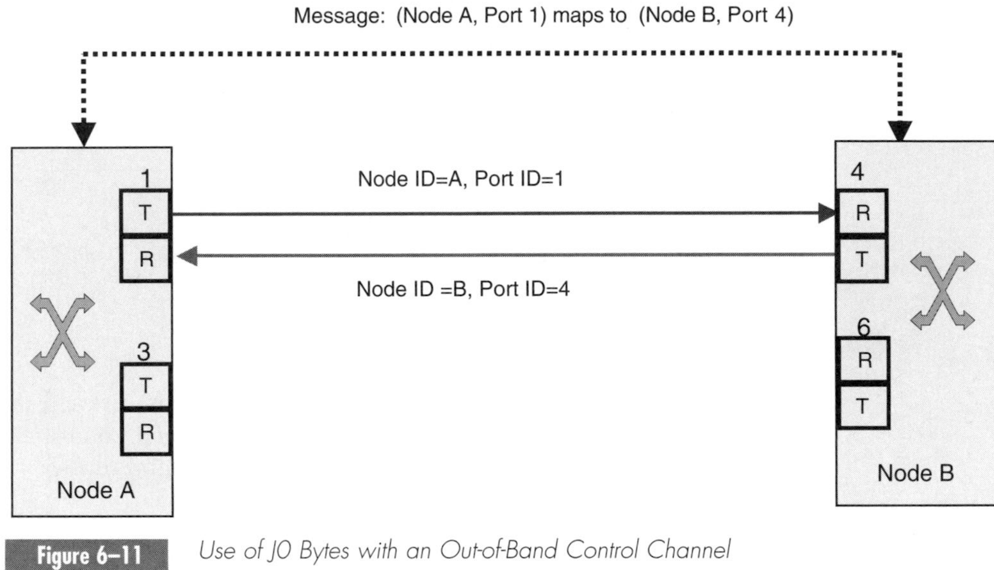

Figure 6–11 *Use of J0 Bytes with an Out-of-Band Control Channel*

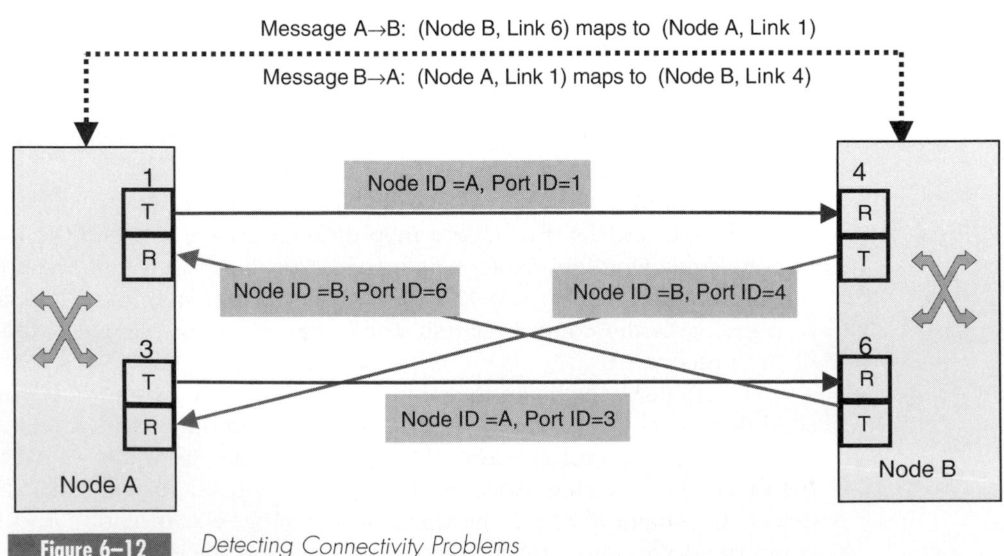

Figure 6–12 *Detecting Connectivity Problems*

Node B. This error is detected when the nodes receive conflicting information over the control channel indicating incorrect association.

6.3.1.2 J0-BASED DISCOVERY WITHOUT AN OUT-OF-BAND CONTROL CHANNEL

Consider Figure 6–11 again, and assume that there is no control channel between the two NEs. In this case, we need another way to establish the link identifier associations. Specifically, consider two nodes A and B that are running the neighbor discovery protocol for a given link. Suppose node A has a numerically higher Node ID. The revised discovery procedure is executed in two passes. In the first pass, node A sends the link identification at its end, and node B reflects the received information. In the second pass, node B sends its information, and node A reflects it back. This allows both nodes to build the link identifier associations and also to detect inconsistencies in wiring. The procedure works as follows:

Both Nodes:

- Determination of status: The node sets the Node ID field to the 8-byte hexadecimal representation of its IP address, and the Port ID field to the 4 byte hexadecimal representation of the identifier of the port over which the message is sent. The flag field is set to the character "R," indicating that the other side should reflect the received information. The sending continues until a correct response is received on the receive port or a timeout occurs. Simultaneously, the node receives J0 messages on the corresponding receive port. If the received Node ID value (after translation) is numerically higher than the node's ID, then the node executes the "Node A" procedure below. Otherwise, it executes the "Node B" procedure.

Node A:

- Sending: Node A sets Node ID to the 8-byte hexadecimal representation of its IP address, and Port ID to the 4-byte hexadecimal representation of the identifier of the port over which the message is sent. The flag field is set to the character "R," indicating that the other side should reflect the received information. The sending continues until a correct response is received on the receive port or a timeout occurs. Simultaneously, node A receives J0 messages over the corresponding receive port.
- Receiving: Node A ignores all received J0 messages until a message with the flag set to "D" is received (which indicates that Node B is reflecting the received information). When such a message is received, Node A sets the flag to "O" in its outgoing J0 messages. This indicates to node B that it can begin sending its node and port information.

- Recording: Node A keeps sending J0 messages with the Flag set to "O." At the same time, it receives and ignores all J0 messages until a message with the flag set to "R" is received. At this point, it notes the received Node ID and Port ID values, and makes an association between the sent and received values. It also copies the received Node ID and Port ID values in its outgoing J0 messages and changes the flag to "D."

Node B:

- Receiving: Node B ignores all received J0 messages until a message with the flag set to "R" is received. When such a message is received, Node B copies the incoming Node ID and Port ID fields in the outgoing J0 messages and sets the flag to "D."
- Recording: Node B notes the received Node ID and Port ID values. It records the association between the received values and its own Node ID, and the ID of the port over which the message was received. It also copies the received Node ID and Port ID values in its outgoing J0 messages and changes the flag to "D."
- Sending: Node B keeps sending J0 messages as above with the flag set to "D." At the same time, it ignores received messages until a message with the flag set to "O" is received. At this point, it starts sending J0 messages with its own Node ID and Port ID, with the flag set to "R." It keeps sending these messages until a message with flag set to "D" is received. When such a message is received, it changes the flag field to "O" in its outgoing message.

An error in port connectivity is indicated if an expected message is not received by either node. The procedure above is illustrated in Figures 6–13a and 6–13b. Figure 6–13a shows the "correct" case, and Figure 6–13b shows the case where there is an error in connectivity. In this case, Node B receives (Node A, Port 3) information on its port 4, and reflects this to A. Node A then detects an error. Node A could report this error to the management system for further action.

6.3.1.3 AN ALTERNATIVE USAGE OF J0 BYTES

So far, we have assumed that only T50 characters can be transported in J0 bytes. Suppose that we do not have this limitation. Then, with 105 usable bits, the local and remote link identifier can be directly coded as follows:

- Local Node Identifier: 32 bits
- Local Port Identifier: 16 bits
- Remote Node Identifier: 32 bits
- Remote Port Identifier: 16 bits

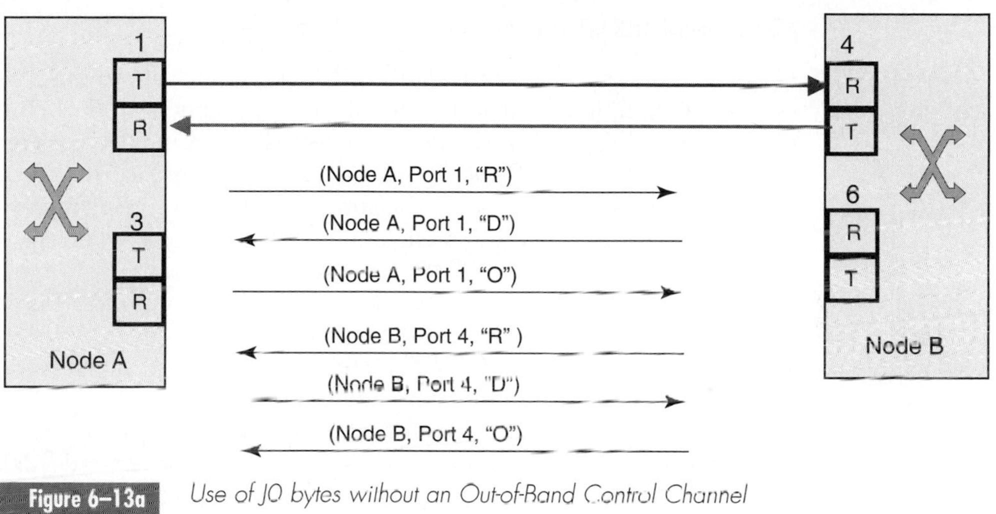

Figure 6–13a *Use of J0 bytes without an Out-of-Band Control Channel*

This representation takes up 96 bits, and there would still be 9 bits left for various flags. With this coding, the discovery protocol would be much simpler than the one described in the previous section. Specifically, each NE could send its own node and port ID along with the received node and port ID over each link. An NE can check for consistency of information received from its neighbor and flag the management system when an inconsistency is detected.

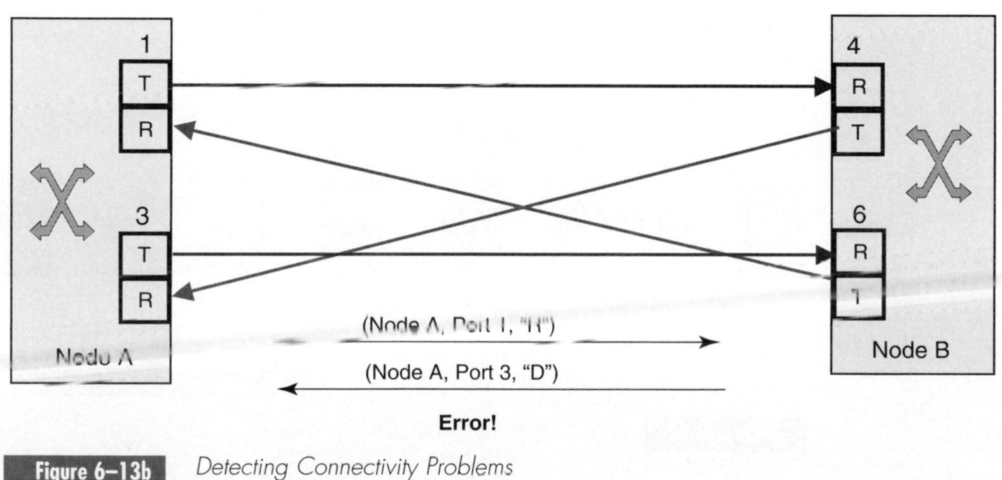

Figure 6–13b *Detecting Connectivity Problems*

6.3.1.4 MULTILAYER NEIGHBOR DISCOVERY

Figure 6–14 shows a chain of SONET NEs operating at various layers. This consists of path, line, and section terminating equipment (PTE, LTE, and STE, respectively) and physical layer regenerators (PLR). A multilayer neighbor discovery procedure utilizes the J0 section trace bytes to discover the LTE, STE, and PLR adjacencies, as shown in Figure 6–14. In terms of hierarchy, the line layer is said to be above the section layer, which, in turn, is above the physical layer.

The purpose of the multilayer neighbor discovery protocol is to allow a network element to find its nearest neighbor at each layer. A neighbor at a given layer may be a number of NEs away with intermediate NEs operating at lower layers (Figure 6–14).

Because linear chains of interconnected NEs are common in the transport environment (e.g., different types of regenerator and add/drop multiplexers), any node in the chain should be able to find out its nearest neighbor without causing disruptions down the chain. The usage of J0 bytes means that some equipment that is normally transparent to this byte must now monitor and write on this byte. This is particularly the case for PLR equipment.

Let us now consider the multilayer neighbor discovery protocol using J0 bytes and an out-of-band control channel. The J0 message format shown in Figure 6–10 would be used, with the Type flag set as follows:

- Type = 0. "Do nothing." Indicates that successive equipment downstream should not respond to this discovery request.
- Type = 1. Physical layer adjacency discovery.
- Type = 2. Section layer adjacency discovery.
- Type = 3. Line layer adjacency discovery.

The protocol given in section 6.3.1.1 is executed, with the following usage for the type field:

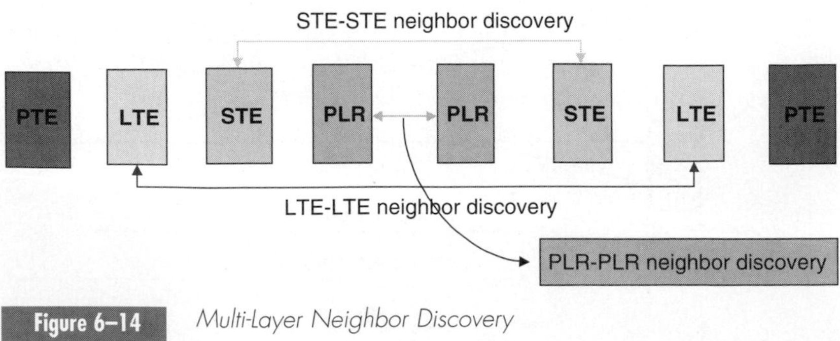

Figure 6–14 *Multi-Layer Neighbor Discovery*

- An NE receiving the J0 message checks to see if it operates at the layer at or above that indicated in the string:
  - If the layer indicated in the message is higher than that at which the NE operates then the message is passed on without modification, that is, the NE will remain "transparent."
  - If the layer indicated in the message is equal to the layer at which the NE operates, then the NE modifies the J0 message by replacing the type field with T = 0 ("do nothing") and passes it on.
  - Suppose the J0 message request remains, that is, it has not changed to a message with T = 0 after a configured amount of time. Then, on the return fiber the NE transmits a J0 message with the type field set to the highest layer at which the NE operates. This message also has its node ID and port ID information.
- The originating NE can now record the received link identifier information contained in the J0 message, and exchange the information over the control channel.
- If a J0 message is not received by the originating NE at the expected layer, then either there is no neighbor at that layer, or the neighbor does not support this procedure. It is also possible in this case that a lower layer neighbor is not transparent to this procedure.

6.3.2 Neighbor Discovery Using the DCC Bytes

The DCC (data communication channel) overhead bytes may be used for realizing a packet communication channel between OXCs as follows:

- SONET Section (SDH Regenerator Section) DCC: This consists of D1, D2, and D3 section overhead bytes (see Chapter 2). Used as a transparent sequence of bytes, this provides a 192 Kbps message channel.
- SONET Line (SDH Multiplex Section) DCC: This consists of D4–D12 line overhead bytes, with 576 Kbps of available bandwidth.

These bytes merely provide a raw data channel. Over this channel, a framing protocol is required to realize a data link. An example is the High-level Data Link Control (HDLC) protocol [Stallings03]. An IP-based Hello protocol can be run over HDLC framing. Another possible choice is the Link Access Procedure-D (LAPD) framing protocol [Tanenbaum02], but LAPD is less commonly used for carrying IP packets. In terms of adjacencies, the line DCC can be used to discover line layer adjacencies, and the section DCC can be used to discover line or section layer adjacencies (see multilayer discovery, above).

The Hello protocol itself is essentially the same as the one described in the beginning of section 6.3. The protocol can either run directly over IP, or it can run over the User Datagram Protocol (UDP) and IP. Regardless of whether UDP is used, the steps to be implemented are as follows. Considering two adjacent nodes running the protocol over each link:

- Sending: Each node forms the Hello message containing its own Node ID and the ID of the port over which the message will be sent. The IP packet containing the message is addressed to the "all-nodes" multicast address, 224.0.0.1, and sent over the DCC.
- Receiving: Each node receiving the Hello message creates the mapping between the received information and the identifier of the logical link on its side. It then appends the received <Node ID, Port ID> values to the Hello message it sends.

The main advantage of using line/section DCC for performing layer adjacency discovery is that UNI 1.0 [OIF01], which has been the subject of successful interoperability tests by multiple vendors, supports this method. The disadvantage is that the use of line/section DCC is not viable for handling the case where two NEs are separated by intermediate multiplexers that may not pass the DCC bytes transparently.

6.3.3 Link Property Correlation

The purpose of neighbor discovery is to determine the local connectivity information from the perspective of each node. Conceptually, with a distributed control plane, the information that a neighbor discovery protocol generates is used to populate the link identification table, as shown in Figure 6–15. In this table, the "local" information is manually configured. This includes Link ID and other parameters pertaining to each link. For example, this could include Shared Risk Link Group ID and other routing metrics (see Chapter 10). The routing-related

Link ID	Status	Other Info. (e.g., port speed, etc.)	Remote Node ID	Remote Link ID	Other Info.
1	Up		IP address	Interface ID	
2	Up		IP address	Interface ID	
3	Down		Unknown	Unknown	

Figure 6–15 *Link Identification Table*

parameters must be identical on both sides of the link. Given that these are manually configured in each NE, it is useful to ensure that the configured values are consistent at both ends of a link. A protocol, running over the control channel, could allow the two NEs to exchange the configured information and raise an alarm if an inconsistency is detected.

6.4 LMP

LMP is a protocol being standardized by the IETF. Its functionality includes:

- Link connectivity verification: Supports the discovery of topological links between adjacent OXCs or PXCs.
- Link parameter correlation: Supports the exchange of link parameters between adjacent NEs.
- Control channel management: Allows the health of the control channel(s) between two adjacent NEs to be monitored.
- Link fault localization: Allows the localization of faults occurring in topological links between PXCs.

LMP has been designed to accommodate OOO switches (PXCs) with their limitations on in-band communication capabilities (i.e., overhead bytes cannot be used for communication). Thus, LMP functions are somewhat more complex than what is required for just SONET/SDH neighbor discovery.

LMP runs as an application over UDP and IP. Thus, LMP requires a means for an NE to send and receive IP packets to/from adjacent NEs. This means that a control channel has to be configured between neighbors *before* LMP begins running. This is in contrast to the SONET/SDH neighbor discovery description earlier, where a control channel was not always required. In the following, we look at various options for realizing control channels.

6.4.1 Control Channels

Control channels between a pair of NEs for carrying IP packets can be realized in two ways:

- In-fiber control channel: The IP packets are carried over a communication channel embedded in the data-bearing topological link between the NEs.
- Out-of fiber control channel: The IP packets are carried over a dedicated communication link between the NEs, separate from the data-bearing topological links.

These options are described further below.

6.4.1.1 IN-FIBER CONTROL CHANNELS OVER SONET/SDH DCC BYTES

The idea of transporting packets over SONET/SDH DCC bytes was described earlier. Suppose there is more than one link between two OXCs, and the DCC bytes on each link could be used to create a control channel. The functional components of the control path between the OXCs in this case are shown in Figure 6–16. Here, an IP packet generated by an NE is first passed to a channel manager. This entity is responsible for selecting one of the possibly many physical communication channels available to its peer. A driver prepares the packet for transmission, and the transmission hardware is responsible for framing the packet, serializing it, and physically transmitting it over the selected overhead bytes to the peer. At the destination, the transmitted frames are extracted from the overhead bytes, and the IP packet is recovered and delivered to the IP destination. Thus, an in-fiber control channel is logically equivalent to a unidirectional point-to-point IP link. The channel manager essentially maintains a collection of such point-to-point links, monitors their status, and determines which link to use when sending a packet to a neighbor. An essential feature of this mechanism is that an IP packet transmitted over any of the available physical channels is received by the destination. This means that there is no coordination required a priori between the transmitter and receiver to determine which of the many physical channels should be used for sending a given packet.

The IP packets sent in this manner must have a destination IP address that refers to the neighboring NE. The automatic discovery by one NE of the other's IP address, the selection and maintenance of the control channel, and so on, are described in section 6.4.2.

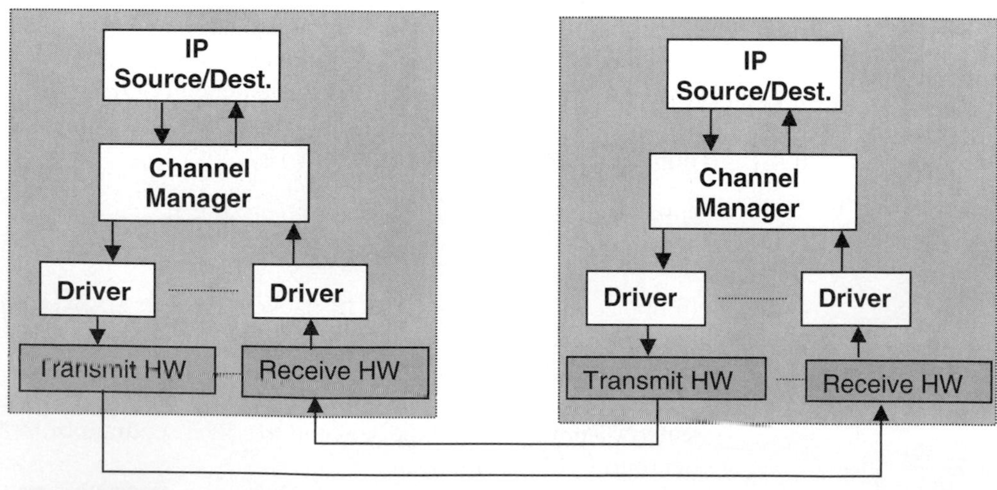

Figure 6–16 *Functional View of In-Fiber Transport*

6.4.1.2 OUT-OF-FIBER CONTROL CHANNELS

In this case, the IP packets are transported over a separate control network that is distinct from the data network. Figure 6–17 illustrates an example where two NEs have points of attachment to two distinct IP networks (also called the Data Communication Network or DCN). In the simplest case, these could be local area networks (LANs). Control messages may be sent over either network without coordination. But each NE must be configured with a routable IP address of the other in order to send packets.

Although two distinct control channel configurations were described, more than one type of control channel may exist between a pair of NEs. For instance, there could be both in-fiber and out-of fiber control channels. Similarly, an NE could have different types of control channels with different neighboring NEs. Thus, NEs must be configured with information indicating which type of control channel is implemented for which set of data links.

6.4.2 LMP Usage with OEO Cross-Connects (OXCs)

In this section, we describe one scenario for LMP usage in SONET/SDH networks with OXCs, where line or section DCC bytes in each link are used for packet communication. The relevant functions are link connectivity verifica-

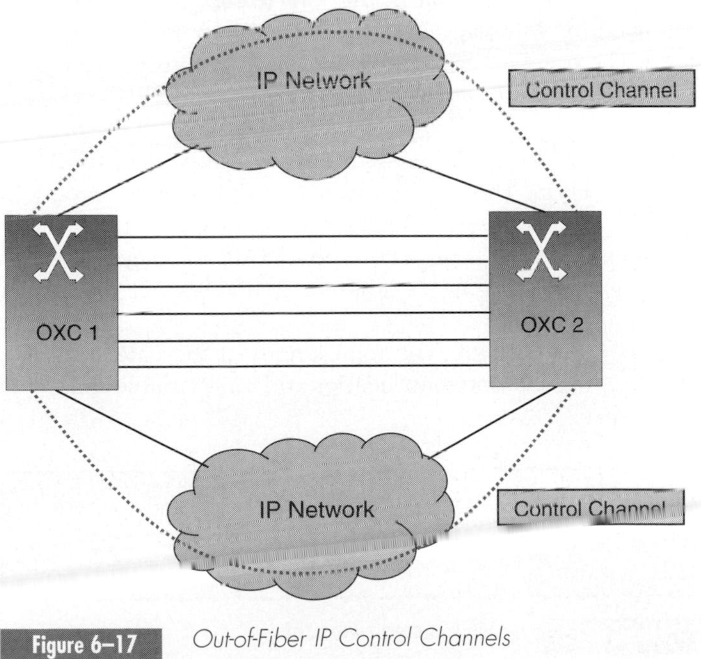

Figure 6–17 *Out-of-Fiber IP Control Channels*

tion, control channel maintenance, and link property correlation. These are described below.

6.4.2.1 BASIC LMP PARAMETERS

The fundamental LMP parameters of importance for neighbor discovery are:

- Node ID: This is a network-wide unique 32-bit identifier assigned to an NE.
- Interface ID: This is an identifier assigned to each interface in an NE. The interface ID must be unique within the scope of a given node. The interface ID could be a 32-bit IPv4 address. The interface ID corresponds to the Port ID we used in earlier descriptions.
- Control Channel ID (CCID): Every control channel terminating at an OXC must be assigned a unique identifier. This is called the CCID, and it is a 32-bit number that is unique within the scope of a Node ID. LMP considers both in-fiber and out-of-fiber control. For in-fiber control channels, the CCID is the same as the interface ID. Out-of-fiber control channels must be assigned their own identifiers. If a node has both in-fiber and out-of-fiber control channels then they must all have unique IDs. Also, the same control channel between two OXCs may be assigned different CCIDs at the two ends.

LMP messages have the following format: <LMP common header> followed by <Message body>. The LMP common header is shown in Figure 6–18. The numbers beside the field descriptions indicate the length of the field in bits. The header consists of the following fields:

- Version: LMP version. The current version is 1.
- Flags: This field indicates various values, depending on the specific LMP message. Details can be found in [Lang+03a].
- Message Type: The type of LMP message. Of relevance to neighbor discovery are Config (1), ConfigAck (2), ConfigNack (4), and Hello (5).
- LMP Length: The total length of the LMP message in bytes, including the common header and any variable-length objects that follow.

Version (4 bits)	Reserved (12 bits)	Flags (8 bits)	Message Type (8-bits)
LMP Length (16 bits)		Checksum (16-bits)	

Figure 6–18 *LMP Common Header*

- Checksum: The standard IP checksum of the entire contents of the LMP message, starting with the LMP message header.

The LMP object format is shown in Figure 6–19. This is similar to the object definition under RSVP (see Chapter 7). The "N" bit indicates whether the parameters encoded in the object are negotiable (N = 1) or not (N = 0).

6.4.2.2 LINK CONNECTIVITY VERIFICATION

This procedure is executed independently for each link. Given that each link supports a packet-based communication channel, initial neighbor discovery is performed through the exchange of LMP Config messages over the channel. This message exchange allows adjacent NEs to determine the logical link end point associations, and to determine errors in connectivity. After this step, Hello messages are repeatedly sent over the DCC channel to keep track of its status ("up" or "down"). When there is a disruption in the Hello protocol (e.g., a Hello message is not received within an expected time period) or when an interface is locally initialized, the Hello protocol is stopped, and the status of the corresponding channel is marked "Down." In this case, configuration messages are exchanged again to determine changes in identification of the topological link.

CONFIG MESSAGE EXCHANGE • This message exchange allows the determination of the link identity and to configure the Hello protocol parameters. The configuration step consists of exchanging two LMP messages: Config, and ConfigAck or ConfigNack. The NE that initiates neighbor discovery sends a Config message to its peer over the control channel. This message contains the link identification information at the sending NE and Hello protocol parameters. An NE receiving a Config message responds with a ConfigAck or a ConfigNack message, indicating the acceptance or the rejection of parameters in the Config message. The reception of a ConfigAck message by the sender of the Config message completes the configuration process. The reception of a ConfigNack message, on the other hand, may terminate the configuration process unsuccessfully, or may result in the transmission of another Config message with revised parameters.

N (1 bit)	C-Type (7 bits)	Class (8 bits)	Length (16 bits)
Object Contents			

Figure 6–19 *LMP Object Format*

A Config message may be sent concurrently by the two NEs to each other. In this case, the NE with a numerically lower Node ID stops sending Config messages and responds to the received Config message. The other NE ignores the received Config messages and waits for a ConfigAck or a ConfigNack message.

The Config Message • The essential contents of the Config message are shown in Figure 6–20. This includes the Node ID of the sending node, the interface ID of the logical link (in the Local CCID field), and parameters pertaining to the Hello protocol that will follow. These parameters are:

- Hello Interval: The frequency with which this NE will send Hello messages over the control channel. This is given as the time between two consecutive Hello messages in milliseconds.
- Hello Dead Interval: The maximum amount of time this NE will wait to receive Hello messages from the other end before declaring the logical link as "down."

Because the NE sending the Config message does not know the identity of the NE at the other end, the destination address of the IP packet containing the message is set to the "all nodes" multicast address, 224.0.0.1.

The ConfigAck Message • The ConfigAck message indicates that the Hello parameters received in the Config message are acceptable to the receiving node. Its essential contents are shown in Figure 6–21. This includes the Node ID of the sending node and the local interface identification (in the Local CCID field), as well as the received Node ID and link identification (in the remote Node ID and the remote CCID fields, respectively).

The ConfigAck message is sent to the source IP address found in the packet containing the Config message. The ConfigNack message is used to reject/negotiate parameters received in the Config message.

Common Header
Local Node ID
Local CC ID
Hello Interval, Hello Dead Interval

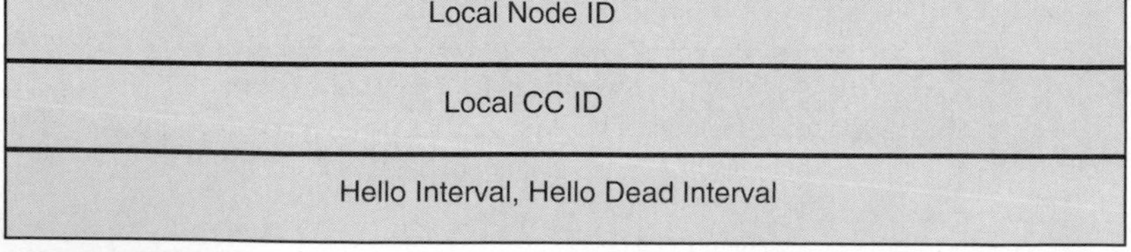

Figure 6–20 *Config Message*

Common Header
Local Node ID
Local CC ID
Remote Node ID
Remote CC ID

Figure 6–21 *ConfigAck Message*

NEIGHBOR DISCOVERY EXAMPLES • Figure 6–22 illustrates neighbor discovery using LMP. The Config message exchange allows each NE to build the "Remote Node ID" and "Remote Interface ID" fields of the link identification table shown in Figure 6–15.

Inconsistent interface connectivity is detected by an NE when either a ConfigAck (or a Nack) message is not received in response to a Config message that has been sent, or when a ConfigAck or a Nack message that it receives does not contain the expected Node ID or link end point identification. This is illustrated in Figure 6–23. Here, the transmit and receive sides of NE-1 interface 1 are connected (wrongly) to receive and transmit sides of NE-2 interfaces 10 and 11, respectively. Thus, in response to a Config message sent over interface 1, NE-1 receives a ConfigAck message with Received CCID = 2. Similarly, in response to a Config message sent over interface 2, the NE receives a ConfigAck message with Received CCID = 1. This allows the detection of inconsistent connectivity.

THE HELLO PROTOCOL • Each NE executing the Hello protocol must periodically send a "Hello" message over the DCC channel. The IP destination address in these messages is set to the Node ID obtained during the configuration procedure. The periodicity of the Hello message is governed by the Hello interval established during the configuration phase.

The Hello message contains a transmit and a received sequence number. The transmit sequence number is the sequence number of this Hello message, and the received sequence number is the sequence number of the last Hello message received by the sender. If an NE is sending Hellos but does not receive any Hellos during the Hello dead interval period, the corresponding channel is declared down. More details of the Hello procedures can be found in [Lang+03a].

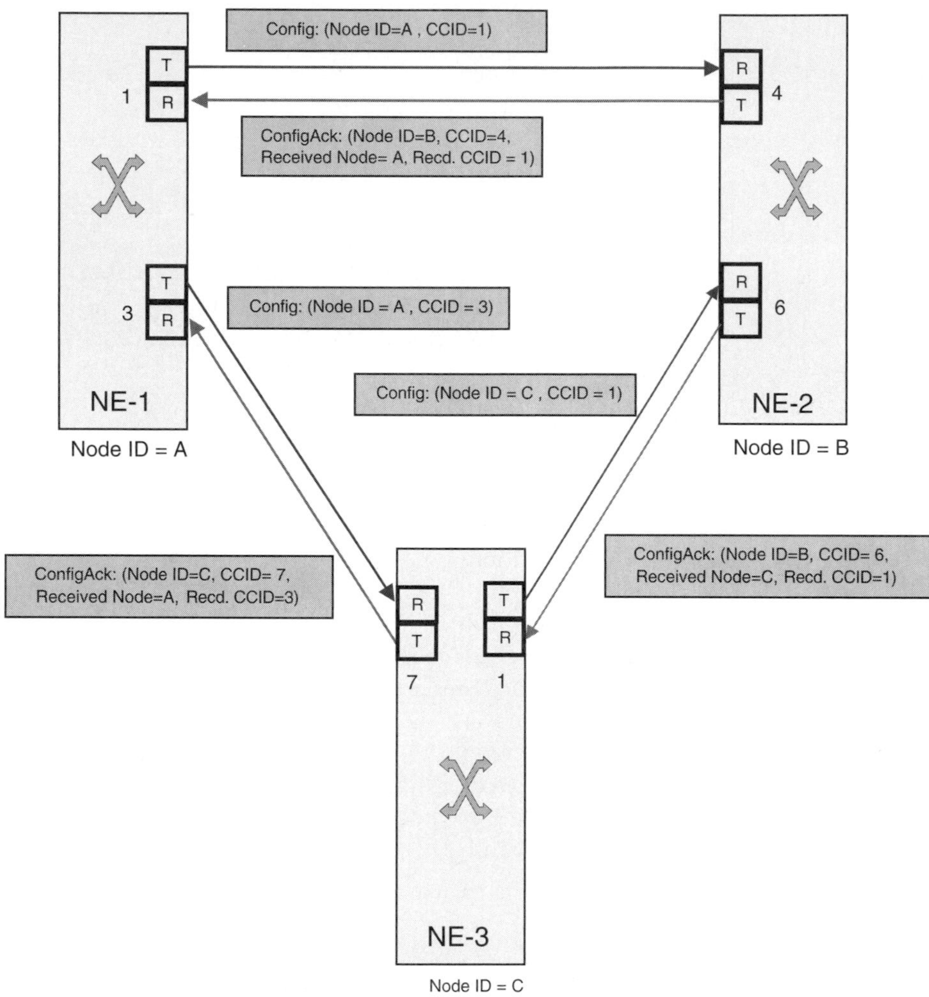

Figure 6–22 *Neighbor Discovery LMP Message Exchange*

6.4.2.3 LINK PROPERTY CORRELATION WITH A DISTRIBUTED CONTROL PLANE

LMP defines three messages for link property correlation. These are Link Summary, Link Summary Ack, and Link Summary Nack messages. Briefly, the Link Summary message is sent by an NE over the control channel (in-fiber or out-of-fiber) to indicate the configured values for an identified link. Note that this message is sent only after neighbor discovery has been completed. The remote NE compares the received values with those configured for the same link on its side. If they match, a Link Summary Ack message is sent.

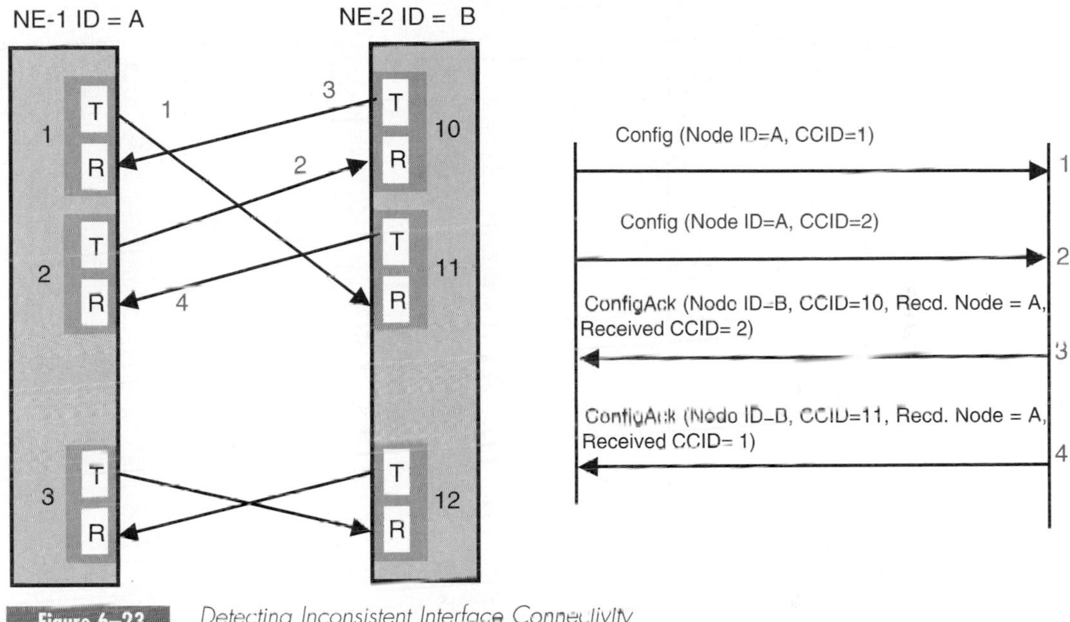

Figure 6–23 *Detecting Inconsistent Interface Connectivity*

Otherwise, a Link Summary Nack message is sent. More details can be found in [Lang+03a].

So far in this section, we have considered neighbor discovery over DCC bytes. What if J0 bytes are used? The LMP procedures in this case would use Test messages over J0 bytes, similar to the Test message usage defined for PXCs next.

6.4.3 LMP Usage with Photonic Cross-Connects (PXCs)

Neighbor discovery is more complicated with PXCs. Specifically, consider automatic link identification. This function requires in-fiber communication capability between PXCs. But PXCs merely switch light from an incoming to an outgoing port and they do not terminate overhead bytes. So what is the solution?

The first step is to introduce additional hardware that allows a PXC to electrically generate and terminate "test" signals that may be used to probe topological links to different neighbors. This is illustrated in Figure 6–24. Here, a signal generating/terminating hardware is permanently connected to one port of each PXC. A "test" message generated by this hardware can be cross-connected to any of the outgoing ports. Similarly, a "test" message received on an incoming port can be cross-connected to the port attached to the test

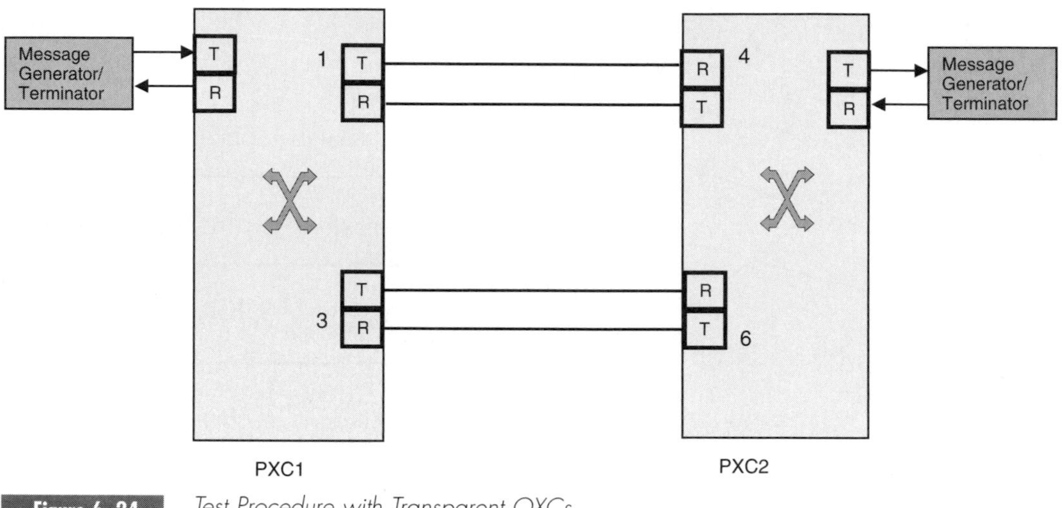

Figure 6–24 *Test Procedure with Transparent OXCs*

generator/terminator. An important assumption here is that the framing and rate of signals carrying "test" messages are compatible with the DWDM transponders to which the output ports of the PXC are connected (see Figure 6–4). This implies homogeneity in the signal rates switched by the OXC.

The use of this hardware to perform link identification is described in more detail next. For the present, let us consider the cost of providing neighbor discovery capabilities in PXCs. First, the test generator/terminator hardware is required. This may be a piece of external equipment or built internally in each PXC. Second, a port in each PXC has to be dedicated for connecting to the "test" generator/terminator. These are in addition to at least one out-of-fiber control channel required between adjacent PXCs. A case, however, can be made that such dedicated hardware and switch resources are also useful for verifying end-to-end connectivity during provisioning. That is, a service provider can verify whether a connection has been properly provisioned, before turning it over to the customer, by generating a "test" message at one end, switching it through the provisioned path, and receiving it on the other end. On the whole neighbor discovery is more complex with PXCs, both from the hardware requirements perspective and from the protocol perspective.

In the following, the neighbor discovery procedure is described in more detail.

6.4.3.1 LINK CONNECTIVITY VERIFICATION

Consider a PXC with a set of topological links to one or more neighboring PXCs. In the opaque (SONET/SDH) network case, the link identification procedure would allow an NE to automatically determine the *complete* identity of each link, that is, the Node ID of the NE at the other end, as well as the remote interface ID. Doing exactly this with PXCs is rather complex. In fact, a lesser goal is often considered. To be specific, suppose the remote Node ID for each link (i.e., the identity of the neighbor) is manually configured in each PXC. Furthermore, let us assume that the out-of-fiber control channel associated with each neighbor is also configured. Then, the link identification procedure can determine the remote interface ID for each link automatically. Clearly, it looks like we are doing half the work manually in this case, and the functionality provided by "automatic" neighbor discovery is rather limited. This is indeed true, and LMP provides only this functionality with PXCs. The usefulness of automatically discovering just the remote interface IDs is debatable. This is especially the case given the requirements for additional hardware and switch resources. Let us, however, consider the procedure for this first and then look at why it is difficult to determine the complete link ID automatically.

6.4.3.2 PROCEDURE

Consider a PXC with the following configured information:

- Its own Node ID.
- The local identities of all topological links (the local interface IDs).
- The identity of each neighbor along with the identity of the out-of fiber control channel to be used to reach the neighbor (see Figure 6–17).
- For each topological link, the Node ID of the neighbor to which the link is connected.

Note that the last two items need not be configured with OXCs. Furthermore, looking at the link identification table (Figure 6–15), what is left to be determined is the remote interface ID. To determine this, the PXC does the following:

1. It selects a neighbor.
2. It sends a message over the control channel to the selected neighbor indicating that it will begin sending a "test" message over each topological link connected to the neighbor.
3. After confirming that the neighbor is willing to receive "test" messages, it selects a link to the neighbor to send these messages.
4. It sends test messages repeatedly over the selected link until the neighbor acknowledges that a message has been received. At this time, the neighbor also indicates the interface ID on its side over which the test message was received.
5. The PXC notes down the remote interface id in its link identification table.
6. It then selects another link, and Steps 4 and 5 are repeated until the remote interface IDs of all the links to the selected neighbor are determined.

7. It notifies the neighbor of the end of link identification.
8. Steps 1–6 are repeated for each neighbor.

Now, from the point of view of the neighbor participating in this procedure, the following events occur:

(a) It receives a request from a neighbor that is going to send "test" messages.
(b) It determines if it can participate in this procedure. For instance, it is possible that its test message terminating hardware (Figure 6–24) is busy because it is participating in a test procedure with another neighbor. It then sends a message back indicating its willingness or inability to participate in the procedure. Suppose it decides to participate. Then,
(c) It checks for a "test" message on each link connected to the neighbor. It does this by sequentially cross-connecting each of the set of incoming ports attached to the neighbor to the outgoing port connected to the test message terminator. After each cross-connect is made, it waits to receive test messages for some time before making the next cross-connect. So, this is a potentially time-consuming sequential process.
(d) If the message terminating hardware detects a "test" message, the local interface ID corresponding to the port over which the message was received is noted.
(e) The "test" message contains the corresponding remote interface id, and this is noted down in the link identification table.
(f) A confirmation message is sent to the neighbor indicating the local interface ID.
(g) Steps c–f are repeated until the remote interface ID is determined for each of the links connected to the neighbor.

In this procedure, all messages other than "test" messages are sent over the control channel. Figure 6–25 illustrates this procedure for a pair of PXCs. Now, let us look at some of the details.

Test Messages • What does a "test" message contain? It should at least have the local interface id of the link over which the message is sent. In addition, it may have the Node ID of the sending PXC, but the same information is also available in the request sent in Step 2 above.

The "test" message can be transported in many ways. With SONET/SDH framing, it can be sent as a string or an IP packet on overhead bytes as described earlier. Another possibility is that the test message is transported as the SONET/SDH payload. If this is the method chosen, then the Packet-over-

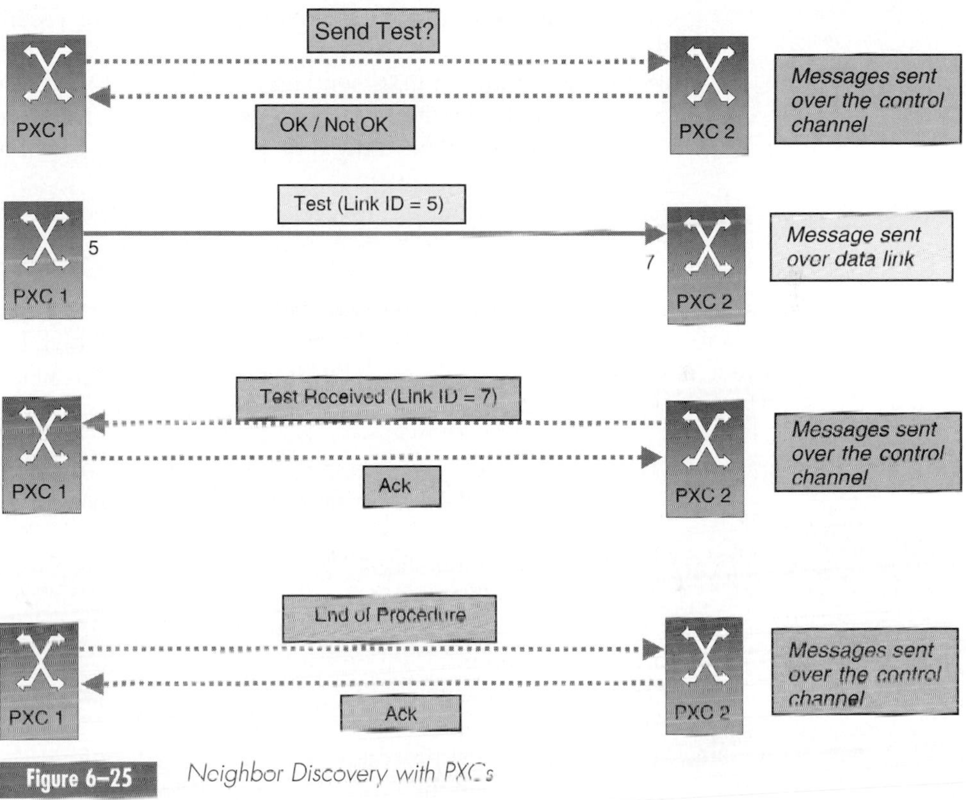

Figure 6–25 *Neighbor Discovery with PXCs*

SONET [Malis+99] encapsulation mechanism defined for IP can be used (see Chapter 3).

Further details on the contents and usage of the test message can be found in [Lang+03a].

OTHER MESSAGES • The other control messages required are as follows:

- A request message from the OXC that is going to send "test" messages to the neighbor that must terminate the "test" messages (Step 2). Under LMP, this message is called "Begin Verify".
- A response from the neighbor to the OXC sending the request (Step b). Under LMP, these messages are called "Begin Verify Ack/Nack."
- A message from the neighbor to confirm the receipt of test messages (Step f). LMP defines the "Test Status Success" message for this. Additionally, LMP also defines the "Test Status Failure"

message to indicate that test messages were not received by the neighbor.

- A message from the OXC sending test message to indicate the completion of link identification procedure (Step 7). The corresponding LMP message is called "End Verify."

As noted before, all these messages are sent over the out-of-fiber control channel.

EXECUTION OF THE NEIGHBOR DISCOVERY PROCEDURE • The description of the neighbor discovery procedure above was very informal and high level. In reality, a number of issues must be addressed in defining an actual protocol. These include:

1. How often should test messages be sent in Step 4?
2. How long should a PXC wait to receive a response from the neighbor in Step 4?
3. Similarly, how long should the neighbor wait to receive a test message in Step c?
4. What happens when two neighboring PXCs simultaneously initiate the test procedure?
5. What happens when a PXC initiates the test procedure, but the neighbor does not want to participate in it?
6. Given that the test procedure actually uses a topological link, it cannot be used when the link is carrying traffic. Then, at what instances should an PXC initiate the test procedure?

The answers to questions 1–3 depends on the time it takes to set up cross-connects in the PXC and the number of links between neighbors. These parameters should be configurable in a protocol.

When two PXCs simultaneously initiate the test procedure, one of them must defer to the other based on some rule. For instance, the PXC with the numerically lower Node ID could defer to the other. If a PXC initiates the test procedure but the neighbor rejects it, then the PXC may wait for some time before initiating the procedure again. The waiting time must be specified in a protocol. Finally, the test procedure should be initiated whenever a link is newly configured, before any user traffic is routed over it. Furthermore, the test procedure must also be initiated when a link recovers from a failure event. This means that it should be possible to do link identification selectively for a set of links rather than the entire set of links to a neighbor. Readers interested in the protocol aspects are referred to the LMP specification [Lang+03a], although this document does not provide answers to all these questions.

6.4.3.3 COMPLEXITY OF COMPLETE LINK IDENTIFICATION

Complete link identification means that a PXC can automatically determine both the Node ID of the neighbor at the other end of a link as well as the remote interface id. The procedures described above were based on the assumption that the remote Node ID was known a priori. Consider the case when this is not true. Then, two problems arise. To completely identify a link, a PXC must potentially interact with *all* its neighbors since any one of them could be terminating the link on the remote end. Second, a neighbor participating in the test procedure must potentially look for test messages on *all* the candidate links (rather than only the subset that are connected to the PXC sending test messages). Other than just the delay this introduces (especially when PXCs support hundreds or thousands of ports), there is protocol complexity. As per the configuration depicted in Figure 6–24, as long as a PXC is engaged in a test procedure with one neighbor, it cannot do the same with another. If different PXCs are initiating the procedure for different links at the same time, the convergence of all these toward the identification of all links becomes an issue. Indeed, the same issue arises even when remote Node IDs are configured, and the link identification procedure described earlier is followed. But this problem is aggravated when the remote Node IDs are not known. As of present date, there is no satisfactory solution to the problem of complete identification of transparent links.

6.4.3.4 LINK PROPERTY CORRELATION

Link property correlation is done using the same messages exchanged over the control channel as described in section 6.4.2.3. This procedure with PXCs is no different than the one described for OXCs. Therefore, we will not describe this any further here.

6.5 Summary

Neighbor discovery is a very practical feature in an optical network whether or not a distributed control plane is used. It solves the messy problem of keeping track of connectivity between adjacent network elements. The protocol mechanisms for neighbor discovery can be very simple if the appropriate overhead bytes are available for use. Neighbor discovery standardization efforts have been progressing in the ITU-T, the OIF, and the IETF. The ITU-T G.7714 recommendation is a formal description of the problem and functional description of the solution. The OIF has specified neighbor discovery procedures to be used across the UNI (see Chapter 7 for a description of the UNI). The IETF has focussed on LMP, whose design is based on accommodating OOO cross-connects (PXCs).

One of the challenges with regard to neighbor discovery is getting an agreement on the usage of a specific set of overhead bytes. J0, J1, and J2 bytes have been proposed, along with section and line DCC bytes for use in neighbor discovery. Given that these bytes are often used for proprietary functions within networks, it has been difficult to get universal agreement on the usage of any of these bytes. It is conceivable that a different set of unused overhead bytes may be dedicated for implementing neighbor discovery in the future.

Neighbor discovery efforts of late have focused on OEO NEs (OXCs). With PXCs, neighbor discovery is complex, and with the waning deployment interest in such network elements this problem has receded to the background (at least temporarily as of this writing).

S E V E N

Signaling for Connection Provisioning

7.1 Introduction

Connection provisioning is the act of establishing a connection between two end points in an optical network. Provisioning has traditionally been in response to a service request received by the optical network operator from an external user. Recent developments in automating this process allow such requests to originate from user equipment directly. In either case, connection provisioning requires the identification of the two connection end points and the desired connection attributes. As an example, Figure 7–1 illustrates an optical network and some of the parameters specified during connection provisioning initiated using a traditional management system. In this figure, all the ports are assumed to be OC-48, and the A-end and Z-end denote the connection end points (which are indicated by <node, port> pairs). After it is initiated, the provisioning process consists of two major steps: First, the specified parameters are used to compute a route for the connection within the

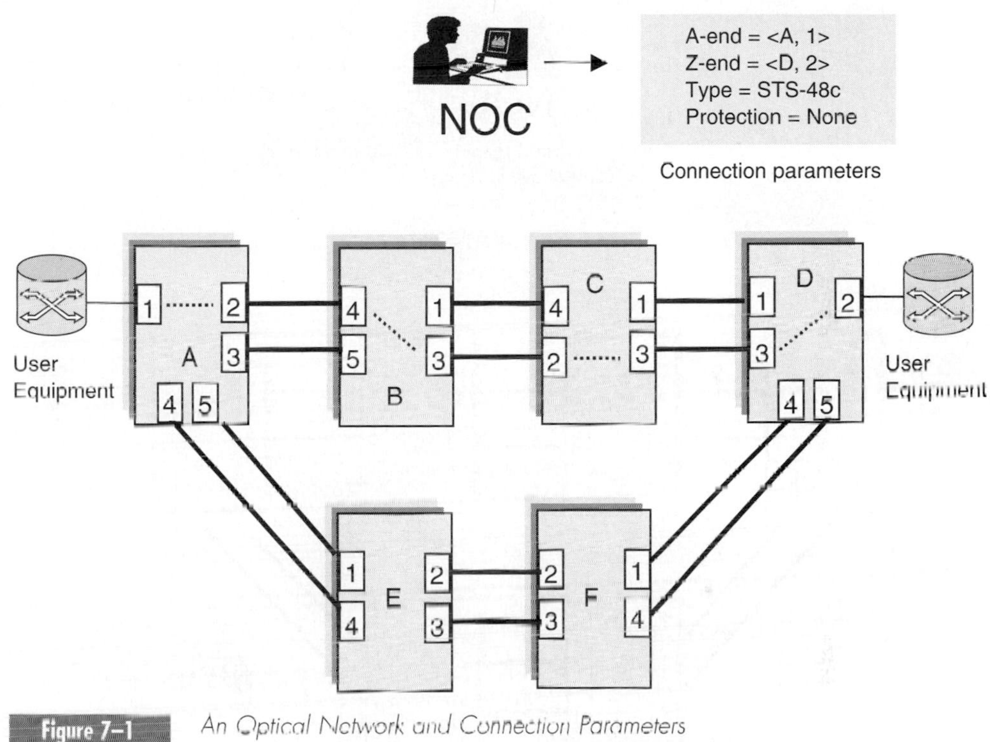

Figure 7–1 *An Optical Network and Connection Parameters*

optical network. The connection route is a function of both the connection parameters and the resources available in the network. The route computation process results in the identification of the sequence of nodes and links in the connection path. Next, the connection is established along the computed route by activating the cross-connects in the appropriate network elements (NE). This is the part of interest in this chapter.

Connection establishment can be realized broadly in one of two ways. Under the first method, each NE in the connection path may be instructed separately by the management system to establish the appropriate cross-connect. In this case, the management system is responsible for computing the complete connection route. This method is illustrated in Figure 7–2 for the connection-provisioning example shown in Figure 7–1. The communication between the management system and the NEs may use protocols such as TL-1 or SNMP, as described in Chapter 13. The second method is to use control communication between NEs in the connection path. This communication is referred to as *signaling*, whereby control messages flow from the source NE to the destination NE via intermediate NEs. A *signaling protocol* defines the syntax and semantics of control messages, as well as rules that govern the

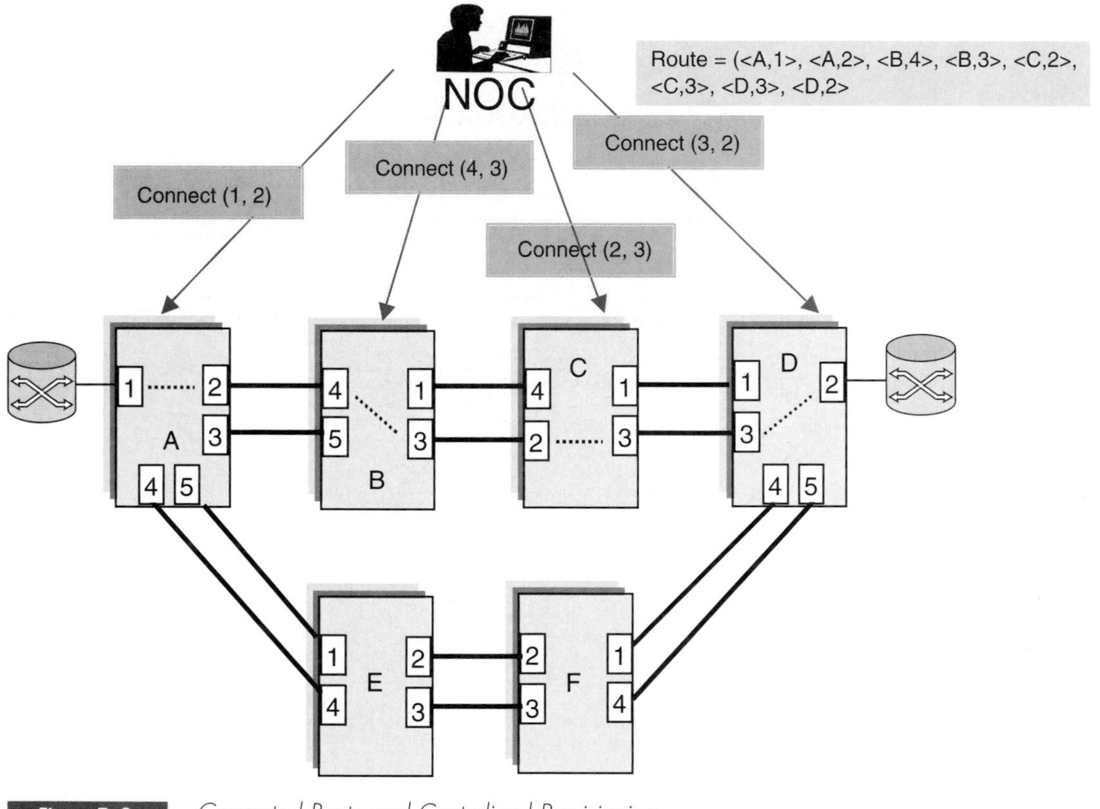

Figure 7–2 *Computed Route and Centralized Provisioning*

transmission, reception, and processing of such messages at each NE. Under many signaling protocols, provisioning requires message flow in two or more passes back and forth between the source and the destination NEs. Figure 7–3 illustrates signaling message flow for provisioning the same connection shown in the previous figures. Even with signaling, connection provisioning may have to be initiated from a management system. The management system in this case triggers the source NE to set up the connection. This NE may compute the connection route, or the route may be computed by the management system and supplied with the provisioning command.

Is one method better than the other? Equipment vendors who use the first method swear by the efficiency and reliability of the method. They point out that a highly reliable management system is required in all networks and that the system must have connectivity to all NEs regardless of whether signaling is used for connection establishment. Furthermore, such a system maintains complete network state information and thus using it for provisioning seems quite

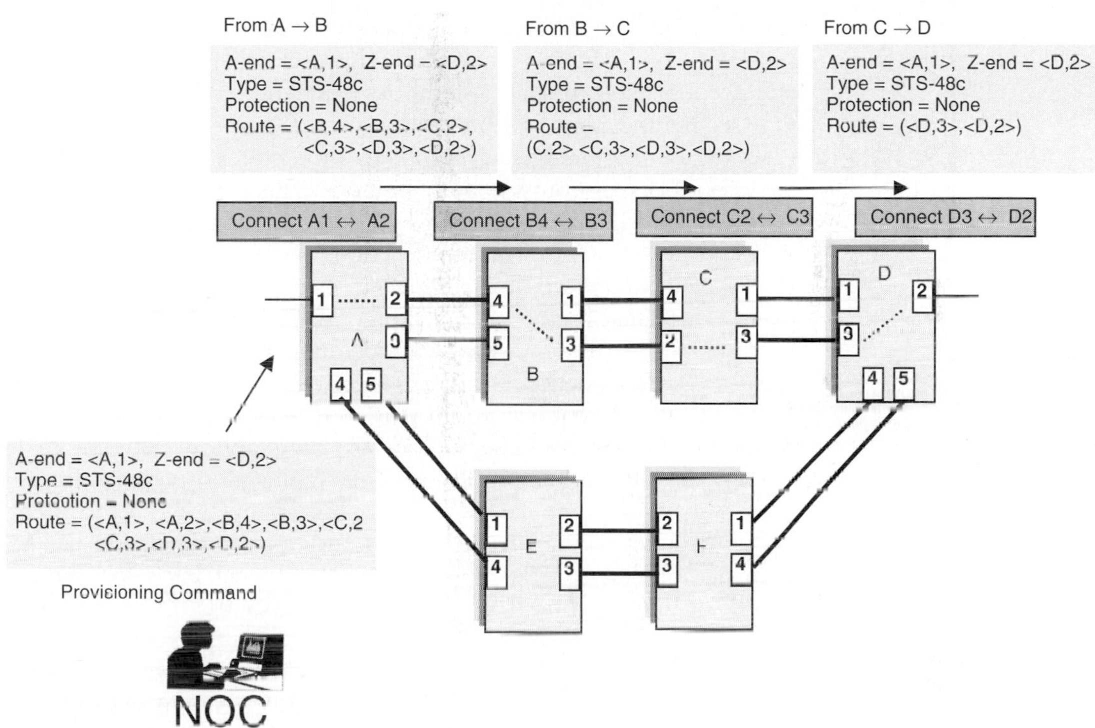

Figure 7–3 *Signaling-Based Connection Provisioning*

natural. On the other hand, the proponents of signaling point out that the management systems are already being overloaded with various tasks (e.g., performance monitoring), and additional network control tasks would strain the system and limit its scalability. Furthermore, signaling capability allows the NEs to speedily react to certain types of failures that require connection reprovisioning (e.g., node failures). Thus, both types of provisioning are here to stay. The focus of this chapter, however, is on provisioning using signaling. Chapter 13 covers management systems.

In this regard, our descriptions so far have been somewhat simplistic in order to explain the basic functionality. In reality, the provisioning problem could be more complex. Specifically, the following issues may arise:

- *End-to-end connection provisioning in a multivendor composite network*: The concept of control domains was described in Chapter 5. In practice, a large optical network may consist of multiple control domains, each consisting of equipment manufactured by a different vendor. Indeed, the provisioning capability within each control domain could be different (e.g., management system based provisioning in one control domain and signaled provisioning in another). A connection in such a composite network consists of connection segments within and between control domains as described in Chapter 5. Provisioning such a connection requires the integration of the control domain provisioning methods. This is indeed the goal of standardized signaling procedures. Different architectural models developed for this purpose are described in the next section.

- *Connection modification*: Parameters of a provisioned connection may be modified by the user of the connection. Effecting the modifications within the network without affecting the existing traffic flow on the connection is called *nondisruptive* connection modification. This may require special procedures.
- *Networks with hierarchical routing*: A large optical network may employ distributed hierarchical routing. Connection provisioning in such a network is similar to provisioning connections in the presence of subnetworks. Specifically, an end-to-end connection has to be provisioned as a series of connection segments, each spanning a region of the network. This is illustrated under the PNNI signaling procedures described in section 7.6.
- *Connection hierarchy*: The concept of layer networks was described in Chapter 5. Specifically, a "link" between two NEs in one (client) layer network could actually be a connection in an underlying (server) layer network. Provisioning a connection in the former network could thus involve provisioning a connection in the latter network. For instance, consider two metro optical networks attached to a core optical network. Suppose the metro networks support STS-1 connection granularity while the core network provides line-transparent STS-48-level switching granularity. Provisioning an STS-1 connection between a node in one metro network and a node in another network might require the provisioning of an STS-48 line-layer connection between two border nodes in these networks, and then accommodating the STS-1 connection within the larger connection. When signaling is used for provisioning, the larger connection may be provisioned dynamically.
- *Provisioning protected connections*: When a connection is protected, a primary and a protection path must be provisioned at the same time. Signaling procedures for provisioning protected connections are described in the next chapter.

Signaling procedures related to provisioning have been standardized by the ITU-T, the OIF and the IETF. Specific architectural models have been developed by these bodies. ITU-T recommendation G.7713 describes distributed call and connection management models pertaining to optical networks. While somewhat abstract, this recommendation formalizes a number of concepts related to signaling. These are described in the next section. The Generalized Multi-Protocol Label Switching (GMPLS) architecture is the product of the IETF, dealing with signaling-related concepts pertaining to optical networks. This is described in section 7.3.

Architectural models are only half the story when it comes to signaling. The actual details are found in signaling protocols themselves. Two protocols of interest are the GMPLS RSVP-TE and the PNNI protocols. The former protocol was originally designed for MPLS networks, but has been adapted to fit both the G.7713 and the GMPLS architectural models. The OIF has also used it as one option for User-Network Interface (UNI) signaling. The latter was designed originally for signaling in ATM networks, but it has been successfully deployed in operational optical networks. It has also been adapted to support the G.7713 architectural framework. These protocols are described in sections 7.5 and 7.6.

7.2 The ITU-T G.7713 Model

7.2.1 What Is G.7713?

G.7713 [ITU-T03a] is an ITU-T recommendation dealing with distributed call and connection management in optical networks conforming to ITU-T G.8080 architecture [ITU-T01d]. The purpose of this recommendation is to describe the parameters and procedures related to signaling independent of any particular signaling protocol. To do this, certain functional requirements and an architectural model for signaling are assumed. The main utility of G.7713 is the specification of the signaling interfaces, and the development of an architectural model that separates the signaling control plane from the data transport plane in optical networks. G.7713 also contains signaling message flow descriptions, and call and connection control finite state machine descriptions. From a practical perspective, these are not as significant, since such features are typically part of established signaling protocols such as RSVP-TE and PNNI.

7.2.2 Architectural Aspects

7.2.2.1 SIGNALING INTERFACES AND THE CONTROL PLANE

Fundamental to the architectural model described in G.7713 are the definitions of the signaling interfaces and the separation of the control plane from the data plane in optical networks. This is illustrated in Figure 7–4, where the optical network shown consists of a series of *n control domains* (or simply, domains). A domain, as described in section 5.2 (in Chapter 5), encloses a part of the overall network. In the simplest case, a domain could consist of a set of interconnected NEs. In the general case, it could be topologically partitioned, consisting of a set of interconnected subnetworks. This is the case depicted in Figure 7–4.The following signaling interfaces are identified in this figure:

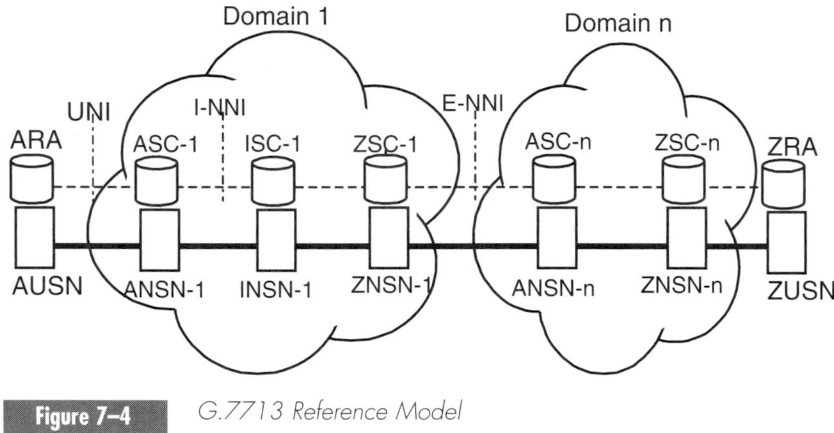

Figure 7–4 *G.7713 Reference Model*

- UNI (User-Network Interface): The signaling interface between the external user (client) network and the optical network.
- I-NNI (Interior Network-Network Interface): The signaling interface between subnetworks within a control domain (in the simplest case, each subnetwork is a single NE).
- E-NNI (Exterior Network-Network Interface): The signaling interface between control domains.

The difference between these interfaces lies in the type and format of information that may be sent across in signaling messages. Specifically, the UNI is the interface over which a client device requests service from the optical network. The signaling messages over this interface pertain to establishing, tearing down, and modifying connections to a remote end point to which a destination client is attached. As mentioned at the beginning of this chapter, the more traditional method is for the client network operator to request service from the operator of the optical network. These two methods result in two different types of connections. When a UNI is used to signal service request, a *switched* connection is provisioned in the network. When the optical network operator provisions a connection through a management system, it is called a *soft permanent* connection.[1] Regardless of how a service request originates, certain parameters are typically associated with subsequent connection provisioning within the optical network. Some of these were shown in Figure 7–1.

[1]Although all connections depend on switching inside the network, the terminology "switched connection" is used to indicate a connection that can be set up and torn down dynamically based on user request. The terminology "soft permanent" is used to indicate a connection that remains up until the network operator explicitly deletes it.

The NNI is the interface across which the actual connection establishment, tear down, and modification messages flow between subnetworks (within or across domains). Unlike the UNI, the NNI messages may carry information about the connection route, endpoint addressing information, and other parameters of use internally within the optical network. The Interior and Exterior NNI differ mainly in the flow of routing and policy related information across the interfaces.

Figure 7–4 also illustrates the separation between the control plane logical functions and its physical realization. The following entities are indicated in the figure. In the following, the notation "A" and "Z" are used to denote the two endpoints of signaling communication:

- *A-RA and Z-RA:* These are the A-end and Z-end Requesting Agents on the user side. An RA is a control plane entity that signals on behalf of an external user subnetwork (which contains the data transport equipment). This is a *logical* entity, that is, this could be physically realized as part of the equipment that has the data plane functionality, or as a separate piece of equipment. In the latter case, a single RA can represent multiple network elements, and there has to be a communication interface between the RA and the network elements it represents. This is necessary in order to coordinate the control plane and the associated data plane functions (e.g., establishment of data plane cross-connects, commencement of data transmission when connection establishment is complete, etc.).
- *A-USN and Z-USN:* These are the A-end and Z-end User Sub-Networks. A USN is the collection of NEs that form the user-side subnetworks. As described earlier, the A-RA and Z-RA implement the control plane functionality for these subnetworks.
- *A-SC, I-SC and Z-SC:* These are the Subnetwork Controllers for the ingress, intermediate, and egress subnetworks within a domain, respectively. As described before, a domain consists of a series of subnetworks (or individual NEs), and an SC represents the logical entity that implements the control plane functions within a subnetwork. As with the A-RA and the Z-RA, an SC can be physically realized as part of an NE, or it can be a separate physical entity. In the latter case, a single SC can represent multiple underlying NEs, and there is a need for a communication interface between the SC and the NEs it represents.
- *A-NSN, I-NSN and Z-NSN:* These are the ingress, intermediate, and egress network-side subnetworks, respectively. The A-SC, I-SC and Z-SC implement the control plane functionality corresponding to these subnetworks.

We have seen that the above architectural model separates the logical control plane functionality from its physical realization. What is the advantage of doing so? The separation mainly addresses a practical issue that arises in dealing with heterogeneous subnetworks. Consider an operator who wants to integrate two subnetworks, one that uses a management system for provisioning and another that uses proprietary signaling. By establishing two subnetwork controllers and using standard NNI signaling between them, the operator can implement end-to-end connection provisioning. This is illustrated in Figure 7–5. But instead, assume that both these subnetworks utilize internal signaling for provisioning. Then, the NNI will be directly between the border nodes in these subnetworks (i.e., the controller functionality will be present directly in the NEs).

7.2.2.2 CALL AND CONNECTION CONTROL

The G.7713 architectural model makes a distinction between a *call* and a connection. A call is a set of related connections between the same two end points. The signaling over the UNI establishes a call from the user perspective. The call is thus relevant to the user equipment at both ends, and to the ingress and egress NEs in the optical network. Within the network, connections are estab-

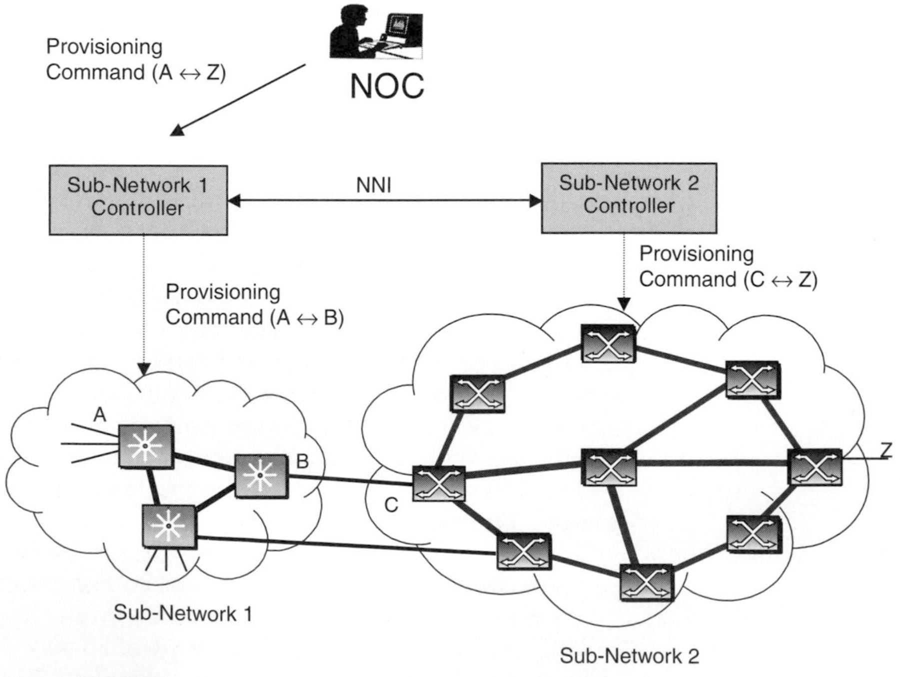

Figure 7–5 *Sub-Network Provisioning*

lished, and the correlation of connections belonging to the same call are done at the ingress and egress NEs. In practical terms, a call is created when the first connection within is created; it is modified when connections within are added, removed, or modified; and it is deleted when the last connection within is deleted.What is the advantage of distinguishing between a call and a connection? As per G.7713, the following features are enabled by this separation:

1. It permits the implementation of nondisruptive connection modification, whereby a new connection is added to a call and an existing connection deleted after traffic is moved from the latter to the former in a "hit-less" manner. Briefly, the ingress and egress NEs in the optical network keep the association between the connections by treating them as part of the same call. Intermediate NEs do not need this association. Readers may refer to the sections on LCAS and Virtual Concatenation in Chapter 3 for applications.
2. Similar to the connection modification feature above, it allows a "working" connection to be related to a "protection" connection, and traffic to be switched from the former to the latter when failures occur.
3. A call with zero connections within is possible. This allows the ingress/egress NEs to maintain "call state" relating to communication that has been disrupted inside the network. For instance, an ingress NE might be looking to reestablish a connection that has been deleted inside the network due to a failure condition.

In essence, the concept of a call formalizes the notion of maintaining state information that correlates connections. The same functionality is accomplished in GMPLS signaling using additional identifiers in connection signaling.

7.2.2.3 CONNECTION PROVISIONING

The connection provisioning procedure under the G.7713 model is illustrated in Figure 7–6. Here, an end-to-end connection is provisioned as a series of segments, some of them over single links and the others within subnetworks. Each controller that processes a signaling message in the first phase of connection provisioning has to determine the next controller to forward the signaling message, as well as local resource assignments for the connections. Routing information to determine the next controller may or may not be present in the signaling message. If it is not present, the controller must compute a partial route. The assignment of local resources would depend on the parameters of the connection. Furthermore, in the case of subnetwork controllers, determining local resources might require the determination of the entire path within the subnetwork for the connection segment.

The detailed functionality implemented for connection provisioning will be clear when we look at specific signaling protocols. The G.7713 recommendation, however, describes only general principles. Specific protocols

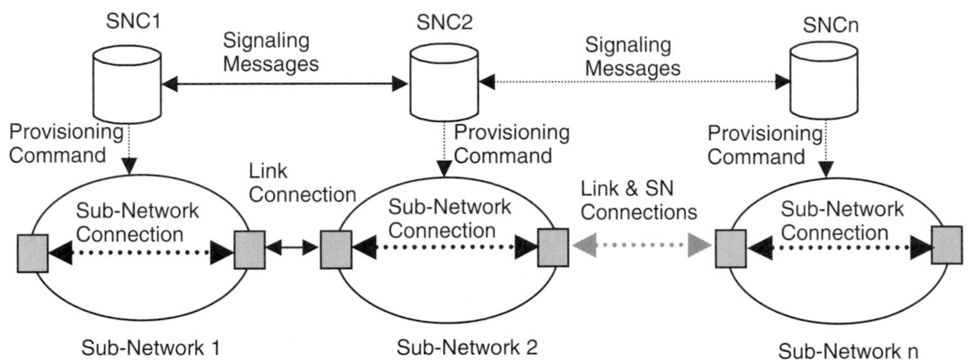

Figure 7–6 *End-to-End Connection Provisioning Across Sub-Networks*

that adhere to this model are separately defined. So far, three existing protocols have been adapted to provide the functionality described in G.7713: P-NNI, RSVP-TE and CR-LDP [ITU-T03b, ITU-T03c, ITU-T03d].

We defer discussion of protocols until later, and look at GMPLS signaling next.

7.3 GMPLS Signaling

Signaling was not part of the original IP network architecture—there was no need to establish a connection in an IP network before sending IP packets. With the advent of traffic engineering based on MPLS (denoted as MPLS-TE, see Chapter 5), the notion of explicitly routed Label Switched Paths (LSPs) came into being. Such LSPs, in essence, are connections over which IP (and potentially other protocol) packets can be carried from a source to a destination. Thus, traffic engineering applications over MPLS have made use of signaling protocols such as RSVP-TE and CR-LDP.

Generalized MPLS (or GMPLS) extends the basic MPLS-TE concepts to cover non-IP networks, in particular, optical networks. The rationale behind GMPLS was described in Chapter 5. In this section, our discussion focuses on GMPLS signaling, as described in [Berger03a].

First of all, as compared with G.7713, the GMPLS signaling specification addresses more concrete issues, such as specific formats of addresses and messages, and signaling actions. Thus, while the GMPLS signaling specification is protocol-neutral, it is only a small step removed from the actual protocols. The two MPLS-TE protocols, RSVP-TE and CR-LDP, are enhanced for use under GMPLS.

GMPLS signaling deals with multiple types of underlying equipment. Generically denoted as Label Switching Routers (LSRs),[2] this includes optical

[2]The term LSR is a remnant of the corresponding usage in MPLS. Denoting an optical switch as an LSR is awkward, but this is the convention followed in the GMPLS specification.

NE such as SONET/SDH cross-connects and transparent optical switches. The GMPLS specification in fact deals with different interfaces, a combination of which is allowed in an LSR. These interfaces are:

1. Packet-Switch Capable (PSC): Interfaces that recognize packet/cell boundaries and can forward data based on the content of the packet/cell header. An MPLS interface on a router is an example of this.
2. Time Division Multiplex capable (TDM): Interfaces that forward data based on the data's time slot in a repeating cycle. An example of this is a SONET/SDH interface.
3. Lambda-Switch Capable (LSC): Interfaces that forward data based on the wavelength on which the data is received. An optical cross-connect that operates at the level of an individual wavelength would have such an interface.
4. Fiber-Switch Capable (FSC): Interfaces that forward data based on a position of the data in physical space. An example of FSC is an interface on a switch that cross-connects one fiber input to another fiber output.

MPLS signaling protocols deal only with (1). Under GMPLS, these protocols are extended to deal with all four. Specifically, GMPLS signaling allows connections to be established, maintained, and torn down over all these interface types. GMPLS signaling allows the provisioning of both working and protection connection paths. Signaling for protection/restoration is covered in the next chapter. In the following, we highlight the essential features of GMPLS signaling.

7.3.1 Basic Signaling Model

The concept of an MPLS label, its allocation, and its usage were described in Chapter 5. To recall, MPLS LSPs are unidirectional, from a source node to a destination node. A node along an LSP is said to be *upstream* from another node if the former is closer to the source than the latter. The latter is then said to be *downstream* from the former. While establishing an MPLS LSP, each node in the path must allocate a label and convey it to the immediate upstream node in the path. When packets begins flowing on the LSP, the first node inserts the label in each packet given by the immediate downstream node. Each node receiving a packet switches the label in the received packet with the one given by the downstream node and forwards the packet over the appropriate interface.

Under GMPLS, a label is no longer carried in the data, but identifies a time slot, wavelength, or port through which the connection data must be switched (depending on the type of interface). The purpose of GMPLS signaling, in essence, is to allow each LSR in the path of a connection to allocate labels pertaining to the connection, communicate the assignment to the appropriate neighbor, and to make the appropriate cross-connect to switch the connection. Whereas MPLS LSPs are unidirectional, GMPLS allows the establishment of bidirectional LSPs. Thus, GMPLS signaling permits the allocation of labels for both directions of data flow concurrently.

Connection provisioning under GMPLS is either initiated through a management system (soft permanent connections) or by a client device through signaling (switched connections). In either case, the trigger is received by the source NE. Assuming that the connection route is available, either computed by the source NE or given in the provisioning trigger, the source NE makes a request to the next NE in the connection route to allocate a label (e.g., identify a port or time slot). The request message contains the connection endpoint identifiers and other parameters. For bidirectional connections, this request also contains the label allocation for the direction of the connection *from* the next NE (the reverse direction). An NE that receives a label allocation request processes the request and sends its own request to the next NE in the path and so on until the request reaches the destination NE. A response is then sent from the destination NE hop by hop toward the source NE. The response contains the label allocated by the downstream NE to its immediate upstream NE for the forward direction. This basic signaling model is illustrated in Figure 7–7. Here, each node allocates the "label" (which actually indicates the port number) for the reverse direction of the connection and solicits the label for the forward direction in the request phase. The forward labels are obtained in the response phase. Under GMPLS signaling, labels are local to the assigning node. Thus, label number 2 (which indicates port 2) sent by node A has to be converted to the corresponding port number at B (port 4). This mapping must either be manually configured in B or automatically obtained through neighbor discovery procedures (Chapter 6). Also, in this example, both directions of the connection are routed over the same path (the same set of links). This is typical in SONET/SDH networks.

Before we proceed further, it is instructive to understand the relationship between the G.7713 model and GMPLS signaling. In essence, G.7713 defines signaling interfaces and functional requirements. GMPLS defines specific signaling messages, objects, and procedures to realize connection provisioning. GMPLS signaling can thus be used at each of the signaling interfaces defined in G.7713. Indeed, this is exactly what has been described in ITU-T recommendations G.7713.2 [ITU-T03c] and G.7713.3 [ITU-T03d], which deal with GMPLS RSVP-TE and GMPLS CR-LDP protocols applied to G.7713 signaling.

It should be noted that under the GMPLS signaling architecture, a distinction is not made explicitly between the UNI and NNI. The same signaling method is applicable regardless of the type of interface, although the information content of signaling messages might be different. Furthermore, GMPLS

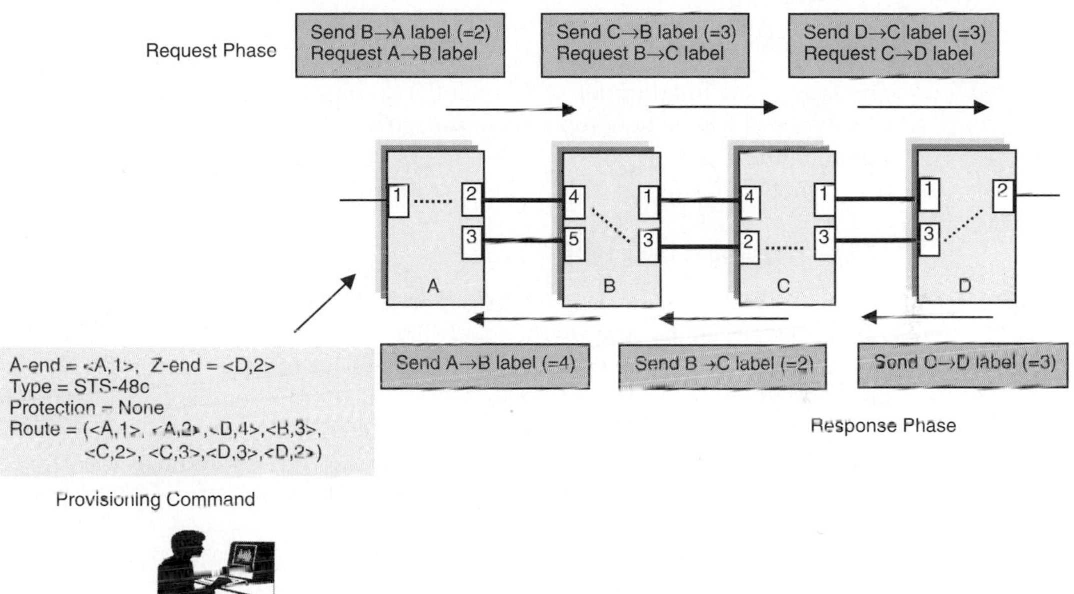

Figure 7–7 *Label Request and Response Phases in Connection Provisioning*

signaling is between peer nodes that are neighbors in the signaling path. These nodes may be neighbors in the data path, or they may be signaling controllers, which represent a group of nodes. In other words, GMPLS does support the control plane/data plane separation, and the protocols are applicable to the model described earlier under G.7713.

Finally, GMPLS utilizes the messages already defined under MPLS-TE protocols (RSVP-TE and CR-LDP) for label request, response, and so on, but it adds new information elements (called *objects*) to these messages along with the corresponding processing rules. Because of the closeness of the GMPLS signaling architectural model to the underlying protocols, it is best to look at the GMPLS-defined extensions in the context of these protocols. Even though there are two such protocols, our focus in this chapter will be on the RSVP-TE protocol [Berger03b] (section 7.4). This protocol is more popular than CR-LDP, and provides identical functionality. Readers who are interested in CR-LDP are referred to [Ashwood-Smith+03].

In the reminder of this section, we look at two important definitions under GMPLS: the new label types and the traffic parameters for SONET/SDH connections. GMPLS extensions pertaining to actually establishing, maintaining, and releasing connections are described in section 7.5.

7.3.2 GMPLS Labels

The label, as defined under MPLS, is a flat 20-bit number. GMPLS allows multiple types of labels, denoted as *generalized labels*. These labels are carried in signaling messages, as shown in the model of Figure 7–7. The following label types, in addition to the MPLS labels, are recognized under GMPLS.

7.3.2.1 PORT OR WAVELENGTH LABEL

This is a 32-bit number. It indicates a port number or a wavelength identifier when fiber switching is used. The label value is of significance only to the allocating node. A node receiving such a label may have to map it onto a locally significant port or wavelength identifier. For instance, consider the example shown in Figure 7–7. When node B indicates (port) label = 4 to node A, node A must map it onto a local port identifier, in this case, 2. Thus, node A knows it must make a cross-connect from its port 2 to its port 1 to provision the connection.

7.3.2.2 WAVEBAND LABEL

Waveband switching allows a set of wavelengths to be switched together. Whereas the fiber/wavelength label allowed the description of a single port/wavelength, the waveband label indicates a set of contiguous wavelength values. The details can be found in [Berger03a].

7.3.2.3 SONET AND SDH LABELS[3]

SONET and SDH each define a multiplexing structure, with the SONET multiplex structure being a subset of the SDH multiplex structure. These two structures are trees whose roots are respectively an STS-N or an STM-N signal and whose leaves are the signals that can be transported and switched via time slots, that is, an STS-x SPE, VC-x or a VT-x SPE. A SONET/SDH label will identify the exact position (i.e., first time slot) of a particular STS-x SPE, VC-x or VT-x SPE signal in a multiplexing structure.

Here, time slots are identified in the sequence in which they appear in the multiplex, not as they appear after any possible interleaving. These multiplexing structures are used as naming trees to create unique multiplex entry names or labels. Since the SONET multiplexing structure may be seen as a subset of the SDH multiplexing structure, the same format of label is used for SONET and SDH.

In the case of contiguous concatenation, only one label appears in the signaling message. This label identifies the lowest time slot occupied by the contiguously concatenated signal, that is, the time slot occupied by the first component signal of the concatenated signal when descending the tree. In the case

---

[3]SDH and SONET labels are defined in [Mannie+03], and the description in this section closely follows the material in [Mannie+03].

of virtual concatenation, the signaling message must indicate the ordered list of all labels pertaining to the concatenated signals. Each label indicates the first time slot occupied by a component of the virtually concatenated signal. The order of the labels must reflect the order of the payloads to concatenate (not the physical order of time slots). In the case of multiplication (i.e., using the multiplier transform, see section 7.3.3), the ordered list of the labels of the constituent elementary signals is carried in signaling messages. In case of multiplication of virtually concatenated signals, the first set of labels indicates the time slots occupied by the first virtually concatenated signal, the second set of labels indicates the time slots occupied by the second virtually concatenated signal, and so on.

It should be noted that when multiple labels are used to describe a signal as in the virtual concatenation and the multiplication case, these labels refer to signals carried on the same link. Thus, it seems like even though the standard definition for virtual concatenation allows component signals to be routed over different paths (see Chapter 3), GMPLS signaling restricts the routing to the same path. But normally, virtually concatenated signals are provisioned independently, and then concatenation is performed at the end points (see Chapter 3). GMPLS defines a feature to provision all the components of a virtually concatenated signal in one shot through the network.

The format of the SONET/SDH label is given in Figure 7–8. The components shown depict an extension of the numbering scheme defined in G.707, that is, the (K, L, M) numbering [ITU-T00a]. The higher order numbering scheme defined in G.707 is not used here. Each letter shown in the figure indicates a possible branch number starting at the parent node in the multiplex structure. Branches are numbered in increasing order from number 1, starting from the top of the multiplexing structure. Figure 7–9 depicts the branching for SONET and gives an example of a SONET label.

When a hierarchy of SONET/SDH connections (LSPs) is established, an LSP with a given bandwidth can be used to carry lower order LSPs. The higher order SONET/SDH LSP behaves as a virtual link with a given bandwidth (e.g., VC-3). A lower order SONET/SDH LSP can be established through that higher order LSP. Since a label is local to a (virtual) link, the highest part of that label is not significant and it is set to zero, that is, the label is "0,0,0,L,M." Similarly, if the structure of the higher order LSP is unknown or not relevant, the lowest part of that label is not significant, and it is set to zero, that is, the label is "S,U,K,0,0." For instance, a VC-3 LSP can be used to carry lower order LSPs. In that case the labels allocated between the two ends of the VC-3 LSP for the lower order LSPs will have S, U, and K set to zero, while L and M will be used to indicate the signal allocated in that VC-3.

S (16 bits)	U (4 bits)	K (4 bits)	L (4 bits)	M (4 bits)

Figure 7–8 *SONET/SDH Label Format*

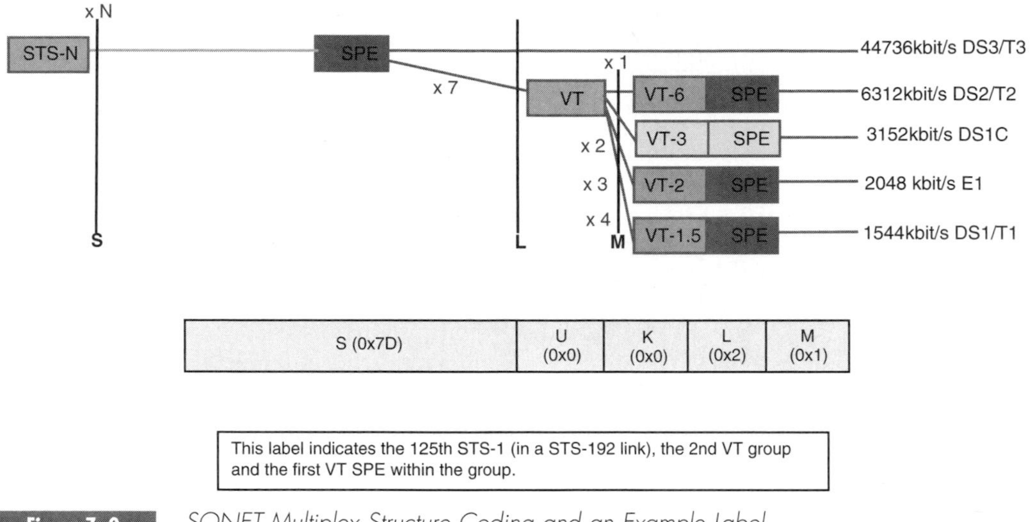

Figure 7–9 *SONET Multiplex Structure Coding and an Example Label*

The possible values of S, U, K, L and M are defined as follows:

1. S = 1…N is the index of a particular STS-3/AUG-1 inside an STS-N/STM-N multiplex. S is significant only for SONET STS-N (N>1) and SDH STM-N (N>0).
2. U = 1…3 is the index of a particular STS-1/VC-3 SPE within an STS-3/AUG-1. U is significant only for SONET STS-N (N>1) and SDH STM-N (N>0).
3. K = 1…3 is the index of a particular TUG-3 within a VC-4. K is significant only for an SDH VC-4 structured in TUG-3s.
4. L = 1…7 is the index of a particular VT Group/TUG-2 within a STS-1 SPE, TUG-3, or VC-3.
5. M is the index of a particular VT-1.5/VC-1, VT-2 or VT-3 SPE within a VT Group/TUG-2. M = 1,2 indicates a specific VT-3 SPE inside the corresponding VT Group; these values are not used for SDH since there is no signal corresponding to VT-3 in SDH. M = 3…5 indicates a specific VT-2 SPE/VC-12 inside the corresponding VT Group/TUG-2. M = 6…9 indicates a specific VT-1.5 SPE/VC-11 inside the corresponding VT Group/TUG-2.

A label is always interpreted along with the SONET/SDH traffic parameters (section 7.3.3), that is, a label by itself does not indicate which signal is being requested. A summary of the S, K, U, L, M values, along with usage examples, can be found in [Mannie+03a].

7.3.3 GMPLS Encoding of SONET/SDH Connection Parameters

The SONET/SDH connection parameters specify the type of SONET/SDH connection being established (e.g., STS-n) and the transparency objectives. Instead of listing all possible connection types and transparency combinations explicitly, the SONET/SDH connection parameters are encoded under GMPLS as a set of parameters that can be used to derive the connection characteristics. These parameters, as depicted in Figure 7–10, are:

- Signal Type: This 8-bit field indicates the type of an *elementary signal*. The elementary signal can be transformed using concatenation, multiplication, and transparency operations to derive the final signal carried in the connection being provisioned. The transforms are all optional, and if indicated, they must be applied strictly in the following order:
  - First, contiguous concatenation (using the RCC and the NCC field values) is applied on the elementary signal, resulting in a contiguously concatenated signal.
  - Second, virtual concatenation (using the NVC field value) is applied either directly on the elementary signal, or on the contiguously concatenated signal obtained from the previous phase.
  - Third, transparency is applied (see Chapter 3).
  - Finally, a multiplication (using the multiplier field value) is applied directly on the elementary signal, or on the contiguously concatenated signal obtained from the first phase, or on the virtually concatenated signal obtained from the second phase, or on these signals combined with some form of transparency.

  The permitted Signal Types for SONET/SDH are listed in Table 7–1.

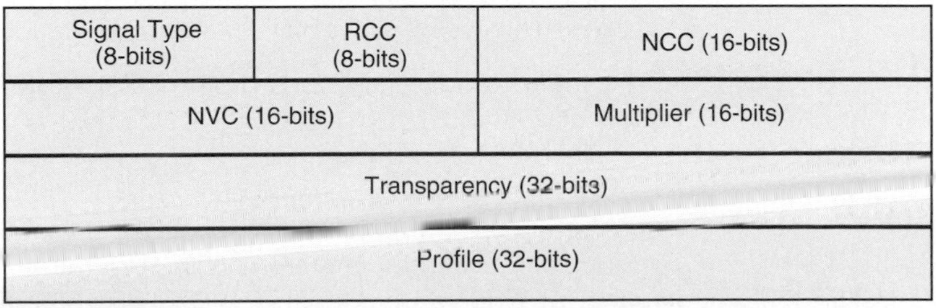

Signal Type (8-bits)	RCC (8-bits)	NCC (16-bits)	
NVC (16-bits)		Multiplier (16-bits)	
Transparency (32-bits)			
Profile (32-bits)			

Figure 7–10 *SONET/SDH Connection Parameters Encoding*

Table 7–1 *SONET/SDH Signals Types*

Signal Type Field	Indicated Elementary Signal (SONET / SDH)	Comments
1	VT1.5 SPE / VC-11	
2	VT2 SPE / VC-12	
3	VT3 SPE	
4	VT6 SPE / VC-2	
5	STS-1 SPE / VC-3	
6	STS-3c SPE / VC-4	
7	STS-1 / STM-0	Only when requesting transparency
8	STS-3 / STM-1	Only when requesting transparency
9	STS-12 / STM-4	Only when requesting transparency
10	STS-48 / STM-16	Only when requesting transparency
11	STS-192 / STM-64	Only when requesting transparency
12	STS-768 / STM-256	Only when requesting transparency

Note that a dedicated signal type has been assigned to the SONET STS-3c SPE rather than coding it as three contiguously concatenated STS-1 SPEs. This has been done in order to provide an easy mapping between SONET and SDH signaling.

- Requested Contiguous Concatenation (RCC): This 8-bit field indicates the required contiguous concatenation of the elementary signal. This field is a vector of flags, with each flag indicating a particular type of contiguous concatenation. Several flags can be set at the same time to indicate a choice. Presently, the following flag is defined:

  - Flag 1 (bit 1, low order bit): Standard contiguous concatenation.

  Flag 1 indicates that the standard SONET/SDH contiguous concatenation as defined in T1.105/G.707 [ITU-T00a] is requested. Other flags are reserved for future use.
- Number of Contiguous Components (NCC): This 16-bit field indicates the number of identical SONET/SDH SPEs/VCs that should be concatenated using the method specified in the RCC field.
- Number of Virtual Components (NVC): This 16-bit field indicates the number of signals that need to be virtually concatenated.

- Multiplier: This 16-bit field indicates the number of identical signals that together form the final signal constituting the connection. These signals can be identical elementary signals, or identical contiguously concatenated signals, or identical virtually concatenated signals.
- Transparency: This 32-bit field is a vector of flags that indicates the type of transparency being requested. Several flags can be combined to request different types of transparency. Not all combinations are necessarily valid. Transparency is only applicable to the fields in the SONET/SDH frame overheads. In the SONET case, these are the fields in the Section Overhead (SOH) and the Line Overhead (LOH). In the SDH case, these are the fields in the Regenerator Section Overhead (RSOH), the Multiplex Section overhead (MSOH), and the pointer fields between the two. With SONET, the pointer fields are part of the LOH.

  Transparency is only applicable when using the following signal types: STM-0, STM-1, STM-4, STM-16, STM-64, STM-256, STS-1, STS-3, STS-12, STS-48, STS-192, and STS-768. At least one transparency type must be specified when requesting such a signal type.

  The different transparency flags are the following:

  - Flag 1 (bit 1, low order): Section or regenerator section layer.
  - Flag 2 (bit 2): Line or multiplex section layer.

  A flag is set to 1 to indicate that the corresponding transparency is requested.

  SONET section/SDH regenerator section layer transparency means that the entire frame must be delivered unmodified. This implies that pointers cannot be adjusted. SONET line/SDH multiplex section layer transparency means that the LOH/MSOH must be delivered unmodified.
- Profile: This field is intended to indicate particular capabilities that must be supported for the connection, for example, monitoring capabilities. Presently, no profile has been defined.

To understand GMPLS-based signaling, it is best to look at a signaling protocol. Our choice, as mentioned earlier, is RSVP-TE. In the following section, we first go through the basic details of RSVP and RSVP-TE. In section 7.5, we look at the GMPLS extensions to RSVP-TE. When describing a protocol, whose specification is rather rich, it is often a difficult to judge how much detail is good enough. Our approach in the following sections is to avoid clutter and look at details that are essential to understand the main features of the protocols pertaining to provisioning. Interested readers can explore further by following the references given.

7.4 RSVP and RSVP-TE

7.4.1 RSVP

7.4.1.1 BASIC MODEL

RSVP was developed to support integrated services (i.e., packet delivery with Quality of Service (QoS) requirements) in the Internet. It is an IETF standard, described in RFC 2205 [Braden+97]. RSVP, in essence, is a signaling protocol. Using RSVP, a source IP host (*sender*) sends a message to a unicast or a multicast IP destination indicating the characteristics of the traffic it will generate. This message is processed by routers in the path from the source to the destination(s) (*receivers*). These routers make note of the reverse path to the sender. Based on the received traffic characteristics, each receiver formulates a reservation request and transmits it to the sender. This request traverses the reverse path maintained by the network routers. Each router along the way processes the reservation request and allocates local resources on the link leading toward the receiver. Thus, unidirectional resource reservation, from the sender to the receiver(s), is established in the network.

RSVP was designed to support both point-to-point and multicast traffic. The adaptation of RSVP, however, for traffic engineering purposes has focused only on the point-to-point application. Thus, in this section, we limit our discussions to the point-to-point case only.

It should be noted that RSVP does not provide route computation functionality. Typically, an IP routing protocol computes forwarding tables, using which RSVP messages are forwarded from the sender to the receiver. RSVP runs directly over IP, with IP protocol number 46. RSVP interactions are between neighboring RSVP-capable entities, called RSVP peers. Under RSVP, unidirectional reservations are made for "sessions," that is, traffic flow to a specific destination. The RSVP model is shown in Figure 7–11. Here, the RSVP process (called RSVP Daemon) communicates with its peer over IP. This process at each node (host or router) interacts with the packet filtering (denoted as *classifier*) and the scheduling modules to establish the appropriate QoS treatment to enforce reservations. In addition, the RSVP process at a router interacts with the routing protocol to determine the next hop to forward an RSVP message.

7.4.1.2 RSVP MESSAGES AND OBJECTS

RSVP defines seven messages:

1. Path
2. Resv (Reserve, pronounced Res-V)
3. PathErr (Path Error)
4. ResvErr (Reserve Error)
5. PathTear

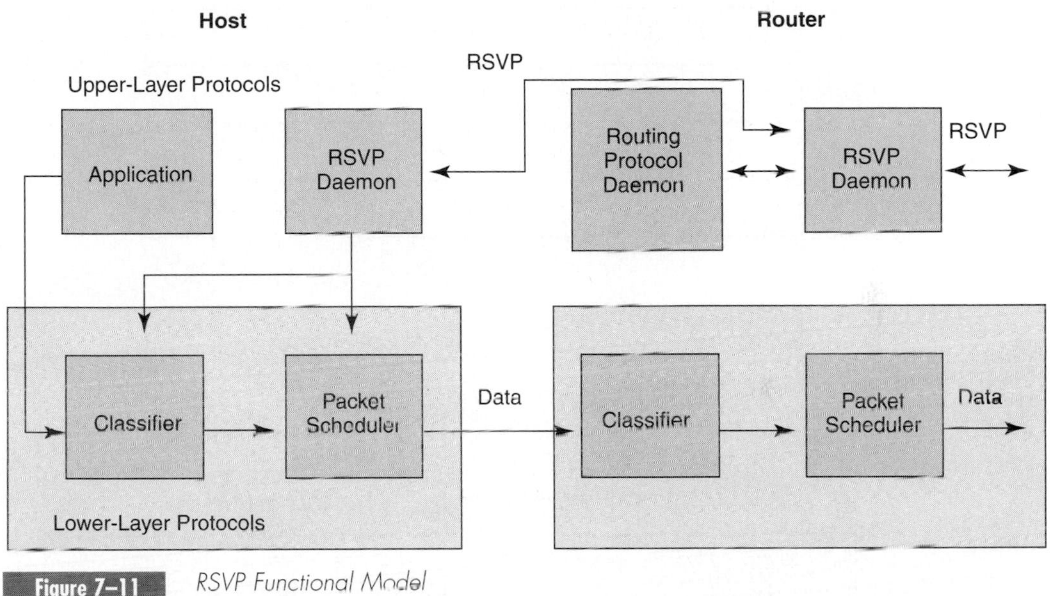

Figure 7–11 *RSVP Functional Model*

6. ResvTear
7. ResvConf (Reserve Confirm)

The Path and the Resv messages are used for establishing reservations for a session. The PathTear and ResvTear messages are used to delete the session state (and the reservation). PathErr and ResvErr are error notification messages. Finally, ResvConf is sent to a receiver to confirm a reservation. Before we describe the usage of these messages for establishing and deleting reservations, it is useful to look at the content of these messages. In aid of this, Figure 7–12 illustrates the RSVP message format. It is seen that RSVP messages carry objects, whose format is shown. The value in the Message Type field of the RSVP common header corresponds to the number indicated above for each message. The objects are coded in a hierarchical way; the Class Number identifies a broad class of similar objects and the Class Type identifies a specific object within the class. The Checksum field in the header covers the entire RSVP message, and the SEND_TTL field contains the IP Time To Live value with which the message was sent (see [Braden+97] for the usage of this field).

The key RSVP objects are as follows.

Session • Conceptually, a session is a uniquely identifiable traffic flow. Under RSVP, reservations are made on a session basis. The session identification consists of the receiver's IP address, protocol ID, and port. This is car-

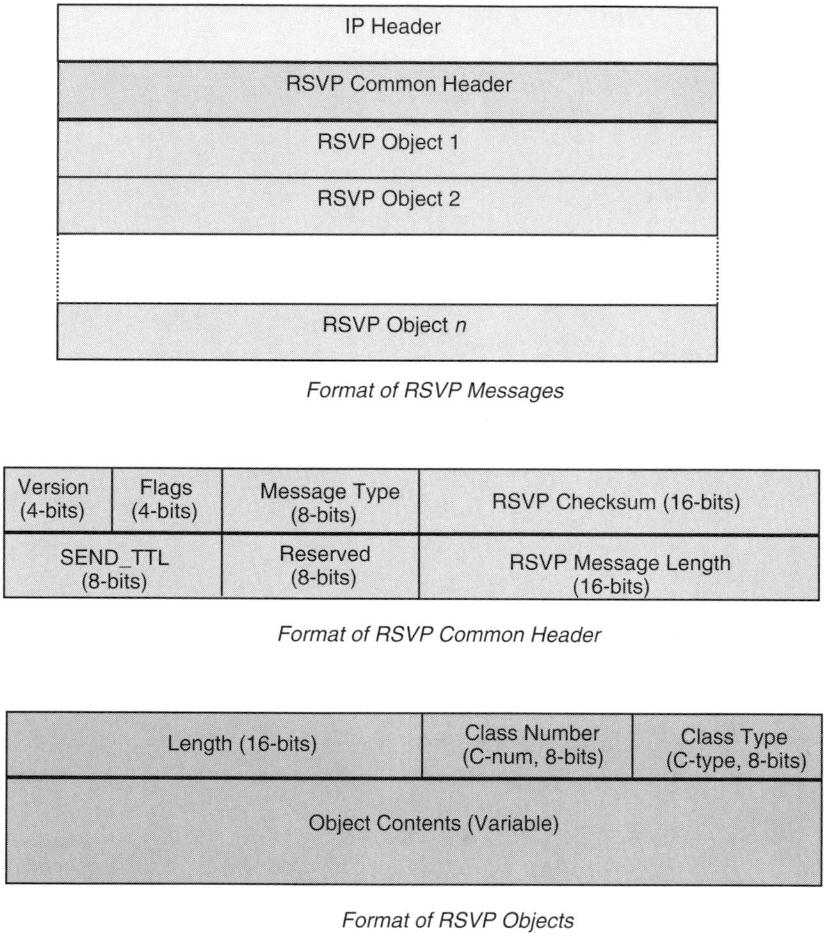

IP Header
RSVP Common Header
RSVP Object 1
RSVP Object 2
RSVP Object *n*

Format of RSVP Messages

Version (4-bits)	Flags (4-bits)	Message Type (8-bits)	RSVP Checksum (16-bits)
SEND_TTL (8-bits)		Reserved (8-bits)	RSVP Message Length (16-bits)

Format of RSVP Common Header

Length (16-bits)	Class Number (C-num, 8-bits)	Class Type (C-type, 8-bits)
Object Contents (Variable)		

Format of RSVP Objects

Figure 7–12 *RSVP Message and Object Formats*

ried as a "session object" in RSVP messages. The format of this object, for an IPv4 destination, is shown in Figure 7–13 (the other possibility is an IPv6 destination, see [Braden+97]). Note that the identity of the sender is not part of the session identification.

SENDER TEMPLATE • The Sender Template identifies the sender of a flow. The format of this object, for a sender with an IPv4 address, is shown in Figure 7-14. The reason this is called a "template" is that the same format is used as a filter to select those packets that receive the QoS treatment (see Filterspec below).

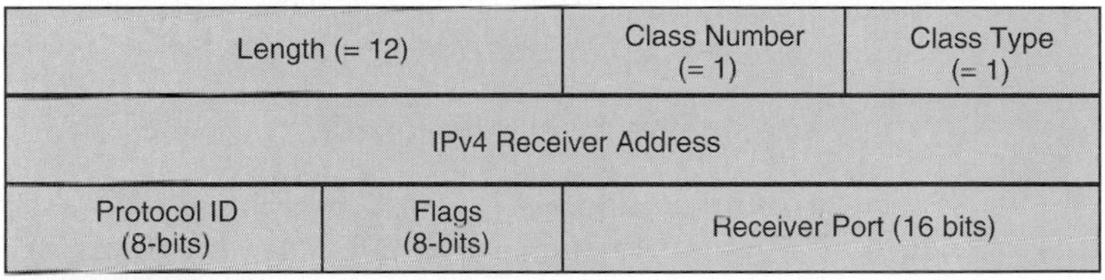

Length (= 12)		Class Number (= 1)	Class Type (= 1)
IPv4 Receiver Address			
Protocol ID (8-bits)	Flags (8-bits)	Receiver Port (16 bits)	

Figure 7–13 *Format of the RSVP Session Object*

SENDER TSPEC • The Tspec indicates the traffic characteristics of the flow being generated by a sender. RSVP itself does not interpret or use this object, but it merely carries this object opaquely. The IETF Integrated Services working group has defined Tspec parameters for different service classes to be used with RSVP [Wroclawski97]. The Tspec is carried from the sender to the intermediate routers, and finally to the receiver.

FLOWSPEC • The Flowspec describes the reservation request. This is carried in Resv messages, from the receiver toward the sender. Intermediate routers use the flowspec to make the reservation. As in the case of the Tspec, RSVP does not interpret or use this object, but delivers it to various nodes.

FILTERSPEC • The Filterspec describes the packets that are to receive the QoS treatment in each node along the path from the sender to the receiver in a given session. The Filterspec is used to set up the packet classifier in each node (see Figure 7–11). The format of the Filterspec object is same as that of the Sender Template.

In addition to these objects, RSVP defines several "reservation styles." A reservation style indicates whether the reservation is dedicated to a flow from a single sender to the receiver, or it is shared among multiple flows from possibly different senders to the same receiver. The typical application in traffic engineering uses dedicated reservation for traffic flows from a single source

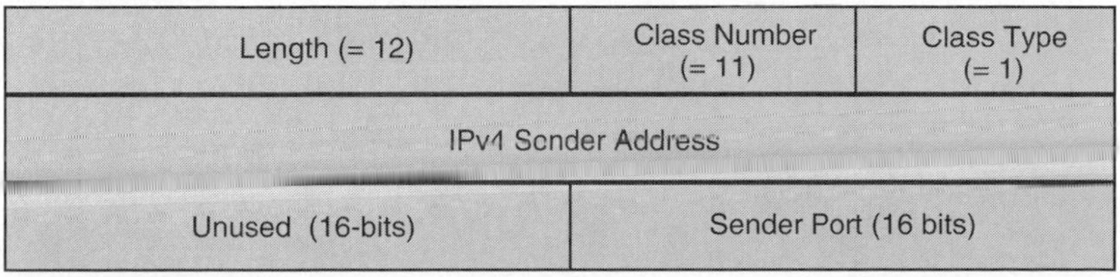

Length (= 12)	Class Number (= 11)	Class Type (= 1)
IPv4 Sender Address		
Unused (16-bits)	Sender Port (16 bits)	

Figure 7–14 *Format of the RSVP Sender Template Object*

to a given destination. Hence, we will not consider reservation styles further. The interested reader is referred to [Braden+97].

7.4.1.3 ESTABLISHING A RESERVATION: PATH AND RESV

The manner in which a reservation is established for a session using RSVP is shown in Figure 7–15. Here, a network of two hosts and five routers is shown. The Path message is originated by the sender host. As shown in Figure 7–16,[4] the Path message contains the identity of the receiver (i.e., Session), the identity of the sender (Sender Template), and the traffic characteristics (Sender Tspec). Recall that RSVP messages are directly carried in IP packets. The IP packet carrying the Path message is addressed directly to the receiver (i.e., receiver's IP address is used as the destination address). This packet follows the normal route to the destination. Each intermediate router that receives the packet, however, creates the *Path State* for the session in a local database, before forwarding the packet to the next hop. The Path State consists of the received Sender Template, Sender Tspec, and Session information, along with the identity of the previous hop toward the source. This previous hop information is received in the RSVP Hop object, as indicated in Figure 7–16. This object, as shown in Figure 7–17, has two fields: the IP address of the previ-

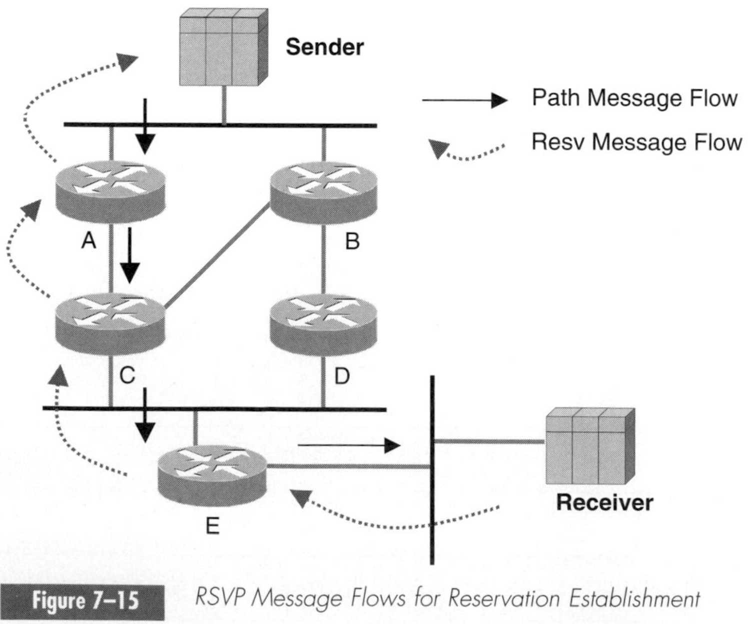

Figure 7–15 *RSVP Message Flows for Reservation Establishment*

[4]Optional objects in the Path message are not shown.

Common Header
Session
RSVP Hop
Time Values
Sender Template
Sender Tspec

Figure 7–16 *Contents of the Path Message*

ous router that forwarded the Path message, and the outgoing interface id (called Logical Interface Handle, LIH) at that router. Each router that forwards the Path message must replace the received RSVP Hop object with a new one containing its own IP address and the identity of the interface over which the packet is forwarded. The message finally reaches the receiver, which also must create the local Path state.

The receiver utilizes the Tspec information in the Path message to formulate a reservation request. It then sends a Resv message to the previous hop in the path. The IP address and the LIH information gathered from the RSVP Hop object in the Path message allow the receiver to determine which local interface should be used to send the Resv message and to which next node the IP packet (carrying the Resv message) must be addressed. A question may arise as to why the Resv message cannot be addressed directly to the sender as the Path message was addressed to the receiver. The problem is that in IP networks, the route from the sender to the receiver may not be the same as the route from the receiver to the sender. Since the reservation is unidirectional from the sender to the receiver, it is necessary for the Resv messages to progress along the same path in reverse as the Path message. Thus, the Resv message is sent hop by hop from the receiver to the sender using the previous hop information stored in each intermediate node.

Length (= 12)	Class Number (= 3)	Class Type (= 1)
IPv4 Next/Previous Hop Address		
Logical Interface Handle (LIH, 32- bits)		

Figure 7–17 *Format of the RSVP Hop Object*

The contents of the Resv message are shown in Figure 7–18.[5] This message has the Session, the Reservation Style, the Filterspec, and the Flowspec objects. Additionally, the RSVP Hop object is used to indicate the node that sent the message. A router that receives the message creates the local *Resv State*, that is, the received Flow and Filterspec information are noted, along with the RSVP Hop information. Furthermore, the Flowspec is used to configure the local packet scheduler corresponding to the appropriate outgoing link, and the Filterspec is used to configure the packet classifier to enforce the reservation for the indicated session. The router then forwards the Resv message to the previous node in the path from the sender, after replacing the RSVP Hop object with its own information. The Resv message finally reaches the sender, which must also make local resource reservation for the flow.

Once a reservation has been established, the data packets can flow from the sender to the receiver. Because the packet classifier and scheduler have been properly configured on the data plane, the traffic flow will receive the appropriate treatment. A question may arise as to what happens when a routing change occurs in the network. Note that the Path message and the data packets constituting the traffic flow, are routed along a path determined by normal destination-based IP routing. But IP routing is dynamic, that is, a failure in the network can result in new routing table entries corresponding to the receiver's address. If this happens, subsequent data packets from the sender will be routed over a new path that does not have resources reserved.

7.4.1.4 THE SOFT STATE APPROACH

In traditional connection-oriented networks, a disruption in the connection path would result in the reestablishment of the connection along a new path before data flow resumes. An example is the telephone network. If a call is dropped in the middle of a conversation (which happens frequently with cel-

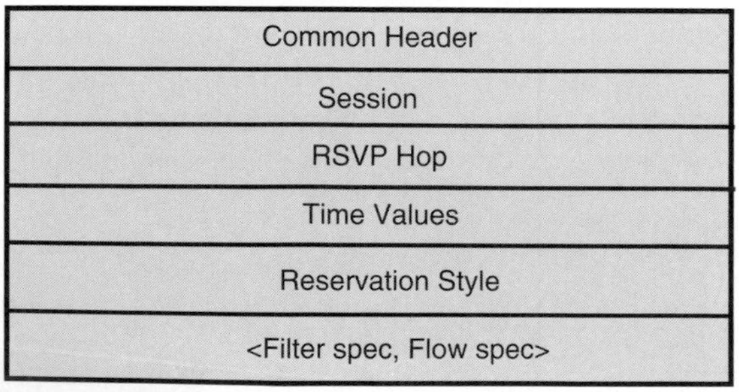

Common Header
Session
RSVP Hop
Time Values
Reservation Style
<Filter spec, Flow spec>

Figure 7–18 *Contents of the Resv Message*

[5] Optional objects in the Resv message are not shown.

lular telephones), the user must redial the call before carrying on the conversation. This approach is referred to as the *hard state* approach, that is, the establishment and maintenance of an explicit connection. This is also the approach followed in optical networks. RSVP, however, follows the *soft state* approach. Under this method, Path and Resv messages are not transmitted reliably, that is, there is no acknowledgment message when a node sends a Path or Resv message to another. Instead, Path and Resv messages are regenerated periodically by each node with "active" Path and Resv states, respectively. This is referred to as *refreshing* the state, and the regenerated messages are called *refresh* messages. The state at a node is considered active if it has been refreshed recently. A Path message thus generated is identical to the original Path message, except it is forwarded to the destination using the currently available IP routing information. The refresh Resv message is identical to the one originally generated by the node, and it is forwarded to the previous node as per the RSVP Hop information kept in the corresponding Path state. A node deletes its Path or Resv state if it does not receive a refresh Path or Resv message, respectively, from the appropriate RSVP peer. When the Path state is deleted, the associated Resv state is also deleted, and a PathTear message is generated. When Resv state is deleted, the corresponding Path state is *not* deleted. A ResvTear message, however, is generated (see below). This soft state approach allows routing changes to be accommodated automatically. If the route changes, the next refresh Path message would follow the new route and establish new Path state (and the corresponding Resv state).

The Time Values field in the Path and Resv messages (Figures 7-16 and 7-18) indicates the refresh time period that will be used by the sender of the message. This allows the receiver of the message to set the time-out period to remove the Path or Resv state. The refresh time period is specified in milliseconds as a 32-bit number.

7.4.1.5 DELETING A RESERVATION: PATHTEAR AND RESVTEAR

A reservation at a node can be deleted in one of the two ways: implicitly when the Path or the Resv state is timed out, or explicitly when a PathTear or a ResvTear message is received. A sender (or an intermediate router) can generate a PathTear message (Figure 7–19[6]) to delete the Path state of a session. As described in the last section, when the Path state is removed at a node, the Resv state is also removed. The PathTear message, like the Path message, is addressed to the receiver of the data flow. An intermediate router that receives the PathTear message removes the local Path and Resv state (it does not generate a ResvTear, however). A PathTear message is not transmitted reliably. If the message is lost, the intended next hop node will eventually time-out and delete its Path and Resv states, as described before.

[6]Optional objects are not shown.

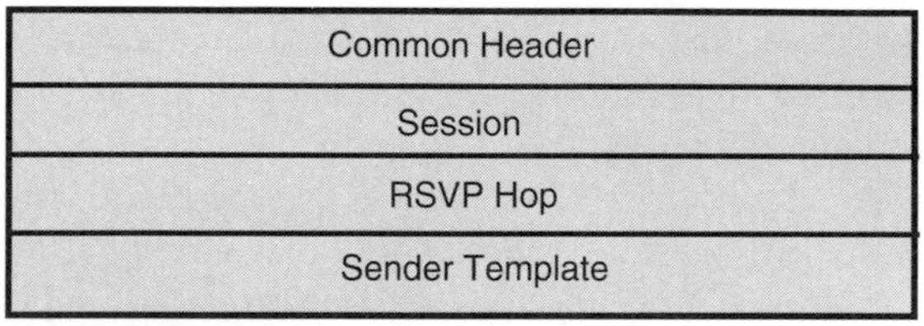

Common Header
Session
RSVP Hop
Sender Template

Figure 7–19 *Contents of the PathTear Message*

The receiver (or an intermediate router) can generate a ResvTear (Figure 7–20[7])to remove the reservation corresponding to a session. The ResvTear, like Resv messages, is transmitted hop by hop. The reception of a ResvTear by a node results in the removal of only the Resv state for the session. The Path state is maintained. Like the PathTear message, ResvTear is not transmitted reliably.

7.4.1.6 PATH AND RESV ERRORS, AND RESERVATION CONFIRMATION

The PathErr and ResvErr messages are used to indicate error conditions. The PathErr message is sent from an intermediate router to the sender using the previous hop information. Other nodes en route do not change their Path state based on this. The ResvErr is sent from an intermediate router to the receiver. Nodes en route may change their Resv state based on this. The PathErr and ResvErr messages contain error codes indicating the problem.

The ResvConf message is sent from the sender or an intermediate router to the receiver to confirm the establishment of the reservation.

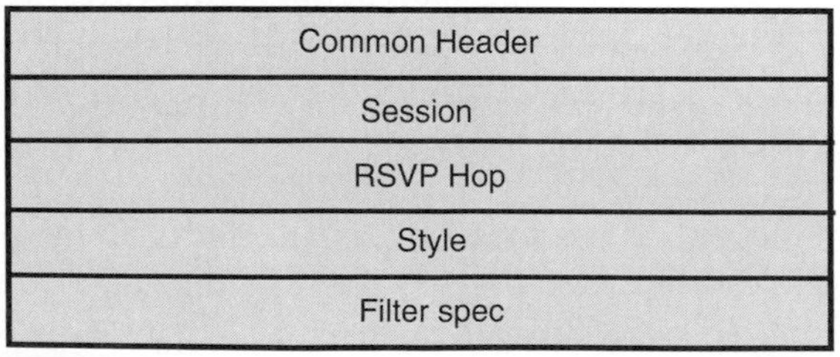

Common Header
Session
RSVP Hop
Style
Filter spec

Figure 7–20 *Contents of the ResvTear Message*

[7]Optional objects are not shown.

These three messages are not central to the discussion that follows. Thus, we do not consider them further. For details on these messages, please refer to [Braden+97].

Finally, although our description so far has focused on the sender and the receiver being hosts, it is possible for the sender and receiver to be routers.

7.4.2 RSVP-TE

RSVP was designed to be a protocol to reserve resources along a preexisting path. With the advent of MPLS-based traffic engineering, there was a desire to reuse the available RSVP implementations to support the creation, maintenance, and deletion of LSPs. The result was RSVP with traffic engineering extensions, or simply, RSVP-TE. These protocol extensions are described in IETF RFC 3209 [Awduche+01b].

The key features of RSVP-TE are:

- The usage of the Path and Resv messages to request and assign labels for LSP establishment
- The ability to specify an explicit route when establishing or rerouting an LSP
- The ability to specify bandwidth and other parameters when establishing an LSP
- The ability to associate related LSPs
- A new Hello protocol for maintaining the adjacency between RSVP peers

The RSVP-TE specification uses the term "LSP tunnel" to denote point-to-point LSPs with or without associated QoS parameters. A number of new objects are introduced in RSVP-TE to support the above features. These are described next, followed by a description of how these objects are used in RSVP-TE to create, maintain and delete LSP tunnels.

7.4.2.1 RSVP-TE OBJECTS

These are as follows:

- Label request
- Label
- Explicit route
- Record route
- LSP tunnel identification in session, sender template, and Filterspec objects
- Session attributes

Label Request • The Label Request object is carried in the Path message. As the name implies, it is used by an upstream node to request a label from the downstream neighbor for the LSP tunnel being established. Under RSVP-TE, three types of labels may be requested: the 20-bit MPLS label, an ATM label within a specified range, or a frame relay label within a specified range. Figure 7–21 illustrates the Label Request object corresponding to the MPLS label. Here, the L3-PID field indicates the type of the layer 3 protocol data units (e.g., IP) that will be carried by the LSP. The other two Label Request object formats are described in [Awduche+01b].

Label • The Label object is carried in Resv messages upstream. This object indicates the label that has been assigned by the downstream neighbor in response to a label request received in the Path message. The format of the Label object is shown in Figure 7–22. The 32-bit label field is wide enough to carry the 20-bit MPLS label, as well as ATM and frame relay labels.

Explicit Route • The Explicit Route Object (ERO) is carried in Path messages during LSP establishment or rerouting. There are basically three kinds of explicit routes:

1. Strict explicit route: This identifies a series of adjacent nodes that describe the complete path from a source to a destination.
2. Loose explicit route: This identifies a series of nonadjacent nodes along the path from a source to a destination. Thus, a loose explicit route has "gaps" that need to be filled to get the complete path.
3. Autonomous system (AS) list: This identifies a series of adjacent autonomous systems (see Chapter 9) that lie along the path from a source to a destination. This is therefore a form of loose explicit route.

The format of the ERO is shown in Figure 7–23. It is a sequence of sub-objects, each sub-object being an IPv4 prefix, an IPv6 prefix, or an AS number. The L bit indicates whether a sub-object indicates a loose hop. With this format, an ERO can be strictly one of the above three types, or it can be a mix of these. For instance, part of the ERO can be a strict sequence of nodes, and a part can be loose, some of them being autonomous systems. The format of the

Length (= 8)	Class Number (= 19)	Class Type (= 1)
Reserved (16-bits)	L3-PID (16-bits)	

Figure 7–21 *Format of the Label Request Object*

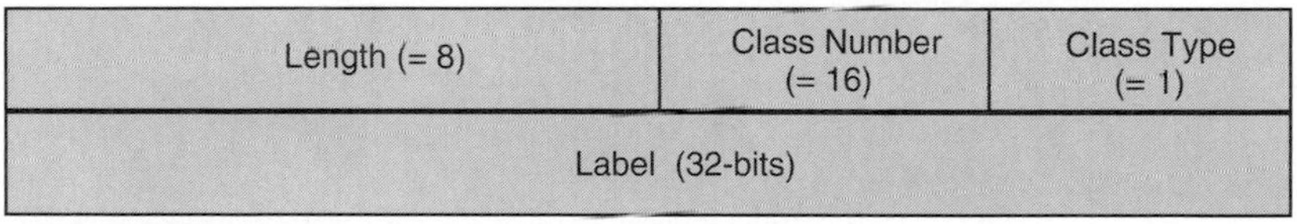

Length (= 8)	Class Number (= 16)	Class Type (= 1)
Label (32-bits)		

Figure 7–22 *Format of the Label Object*

IPv4 ERO sub-object is also shown in Figure 7–23. Here, the IPv4 address field could contain an IP address prefix of length less than 32 bits. Such a prefix is possible when the ERO hop is loose. The prefix length field indicates this.

With the ERO being present in Path messages, the forwarding of these messages is now different from the way they were handled under RSVP.

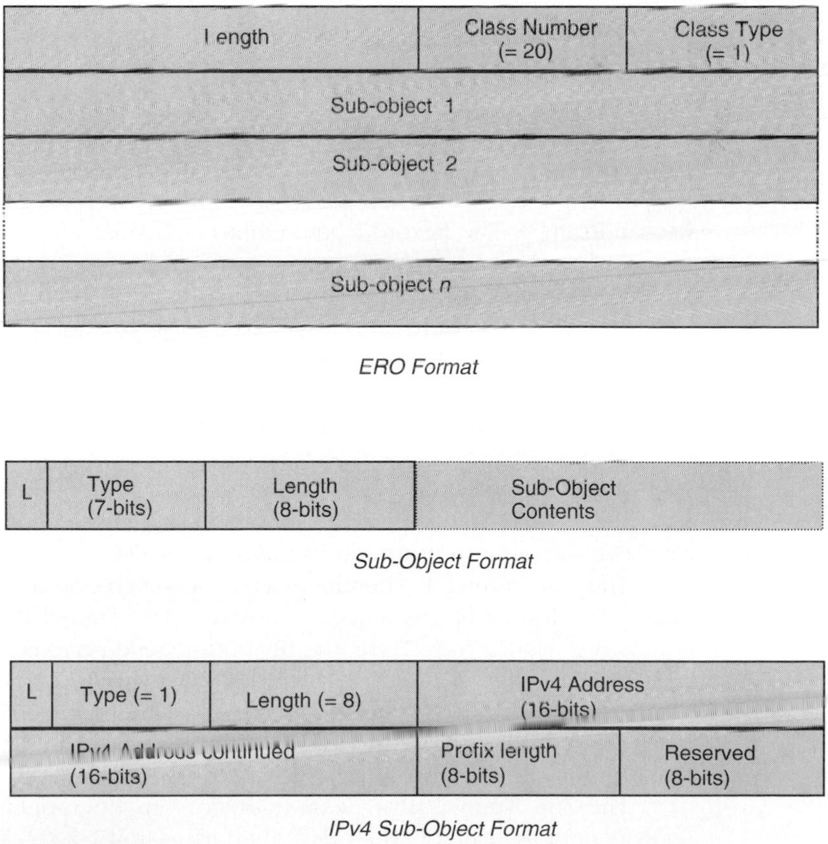

Length	Class Number (= 20)	Class Type (= 1)
Sub-object 1		
Sub-object 2		
Sub-object *n*		

ERO Format

L	Type (7-bits)	Length (8-bits)	Sub-Object Contents

Sub-Object Format

L	Type (= 1)	Length (= 8)	IPv4 Address (16-bits)
IPv4 Address continued (16-bits)		Prefix length (8-bits)	Reserved (8-bits)

IPv4 Sub-Object Format

Figure 7–23 *ERO Format Details*

Suppose a node receives a Path message with an ERO in which the node is listed in the first sub-object (a strict hop to this node from the previous node). It determines the next node to forward the message as follows:

1. The second sub-object in the ERO indicates a directly reachable neighbor: The node strips off the first sub-object and forwards the Path message to the neighbor.
2. The second sub-object indicates a remote node not directly connected: The node strips off the first sub-object and either forwards the Path message to the next hop toward the remote node as determined from its IP routing table, or computes a strict or loose explicit route to the remote node, prefixes the existing ERO with the computed explicit route, and then forwards the path message to the next node in the computed route.
3. The second sub-object indicates an AS: The node strips off the first sub-object and determines the border node in its AS or a neighboring AS (if the node itself is a border node in its AS) to forward the Path message. Once the next node is determined, the choices for forwarding are the same as in (2).

This description is a simplification of the actual procedures that may be employed in processing an ERO. More details are given in [Awduche+01b].

Record Route • The Record Route Object (RRO) is carried in Path messages. It is used to record the actual sequence of nodes (or interfaces) traversed by an LSP being established. The label assignment on various hops may also be recorded. This object provides a way to monitor the paths of LSPs, as well as to detect loops when loose explicit routing is used to set up LSPs. This object is not central to the discussion that follows, and hence we do not describe it further here. The interested readers can refer to [Awduche+01b].

LSP Tunnel Identification • LSP tunnel identification is treated separately for IPv4 and IPv6 addressing. In the following, we consider only the IPv4 case. The IPv6 formats can be found in [Awduche+01b].

The LSP tunnel is identified as a new sub-object under the session object. The format of this object (denoted as LSP Tunnel IPv4 Session object) is shown in Figure 7–24. Here, the IPv4 tunnel end point address indicates the address of the egress node (destination) at which the LSP tunnel terminates. The tunnel ID is a 16-bit number assigned by the source. The extended tunnel ID is an additional 32-bit field that can be optionally used to expand the tunnel ID field. The typical use is to place the IP address of the source here.

The LSP Tunnel IPv4 Session object can be roughly considered the equivalent of the call identifier described in section 7.2.2.2. This object can be common across multiple related LSPs, thereby providing the LSRs in the net-

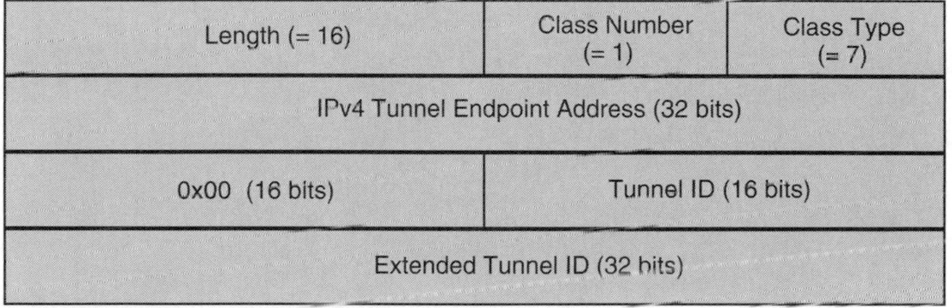

Figure 7–24 *LSP Tunnel IPv4 Session Object*

work a means to associate these LSPs. This association is useful in certain applications such as non-disruptive modification of LSP bandwidth. This is described further in [Awduche+01b].

The equivalent of the connection identifier described in section 7.2.2.2 is the LSP identifier. This identifier is carried in the Sender Template object as a sub-object. This new sub-object is called LSP Tunnel IPv4 Sender Template object, and its format is shown in Figure 7–25. The LSP identifier is a combination of the IP (v4) address of the source and a 16-bit suffix (denoted as LSP ID) assigned by this source. The same format is used to define the LSP Tunnel IPv4 Filterspec, which is sent in Resv messages to identify the specific LSP to the packet classifier function. Two LSPs between the same source and destination pair may have the same values for the LSP Tunnel IPv4 Session object (the call ID) while having distinct values for the LSP identifiers (the connection IDs).

SESSION ATTRIBUTES • The session attributes object is carried in Path messages. It describes further parameters related to the session in addition to the QoS parameters described in the Tspec. There are two formats defined for the session attributes, one of them a superset of the other. This is the format illustrated in Figure 7–26. Here, the fields have the following meaning:

Length (= 16)	Class Number (= 11)	Class Type (= 7)
IPv4 Tunnel Sender Address (32 bits)		
0x00 (16 bits)	LSP ID (16 bits)	

Figure 7–25 *LSP Tunnel IPv4 Sender Template Object*

Length (= 16)		Class Number (= 207)	Class Type (= 1)
Exclude Any (32 bits)			
Include Any (32 bits)			
Include All (32 bits)			
Setup Priority (8 bits)	Holding Priority (8 bits)	Flags (8 bits)	Name Length (8 bits)
Session Name (Variable)			

Figure 7–26 *Session Attributes Object*

- Exclude Any: This is a 32-bit field of flags, each bit indicating a specific link "color." The color parameter groups links according to some administrative criteria (e.g., all low-speed links are assigned color 1). The LSP cannot be routed over any link that has been assigned a color corresponding to a bit set to 1 in the Exclude Any field.
- Include Any: This is a 32-bit field of flags, each indicating a specific link color. The LSP should be routed only over links that have at least one of the indicated colors assigned.
- Include All: This is a 32-bit field of flags, each indicating a specific link color. The LSP should be routed only over links that have all of the indicated colors assigned.
- Setup Priority: This 8-bit field defines the priority of the LSP with respect to other LSPs when obtaining resources. Eight priority levels, from 0 to 7, are defined (with 0 being the highest priority). When establishing an LSP with set-up priority s, another LSP with holding priority $> s$ can be preempted to make room for the former.
- Holding Priority: This 8-bit field defines the priority of the LSP with respect to other LSPs in retaining resources. Eight priority levels, from 0 to 7, are defined (with 0 being the highest priority). An established LSP with a holding priority h can be preempted by another LSP with setup priority $< h$. The holding priority of an LSP should always be higher than its setup priority, that is, the holding priority value h should be less than the setup priority value s).

- Flags: This is a 8-bit vector of flags. Three flags are defined. Of these, the one that is of interest to us is the "Local Protection Desired" flag, which is activated by setting bit 1 (low order). This flag indicates that an intermediate LSR can reroute an LSP upon a failure regardless of the route specified in the original ERO. Other flags are described in [Awduche+01b].
- Name Length: This is an 8-bit field indicating the length (in bytes) of the Session Name field.
- Session Name: Character string indicating the name of the session.
- Having described these objects, it remains for us to show how these are used in establishing, maintaining, and deleting LSPs. This is our objective in the next section.

7.4.2.2 ESTABLISHING AN LSP TUNNEL

We saw that RSVP-based reservations could be established from host to host. An LSP tunnel, however, is typically created between an ingress LSR and an egress LSR within a network (recall that the application of RSVP TE is for traffic engineering). The establishment of this tunnel is typically triggered by administrative action, for example, a command from the network management system to the ingress LSR. Based on the available routing information, the required QoS and the session attributes, an ERO is first computed. This computation could be done either in the management system, for example, or by the ingress LSR. The ingress LSR then constructs a Path message addressed to the appropriate IP destination (the egress LSR). This message contains the ERO, a Label Request object, the tunnel identification, session attributes, and, optionally, the RRO. The progress of the Path message further downstream is similar to the way it happens under RSVP (section 7.4.1.3). An LSR that receives the Path message creates the local Path state. This Path state includes the received ERO, session attributes, and so on. The LSR then determines the local resource allocations for the LSP, and determines the next LSR to forward the Path message by examining and perhaps expanding the ERO (see section 7.4.2.1). It sets the RSVP Hop information (and RRO, if required) appropriately and then forwards the Path message to the next LSR. The Path message ultimately reaches the egress LSR.

The Resv message is sent by the egress LSR in response to the Path message received. The progression of this message is similar to the RSVP case (section 7.4.1.3), except that each LSR also sends the label assigned for the LSP in the Resv message. An LSR that receives the Resv message uses the label assigned by the downstream LSR and the label it has assigned to its upstream to set up its MPLS forwarding table appropriately. Furthermore, at this stage, an LSR actually commits the required local resources to the LSP. Finally, the Resv message reaches the ingress LSR and the LSP is established.

Figure 7–27 shows an example of LSP tunnel establishment in a small network of five MPLS LSRs. The LSP is established from LSR R1 to LSR R4, with a bandwidth of 500 Kbps, setup priority of 3, and holding priority of 2. Figure 7–28 shows some of the details of the process. Here, R1–R4 indicates the IP address of the respective LSRs. Furthermore, the LSRs are assumed to be connected by unnumbered point-to-point links whose interface identifiers are marked. LSR R1 computes the ERO, given by <R1, R2, R3, R4>, and each LSR is assumed to choose the local interface to reach the next LSR in the path. The messages show the contents of the significant fields. Not shown in this figure are the Path and the Resv states created at each LSR.

7.4.2.3 RSVP-TE SOFT STATE

RSVP-TE relies on the basic soft state mechanism provided by RSVP. The Path and Resv state must be refreshed periodically as described in section 7.4.1.4. Recall, however, that the LSP establishment was controlled by an explicit route. Thus, an interesting question is, how does this work with soft state refreshes? Note that in the case of RSVP, the refresh messaging adapted to route changes, that is, a Path refresh message is sent to the current next hop toward the destination. Under RSVP-TE, consider the case of an LSR A that has to send a Path refresh message to a downstream LSR B as given by the ERO. Several scenarios are possible:

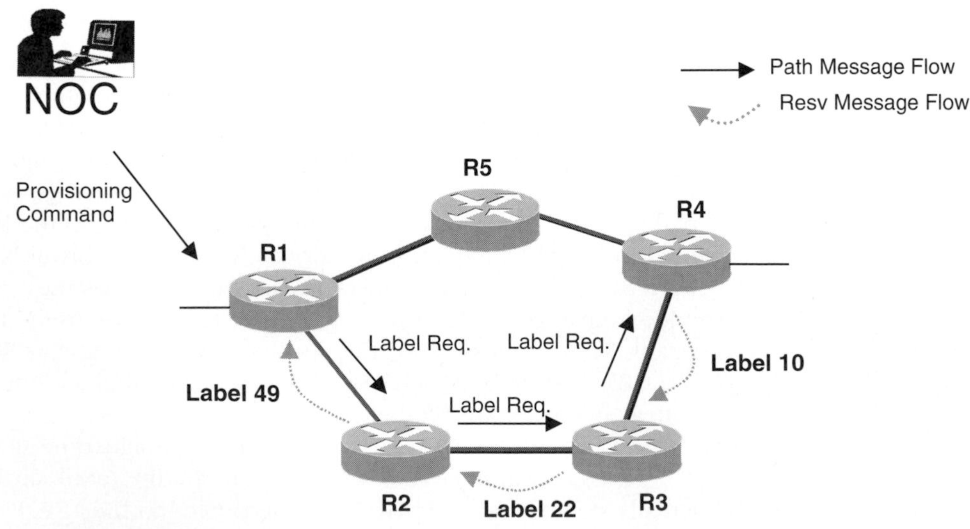

Figure 7–27 *LSP Tunnel Establishment Example*

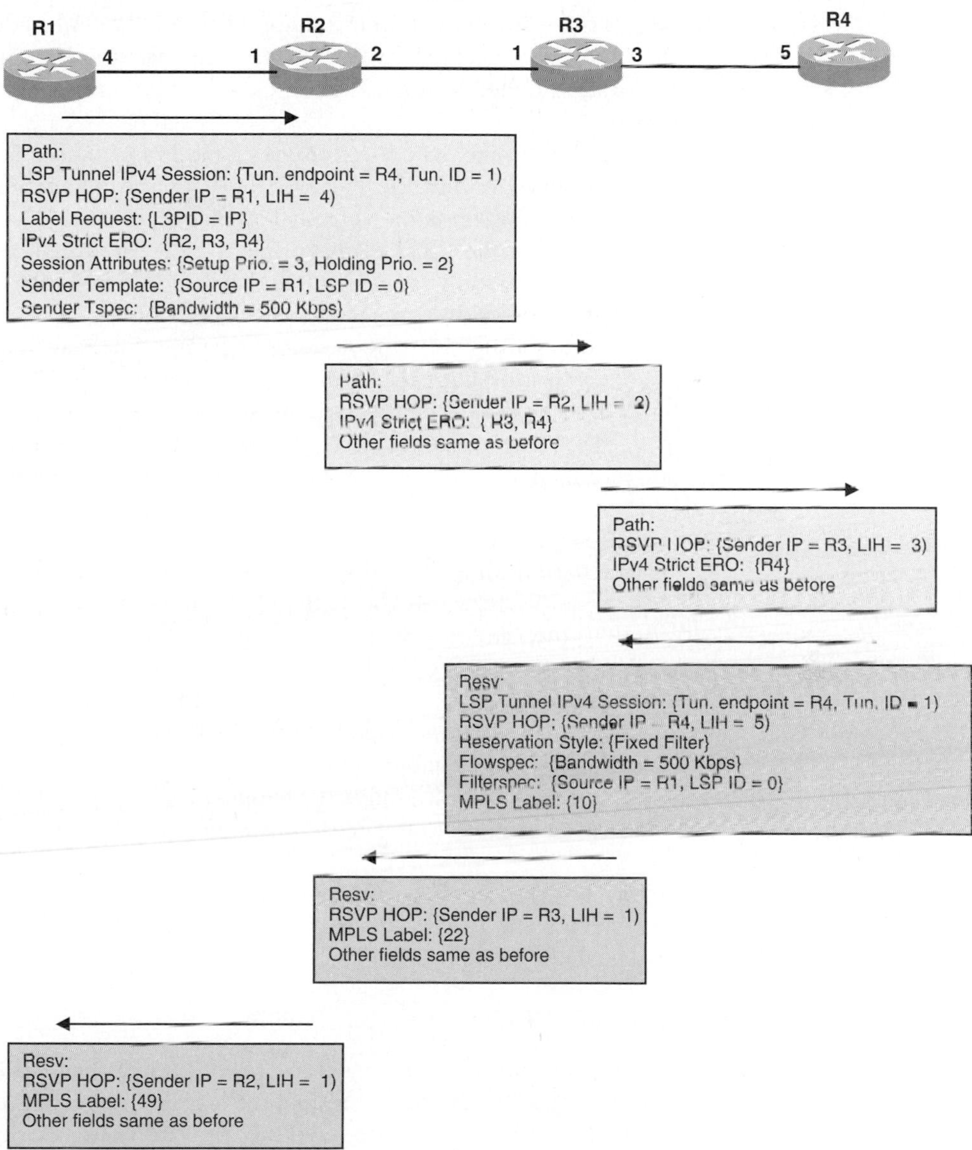
R1
R2
R3
R4
4
1
2
1
3
5
Path:
LSP Tunnel IPv4 Session: {Tun. endpoint = R4, Tun. ID = 1)
RSVP HOP: {Sender IP = R1, LIH = 4)
Label Request: {L3PID = IP}
IPv4 Strict ERO: {R2, R3, R4}
Session Attributes: {Setup Prio. = 3, Holding Prio. = 2}
Sender Template: {Source IP = R1, LSP ID = 0}
Sender Tspec: {Bandwidth = 500 Kbps}
Path:
RSVP HOP: {Sender IP = R2, LIH = 2)
IPv4 Strict ERO: { R3, R4}
Other fields same as before
Path:
RSVP HOP: {Sender IP = R3, LIH = 3)
IPv4 Strict ERO: {R4}
Other fields same as before
Resv:
LSP Tunnel IPv4 Session: {Tun. endpoint = R4, Tun. ID = 1)
RSVP HOP: {Sender IP = R4, LIH = 5)
Reservation Style: {Fixed Filter}
Flowspec: {Bandwidth = 500 Kbps}
Filterspec: {Source IP = R1, LSP ID = 0}
MPLS Label: {10}
Resv:
RSVP HOP: {Sender IP = R3, LIH = 1)
MPLS Label: {22}
Other fields same as before
Resv:
RSVP HOP: {Sender IP = R2, LIH = 1)
MPLS Label: {49}
Other fields same as before

Figure 7–28 *LSP Tunnel Establishment Example Details*

1. LSR B is the strict next hop LSR in the ERO, and LSR A has determined that B is unreachable (e.g., from available routing information or using the Hello protocol, see below): There are two possibilities here:
   (a) Local reroute: LSR A determines a route around the failure (taking into account the LSP QoS and session parameters) to LSR B. It then sends the refresh Path message along this route by prefixing the route to the original ERO. Note that this type of local rerouting cannot be used if LSR B itself fails (see Hello protocol below).
   (b) Reestablishment: LSR A sends a PathErr or ResvTear message toward the ingress LSR indicating inability to establish the LSP. The ingress, hopefully, will reestablish the LSP with a new ERO that avoids the problem segment. The LSRs in the old ERO (and not in the new ERO) will time out their Path and Resv states.
2. LSR B is a loose next hop in the ERO: In this case, the Path refresh is exactly the same as in the RSVP case when route changes occur. LSR A simply forwards the Path refresh message along the current route to the (remote) next hop LSR in the ERO.
3. LSR A stops receiving Path refresh messages: As per the RSVP soft state procedure, LSR A removes the local Path and Resv states after sending a PathTear message toward LSR B. There is no consequence if LSR B is not reachable.
4. The ingress LSR determines a change in route affecting the ERO: This case is similar to the reestablishment case in (1).

These scenarios are not spelled out in RFC 3209 [Awduche+01b]. Protocol implementers have some latitude in determining how to handle failure situations using standard messaging.

7.4.2.4 RSVP-TE HELLO PROTOCOL

RSVP-TE introduces a new RSVP message called "Hello." Each LSR sends a Hello to each of its RSVP-TE peers frequently (default is once every 3 seconds). This message serves as a keep-alive mechanism to rapidly detect node failures. An LSR considers its peer as failed if it does not receive a Hello message from the peer within a certain time period (default is 12 seconds). The details of the Hello protocol are described in [Awduche+01b].

7.4.2.5 REMOVING AN LSP TUNNEL

An LSP tunnel is removed either due to soft state time-out or by explicit action by one of the LSRs in the path. The orderly removal process consists of the ingress LSR sending a PathTear message toward the egress. The format of this message is similar to the RSVP PathTear but with the enhanced session object (with the tunnel identification). The PathTear is forwarded based on the Path state available at each LSR. An LSR receiving the PathTear removes both the Path and the Resv states, after forwarding the PathTear to the next LSR.

A ResvTear can be sent by the egress LSR or any intermediate LSR. This results in only the Resv state being removed in intermediate LSRs.

7.4.2.6 RSVP REFRESH REDUCTION

A problem with the soft state approach is the need to refresh the Path and Resv state corresponding to each LSP independently. Since RSVP messages are not transmitted reliably, the refreshing has to be done fairly frequently to both ensure that LSPs are established quickly and to improve failure response. This frequent refresh activity, multiplied by the number of LSPs, could pose a problem to LSRs. A solution to alleviate this problem is RSVP refresh reduction. This is described in IETF RFC 2961 [Berger+01]. This RFC introduces three capabilities:

1. A way to bundle messages pertaining to multiple LSPs in a single message
2. A reliable messaging mechanism between RSVP peers, and
3. A way to abbreviate refreshed information by using a short identifier

The first capability is realized by introducing a new "bundle" message that can carry multiple messages (Path, Resv, etc.) from one LSR to another. The constituent messages in a bundle may pertain to different LSPs. This message is an optimization. The second capability essentially eliminates the RSVP characteristic of unreliable message transmission between peers. This allows the refresh frequency to be reduced. The third capability eliminates the need to send entire Path or Resv message when refreshing. All these capabilities are optional, that is, an RSVP node need not support these capabilities to interact with those that do. Indeed, two RSVP peers invoke these capabilities only if both of them support the capabilities. We refer the interested reader to [Berger+01] for further investigation of the RSVP refresh reduction capabilities.

Now that we seen the essential elements of RSVP and RSVP-TE, we can next look into how these are used in the GMPLS context.

7.5 GMPLS Extensions to RSVP-TE

At a first glance, the GMPLS extensions to RSVP-TE consist of a few new objects, a new message, and associated procedures. If we look deeper, it becomes apparent that GMPLS brings significant changes to the usage of RSVP-TE. These are:

- Enforcement of the separation between the data plane and the control plane. In particular, the RSVP model where the control messaging is tied to specific data plane interfaces (see section 7.4.1.3) is eliminated.
- The dilution of the soft state model. As described in sections 7.4.1.4 and 7.4.2.3, failures or miscommunication in the control plane lead to data plane actions under RSVP and RSVP-TE. GMPLS extensions aim to ensure that control plane failure events do not affect the fate of connections whose data plane is perfectly operational. This is done by quietly moving away from the spirit of the soft state model and by instituting control plane recovery procedures.
- Emphasis on control plane recovery procedures. GMPLS extensions allow two RSVP-TE peers to coordinate the recovery of state information after a control plane failure event. During this recovery process, existing data plane connections are left intact.
- Support for bidirectional connections. RSVP-TE supports unidirectional LSPs. GMPLS extensions allow bidirectionality.
- Introduction of a remote notification mechanism. RSVP-TE messaging follows the connection path. GMPLS introduces a notification extension that allows messaging between remote nodes along routes that are not tied to the connection path.

Let us now examine the GMPLS extensions themselves. As before, we look at the new objects and messages introduced, and then the procedures for connection establishment, maintenance, and removal. From here on, we use the term "GMPLS RSVP-TE" to denote GMPLS extensions to RSVP-TE. Furthermore, we use the term "connection" and "network element (NE)" to denote what are called LSPs and LSRs, respectively, in GMPLS RSVP-TE. Our usage corresponds to the terminology in use in optical networking.

7.5.1 GMPLS RSVP-TE Objects

7.5.1.1 GENERALIZED LABEL REQUEST

This object is carried in the Path message, and it replaces the label request object (section 7.4.2.1). This object carries the following connection parameters, and its format is depicted in Figure 7–29:

1. LSP encoding type: Indicates the type of connection, for instance, SONET/SDH, PDH, etc.
2. Switching type: This information indicates the type of switching (e.g., packet, TDM, fiber, etc.) that needs to be performed at each interface that the connection is switched through.

Length (= 8)		Class Number (= 19)	Class Type (= 4)
LSP Encoding Type (8 bits)	Switching Type (8 bits)	G-PID (16 bits)	

Figure 7–29 *Format of the Generalized Label Request Object*

3. Generalized Protocol ID (G-PID): The type of payload being carried in the connection (e.g., packet over SONET).

Additional information fields pertaining to the connection are carried in the existing RSVP-TE objects. These are:

4. Source and destination end point identification: These are either IPv4 or IPv6 addresses.
5. Bandwidth: This is the bandwidth required by the connection. A set of discrete values, covering the range from DS-0 to OC-768/STM-256, have been defined using the IEEE 32-bit floating point format.

The source address information is carried in the Sender Template object, the destination address is carried in the Session object, and the bandwidth is carried in the Tspec object. In addition, when a SONET/SDH connection is established, the related traffic parameters are encoded as described in section 7.3.3. The traffic parameters are carried in the new SONET/SDH Sender Tspec and SONET/SDH Flowspec objects [Mannie+03a].

7.5.1.2 GENERALIZED LABEL

Different label types defined under GMPLS were described in section 7.3.2. Under GMPLS RSVP-TE, the Generalized Label object replaces the Label object (section 7.4.2.1) in the Resv message. The format of this object is shown in Figure 7–30. The Label field can contain various label types, including the MPLS label (Figure 7–22) and the SONET/SDH label (Figure 7–8).

7.5.1.3 SUGGESTED LABEL

Suggested Label is carried in the Path message. As described in the example of Figure 7–7, the downstream NE assigns the label for the source-to-destination direction of the connection. The Suggested Label feature allows an NE to "suggest" to its immediate downstream neighbor the generalized label to be returned during the response phase. The rationale given for introducing the suggested label feature is as follows. Typically, during the response phase, an NE receives a label from its downstream neighbor, sets up its cross-connect based on the received value (see Figure 7–7), and then passes on its own label

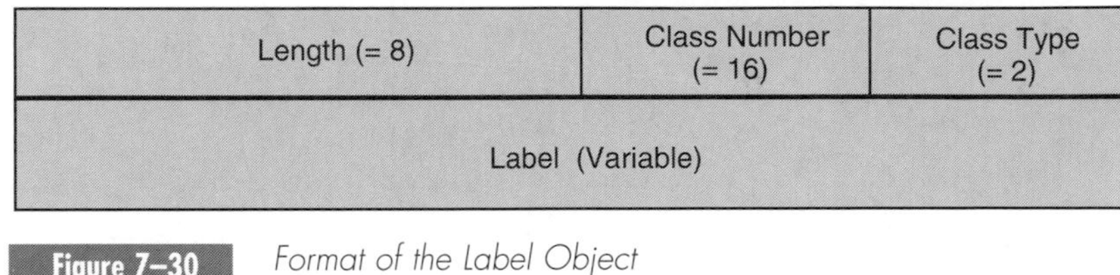

Figure 7–30 *Format of the Label Object*

assignment to its upstream neighbor. With certain all-optical fabrics, establishing a cross-connect might take several tens of milliseconds thus delaying connection provisioning. If an NE can choose a label and make the cross-connect during the request phase, it can eliminate the delay during the response phase.

A suggested label has the same format as the generalized label. Furthermore, a downstream NE need not accept a suggested label, that is, it may return a different label in the response phase. In this case, the upstream NE may have to reestablish the cross-connect. Finally, given that connection provisioning does not have pressing time constraints like protection switching, the value of suggested label during provisioning is rather dubious. It may, however, be of use when connections are dynamically reprovisioned after failures.

7.5.1.4 UPSTREAM LABEL

Upstream Label is carried in the Path message. This label is present if a bidirectional connection is being provisioned. As described before, the downstream NE assigns the label for the forward (source to destination) direction of the connection during the response phase of provisioning (Figure 7–7). This is carried as a generalized label in the Resv message. An upstream label, on the other hand, indicates the label selected by the upstream for the reverse (destination to source) direction of the connection. The upstream label has the same format as the generalized label. Clearly, the specific type of label must match for the two directions of the connection. Furthermore, the parameters have to be the same for both directions of the connection.

7.5.1.5 LABEL SET

Label Set is carried in the Path message. It is used by an upstream NE to control the selection of labels by downstream NEs. That is, an NE indicates the set of labels that are acceptable to it in the request message. A downstream NE must then select a label from this set. For instance, consider the case of provisioning a wavelength connection through an all-optical network where the switches cannot perform wavelength conversion. Here, the source NE would indicate a set of wavelengths it has available for the connection in the Label Set object. As the request message traverses toward the destination, each intermediate NE would look at the received label set, consider the wavelengths locally available, potentially decrease the set of available labels by modifying the Label Set object, and forward the object to its downstream neighbor. When the request reaches the destination NE, it can choose one of the permitted labels (wavelengths) for the connection and indicate this in the response message. The same label is then propagated to the source NE.

The format of the label set object is given in Figure 7–31. Here, the "Action" field indicates the following:

- Action = 0 (Inclusive list): Explicitly indicates each label included in the set. An NE can choose only a label that is listed.
- Action = 1 (Exclusive list): Explicitly indicates each label excluded from consideration. An NE can choose any label *except* those listed.
- Action = 2 (Inclusive range): Indicates a range of labels included in the set. An NE can choose only a label included in the range. The label set object thus contains two labels, one each for the start and the end of the range.
- Action = 3 (Exclusive range): Indicates a range of labels excluded in the set. An NE cannot choose a label included in the range. The label set object thus contains two labels, one each for the start and the end of the range.

The "Label Type" field indicates the type of label.

7.5.1.6 ACCEPTABLE LABEL SET

Acceptable Label Set is carried in certain PathErr, ResvErr, and Notification (see below) messages. When an NE cannot accept a given label, it may generate an error message with the set of acceptable labels. The Acceptable Label Set object has the same format as the Label Set object.

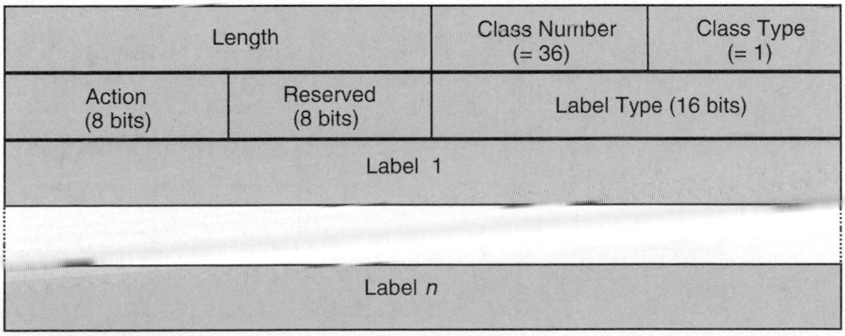

Length		Class Number (= 36)	Class Type (= 1)
Action (8 bits)	Reserved (8 bits)	Label Type (16 bits)	
Label 1			
Label *n*			

Figure 7–31 *Format of the Label Set Object*

7.5.1.7 PROTECTION INFORMATION

Protection Information is carried in the Path message. This object indicates the protection desired for the connection *on each link* in the connection path. This object may be present when provisioning both the working and the protection paths of an end-to-end path-protected connection. The format of the Protection Information object is illustrated in Figure 7–32. The following fields are present:

- Secondary (S) Bit: This 1-bit field indicates whether the connection being provisioned is primary (working, S = 0) or secondary (protection, S = 1). The protection mode request that follows is applicable only to primary connections.
- Link Flags: This 6-bit field is a vector of flags. A bit that is set indicates that a specific protection mode is requested. More than one bit may be set if more than one protection mode is acceptable. The selection of the specific protection mode is then a local decision at each NE.
    - Bit 5 (high order): Enhanced protection.
      This indicates that better protection than 1 + 1 is desired. Typically, this bit would be set to request 4-fiber BLSR/MS-SPRING-type protection.
    - Bit 4: 1 + 1
      This indicates that 1 + 1 protection is desired.
    - Bit 3: 1:1
      This indicates that 1:1 protection is desired.
    - Bit 2: Shared
      This indicates that 1:N or M:N protection is desired.
    - Bit 1: Unprotected
      This indicates that the connection should not be protected on each link.
    - Bit 0: Extra traffic
      This indicates that the connection may be routed as extra traffic on each link, that is, it may be preempted to protect other connections.

Clearly, only the Unprotected mode can be requested for secondary connections (when S = 1). That is, the rest of the protection modes are not

Length (= 8)		Class Number (= 37)	Class Type (= 1)
S	Reserved (25 bits)		Flags (6 bits)

Figure 7–32 *Format of the Protection Information Object*

applicable to a secondary (protection) connection that provides end-to-end path protection to a primary (working) connection.

7.5.1.8 ADMINISTRATIVE STATUS

The administrative status object is used in signaling messages to indicate that a connection is being administratively "downed," deleted, or being put in a test mode. GMPLS signaling provides a way to signal these administrative actions. This ensures that NEs in the connection path will not mistake administrative actions for failure events and trigger protection actions. The format of the administrative status object is illustrated in Figure 7–33. The following fields are present:

- Reflect (R): This bit indicates that the received administrative status object must be reflected back by the receiving node in an appropriate message. The usage of this bit will become clear when we look at connection deletion in section 7.5.4.
- Testing (T): This bit indicates that the connection is being set in the testing mode. The actions to be taken at each node receiving the administrative status object with the T bit set is not specified.
- Administratively Down (A): This bit indicates that the connection is being taken down administratively.
- Deletion in progress (D): This bit indicates that the connection is being deleted. The usage of the D bit during connection deletion is described in section 7.5.4.

7.5.1.9 INTERFACE IDENTIFICATION

Under MPLS-TE, signaling messages are sent over the same links that data flows. Thus, the labels that are assigned are specific to the interfaces over which signaling messages are received. Under GMPLS, the control channels over which signaling messages are sent may be distinct from the data links. For instance, there could be an out-of-band control link (e.g., Ethernet) connecting two optical switches. Signaling messages pertaining to connection provisioning over all the data links may be sent over this out-of-band link.

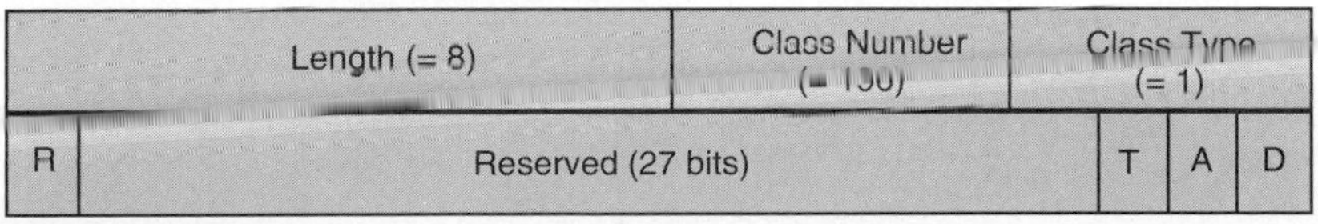

<table>
<tr><td colspan="3">Length (= 8)</td><td>Class Number (= 196)</td><td colspan="3">Class Type (= 1)</td></tr>
<tr><td>R</td><td colspan="3">Reserved (27 bits)</td><td>T</td><td>A</td><td>D</td></tr>
</table>

Figure 7–33 *Format of the Administrative Status Object*

Thus, it must be possible in signaling messages to explicitly identify the data link on which labels are being assigned. The interface identification object does this.

Generally, under GMPLS, interfaces can have different types of addressing, as shown in Figure 7–34.[8] This figure depicts two adjacent NEs with their IP addresses (chosen arbitrarily for this example). Four types of links are shown:

- A numbered link bundle (also called a "TE link," see Chapter 10): This bundled link consists of multiple component links. The bundled link itself has an IP address at each end, shown in the figure. The component links are identified by locally distinct identifiers at each end.
- An unnumbered link bundle: Same as above, except that the link bundle does not have an IP address assigned at either end. Instead, a locally distinct identifier is used at either end to identify the bundle.
- A numbered individual link: This is a point-to-point link with an IP address assigned at each end.
- An unnumbered individual link: This is a point-to-point link with a locally distinct identifier at each end.

The bundling concept is used to reduce the routing overhead, as discussed in Chapter 10. During signaling, however, the precise link for label allocation must be identified even if it is part of a bundled link. The inter-

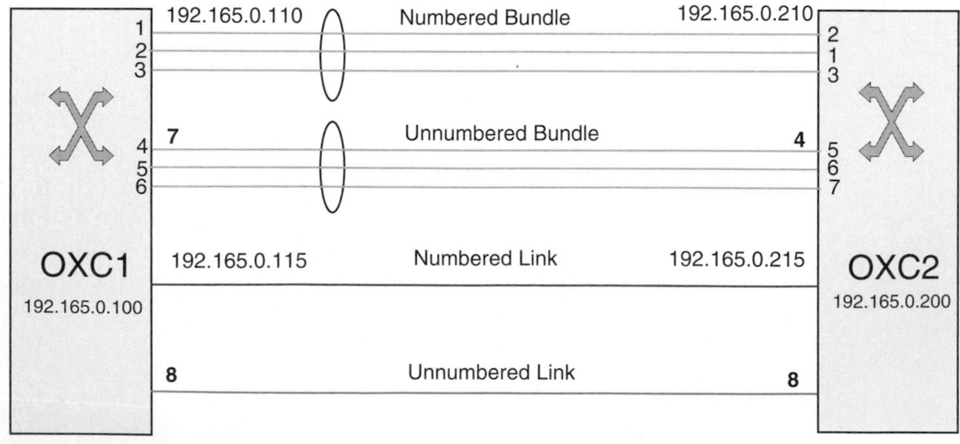

Figure 7–34 *Different Interface Addressing Schemes*

[8]Not all of these addressing modes may be used in practice.

face identification object (called the IPv4 IF_ID_RSVP_HOP object) serves this purpose. This object is used in place of the RSVP Hop object in GMPLS RSVP-TE. The format of this object is shown in Figure 7–35. To understand how this object is used, note that in Figure 7–34, each interface terminating a link (whether individual or component link) has a distinct identifier at an NE. This is the identifier signaled using the interface identification object.

With this object, both the control plane address from which the GMPLS RSVP-TE message is sent, and the data plane component link identifier are captured. The former is captured in the IPv4 previous/next hop address and the LIH fields as in the case of regular RSVP-TE. The latter is captured as follows. If the data link is numbered, the IPv4 address of the link is used as

Length	Class Number (= 3)	Class Type (= 3)
IPv4 Next/Previous Hop Address (32 bits)		
Logical Interface Handle		
TLVs (Variable)		

Interface Identification Object Format (IPv4 IF_ID_RSVP_HOP)

Type (= 1, IPv4) (16 bits)	Length (= 8) (16 bits)
Value (= IPv4 address) (32 bits)	

TLV Format for Numbered Links

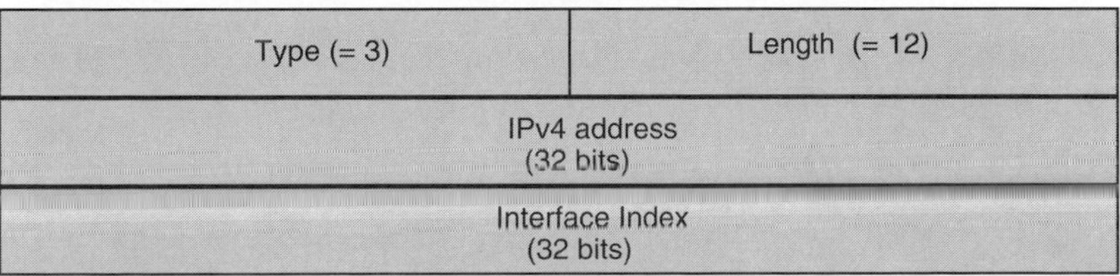

TLV Format for Unnumbered Links

Figure 7–35 Interface Identification

shown in the first TLV. If the data link is unnumbered, then the IPv4 address of the NE and the distinct interface identifier are captured as shown in the second TLV. This usage is further described in section 7.5.3.

7.5.1.10 NOTIFICATION REQUEST

The Notification Request object may be present in Path messages. This object indicates the IP address to which failure-related notifications (see below) should be sent. Each NE that processes the Path message may note this information for notification purposes.

7.5.2 The Notify Message

The Notify message is a new message introduced under GMPLS RSVP-TE. It provides a mechanism for an NE to inform a remote NE (usually the ingress or the egress) about an event related to the connection (usually a failure event). An NE generates a Notify message if it had received a Notify Request object in the Path message. The notify message is different from PathErr and ResvErr in that it can be targeted to a node other than the immediate upstream or downstream neighbor and routed independently of the connection path. The notify message does not replace these error messages. This message contains an error code and a Message ID object.

The receipt of the Notify message is acknowledged by the receiver with an Ack message, which is a Notify message with a Message ID Ack object.

Now that we have examined all the objects, and the new message, defined under GMPLS RSVP-TE, it just remains to be seen how these objects are used in signaling. This is described next.

7.5.3 Connection Establishment under GMPLS RSVP-TE

Having gone through the LSP tunnel establishment procedure under RSVP-TE, it should not be hard to guess as to how connection provisioning would work under GMPLS RSVP-TE. In essence, the Path and Resv messages are used for the request and response phase of provisioning (illustrated in Figure 7–7). There are some differences, however, between the way RSVP-TE is used for LSP establishment in MPLS networks and GMPLS RSVP-TE is used to provision connections in optical networks. Specifically,

- Whereas RSVP-TE signaling occurs over the same links on which the corresponding LSP is established, a separate signaling control link is required between GMPLS RSVP-TE peers. This control link is realized as part of the Data Communication Network (DCN). The DCN could be implemented in-band, for example, using SONET/SDH overhead bytes (see Chapter 6), or it could be an out-of-band network (e.g., an IP network).

- When using GMPLS RSVP-TE, the reliable messaging mechanism described in section 7.4.2.6 is typically used.
- Control plane restart procedures (see section 7.5.5) are implemented when using GMPLS RSVP-TE.

The connection establishment procedure is best described with the aid of an example. Figures 7–36a and 7–36b expand the provisioning example in Figure 7–7 with the details of the Path and Resv messages, respectively. Consider Figure 7–36a first. Here, a network of four NEs is shown. Each NE has an IP address, and other than one of the links between NEs A and B, all other links are unnumbered. Furthermore, all the links are assumed to be OC-48 links. In addition to the data links, the control link between the NEs are shown as dotted lines. Furthermore, each control link interface is identified by the IP address of the corresponding NE and an interface id (LIH) shown next to it.

NE A receives a provisioning trigger to establish a bidirectional STS-48c connection between its interface 1 (with IP address 192.165.1.85) and NE D (IP address = 192.165.4.30), interface 2 (IP address = 192.165.4.45). Based on available routing information, NE A computes an explicit route passing through NEs B, C, and D. In this case, each NE would be responsible for picking the actual link to the next NE when the connection is provisioned.

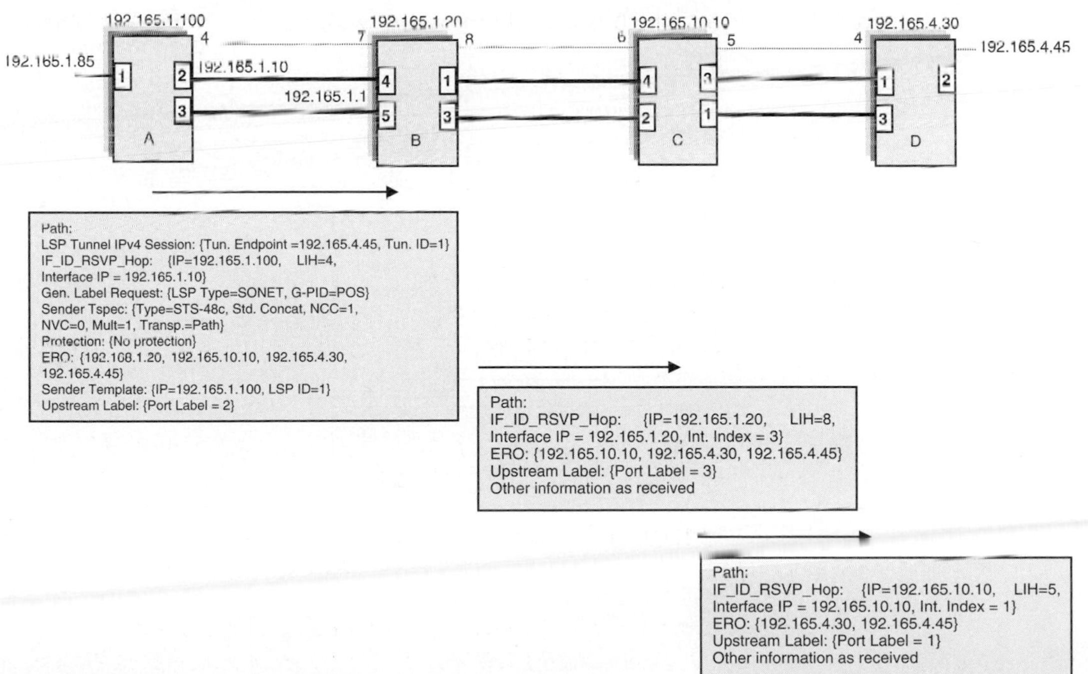

Figure 7–36a *Path Message Flow under GMPLS RSVP-TE*

The Path message generated by NE A is shown. This message has the LSP Tunnel IPv4 Session object set to indicate the remote destination and the locally assigned tunnel ID. The ERO lists the IP address of NEs in the path. The Interface identification object (IF_ID_RSVP_HOP) indicates both the control channel id (IP address and LIH) and the data link ID (IP address for numbered, and IP address plus interface index for unnumbered links). The Generalized Label object lists the type of LSP as SONET and the G-PID as Packet over SONET (POS). The SONET traffic parameters are given in the Sender Tspec. The Sender Template lists the IP address of NE A and the locally assigned LSP ID. Finally, the Upstream Label object indicates the label selected for the D to A direction of the connection. Since the links are OC-48, they can each accommodate only one STS-48c connection and hence, the label type is indicated as port label rather than SONET label.

As the Path message progresses, each intermediate NE creates its Path state, and propagates the Path message to the next NE after modifying the ERO, the upstream label information, and the interface identification information. The message finally reaches NE D, which notices that the destination is local and thus terminates the message.

The corresponding Resv message flow is shown in Figure 7–36b. The Resv message generated by D contains the (port) label for the connection segment from C to D. The Flowspec information essentially reflects the traffic parameters

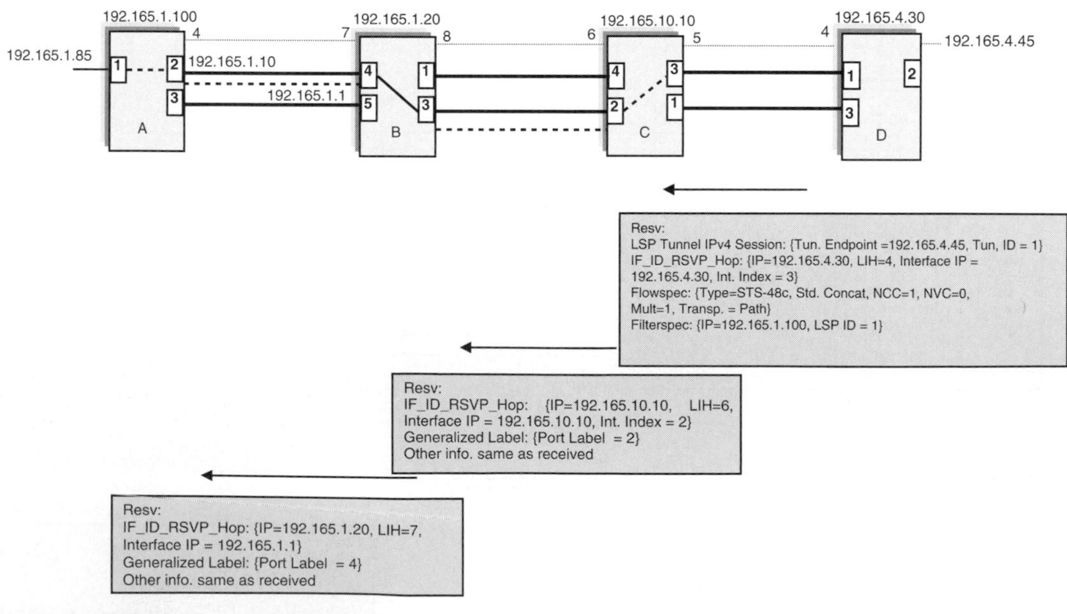

Figure 7–36b *Resv Message Flow under GMPLS RSVP-TE*

received in the Tspec. The progression of the Resv message is shown in the figure. As each NE processes the Resv message, it sets the appropriate cross-connects to establish the two directions of the connection. Connection provisioning is completed when A receives the Resv message and sets the appropriate cross-connects. The end-to-end connection is shown in the figure using dotted lines.

Not shown in Figure 7–36 is the reliable delivery of Path and Resv messages. This option was described in section 7.4.2.6, and its use is typical in optical network. The usage of this option means that the soft state refreshes can be infrequent. The soft state mechanism is not entirely eliminated (it is part of the RSVP definition), but the time period between refreshes is typically set to a high value. Disruptions in the connection path are typically determined by built-in SONET/SDH mechanisms, and thus a high refresh timer value does not affect the responsiveness of GMPLS RSVP-TE to react to connection failures.

7.5.4 Connection Deletion under GMPLS RSVP-TE

Under RSVP-TE, a source deletes an LSP tunnel by sending a PathTear. As the PathTear progresses, intermediate LSRs simply remove their Path and Resv states. The same procedure cannot be used in an optical network. As soon as an upstream NE deletes its state (and removes the cross-connect), downstream NEs may detect a connection failure and resort to protection action or send out unnecessary alarms. Thus, GMPLS RSVP-TE introduces extra phases in connection deletion such that NEs along the connection path are aware of a deletion in progress before the actual deletion occurs. The Administrative Status object (Figure 7–33) is used in this procedure.

Let us consider the connection that was set up earlier in the example depicted in Figure 7–36. The message sequence for the deletion of this connection when initiated by the source (NE A) is shown in Figure 7–37a. Here, NE A first sends a Path message to initiate deletion. This message is similar to the periodic Path messages sent for the connection except that it has the Administrative Status object with the R and D bits set to 1. As this message progresses along the connection path, each intermediate NE notes that the connection is in the process of being deleted (thus, they will not initiate protection actions if they observe faults along the connection path). When the destination (NE D) receives the Path message, it generates a Resv in response. Since the R bit was set in the received Administrative Status object, NE D *reflects* the object back in the Resv message with R bit set to 0 and D bit set to 1 (see section 7.5.1.8). When NE A receives the Resv message with the Administrative Status object, it sends a usual PathTear message. As this message progresses along the connection path, the NEs en route remove the Path and Resv state associated with the connection.

The message sequence when deletion is invoked by the destination (NE D) is shown in Figure 7–37b. Here, the NE D first sends a Resv message with the Administrative Status object. The R and D bits in this object are set to 1.

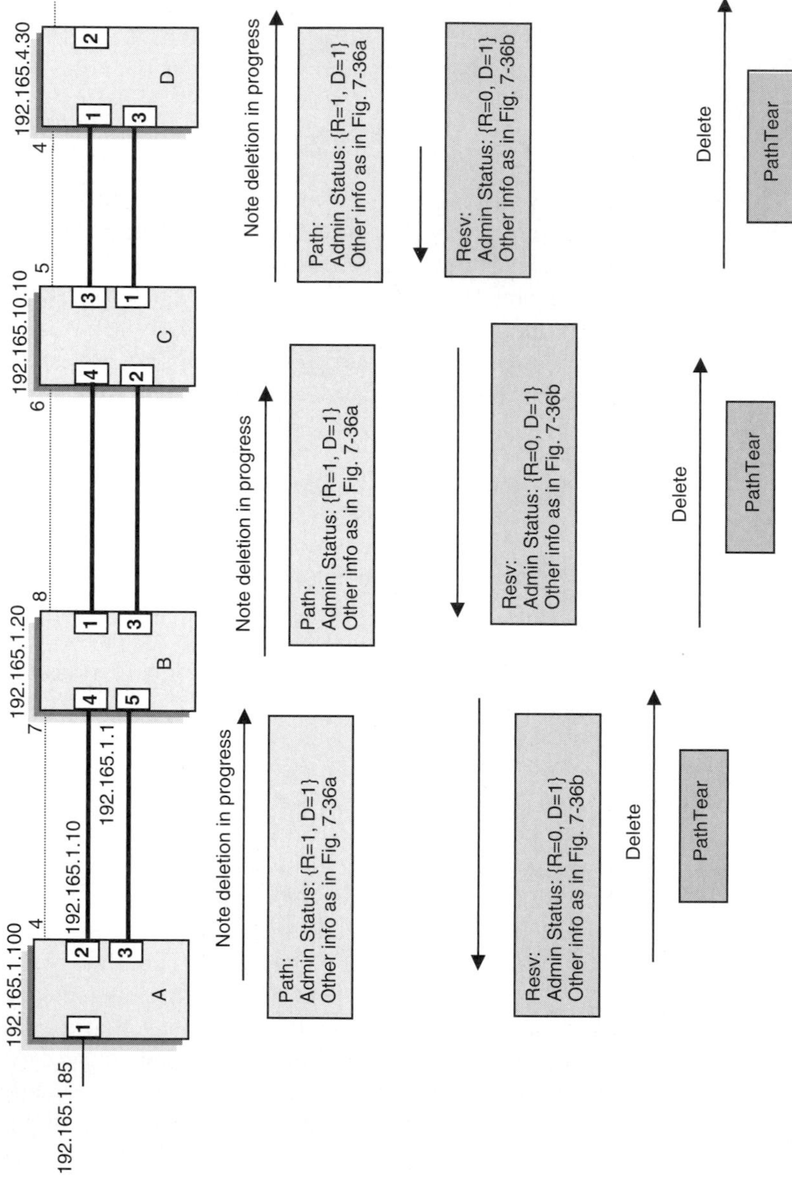

Figure 7–37a *Delection Initiated by the Source*

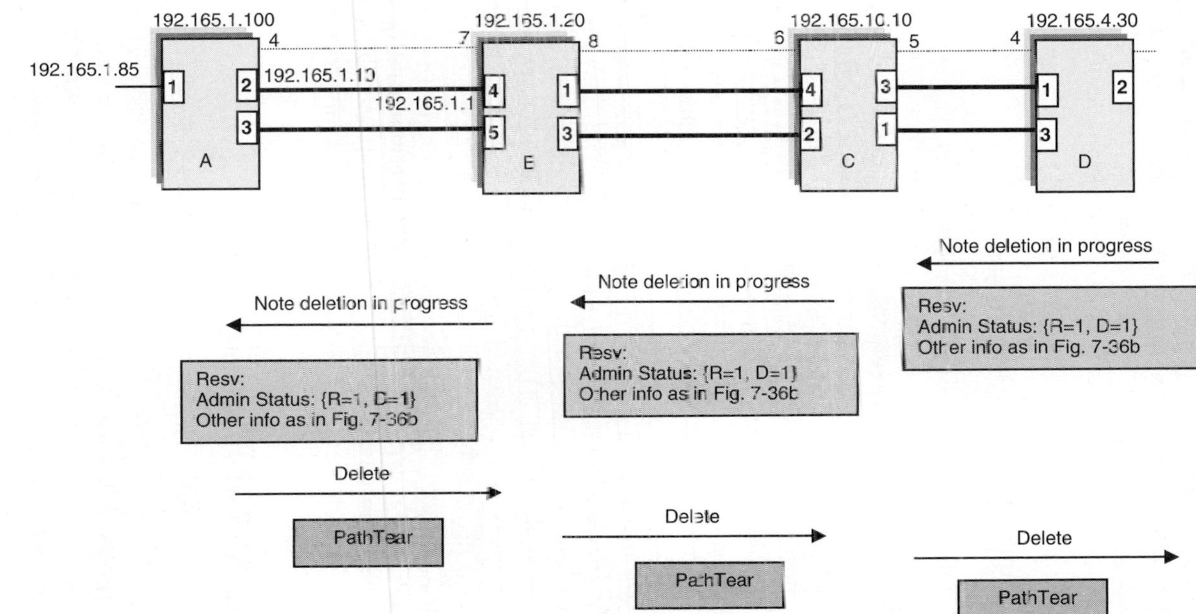

Figure 7–37b *Delection Initiated by the Destinction*

This message is propagated toward the source (NE A), and each intermediate NE notes that the connection is about to be deleted. When NE A receives the message, it generates a PathTear as before.

As before, reliable messaging is not shown in Figure 7–37 to simplify the description.

7.5.5 GMPLS RSVP-TE Restart Procedures

A result of the separation of the control and data planes is that failures in the control plane do not imply failures in the data plane. Consider Figure 7–36 again. The control link between NEs is shown as a dotted line. As mentioned before, this link could be a separate out-of-band link or an in-band control channel. In either case, a failure in the control link or the failure of the signaling software process does not imply that any of the previously established data plane connections have been affected. Thus, under GMPLS RSVP-TE, data connections are not removed when control communication is disrupted (whereas under RSVP-TE, the nonreceipt of Path refresh messages will lead to the removal of Path and Resv state at an LSR). Instead, GMPLS RSVP-TE introduces control plane restart procedures. That is, a node that loses the control link to another will attempt to synchronize its Path and Resv state when the control link is reestablished. Meanwhile, connections may themselves be deleted manually or fail. The synchronization process aims to assure that RSVP-TE peers have a consistent view of the connections when they recover from control plane failures.

Thus, we note that deletion of connections in optical networks using GMPLS RSVP-TE is typically the result of an administrative action or a data plane failure. Temporary disruptions in control plane communication do not lead to such deletion. The control plane restart procedures are further described in [Berger03b].

7.5.6 GMPLS RSVP-TE Signaling at the UNI and the NNI

So far, our discussion has been on using GMPLS RSVP-TE as an end-to-end signaling protocol in a network where all the NEs run the protocol. Now consider Figure 7–4, where the UNI and the NNI are shown. One of the main features of the model shown in Figure 7–4 is that signaling at the UNI is independent of signaling within the network. Therefore, when GMPLS RSVP-TE is used for signaling at the UNI, it is possible that a different signaling protocol (or management-system-based provisioning) is used within the network. Also, in the model shown in Figure 7–4, domains are treated like black boxes, that is, one cannot assume that specific signaling protocols are supported for provisioning within a domain. Thus, signaling across the E-NNI is independent of the signaling used within domains.

These assumptions require modifications to GMPLS RSVP-TE if this protocol were to be used for UNI and NNI signaling. Specifically, note that RSVP-TE signaling session destination is the actual end point of the connection being provisioned. In the case of UNI signaling, the GMPLS RSVP-TE session from the source client has to be terminated at the ingress NE, and another session has to be run between the egress NE and the destination node. The continuity of the information transfer must be ensured by the provisioning mechanism used within the network. In addition, UNI signaling requires that certain UNI-specific connection parameters must be carried in signaling messages. The connection model and details can be found in the UNI signaling specifications from the Optical Interworking Forum (OIF) [OIF01].

Now, note that E-NNI signaling is part of provisioning a connection within a network. Thus, provisioning-oriented signaling originates from an ingress node and terminates in an egress node as we have discussed so far. E-NNI signaling occurs where the connection crosses the boundary between domains. If the provisioning of the connection segment within a domain uses a different signaling protocol (or management-system-based provisioning), a problem similar to UNI signaling may arise. This is the case if the signaling controllers are present in border nodes of domains. In this case, the end-to-end signaling has to be "patched up" within domains. The details of E-NNI signaling using GMPLS RSVP-TE can be found in [ITU-T03c].

We have so far focused on the GMPLS RSVP-TE and its precursors. The ATM P-NNI signaling protocol has been adapted for optical network signaling, and it has been successfully deployed. This protocol is described next.

7.6 P-NNI Signaling Adaptations for Optical Networks

The P-NNI hierarchy, addressing, and peer group identification were discussed in Chapter 5. In the following, we look at P-NNI signaling features and their adaptation for signaling in optical networks. The peer group hierarchy depicted in Figure 5-15 is useful for the discussion below and hence it is reproduced as Figure 7–38.

7.6.1 P-NNI Signaling Communication

The signaling communication protocol model under P-NNI is shown in Figure 7-39. Here, the P-NNI protocol entities in peer nodes utilize a signaling ATM adaptation layer (SAAL) which consists of the following:

- A Service Specific Coordination Function (SSCF) specified in ITU-T recommendation Q.2130. This function maps the services of the lower layer, the Service Specific Connection Oriented Protocol (SSCOP), to the requirements of the P-NNI signaling procedures.

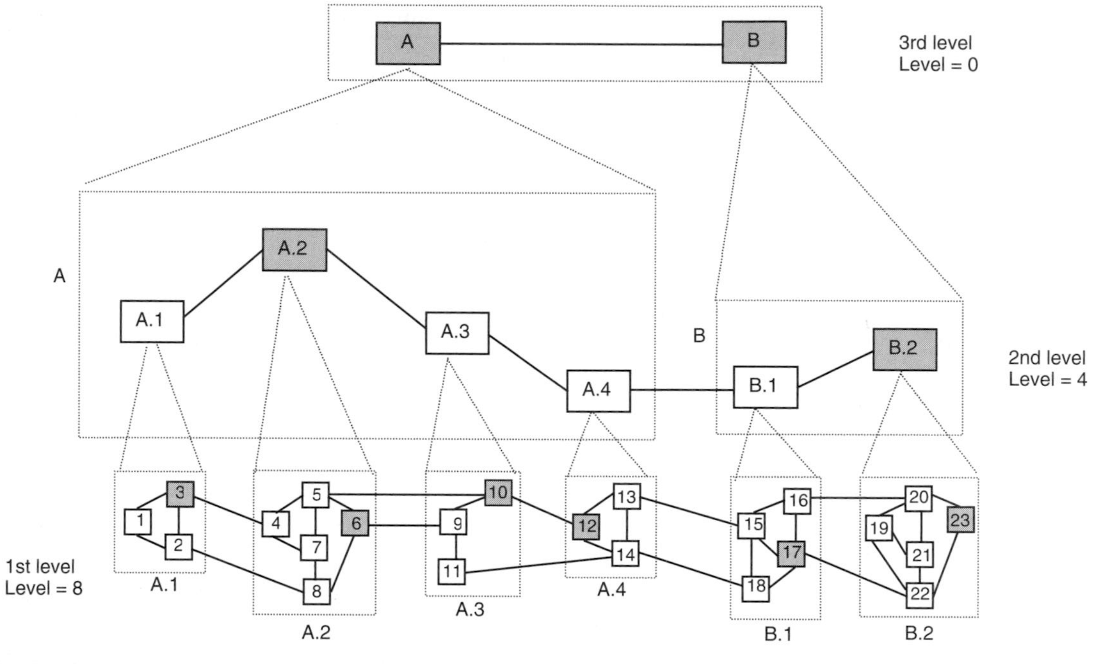

Figure 7–38 *P-NNI Hierarchy*

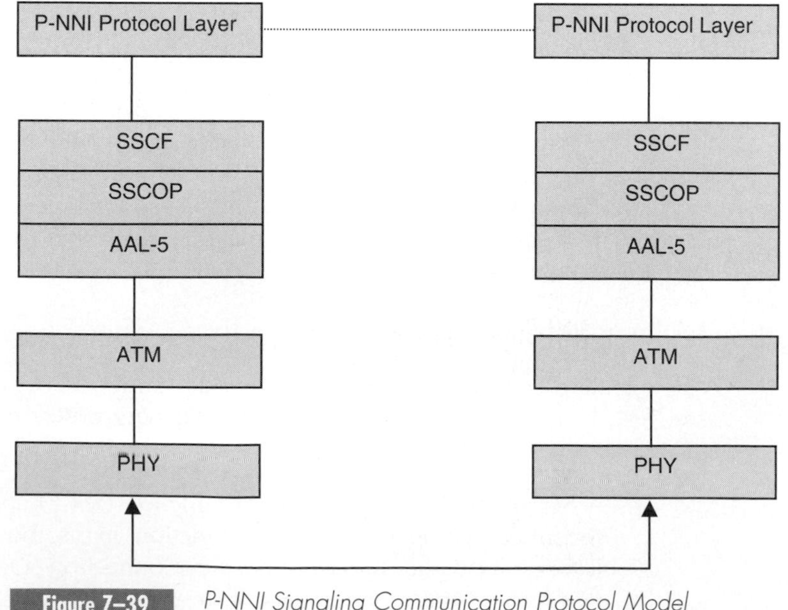

Figure 7–39 *P-NNI Signaling Communication Protocol Model*

- SSCOP, which is specified in ITU-T recommendation Q.2110. This protocol provides a reliable delivery service between two (SSCOP) peer entities.
- The ATM Adaptation Layer Type 5 (AAL-5) functions as specified in ITU-T recommendation I.363. This function provides segmentation and reassembly of signaling protocol data units.

In short, P-NNI signaling utilizes a reliable transport protocol between signaling peers, over a physical or logical link. This is in contrast to RSVP-TE reliable messaging, which uses an underlying unreliable messaging procedure with protocol additions for reliability.

7.6.2 The Designated Transit List

The Designated Transit List (DTL) is the equivalent of the ERO in RSVP-TE (see section 7.4.2.1). The DTL indicates the route for a connection being provisioned within a single peer group. A sequence of DTLs are used to indicate the end-to-end route. The DTL is encoded as a list of nodes and (optionally) links to be visited, physical or logical, with a pointer indicating the next entity in the route. The contents of the DTL information element are indicated in Figure 7–40a. Here, the Current Transit Pointer field indicates the beginning of the next element to be processed in the list. The port identifier is set to 0 if only a node identifier is specified as the next element.

Figure 7–40b shows the complete sequence of DTLs for a connection being provisioned from node 1 to node 23 in Figure 7–38 (also see Figure 5–16). When processing the connection setup, the sequence of DTLs is treated as a stack, the topmost DTL in the stack indicating the route in the first level peer group, the next DTL below that indicating the route in the second-level peer group, and so on. In this example, the DTLs consist only of logical nodes (port identifier set to 0).

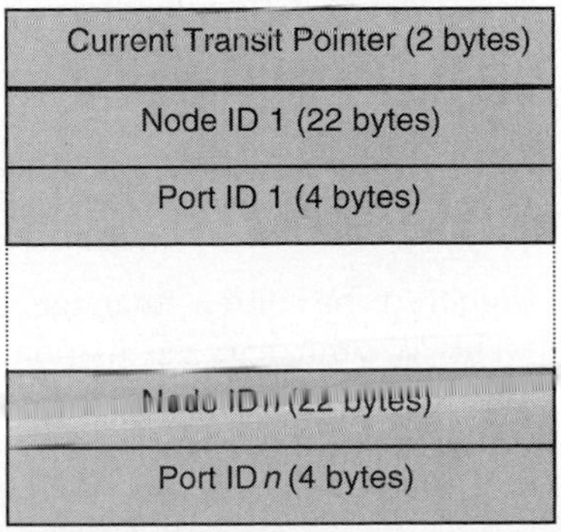

Current Transit Pointer (2 bytes)
Node ID 1 (22 bytes)
Port ID 1 (4 bytes)
Node ID *n* (22 bytes)
Port ID *n* (4 bytes)

Figure 7–40a *DTL Contents*

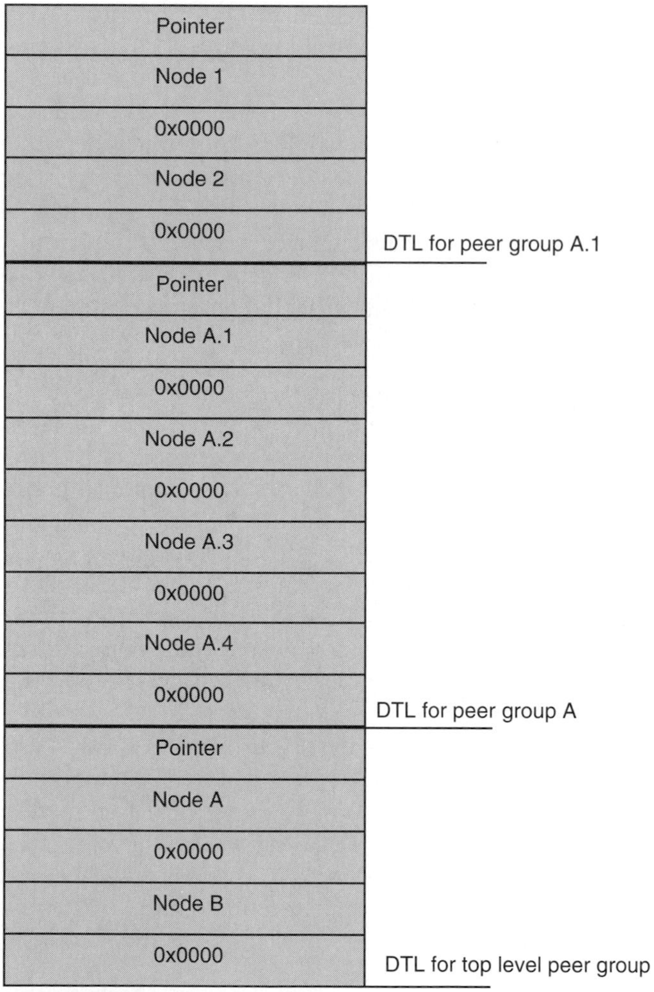

Pointer
Node 1
0x0000
Node 2
0x0000
Pointer
Node A.1
0x0000
Node A.2
0x0000
Node A.3
0x0000
Node A.4
0x0000
Pointer
Node A
0x0000
Node B
0x0000

Figure 7–40b *DTL Stack for the Route from Node 1 to 23*

7.6.3 Connection Establishment and Deletion

Connection establishment is triggered by either management action or a request received over the UNI. This is similar to the manner in which provisioning triggers are received under RSVP-TE. Once the trigger is received, the ingress node computes a route to the destination and initiates P-NNI signaling to establish the connection. This is also similar to the RSVP-TE connection provisioning case described earlier. To look at more details, we can use the network shown in Figure 7–38. Suppose a connection is to be provisioned from node 1 to node 23. The provisioning request contains the connection attributes. Node 1 then computes a route for the connection and constructs a sequence of DTLs. This sequence was illustrated in Figure 7–40b. The node initiates signaling by sending a SETUP message to the next node (2) in the route. This message contains the connection parameters and the DTL. Node 2, after processing the message, returns a CALL PROCEEDING message to 1. This message, among other things, contains the ATM VPI/VCI values for the connection. This is similar to label assignment under RSVP-TE, except that the assignment happens hop by hop as the SETUP message proceeds rather than in a separate reverse phase as in RSVP-TE. The assigned VPI/VCI value can be used for both directions of the connection in case of a bidirectional connection. The SETUP message then proceeds to the next node, as shown in Figure 7–41. The interesting thing to note is that the DTL shown in Figure 7–40b ends with node 2 in peer group A.1, and continues with logical node A.2. Node 2 is able to send a SETUP message to node 8 in A.2, since it is directly connected to this node. The DTL sent in the SETUP message would start with A.2 and carry the rest of the DTLs shown in Figure 7–40b. Node 8 becomes responsible for expanding the DTL to include node 6 on the way to the next DTL element in the peer group, that is, A.3 Thus, the DTL gets expanded when the SETUP message hits a border node that has more information about the internals of a peer group whose logical identifier is included in the DTL. The SETUP message ultimately reaches node 23. The final route for this message is <1, 2, 8, 6, 9, 10, 12, 14, 18, 17, 22, 23>.

When the SETUP message has been accepted by node 23, it sends a CONNECT message to its predecessor (node 22). The CONNECT progresses in the reverse direction as the SETUP. A node receiving a CONNECT message sends a CONNECT ACK, as shown in Figure 7–41. When Node 1 receives the CONNECT message, the connection establishment is complete and data transmission can begin.

As in the RSVP-TE case, connection state is created in intermediate nodes when SETUP and CONNECT messages are processed. The details of this are not absolutely necessary for subsequent discussion, but we note that the state created is hard, that is, it is not deleted until the connection is deleted (either due to network action or from the end point). This is in contrast to RSVP-TE soft state.

Finally, a long list of ATM-specific connection attributes is carried in the SETUP and the CONNECT messages. The interested reader can refer to [ATMF02] for details.

The message sequence for the deletion of the connection that was set up in the last example is shown in Figure 7–42. The deletion is triggered by node 1, which sends a RELEASE message to the next node (2). This message identifies the connection to be deleted. After receiving the message, node 2 responds with a RELEASE COMPLETE message. The receipt of this message causes the connection state to be cleared in node 1. The same action is

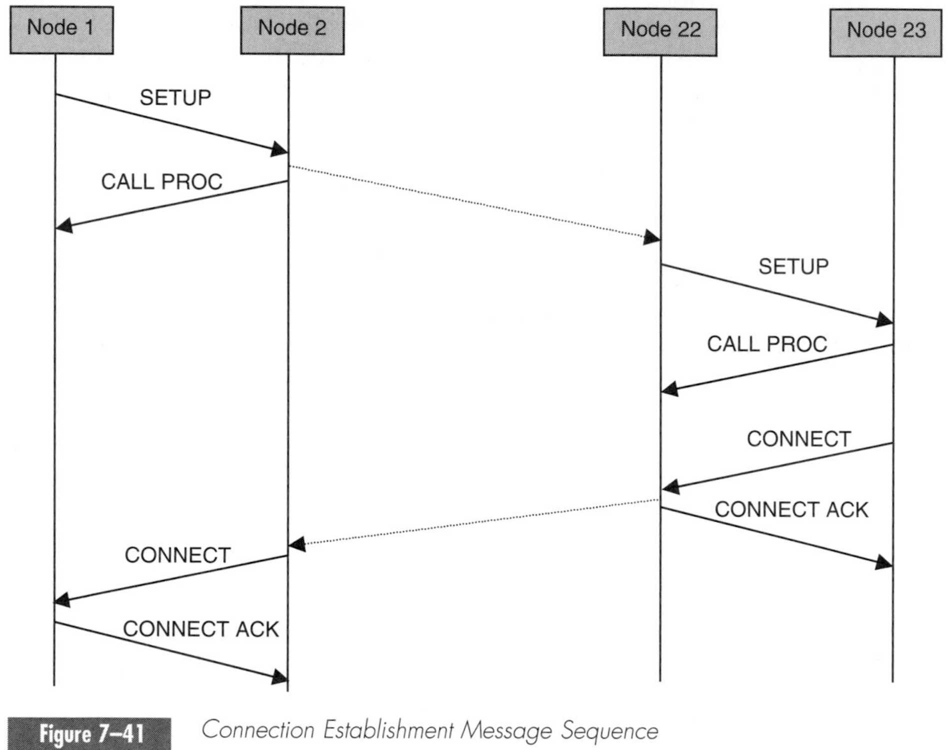

Figure 7–41 *Connection Establishment Message Sequence*

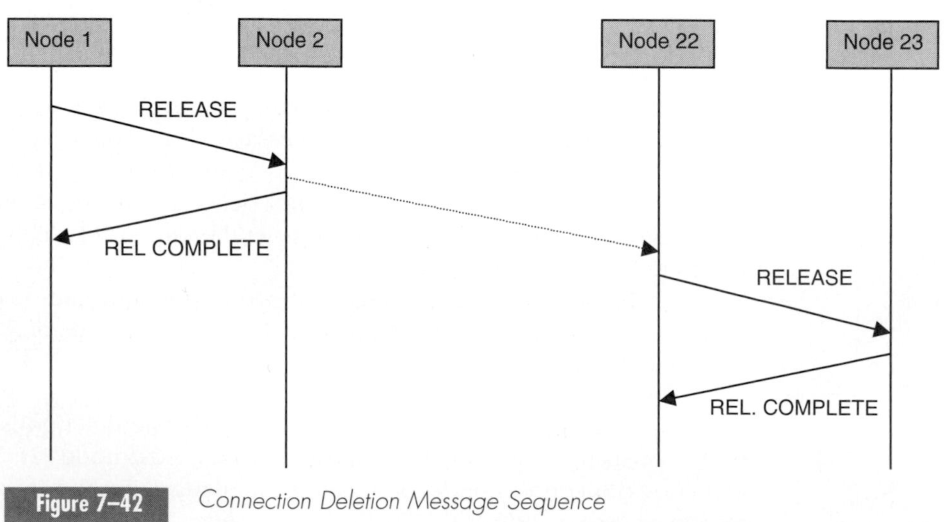

Figure 7–42 *Connection Deletion Message Sequence*

repeated along the connection path until the destination, node 23, receives the RELEASE and responds to it. More details on the contents of these messages, as well as details of other signaling messages defined under P-NNI can be found in [ATMF02].

7.6.4 P-NNI Adaptations for Signaling in Optical Networks

The changes to P-NNI required for signaling in optical networks consist of new information elements in signaling messages and insulation between the control and data planes. These are summarized below:

- Connection identification: As described in section 7.6.3, ATM VPI/VCI values are used during connection establishment as labels (this information is carried in the connection identifier information element). This must be substituted with the generalized label information pertaining to optical networking (e.g., a time slot, lambda, or port number).
- Traffic descriptors: P-NNI signaling messages carry ATM-specific traffic description parameters (similar to RSVP Sender Tspec). These must be replaced by optical network related connection parameters, such as the SONET/SDH parameters described in section 7.3.3.
- Separation of control and data planes: P-NNI signaling would release the connection if there is a disruption in the signaling path. What is required in optical networks, however, is the ability to keep data connections up if failures occur only in the control plane. This is the same issue with RSVP-TE, as described in section 7.5.
- Graceful deletion: Note that the P-NNI signaling deletion sequence shown in Figure 7–42 is similar to the RSVP-TE sequence where the source sends a deletion message that results in the removal of connection state at each hop. In optical networks, connection deletion in this manner may result in protection actions in downstream nodes. GMPLS RSVP-TE used extra phases in deletion-related signaling, utilizing the administrative status object (see Figure 7–37). A similar extension to signaling is needed with P-NNI.

On the plus side, P-NNI already supports certain procedures that are useful in connection-oriented networks. These include hard state and the ability to try alternate paths during signaling when the specified explicit route (DTL) is found to be infeasible.

7.7 Summary

In this chapter, we gave an overview of features required for signaling in optical networks and the details of GMPLS RSVP-TE and the P-NNI protocols. Our description has covered only the essential features of these protocols. An in-depth discussion would probably fill a whole book. Fortunately, the publicly available specification of these protocols can help the reader in obtaining further information.

Both GMPLS RSVP-TE and P-NNI protocols have been implemented by vendors for use in networks consisting of their own switches. There have also been demonstrations of interoperable UNI and NNI implementations. It remains to be seen when widespread deployments of these protocols in operational networks would occur.

E I G H T

Signaling for Protection and Restoration

8.1 Introduction

Protection and restoration are two methods whereby traffic affected by network failures is automatically rerouted over alternate resources. As per the definitions in Chapter 4, the term protection denotes the paradigm whereby a dedicated backup resource is used to recover the services provided by a failed resource. In contrast, the term restoration is used to denote the paradigm whereby backup resources are not dedicated to specific primary resources, but allocated dynamically based on availability. This may result in longer recovery times as compared with the protection case, but with possible improvements in network utilization.

Protection is a well-established feature in SONET/SDH networks. In Chapter 4, the details of Linear Automatic Protection Switching (LAPS) and ring protection schemes were described. These protection schemes utilized certain SONET/SDH overhead bytes (K1 and K2) for communication between network elements (NEs). The resulting protocols are said to be *bit-oriented*, since the communication does not rely on any additional framing procedure or transport protocol. With the advent of mesh networking, the existing LAPS schemes, which work between adjacent NEs, have been augmented with new mesh protection schemes. These are end-to-end protection schemes and include both dedicated protection (e.g., 1 + 1), as well as shared protection. Furthermore, newer LAPS-like link protection schemes have also been proposed. Like LAPS, these new protection schemes require signaling between NEs.

A question is whether the signaling for the new protection schemes should be bit-oriented (i.e., directly using SONET/SDH overhead bytes) or based on a higher-level protocol (e.g., RSVP-TE). Bit-oriented protocols are generally fast and can be optimized to the internal architecture of NEs. On the other hand, signaling based on a higher-level protocol allows the development of new protection schemes rather quickly due to the richer set of messaging constructs available. The use of higher-level protocols also facilitates interoperability when multiple subnetworks are interconnected to form a larger optical network (Figure 8–1). Finally, higher-level protocols are required in networks with OOO switches (i.e., PXCs) where bit-oriented protocols are not usable.

Now, restoration was briefly considered in Chapter 4, with emphasis on the efficiency aspects of restoration procedures. Aside from efficiency, restoration must be considered when end-to-end protection does not succeed or cannot be provided. For instance, shared mesh protection is designed to protect against single failure events (see section 8.4). If more than one failure occurs concurrently, mesh protection may not succeed for some connections. In this case, the failed connections could be subject to restoration procedures. As an example of the case where end-to-end protection is not possible, consider an optical network consisting of multiple, interconnected subnetworks (Figure 8–1). Suppose that standard NNI signaling (see Chapter 7) is implemented between the subnetworks, but the routing scheme used does not provide adequate information to determine end-to end diverse paths (see Chapter 12). In this case, end-to-end path protection for a connection may be realized as shown in Figure 8–1. Here, the connection segment within each subnetwork is protected using end-to-end protection within that subnetwork, and the segment between two subnetworks is protected using LAPS. In this scenario, it is clear that the border nodes through which both the working and protection paths are routed are points of vulnerability. Failure of one of these nodes will render the connection unprotected. In this case, restoration may be used as a method of last resort to recover from node failures.

From a signaling point of view, restoration is tantamount to reprovisioning a connection after a failure. In Chapter 7, we saw that provisioning can be through a management system or signaling based. Since restoration needs to be completed as quickly as possible, the common wisdom is that restoration

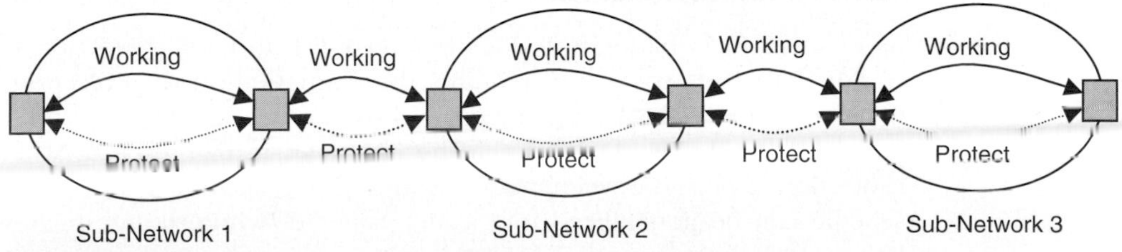

Figure 8–1 *Segmented Protection*

must be based on signaling. Thus, while connection provisioning may or may not need a distributed control plane, protection and restoration do.

In the rest of this chapter, we describe the new mesh protection schemes, their signaling requirements, and the various options for realizing the signaling. As mentioned earlier, we consider two broad categories of new protection schemes in mesh networks: span or link protection, and end-to-end or path protection. Span protection refers to the protection of a link (and hence all the connection segments routed over the link) between two neighboring NEs. End-to-end protection refers to the protection of an entire connection path from the ingress to the egress points in a network. A connection may be subject to both span protection (for each of its segments) and end-to-end protection (when span protection does not succeed or is not desired). In this context, the link and the connection are typically bidirectional consisting of a pair of unidirectional entities (see Chapter 6). Under span and end-to-end protection schemes, it may be required that when a failure affects any one direction of the connection, both directions of the connection are switched to a new link or path, respectively.

In the next section, we examine the new span protection scheme and the signaling protocol mechanisms suitable for implementing it. Following this, in section 8.3, we describe dedicated end-to-end mesh protection schemes and the associated signaling mechanisms. In section 8.4, shared mesh protection is described. It should be noted that mesh protection is still implemented in a proprietary manner by different equipment vendors. As of this writing, standards are evolving on protection and restoration protocols [Papadimitriou+02, Lang+03b]. Thus, our descriptions in sections 8.2–8.4 are based on work in progress. Now, questions are often raised as to the relationship between the signaling procedures used in optical networks for protection and restoration versus those used in MPLS networks for the same functions. We discuss this in section 8.5.

8.2 Span Protection

8.2.1 Functional Description

As described in Chapter 4, LAPS supports 1 + 1 and 1:N protection schemes. Under LAPS, 1:N protection requires the configuration of *protection groups*, that is, groups of N+1 links, where N links are designated as working links and 1 link as the protection link. This is shown in Figure 8–2a, where three protection groups between nodes A and B are shown. The 1:N protection scheme can be generalized into a M:N scheme, where there are N working links and M protection links, M < N. Thus, if a failure affects more than M working links in a protection group, only M of them can be protected even if

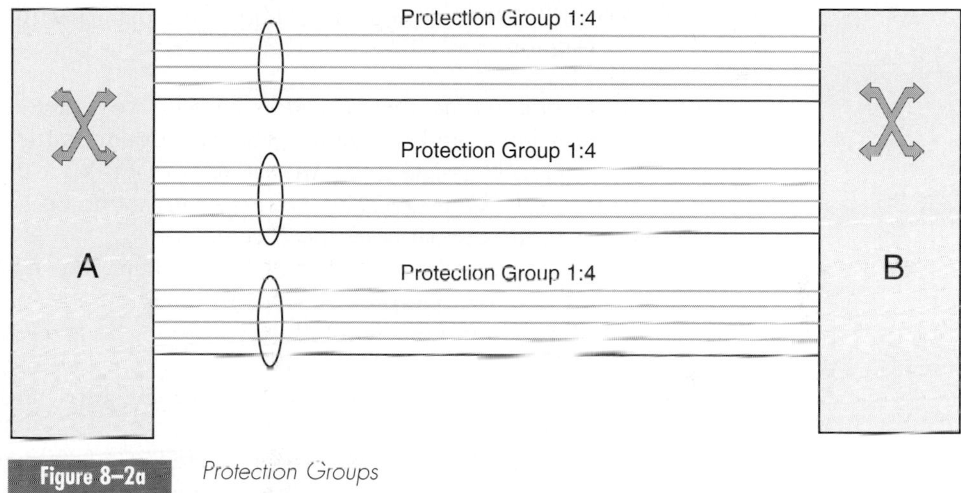

Figure 8–2a Protection Groups

there are free protection links in other groups. A further generalization of this scheme is to pool all protection links into a single group. That is, a protection link can protect any working link. This is shown in Figure 8–2b. In effect, this is similar to having a single M:N protection group, except that there is flexibility in choosing the values of M and N, and the ability to not preassign links as working or protection (if so desired). This type of protection can also be used with OOO NEs (i.e., PXCs) if failures can be localized.

Figure 8–2b Pooling of Protection Links

Considering two neighboring NEs A and B, the details of this protection scheme are as follows:

- At any point in time, there are M+N links between A and B of which at most N links can be assigned to carry working traffic and at most M links can be assigned to carry protection traffic. A link is said to be "free" if it has no working or protection traffic on it, or it is carrying extra traffic that could be preempted.
- When a working link is affected by a failure, the traffic on it is diverted to a free link provided that the total number of links being used for carrying protection traffic (referred to as *protection links*) is less than M. Note that the failed link could be carrying more than one connection, for example, an OC-192 link carrying four STS-48 link connections.
- More than one working link may be affected by a failure event. In this case, there may not be an adequate number of free links to assign to protection traffic (i.e., the number of protection links exceeds M). The set of affected working links that are actually restored is then subject to policies (e.g., based on relative priority of working traffic).
- Each node is assumed to have an identifier, called the Node ID. Each node is also assumed to have the mapping of its local link (or port) ID to the corresponding ID at the neighbor. This mapping could be manually configured, or obtained automatically using a neighbor discovery procedure (see Chapter 6). When traffic must be diverted from a failed working link to a free link, the decision as to which free link is chosen is always made by one of the nodes, A or B. To do this, the node with the numerically higher Node ID is considered the "master," and it is required to both apply any policies and select specific free links to divert working traffic. The other node is considered the "slave." The determination of the master and the slave may be based on manually configured information, or as a result of running a neighbor discovery procedure.
- Failure events themselves may be detected using SONET/SDH mechanisms where applicable (see Chapter 3). Since a bidirectional link is realized using a pair of unidirectional links, a failure in the link from A to B is typically detected by B, and a failure in the opposite direction is detected by A. It is possible for a failure to simultaneously affect both directions of the bi-directional link. In this case, A and B will concurrently detect failures, in the B-to-A direction and in the A-to-B direction, respectively.

The basic steps in this span protection scheme are as follows:

1. If the master detects a failure of a working link, it autonomously invokes a process to allocate a free link to protect the affected traf-

fic. This process must take into account any policies in protecting working traffic and ensure that the total number of protection links does not exceed M.

2. If the slave detects a failure of a working link, it must inform the master of the failure. The master then invokes the same procedure as above to allocate a free link. (It is possible that the master has itself detected the same failure, for example, a failure simultaneously affecting both directions of a link.)
3. Once the master has determined the availability and the identity of the free link for carrying protection traffic, it indicates this to the slave and requests the switchover of the traffic. Prior to this, if the selected link was carrying extra traffic, the master stops using the link for this traffic (i.e., the traffic is not forwarded into or out of the link).
4. The slave sends an acknowledgment to the master. Prior to this, if the selected link was carrying traffic that could be preempted, the slave stops using the link for this traffic (i.e., the traffic is not forwarded into or out of the link). It then starts sending and receiving the (failed) working link traffic over the newly assigned protection link.
5. When the master receives the acknowledgment, it starts sending and receiving the (failed) working link traffic over the new protection link.

It is clear from the description above that this span protection scheme may require up to three messages for each working link being switched: a failure indication message, a switchover request message, and a switchover response message. The functional requirements pertaining to these messages are as follows.

8.2.2 Messages

8.2.2.1 FAILURE INDICATION MESSAGE

This message is sent from the slave to the master to indicate the ID of one or more failed working links. The number of links included in the message would depend on the number of failures detected within a window of time by the sending node. A node may choose to send separate failure indication messages in the interest of completing the restoration for a given link within an implementation-dependent time constraint.

The ID of a failed link is the identification used by the slave node. The master must convert this to the corresponding local ID.

8.2.2.2 SWITCHOVER REQUEST MESSAGE

This message is sent from the master to the slave to indicate that the connections on the (failed) working link can be switched to an available free link. This message contains one or more entries of the form, <Protection link ID, Working link ID>, each indicating a newly assigned link to protect a failed working link. The IDs are based on the identification used by the master. The slave must convert them to the corresponding local IDs.

The master may not be able to find a free link to protect a failed working link. Thus, the set of restored links indicated in this message may be a subset of all failed links. Also, depending on time constraints, the master may switch the set of failed links in smaller batches. Thus, a failure event may result in the master sending more than one switchover request message to the slave node.

8.2.2.3 SWITCHOVER RESPONSE MESSAGE

This message is sent from the slave to the master to indicate the completion (or failure) of switchover at the slave. It contains the IDs of the new protection links that the slave has switched over to. In this message, the slave may also indicate that it cannot switch certain failed links to protection links (for unspecified reasons). The action to be taken by the master in this case is not explicitly defined (e.g., the master may abort the switchover of these links, and perhaps trigger end-to-end path protection for the affected connections).

Figure 8–3 illustrates how this protection scheme works. Here, node A is the master and B is the slave. Also, M = 2 and N = 5, and the links have different identification on the two sides. A failure event affects links 3 and 4, as identified by node B, in the A→B direction. The failure indication message from B to A carries these identifiers. Node A maps these identifiers to the local values, that is, 1 and 2. It then decides to switch traffic on links 1 and 2 to free links 6 and 7, respectively. The switchover request message from A to B carries this information. At B, the link identifiers 6 and 7 are mapped to the local identifiers 2 and 6, respectively. Node B switches the traffic to these links and indicates the successful switchover in the switchover response message sent to A.

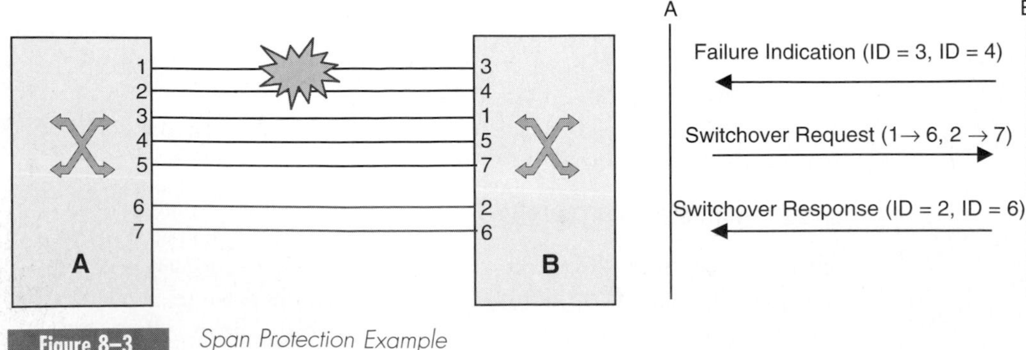

Figure 8–3 Span Protection Example

8.2.3 Preventing Unintended Connections

An unintended connection occurs when traffic from the wrong source is delivered to a receiver. This must be prevented during protection switching. This is primarily a concern when the protection link is being used to carry extra traffic (i.e., traffic that can be preempted). In this case, it must be ensured that the connection traffic being switched from the (failed) working link to the protection link is not delivered to the receiver of the preempted traffic. Thus, in the message flow described above, the master node must disconnect any preempted traffic on the protection link before sending the switchover request. The slave node should also disconnect preempted traffic before sending the switchover response. In addition, the master node should start receiving traffic for the protected connection from the protection link. Finally, the master node should start sending protected traffic on the protection link upon receipt of the switchover response.

8.2.4 Reversion

With conventional protection groups, it is common to revert traffic from a protection link to the working link when a failure is repaired. With the span protection scheme described earlier, reversion is not necessary as any free link can be used for protection purposes subject to the limit on the numbers.

8.2.5 Signaling Mechanisms

Signaling for span protection requires the exchange of the three messages described earlier. There are essentially two ways in which the signaling can be done. Bit-oriented signaling, as used in LAPS (see Chapter 4), is one choice when dealing with SONET/SDH networks. But the K1/K2-byte based procedure described for LAPS in Chapter 4 cannot handle a large number of links interconnecting neighboring NEs. Specifically, this procedure cannot identify more than 15 channels within a protection group. Furthermore, the procedure described in section 8.2.1 requires the master-slave relationship to be able to make switching decisions consistently at one end of the link. Thus, if bit-oriented signaling is to be used, then additional overhead bytes are needed to carry the link identification information. Also, the protection protocol must be defined to correspond to the functional description above.

The other choice for signaling is to use a higher-level protocol. This option is suitable with both OOO and OEO NEs. With this option, the two neighboring NEs participating in span protection are signaling peers, running a protocol over a control channel. The signaling protocol itself could be based on a protocol used for provisioning, such as GMPLS RSVP-TE. But a problem with this approach is that the provisioning protocols are used for establishing end-to-end path layer connections, and their usage for span protection may lead to some complexity. To see this, consider the usage of GMPLS RSVP-TE to realize the messaging described in section 8.2.2. At a first glance, the following realization may look suitable:

- Failure indication: With SONET/SDH networks, the remote defect indication feature described in Chapter 3 could be used to achieve the functionality of this message. Where this is not possible, the notify message (see section 7.5.2) can be used. The "error" reported by this message could consist of the identification of failed links.
- Switchover request: It seems like the Path message with the label request object could be used as an implicit switchover request (see section 7.5.3). The Path message, however, pertains to individual connections and not a link. Thus, if more than one connection is being routed over a failed link, a separate Path message must be generated for each such connection to switch it over to a protection link. But from section 8.2.1, we see that there is a need to designate one of the NEs engaging in span protection as the master. This is the node that should generate the Path message during protection. Path messages, however, flow from the node that was upstream to the node that was downstream during provisioning. If a failed link between two NEs A and B was carrying multiple connections, it is possible that for some connections A is the upstream node and for others B is the upstream node. This is shown in Figure 8–4. Here, the Path message for the connection provisioned from S1 to D1 flows from A to B. On the other hand, the Path message for the connection provisioned from S2 to D2 flows from B to A. In this case, it is difficult to uniquely designate one of the NEs as the master.

  A solution to this problem could be use a different GMPLS RSVP-TE message for switchover request. For instance, it is possible to use the Notify message with additional information elements to indicate the IDs of protection links. Since the notify message can be

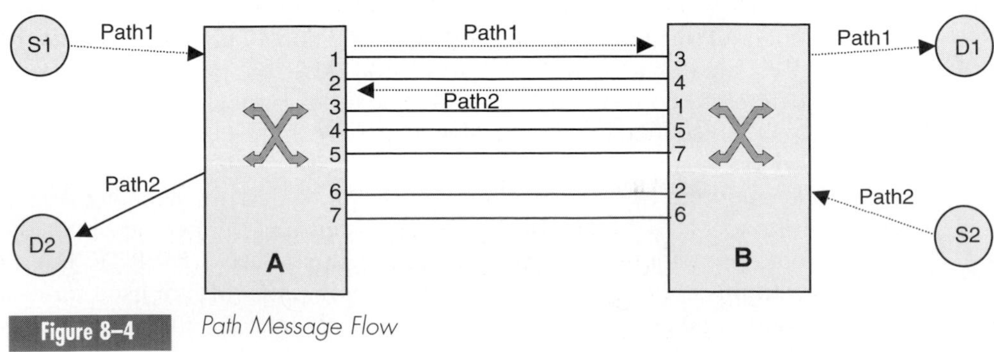

Figure 8–4 *Path Message Flow*

sent both upstream or downstream, this would work. But then, this usage can hardly be considered as the use of the RSVP-TE protocol. Rather, the messaging would be an overlay over RSVP-TE.

- Switchover response: The Resv message with the Label object (see section 7.5.3) can be used as an implicit switchover response. As in the case of the Path message, the Resv message pertains to individual connections. Thus, the same complexities outlined above arise with this usage. The solution is to use the Notify message with additional information elements. In this case, we are essentially using an overlaid protocol, as mentioned earlier.

In summary, it is definitely possible to use the control plane to realize span protection, but enhancements to the semantics of GMPLS signaling protocols would be required to do this. Path protection, however, falls more naturally within the framework of the GMPLS signaling protocols. This is described next.

8.3 End-to-End Dedicated Mesh Protection

End-to-end path protection and restoration refer to the recovery of an entire connection from the ingress to the egress port in a network. Suppose the working path of a connection is routed from a source NE A to a destination NE B through a set of intermediate NEs. In this and in the next section, we define end-to-end 1 + 1 protection modes, describe their functionality, and the signaling mechanisms needed to implement them.

8.3.1 Unidirectional 1 + 1 Protection

Under this protection mode, a dedicated, resource-disjoint alternate path is preestablished to protect the working path of the connection. Traffic is simultaneously sent on both paths and received from one of the functional paths by the end nodes A and B. This is similar to the unidirectional 1 + 1 protection scheme described in Chapter 4. There is no explicit signaling involved with this mode of protection, and therefore we do not consider this further.

8.3.2 Bidirectional 1 + 1 Protection

8.3.2.1 FUNCTIONAL DESCRIPTION

Under this protection mode, a dedicated, resource-disjoint alternate path is preestablished to protect the working path of the connection. Traffic is simultaneously sent on both paths. Under normal conditions, the traffic from the working path is received by nodes A and B (in the appropriate directions). A failure affecting the working path results in both A and B switching to the traffic on the protection path in the respective directions. Note that this requires signaling between the end nodes to coordinate the switch to the protection path. The basic steps in bidirectional 1 + 1 path protection are as follows:

- Failure detection: Suppose a node in the working path detects a failure event. Such a node must send a failure indication signal toward the upstream or/and downstream end of the connection (node A or B). In Chapter 3, we saw the usage of the Alarm Indication Signal-Path (AIS-P) when line-layer failures occur. Specifically, an NE detecting a failed link (for example) would generate an AIS-P signal in the downstream direction. Similarly, a Path Terminating Equipment (PTE) noting path layer failures would send a Remote Defect Indication-Path (RDI-P) upstream to its peer. These signals *could* be noted by an end node (A or B, or both depending on the direction of the failure) to initiate path protection.

  Now, suppose both span protection and path protection are being used. When a failure occurs, an AIS-P (and/or RDI-P) would be generated, but the end node must not initiate path protection until it is certain that span protection did not succeed. In this case, an explicit failure indication message needs to be used. This message may be forwarded along the working path, or routed over a different path if the network has general routing intelligence.
- Switchover: When an end node detects a failure in the working path, it starts using the protection path for sending and receiving the traffic. At the same time, it sends a switchover request message to the other end node. When an end node receives a switchover request message, it starts using the protection path to send and receive traffic (if it is not already doing so). At the same time, it sends a switchover response message to the other end to acknowledge the receipt of the request.

8.3.3 Messages

To describe the signaling messages in detail, we have to first introduce certain identifiers. These are the Connection ID, which uniquely identifies each connection, and the Node ID, which uniquely identifies each node in the network. Furthermore, each node on the working or the protection path of a connection must know the connection identifier, the previous and next nodes in the connection path, and the type of protection being afforded to the connection (i.e., 1 + 1 or shared). This is so that restoration-related messages may be forwarded properly.

The nodal information may be assembled when the working and protection paths of the connection are provisioned using signaling, or may be configured in the case of management system based provisioning (see Chapter 7). The information must remain until the connection is explicitly deleted.

8.3.3.1 END-TO-END FAILURE INDICATION MESSAGE

This message is sent by an intermediate node toward the source of a connection. For instance, such a node might have attempted local span protection and failed. This message is necessary only when SONET/SDH mechanisms are not used.

Consider a node detecting a link failure. The node must determine the identities of all the connections affected by the link failure, and send an end-to-end failure indication message to the source of each connection. Each intermediate node receiving such a message must determine the appropriate next node to forward the message so that the message would reach the connection source. Furthermore, if an intermediate node is itself generating a Failure Indication message (e.g., multiple unidirectional failures have occurred), there should be a mechanism to suppress all but one source of these messages. Finally, the Failure Indication message must be sent reliably from the node detecting the failure to the connection source. Reliability may be achieved, for example, by retransmitting the message until an acknowledgment is received.

8.3.3.2 END-TO-END FAILURE ACKNOWLEDGE MESSAGE

The source node sends this message in response to an end-to-end failure indication. This message is sent to the originator of the Failure Indication message. The acknowledge message is sent in response to each Failure Indication message received.

Each intermediate node receiving the Acknowledge message must forward it toward the destination of the message.

8.3.3.3 END-TO-END SWITCHOVER REQUEST MESSAGE

The source node generates this message. It is sent to the destination node along the protection path, and it carries the ID of the connection being restored. This message must indicate whether the source is able to switch over to the protection path. If the source is not able to switch over, the destination may not also switch over.

The End-to-End Switchover message must be sent reliably from the source to the destination of the connection.

8.3.3.4 END-TO-END SWITCHOVER RESPONSE MESSAGE

The destination node sends this message after receiving an End-to-End Switchover Request message. It is sent toward the source of the connection along the protection path. This message should indicate the ID of the connection being switched over. This message must be transmitted in response to each End-to-End Switchover Request message received.

8.3.4 Signaling Procedures

As in the case of span protection, both bit oriented as well as control plane signaling may be considered for end-to-end bidirectional 1 + 1 protection. With bit-oriented signaling, a set of overhead bytes has to be selected, and the signaling syntax and semantics for processing and forwarding these bytes have to be defined. Alternatively, we could examine the applicability of GMPLS signaling mechanisms for 1 + 1 path protection, as considered below. It should be noted that the discussion below is not based on any proposed standard, but it is an examination of possibilities.

8.3.4.1 PROVISIONING THE PROTECTION PATH

The working and protection paths can be routed as described in Chapter 10 and signaled using GMPLS RSVP-TE as described in section 7.5.3. In essence, these paths are provisioned separately, as if they are independent connections (albeit with the same attributes). In doing so, it is necessary for the source NE to somehow indicate to the destination NE that the working and protection connections are in fact related. The RSVP-TE LSP ID can be used for this purpose, as described in section 7.4.2.1. The notification request must be enabled for the working and the protection connections, as described in section 7.5.1.10. Once these connections are established, both end points send traffic on both connections, but receive only on the working connection.

8.3.4.2 END-TO-END FAILURE INDICATION AND ACKNOWLEDGMENT

The GMPLS RSVP-TE Notify message can be used for this purpose. The NE detecting the failure on the working path sends this message to the source of the connection. This message identifies the failed connection, using the LSP ID. If more than one connection from the same source is affected by a failure, a single Notify message can carry the IDs of all these connections. After receiving the Notify message, the source sends an acknowledgment back, as described in section 7.5.2.

8.3.4.3 END-TO-END SWITCHOVER REQUEST AND RESPONSE

End-to-end switchover request is essentially a communication between the source and the destination NEs. Intermediate NEs need only to forward this message. The usage of the Path message may be considered for this purpose, but this message is typically processed at each hop. Furthermore, the Path message does not indicate that the destination must start receiving from another connection (in this case, the protection connection). Thus, some new semantics needs to be introduced if the Path message is used. The Administrative Status object (Figure 7-33) can be used for this purpose. Specifically, one of the reserved bits in the object can be used to indicate that protection switching must be performed at the end point. Let us call this the P bit. The R bit must be set to indicate that the receiver must reflect the object in a Resv message that acts as the End-to-End Switchover Response message.

Figure 8–5 illustrates the GMPLS RSVP-TE signaling for bidirectional 1 + 1 protection. Here, an intermediate node generates the Notify message with the appropriate connection ID (LSP ID). The subsequent Path message is sent from A to B along the protection path, with the connection ID and the Administrative Status object. The corresponding Resv message flows from B to A (hop by hop). An alternative to this is the use of Notification messages for end-to-end switchover request and response, which we have not shown.

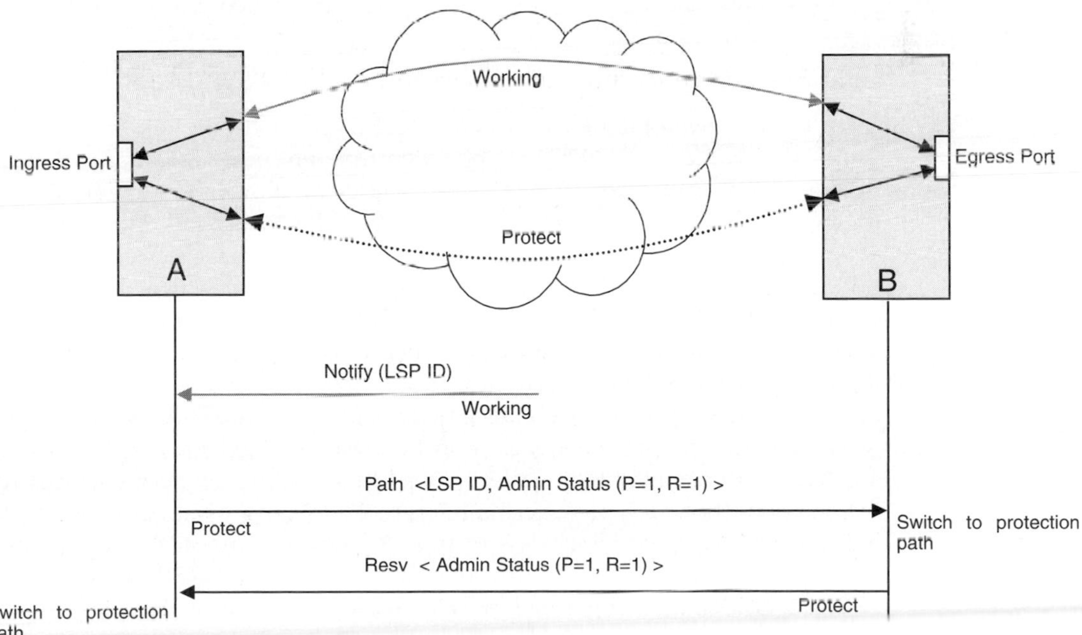

Figure 8–5 *Bi-Directional 1+1 Using GMPLS RSVP-TE*

8.4 End-to-End Shared Mesh Protection

8.4.1.1 Functional Description

Shared mesh protection refers to an end-to-end protection scheme whereby network resources are shared by multiple protection paths. Typically, protection paths of connections whose working path are resource-disjoint (e.g., link disjoint) share resources. The idea is that with a *single* failure, at most one of the working paths will be affected, and hence the protection path of the corresponding connection may be activated. In this regard, we have to understand what a "single" failure means. To do this, first consider the types of failures that may occur:

1. Failure of a single transmit/receive interface hardware: This affects all the connections on the corresponding link.
2. An amplifier failure that may cause multiple link failures: This affects all the connections that are routed over the affected links.
3. A conduit/cable cut that may translate to multiple fiber cuts within the same conduit/cable: This may cause near-simultaneous link failures between multiple node pairs, and hence affect a number of connections.
4. A node failure: Affects all the connections routed through the node.

Thus, a given failure event may affect more than one link between the same pair of nodes or even links between different node pairs. The concept of Shared Risk Link Group (SRLG, see Chapter 6) allows the network operator to assign a unique identifier to each entity that could fail due to a given event. For example, considering item (1) above, each link between a pair of nodes could be assigned an SRLG value. Similarly, considering item (3) above, each link that is routed over the same conduit could be assigned a distinct SRLG value. Thus, a link could have multiple SRLG values assigned, depending on the types of failures that are recognized.

A working path of a connection is said to be SRLG-diverse from the working path of another connection if the corresponding routes do not share any links with common SRLG values. Depending on the failure modes against which connections are protected, different SRLG values would be assigned to links. Then, if the working paths of two connections are SRLG-diverse, then any of the above types of failures that are covered by the SRLG assignment can be considered a "single" failure. That is, such a failure will not affect both connections simultaneously. Figure 8–6 illustrates this. Here, the two protection paths P1 and P2 share the bandwidth on the link between C1 and C2. The corresponding working paths are shown to be node disjoint.

Mesh protection requires prior *soft-reservation* of capacity along the protection path. Soft-reservation means that capacity is reserved but not allocated

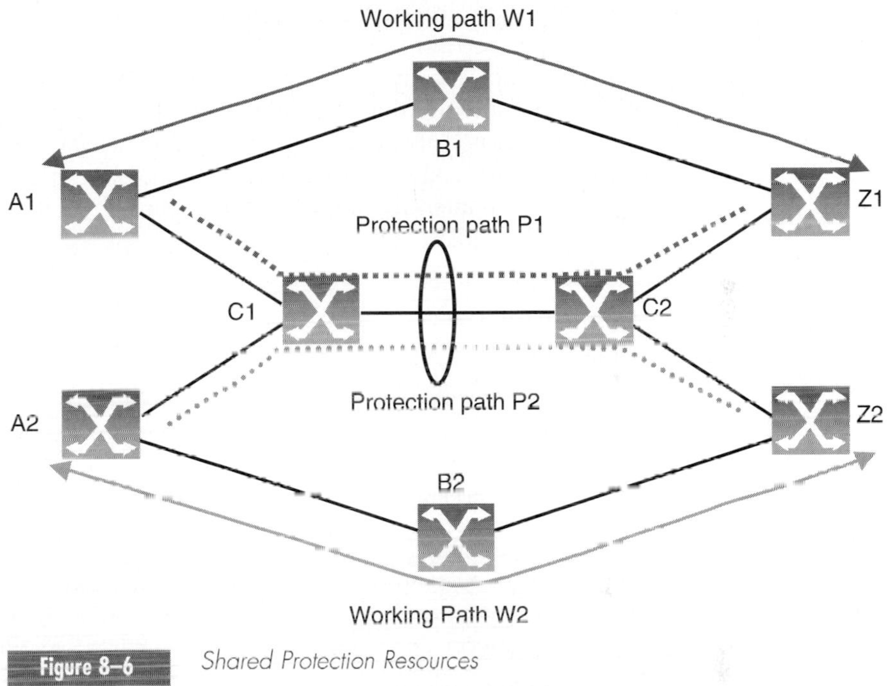

Figure 8–6 *Shared Protection Resources*

to a specific connection (i.e., no cross-connections are made in NEs to activate a specific protection path). The protection capacity may be kept idle or allocated to extra traffic that can be preempted. The protection path is explicitly activated after a failure event. Thus, unlike the 1 + 1 case, shared mesh protection requires actions at each intermediate node along the protection path during protection switching. It is possible that a protection path of a connection may not be successfully activated when multiple, concurrent failure events occur. In this case, the shared protection capacity can be assigned to at most one connection whose working path failed.

Shared mesh protection requires nodes and connections identified as described in section 8.3.3. Furthermore, each node in the working and protection path of a connection must know the identities of its upstream and downstream neighbors. Each node in the protection path of a connection must also know the cross-connection needed to establish the data plane. This information could be of the following form:

{Connection ID, <Incoming Port, Channel, etc.>, <Outgoing Port, Channel, etc.> }

The precise nature of the Port, Channel, etc. information would depend on the type of node and connection.

Under mesh protection, failure detection and indication are similar to the procedures described for end-to-end 1 + 1 protection. Once the source NE learns of the failure, it activates the protection path by sending an end-to-end switchover request along the protection path. This message results in certain actions in the intermediate nodes. The destination activates the protection path and sends an end-to-end switchover response message. This activates the protection path in each intermediate NE and the source. The details are as follows.

8.4.2 Messages

8.4.2.1 END-TO-END FAILURE INDICATION AND ACKNOWLEDGMENT

The end-to-end failure indication and acknowledgment procedures and messages are as defined in section 8.3.3.

8.4.2.2 END-TO-END SWITCHOVER REQUEST

This message is generated by the source node after receiving an indication of failure in the working path. It is sent to the connection destination along the protection path, and it carries the ID of the connection being restored. This message must allow intermediate nodes to record whether they are able to activate the protection path. Suppose that some intermediate node is not able to establish the cross-connects for the protection path. It is then desirable that no other node in the protection path establishes cross-connects for the path. This would allow shared mesh protection paths to be efficiently utilized. This requirement implies that the switchover to the protection path should occur in two phases: In the forward phase, the Switchover Request message indicates the impending protection switch to the intermediate nodes in the protection path and collects information as to their ability to switch. In the reverse phase, the actual protection switching occurs if all nodes in the path indicate their ability to switch over.

8.4.2.3 END-TO-END SWITCHOVER RESPONSE

The destination node sends this message in response to each End-to-End Switchover Request it receives. This message is sent along the protection path toward the source of the connection. This message indicates the ID of the connection being switched over, and whether all the intermediate nodes have agreed to switch over (as determined in the forward phase using the Switchover Request message).

8.4.2.4 REVERSION

Reversion refers to the process of moving traffic back to the working path from its protection path after the former is repaired. With shared mesh protection, reversion is desired for the following reasons. First, the protection route may not be as efficient as the route of the working path. Second, moving a connection to its working path allows the protection resources to be used to protect other connections.

Reversion requires the following steps:

1. Reestablishing the working path: The working path must be operational following the repair of the failure. This might require the working path to be completely reprovisioned.
2. Bridging at the source: The source node must bridge the transmitted signal onto both the working and protection paths.
3. Switchover request: The source must send an End-to-End Switchover Request to the destination along the working path. This message contains the connection ID. Upon receipt of this message, the destination selects the signal from the working path. At the same time, it bridges the transmitted signal onto both the working and the protection paths.
4. Switchover response: The destination must send an End-to-End Switchover Response message to the source confirming the completion of the operation. This message is sent along the working path. When the source receives this message, it switches to receive from the working path, and stops transmitting traffic on the protection path.
5. Switchover completed: The source then sends a Switchover Completed message to the destination confirming that the connection has been reverted. Upon receipt of this message, the destination stops transmitting along the protection path and deactivates the connection along this path.
6. Release protection resources: The resources allocated for the connection along the protection path (including the cross-connects made) must be released.

We shall see how the reversion signaling could be realized in section 8.4.3.4.

8.4.3 Signaling Procedures

As before, signaling can be bit-oriented or based on a higher-level protocol. Similar functionality has to be achieved in either case. In the following, we consider the possible use of GMPLS RSVP-TE signaling for shared mesh protection. As before, this discussion is not based on any specific standard that has been proposed for protection signaling, but merely an examination of the possibilities.

8.4.3.1 PROVISIONING THE PROTECTION PATH

Unlike the 1 + 1 case, the protection path is distinct from the working path in that resources are reserved but not allocated to the connection along the protection path. Such a shared protection path can be established by using the GMPLS RSVP-TE Path message with the appropriately set protection object (see section 7.5.1.7). Specifically, in the protection object, the S (Secondary) bit and bit 2 of the link flags must be set to indicate shared mesh protection. As in the case of 1 + 1 protection, the working and protection paths must be associated using the same LSP ID (see section 7.4.2.1). Finally, the Path state in each node in the protection path must reflect the fact that the path is not active. This requires some extensions to the existing RSVP-TE scheme.

8.4.3.2 END-TO-END FAILURE INDICATION AND ACKNOWLEDGMENT

The Notify message can be used in the same manner as described for 1 + 1 protection in section 8.3.4.2.

8.4.3.3 END-TO-END SWITCHOVER REQUEST AND RESPONSE

The Path message can be used as the End-to-End Switchover Request mechanism. As described in section 8.4.2.2, the intermediate NEs along the protection path must record their ability to activate the protection path in this message. As in the 1 + 1 case, the Administrative Status object can be used to both indicate that the protection path is being activated and to record the inability of an intermediate node to activate the path. To do this, the P bit in the object is set to 1 to indicate protection switching as before. The R bit is set to 1 to request the receiver to reflect the received Administrative Status object. A new bit is used to indicate whether all NEs can activate the protection path. Let us call this the N bit. The new Administrative Status object is depicted in Figure 8–7. The N bit is set to 0 by the source, and an intermediate NE sets it to 1 if it cannot activate the protection path. If the receiver sees the N bit set to 0, it activates the protection path. Regardless of the status of the N bit, the receiver reflects the received Administrative Status object in a Resv message. This message acts as the End-to-End Switchover Response and traverses to the source along the protection path. Each intermediate NE examines the N bit, and if it is 0, activates the protection path.

The message sequence for shared mesh protection is similar to that shown in Figure 8–5, except for the addition of the N bit to the Administrative Status object.

Length (= 8)		Class Number			Class Type (= 1)	
R	Reserved (25 bits)	P	N	T	A	D

Figure 8–7 *Enhanced Administrative Status Object*

8.4.3.4 REVERSION

With GMPLS RSVP-TE, reversion is realized as follows:

1. The working path is reestablished using Path and Resv message exchanges.
2. The traffic is switched from the protection path to the working path using Path and Resv messages with Administrative Status objects, as described in section 8.3.4 for bidirectional 1 + 1 protection.
3. The protection path resources are deallocated as follows. The source NE sends a Path message to the destination along the protection path. This message has an Administrative Status object with the D and R bits set to 1. The destination returns a Resv message in response along the reverse path. In this message, the Administrative Status object has the D bit set to 1, and the R bit is set to 0. Each intermediate node then releases the cross-connections and makes the shared protection capacity available to other connections.

8.5 Discussion

8.5.1 Performance Aspects and MPLS Fast Reroute

How fast can a protection scheme be if implemented using GMPLS signaling? Note that the bit-oriented protection protocols have the advantage of speed. There is no higher-level protocol processing, and message propagation through intermediate NEs is very quick. The corresponding delay measures for GMPLS signaling have not been highlighted by any study as of this writing. It has, however, been shown that LSP protection in MPLS networks using a feature called "fast reroute" can be accomplished within 50 ms time limit. Thus, an association is sometimes made between MPLS fast reroute and GMPLS-based protection in optical networks to imply that the latter can be responsive too. MPLS fast reroute, however, is not the same as protection in optical networks. Our objective in this section is to describe the distinction. The following descriptions are based on work in progress at the IETF [Pan+03].

As described in [Pan+03], MPLS fast reroute primarily provides "local repair" functionality. Local repair is illustrated in Figure 8–8. Here, the primary LSP is established from LSR A to LSR F, along the path A-B-C-D-E-F. At each LSR, a "detour" LSP is established to bypass the next hop LSR. Thus, a detour LSP connects LSR A to LSR C, LSR B to LSR D, and so on. There may be intermediate nodes along the path of the detour LSP. This is not shown in the figure. A detour LSP starts at the source or intermediate LSR in the path and ends at another intermediate or destination LSR. The starting point is called the

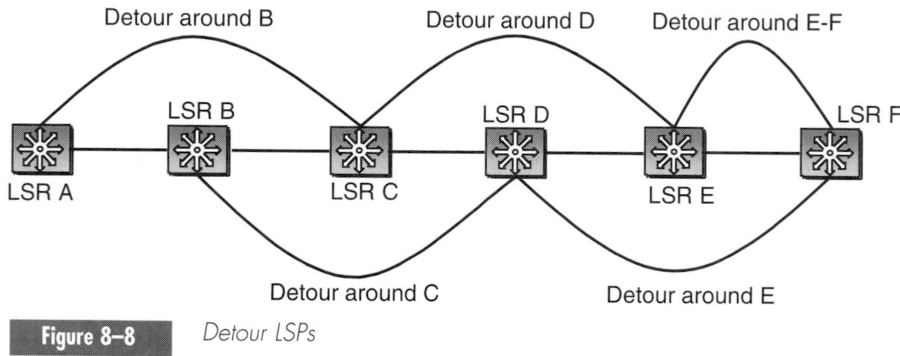

Figure 8–8 *Detour LSPs*

point of local repair (PLR), and the ending point is called the merging point (MP). As the name implies, the MP represents the point at which the detour LSP is "merged" with the primary LSP.

Suppose a link fails along the path of the primary LSP. The LSR immediately upstream of the link diverts the LSP traffic onto the detour LSP. The traffic thus bypasses the failed link and reaches the MP. The LSR at the merging point then forwards the traffic along the primary LSP. For instance, considering Figure 8–8, suppose the link B-C fails. LSR B, after detecting the failure, starts forwarding the LSP traffic over the detour LSP along the path B-D. This is shown in Figure 8–9. The same action can be achieved when a node failure occurs, since detour LSPs can bypass nodes along the primary LSP as shown in Figure 8–8.

Detours can be established to protect individual LSPs or all the LSPs traversing a facility. The example in Figure 8–8 illustrates the former type of detour, also called one-to-one backup. A facility backup, on the other hand, is realized by establishing LSP tunnels with sufficient capacity between the PLR and the MP to accommodate traffic on all LSPs routed between the PLR and the MP along their primary paths. Figure 8–10 illustrates the case where there are two primary LSPs, one from LSR A to F (dotted line), another from

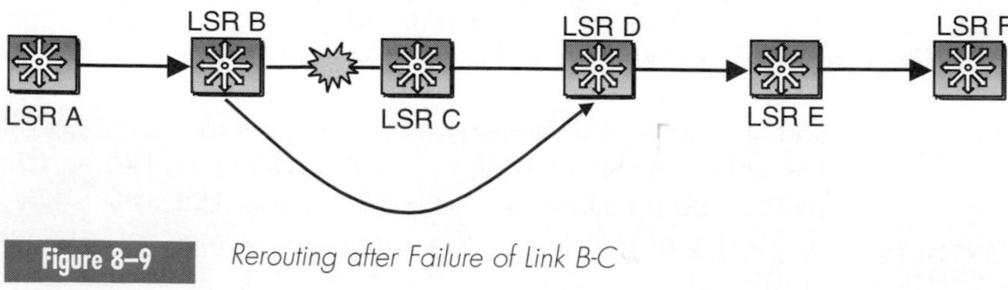

Figure 8–9 *Rerouting after Failure of Link B-C*

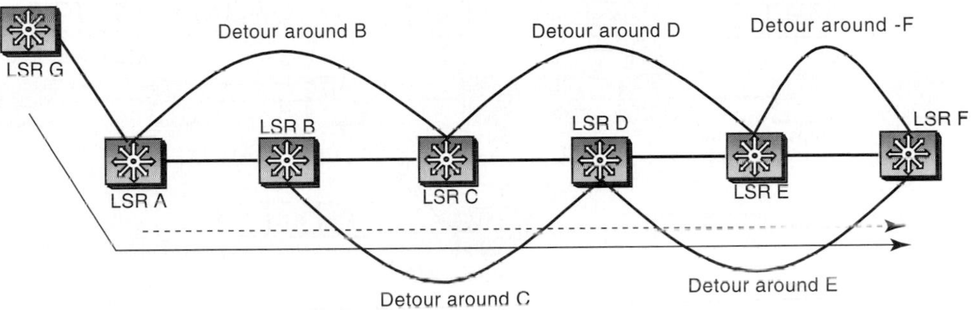

Figure 8–10 *Facility Backup Example*

LSR G to F (solid line). Both these LSPs traverse the common route from LSR A to LSR F. Each detour shown is a facility backup where the detour LSP tunnels protect both primary LSPs.

The manner in which protection is accomplished in the case of one-to-one backup is illustrated in Figure 8–11. As shown in the figure, the LSP route before the failure was A – B – C – D – E – F. An incoming packet is assigned a label 10 by LSR A. The label is switched from 10 to 40 by B, 40 to 9 by C, 9 to 13 by D, 13 to 11 by E, and finally the packet is delivered to the destination by F. When link B-C fails, LSR B immediately switches incoming packets toward LSR G, after switching the label from 10 to 20. LSR G switches the label from 20 to 17 before forwarding the packets to D. The alternate path and the labels to be assigned to incoming packets are preconfigured. At D, the packets are assigned a label 13 and forwarded to E as before.

Figure 8–12 illustrates label switching under the facility backup case. Here, a detour LSP tunnel is preprovisioned along the path B-G-D. This tunnel can carry traffic on multiple "inner" LSPs. As before, packets along an

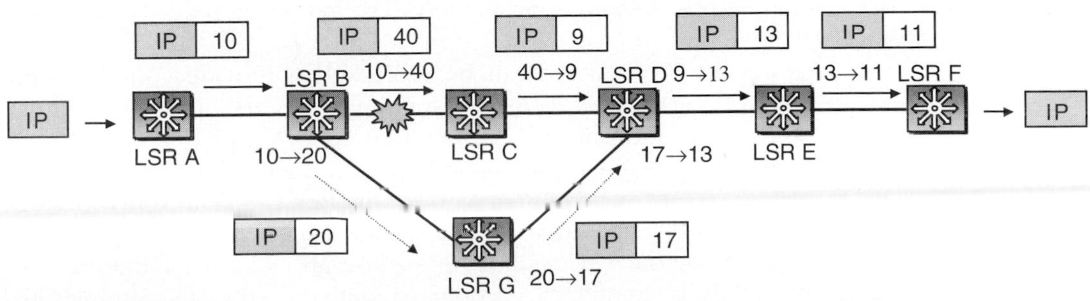

Figure 8–11 *Label Switching with One-to-One Backup*

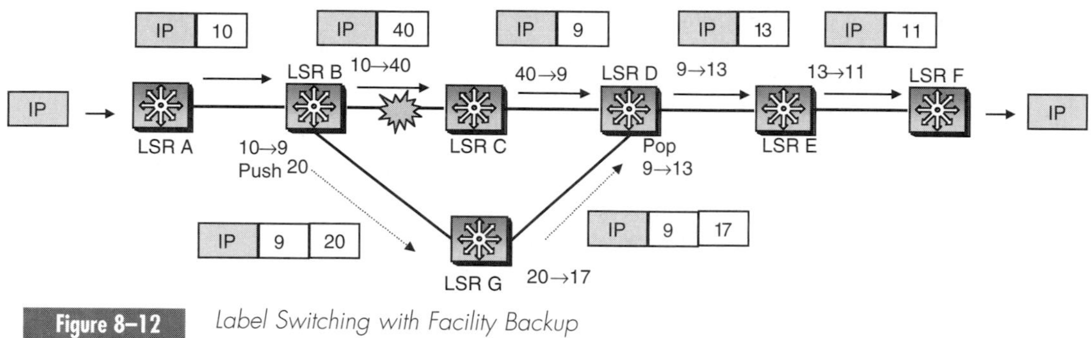

Figure 8–12 *Label Switching with Facility Backup*

LSP before the failure event are shown on top. After link B-C fails, the traffic is diverted onto the detour LSP tunnel. This is done using MPLS label stacking (see section 5.4.1). LSR B switches the incoming label (10) to the label that would have been seen by LSR D along the primary path (i.e., 9). LSR B also pushes a new top-level label, 20, corresponding to the detour LSP tunnel. Note that for other LSPs traversing the path B – C – D, LSR B would switch incoming labels to the values expected at D and push the same top-level label, 20. At LSR G, the top-level label is switched from 20 to 17. Finally, at D, the top-level label is popped to expose the original label placed by B, that is, 9. From here on, D switches the packet as if it arrived on the primary path.

From the descriptions above, it is clear that there is no internode signaling involved to effect LSP local repair. All the information needed to establish the alternate path is preconfigured. The RSVP-TE signaling for provisioning detour LSPs is described in [Pan+03]. We will not get into the details of this, but just note here that the signaling is somewhat complex. This is because a single primary LSP requires the establishment of multiple detour LSPs, and depending on the topology of the network, the detours have to be merged appropriately. The interested reader can refer to [Pan+03].

The detour LSP concept can be extended to provide complete end-to-end detour. This aspect is not covered in [Pan+03], but illustrated in Figure 8–13. Here, the primary LSP between LSRs A and F is routed as in the previous examples. A node-disjoint detour is established along the path A – G – H – I – F. When a failure occurs on the link C – D, a Notify message is sent by C to the source, that is, LSR A. LSR A then immediately switches traffic along the detour LSP as shown. Because MPLS LSPs are unidirectional, this procedure is simplified. As compared with the previous examples, the addition here is the use of the Notify message.

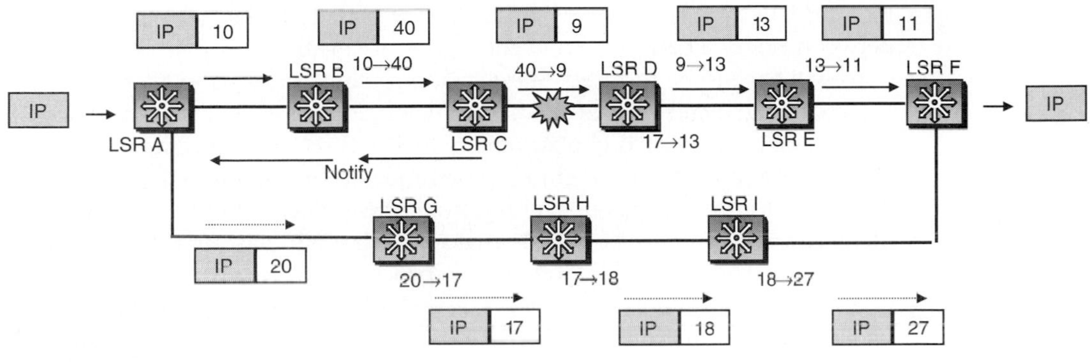

Figure 8–13 *End-to-End LSP Protection*

In summary, MPLS fast reroute based on local repair may not require any signaling during protection switching if the underlying link layer provides an upstream notification mechanism (e.g., RDI-L, see Chapter 3). Otherwise, a notification mechanism is required. End-to-end detour does require a notification mechanism, but it does not require the establishment of LSP mappings dynamically after a failure event. Furthermore, none of these protection mechanisms require coordination between the end nodes. In contrast, bidirectional 1 + 1 protection in optical networks requires a failure indication mechanism and end-to-end coordination. In addition, shared mesh protection requires the dynamic establishment of cross-connections at intermediate nodes. Thus, it is not meaningful to directly extrapolate performance observed in MPLS networks to optical networks even if a common protocol base (e.g., RSVP-TE) is used.

8.5.2 Restoration

We have focused on protection so far in this chapter. We stated in the introduction that restoration is tantamount to reprovisioning. The implication was that restoring a connection requires the same signaling procedures used during provisioning. Although this is largely true, certain issues that arise with restoration must be highlighted. First, the time to provision a connection is not as critical as the time to restore. This has some repercussions. Consider an optical network in which distributed routing is used. Suppose a failure affects a number of connections with different sources. Each of these sources will concurrently attempt to restore the connection along different paths. Because of the distributed routing, the view of the network resources at these source nodes may become temporarily out of date due to the restoration activity.

This is illustrated in Figure 8–14. Here, there are two connections, one from node A to node G, and another from node B to node H. The latter is indicated by dotted lines. Suppose there is a failure that affects both links between nodes D and G. From the figure, it can be seen that both connections will have to be restored. Suppose the routing information at nodes A and B indicate the availability of link E – G. Then, it is possible that A chooses the path A – E – G, while B chooses the path B – E – G – H. Assuming that only one of these connections can be accommodated on the link E – G, the route computed for the other connection is not correct. Because of the need to complete restoration quickly, an alternate detour path has to be dynamically computed. This requires *crank-back* procedures (see PNNI signaling in Chapter 7). Referring to Figure 8–14 again, suppose the connection from B to H is routed over the link E – G. The connection from A to G is cranked back to node A and the alternate detour path A – C – I – G is chosen. In contrast to restoration, if a provisioning request does not succeed in a network with distributed routing, the connection can be provisioned a little later after the routing information stabilizes.

Second, a network that relies entirely on restoration requires a mechanism for reoptimizing connection routing periodically. To see this, consider the example in Figure 8–14 again. The initial path for connection from A to G was A – D – G, and the restoration path was A – C – I – G. Suppose the failed links between D and G is repaired. This makes the better path available once again, to which the connection can be moved. This is similar to reversion in protection switching, but it may be implemented as part of a global reoptimization process.

Finally, restoration requires a fast notification mechanism to indicate failures along the path of a connection to the source. Where such notification is available from the SONET/SDH layer, this is not an issue, but the messaging described in earlier sections will be required otherwise.

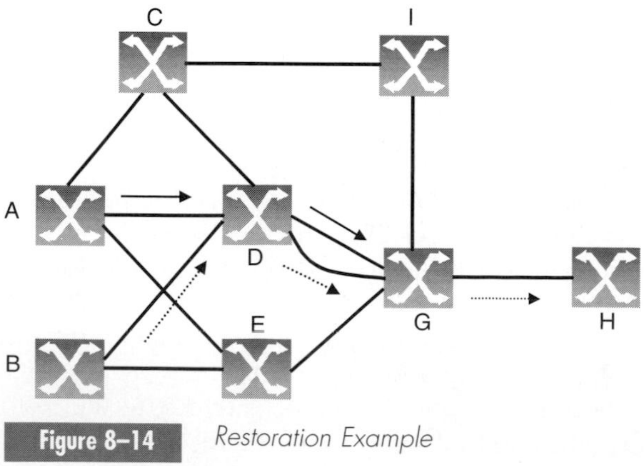

Figure 8–14 *Restoration Example*

8.6 Summary

In this chapter, we examined signaling for protection and restoration in mesh optical networks. The mesh architecture introduces certain new requirements for protection switching as compared with rings. Chief among these is the need for signaling mechanisms to notify failures and activate the protection path. In this regard, two broad choices for signaling were described: bit-oriented and message-based signaling. The bit-oriented method may have the advantage of speed and simplicity over the message-based method. It is, however, likely that the message-based method may be easier to deploy from an interoperability perspective. The performance of either signaling method in mesh networks is still an area of debate. In ring networks, the 50 ms latency requirement on protection switching is common. In mesh networks, dedicated 1 + 1 type protection switching can be achieved in 50 ms, but shared mesh protection is typically subject to higher latencies (e.g., 200 ms in certain vendor implementations). Message-based signaling in this case may lead to higher latencies than bit-oriented signaling. Another concern with message-based signaling is the possibility of signaling message "storms," that is, large number of signaling messages generated as a result of failure events, due to the requirement on signaling reliability. It is expected that more insights will be obtained on message-based signaling as studies are performed and deployments occur.

N I N E

Routing Overview

9.1 Introduction

Routing refers to the process whereby a node finds one or more paths to possible destinations in a network. Routing consists of several components: neighbor discovery, topology discovery, and path selection. Neighbor discovery is typically the first step of routing whereby the nodes in a network discover the identity of their immediate neighbors and how they are connected to these neighbors. Topology discovery is the process by which a node discovers other nodes in the network and how they are connected to each other. Once the network topology is known, paths from a source to a destination can be computed using path computation algorithms.

Due to the tremendous popularity of the Internet, routing today has become synonymous with IP routing, or routing in the IP (network) layer [Stallings03]. Optical networks are different from IP networks in many ways. But IP routing protocols, with some adaptations and extensions, can be used to dynamically route connections in optical networks. Routing in optical networks is also related to routing in telephone networks and Asynchronous Transfer Mode (ATM) networks.

In this chapter, we review the routing architectures and protocols in different networks. Given the popularity of IP and the Internet, we discuss IP routing protocols in detail. We also briefly discuss routing in telephone networks and in ATM networks. In the chapters that follow, we discuss how the IP routing protocols can be extended and enhanced to handle connection routing in dynamic optical networks.

In this and the following chapters, we distinguish between routing within a network controlled by one administrative entity and routing across networks controlled by different administrative entities. The primary focus of the next chapter is routing within a network managed by a single administrative entity, also known as *intradomain* routing. Routing across networks managed by different administrative entities, known as *interdomain* routing, is the subject of Chapter 12.

9.2 History of Routing

In this section, we review the routing architectures and their evolution in two of the largest networks in existence—the telephone network and the Internet. Routing in the circuit-switched telephone network is in many ways similar to routing connections in an optical network, which is also a circuit-switched network. Although some aspects of routing in the packet-switched Internet are similar to those of routing in telephone and optical networks, many differences exist. Different standards bodies are working on defining more sophisticated IP-centric routing protocols for routing connections in optical networks.

9.2.1 Routing in the Telephone Network

Figure 9–1 shows the architecture of today's telephone network [Briley83]. As shown in the figure, it is a three-layer hierarchy consisting of central offices (CO), local exchange carriers (LEC), and fully connected wide-area core networks. LECs may connect to multiple wide-area cores. If the two end points of a call are in the same CO, then they are directly connected. If the two end points are in different COs within the same LEC, then the call is routed over the single-hop path between the COs. If the two end points are in different LECs, then the call is routed through the core. In the following we discuss the evolution of routing in telephone networks.

Routing in the core uses either one-hop or two-hop paths. Note that the core is fully connected. The direct one-hop path between the originating and the terminating switch is considered to be the primary path between them. If the primary path between a pair of switches is available, then the call is routed over that path. If the primary path is not available, then the call is routed over

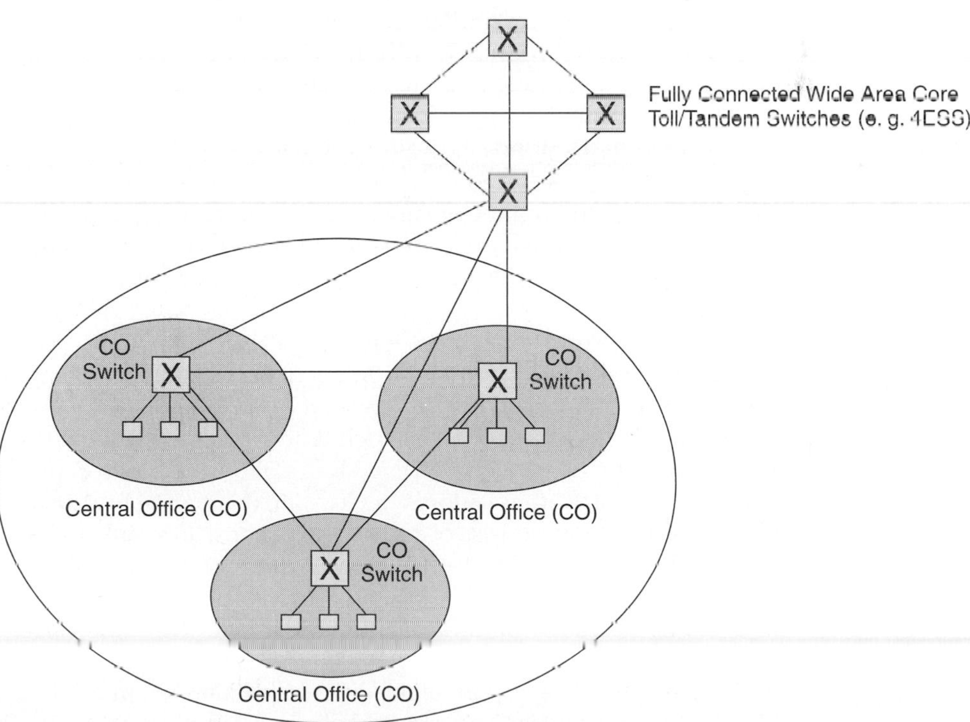

Figure 9–1 *Telephone Network Architecture*

one of the alternative two-hop paths. In that case the routing problem boils down to which two-hop path to use.

The early telephone network relied on static one-hop routing in the core. Under this scheme the path between the source and the destination switches remained fixed independent of the state of the network. The network was overprovisioned since a given fixed route had to be dimensioned to handle the peak-hour traffic. A call was dropped if the selected path was busy. Static routing in the telephony network was found to be too rigid and inefficient.

After the introduction of digital switches, static routing in the core was replaced by dynamic routing. Dynamic routing alleviated the routing inflexibility with static routing so that the network would operate more efficiently. Dynamic routing also improved network resilience by permitting the calculation of routes on a per-call basis and the periodic updating of routes. Three types of dynamic routing schemes have been designed for use in the telephone network. These are:

1. **Time-Dependent Routing (TDR):** Under TDR, regular variations in traffic loads based on the time of the day or the day of the week are exploited in planning the routing tables.
2. **State-Dependent Routing (SDR):** Under SDR, routing tables are updated in real time according to the current state of the network, for example, traffic demand, utilization, and so on.
3. **Event Dependent Routing (EDR):** Under EDR, routing changes are triggered by events such as call set-up attempts failing due to congested or blocked links. In these instances, new routes are established using learning models. EDR methods are real-time adaptive, but, unlike SDR, they do not require global state information.

Dynamic Non-Hierarchical Routing (DNHR) [Ash97] is an example of TDR. DNHR was introduced in the AT&T network in the 1980s to respond to time-dependent information such as load variations. Under DNHR, a day is divided into ten time periods. For each time period, each switch is assigned a primary one-hop path and an ordered list of alternate two-hop paths for every destination. DNHR thus adopts a "two-link" approach described earlier, whereby a path can consist of at most two hops. If a call cannot be routed over a selected route due to the unavailability of resources, the originating switch selects the next route in the list, and so on, until the call is routed or there are no alternate routes available. In the latter case, the call is blocked.

Route assignment in DNHR takes into account the network load over different time scales. Correspondingly, different routing schemes are used to preplan the routing tables. The *network design* algorithm operates over yearly intervals while the *demand-servicing* algorithm operates on a weekly basis to fine-tune link sizes and routing tables. At the smallest time scale, the routing algorithm is used to make limited adjustments based on daily traffic variations.

DNHR works well when traffic is predictable. For bursty and unpredictable traffic, the network may enter into a situation where spilled calls from overloaded links can block calls on direct links. This problem is addressed by using *link reservation,* whereby some links are reserved for direct calls only.

Real Time Network Routing (RTNR) [Ash97] is another dynamic routing algorithm used in today's telephone network. Under RTNR, each switch maintains a list of lightly loaded links that terminate on that switch. The intersection of the lists at the source and the destination switches is the set of lightly loaded paths between the source and the destination. For example, consider two switches—1 and 2. Let us assume that the set of lightly loaded links terminating on switch 1 are 1-3, 1-4, and 1-5, where 3, 4 and 5 are other switches. Hence, switch 1 maintains the list, {3,4,5}. Let us also assume that the set of lightly loaded links terminating on switch 2 are 2-3, 2-6, and 2-7, where 6 and 7 are two other switches. Consequently, the list maintained by switch 2 is {3,7,8}. Now, if a call has to be routed from switch 1 to switch 2, switches 1 and 2 exchange their lists with each other. The intersection between the two lists is switch 3. Hence, 1-3-2 is a good alternate (two-hop) path between switches 1 and 2. RTNR works very well in practice resulting in very few blocked calls.

Despite their common roots in circuit switching, routing in telephone and optical networks are subject to different requirements. The topology of telephone networks is rather restricted, that is, complete mesh in which the routes are at most two hops long. An optical network, on the other hand, can have a general mesh topology with routes longer than two hops. In this regard, optical networks are similar to IP networks. This is one of the reasons why IP routing protocols, rather than telephony routing protocols, have been extended to route connections in optical networks.

9.2.2 Routing in the Internet

Unlike telephone networks, the Internet does not have a rigid structure. It is a collection of networks that are interconnected at various peering points (see Figure 9–2) [Halabi+00]. Different Internet Service Providers (ISPs) manage this collection of networks. The peering points are the points where the ISPs exchange traffic from each other. Depending on the size and the reach of their networks, ISPs can be classified into different tiers. Tier 1 ISPs are the Global/National ISPs that are the top of the ISP hierarchy. Tier 1 ISP networks are connected to each other at various public and private peering points and form the backbone of the global Internet. Tier 2 and Tier 3 ISPs are typically the regional and local service providers and their networks are connected to the Internet through Tier 1 providers. Tier 2 and Tier 3 providers also peer with each other at different private and public peering points. We should note here that the peering relationship is typically an agreement of equals, whereby service providers exchange traffic from each other when the volume of traffic flowing in each direction is approximately equal. For asymmetric traffic

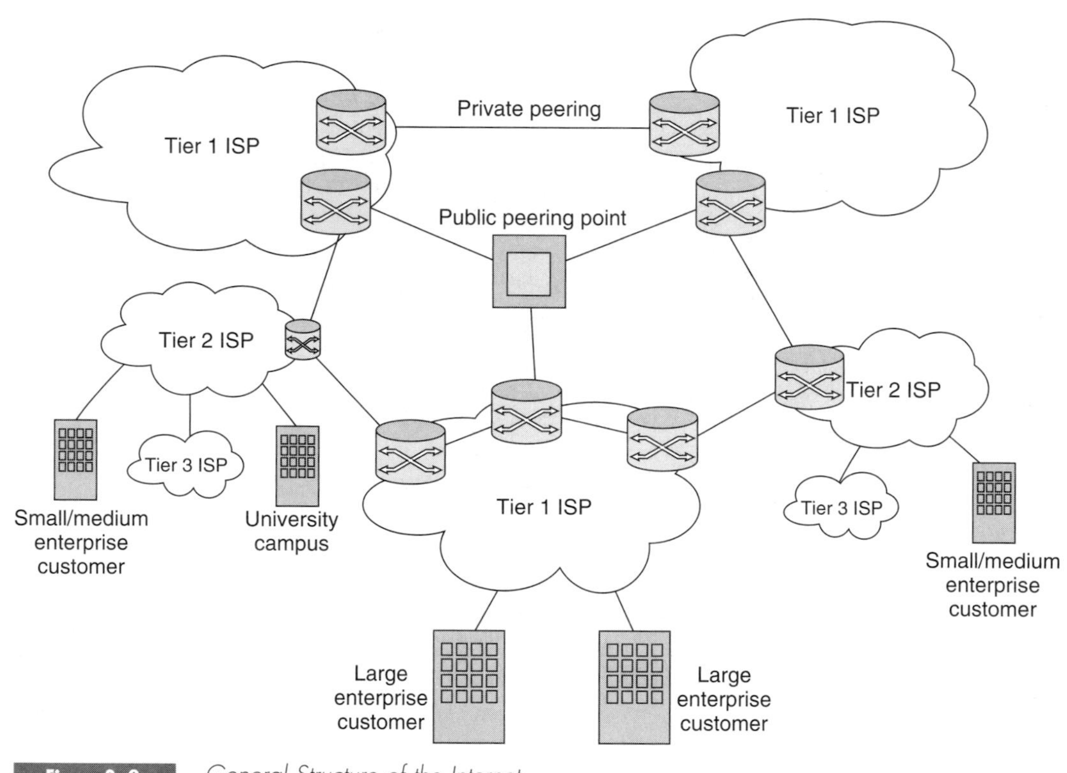

Figure 9–2 *General Structure of the Internet*

flow, ISPs often strike transit relationships, whereby a smaller ISP sends traffic through a lager service provider for a transit fee. Businesses and individual customers are connected to the Internet through ISPs. Businesses are often connected to multiple service providers for reliability.

From a more technical point of view, the Internet is a collection of "autonomous systems" or ASs. From a control plane point of view, an AS is similar to a control domain described in Chapter 5. It is defined to be the collection of IP networks managed by a single organization. The definition of an organization is fairly loose. It can be a service provider, a company, or a university. Many organizations span multiple ASs. Some organizations do have their own AS(s). Neighboring ASs are connected to each other as peers through private and public Internet exchange points. Two ASs may also have a customer and a provider relationship when traffic from the customer AS transits through the provider AS. Neighboring ASs may exchange information about reachable destinations with each other. They do not, however, exchange internal topology information. There is a large number (approximately 11,500) of ASs with different sizes in the Internet.

9.3 Routing Protocol Basics

9.3.1 Routing and Forwarding

In the context of the Internet, the term "routing" is used loosely to identify both control and data plane functions. It is, however, important to differentiate between these functions. The role of the control plane is to allow nodes to discover the topology of the network and compute routes to other nodes. This is accomplished by running a routing protocol that advertises topology and reachability information throughout the network. The reachability information disseminated by the routing protocol is consolidated in a *forwarding table* at each node, which contains the identity of the next node and the outgoing interface to forward packets addressed to each destination.

The data plane function at a router consists of forwarding incoming IP packets (or datagrams) toward their destinations, using the information contained in the forwarding table. More specifically, forwarding an IP datagram involves examining the destination IP address of the datagram, searching the forwarding table to determine the next hop and the corresponding outgoing interface, and then forwarding the datagram to the next hop. Forwarding also involves other functions, such as examining and decrementing the time-to-live (TTL) field of the packet and examining and adjusting the header checksum (see Figure 5-11) [Tanenbaum02]. If quality of service (QoS) features are implemented, then the forwarding function may include packet classification based on the source address, destination address and other fields found in the IP header, and perhaps even the IP payload [Braden+97, Wroclawski97].

It should be noted that only the control plane of IP routing is adapted for use in optical networks. The packet forwarding function of IP routing is not relevant in these networks.

9.3.2 Routing Protocol Design Tenets

The following principles are generally followed in the design of IP routing protocols:

- **Simplicity:** Routing algorithms are designed to be as simple as possible. In other words, a routing algorithm is ideally designed to function efficiently, incurring the minimum computational and communication overhead. Efficiency is particularly important when the routing software must run on a processor with limited resources.
- **Scalability:** Scalability is the ability of a routing protocol to accommodate a large number of routers and end-systems without incurring excessive overheads. This is one of the most important design

tenets of any IP routing protocol. There are different ways of achieving scalability, such as employing a routing hierarchy or performing route aggregation (see Chapters 10 and 12). Both these techniques help contain the size of the routing databases. Another common technique for achieving scalability is to reduce the number of routing updates using thresholding schemes. This is further described in Chapter 10.

- **Optimality and accuracy:** Optimality refers to the ability of a routing algorithm to select the best route, as defined by some metric (see Chapter 11). As an example, a routing algorithm may use the number of hops and total delay as metrics, but may weight delay more heavily in the calculation of routes. Naturally, routing metrics must be defined precisely for the type of optimization to be performed.
- **Robustness and stability:** Routing algorithms must be robust, which means that they should perform correctly under adverse circumstances, such as when hardware failures, high load conditions or incorrect implementations are encountered. Because routers are located at network junction points, they can cause significant problems when they fail. The best routing algorithms are often those that have withstood the test of time and have proven stable under a variety of network conditions.
- **Convergence:** In addition to being robust, routing algorithms must converge rapidly. Convergence is the process by which all routers agree on optimal routes. When a network event causes existing routes to become unavailable or new routes to become available, routers distribute routing update messages throughout the network. This results in the recalculation of optimal routes by some or all routers. Routing algorithms that converge slowly can cause routing loops or network outages.

  Figure 9–3 illustrates the looping problem in a network consisting of eight routers (R1-R8). Here, a packet destined to R8 arrives at R1. The shortest path from R1 to R8 is the direct link. But that link is down as shown. Suppose that R1 has already recomputed the optimal route to R8 as (R2-R3-R4-R8). It therefore forwards the packet to R2. Suppose that R2 has not yet received the information about the failed link and it still has R1 listed as the next hop to R8 (along the path R2-R1-R8). R2 therefore forwards the packet back to R1, and the packet continues to bounce back and forth between the two routers until R2 receives the routing update.
- **Flexibility:** Routing protocols should be flexible, that is, they should accommodate different metrics, support one or more routes to destinations, multiple routing hierarchies, and most importantly future extensions.

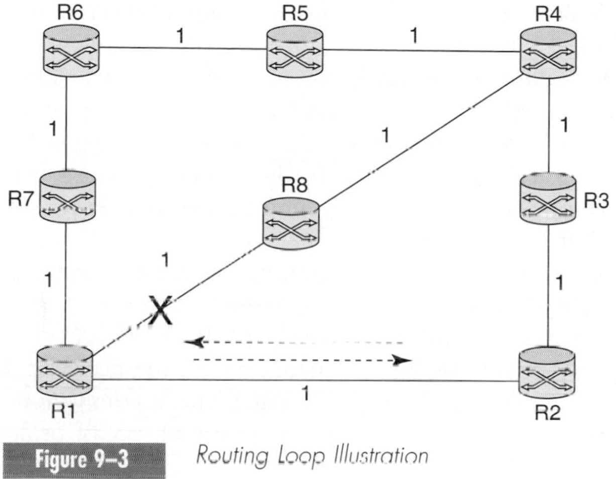

Figure 9–3 *Routing Loop Illustration*

9.3.3 Different Types of IP Routing Protocols

There are two basic types of IP routing protocols: distance-vector and link-state. Under the distance-vector approach, each node maintains the distance (e.g., hop count) to each destination through each of its neighbors. The next hop to a destination is taken to be the neighbor through which the distance to the destination is minimum. Under the link state approach, each node maintains the complete view of the network topology. To keep this view up-to-date, each node broadcasts the details of its local links to other nodes in the network. Nodes compute paths to different destinations based on the topology view. These routing approaches are described further below.

9.3.3.1 DISTANCE VECTOR ROUTING

Under the distance vector approach, each node maintains the cost (or distance) to each destination through each of its neighbors. A node selects the neighbor through which the cost to a destination is minimum as the next hop for that destination. The intention is that from any node the succession of next hops would lead to the destination. The cost of a path from a source to a destination is the sum of the costs of the links in the path. The network administrator typically provisions link costs, although it is possible to automatically map certain link characteristics into costs. A change in the link cost occurs when the link fails, or when the cost is updated. A change in the cost of the link would result in the change in the cost of all paths that use the link. This change would first be observed by the two end points of the link. These nodes would then update the costs to different destinations that are reachable over the link. If a node determines a change in the minimum cost to a destination, it sends the new minimum distance to its neighbors. If the minimum distances to different destinations maintained by a neighbor change due to these updates, the process is repeated [Tanenbaum02].

It is well known that classical distance-vector algorithms such as distributed Bellman-Ford [Bellman58, Ford+62] may produce both short-lived and long-lived loops (Figure 9–3). Routing Information Protocol (RIP) [Hedrick88] is an example of a routing protocol that uses the distributed Bellman-Ford algorithm (see Chapter 11). New generations of distance vector algorithms, such as Merlin-Segall algorithm [Merlin+79], avoid looping. A variation of the distance vector approach, known as *path vector*, utilizes information about the entire sequence of "next hops" to a destination (i.e., the nodes in the path) to detect and avoid routing loops [Rajagopalan+91]. The Border Gateway Protocol (BGP) [Stewart99, Rekhter+95] is an example of a path vector protocol.

9.3.3.2 LINK STATE ROUTING

Under the link-state approach, each node maintains a view of the network topology and link costs. When the state of a link changes (up to down or vice versa, or a change in link cost), a notification, called a *Link State Advertisement (LSA)* is flooded throughout the network. All the nodes note the change and recompute their routes accordingly. Note that a node's view of the link state may not be the same as another node's due to long propagation delays, partitioned networks, and so on. Such inconsistent views of network topology at different nodes may lead to routing loops. These loops, however, are short-lived, and they disappear after the link-state updates are received by all the nodes. Link state routing protocols are more scalable and less bandwidth-intensive than distance vector routing protocols. They are, however, more complex, and more compute- and memory-intensive.

The first link-state routing protocol, called Shortest Path First (SPF), was developed for use in the ARPANET (Department of Defense's Advanced Research Project Agency, now called DARPA) packet switching network. It was the starting point for all other link state protocols developed later. The homogeneous ARPANET environment, that is, single-vendor packet switches connected by synchronous serial lines, simplified the design and implementation of the original protocol. Over time, the protocol matured with many enhancements. These enhancements dealt with improving the fault tolerance and convergence of the routing protocol. Among other things, this included the addition of a checksum to LSAs (thereby detecting database corruption). It also included means for reducing the routing traffic overhead. This was accomplished by introducing mechanisms, which enabled the interval between LSA originations to be increased by an order of magnitude.

The Internet Engineering Task Force (IETF) extended the SPF work to develop the Open Shortest-Path First (OSPF) routing protocol [Moy98]. OSPF is a hierarchical link state routing protocol that supports multiple routing areas.

This enables routing scalability through information hiding and summarization. OSPF also includes specific features for efficient operation in internets consisting of broadcast Local Area Networks (LANs) and other multiple access networks. A somewhat similar link state protocol, called IS-IS (Intermediate System to Intermediate System), was specified by the International Standards Organization (ISO), and adopted by the IETF for IP routing [Callon90].

9.4 Internet Routing Protocols

As mentioned earlier, Internet routing protocols can be classified into interdomain and intradomain routing protocols. Interdomain routing protocols are also referred to as *Exterior Gateway Protocols* or EGPs, based on early Internet terminology. BGP is the most popular example of an EGP. In fact, it is the only EGP that is in use in the Internet today. Intradomain routing protocols, on the other hand, are referred to as *Interior Gateway Protocols* or IGPs. Examples of IGPs include OSPF, IS-IS, and RIP. Figure 9–4 gives an overview of different routing protocols running in the Internet.

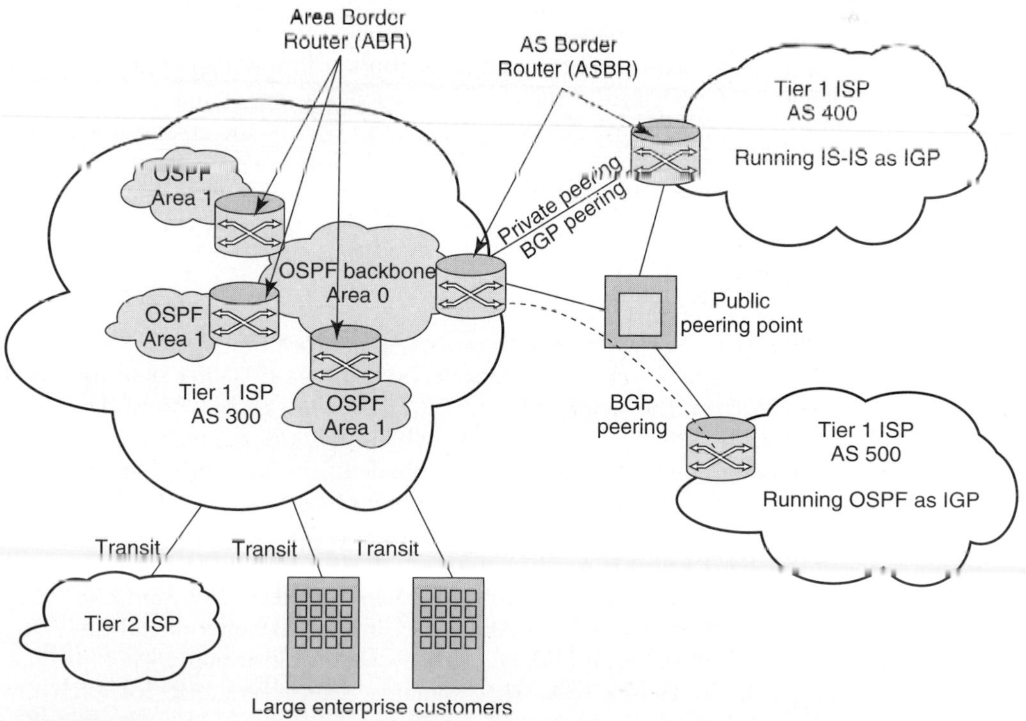

Figure 9–4 *IGPs and EGP in the Internet*

9.4.1 Intradomain Routing Protocols

9.4.1.1 RIP

RIP is an IGP based on the distance vector routing paradigm. It is also known by the name of its Unix implementation, *routed* (pronounced route-d), which was originally designed at University of California at Berkeley to provide consistent routing and reachability information among machines on a LAN. RIP's popularity is not necessarily based on its technical merits, but due to the fact that U.C. Berkeley distributed *routed* along with their popular BSD UNIX systems. Thus, many Internet sites adopted and installed *routed* without even considering its technical merits and limitations. Once installed and running, it became the basis for local routing.

Typical of a distance vector algorithm, RIP works fine for small, stable, high-speed networks. Routers running RIP broadcast their entire routing database periodically, typically every 30 seconds. This message lists each destination along with a "distance" to that destination, measured in number of router hops. Each router selects as next hop the neighbor whose distance is the shortest to a given destination, and advertises its own distance to all its neighbors.

Because every router is broadcasting its entire routing table, it takes a while for these tables to converge in times of network instability. Under RIP, there is no explicit protection from routing loops. Rather, a route is rejected when the associated distance (cost) reaches a maximum. Due to this, RIP suffers from slow convergence; when a loop occurs, the corresponding path cost tends to slowly increase, and the routing loop persists until the cost reaches the maximum value. In large networks or networks with slow links, some routers may still advertise a route that has ceased to exist.

9.4.1.2 OSPF

OSPF is a link state routing protocol. In contrast to a distance vector protocol, where a router "tells all neighbors about the world," link state routers "tell the world about the neighbors." OSPF LSAs allow routers to update each other about the LAN and WAN links to which they are connected. When a change is made to the network, LSAs are broadcast throughout the network. Five different types of LSAs are defined in OSPF. They are:

1. **Router LSA:** This contains the state and the cost of all point-to-point links that terminate on a router. There is only one router LSA associated with a router. (Note: In optical networks all links are point-to-point and hence can be captured in router LSAs.)
2. **Network LSA:** This contains a representation for each broadcast network, e.g., Ethernet. (Note: Network LSA is not necessary in optical networks.)

3. **Summary LSA:** For reasons of scalability, OSPF networks are often divided into multiple areas. Router and network LSAs pertaining to nodes and links in an area are contained within the area. Information about reachable destinations within an area is sent in summary LSAs to nodes outside the area. (Note: Summary LSAs may be used in optical networks with multiarea routing.)
4. **External LSA and ASBR LSA:** Routes learned form other ASs are distributed using external and ASBR (AS Border Router) LSAs.
5. **Opaque LSA:** Opaque LSAs provide a standard way to extend OSPF. We will see in Chapter 10 how opaque LSAs are used to extend OSPF for routing in optical networks.

OSPF routers receive LSAs and store them in a topology database, known as the *Link State Database* (LSDB). The typical LSDB contains a representation of every link and router in the network. The LSDB is used to calculate a forwarding table that lists the next hop to each destination. Each router uses an *identical* procedure, called Dijkstra's algorithm [Dijkstra59] (see Chapter 11), to compute consistent forwarding tables.

OSPF addresses all of the shortcomings of RIP and it is therefore better suited for routing in large, dynamic networks. For example, instead of sending its entire routing table to its neighbors every 30 seconds under RIP, a router broadcasts its local link state information every 30 minutes under OSPF. OSPF can get away with this large update interval, because OSPF routers also broadcast small update messages (typically less than 75 bytes) whenever they detect a change in the network (e.g., a failure or a new link). When routers exchange updates that reflect changes in the network, they converge to a new representation of the topology quickly and accurately.

Although it improves upon RIP, OSPF itself had to address the following issues. First, the number of LSAs that flow between routers can become an issue in large configurations. For instance, in a network with over a hundred routers, a single link change can precipitate a flood of LSAs that propagate across the entire network. Next, each time there is a change in the network, routers must recompute routes. In very large OSPF networks, topology convergence can be delayed while routers exchange link-state messages, update databases, and recalculate routes.

OSPF addresses these issues by incorporating the notion of areas (see Figure 9–5). OSPF areas are simply logical subdivisions of an OSPF network. Typically, an enterprise is divided into areas that correspond to buildings, campuses, regions, etc. An enterprise can have a large number of areas.

OSPF routers within one area do not exchange detailed topology information with routers in other areas. When a LAN or WAN link is added to one area, topology updates flow only to routers within that area. This reduces the number of updates that flow through the network and the size of the topology databases in each router. In an enterprise with 500 routers, the creation

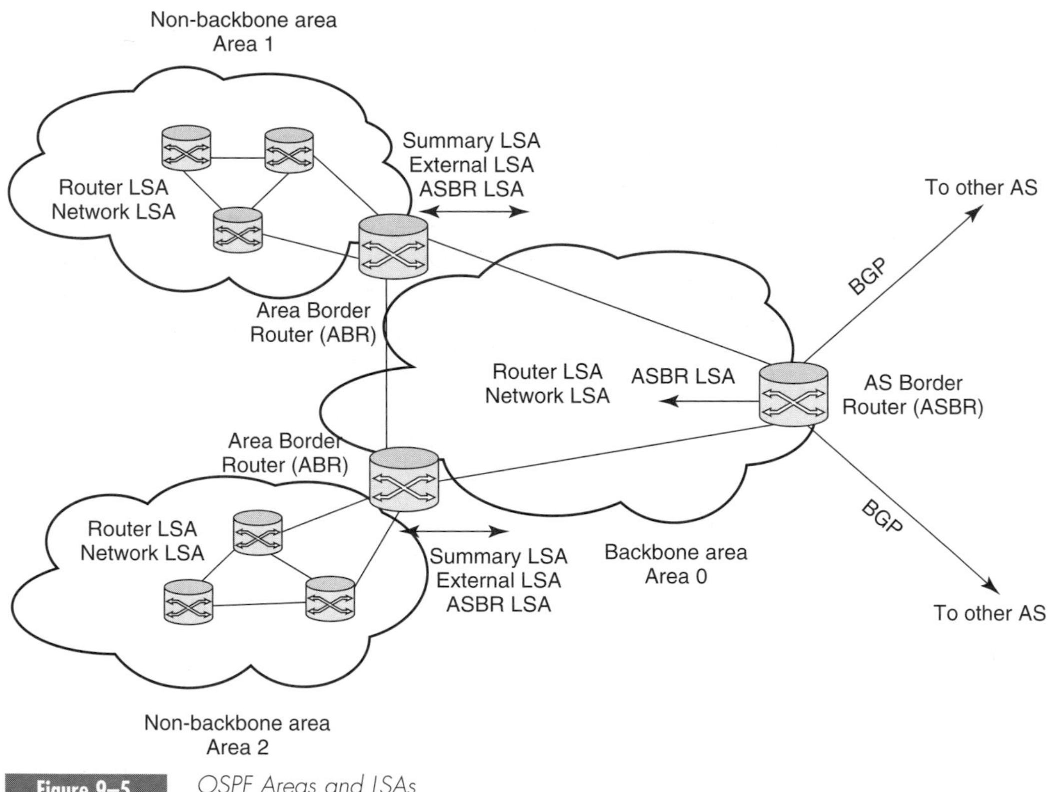

Figure 9–5 *OSPF Areas and LSAs*

of 10 areas of 50 routers means that each router only needs to store link information for 50 routers, and not for all 500. OSPF areas are connected to each other by means of a *backbone* area that is just another area by itself. A router that connects its area to the backbone area must maintain the topology databases for both areas. These special multiarea routers are called Area Border Routers (ABRs), and they serve as a filter for the routing information that moves between the other areas and the backbone. ABRs send summary LSAs that contain a summarization of the reachability information pertaining to their areas.

This technique of hierarchical routing reduces the complexity of an OSPF network, as a router need not know the internal details of all the areas. Each ABR sends out summary LSAs that advertise the IP address prefixes reachable within its area. Other ABRs store these summarization messages and use them to compute routes for the interarea traffic. While summarization of IP addresses as prefixes reduces the routing overhead, it does introduce an administrative overhead. Specifically, summarized prefixes must be administratively configured in ABRs. This task is similar to the configuration of router traffic filters or priorities.

A good example of the benefits of OSPF areas can be seen in a campus environment, where each building is defined as an area. Let us take a campus where each building has multiple floors and a router on each floor. Without OSPF areas, routers would have to exchange updates with every other router on the campus. When areas are configured, routers only exchange link state information with routers in the same building. An ABR in each building forms a link between the building and the campus backbone.

Another example of the application of OSPF areas is a national network that is divided into areas corresponding to different regions of the country. For example, all the routers in the New York area would have identical databases that cover the New York region only, and the same would apply to other regions as well. In each area, an ABR is attached to the national backbone. This approach eliminates the need to propagate router update messages across the entire national network.

OSPF is the de facto industry standard protocol because of its robustness. It supports the requirements of larger networks such as special service requests and authentication of routing protocol messages. OSPF is an efficient protocol, supporting speedy recovery from topology changes. OSPF also minimizes overhead traffic by only sending updates on changes rather than the entire routing table.

9.4.1.3 IS-IS

IS-IS is also a link state routing protocol that offers similar services as OSPF. IS-IS, however, was developed by ISO as a part of the Open System Interconnection (OSI) network architecture [Tanenbaum02]. IS-IS was originally developed for routing within ISO Connectionless Network Protocol (CLNP) networks. It was later extended to support IP routing [Callon90].

In OSI terms, an *end system* (*ES*) refers to any network node that does not perform routing (e.g., a host) whereas an *intermediate system* (*IS*) is a router. Thus, the ES-IS protocol allows ESs and ISs to identify each other while IS-IS supports routing between ISs.

IS-IS periodically floods the network with link state information, allowing each router to maintain a complete picture of the network's topology. Optional path metrics available with IS-IS are based on delay, expense, and error. The delay metric represents the amount of delay on a particular link. Expense relates to the communications costs of using the link. The error metric represents the error rate of the link. The use of these metrics allows IS-IS to respond to the quality of service (QoS) field in the CLNP packet header. These mappings tell the IS-IS protocol to compute a path that best matches requested QoS.

IS-IS uses three basic packet types: *Hello*, *Link State*, and *Sequence Number*. For further details on IS-IS, refer to [Callon90, ISO90].

9.4.2 Interdomain Routing Protocols

The goal of interdomain routing is to exchange routing information across ASs. An AS is typically a collection of networks with the same routing policy and usually under single ownership, trust, and administrative control. An AS consists of one or more border routers, which exchange routes with border routers in other ASs. In addition, border routers may participate in intradomain routing within the AS.

9.4.2.1 BGP

BGP is the de facto standard interdomain routing protocol in the Internet. It was first specified in 1989. BGP version 4, the most recent version of BGP, was first specified in 1994 and updated in IETF RFC 1771 [Rekhter+95]. There also have been a number of other documented extensions to BGP.

The BGP protocol instance running in a border router establishes peer relationships with adjacent border routers, referred to as neighbors. Unlike OSPF and ISIS, which automatically discover the routing neighbors, BGP has to be configured with the peers' IP addresses and their AS Numbers (ASNs) over the appropriate interfaces. BGP peers send small keep-alive messages to each other. If a neighbor stops receiving keep-alive messages for a predefined hold time, it will update its routing table to reflect the loss of available routes through the corresponding peer. A router running BGP also sends incremental updates to its peers when routes become unavailable. Otherwise, the full routing tables are exchanged only when two routers first establish or reestablish a peering relationship.

BGP is a path vector protocol, which is similar to a distance vector protocol, but with a key difference. A distance vector protocol advertises only the cost of the path to a destination. A path vector protocol advertises both the cost of the path as well as the sequence of nodes in the path [Rajagopalan+91]. Under BGP, the path information is described at the level of ASs rather than individual nodes. A router running BGP chooses a route that traverses the least number of ASs to a destination. To enable this, a router that first advertises reachability to a destination includes its own AS number in the advertisement. Each router that receives this advertisement and propagates to other routers appends its AS number to the path information. By default, the path with the fewest ASs to a destination network is stored in the routing table. Since the path to a given destination can traverse multiple routers within an AS, the actual hop count may be higher than what the AS path indicates. The path information also helps in avoiding routing loops; a router that receives an external advertisement that includes its own AS number will reject the advertisement.

One of the advantages of BGP is its built-in flexibility to enhance the default behavior. For instance, it may be desirable to control the path taken by the traffic leaving a network. By default, BGP determines the optimal path by picking the route that has the fewest number of ASs. Because BGP does not take link speed or network load into consideration when computing paths, the shortest path may not be the optimal one. BGP's Local Preference attribute [Stewart99] allows some control over route selection. This attribute forces BGP to choose a particular route out of an AS when there are multiple choices. Another BGP attribute, Multi-Exit Discriminator (MED) [Rekhter+95], helps control the path taken by traffic coming into an AS.

BGP routing can be controlled through the Community attribute that identifies a group or community of routes. A BGP router takes a predefined action based on the value of the attribute. This value can be defined by the network administrator, but a well-known value corresponds to the predefined community, called No-Export. When a BGP router sees a route come in with the No-Export community, it will not advertise the route outside its own AS. This can be handy for balancing incoming traffic.

9.5 P-NNI

P-NNI routing and signaling protocols are used to discover an ATM network topology, create a database of topology information, and route ATM virtual circuits over the discovered topology [ATMF02]. Under the P-NNI model, the network is viewed as a multilevel hierarchy. Each level in the hierarchy consists of one or more entities known as the peer group. The constituents of the peer group vary depending on the level of the hierarchy. At the lowest level of the hierarchy, the peer groups consist of network elements, namely, the switches. As we move up in the hierarchy, the peer groups consist of abstract nodes representing peer groups at the lower layers. The structure of the P-NNI hierarchy, P-NNI peer groups, peer group leader, and border nodes were described in Chapter 5. P-NNI signaling was described in Chapter 7. In the following, we look at P-NNI routing briefly.

9.5.1 P-NNI Routing

P-NNI routing follows the link state paradigm, and it is hierarchical. Neighboring nodes form a peer group by exchanging their peer group identifiers (PGIDs) in Hello packets using a protocol that makes the nodes known to each other. If the nodes have the same PGID, they belong to the peer group defined by that particular ID. If their PGIDs are different, they belong to different peer groups. A border node has at least one link that crosses the peer group boundary. Hello protocol exchanges occur over logical links.

P-NNI defines the creation and distribution of a topology database that describes the elements of the routing domain as seen by a node. This database provides all the information required to compute a route from the node to any address that is reachable in or through that routing domain. Nodes exchange database information using P-NNI Topology State Elements (PTSE). PTSEs contain topology characteristics derived from link or node state parameter information. The state parameter information could be either metrics or attributes. PTSEs are grouped to form the P-NNI Topology State Packet (PTSP). PTSPs are flooded throughout the peer group so that all the nodes in a peer group can converge to identical databases.

As described in Chapter 5, every peer group has a peer group leader (PGL). There is at most one active PGL per peer group. The PGL will represent the peer group in the parent peer group as a single node. The PGL also floods the PTSEs received in the parent peer group into its own peer group. Apart from its specific role in aggregation and distribution of information for maintaining the P-NNI hierarchy, the PGL does not have any special role in the peer group.

P-NNI routing works in conjunction with P-NNI signaling during connection establishment. Specifically, the crank-back feature in the signaling protocol allows inaccuracies in summarized routing information to be compensated for during connection establishment. Connection establishment under P-NNI, which was described in Chapter 7, consists of two operations: the selection of a path and the setup of the connection state at each node along that path. If the computed path is not correct (due to inconsistencies in the summarized view and the actual state), the connection set-up attempt may be blocked en route. The crank-back feature allows the path to be partially or fully recomputed by nodes en route.

In summary, P-NNI routing is highly scalable due to the large number of hierarchical levels allowed. Furthermore, it incorporates multiple link and node metrics, and mechanisms to summarize peer group topology and attributes. Some of these concepts have been used to define interdomain routing in optical networks, as described in Chapter 12.

9.6 Summary

In this chapter, we reviewed routing protocols used in different types of networks. Specifically, we covered the evolution of routing in the telephone network, described intradomain and interdomain IP routing protocols, and briefly discussed ATM P-NNI routing. This background information is necessary to understand the topics covered in the following chapters on intradomain and interdomain routing in optical networks.

T E N

Intradomain Optical Routing

10.1 Introduction

Today, routing a connection in a traditional optical transport network involves a number of steps. Many of these involve manual actions, and hence painstaking and error-prone. Also, the routing infrastructure is predominantly centralized. A centralized Element or Network Management System (EMS/NMS) acts as the repository of the network topology database. The entries in the topology database are often entered and updated manually. Routers are computed automatically, but with manual intervention. There is a strong desire among the network operators to transition from this centralized and manual approach to a more distributed and automated routing system. In this chapter, we discuss a distributed routing architecture for optical networks that has been endorsed by different standard bodies, as well as user communities.

The primary focus of this chapter is on intradomain routing. Interdomain routing is the subject of Chapter 12. Also the emphasis in this chapter is on protocols for network topology discovery and dissemination. The path computation aspect of routing is covered in Chapter 11. Much of the discussion in this chapter is based on the work in the Internet Engineering Task Force (IETF), the International Telecommunications Union (ITU-T), and the Optical Interworking Forum (OIF). These proposals are generally extensions of intradomain IP routing protocols, such as OSPF and IS-IS, to handle routing of connections in optical networks.

10.2 Differences between IP and Optical Routing

Although IP routing protocols are being extended for routing connections in optical networks, there are major differences between routing in circuit switched optical networks and routing in packet switched IP networks.

- IP routing involves both control and data plane functionality. The function of the control plane is twofold: to distribute topology information throughout the network (link state routing) and to compute a forwarding table from the topology information. The actual forwarding of IP packets, using the forwarding table, is the function of the data plane. No connection is established ahead of time, and packets are forwarded hop by hop from the source to the destination. In optical networks, as in other circuit-switched networks, the data plane is not involved in connection routing. In these networks, end-to-end connections are explicitly established based on the network topology and resource information. Once a connection is established, data is transferred over that connection without further involvement of the routing engine.

- In IP networks, the routing protocols are intimately involved with data plane forwarding decisions and hence their failure adversely impacts the services offered to end users. Due to the separation of control and data planes, routing protocol failures in optical networks do not adversely impact existing connections. This does not imply routing is less critical in the optical case, only that its service-impacting effect is secondary. For example, topology and resource status inaccuracies will affect the establishment of new connections, but will not (and should not) cause an existing connection to be torn down.
- Since a connection has to be established and appropriate resources have to be reserved in advance of data transfer, routing in an optical network requires knowledge of the availability of different resources in the network. Current versions of intradomain IP routing protocols do not handle resource availability information. Recent routing extensions for IP traffic engineering address this issue. Further enhancements are necessary to handle detailed resource availability information required for routing connections in optical networks. Also in optical networks, a connection establishment could be blocked if resources are not available, whereas some level of overloading (and temporary congestion) is tolerated in IP networks. In other words, statistical multiplexing is a feature not applicable in optical networks.
- Another difference between routing in IP and optical networks is that IP routing is hop-by-hop while routing in optical network is typically source-directed. In other words, with IP routing each node on the path from a source to a destination independently decides the next hop to forward a packet. Hence, it is important that all nodes in the network have consistent topological view and they all use the same route computation algorithm. In optical networks, the source node is responsible for computing the entire path from the source to the destination. Hence, as long as the source has the right topological information of the network, it can compute the best path. Also, it is not necessary for all nodes to use the same route computation algorithm.
- Finally, another important difference in routing arises due to protection and restoration requirements. In IP networks, traffic is typically forwarded over the shortest path. If there is a failure in the network, the routing scheme discovers alternate paths and packets are routed around the failure. In other words, network failures are handled in a reactionary fashion. On the other hand, one of the basic features of optical networks is the protection of connections using precomputed and often preprovisioned, facility-diverse backup paths (see Chapter 8). Facility diversity ensures that the working and the protection paths are not concurrently affected by the same failure. In order to compute facility-diverse working and protection paths, switches in the

network need to have access to physical plant information. The physical diversity information is not available in IP routing.

In the following, we discuss some of the network characteristics that make routing in optical networks different from routing in IP networks. We also address how these specific characteristics can be abstracted and distributed using the mechanisms provided by link state IP routing protocols.

10.3 Routing with Physical Diversity

Route diversity is an important constraint often imposed on multiple connections between the same end points in an optical network. In particular, the requirement on link diversity is common, that is, two connections may not be routed over a common link. Occasionally, a more stringent node diversity requirement might arise, that is, two connections may not be routed via any common node.

Physical diversity between connections is driven by the need to prevent connections from being affected by the same failure. Two connections are said to be diverse if no single failure would affect both of them. In traditional transport networks, the dominant failure mode is a failure in the interoffice plant, such as a fiber cut. Data network operators have relied on their private line providers to ensure diversity so that IP routing protocols do not have to deal directly with the problem.

The concept of Shared Risk Link Group (SRLG) [Hjálmtysson+00] is used to capture diversity. An SRLG identifier is a number assigned to a set of links that are realized over the same physical resources and hence subject to the same failure. A given link may be assigned more than one SRLG identifier depending on the underlying physical resources. The SRLGs associated with a link can thus be viewed as an abstraction of different physical resources whose failure may affect the service on that link. The following are different forms of physical diversity captured by SRLGs:

- **Cable (conduit) diversity.** A cable (conduit) is a physical enclosure for a collection of fibers. Two fibers are said to be cable (conduit) diverse if they are carried over different cables (conduits). Two connections are cable (conduit) diverse if they are routed over fibers that are cable (conduit) diverse. This type of diversity helps to protect against the vulnerability of connections to "ordinary" cable cuts (technically known as *backhoe fades*). A set of cable (conduit) diverse paths may be computed by associating a unique SRLG identifier to each cable (conduit), assigning that SRLG value to each link realized over that cable (conduit) and choosing links with different SRLG values for each path.

- **Right of way (ROW) diversity.** ROW denotes the physical path (terrestrial or underwater) of one or more conduits. ROW diversity helps to protect against larger scale disasters such as ship anchor drags, train derailments, and so on. A set of ROW diverse paths may be computed by associating a unique SRLG identifier to each ROW, assigning that SRLG value to each link traversing that ROW, and choosing links with different SRLG values for each path.
- **Geographic route diversity.** This type of diversity helps to protect against various larger scale disasters such as earthquakes, floods, tornadoes, hurricanes, and so on. For this purpose, geography can be approximately described by a piecewise set of latitude/longitude or Universal Transverse Mercator (UTM) coordinate pairs. A set of geographic route diverse paths may be computed by associating a unique SRLG identifier to each geographic area, assigning that SRLG value to each link traversing that area, and choosing links with different SRLG values for each path.

The SRLG concept can be adopted to cover node diversity. In this case, a "node" can be one network element, a set of network elements, or even an entire network. From the point of view of node diverse routing, specific entities of interest include nodes, physical points of presence (e.g., a switching center), geographic areas, service provider networks, and so on. A set of node diverse paths may be computed by assigning a unique SRLG identifier to each node and choosing nodes with different SRLG values for each path.

Dealing with diversity is an unavoidable requirement for routing in optical networks. It requires the ability to deal with constraints in the routing process but, more importantly, additional state information. Specifically, the SRLG relationships between links and the precise paths of existing circuits must be available so that a diverse path for a new circuit can be computed.

At present, SRLG information cannot be self-discovered. Instead, the information must be manually configured for each link. Furthermore, in a large network it is very difficult to maintain accurate SRLG information. The problem becomes particularly daunting when multiple administrative domains are involved, for instance, after the acquisition of one network operator by another.

10.4 Routing with Constraints

As discussed earlier in the chapter, routing in optical networks needs to be cognizant of different resource types and resource constrains. In particular, types and capabilities of optical links and switching nodes are of interest. Also important are some of the optical constraints that need to be met for error-free data transfer over the connections. In the following, we discuss some of the important resources, and the associated characteristics and constraints.

10.4.1 Link Characteristics

10.4.1.1 ENCODING, SWITCHING CAPABILITY, AND CAPACITY AVAILABILITY

A node computing an end-to-end path needs to know the characteristics of different types of links that are available. Some of the parameters that define the characteristics of a link are:

- **Link encoding:** One of the important characteristics of a link is the type of payload it can carry. For example, a link can be completely transparent and can carry any traffic irrespective of its format or bit-rate. Transparent links are available in all-optical (OOO, see Chapter 1) networks only, which are still not widely deployed. In most optical networks, links are opaque and carry specific types of payload. For example, a link can carry SONET, SDH, Gigabit Ethernet, or Fiber Channel payloads. It is also possible for a link to carry more than one type of payload.
- **Interface switching capability:** The payload type by itself does not completely characterize a link. It is also important to identify the switching capabilities of the nodes on both sides of the link. It is possible that the switching nodes on two sides of the link have different switching capabilities. Switching capabilities are associated with switch interfaces and are referred to as interface switching capabilities. The interface switching capabilities that are relevant to optical routing are:
    - **Time-Division Multiplex (TDM) capable:** A node receiving data over a TDM capable interface can multiplex or demultiplex channels within a SONET/SDH payload. For TDM capable interfaces, additional information such as switching granularity and support for different types of SONET/SDH concatenation must also be indicated.
    - **Lambda-switch capable:** A node receiving data over a lambda-switch capable interface can recognize and switch individual wavelengths (lambdas) within the interface. Additional information, such as data rate, must be indicated for these interfaces. For example, a lambda-switch capable interface could support the establishment of connections at both OC-48c and OC-192c data rates.
    - **Fiber-switch capable:** A node receiving data over a fiber-switch capable interface can switch the entire contents to another interface (without distinguishing lambdas, channels, or packets). That is, a fiber-switch capable interface switches at the granularity of an entire interface and cannot extract individual lambdas within the interface.

- **Available capacity:** Available capacity is an important parameter that determines whether a specific connection can be carried on a link. Capacity of links bound by TDM-, lambda-, or fiber-switch capable interfaces is defined in discrete units (e.g., number of available time slots on a TDM link). Besides the total available capacity on a link, additional information such as minimum and maximum units of available capacity may be indicated. All of these are important for making routing decisions.

10.4.1.2 PROTECTION CAPABILITY

Links in an optical network may have different protection capabilities. During path selection, this information is used to ensure that the protection requirements of the connection will be satisfied by all the links en route. Typically, the *minimum* acceptable protection is specified at path instantiation, and the path selection algorithm finds a path that satisfies at least this level of protection. The following are possible protection capabilities that could be associated with a link:

- **Preemptible:** This indicates that the link is a protection link, that is, it protects one or more other links (see Chapter 8). The traffic carried on a protection link will be preempted if any of the corresponding working links fail and traffic is switched to the protection link. This means that only extra traffic can be routed over this link.
- **Unprotected:** This indicates that there is no other link protecting this link. The connections on a link of this type will not be protected if the link fails.
- **Protected:** This indicates that there are one or more links that are protecting this link. There can be different flavors of protection. A link that is protected by another dedicated link is said to have dedicated protection. Multiple links, which are protected by one or more common protection links, are said to have shared protection.

10.4.2 Optical Constraints

Routing in all-optical networks is subject to additional constraints. Specifically, the routing protocols and algorithms need to ensure that signal impairments are kept within acceptable limits.

As discussed in Chapter 1, impairments can be classified into two categories, linear and nonlinear. Linear effects are independent of signal power and affect wavelengths individually. Amplifier spontaneous emission (ASE), polarization mode dispersion (PMD), and chromatic dispersion are examples of linear impairments [Stern+99]. Nonlinear impairments are significantly more complex and generate not only impairments on each channel, but also cross talk between channels. In the following, we briefly discuss different types linear and nonlinear impairments and how they can be abstracted for the purpose of routing.

- **Polarization Mode Dispersion (PMD):** PMD degrades signal quality and limits the maximum length of a transparent segment. With older fibers, the maximum length of the transparent segment should not exceed 400 km and 25 km for bit rates of 10Gb/s and 40Gb/s, respectively. Due to recent advances in fiber technology, the PMD-limited distance has increased dramatically. With newer fibers, the maximum length of the transparent segment without PMD compensation is limited to 10,000 km and 625 km for bit rates of 10 Gb/s and 40 Gb/, respectively. Typically, the PMD requirement is not an issue for most types of fibers at 10 Gb/s or lower bit rate. It cannot be ignored, however, at bit rates of 40 Gb/s and higher. The only link dependent information needed by the routing algorithm is the square of the link PMD, denoted as link-PMD-square. It is the sum of the span-PMD-square of all spans on the link.
- **Amplifier Spontaneous Emission (ASE):** ASE degrades the optical signal-to-noise ratio or OSNR. OSNR level depends on the bit rate, transmitter-receiver technology (e.g., availability of forward error correction [FEC]), and margins allocated for the impairments, among other things. OSNR requirement can translated into constraint on maximum length of the transparent segment and number of spans. For example, current transmission systems are often limited to 6 spans each 80 km long. The only link-dependent information needed for ASE by the routing algorithm is the link noise, which is the sum of the noise of all spans on the link. Hence, the ASE constraint that needs to be satisfied is that the aggregate noise of the transparent segment, which is the sum of the link noise of all links, cannot exceed the ratio of transmit power and OSNR.

There are many other types of impairments that affect signal quality. Most of the impairments generated by network elements such as OXCs or OADMs (see Chapter 1) can be approximated using a network-wide margin on the OSNR.

Besides linear impairments, there are many nonlinear impairments, which affect optical signal quality [Stern+99]. It is extremely difficult to deal with nonlinear impairments in a routing algorithm because they lead to complex dependencies, for example, on the order in which specific fiber types are traversed. A full treatment of the nonlinear constraints would likely require very detailed knowledge of the physical infrastructure. An alternative approach is to assume that nonlinear impairments are bounded and result in a margin in the required OSNR level for a given bit rate.

10.5 Link Bundling

Link bundling has been proposed in the context of optical networks to improve the scalability of routing protocols. Neighboring nodes in an optical network are often connected by a large number of parallel links/fibers between them. With traditional IP routing protocols, each physical link between a pair of neighboring nodes constitute a routing adjacency. Hence, if there are *N* parallel links between two nodes, it will result in *N* routing adjacencies between them. Multiple parallel adjacencies severely limit scalability of routing protocols by creating unnecessary computational load on the network elements and superfluous control traffic.

In order to understand this problem better, let us consider the example in Figure 10–1, where two neighboring switching nodes in an optical network are connected by eight parallel links. Let us also assume that they are running the OSPF routing protocol. These eight parallel links between the nodes will result in eight routing adjacencies between them, with the OSPF Hello protocol running over each adjacency. Furthermore, anytime a node receives an LSA, it will send a copy to its neighbor over each of the eight parallel links. The neighboring node will accept only the first of these LSAs, discarding the rest. Clearly, this is a waste of network bandwidth and computing resources on the nodes.

Link bundling eliminates this inefficiency by aggregating several (or all) of the parallel links between two neighboring nodes into a single logical link. The resulting logical link is called a *bundled* link (also known as a traffic engineering (TE) link in GMPLS OSPF/IS-IS terminology) [Kompella02a, Kompella02b], and the constituent physical links are called *component* links.

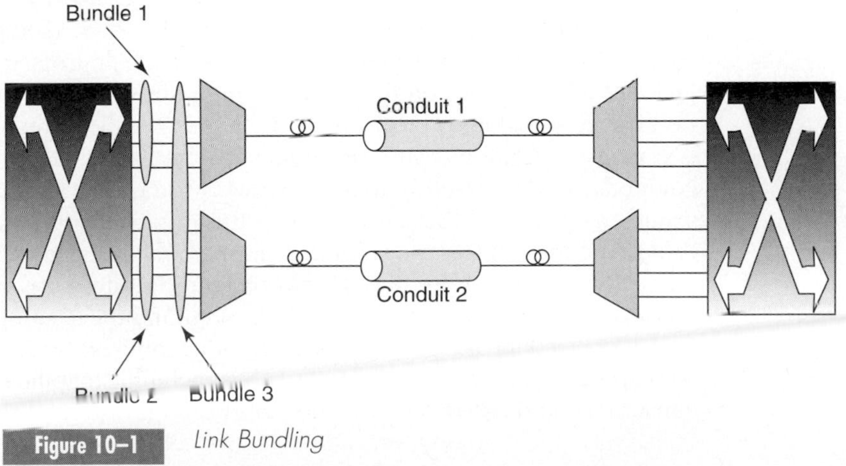

Figure 10–1 *Link Bundling*

This aggregation improves routing scalability by reducing the amount of routing information exchanged between neighboring nodes. As with any aggregation technique, link bundling may result in loss of information. In order to limit this loss, some restrictions on link bundling have been put in place.

For example, consider the scenario in Figure 10–1. The two switches in the figure are connected by two DWDM systems, each carrying four wavelengths. Note that the DWDM systems are connected by fibers that pass through two different conduits. Now, it is possible to bundle all eight links (wavelengths) between the two switches into a single bundle as shown (bundle 3). This bundling, however, fails to capture the fact that the links go over two different DWDM systems and through two different conduits, and hence form two different risk groups. A better approach would be to create two different bundles, bundle 1 and bundle 2, each consisting of links that use the same DWDM system and conduit.

All component links in a bundle must begin and end on the same pair of nodes. All component links must have the same link characteristics, for example, the same TE metric (i.e., an administrative cost). Although not mandatory, they should also belong to the same set of SRLGs. Aggregation rules can be defined for other parameters, such as the maximum bandwidth available on the link, the maximum bandwidth that can be allocated to a connection traversing the link, and so on. Bundling may also be applied recursively, that is, a component link may itself be a bundled link.

10.6 Source Routing

Routing of an optical layer connection requires that the entire path for connection be computed at the ingress node and signaled to other nodes in the path. In order to accomplish this, the ingress node computes an explicit route, also known as a source route, from the ingress to the egress that includes all the nodes on the path. During path setup, the entire route is carried by the signaling protocol from the ingress to the egress node as the path is established. The intermediate nodes on that route do not perform routing computations, but merely use the explicit route information to forward the setup message (see Chapter 7). Since the ingress node computes the entire route, the possibility of a routing loop is eliminated. Consequently, the restriction that all nodes should run the same routing algorithm can also be relaxed. But as noted in the previous sections, the routing algorithm must take into account issues such as computing physically diverse primary and backup paths, additional constraints on switching capabilities, optical domain constraints, and so on.

10.7 Optical Intradomain Routing

Different standards bodies, such as the IETF, the OIF and the ITU-T, are working on enhancing intradomain routing protocols such as OSPF and IS-IS, for routing and topology discovery in networks that consist of optical or other circuit switches. In this section, we discuss the work in progress in different standards bodies, using OSPF as an example.

Over the last several years, the OSPF routing protocol [Moy98] has been widely deployed throughout the Internet. As discussed in the last chapter, OSPF is a link state routing protocol. OSPF specifies a class of messages called LSAs that allow nodes in the network to update each other about their local links. Five different types of LSAs are defined in OSPF, as described in the last chapter.

As discussed earlier in this chapter, routing in IP and optical networks is not quite the same, and hence OSPF needs to be enhanced to route connections in optical networks. For example, in optical networks, the links are always point-to-point. Hence, network LSAs are not required. On the other hand, the link state information contained in router LSAs do not include detailed information on link characteristics, such as resource availability, physical diversity, and so on. Consequently, extensions to LSAs are required. Instead of enhancing the router LSA, these enhancements have been accommodated using opaque LSAs, which provide a generalized mechanism to extend OSPF.

Opaque LSAs consist of a standard LSA header (Figure 10–2) followed by a application-specific information field [Coltun98]. Like other LSAs, the opaque LSA is distributed using the OSPF flooding mechanism. The manner in which an opaque LSA is flooded depends on the flooding *scope* of the LSA. The following describes different flooding scopes:

- **Link local flooding:** In this case, the LSA is only transmitted over a single point-to-point or broadcast link.

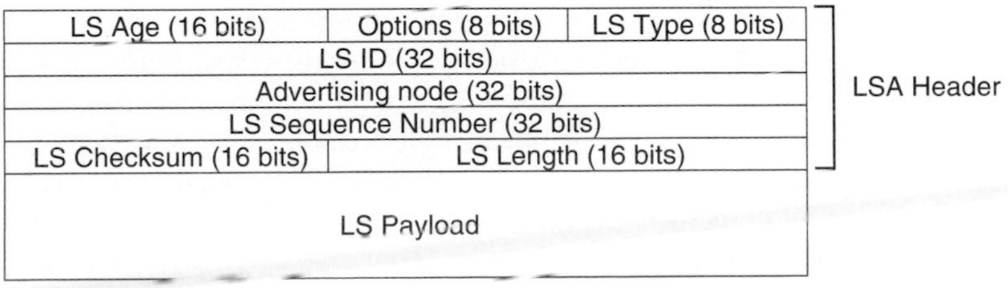

LS Age (16 bits)	Options (8 bits)	LS Type (8 bits)
LS ID (32 bits)		
Advertising node (32 bits)		
LS Sequence Number (32 bits)		
LS Checksum (16 bits)	LS Length (16 bits)	
LS Payload		

LSA Header (bracket: first five rows)

Figure 10–2 *Link State Advertisement (LSA) Format in OSPF*

- **Area local flooding:** In this case, the opaque LSA is flooded only in the area where it originated.
- **Autonomous system (AS) wide flooding:** In this case, the LSA is flooded throughout the AS.

In the following sections, we describe how opaque LSAs have been used to extend OSPF for optical routing. Specifically, we describe routing within a single OSPF area, as well as routing across multiple areas. As one can possibly anticipate, routing across multiple areas is much more complex than routing within a single OSPF area. Consequently, it does not come as a surprise that the current state of the art for routing in a single area is more mature as compared with routing across multiple areas.

10.7.1 Routing in a Single Area

OSPF enhancements in support of MPLS TE [Katz+02] were already underway when the IETF started its work on routing in optical networks. It turned out that the requirements driven by MPLS TE extensions have a lot of overlap with those driven by routing in optical networks. As a result, these two efforts have been aligned under the umbrella of GMPLS OSPF TE extensions or, simply, GMPLS OSPF-TE. In the following, we discuss this work and how it addresses the requirements for routing in an optical network. A similar initiative is also underway to enhance IS-IS [Callon90, Kompella02b].

The extensions to OSPF have been brought about by extending the notion of a link. In addition to advertising "regular" point-to-point links using router LSAs, OSPF-TE also allows a node to advertise TE links. A TE link is a single or a bundled link with associated characteristics. The properties of the link pertaining to shortest path first (SPF) computation (e.g., link cost) are advertised using router LSAs. The other characteristics of a TE link are advertised using opaque LSAs. Opaque LSAs carrying such TE information are also known as TE LSAs. In summary, a TE link is a "logical" link that has several properties and it may or may not have one-to-one correspondence to a "regular" point-to-point link.

The liveness of a TE link, that is, whether the link is functional, is determined by the liveness of each its component links. A bundled link is said to be alive when at least one of its component links is functional. The liveness of a component link can be determined by using any of several means: routing protocol (e.g., IS-IS or OSPF) Hello[1] messages over the component link, signaling protocol (e.g., RSVP) Hellos (see Chapter 7), link management protocol (LMP) Hellos (see Chapter 6), or from link layer indications (see Chapter 3). Once a bundled link is determined to be alive, it can be advertised using OSPF LSA flooding.

[1]Even if IS-IS/OSPF hellos are run over the all component links, IS-IS/OSPF flooding can be restricted to just one of the component links.

The characteristics of a single component link, include the following [Kompella02a]:

- **Maximum bandwidth:** This parameter specifies the absolute maximum bandwidth usable on the link. This is the capacity of the link.
- **Unreserved bandwidth:** This parameter specifies the amount of bandwidth not yet reserved on the link. Unreserved bandwidth values can be advertised separately for different priority levels. Currently, eight priority levels are supported. For a bundled TE link, the unreserved bandwidth is the sum of unreserved bandwidths of all the component links.
- **Maximum and minimum connection bandwidth:** These parameters determine the maximum and minimum bandwidth that can be allocated to a connection on the link. The maximum bandwidth that can be allocated is less than the unreserved bandwidth on the link. The minimum bandwidth that can be allocated depends on the granularity of switching supported by switching nodes. The maximum connection bandwidth of a bundled link is defined to be the maximum of the maximum connection bandwidth of all the component links.

  For example, suppose there are two unreserved OC-192 channels or component links in a TE link. The unreserved bandwidth is then 2 × 10 Gbps or 20 Gbps. The maximum bandwidth that can be allocated to a connection, however, is only 10 Gbps. Assuming that the switches support only STS-48c or 2.5 Gbps switching granularity, the minimum bandwidth that can be allocated to a connection is 2.5 Gbps.
- **Link protection type:** This describes the protection capabilities of the link. Some of the supported protection types are preemptible, unprotected, shared, dedicated 1:1 and dedicated 1+1, as described earlier.
- **SRLG:** This is an unordered list of numbers that are the SRLG identifiers associated with the link.
- **Interface switching capability descriptor:** This includes the following parameters:

  Switching capability: This parameter identifies the switching capabilities of the interfaces associated with the link. The following values are relevant to optical switching: Time-Division-Multiplex (TDM) capable, lambda-switch capable, and fiber-switch capable. These were defined earlier.

  Switching-capability-specific information: The switching-capability-specific information depends on the switching capability parameter. For example, when the switching capability parameter is TDM, the specific information includes switching granularity, an indication of whether the interface supports standard or arbitrary SONET/SDH concatenation, and so on.

10.7.2 An Example

Consider the network shown in Figure 10–3, consisting of four optical switches, nodes A–D, and six TE links, 1–6. We assume that the switches are TDM-switching capable at STS-48c granularity. Let us also assume that TE links are link bundles with the following properties:

Link 1: 4 OC-48 component links, 2 used and 2 unused, unprotected, and SRLG ID = 123

Link 2: 4 OC-48 component links, 2 used and 2 unused, unprotected, and SRLG ID = 234

Link 3: 4 OC-48 component links, 2 used and 2 unused, unprotected, and SRLG ID = 345

Link 4: 4 OC-192 component links, 2 used and 2 unused, unprotected, and SRLG ID = 456

Link 5: 4 OC-192 component links, 2 used and 2 unused, unprotected, and SRLG ID = 567

Link 6: 4 OC-192 component links, 2 used and 2 unused, unprotected, and SRLG ID = 678

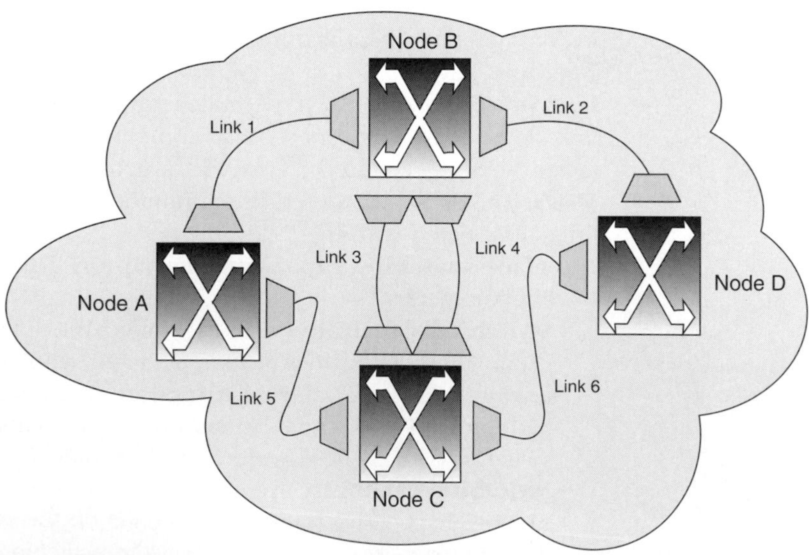

Figure 10–3 *Example of an Optical Network Configured as a Single OSPF Area*

Table 10–1 *Router LSAs for the Example Network in Figure 10–3*

LS Type	LS ID	Advertising Node	Comments
Router LSA	Node ID of A	Node A	SPF properties of Links 1 and 5
Router LSA	Node ID of B	Node B	SPF properties of Links 1,2,3, and 4
Router LSA	Node ID of C	Node C	SPF properties of Links 3,4,5, and 6
Router LSA	Node ID of D	Node D	SPF properties of Links 2 and 6

Let us assume that the network is configured as a single OSPF area. Consequently, no summary LSAs are required. Because we only have point-to-point links, no network LSAs are necessary. Let us also assume that there are no external routes, and hence no external LSAs are required either. The link state database of each node will consist of only router LSAs and TE LSAs. Because there are four nodes, only four router LSAs, one originated by each node, will be present. There will be twelve TE LSAs, two each for every TE link since both end points advertise the link between them. Table 10–1 shows the router LSAs maintained by each node and Table 10–2 shows the TE LSAs (see also Figure 10–2).

Table 10–2 *TE LSAs for the Example Network in Figure 10–3*

LS Type	LS ID	Advertising Node	Comments
TE LSA	Link ID of link 1	Node A	TE properties of link 1 as seen by A
TE LSA	Link ID of link 1	Node B	TE properties of link 1 as seen by B
TE LSA	Link ID of link 2	Node B	TE properties of link 2 as seen by B
TE LSA	Link ID of link 2	Node D	TE properties of link 2 as seen by D
TE LSA	Link ID of link 3	Node B	TE properties of link 3 as seen by B
TE LSA	Link ID of link 3	Node C	TE properties of link 3 as seen by C
TE LSA	Link ID of link 4	Node B	TE properties of link 4 as seen by B
TE LSA	Link ID of link 4	Node C	TE properties of link 4 as seen by C
TE LSA	Link ID of link 5	Node A	TE properties of link 5 as seen by A
TE LSA	Link ID of link 5	Node C	TE properties of link 5 as seen by A
TE LSA	Link ID of link 6	Node C	TE properties of link 6 as seen by C
TE LSA	Link ID of link 6	Node D	TE properties of link 6 as seen by D

Now let us examine the TE LSA pertaining to link 1, advertised by node A. Among other items, it will include the following pieces of information:

1. Maximum bandwidth (i.e., absolute capacity) is 4 × 2.5 Gbps or 10 Gbps since there are four OC-48 component links in the TE link.
2. Maximum available or unreserved bandwidth is 2 × 2.5 Gbps or 5 Gbps since only two OC-48 component links are available.
3. Maximum connection bandwidth is 2.5 Gbps since the component links are OC-48.
4. Minimum connection bandwidth is 2.5 Gbps since the switching is at the granularity of STS-48c.
5. The protection type of the links are "unprotected" and the associated SRLG list contains only one SRLG ID, that is, 123.
6. The switching capability of the interface is TDM since the switches are TDM-capable. Switching granularity is STS-48c.

Using the information contained in the router and the TE LSAs, each node can easily construct a topology database that contains the information shown in Table 10–3. Note that Table 10–3 shows only a subset of different fields; the actual topology database will contain other information fields. As shown in Table 10–3, the topology database contains detailed information about different TE links between nodes. This information is used by the route computation module to compute explicit routes to different destinations.

The link information presented in Table 10–3 is sufficient to compute unprotected and 1 + 1 protected paths. It is not, however, sufficient to compute shared mesh protected paths (Chapter 8). Recall that under shared mesh protection, multiple backup paths may share protection links as long as the corresponding primary paths do not have any common SRLGs. Note that Table 10–3 does not provide any information about shared backup links and the connections that can potentially use them.

In the absence of any additional information, simple heuristics can be used to compute shared backup paths. For example, a physically diverse protection path can be computed first. Then, sharing can be attempted on as many links as possible during signaling, using information available at each node along the protection path (see [Sengupta+02]). We do not consider this topic further here.

10.7.3 Routing in All-Optical Networks

Routing in an all-optical network without wavelength conversion raises several additional issues that have not been addressed in the OSPF enhancements discussed earlier. First, since the route selected must have the chosen wavelength available on all links, this information needs to be considered in the routing process. Consequently, wavelength availability information needs to

Table 10–3 *Topology Database for the Network in Figure 10–3*

	Node A	Node B	Node C	Node D
Node A		**Link 1:** Max capacity 10 Gbps; available capacity 5 Gbps; switching capability SONET, switching granularity 2.5 Gbps; unprotected; SRLGs {123}; max connection bandwidths 2.5.Gbps; min connection bandwidth 2.5Gbps.	**Link 5:** Max capacity 20 Gbps; available capacity 10 Gbps; switching capability SONET; switching granularity 2.5 Gbps; unprotected; SRLGs {567}; max connection bandwidth 10 Gbps; min connection bandwidth 2.5Gbps.	
Node B	**Link 1:**		**Link 3:** Max capacity 10 Gbps; available capacity 5 Gbps; switching capability SONET, switching granularity 2.5 Gbps; unprotected; SRLGs {345}; max connection bandwidth 2.5 Gbps; min connection bandwidth 2.5.Gbps. **Link 4:** Max capacity 20 Gbps; available capacity 10 Gbps; switching capability SONET; switching granularity 2.5 Gbps; unprotected; SRLGs {456}; max connection bandwidth 10 Gbps; min connection bandwidth 2.5Gbps.	**Link 2:** Max capacity 10 Gbps; available capacity 5 Gbps; switching capability SONET; switching granularity 2.5 Gbps; unprotected; SRLGs {234}; max connection bandwidth 2.5.Gbps; min connection bandwidth 2.5Gbps.
Node C	**Link 5:**	**Link 3:** **Link 4:**		**Link 6:**
Node D		**Link 2:**	**Link 6:** Max capacity 20 Gbps; available capacity 10 Gbps; switching capability SONET; switching granularity 2.5 Gbps; unprotected; SRLGs {678}; max connection bandwidth 10 Gbps; min connection bandwidth 2.5Gbps.	

be advertised by the routing protocols. An alternative is to "hunt" for available wavelengths during signaling using the GMPLS Label Set feature (see Chapter 7), but relying on this alone may not be efficient.

Next, link-specific information for each type of impairment that has the potential of being limiting for some routes needs to be advertised. Routing constrains imposed by PMD and ASE fall in this category. Other link-dependent information includes span-length, cross talk, and so forth. In addition to the link-specific information, bounds on each of the impairments need to be quantified. Since these are system dependent, they are determined by the system designer's impairment allocations.

Finally, as optical transport technology evolves, the set of constraints that need to be considered may change. The routing and control plane design should therefore be as open as possible, allowing parameters to be included as necessary.

10.8 Routing across Multiple Areas

The OSPF extensions discussed earlier apply to a single OSPF area. For reasons of scalability, an OSPF routing domain may consist of multiple areas. In this section, we discuss how optical routing extensions to OSPF can be extended to multiple OSPF areas.

10.8.1 Packet Forwarding in IP Networks

Let us first consider how basic packet routing works in a two-level OSPF hierarchy. This hierarchy was described in the last chapter, where the notion of OSPF areas was discussed. Specifically, the OSPF protocol requires that each of the areas (including the backbone area) be internally connected. Following this rule, there are two general OSPF topology configurations possible. The first is the strictly hierarchical configuration, shown in Figure 10–4. Here, there are three areas, numbered in the usual OSPF fashion, 0.0.0.1 to 0.0.0.3. In addition, there is a backbone area, numbered 0.0.0.0. The path from a node in one area to a node in another area crosses no intermediate area other than the backbone. The second is a more general configuration, shown in Figure 10–5. Here, some of the backbone links are actually *virtual* links (shown as dotted lines between nodes B2–B6, C1–C4, and D2–D3). A path in the backbone area might consist of paths through intermediate areas. Thus, an end-to-end path may traverse one or more intermediate areas. The selection of a particular topological organization has implications on the manner in which areas are managed and end-to-end connections are provisioned in the case of an optical network.

Under the OSPF protocol, each node generates LSAs that are flooded to all nodes in its area. This happens in each area independently, including the

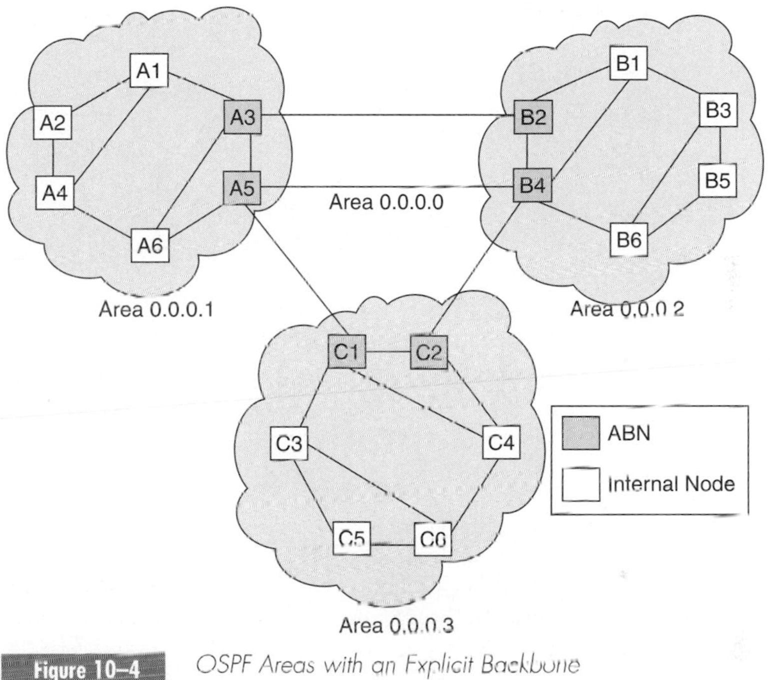

Figure 10–4 *OSPF Areas with an Explicit Backbone*

backbone area. The area border nodes[2] (ABNs) are responsible for creating summary information regarding the areas they serve (other than the backbone area). In IP networks, the summary information consists of IP address prefixes, and associated cost information. Each ABN floods the summary information into the backbone area. Each ABN also floods the summary information regarding external areas into the area it serves. These procedures allow an internal node in an area to maintain the complete link state information pertaining to its area and summary information pertaining to external areas. This type of information abstraction is adequate for packet forwarding in IP networks. Specifically, for a destination in an external area, an internal node merely computes a path to one of the ABNs advertising the destination. Similarly, an ABN computes a path to an external destination by computing a path to another ABN in the destination area. Finally, the ABN in the destination area computes a direct path to the destination node.

Thus, packet forwarding from node A2 to node B5 in the network shown in Figure 10–4 works as follows:

[2]Under OSPF, the term area border router (ABR) is used. We use the term ABN to generalize this concept to optical networks.

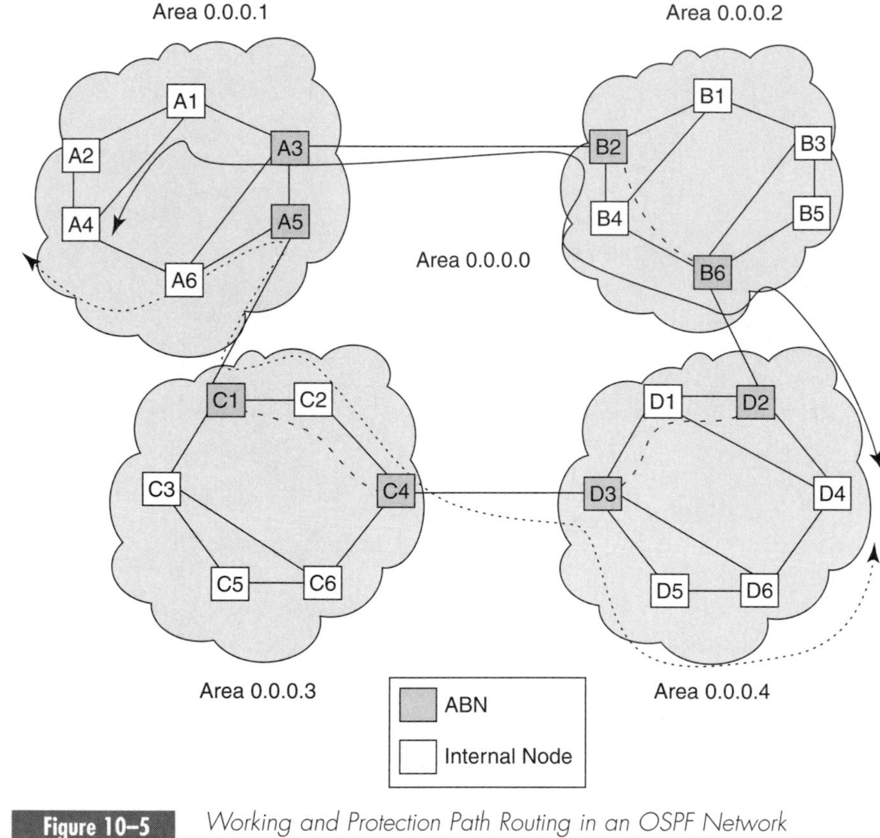

Figure 10–5 *Working and Protection Path Routing in an OSPF Network with Virtual Backbone Links*

1. A2 routes the packet toward ABN A5, which had advertised a path to an IP prefix that includes the address of B5 (it is assumed that each intermediate node in Area 0.0.0.1 has selected ABN A5 as the egress towards node B5 using the standard OSPF forwarding table computation procedure, see Chapter 9).
2. ABN A5 routes the packet to ABN B4 in Area 0.0.0.2.
3. ABN B4 routes the packet to B5 (it is assumed that each intermediate node in Area 0.0.0.2 has computed a consistent forwarding table using the standard OSPF procedure).

Packet forwarding from node A4 to node D4 in the network shown in Figure 10–5 works as follows:

1. A4 routes the packet toward ABN A3, which had advertised a path to an IP prefix that includes the address of D4 (it is assumed that each intermediate node in Area 0.0.0.1 has selected ABN A3 as the

egress toward node D4 using the standard OSPF forwarding table computation procedure).

2. ABN A3 routes the packet to ABN D2 in Area 0.0.0.4. The forwarding table at each ABN is computed based on the (virtual) backbone topology maintained by each ABN. The next node selected is ABN B2.
3. ABN B2 determines that the next node in the backbone area toward ABN D2 is ABN B6. Since link B2-B6 in the backbone is virtual, B2 utilizes the forwarding table computed for Area 0.0.0.2 to forward the packet to ABN B6. Each intermediate node in Area 0.0.0.2 is assumed to have selected ABN B6 to reach node D4 (therefore, the packet need not be *tunneled* from B2 to B6, i.e., carried within another packet originating at B2 and terminating at B6).
4. ABN B6 forwards the packet to ABN D2 in Area 0.0.0.4.
5. ABN D2 routes the packet to D4 (it is assumed that each intermediate node in Area 0.0.0.4 has computed a consistent forwarding table using the standard OSPF procedure).

10.8.2 Summarizing Resource Information

The summary reachability information advertised via the backbone into each area is adequate to forward IP packets. To establish optical connections, however, path computation procedures must take into account resource availability information. But summarization of resource availability information is rather awkward. The main problem is that the resource availability information advertised into an area must be sufficiently detailed to result in successful path computation most of the time, while not affecting the scalability of the routing scheme. This problem has been dealt with in the PNNI routing protocol that advertises (succinct) abstract topologies of external peer groups. Using this method, for instance, the topology of the backbone network may be summarized by an abstract topology where the ABNs are nodes and the links represent the resource availability in the paths between ABNs.

In general, topology summarization using the available OSPF mechanisms may be complex. Additionally, it may not be really necessary to do this. An approach for resource summarization may be as follows:

1. Each link is characterized by a hop count (h) and a bandwidth (b) parameter.[3] h and b for a virtual link are computed by the ABNs at the two ends using a shortest path algorithm that finds the minimum-hop path with the maximum available bandwidth (*shortest widest* path, see Chapter 11). This algorithm is run on the internal topology of the area that contains the virtual link.

[3]In fact, the "bandwidth" parameter could characterize minimum and maximum bandwidths, etc., as described in section 10.7. To simplify the discussion of multiarea routing, we assume that the parameter merely describes an estimate of available bandwidth on a link. The hop count is assumed to be 1 for direct links.

2. Each IP prefix advertised into the backbone by an ABN is characterized by *h* and *b* parameters. These parameters are *estimated* by the ABN using a heuristic algorithm, or from configured information.
3. Each IP prefix advertised into an area by an ABN is characterized by *h* and *b* parameters. These parameters are computed by combining the information advertised in step (2) and step (1).

It is assumed that virtual backbone area links are configured by the operator (i.e., the ABNs at the ends of the links are configured with the virtual adjacency information). The *b* and *h* parameters for virtual links may be determined dynamically by the ABNs at both ends (using a consistent procedure) or they may be configured. Considering the network shown in Figure 10–5, the reachability of D4 is advertised into Area 0.0.0.1 in the following manner:

1. ABN D2 computes $h = 1$ and $b = 10$ for the IP prefix that includes D4 (the *b* values in this example are arbitrary, for illustration purposes). Similarly, ABN D3 computes $h = 2$ and $b = 10$ for the same prefix. Both of these ABNs advertise the same prefix with the computed *h* and *b* parameters into the backbone area.
2. Virtual links C4-C1 and B2-B6 are assigned $h = 2$, $b = 15$, and $h = 2$, $b = 5$, respectively, by the ABNs at their end points. The OSPF LSAs for these links, flooded in the backbone, carry these parameters.
3. ABN A3 advertises the IP prefix that includes D4 into Area 0.0.0.1, with $h = 5$ (addition of all *h* values to reach D4 along the minimum hop path, A3-B2-B6-D2-D4) and $b = 5$ (the minimum of all *b* values along the path to D4).
4. ABN A5 advertises the IP prefix that includes D4 into Area 0.0.0.1, with $h = 6$ (A5-C1-C4-D3-D6-D4) and $b = 10$.

10.8.3 Provisioning in a Multiarea Network

The provisioning model is based on dividing an end-to-end provisioning event into a sequence of provisioning events in each area. Because the complete topology of the network is unavailable to any node, the provisioning proceeds from the source node to an ABN in the source area, from this ABN to an ABN in the destination area, and, finally, from the last ABN to the destination node. In the backbone area, provisioning may be carried out inside other areas where virtual links were configured. As an example, consider provisioning a connection from A4 to D4 in the network shown in Figure 10–5. Suppose that as described earlier ABNs A3 and A5 have advertised $h = 5$, $b = 5$, and $h = 6$, $b = 10$, respectively, for an IP prefix containing D4 into Area 0.0.0.1.

1. Node A4 computes $h = 2$, $b = 8$ for destination A3, and $h = 2$, $b =$ 10 for destination A5 within Area 0.0.0.1. Combining the *h* and *b* values advertised for D4 by these ABNs, A4 determines that the path

via A3 to D4 will lead to $h = 7$ and $b = 5$. Similarly, the path to D4 via A5 is found to be $h = 8$ and $b = 10$. A4 decides to use A3 as the egress ABN in Area 0.0.0.1 to reach D4.

2. A4 signals a connection establishment request to A3, with D4 as the ultimate destination. Let us assume that this is a RSVP-TE Path message with Label Request, Upstream Label and other objects (see Chapter 7). This message contains the strict explicit route from A4 to A3, and a loose route from A3 to D4 (the loose route need not list any nodes between A3 and D4). The Upstream Label indicates the label allocated for the reverse direction of the connection.
3. ABN A3 determines that it has to reach ABN D2 to reach D4, based on the backbone topology database. It then expands the loose route A3-D4 as A3-B2-B6-D2-D4 and forwards the Path message to the next node, B2, with Label Request, Upstream Label and other objects.
4. From the explicit route information in the Path message, ABN B2 determines that the next hop toward D4 is B6. The link B2-B6, however, is a virtual link. B2 therefore computes a (bidirectional) path to B6, which satisfies the required bandwidth. This explicit route turns out to be B2-B4-B6. Thus, B2 expands the received explicit route as B2-B4-B6-D2-D4, places it in the Path message, and forwards the message to B4. This explicit route is strict from B2 to D2, and loose from D2 to D4.
5. ABN D2 receives the Path message with the indication that D4 is the ultimate destination. It computes a path to D4 with the requested bandwidth. The explicit route found is D2-D4. This route is placed in the Path message and forwarded to D4.
6. D4 receives the Path message and generates a Resv message back toward A4.
7. The Resv message is forwarded in the reverse path to the source. Each node en route allocates a label for the forward direction of the connection and sends it in the Label object. The connection setup is completed when A4 receives the Resv message, as described in Chapter 7.

The resulting path, <A4-A1-A3-B2-B4-B6-D2-D4>, is shown in Figure 10–5 (solid line).

10.8.4 Shared Mesh Protection in a Multiarea Network

End-to-end shared mesh protection requires that a protection path be established a priori for each (protected) working path (see Chapter 8). Recall that a protection path should be physically (SRLG-wise) diverse from the working path. Thus, the computation of protection paths requires both the information about the SRLGs associated with the network links and the information on the actual routes of the working paths. It was illustrated in section 10.7.2 how the SRLG information is propagated under single-area OSPF. Although the topology database information depicted in Table 10–3 does not show it, each node is assumed to keep track of the entire route of working paths originating from that node, along with the SRLGs associated with that path. Thus, a node under single-area OSPF can compute the protection path based on available information.[4]

With multiple areas, a node has neither detailed topology (and SRLG) information nor working path information outside of its own area. How then to establish a protection path? In the following, we describe various procedures for doing this. First, in section 10.8.4.1, an approach based on using "route servers" is described. Next, in section 10.8.4.2, an incremental protection path establishment procedure is described. Finally, in section 10.8.4.3, area-wise protection is described.

10.8.4.1 PROTECTION PATH COMPUTATION USING ROUTE SERVERS

Under this model, it is assumed that a "route server" participates in OSPF routing in *all* the areas. That is, the route server maintains the topology and resource information pertaining to the entire network. The route server may thus treat the multiarea network as a single large OSPF area and use the same protection path computation methods developed for single-area networks.

Clearly, since the route server has complete information, it can compute both working and protection paths. But for reasons of robustness and scalability, working path computation and establishment may be decentralized, using the procedures described in sections 10.8.2 and 10.8.3. Suppose this is the case. Then, each node is responsible for establishing the working path. Once the working path is established, it is assumed that the originating node has detailed knowledge about the route taken by the working path, along with the SRLGs traversed. Note that this information will not be propagated by OSPF itself, but has to be obtained during signaling (e.g., this information may be collected using RSVP-TE RRO, see Chapter 7). The orginating node can then supply the detailed working path information to the route server, which can then compute a full protection path. The establishment of the protection path would be similar to the procedure described in section 10.8.3, except that a strict explicit route will be used (i.e., no need for ABNs to expand loose hops).

[4]A related problem, which we will not consider here in detail, is that of optimizing the sharing of protection capacity in the network. This requires that a node computing the protection path be aware of the routes of *all* the active working paths. To realize this requirement, the working path information must be flooded throughout the network, which will adversely affect the scalability of routing. Heuristic methods, however, have been proposed to avoid this need [Kodialam+00]. Briefly, these methods rely on additional link parameters to indicate the presence of shared protection bandwidth, and the usage of this information during protection path computation.

The route-server-based based protection path computation approach does not require SRLG information to be summarized along with other resource information (as described in section 10.8.2). On the other hand, this approach is at best an interim step toward the final solution that takes into account only area-level information to compute protection paths.

10.8.4.2 INCREMENTAL PROTECTION PATH ESTABLISHMENT

Under this approach, the working path is established using multiarea OSPF and signaling as described in section 10.8.3. After the working path is established, it is assumed that the source node has detailed knowledge about its route and the SRLGs traversed, as described earlier. This information is used to compute the end-to-end (shared) protection path in each area incrementally as follows.

Consider the working path between nodes A4 and D4 established under the example in section 10.8.3. This path, <A4-A1-A3-B2-B4-B6-D2-D4>, is shown in Figure 10–5. The following steps are used to compute a *node-disjoint* protection path (which can be considered in terms of SRLG-disjointedness, as described in section 10.3):

1. Utilizing the resource availability information and the SRLG information pertaining to the working path in Area 0.0.0.1, node A4 determines that the protection path segment in that area should exit through ABN A5. It thus computes a protection path segment, <A4-A6-A5> that is (node) SRLG-disjoint from the working path segment within Area 0.0.0.1.
2. A4 signals a connection establishment request to A5, with D4 as the ultimate destination. Let us assume that this is a RSVP-TE Path message with Label Request and other objects (see Chapter 7). This message contains the strict explicit route from A4 to A5, and a loose route from A5 to D4, that is, <A4-A6-A5-D4>. The Path message also carries the SRLGs associated with the working route (this feature requires extensions to RSVP-TE).
3. Using the SRLG information contained in the Path message, ABN A5 expands the loose hop <A5-D4> as the (SRLG-disjoint) explicit route, <A5-C1-C4-D3-D4>, and forwards the Path message to the next node, C1.
4. From the explicit route information in the Path message, ABN C1 determines that the next hop toward D4 is C4. The link C1-C4, however, is a virtual link. C1 therefore computes an SRLG-disjoint path to C4, which satisfies the required bandwidth. This explicit route turns out to be C1-C2-C4. Thus, C1 expands the received explicit route as C1-C2-C4-D3-D4, places it in the Path message, and forwards the message to C2. This explicit route is strict from C1 to D3, and loose from D3 to D4.

5. ABN D3 receives the Path message with the indication that D4 is the ultimate destination. Using the working path SRLG information, it computes a (SRLG) disjoint path to D4 with the requested bandwidth. The explicit route found is D3-D5-D6-D4. This route is placed in the Path message and forwarded to D4.
6. D4 receives the Path message and generates a Resv message back toward A4.
7. The Resv message is forwarded in the reverse path to the source. The protection path establishment is completed when A4 receives the Resv message, as described in Chapter 7.[5]

The protection path thus established is shown in Figure 10–5 (dotted line). It should be noted that because this is an incremental procedure, it is possible that some intermediate node may fail to find a suitable route. In this case, an alternate path has to be found, for instance, using a crank-back procedure [Farrel+03].

10.8.4.3 AREA-WISE PROTECTION

Area-wise protection refers to the approach where protection signaling is limited to the area in which the primary path segment failed (see Chapter 8). To do area-wise protection, it is required that the working and the protection path segments within an area originate and terminate at the same nodes. In this regard, the ABNs become the junction nodes for working and primary paths, as shown in Figure 10–6. Here, the working and protection path segments are shown as solid and dotted lines, respectively. For instance, within Area 0.0.0.1, the working path segment is <A4-A1-A3>, and the protection path segment is <A4-A6-A3>. The failure of the working path within Area 0.0.01 will be handled by activating the protection path segment within Area 0.0.01 while keeping the working path segments in other areas in place. Under this arrangement, when the backbone area has virtual links, the protection path segments within certain areas may be established twice: one to protect the working path segment within the area and the other to protect the working path segment in the backbone area.

Protection path routing for area-wise protection can be described with reference to Figure 10–6. Suppose that A4 has established the working path, <A4-A1-A3-B2-B4-B6-D2-D4>, as shown in the figure. The protection path is established as follows:

1. Node A4 first determines that the exit ABN in Area 0.0.0.1 for the working path is A3. Utilizing the resource availability information

[5]In this example, each node along the protection path only allocates shared protection resources during signaling. The activation of the protection path occurs after a failure, as described in Chapter 8.

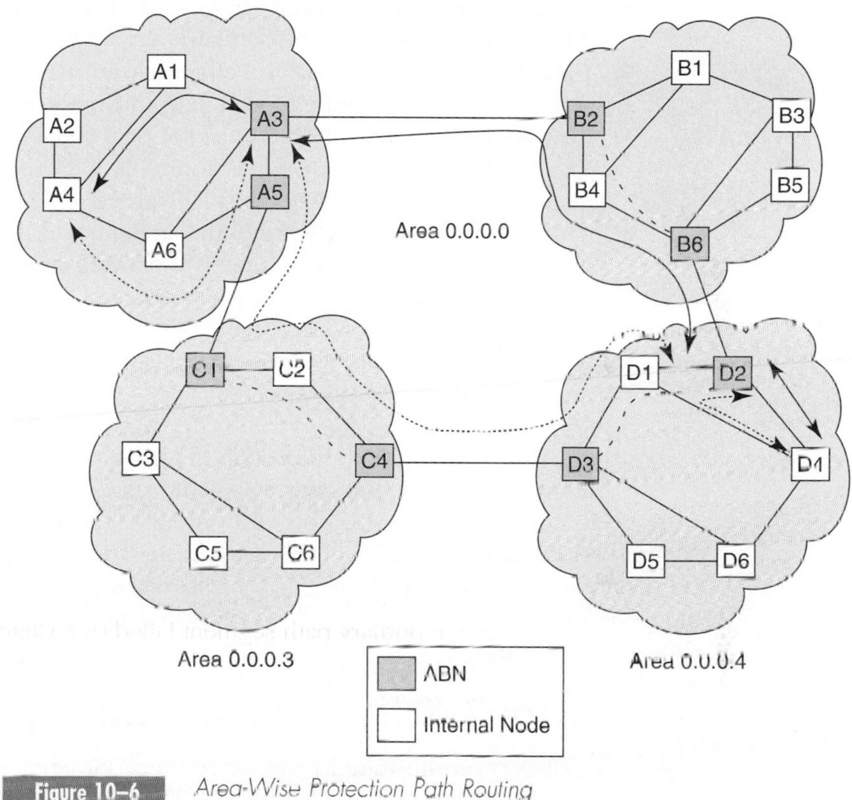

Figure 10–6 *Area-Wise Protection Path Routing*

and the SRLG information pertaining to the working path segment in Area 0.0.0.1, node A4 then computes the protection path segment, <A4-A6-A3> that is (node) SRLG disjoint from the working path segment.

2. A4 signals a connection establishment request to A3, with D4 as the ultimate destination. Suppose that this is a RSVP-TE Path message with Label Request and other objects. This message contains the strict explicit route from A4 to A3, and a loose route from A3 to D4, that is, <A4-A6-A3-D4>. The Path message also carries the entire working route information and the SRLGs associated with the working route.
3. Using the working route information, ABN A3 determines that the egress ABN is D2. Using the SRLG information contained in the Path message, ABN A3 expands the loose hop <A3-D4> as the (SRLG-disjoint) explicit route, <A3-A5-C1-C4-D3-D2-D4>, and forwards the Path message to the next node, A5.

4. ABN D3 receives the Path message and expands the loose hop <D3-D2> into <D3-D1-D2> and forwards the message to D2.
5. ABN D2 finally receives the Path message with the indication that D4 is the ultimate destination. Using the working path SRLG information, it computes a (SRLG) disjoint path to D4 with the requested bandwidth. The explicit route found is D2-D1-D4. This route is placed in the Path message and forwarded to D1.
6. D4 receives the Path message and generates a Resv message back toward A4. The Resv message is forwarded in the reverse path to the source. Ingress and egress nodes in each area perform the appropriate actions to associate the working and protection path segments. The protection path establishment is completed when A4 receives the Resv message.

It is clear that the procedure described above may result in some inefficiency. This was seen in (4) above, where the protection segment had to go from D3 to D2. Instead, an SRLG-disjoint protection segment could have been established directly from D3 to D4, which is the final destination. As before, because this is an incremental procedure, it is possible that some intermediate node may fail to find a suitable protection route. In this case, the procedure has to be retried.

10.8.5 Multiarea Traffic Engineering Based on OSPF

The above discussion illustrated proprietary, heuristic approaches for routing and connection provisioning using multiarea OSPF. Standards-based multiarea OSPF-TE is still at its infancy. A number of proposals have been made in the IETF for traffic engineering across multiple areas [Cheng03, Kompella+02c, Srisuresh+03]. Based on the flooding scope of TE LSA, these proposals can be categorized as follows:

1. **TE LSAs restricted to area local flooding scope:** In this case, the TE LSAs are broadcast only in the local area and do not cross area boundaries. The advantage of this approach is that it is almost as scalable as the original OSPF. The obvious disadvantage is that the nodes do not have access to the TE information outside their local area except for the ABNs. These have access to the TE information in the areas they border with.
2. **TE LSAs are broadcast across area boundaries:** Under this approach, the TE LSAs are broadcast beyond the local area. The obvious advantage is that nodes outside the local area also have TE information available to them. The price paid is the scalability. One possible compromise is to broadcast the TE LSAs within the local area and broadcast only summary TE LSAs across area boundaries.

Another possible alternative is to limit the broadcast, for example, from backbone area to other areas, but not vice versa.

When TE LSAs are broadcast only within the local area, there are different approaches to compute end-to-end paths.

- **Per-area path computation:** Under this approach, the source node computes a strict explicit route from itself to the ABN within its own area. It then initiates path establishment. Once the path setup request reaches the ABN in the source area, the ABN uses the topology and TE information of the backbone area to compute a strict explicit route to an ABN in the destination area. The destination ABN uses the topology and TE information of the destination area to compute a strict explicit route to the destination node. This procedure was illustrated in section 10.8.3.

  The choice of the ABN in the source area is determined only by the information in that area. Thus, the inability to find a route via a given ABN does not imply that no other routes exist. Specifically, it would be necessary to try other ABNs to find an alternate route [Farrel+03]. This procedure, therefore, is inherently iterative.
- **Path computation by a route server:** Under this approach, a route server participates in topology discovery using OSPF TE along with the NEs. It is assumed that the route server has the complete topology and TE information of the entire autonomous system (all OSPF areas). The source node then requests the route server to compute the entire path from the source to the destination. Once the route is obtained, the source node initiates the path set-up process. This procedure was described in section 10.8.4.1.

  A variation in the above method is to use multiple, redundant route servers for fault tolerance. Thus, every node participates in the hierarchical topology distribution phase, but a few specialized nodes get the complete topology information.

Various proposals for extending the scope of TE LSA broadcast are under consideration. One such proposal recommends broadcasting TE LSAs from the backbone area into nonbackbone areas [Cheng03]. There are other proposals recommending creation of summary TE LSAs to be broadcast across the entire AS [Srisuresh+03]. In the following, we discuss end-to-end path computation under both approaches.

- **Backbone TE LSAs broadcast across area boundaries:** Under this approach, the source node obtains the TE information from the backbone area, and uses it to compute the path all the way from itself to the ABN in the destination area. That ABN computes the rest of the path to the destination node. In certain cases, it may be desirable to "preengineer" the backbone area by constructing a set of paths that would be used as traverse the backbone area. With a preengineered backbone area, it is possible to restrict the backbone TE LSAs leaked to nonbackbone areas to contain only the information associated with the preengineered paths.

- **Summary TE LSA broadcast across area boundaries:** Under this approach, TE information from within an area is summarized and then broadcast to other areas. Specifically, the ABNs perform the TE attribute summarization, for example, summarization of bandwidth, delay, and so on. The summarized metric advertised by an ABN represents the best possible value considering all the paths from the ABN to the destination in question. This procedure was illustrated in section 10.8.2. Since these summaries provide a clearer picture of the resources available in external areas, the probability of encountering a node (in another area) where resources cannot be allocated to a connection is minimized. The summarized TE resource availability information also helps in determining the ABN that is "closest" to the destination in terms of the resources required for the connection. This determination is similar to the route calculation based on summarized routes across areas under regular OSPF [Moy98].

10.9 Issues

One of the consequences of defining different OSPF TE extensions is that the frequency and the volume of routing updates may increase significantly as compared with regular OSPF. With traffic engineering extensions, link state advertisements capture resource availability. This information must be refreshed frequently enough to maintain fidelity. At the same time, they should not be generated too frequently, for instance, to reflect minor changes in resource status. A configurable thresholding scheme can be used whereby a node would generate an LSA update only if the resource information changes "significantly." This modification reduces the number of TE LSA updates.

In the absence of any change in the network state, the TE LSAs are refreshed at regular refresh intervals of thirty minutes, just like other LSAs. In addition to regular refreshes, LSAs need to be updated to reflect changes in the network state (topology and resource information). The following configurable mechanisms can be used to reduce the number of TE LSA updates:

- **Relative change based triggers:** Under this scheme, an update is triggered when the relative difference between the current and the previously advertised link state exceeds a certain threshold expressed as a percentage value. For example, anytime the percentage of available bandwidth in a TE link increases or decreases by more than the specified thresholds, an update may be generated.

- **Absolute change based triggers:** This scheme differs from the relative change based scheme described above in that the measure of change is absolute. For example, in this scheme an update is triggered when the number of available component links in a link bundle crosses a certain configurable constant.
- **Timer based triggers:** Timer based triggers may be used to generate updates at fixed intervals or used to enforce minimum spacing between two consecutive updates. The latter is referred to as a hold-down timer and is used in conjunction with threshold or absolute change based triggers to control the volume of link state updates.

Figure 10–7 shows bandwidth requirement for optical TE and router LSA updates for OSPF areas of different sizes under different connection holding times [Sengupta+02]. In this figure, we assume that an optical TE LSA is generated as soon as there is a change in link state due to change in resource availability (e.g., note that this an extreme situation reflecting the upper bound on the bandwidth requirement). Figure 10–8 shows the bandwidth usage for networks of different sizes and for different triggering thresholds. These results show that bandwidth requirement for LSA update is modest even under extreme conditions, with very small connection holding time and in very large networks.

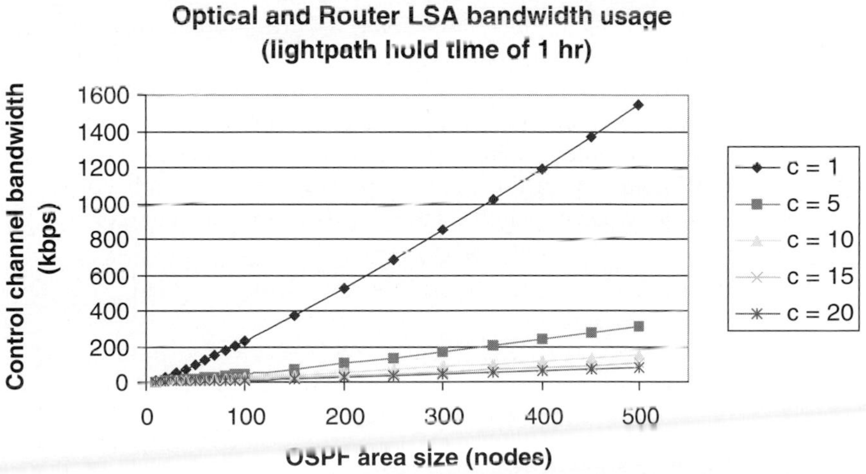

Figure 10–7 *Bandwidth Requirements for TE/Optical and Router LSA Updates for Different Connection Holding Times and Different Network Sizes*

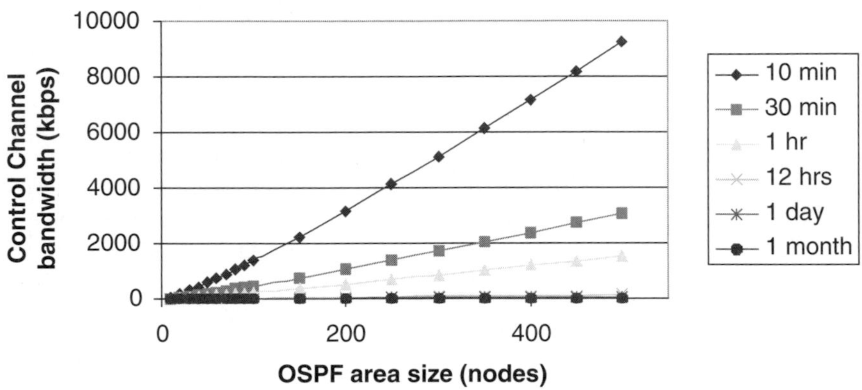

Figure 10–8 *Bandwidth Requirements for TE/Optical and Router LSA Updates for Different Triggering Thresholds and Different Network Sizes*

10.10 Summary

In this chapter we described intradomain optical routing. Specifically, we discussed the difference between intradomain IP and optical routing. We then discussed different requirements that are specific to optical networks and optical routing. We also covered extensions to OSPF necessary to handle optical routing in a single area. State of the art in multiarea OSPF extension was addressed next followed by a brief discussion of the performance impact due to these extensions. Although a single routing protocol base (i.e., OSPF) for multiarea, intradomain routing was considered in this chapter, the general issue of interdomain routing in a heterogeneous environment is examined in Chapter 12. In the next chapter, we discuss path computation algorithms, a topic closely related to the discussion in this chapter.

ELEVEN

Route Computation and Path Selection

11.1 Introduction

As each connection request is presented to an optical network, a route is calculated and a path is selected through the network from the source to the destination. Path selection in optical networks can be contrasted with the procedure used in IP networks. In IP networks, each router independently makes a forwarding decision based on the destination address of each packet. This independence of routing decision at each network node may result in routing loops (see Chapter 9). Thus, to avoid loops, all the routers in a network are required to have identical topology information and use the same algorithm for route computation. Routing loops are not an issue in connection-oriented networks, where connection routes are explicitly specified. An example is the usage of the explicit route object during LSP establishment under MPLS-TE (Chapter 7). Thus, there is a much weaker coupling between path selection and other routing functions such as topology/resource discovery in connection-oriented networks as compared with connectionless (packet) networks. This allows us to consider a wider range of route optimization criteria in connection-oriented networks.

Suppose that topology and resource information pertaining to an optical network are available from either a distributed routing protocol or a network management system. A range of criteria can then influence the selection of a connection path from a source to a destination. These include:

1. Desired connection bandwidth: This can be specified in two ways: as an exact value, or as a range, $[b_{min}, b_{max}]$, where b_{min} is the minimum bandwidth required and b_{max} is the maximum required. In the latter case, it is expected that the maximum possible bandwidth between b_{min} and b_{max} would be allocated.
2. Time delay: This can be a constraint on the absolute delay along the path from the source to the destination, or a differential quantity with respect to another path or group of paths. This delay bound would apply both to propagation and processing delays. Note that as compared with packet networks, queuing delays do not play a role in optical networks.
3. Reliability (protection and restoration properties): Typically, a minimum assurance regarding the reliability for the path may be desired. Or, specific protection or restoration time limits (e.g., 50 ms) may be specified.
4. Degradation: This constraint applies to path computation specifically in transparent optical networks (see Chapter 10). In these networks, attenuation along various routes is an issue. It may be required to minimize the degradation or keep it below some prescribed level.

5. Distance: To limit propagation delay or cost, the maximum length of the route may be specified. This may be in terms of miles or kilometers, or in terms of hop count.
6. Diversity: It may be required that the connection path is physically diverse from the path(s) of other connections, or avoid certain geographic areas entirely (see Chapter 10). Diversity constraints ensure that working and protection paths are not affected by the same failure(s).
7. Resource sharing: How the connection is routed can impact resource sharing in the network. For example, under mesh protection, working paths must be routed in such a manner as to maximize resource sharing among protection paths [Labourdette+02, Bouillet+02a] (see Chapter 10).
8. Network optimization: It may be desired that the overall network utilization is optimized. Thus, connection routing must be such that the use of network resources (capacity) is optimized or network costs are minimized [Labourdette+02].

It is clear from the above list that there are multiple dimensions to the problem of choosing a good route for a connection. Depending on the specific optical technology, some of these will be more important than others. For example, the Bit Error Rate (BER) in modern SONET/SDH networks is so low that signal degradation would not be a criterion for route selection. In transparent optical networks, however, there are a number of measures of degradation besides BER that have to be considered during route selection. In the following, we give an overview of route computation/path selection techniques and illustrate their applicability to optical networking.

11.2 Shortest Path Computation

Given the graph of a network with a *distance* (cost) assigned to each link, *shortest path* algorithms find the least cost path between a selected node and all other nodes in the network [Bertsekas98, Gibbons85].

Before we delve into the applicability of this technique to optical path selection, we first need to introduce some terminology and notation. A network can be represented by a graph $G = (N, A)$, where N is the set of nodes (also called *vertices*) and A is the set of links. $(i, j) \in A$ if there is a link from node i to node j. Note that for complete generality, each link is considered to be unidirectional. If a link from node i to node j is bi-directional, then $(i, j) \in A$ and $(j, i) \in A$. For a link $(i, j) \in A$, the cost of the link is denoted by $a_{i,j}$. Given two nodes s and t, a shortest path algorithm finds a path P with

s as the start node and t as the termination node such that $\sum_{(i,j)\in P} a_{i,j}$ is minimized.

At a first glance, the shortest path technique may seem rather limited in its optimization capabilities. Different measures of path performance, however, can be optimized by appropriately setting the link costs, $a_{i,j}$. In fact, one can get quite creative here and a different set of weights can be chosen for optimizing under different criteria. For example, the link weights $a_{i,j}$ could be set to:

1. Dollar cost of link (i, j), which results in the minimum cost path.
2. Distance in miles between i and j, which results in the shortest distance path. Such a routing criterion could be used where dollar costs are proportional to distances, which is typically the case in some types of optical transport networks.
3. 1 for all $(i, j) \in A$, which results in a minimum hop path. This type of measure was used in the early days of data networking where queuing and processing delays dominated.
4. ln $(p_{i,j})$, where $p_{i,j}$ is the probability of failure of link (i, j). Using this measure, the path with the lowest probability of failure is obtained.
5. $-10\log(Attenuation_{i,j})$, where $Attenuation_{i,j}$ is the optical attenuation on link (i, j). Such a link weight would be useful in transparent optical networks to determine the path with the least attenuation.

11.2.1 The Bellman-Ford Algorithm

A variant of the Bellman-Ford Algorithm was used early in the Routing Information Protocol version 2 (RIPv2) for IP routing [Malkin98]. This is an iterative algorithm that computes the shortest paths from a given node to all the other nodes in the network. In computing these paths, the algorithm assigns to each node j in each iteration k, a label d_j^k Let us assume that there are a total of N nodes in the network and that the origin node is 1. Then the algorithm can be defined as follows:

Initialization

$$(k = 0):\ d_1^0 = 0,\ d_j^0 = \infty,\ \forall j \neq 1$$

Iteration

$$(k = 1,2,3,\ldots):\ d_1^k = 0,\ d_j^k = \min_{(i,j)\in A}\left\{d_i^{k-1} + a_{i,j}\right\},\ \forall j \neq 1.$$

The above algorithm has the following properties:

1. For all $j \neq 1$ and $k \geq 1$, d_j^k is the shortest distance from node 1 to node j using paths with k links or less, where $d_j^k = \infty$ means that all paths from node 1 to node j use more than k links.
2. Given that $a_{i,j} \geq 0$ for all $(i,j) \in A$, the algorithm terminates in at most N iterations, that is, $d_j^k = d_j^{k-1}$ for some $k < N$ and all j.

Close examination of the iteration equation above shows that in each iteration, each node is examined to see which neighbor's cost, combined with the cost of the link from that neighbor, yields the shortest cost path from node 1. Hence, for each node, the node t in the iteration that resulted in the minimum distance will be the previous hop along the shortest path from node 1. It should be noted that by substituting $a_{j,i}$ for $a_{i,j}$ in the iteration equation, the cost of the shortest path *from* each node *to* node 1, and the identity of the *next* hop in the path can be obtained. Clearly, if link costs are symmetrical, that is, $a_{i,j} = a_{j,i}$, then the procedure above gives the cost of the shortest path in both directions.

11.2.1.1 BELLMAN-FORD ALGORITHM EXAMPLE

Consider the network represented by the graph shown in Figure 11–1. In this figure, the cost of a link is indicated in the middle of the link. The iterations of the Bellman-Ford algorithm are shown Table 11–1. As per the properties of the algorithm, for $k = 1$ we see that the shortest path from node 1 to node 2 with 1 or fewer links is simply the direct link between nodes 1 and 2. The cost of this path is 4. In the next iteration ($k = 2$), we get the shortest paths with two or fewer links, and it turns out that it is more cost effective to go to node 2 via node 3, rather than using the direct link. Also note that the algorithm stops before $k = 7$, the total number of nodes in the network.

11.2.2 Dijkstra's Algorithm

Dijkstra's algorithm [Dijkstra59] for finding shortest paths is used in what is probably the most popular intradomain IP routing protocol, OSPF [Moy98] (see Chapter 9). Like the Bellman-Ford algorithm, Dijkstra's algorithm assigns a label, d_i, to each node i. It, however, does not iterate over these labels. Instead, it keeps a list, V, of candidate nodes that is manipulated in its iteration procedure. Once again, without loss of generality, we will assume that we are interested in finding the shortest path from node 1 to all the other nodes in a network of N nodes.

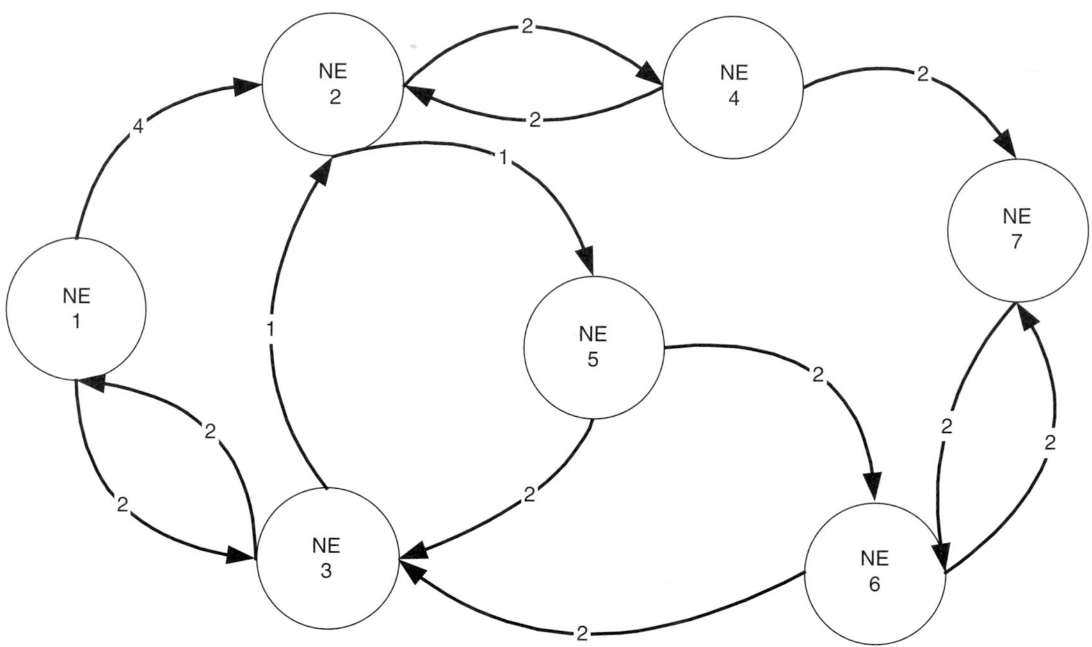

Figure 11–1 Network Graph for Illustrating the Shortest Path Algorithm

Initialization

$$V = \{1\},\ d_1 = 0,\ d_j = \infty,\ \forall j \neq 1$$

Iteration

(a) Remove from V a node i such that $d_i = \min_{j \in V} d_j$.

(b) For each link $(i,j) \in A$ if $d_j > d_i + a_{i,j}$, then set $d_j = d_i + a_{i,j}$ and add j to V if it is not already in V.

Table 11–1 Bellman-Ford Iterations for the Graph of Figure 11–1

Iteration (*k*)	Label List (d1, ..., d7),	Previous Node List (NE1, ..., NE7)
0	(0, ∞, ∞, ∞, ∞, ∞, ∞)	(x, x, x, x, x, x, x)
1	(0, 4, 2, ∞, ∞, ∞, ∞)	(x, 1, 1, x, x, x, x)
2	(0, 3, 2, 6, 5, ∞, ∞)	(x, 3, 1, 2, 2, x, x)
3	(0, 3, 2, 5, 4, 7, 8)	(x, 3, 1, 2, 2, 5, 4)
4	(0, 3, 2, 5, 4, 6, 7)	(x, 3, 1, 2, 2, 5, 4)

The algorithm above has the following properties:

1. Given that $a_{i,j} \geq 0$ for all $(i,j) \in A$, the algorithm will terminate in at most N iterations.
2. All the nodes with a final label that is finite will be removed from the candidate list exactly once, in the order of increasing distance from node 1.

As the properties indicate, once a node is removed from the candidate list its distance from node 1 is known. The value of i in step (b) that led to the final value of the label indicates the previous hop in the path from 1.

11.2.2.1 DIJKSTRA'S ALGORITHM EXAMPLE

Considering the network represented by the graph in Figure 11–1 again, Table 11–2 shows the iterations of Dijkstra's algorithm. In this table, we show the labels, candidate list, and previous hop. Note that when a node is removed from the candidate list, its label and previous node value no longer change (as described by the properties). Hence, if we are only interested in getting to a particular end node rather than all possible end nodes, then we can stop the algorithm as soon as that node is removed from the candidate list.

11.2.3 A Comparison of Bellman-Ford and Dijkstra Algorithms

We described two different shortest-path algorithms in the last two sections. One might ask "which one is better?" The answer to this question depends on the context.

Table 11–2 *Dijkstra's Algorithm Iterations for the Graph of Figure 11–1*

Iteration	Label (d1, …, d7)	Candidate List, V	Previous Node (NE1, …, NE7)
0	(0, ∞, ∞, ∞, ∞, ∞, ∞)	{1}, remove 1	(s, x, x, x, x, x, x)
1	(0, 4, 2, ∞, ∞, ∞, ∞)	{2, 3}, remove 3	(x, 1, 1, x, x, x, x)
2	(0, 3, 2, ∞, ∞, ∞, ∞)	{2}, remove 2	(x, 3, 1, x, x, x, x)
3	(0, 3, 2, 5, 4, ∞, ∞)	{4, 5} remove 5	(x, 3, 1, 2, 2, x, x)
4	(0, 3, 2, 5, 4, 6, ∞)	{4, 6}, remove 4	(x ,3, 1, 2, 2, 5, x)
5	(0, 3, 2, 5, 4, 6, 7)	{6, 7}, remove 6	(x, 3, 1, 2, 2, 5, 4)
6	(0, 3, 2, 5, 4, 6, 7)	{7}, remove 7	(x, 3, 1, 2, 2, 5, 4)

Consider the distributed, asynchronous version of the Bellman-Ford algorithm used in RIPv2 [Malkin98]. It divides up the shortest path computation amongst the routers participating in the protocol. This robustness is important in the Internet. Unfortunately, with the Bellman-Ford technique, the iterations must continue until the labels stop changing. With Dijkstra's algorithm, the procedure can stop once the desired destination node(s) are removed from the candidate list. This property is useful if the paths to only a subset of nodes need to be computed. Other properties can influence the choice in particular network situations. For example, the Bellman-Ford algorithm can be significantly faster with sparse networks, that is, networks where the number of links is much less than N^2, where N is the number of nodes. It was seen that when the Bellman-Ford algorithm and Dijkstra's algorithm were applied to the network of Figure 11–1, the former terminated with fewer iterations. For more information, analysis, and comparison of these algorithms, see [Bertseka98].

11.3 Routing with Simple Constraints

The shortest path algorithms described above allow us to select an optimal path based on a set of chosen link weights. We can combine the shortest path technique with a simple graph pruning approach to include certain classes of constraints. In general, this approach is applicable when specific nodes or links can be excluded from the path based on their attributes. This is illustrated in the following examples.

11.3.1 Link Protection Constraints Example

Consider the network shown in Figure 11–2, where each link is assigned a cost and unprotected links are indicated by dashed lines. The shortest path from NE 1 to NE 7, regardless of individual link protection capabilities, is (NE 1, NE 3, NE 6, NE 7), as shown.

If, however, it is desired that a path be found from NE 1 to NE 7 that only traverses protected links, then the unprotected links must first be pruned from the graph. This pruned network graph is shown in Figure 11–3 along with the new least cost protected path from NE 1 to NE 7, that is, the path (NE 1, NE 2, NE 4, NE 7).

11.3.2 Bandwidth Constraints

Consider the network shown in Figure 11–4, consisting of OC-192 links. There is initially no traffic in this network. Suppose that at time t_0, a request is received to establish an STS-1 connection from NE 1 to NE 7. Based on the economic link costs, the shortest path is computed as (NE 1, NE 3, NE 6, NE

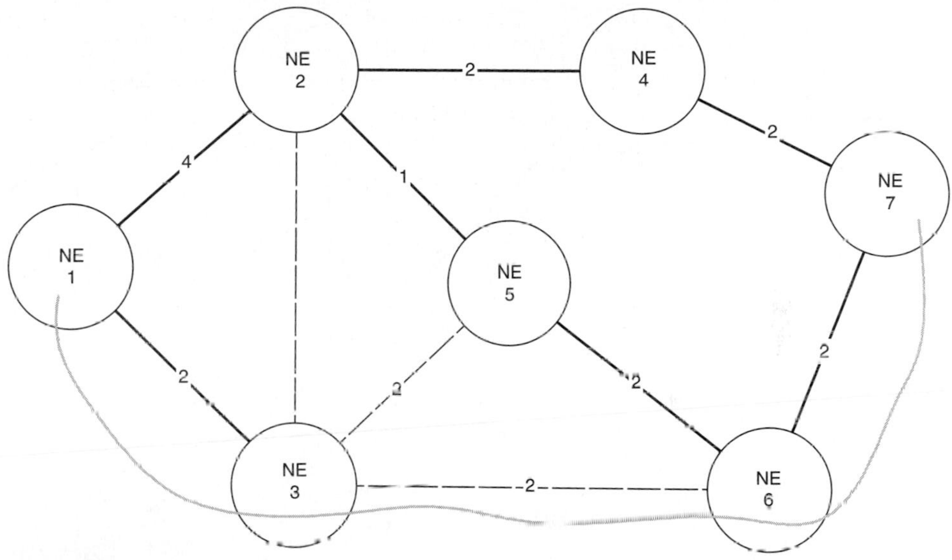

Figure 11–2 *Network Graph with Unprotected Links Indicated by Dashed Lines*

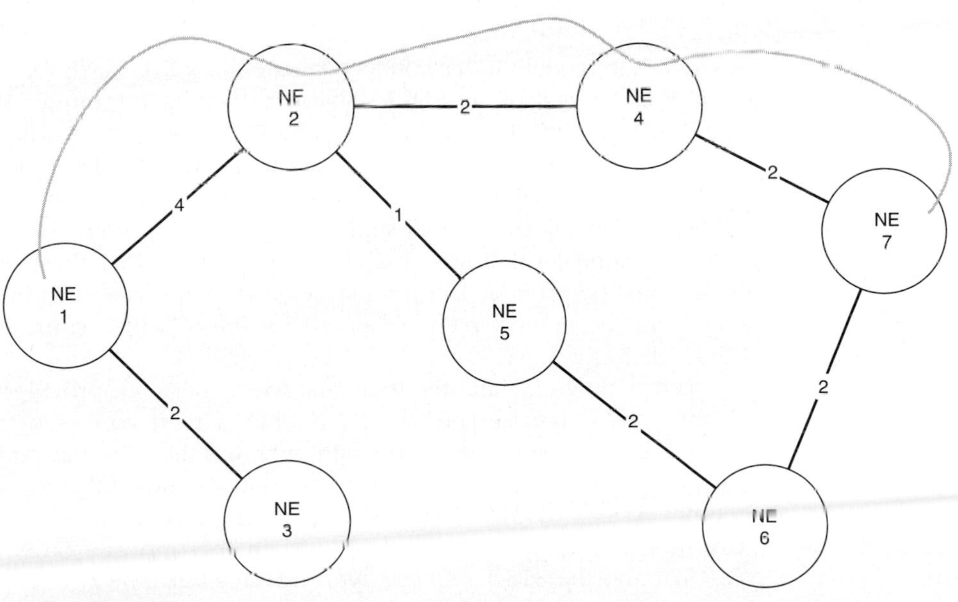

Figure 11–3 *Graph after Pruning the Unprotected Links in Figure 11–2*

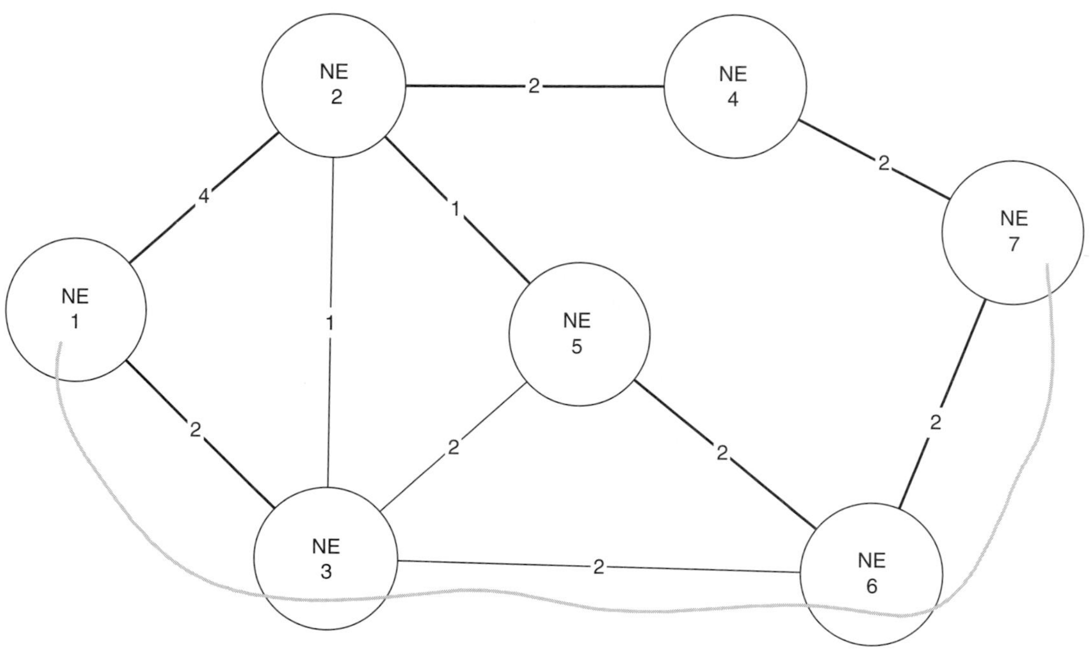

Figure 11–4 An OC-192 Mesh Network with Initially No Traffic

7). Hence, after routing this connection, the links (NE 1, NE 3), (NE 3, NE 6), and (NE 6, NE 7) carry an STS-1 signal and they have room for 191 additional STS-1s.

Now suppose at a later time t_1, another request is received to establish an STS-192c connection from NE 1 to NE 7. This signal needs 192 STS-1 slots and hence any link that cannot support it should be pruned from the network graph. In particular, the links that are carrying the STS-1 that were set up at time t_0 must be pruned. The pruned network graph is shown in Figure 11–5 along with the optimal path computed for the STS-192c connection, that is, (NE 1, NE 2, NE 4, NE 7).

Let us now examine the total cost to the network provider of supporting these two signals. The STS-1 path has a total cost of 6, obtained by adding the link weights along the path, whereas the STS-192c path has a total cost of 8. If we consider the total cost times bandwidth, we have (6 cost units)*(1 STS) + (8 cost units)*(192 STS) = 1542 (cost units*STS). Now suppose that the connection requests came in the opposite order, that is, the STS-192c and the STS-1 requests were received at time t_0 and t_1, respectively. It then turns out that the STS-192c will be routed over the path (NE 1, NE 3, NE 6, NE 7), and the STS-1 will be routed over the path (NE 1, NE 2, NE

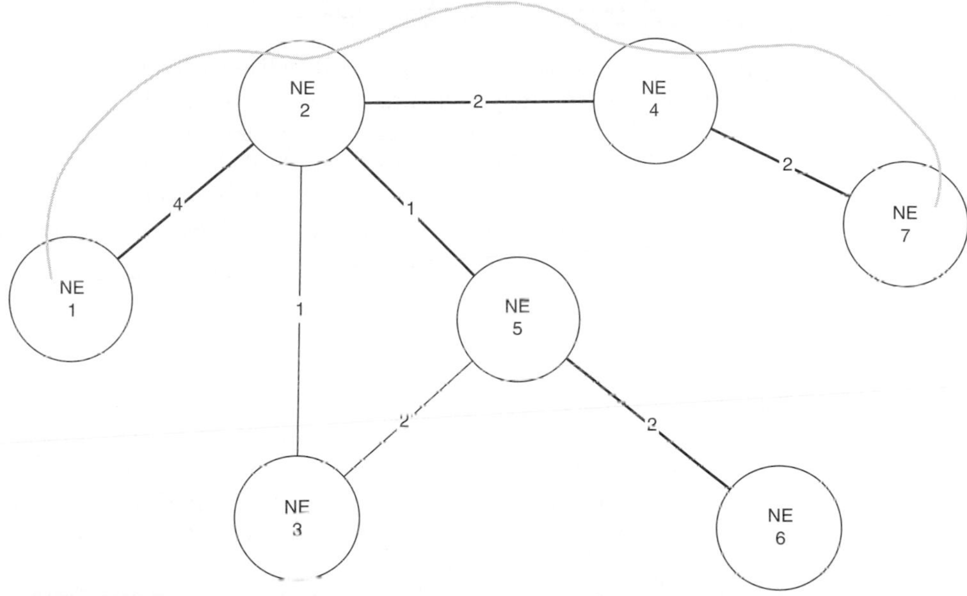

Figure 11-5 *Network of Figure 11-4 with All Links that Cannot Support an STS 192c Removed*

4, NE 7). In this case, the total cost times bandwidth product will be (6 cost units)*(192 STS) + (8 cost units)*(1 STS) = 1160. Hence, the order in which connections are established can be important to the overall economic efficiency of the network.

11.4 Path Selection for Diversity

Multiple optical connections are often set up between the same end points, for example, working and protection connections (see Chapter 8). An important constraint on these connections is that they must be diversely routed. In particular, they may have to be routed over paths that are link diverse, that is, which do not share any common link, or node diverse, that is, which do not share any common node. Note that node diversity is a stronger criterion, and it also implies link diversity.

When multiple physical and electronic levels are considered, ensuring link diversity is complicated by the possibility of two paths being diverse at one layer but not at another. Different types of link and node diversity requirements were described in section 10.3. In the following, the computation of link diverse paths is examined.

11.4.1 Link Diverse Routing Algorithms

Suppose it is required to compute two link diverse paths between a source and a destination. A straightforward approach that could be employed is as follows. First, the shortest path between the source and the destination is computed using one of the previously described algorithms. Next, all the links in this path are pruned from the graph, and another shortest path is computed using the modified graph. By construction, these two paths will be link diverse.

11.4.1.1 NONOPTIMAL DISJOINT PATHS VIA PRUNING

Consider the application of the pruning method to find two minimum cost link disjoint paths between NE 1 and NE 6 shown in Figure 11–6. The shortest path is computed as (NE 1, NE 4, NE 3, NE 6), with a total link cost of 3. This is indicated in the figure. The links along the shortest path are pruned from the graph to derive the graph shown in Figure 11–7. The shortest path (NE 1, NE 2, NE 8, NE 6), with a cost of 12, is then computed. This path, shown in Figure 11–7, is link-diverse from the first path.

While the pruning approach allowed the determination of two link disjoint paths in this example, it did not incorporate a means to minimize the *total* cost of the two paths found. In fact, there exists two link disjoint paths

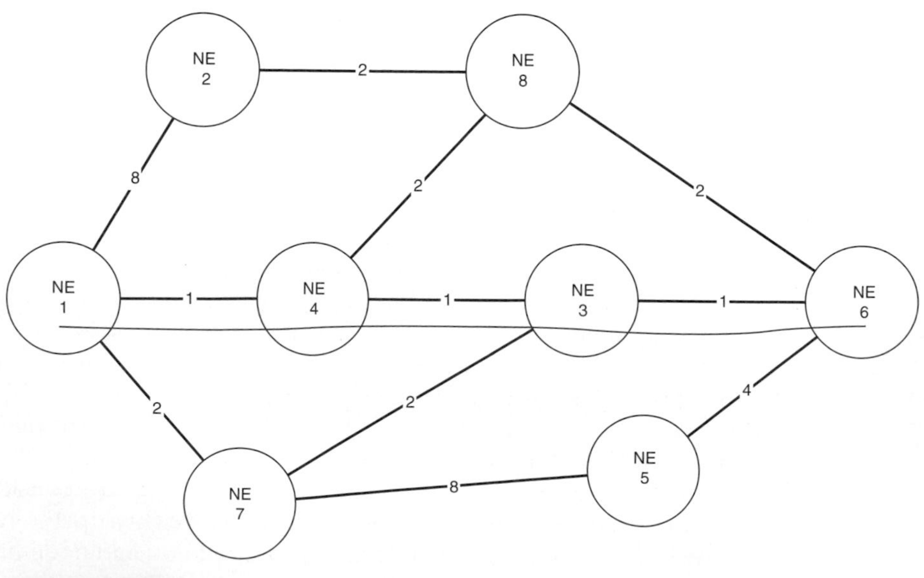

Figure 11–6 *Finding the Shortest Path*

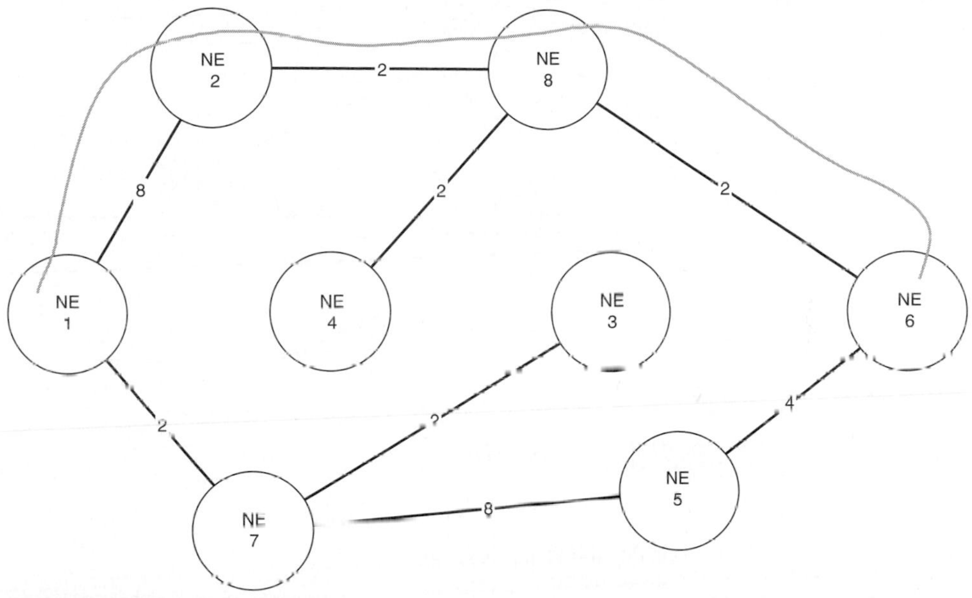

Figure 11–7 Finding the Second Link Diverse Path via the Pruned Network Graph

whose total cost is 10 whereas the total cost of the paths found above was 15 (these paths are (NE 1, NE 4, NE 8, NE 6) and (NE 1, NE 7, NE 3, NE 6)). The pruning approach can perform much worse, as the following example shows.

Consider the network shown in Figure 11–8 in which it is desired to find two minimum cost disjoint paths from NE 1 to NE 6. The shortest path from NE 1 to NE 6 is (NE 1, NE 4, NE 3, NE 6), and it is shown in Figure 11–8. When the links in this path are pruned, the network shown in Figure 11–9 is obtained.

We can immediately see from this figure that we have a problem. In particular, the network is no longer connected, and hence a second path from NE 1 to NE 6 cannot be found. Two link disjoint paths, (NE 1, NE 2, NE 3, NE 6) and (NE 1, NE 4, NE 5, NE 6), indeed exist, but the pruning approach cannot be used to find them.

11.4.2 Shortest Link Diverse Paths Algorithm

The two previous examples have shown that the pruning technique does not guarantee the discovery of either the optimal or even a feasible pair of disjoint paths. A very straightforward and efficient algorithm does exist for finding a pair of link-disjoint paths with the lowest total cost [Bhandhari99]. This algorithm does not require significant additional computation as compared with the pruning method, and it is described below.

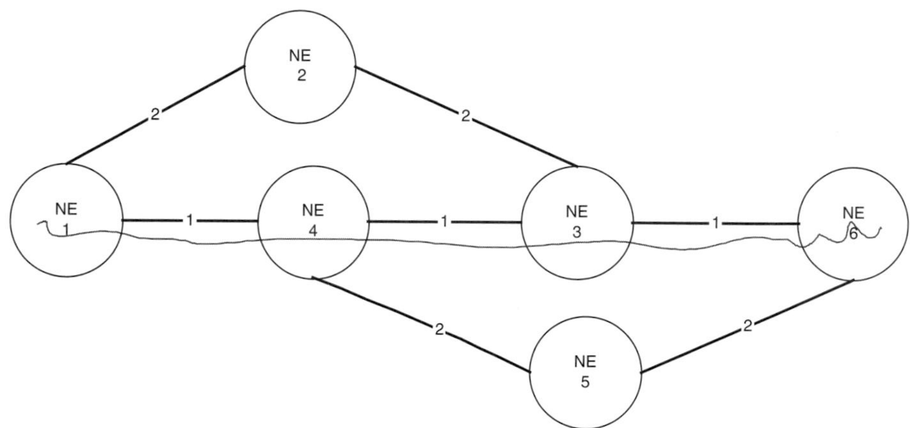

Figure 11–8 Network where Pruning Fails to Find Disjoint Paths

11.4.2.1 LINK DISJOINT PATH PAIR ALGORITHM

Given: A source node, *s*, a destination node, *d*, and a network represented by an undirected weighted graph with positive weights, that is, we are assuming bidirectional connections and bidirectional links.

1. Obtain the shortest path between *s* and *d*. Denote the set of links in this path as S_1.
2. Modify the original network graph by: (a) making each bidirectional link in S_1 unidirectional in the direction from *d* to *s*, and (b) set the link weights along this direction to be the negative of the original link weights.

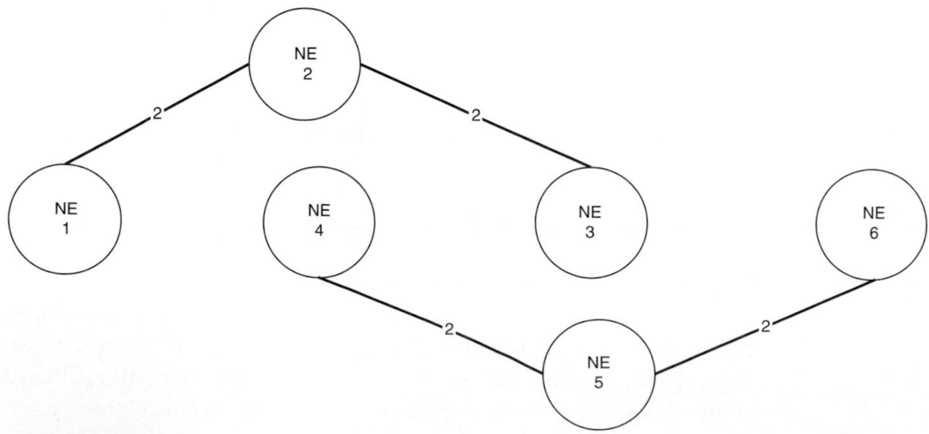

Figure 11–9 Graph of Network of Figure 11–8 with Shortest Path Links Removed

3. Compute the shortest path from s to d in the modified graph obtained in step 2. Denote the set of links in this path as S_2.
4. Remove links that occur in both S_1 and S_2. Denote this set of links as $S_3 = S_1 \cap S_2$.
5. Group the remaining links in $S_1 \cup S_2 - S_3$ into two disjoint paths.

Suppose we apply this algorithm on the network shown in Figure 11–8, which also depicts the shortest path from NE 1 to NE 6. The set of links, S_1, in this path are { (NE 1, NE 4), (NE 4, NE 3), (NE 3, NE 6) }. This path is modified according to step 2 above, and a new shortest path is computed on the modified graph. This is shown in Figure 11–10, with the new path highlighted. The set of links, S_2, in this path are { (NE 1, NE 2), (NE 2, NE 3), (NE 3, NE 4), (NE 4, NE 5), (NE 5, NE 6) }. The set, S_3, of links that are in the intersection of the two shortest paths is { (NE 4, NE 5) }. After removing this link, the set of links that remain (i.e., $S_1 \cup S_2 - S_3$), is { (NE 1, NE 2), (NE 1, NE 4), (NE 2, NE 3), (NE 4, NE 5), (NE 3, NE 6), (NE 5, NE 6) }. These links are used to form the two disjoint paths, (NE 1, NE 2, NE 3, NE 6) and (NE 1, NE 4, NE 5, NE 6). Figure 11–11 depicts these links as dashed lines, along with the two disjoint paths.

Let us now apply this algorithm on the network shown in Figure 11–6, which also depicts the shortest path (S_1) from NE1 to NE6. This path is modified according to step 2 above, and a new shortest path (S_2) is computed on the modified graph. This is shown in Figure 11–12, with the new path (NE 1, NE 7, NE 3, NE 4, NE 8, NE 6) highlighted. Now the link that is in both paths (S_3) is (NE 4, NE 3). After removing this link, the set of links that remain (i.e., $S_1 \cup S_2 - S_3$) is { (NE 1, NE 7), (NE 1, NE 4), (NE 4, NE 8), (NE 7, NE 3), (NE 3, NE 6), (NE 8, NE 6) }. These links are used to form the two disjoint

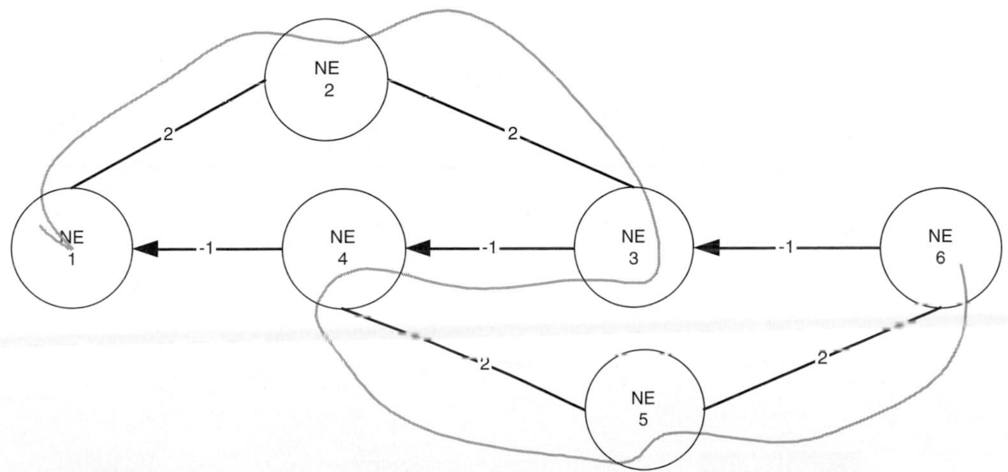

Figure 11–10 *Network of Figure 11–8 Transformed, with Shortest Path Indicated*

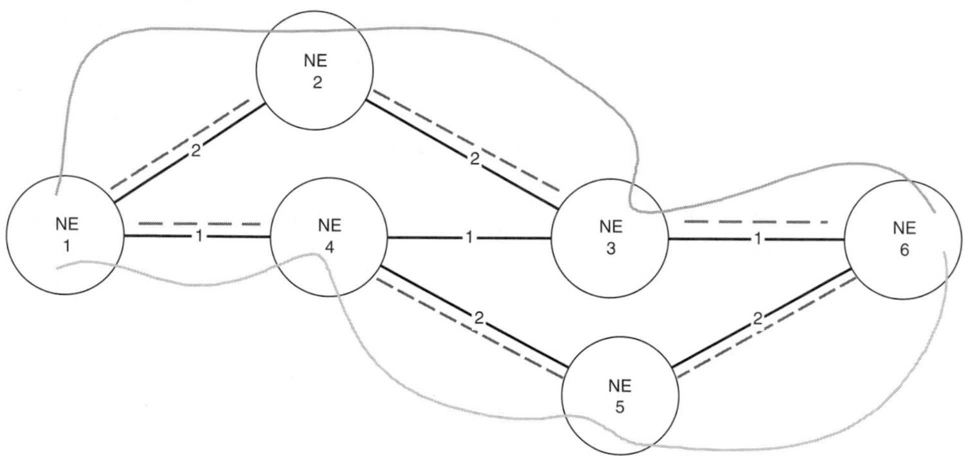

Figure 11–11 *The Set of "Useful" Links Along with the Two Disjoint Paths They Generate*

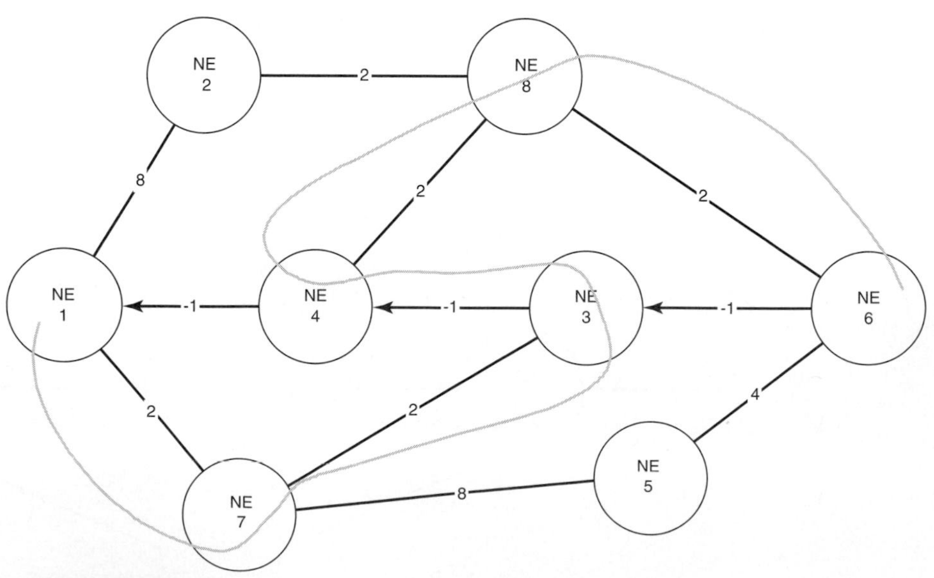

Figure 11–12 *Modified Graph of the Network of Figure 11–6*

paths, (NE 1, NE 7, NE 3, NE 6) and (NE 1, NE 4, NE 8, NE 6). Figure 11–13 depicts these links as dashed lines, along with the two disjoint paths.

A proof that the above algorithm converges and finds two diverse paths with the least total cost (if they exist) can be found in [Bhandhari99]. In both the examples given above, the two link-diverse paths were also node-diverse. This generally may not be the case. By applying additional transformations to the network graph, an algorithm for finding two node disjoint paths of least total cost can be obtained [Bhandhari99]. Finally, it turns out that the previous algorithm can be extended to find K lowest cost link disjoint paths.

11.5 Network Optimization

The next level of generalization comes when we consider one of the following:

1. Concurrent routing of multiple connection requests between different sources and destinations in some "optimal" fashion.
2. Optimization of some measure while simultaneously ensuring that a minimum acceptable quantity of another measure is satisfied.
3. A combination of the previous two.

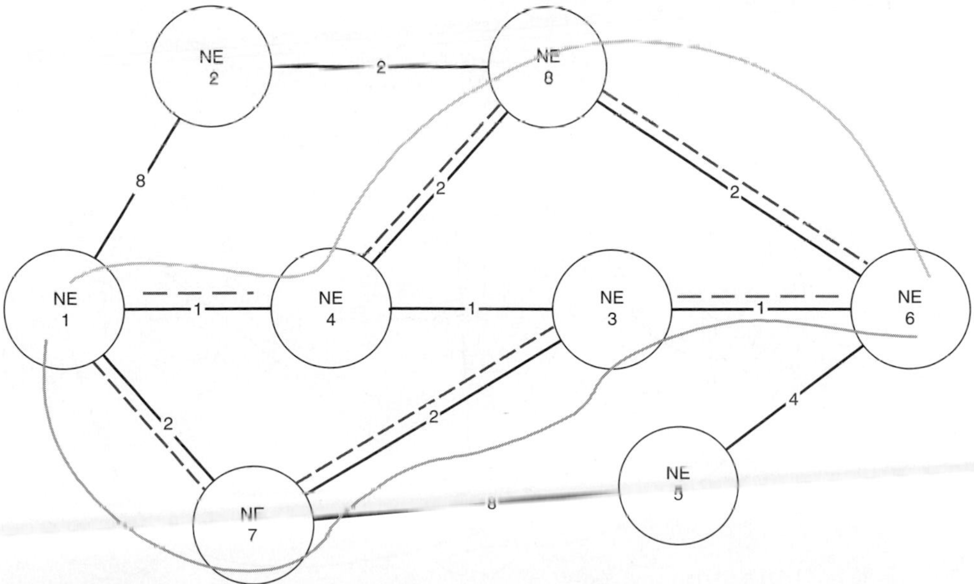

Figure 11–13 *The Set of "Useful" Links along with the Two Disjoint Paths Generated*

As an example of case 2, consider an optimization to find the least cost path based on economic link weights while simultaneously ensuring that the path has a failure probability below a given threshold (based on the individual link failure probabilities). To see why case 1 is important, consider the following example illustrated in Figure 11–14. This figure depicts a network consisting of OC-192 links interconnected via switching nodes or ADMs. Assume that the network is not carrying any traffic initially, and that the following requests for STS-192c connections are received subsequently in the order shown:

1: from NE2 to NE3,
2: from NE1 to NE4,
3: from NE3 to NE4, and
4: from NE4 to NE5.

Suppose that each of these connections have be routed over the shortest path, that is, we want to optimize the placement of connections in some respect. Unfortunately, due to the scarcity of bandwidth, setting up the first connection (from NE2 to NE3) over the shortest path prevents the establishment of the second connection (from NE1 to NE4). In addition, the third connection request (from NE3 to NE4) being accepted prevents the fourth (from NE4 to NE5) from being satisfied. Hence, only half of the STS-192c connection requests can be satisfied. Could things have been different? Yes.

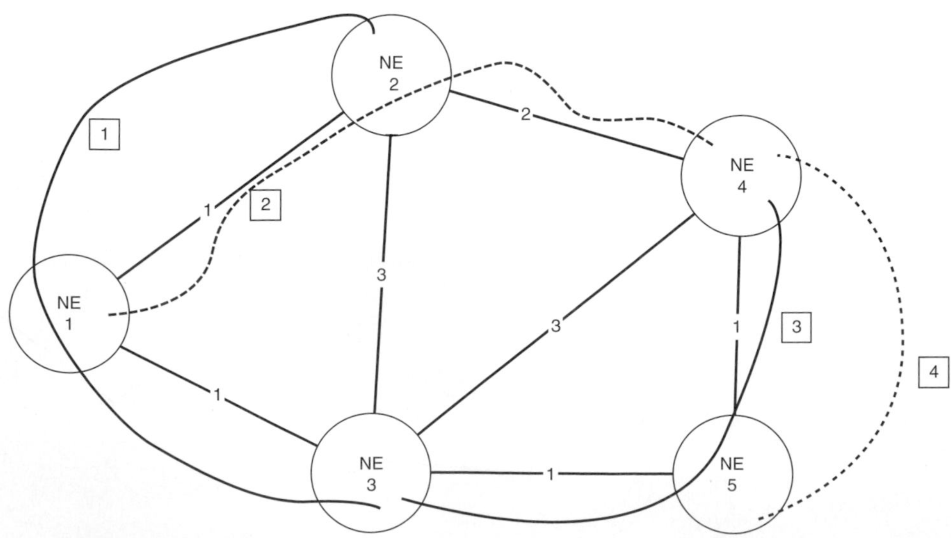

Figure 11–14 *Network of OC-192 Links Supporting Only 2 of 4 STS-192c Connection Requests*

Figure 11–15 depicts the result of successive shortest path placements if the connection requests are received in the following order: (from NE 4 to NE 5), (from NE 1 to NE 4), (from NE 2 to NE 3) and (from NE 3 to NE 4). In this case, all the connections are successfully routed.

It is seen from this example that if connections are routed along the shortest path independently of each other, then the order in which a set of connection requests are processed could determine the number of requests that are satisfied. When connection requests are received over a long period of time, it may be necessary to *reoptimize* connection routing to maximize the number of accepted connections [Bouillet+02b]. Reoptimization means that existing connections are periodically reordered and rerouted to optimize network utilization. Reoptimization requires more sophisticated techniques than the shortest path schemes discussed so far.

11.5.1 Batch Processing

The placement of multiple connections concurrently requires the application of certain optimization techniques. In this regard, the optimization problem to be solved can be expressed in standard mathematical language. In general, the problem consists of maximizing or minimizing some function of several variables subject to a number of constraints on those variables. Such a prob-

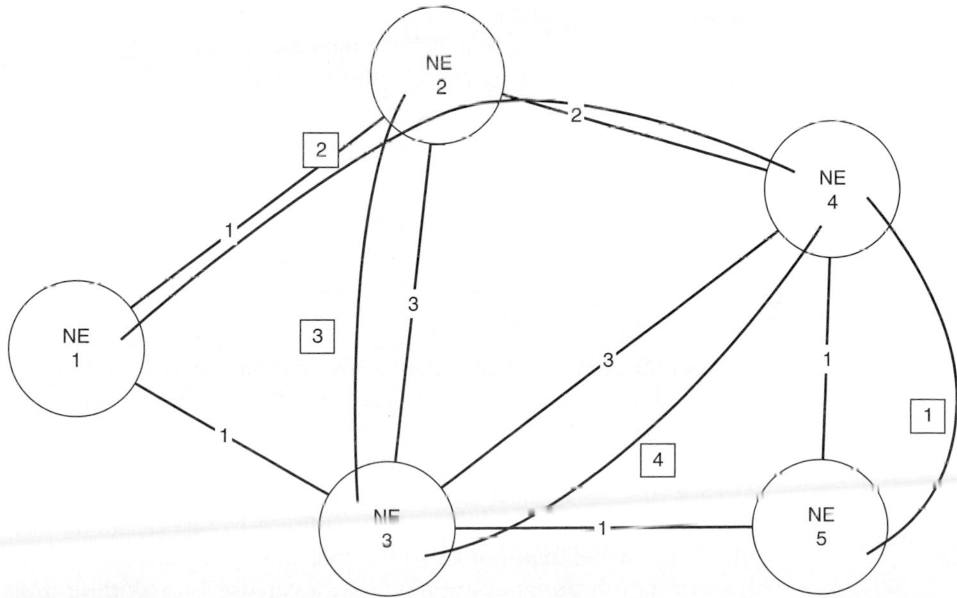

Figure 11–15 *Network of Figure 11–14 with STS-192c Connection Requests Arriving in a Different Order*

lem is usually called a *mathematical programming* problem, and there is a great deal of work devoted to various classes of these problems and their solutions. Before describing the general batch processing approach, we first return to the shortest path problem and show how to formulate the mathematical equations describing it.

11.5.2 Shortest Path: Mathematical Formulation

Given a directed graph with link weights $a_{i,j}$, let $x_{i,j}$ denote the amount of *flow* on link (i, j) from node i to node j. The first set of constraint equations capture the requirement that the flow variables are non-negative, that is.,

$$x_{i,j} \geq 0, \forall (i, j) \in A \tag{1}$$

With this assumption, we are interested in minimizing the following function:

$$\sum_{(i,j) \in A} a_{i,j} x_{i,j} \tag{2}$$

At the source node, we have:

$$\sum_{(s,j) \in A} x_{s,j} - \sum_{(i,s) \in A} x_{i,s} = b_s \tag{3}$$

where b_s is the amount of flow entering the network at the source node. This simply indicates that the traffic from the source to the destination enters at the source node and it is equal to b_s. In the case of the shortest path problem, $b_s = 1$. Similarly, at the destination node, the net outflow from the node is given by:

$$\sum_{(d,j) \in A} x_{d,j} - \sum_{(i,d) \in A} x_{i,d} = -b_s \tag{4}$$

Finally at intermediate nodes, i, we have:

$$\sum_{j(i,j) \in A} x_{i,j} - \sum_{j(j,i) \in A} x_{j,i} = 0, \ i \in V, i \neq s, d \tag{5}$$

This equation just indicates that at intermediate nodes there is no loss or gain of flow. Equations (3–5) are called *node balance* equations.

For example, considering the network shown in Figure 11–1, there are 13 links and 7 nodes. Hence, with the above formulation, a linear equation in 13 variables subject to 20 constraint equations (13 non-negativity constraints and the 7 node balance equations) has to be mimimized. Given the efficiency of Bellman-Ford and the Dijkstra algorithms, it is little wonder that this non-graph-oriented approach is never used for finding individual shortest paths.

11.5.3 Multicommodity Flow: Mathematical Formulation

Now, let us consider the case where a batch of connections has to be set up between various source and destination pairs. Since each connection is unique between a given source-destination pair, it can be considered as a separate "commodity" in our model. Hence, we will deal with the flow variables $x_{i,j}(k,m)$ where $(i,j) \in A$, ranges over the links in the network and (k,m) ranges over all the source-destination pairs. As before, the non-negativity constraint is

$$x_{i,j}(k,m) \geq 0 \tag{6}$$

And, the set of N (source, destination) node balance constraint equations are

$$\sum_{(s,j)\in A} x_{s,j}(s,m) - \sum_{(i,s)\in A} x_{i,s}(s,m) = b_{s,m}, \tag{7}$$

$$\sum_{(d,j)\in A} x_{d,j}(k,d) - \sum_{(i,d)\in A} x_{i,d}(k,d) = -b_{k,d}, \tag{8}$$

$$\sum_{j(i,j)\in A} x_{i,j}(k,m) - \sum_{j(j,i)\in A} x_{j,i}(k,m) = 0, \; i \in V, i \neq k, m. \tag{9}$$

To make it easier to keep track of constraints and the minimization function, we introduce the flow variable, (i,j), $y_{i,j}$, for each link (i, j). This is related to the $x_{i,j}(k,m)$ variables as follows:

$$y_{i,j} = \sum_{\substack{(k,m)\in \text{ all} \\ \text{source-destination} \\ \text{pairs}}} x_{i,j}(k,m). \tag{10}$$

The bandwidth constraints for the links can be written as

$$0 \leq y_{i,j} \leq c_{i,j} \quad (i,j) \in A. \tag{11}$$

and the function to be minimized is then

$$\sum_{(i,j)\in A} a_{i,j} y_{i,j}, \tag{12}$$

If the signals and links are bidirectional, then we will also have the additional symmetry constraints

$$x_{i,j}(k,m) = x_{j,i}(m,k). \tag{13}$$

As an example, consider the network depicted in Figure 11–14. This network has 7 bidirectional links (SONET OC-192), which have to be formulated as 14 unidirectional links in the above equations. There are 4 bidirectional (source, destination) connection pairs, or 8 unidirectional (source, destination) pairs. Thus, there are a total of 112 flow variables. There are also 14 link constraint equations and 40 node balance equations. This formulation is quite impractical to solve by hand. The approach, clearly, should be to automate the solution procedure as described next.

11.5.4 Formulating and Solving Multicommodity Optimizations

In the previous section, the batch path computation problem was formulated in terms of a mathematical programming problem. It was seen that even with a small network consisting of a small number of source-destination pairs, this formulation could produce too many equations and variables to be amenable to manual solution. In general, there are two main parts to solving these problems: (1) setting up the equations, and (2) solving the resulting optimization problem based on these equations.

Descriptions of techniques for solving optimization problems such as these can be found in many books on linear programming [Chvátal83]. A fairly sophisticated and thorough coverage of algorithms is given in [Bertsekas98]. We will therefore not attempt to cover any of this material here.[1]

In a reasonably sized, multicommodity network problem, it would not be unusual to deal with tens to hundreds or thousands of variables and equations. Hence, generating these equations can be somewhat tricky. Although custom software can be written to do this, special purpose languages can make the job significantly easier and quicker.[2] As an example, the following program, coded in the language *AMPL* [Fourer+93], formulates the multicommodity flow equations (6–13).

In this program, the network-specific information and connection demands have been separated from the general model formulation. First, the fundamental variables are defined, that is, the set of *NODES* (line 3), the set of source-destination pairs, *SD_PAIRS,* (line 6), and the set of *LINKS* (line 12). The specific values that these variables will assume are taken from a separate data file. Next, the "demand" parameters for each source destination pair (line 8) are defined. These are the $b_{i,j}$ variables in equations 7 and 8. The *flow* vari-

[1]It should be noted that the linear programming problems mentioned here are actually integer linear programs since the variables can only assume integer values.

[2]Easier after the "learning curve" of yet another computer language has been scaled.

ables in line 18 are just the $x_{i,j}(k,m)$ parameters of equation 6. The link weights have been named *usage_cost* and are defined on line 32. The values for these are specified in a separate data file. In this example, the total usage cost of the network is being minimized (see lines 34 and 35). Finally, the node balance equations and link capacity constraint equations are given in lines 36–49. Comments start with '#'.

```
1  #    The nodes in the network will be listed in a data
2  #    file.
3  set NODES;
4  #    The set of source-destination pair traffic demand to
5  #    be routed
6  set SD_PAIRS within {NODES, NODES};
7  # The traffic demand between the source and destination
8  param demand {SD_PAIRS};
9  check {(s,d) in SD_PAIRS }: demand[s,d] = demand[d,s];
10 #    The set of unidirectional links. This must be a sym-
11 #    metric set.
12 set LINKS within {NODES, NODES};
13 check {(i,j) in LINKS }: ( (j,i) in LINKS);
14 #(i,j) in LINKS and
15 #    The set of flow variables, i.e., the amount of traf-
16 #    fic on a particular link dedicated to a particular
17 #    source-destination communication path.
18 var flow {LINKS, SD_PAIRS}>=0;
19 #    Bi-directional constraint, the flow between s and d
20 #    over link (i,j) must be the same as the flow between
21 #    d and s over link (j,i).
22 subject to Bidirectional {(s,d)in SD_PAIRS, (i,j) in LINKS }:
23       flow[i,j,s,d] = flow[j,i,d,s];
24 var total_flow {LINKS} >= 0;
25 #    Total flow variable is just the flow over the link.
26 subject to TotalFlow { (i, j) in LINKS }:
27       total_flow[i,j] = sum { (s, d) in SD_PAIRS }
28       flow[i,j,s,d];
29 #     Minimize over the sum of all flows:
30 param usage_cost{LINKS} >= 0;
31 # Normal cost of using the link
32 param link_size > 0;
33 # Size of the links, e.g., 48  for OC-48
```

```
minimize UsageCost: sum {(i,j) in LINKS}
      usage_cost[i,j]*total_flow[i,j];
#   Node balance equations.  These are needed at every
#   node for every source-destination pair.
Subject to BalanceNull {n in NODES, (s,d) in SD_PAIRS:
s<>n and d<>n }:
sum {(n, i) in LINKS} flow[n,i,s,d] - sum {(i,n) in
LINKS} flow[i,n,s,d] = 0;
subject to BalanceSource {n in NODES, (n,d) in SD_PAIRS}:
sum {(n, i) in LINKS} flow[n,i,n,d] - sum {(i,n) in
LINKS} flow[i,n,n,d] = demand[n,d];
subject to BalanceDest {n in NODES, (s, n) in SD_PAIRS}:
sum {(n, i) in LINKS} flow[n,i,s,n] - sum {(i,n) in
LINKS} flow[i,n,s,n] = -demand[s,n];
subject to LinkConstraint {(i, j) in LINKS }:
total_flow[i,j] <= link_size;
```

The next AMPL code segment describes the network of Figure 11–14, along with demands for two (bidirectional) connections, one from NE 2 to NE 3 and the other from NE3 to NE 4.

```
set NODES := N1 N2 N3 N4 N5;
set SD_PAIRS := (N2, N3) (N3, N2) (N3, N4) (N4, N3) ;
set LINKS := (N1, N2) (N2, N1) (N1, N3) (N3, N1) (N2, N3)
(N3, N2) (N2, N4) (N4, N2) (N3, N4) (N4, N3) (N3, N5)
(N5, N3) (N4, N5) (N5, N4);
param demand :=
      N2 N3 192
      N3 N2 192
      N3 N4 192
      N4 N3 192;
param usage_cost :=
      N1 N2 1
      N2 N1 1
      N1 N3 1
      N3 N1 1
      N2 N3 3
      N3 N2 3
      N2 N4 2
      N4 N2 2
      N3 N4 3
      N4 N3 3
```

```
        N3 N5 1
        N5 N3 1
        N4 N5 1
        N5 N4 1;
param link_size = 192;
```

The following code sample shows the results of running the network flow model and the above data through *AMPL* and a solver/optimizer called *MINOS 5.5*. The results are displayed in terms of the links involved with a particular source destination flow. The display is in the form of a matrix in which the row *Ni* and column *Nj* define the link (*NE i, NE j*). For example, for the NE 2 to NE 3 connection, the links (NE 1, NE 2) and (NE 1, NE 3) are used while for the NE3 to NE4 connection, links (NE 3, NE 5) and (NE 4, NE 5) are used. Note that these are the paths shown in Figure 11–14.

```
ampl: model c:\Greg\design\Mps\fifth.mod;
ampl: data c:\Greg\design\Mps\fourth.dat;
ampl: solve;
MINOS 5.5: optimal solution found.
8 iterations, objective 1536
ampl: display flow;
flow [*,*,N2,N3]
:       N1    N2    N3    N4    N5    :=
N1      .     0     192   .     .
N2      192   .     0     0     .
N3      0     0     .     0     0
N4      .     0     0     .     0
N5      .     .     0     0     .
 [*,*,N3,N4]
:       N1    N2    N3    N4    N5    :=
N1      .     0     0     .     .
N2      0     .     0     0     .
N3      0     0     .     0     192
N4      .     0     0     .     0
N5      .     .     0     192   .
```

The results obtained in the previous example were not all that surprising. In particular, since the two connection requests did not interfere with each other, these results correspond to running a shortest path algorithm twice. Now, suppose that all four connection requests shown in Figure 11–14 are presented together. The following code shows the network model with the demands enlarged to include four bidirectional connections requests.

```
set NODES := N1 N2 N3 N4 N5;
set SD_PAIRS := (N1,N4) (N4, N1) (N2, N3) (N3, N2) (N3,
N4) (N4, N3) (N4, N5) (N5, N4);
set LINKS := (N1, N2) (N2, N1) (N1, N3) (N3, N1) (N2, N3)
(N3, N2) (N2, N4) (N4, N2) (N3, N4) (N4, N3) (N3, N5)
(N5, N3) (N4, N5) (N5, N4);
param demand :=
      N1 N4 192
      N4 N1 192
      N2 N3 192
      N3 N2 192
      N3 N4 192
      N4 N3 192
      N4 N5 192
      N5 N4 192;
param usage_cost :=
      N1 N2 1
      N2 N1 1
      N1 N3 1
      N3 N1 1
      N2 N3 3
      N3 N2 3
      N2 N4 2
      N4 N2 2
      N3 N4 3
      N4 N3 3
      N3 N5 1
      N5 N3 1
      N4 N5 1
      N5 N4 1;
param link_size = 192;
```

The results of running the network flow model with the above data through *AMPL* and a solver are shown below. As before, the matrices display the flow on the links corresponding to each connection.

```
ampl: model c:\Greg\design\Mps\fifth.mod;
ampl: data c:\Greg\design\Mps\fourth2.dat;
ampl: solve;
MINOS 5.5: optimal solution found.
16 iterations, objective 3840
```

```
ampl: display flow;
flow [*,*,N1,N4]
:      N1     N2     N3     N4     N5      :=
N1      .    192      0      .      .
N2      0      .      0    192      .
N3      0      0      .      0      0
N4      .      0      0      .      0
N5      .      .      0      0      .
[*,*,N2,N3]
:      N1     N2     N3     N4     N5      :-
N1      .      0      0      .      .
N2      0      .    192      0      .
N3      0      0      .      0      0
N4      .      0      0      .      0
N5      .      .      0      0      .
[*,*,N3,N4]
:      N1     N2     N3     N4     N5      :=
N1      .      0      0      .      .
N2      0      .      0      0      .
N3      0      0      .    192      0
N4      .      0      0      .      0
N5      .      .      0      0      0
[*,*,N4,N5]
:      N1     N2     N3     N4     N5      :=
N1      .      0      0      .      .
N2      0      .      0      0      .
N3      0      0      .      0      0
N4      .      0      0      .    192
N5      .      .      0      0      .
```

From this, we see that the connection from NE 4 to NE 5 is supported by the link, (NE 4, NE 5); the connection from NE 3 to NE 4 is supported by the link, (NE 3, NE 4); the connection from NE 1 to NE 4 is supported by links (NE 2, NE 4) and (NE 1, NE 2); and the connection from NE 2 to NE 3 is supported by the link (NE 2, NE 3). Note that this solution is the same as that shown in Figure 11–15, which was obtained using a different ordering of the connection requests into a shortest path algorithm. Changing the order of connection requests into a shortest path algorithm, however, is in general not a useful way to find an optimal solution. This is because the number of permutations of the ordering grows exponentially, that is, as *N*!, where *N* is the number of connection requests.

Although the last example involves 112 flow variables, 14 link constraint equations and 40 node balance equations, it would only take a second or less to run on a typical desktop PC. This is partly due to the fact that the equations generated for realistic networks tend to be rather sparse, that is, they contain mostly zero entries. This reflects the fact that the average *degree* of a node in a network graph, that is, the number of links connected to the node, tends to be much less than the number of nodes in the network. Another aspect of the problem, as formulated in equations (6)–(13), is that it only involves linear functions and linear constraints of real valued variables. The sparseness, combined with the linearity of these equations, allows for extremely efficient numerical solution via linear programming methods and sparse matrix techniques.

11.6 Summary

Path computation algorithms play a key role in optical network routing [Ellinas+02]. While traditional shortest-path algorithms can be directly used in IP routing, additional constraints have to be considered in optical routing. Furthermore, finding physically diverse paths requires the application of new algorithms. Many vendors today use centralized path computation for provisioning connections. This is due to the need to optimize connection routing and also to reduce the complexity of implementations. Distributed path computation will be the norm with the newer control plane technologies [Bouillet+02c]. Some aspects of distributed path computation in large, multi-area networks were described in Chapter 10. The next chapter deals with routing in heterogeneous environments, where the challenge is to capture sufficient information about the structure of the network and available resources for efficient path computation.

T W E L V E

Interdomain Control

12.1 Introduction

As carriers build global and national networks, it becomes necessary to systematically partition these networks into *control domains*, that is, subnetworks in which a particular control paradigm or protocol is employed. Control domains are often referred to simply as *domains* (see Chapter 5).

From a network control perspective, the motivations for dividing a network into domains are:

- To define administrative boundaries
- To allow for scalability of routing and signaling
- To isolate portions of the network for security or reliability, and
- To accommodate technology differences between systems, for example, by partitioning a single carrier's network into separate single vendor subnetworks

Figure 12–1 illustrates the partitioning of a network into three domains. An *interdomain interface* is the signaling and routing interface between two

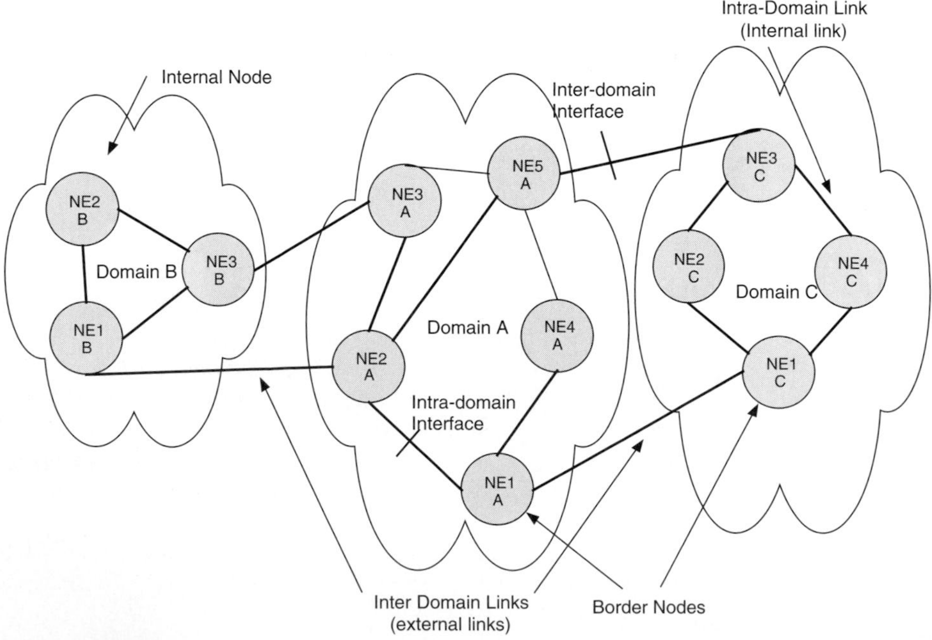

Figure 12–1 *Partitioning a Network into Domains*

network elements (or controllers, see Chapter 7) in different domains.[1] An *intradomain* interface is the signaling and routing interface between two network elements in the same domain. These interfaces are illustrated in Figure 12–1. An interdomain interface is likely to have different characteristics than an intradomain interface as the domain boundary exists for the purpose of hiding certain aspects of the domain from the outside world.

The domain concept as used here is orthogonal to the concept of layering in transport networks. In the transport network, layers are technology specific and are used for multiplexing, performance monitoring, and fault management, with different layers providing different capabilities in each of these areas. A routing protocol for optical networks must include information particular to the technology layer in which it is being used.

In the rest of this chapter, we describe interdomain control requirements and routing architectural models. Presently, interdomain control is at early stages of standardization and experimentation [ITU-T02b]. Thus, the following descriptions are conceptual and high-level rather than being protocol oriented as in earlier chapters.

12.2 Interdomain Control Requirements

There are several reasons why a large network may be partitioned into domains. In each application, there are specific requirements on signaling and routing across interdomain interfaces. In this section, we explore these issues.

12.2.1 Scalability

As networks grow, the scalability of the control plane becomes an issue. Specifically, the complexity of transmission, storage, and processing of routing information increases with the size of the network. It therefore becomes necessary to partition a carrier's network into multiple domains between which the flow of routing information is limited in some fashion. This reduces the amount of information exchanged across the network, and reduces the convergence time of routing protocols within a domain. Thus, for scalability, the internal topology and resource information of a domain is abstracted when sent outside, while the overall interdomain topology and resource information is made available to allow diverse path computation. Note that the general domain capabilities as well as reachability of destinations across domains need to be shared as completely as possible.

Current IP routing protocols provide for scalability by allowing topological partitioning (see Chapter 5). An example is OSPF's multiple area capabil-

[1]Such nodes are also called border nodes (see Figure 12–1).

ity (see Chapter 9). Consider Figure 9-5 again, which depicts the use of OSPF areas for routing scalability. The figure shows three OSPF areas. The backbone area (area 0) has special properties, and all the other areas must be attached to it. Note that the traffic *between* these OSPF areas must traverse the backbone area. Also note that an Area Border Router (ABR) must be a member of two areas, that is, its own area and the backbone area. Only reachability information, and not topology information, is exchanged between areas (including the backbone area). This results in a significant reduction in information transferred between areas and hence promotes scalability. The lack of topology information exchange across areas, however, means that sufficient information is not available to perform diverse route calculations.

12.2.2 Intervendor Interoperability

An important application of the optical control plane is the promotion of interoperability between vendors. From a carrier's perspective, the use of domains can provide a clean way to isolate "clouds" of equipment belonging to different vendors, with a well-defined interface between the domains for interoperability. This is shown in Figure 12–2. In this case, two specific requirements arise:

1. The protocols used between the domains for signaling and routing must be independent of any protocols used within the domains, and
2. The internal operation of a domain must be hidden from entities in other domains.

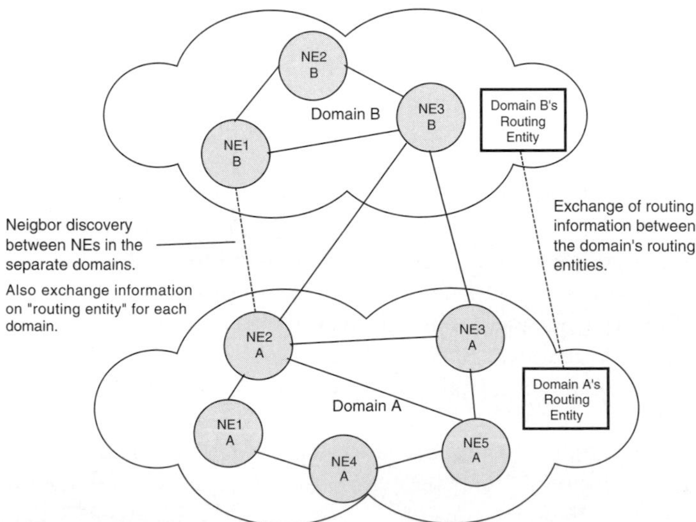

Figure 12–2 *Intracarrier Intervendor Routing Domains*

These requirements arise because vendors typically develop routing and management methods independently, often using proprietary mechanisms. Creating vendor-specific domains allows the accommodation of these differences, while allowing standardized communication across interdomain interfaces. For example, the routing entity in each domain shown in Figure 12–2 could obtain the internal topology and resource information by participating in a routing protocol like OSPF, by querying the domain's management system, or by simply having the required information manually configured into it.

With reference to Figure 12–2, the following scenarios are possible:

1. A proprietary distributed routing protocol is implemented in each domain
2. As is the case with a number of existing installations, a management-system-based (centralized) topology/resource discovery and routing schemes are implemented in both domains.
3. Centralized routing is implemented in one domain while distributed routing is used in the other.

The two requirements listed earlier capture interoperability needs in all these three cases.

A similar interoperability scenario comes up in the IP world when considering routing between different Internet service providers (ISPs). An ISP typically uses either the IS-IS or the OSPF protocol for routing within its own network. Although similar in function (both are link state routing protocols), these protocols do not interoperate. When ISPs establish peering agreements, that is, agree to carry traffic from each other, they use another protocol, BGP, which is neutral to the internal routing protocol running in each ISP's domain. This situation is illustrated in Figure 12–3.

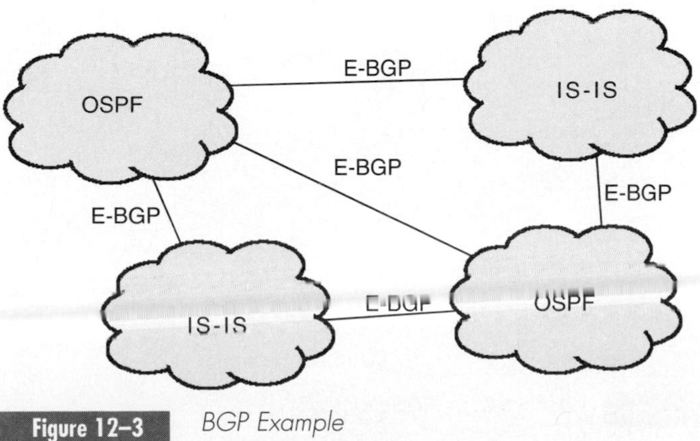

Figure 12–3 *BGP Example*

12.2.3 Administrative Partitioning

A slightly different but interesting application of the domain concept occurs when a carrier has multiple administrative domains under the purview of independent business units (BUs). This is illustrated in Figure 12–4.

Different BUs may represent independently administered cost centers. Being autonomous entities, BUs may allow only limited information sharing between networks run by each other. For instance, topology may be exchanged without detailed resource usage information. This scenario illustrates another form of limited information sharing; namely, complete sharing of topology while restricting the disclosure of resource availability information.

12.2.4 Deployment and Operations Considerations

The domain concept allows heterogeneous control methods to coexist in a large network, while permitting interoperability via a standard interdomain interface. An alternative to this approach is to have a single standardized protocol (e.g., OSPF), with its own scaling mechanism (e.g., OSPF areas), running in all the nodes. The problem with such an idea becomes apparent, when we consider it in the context of a large optical network. In essence, the same protocol needs to be implemented in different types of nodes (perhaps from dif-

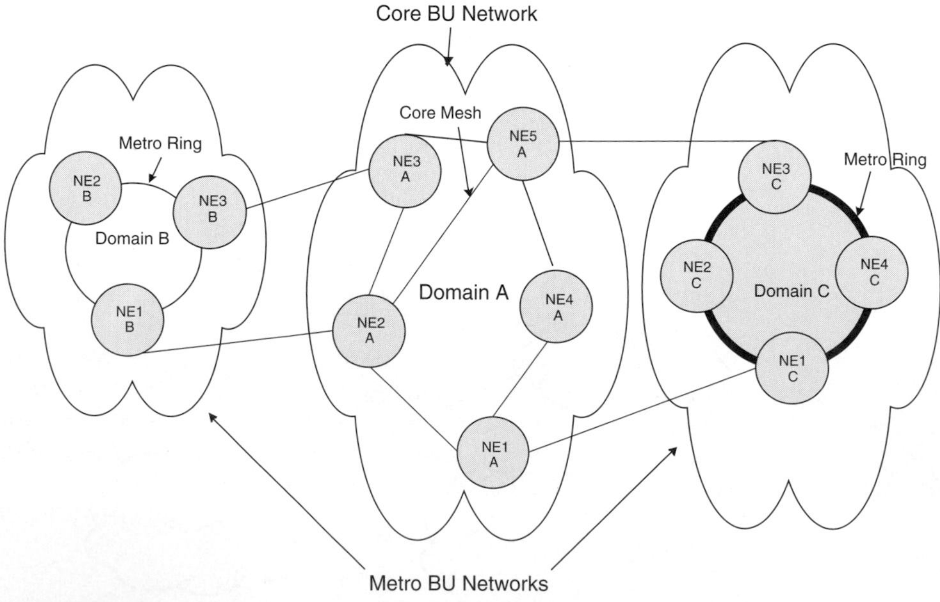

Figure 12–4 *Administrative Partitioning*

ferent vendors) in a truly interoperable manner. This may not be feasible if some nodes are simply not designed to operate under a distributed control plane. With others, this may require a major software upgrade. In short, this is not a practical proposition. On the other hand, with the domain approach new protocols run between domains and not between each node in a domain. This allows the existing functionality of nodes within a domain to be maintained and does not require a carrier to "revamp" all the nodes within the domain.

From an operations perspective, it is desirable to limit the interactions between nodes across domain boundaries. In particular, signaling and routing generate a variety of information flows. Too much information flowing can cause problems, as in "signaling storms" encountered in telephone networks or "route flapping" in IP networks. One approach to monitoring, suppressing, and possibly preventing such disruptive phenomena is to let entities representing an entire domain rather than individual nodes exchange information, as shown in Figure 12–2.

A domain's routing entity (Figure 12–2) could apply flooding and summarization mechanisms as if it is a switching system. The functions of the routing entity could include (a) exchanging reachability information (i.e., which NEs can be directly reached from this domain), (b) verification of domain connectivity (i.e., understanding how a domain is directly connected to other domains), (c) exchanging summarized domain topology information, and (d) exchanging topology information concerning other domains.

12.3 Domain Hierarchies

We have seen that (topological) hierarchies are used with various routing protocols (OSPF, IS-IS, and ATM's PNNI routing) to enhance scalability. In transport networks and other types of circuit switched networks (e.g., the telephone network), hierarchies are also used to demarcate specific boundaries of networks (from the policy perspective). This is particularly the case when networks cross geopolitical boundaries. For example, a transport network may be composed of metropolitan networks interconnected by a state (or province)-wide core network. These state-wide core networks may be interconnected by a regional core network. These regional networks might then be interconnected by a country or continent-wide core network. Finally, international core networks may tie together various levels of international networks. Due to different regulatory, operational, or business influences, these networks may be administered somewhat autonomously, and hence a hierarchical assemblage of control domains is highly desirable, independent of scalability concerns.

Let us consider the use of hierarchy for structuring a carrier's network strictly for scalability. Suppose that a routing protocol can deal with 200 nodes at any given layer in a hierarchy. How many physical nodes (lowest level nodes) can be accommodated in total by (a) two, (b) three, or (c) four levels of hierarchy? Given that N nodes can be accommodated per hierarchical level, a two-level network would have N second level logical nodes each representing N physical nodes, resulting in a total of N^2 physical nodes. Repeating this process we get the following results: (a) N^2= 40,000 nodes; (b) N^3= 8,000,000 nodes; (c) N^4= 1,600,000,000 nodes. From this, we see why those who need hierarchy for scalability alone question the need for more than three levels of hierarchy, while those who require hierarchical structuring of networks based on geopolitical boundaries cannot get by with just three levels of hierarchy.

12.3.1 Relationship to Signaling

As seen in Chapter 7, signaling protocols already contain provisions for "loose explicit routes" or "abstract nodes" which allow them to accommodate hierarchical domains. Thus, our focus later is on modifications and extensions to routing protocols for interdomain use.

Routing in optical networks involves calculating the entire route of the connection (albeit a loose route in some cases) at the source. As a connection set-up request crosses different domains, the signaling entity in each domain can take the loose routing information, and, based on detailed information about the internal topology of the domain, compute a specific intradomain path. This process can be repeated within each domain, with the routing entity in each domain using a potentially different algorithm to calculate the portion of the path passing through its domain.

For example, in the network of Figure 12–1, a route between NE4 in domain C and NE2 in domain B could be specified simply as a sequence of domains {C, A, B} to be traversed by the set-up request for the connection to be established between these nodes. This route could then be locally expanded in domains A and B, either by a border node or by an appropriate entity in the domain responsible for resolving the route, to the exact sequence of hops through that domain. For instance, within domain C, the route may be resolved as NE4→NE1. The border node NE1 in domain A may resolve the local route to be NE1→NE2→NE3. Finally, border node NE3 in domain B may resolve the route (due to its local constraints) to be NE3→NE2→NE1. Once the connection is established and the source node receives the corresponding acknowledgment, the connection is deemed available to carry data (possibly after the completion of other end-to-end connectivity tests conducted by the carrier).

12.3.2 Routing Hierarchies

To aid our discussion of domain hierarchies, we introduce below a subset of the definitions used in the ITU-T optical routing architecture and requirements document [ITU-T02b]. These pertain to *Routing Controllers, Routing Areas, Routing Control Domains*, and *Link Resource Manager*.

Routing Controller (RC): This is an entity that computes routes across a routing area. There could be multiple, cooperating RCs within a routing area. For example, when a routing protocol like OSPF is used, every node running OSPF would be an RC. On the other hand, with centralized routing of the sort typically used in legacy transport networks, there would be a single RC, perhaps implemented in the Element Management System (EMS). In general, there could be one or more RCs in a routing area, either implemented directly on NEs or on separate equipment. The RCs implement interdomain routing.

Routing Area (RA): Abstractly, an RA is a collection of nodes and links that define the topology over which RCs compute paths. At the lowest level of the domain hierarchy, an RA represents a control domain, that is, the nodes represent physical NEs and the links represent the interconnections between the NEs. The nodes and links in an RA can also be "abstract," that is, each node itself representing an RA and the links representing the interconnections between these RAs. This will be the case at the higher levels of the domain hierarchy RCs work with each other within a single RA (and within that RA only). For example, Figure 12–5 depicts three distinct RAs, identified as 2112, 505, and 417, in the first level of a domain hierarchy. Each of these RAs could be a control domain, for instance, a vendor "cloud" with its own internal control and management mechanisms. The RCs within the scope of RA 2112, that is, RC 3 and RC 7, interact with each other, but not with RC 11 in RA 505. This notion of an RA is somewhat different from the OSPF [Moy98] notion of a routing area in that

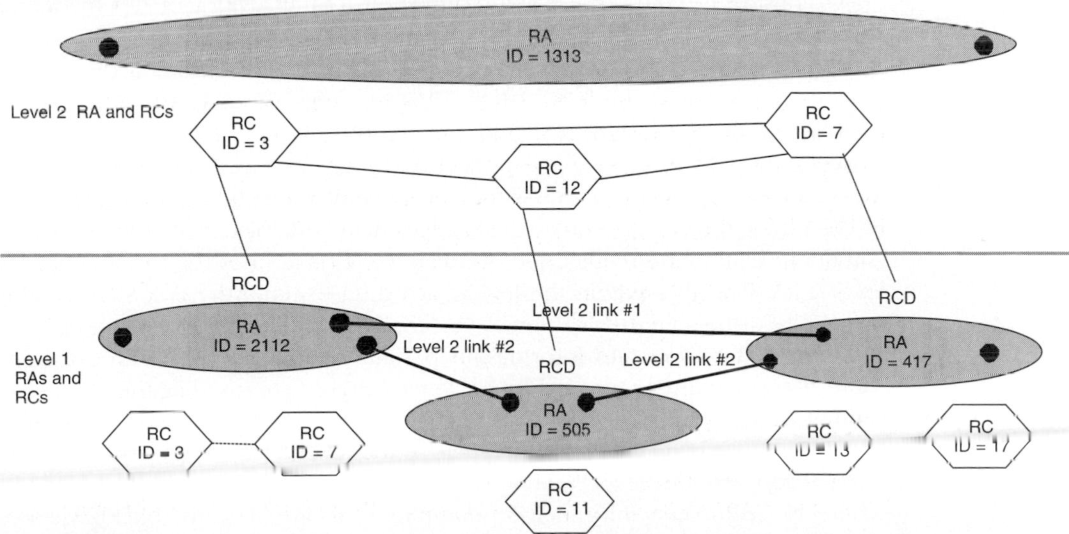

Figure 12–5 *An Example Hierarchical Network Illustrating RAs, RCs, and RCDs*

it does not imply anything about how entities in different RAs interact (unlike OSPF's requirement on communications via the backbone area).

Routing Control Domain (RCD): Each RC represents a routing control domain, that is, a logical region whose properties are characterized by the RC. When a domain hierarchy is created, an RA in level N-1 is represented as an RCD in level N by a level N-1 RC. Thus, an RCD is what appears as the abstract node in higher-level RAs, as described earlier. For example, Figure 12–5 depicts level 1 routing areas 2112, 505, and 417 being represented as RCDs by RCs 3, 12, and 7, respectively, within the level 2 routing area (identifier 1313). To summarize, a routing area defines the scope of a set of cooperating routing controllers while a routing control domain is associated with a single routing controller.

Link Resource Manager (LRM): A link resource manager is a logical entity responsible for allocating and deallocating link resources, that is, time slots, wavelengths, and so on. In addition, it is responsible for providing link status information to the appropriate RC. Figure 12–5 shows several links (e.g., optical fibers) interconnecting the level 1 routing areas. Since these links are *between* level 1 routing areas, they do not fall under the management of any level 1 RC. Hence, the LRM associated with each of these links will need to communicate link status information to the appropriate level 2 RC.

Thus, the RCs within an RA represent either a single control domain or a hierarchy of such domains. Abstractly, these RCs are "nodes" within an RA, and they execute a link state routing protocol within the RA. This is similar to the manner in which routers in an OSPF area implement intraarea OSPF routing. Now, consider a collection of interconnected RAs at level 1 of the hierarchy. Each of these RAs is treated as a separate routing control domain and represented by a single RC ("node") in a level 2 RA. This RC is thus a member of both the level 1 and the level 2 RAs. This is similar to an OSPF ABR being a member of both its own area and the backbone area. The interconnection between the RAs in level 1 is captured by "links" between the corresponding RCs ("nodes") in level 2. These links could be links directly connecting the RCs in the physical topology, or (logical) adjacencies established between the RCs (similar to OSPF virtual links, see Chapter 10). This defines the topology of the level 2 RA. The RCs within the level 2 RA then execute the link state routing protocol. Further hierarchical levels are constructed in the same manner.

Now, the link state information pertaining to level N+1 is required to route a connection between RAs in level N. This means that the RC representing a level 1 RA in a level 2 RA must abstract and inject its level 1 RA information into the level 2 RA, and summarize the level 2 (topology and resource) information into its level 1 area. This is similar to interarea OSPF routing, where an ABR injects information pertaining to its area into the backbone area and propagates reachability information received in the backbone area (from other ABRs) into its area.

12.3.3 Identification of Components within a Hierarchy

To implement hierarchical routing as described, RCs and RAs need to be identified in the interdomain routing protocol. An *RC identifier (RC-ID)* uniquely identifies an RC within a given routing area. There is no separate RCD identifier, since each RCD is uniquely associated with an RC. Thus, the RC-ID is synonymous with the corresponding RCD identifier.

Before two RCs communicate with each other, they should verify that they are in the same routing area. Hence, it is useful to have an identifier for RAs, that is, *RA identifiers (RA-IDs)*. Another way of thinking about this is that an RA-ID identifies the scope or context within which one or more RCs interact. An RC-ID must be unique only within its containing RA. Such a situation is shown in Figure 12–6, where the RC-IDs used in level 2 are the same as those used within some of the level 1 RAs. RC-IDs, however, can be globally unique.

12.3.3.1 OSPF EXAMPLE

The format of the OSPF packet header is shown in Figure 12–7 [Moy98]. This header contains an Area ID and a Router ID. These correspond to the RA-ID and the RC-ID, respectively. The concepts discussed earlier can be used to model OSPF's hierarchical interactions. In particular, OSPF maintains separate

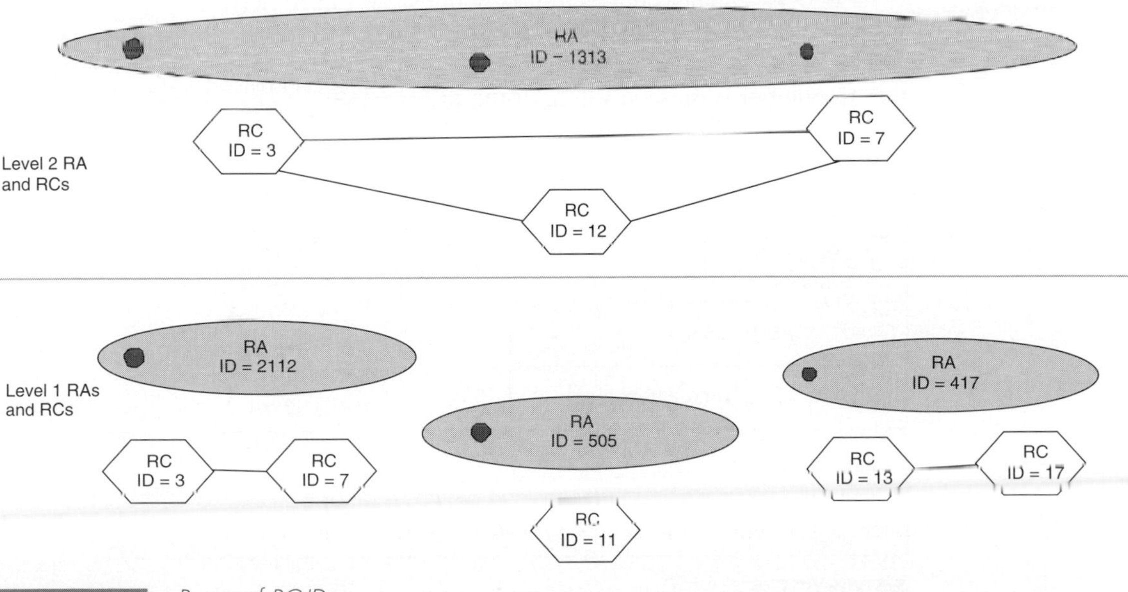

Figure 12–6 *Reuse of RC-IDs*

Version # (8-bits)	Type (8-bits)	Length(16-bits)	
Router ID (32-bits)			
Area ID (32-bits)			
Checksum(16-bits)		Auth Type(16-bits)	
Authentication			

Figure 12–7 *OSPF Header*

routing interactions in each of its areas, and the Area ID is used to tell these apart when a router participates in multiple areas.

12.3.3.2 BGP EXAMPLE

BGP-4 [Rekhter+95] runs over TCP. Once a TCP session is established between two BGP speakers (i.e., the equivalent of RCs), each speaker sends an *Open* message. The format of this message, containing the AS number, is shown in Figure 12–8.

BGP essentially defines the second level RA in IP networks. That is, each AS running E-BGP with another AS (see Figure 12–3) can be considered as a first level RA, and hence represented as an RCD in the second level RA. Thus, the AS number is the equivalent of the RCD identifier in the domain hierarchy.

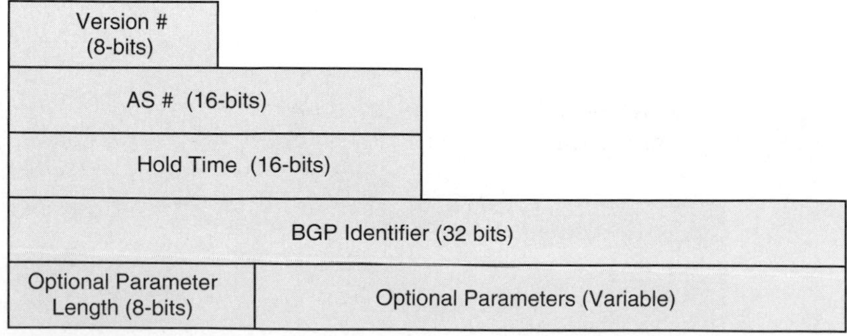

Figure 12–8 *BGP Message Format*

12.3.3.3 OPERATIONAL ISSUES ARISING FROM RA IDENTIFIERS

The containment relationship between routing areas may need to change from time to time in an optical transport network. Such changes may come about due to incremental network growth, mergers, acquisitions and/or divestitures. The following capabilities are needed to support these changes:

- Splitting an area into two
- Merging two areas into one
- Adding a new area between two levels in the hierarchy
- Adding a new area to the top of the hierarchy

These changes should have minimal impact on the operation of the network. The following efficient methods for dealing with these changes are described in [ITU-T02b].

SPLITTING/MERGING AREAS • The splitting and merging of RAs can be best handled by allowing an RA to have multiple synonymous RA-IDs at the same time. The process of splitting can then be accomplished by the following sequence of actions:

1. Add the second identifier to all the RCs in the new area.
2. Ensure that at least one adjacency exists between RCs in the two RAs being formed.
3. At a specified time, drop the original RA identifier from the RCs being placed in the new RA.

A similar sequence can be used to merge two areas into one:

1. The RA-ID of the merged area is selected to be the ID of one of the RAs being merged.
2. The selected RA-ID is added to the RCs in the other area.
3. The original RA-ID is removed from the RCs modified in Step (2).

INSERTING NEW AREAS AT THE TOP OR IN THE MIDDLE OF THE HIERARCHY • Adding a new area at the top of the hierarchy or between two existing areas in the hierarchy can be accomplished by using methods similar to splitting and merging areas. The extent of reconfiguration needed, however, is dependent on how an RA is identified. Two different approaches exist for defining an RA-ID:

1. Relative identifiers: Each RA is identified relative to its position in the hierarchy. Thus, the RA-ID consists of a string of identifiers starting at the root of the hierarchy. This is similar to UNIX file names.

The parent/child relationship that exists between two RAs is implicit in such an identifier.

2. Absolute identifiers: Each RA is independently and uniquely identified. The parent/child hierarchical relationship cannot be determined by just examining the identifiers.

Because an RC has to use the RA-ID to identify if adjacent RCs are located in the same RA, the RA-ID has to be provisioned in each RC prior to forming adjacencies. If the first method is used, then insertion of a new area changes the IDs of all the RAs below the point of insertion. This will require the new RA-ID to be provisioned in all the RCs in all the areas below the point of insertion, and the old RA-ID to be removed. As the point of insertion is moved up in the hierarchy, the number of nodes to be reconfigured can grow exponentially.

If RA-IDs are absolute, then the amount of reconfiguration is greatly reduced. Instead of the RCs in all the areas below the point of insertion being reconfigured, only the RCs affected by the insertion need to be reconfigured.

12.3.4 Diversity Services and Domain Representation

Although it is not necessary and frequently not desired, there are certain situations in which revealing something about the internal topology and resources of a domain can be advantageous. This may be done, for instance,

1. To promote efficiency in traffic engineering
2. When a domain offers some form of diverse transit service
3. When a domain offers diverse connection origination and termination services for end systems

Figure 12–9 depicts the network of Figure 12–1, with each domain represented by an abstract node. To realize better traffic engineering across an abstract node (domain), the propagation of abstract (i.e., approximate) internal link connectivity information is necessary. Such internal abstract links are shown for domain A (abstract node A) in Figure 12–9. Note that these abstract links do not necessarily correspond to internal physical links within the domain. In addition to helping in traffic engineering, the abstract link representation is also useful if a domain provides diverse transit service. An example of this service is also shown in Figure 12–9. In this case, the internal abstract links of domain A are advertised, along with their SRLGs, to the rest of the network so that diverse paths can be computed. Two connections that originate at location A in domain B and terminate at location Z in domain C can be routed over diverse paths across domain A.

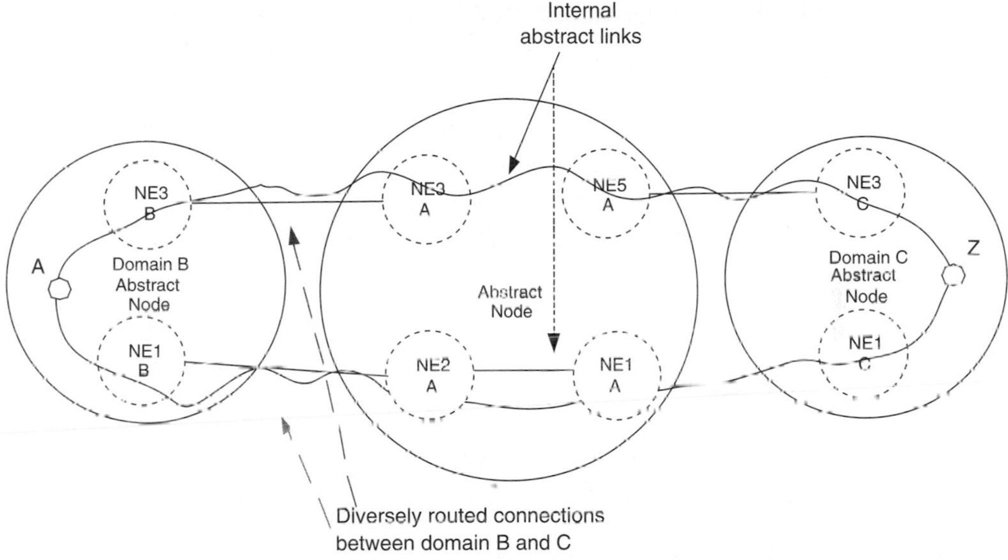

Figure 12–9 *Abstract Node and Link Representation to Support Diverse Transit Service*

12.4 Interdomain Routing

The only true domain-to-domain protocol in use in the Internet today is the BGP protocol. BGP usage is not predicated on the use of specific routing protocols within domains. For example, BGP is frequently used between domains running different and incompatible internal routing protocols (typically, OSPF or IS-IS). Unfortunately, BGP does not have mechanisms to deliver the topology and link status information that is important in computing routes in optical networks. Nor does it have mechanisms for dealing with multiple hierarchical levels. In this section, we examine how a hierarchical link state protocol can be used for interdomain (i.e., domain-to-domain) routing.

12.4.1 Routing Information Categorization

Different applications of interdomain optical routing call for different types of information to be shared between domains. We can broadly categorize this information into two categories: topology and resource information, and node and domain information.

12.4.1.1 TOPOLOGY AND RESOURCE INFORMATION

Under this category, the attributes associated with each link are:

- Link identifier (typically, a pair of IDs, one for each end)
- Available capacity
- Other metrics
- Protection and restoration support
- Associated SRLG

A link may be interdomain (external) or intradomain (internal). It may correspond to a component link, a link bundle (TE link, see Chapter 10), or an abstract link.

Topology • The link identifier indicates the two ends of the link, typically the nodes that terminate the link. The SRLG parameter indicates the failure dependencies between links.

As discussed in Chapter 11, link attributes may be captured by administratively established metrics. A link may have more than one metric associated with it. The topology of the network is defined by the collection of links identified.

Link Capacity • The bandwidth accounting needed in optical networks is significantly different as compared with packet networks. In packet networks, for instance, with ATM or MPLS-TE, complex statistical measures are used to characterize the load on a link. These measures are not exact, but the "compressibility" of statistically multiplexed traffic minimizes the impact of small errors in characterization. By contrast, if an OC-192 link has just one STS-1 path occupied (less than 1% of the link bandwidth), it cannot accommodate an STS-192c path. Due to the relatively simple multiplex structures used, tracking bandwidth resources is much easier in optical networks than in packet switched networks. Much stricter bandwidth accounting, however, is required for optical links. For instance, while an individual optical link can be fully utilized, a packet link is typically run at less than full capacity to accommodate bursts. Such basic differences restrict the direct applicability of some of the packet network traffic engineering mechanisms in optical networks.

Although the multiplex structures in optical transport networks are fairly straightforward, there are a number of issues that prevent a single number from representing the available capacity on a fiber. For example, in a SONET system, it is not generally possible to represent the capacity at the STS path level by the number of empty STS-1 time slots on a line. This is due to the placement rules concerning STS-Nc, that is, concatenated signals (see

Chapter 2). Instead, it is much easier to list the available capacity for each type of signal that may be carried on a link.

To illustrate this, consider Figure 12–10, which shows the time slots of an OC-48 line that is carrying a combination of STS-1, STS-3c, and STS-12c path-level signals. Under the rules of standard concatenation, this link can further accommodate 24 STS-1s, 6 STS-3cs, and no STS-12cs. Note how a single number cannot characterize the available capacity.

We saw in Chapter 2 that a VC-3 signal can be used to carry a number of smaller-capacity signals known as lower order VCs (or virtual tributaries in SONET). These are multiplexed using an intermediate structure known as a TUG-2. A VC-3 can hold seven TUG-2s (see Chapter 2). A TUG-2 can only hold one type of signal, (VC-11, VC-12, VC-2), but in the case of VC-11 and VC-12, it can hold either 4 or 3 of these signals, respectively. As in the previous example, a better description than a single number is needed to capture the capacity. For example, consider a VC-3 that has 2 TUG-2s occupied with 2 VC-11s each, and 2 TUG-2 each with 1 VC-12, with the remaining TUG 2 unoccupied. We can easily and compactly represent the bandwidth available by indicating that the VC-3 has the capacity for 3 TUG 2s, 4 VC-11s, and 4 VC-12s. No single number, however, can represent the available capacity.

Underlying Protection • The protection features supported on a link are useful to characterize. For instance, such information could indicate whether the link is protected and, if so, the type of protection scheme (e.g., linear 1+1, linear 1:N, 4F-BLSR, etc.). This information can be used both in path selection and in advanced multilayer recovery methods (see Chapters 7 and 10).

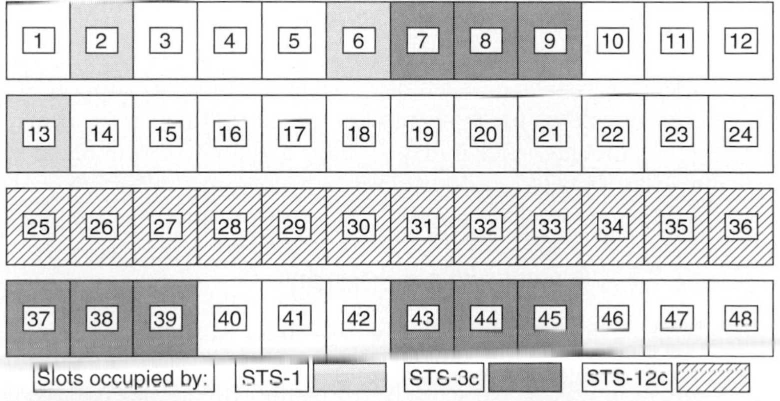

Figure 12–10 *An OC-48 Link Carrying STS-1, STS-3c, and STS-12c Signals*

12.4.1.2 DOMAIN AND NODE-RELATED INFORMATION

Reachability information indicates which end systems or network nodes are directly reachable from a particular domain. Suppose that in domain B of Figure 12–1, each of the network elements, NE1–NE3, is attached to end systems. Then, the addresses of all the attached end systems and those of the three NEs would form the reachability information for domain B.

Subnetwork capability information describes the capabilities or features offered by the domain as a whole. This information is used in applications where sharing the internal topology and resource information is inappropriate. This information can include (a) switching capabilities, (b) protection capabilities, (c) an overall available-capacity measure, and (d) reliability measures. For example:

- In a SONET network, one subnetwork may switch at STS-3c granularity while another switches at STS-1 granularity. Understanding which types of signals within a SDH/SONET multiplex structure can be switched within a subnetwork is important.
- Some networking technologies, particularly SONET/SDH, provide a wide range of standardized protection techniques, but not all domains may offer all the protection options. For example, a 2/4-F BLSR based subnetwork could support extra data traffic, ring protected traffic, and non-preemptable unprotected traffic (NUT), while a mesh network might offer shared, line layer linear protection and mesh protection.
- Some domains may be in locations that have lower incidences of link failure. Such information could be helpful in computing routes to statistically "share the pain."

Although properties of the subnetwork are very important for routing a connection, end systems also possess a wide variety of capabilities. Allowing end system capabilities (such as a system's ability to support SONET/SDH virtual concatenation) to be distributed into a routing protocol may not be advantageous though, since it may counter the ability to summarize reachability information. Detailed end-system information may alternatively be obtained using a directory service or some type of direct query between the end systems.

12.4.2 Routing within a Hierarchy

When a hierarchy of RAs is established, RCs must be configured at least with information that allows them to determine which RAs they belong to. The question arises, particularly from the operational context, as to how much information can flow automatically between different levels in a routing hierarchy.

In this section, we look at automation of information flow up and down the routing hierarchy. In the following section, we look at the role neighbor discovery (Chapter 6) can play in automating the routing configuration process.

12.4.2.1 ROUTING INFORMATION FLOW UP THE HIERARCHY

The primary entities of interest at level N of a routing hierarchy are the links between the RCDs (represented by the RCs) in that level and the reachable addresses within each RCD. The properties of an RCD are represented by the "nodal" properties of the corresponding RC. These are in turn derived from the corresponding level N-1 (next lower level) RA that the RCD represents. The links between level N-1 RAs are actually level N RA links (or higher) as shown in Figure 12–11. In addition, in some cases it may be very useful for an RC to offer some approximate representation of the internal topology of its corresponding RCD. Figure 12–11 shows information flow between RC 11 in RA 505 and RC 12 in RA 1313.

12.4.2.2 ROUTING INFORMATION FLOW DOWN THE HIERARCHY

An RC at a lower level of the hierarchy needs information pertaining to higher levels to be able to compute an end to end path. For example, RCs in RA 2112 need to know the interconnection between level N-1 RAs to be able to compute a path across these RAs. But this interconnection information is avail

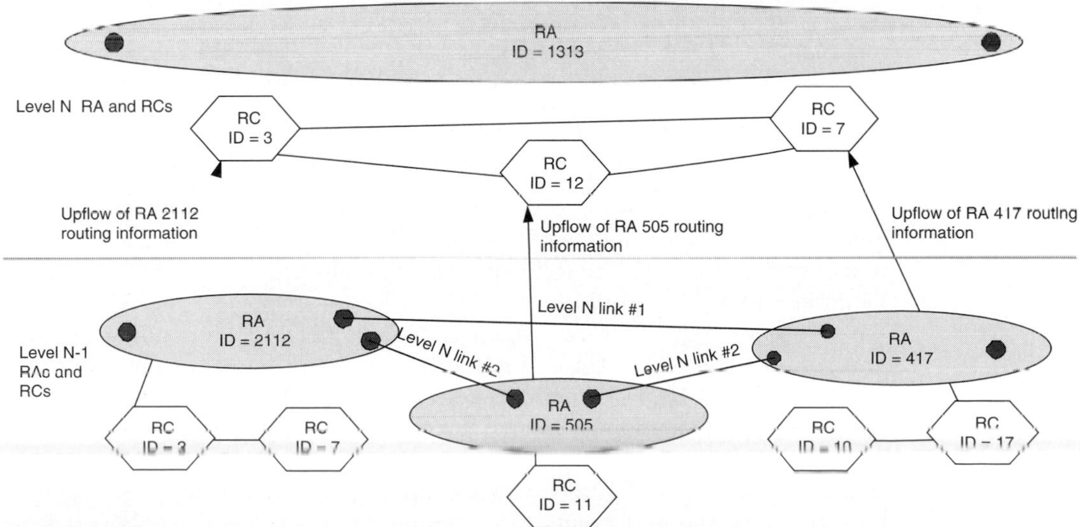

Figure 12–11 *Example Hierarchy with Up Flow of Information from RCs*

able only at level N. Thus, there is need for routing information to flow down the hierarchy. There are two approaches for realizing this flow.

In the path computation server approach, a higher-level RC is consulted to find an appropriate route between the source and the destination RAs. This would give a coarse route, that is, in terms of a list of RAs at a given level to be traversed. Under this approach, the contacted RC must belong to an RA within whose scope both the end points lie.

Instead of contacting an RC at another level, the higher-level topology information may be propagated downward to all the lower level RAs. Such an approach was taken in hierarchical PNNI routing [ATMF02] (see Chapter 9).

12.5 Discovery Processes and Hierarchy

12.5.1 Interdomain Discovery

The neighbor discovery process described in Chapter 6 was used by a node to automatically discover its connectivity to its neighbors. A portion of the discovery process must run in-fiber as discussed in Chapter 6.

To facilitate interdomain optical control, it is possible to incorporate the following information in the neighbor discovery process running over a link between nodes in different control domains:

1. The lowest level routing area that contains both end points of the link.
2. Additional domain capability information including information concerning types of routing or signaling protocols supported on the interdomain interface, or other domainwide properties such as SRLG information.

Knowing (1) allows two end points, which are in different lowest-level areas, to notify their respective RCs. These RCs may or may not choose to set up a control adjacency. The following example illustrates how the lowest level common routing area could be found.

Consider Figure 12–12, which depicts a network containing six RAs arranged in a hierarchy. Let us look at how the end points of links B and C can determine the appropriate lowest level common RA for each link. For link B, the two RA containment hierarchies, starting from the lowest level RA-ID to the highest level RA-ID are (2112, 113, 1313) and (505, 113, 1313). Suppose each end point is configured with the appropriate area list. By exchanging these two lists, the end points can determine that RA 113 is the lowest level common RA. For link C, the RA lists for the two ends are (505, 113, 1313) and

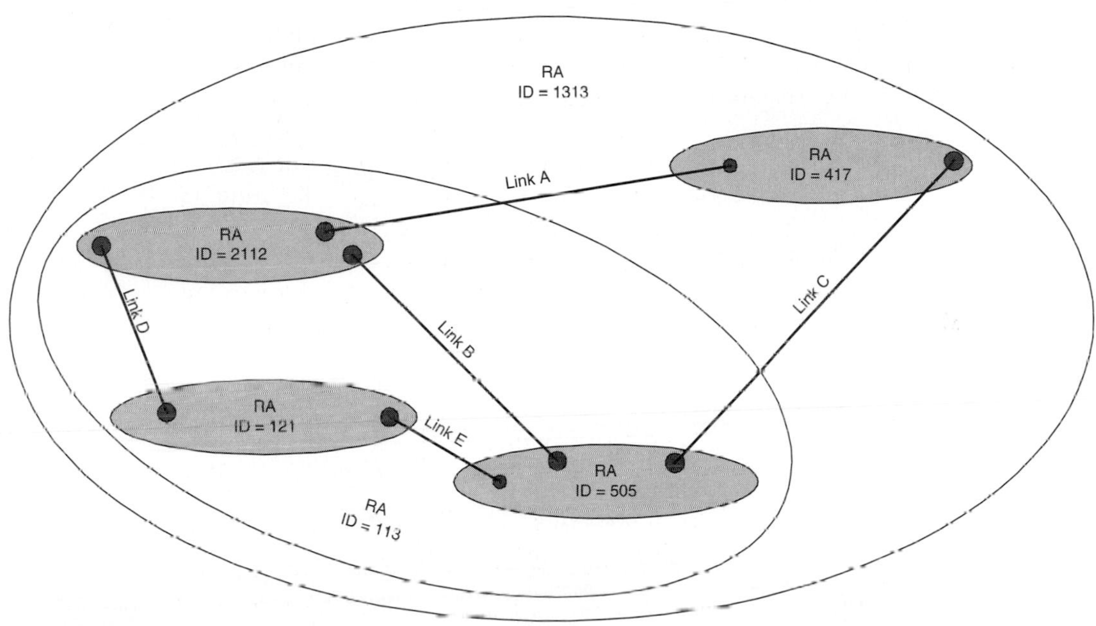

Figure 12–12 *Discovery of the Appropriate RA for Each Link*

(417, 1313). By exchanging these lists, the end points can determine that RA 1313 is the lowest level common RA.

After determining the lowest level common RA, the link end points can exchange information on the identities of the RCs between which a control adjacency should be established.

12.6 Summary

Interdomain routing control is a challenging topic that addresses scalability and heterogeneity requirements in large optical networks. The addition of administrative constraints on information exchange adds to the complexity of the problem, as does the need for flexible network organization. While intradomain routing has been studied in detail, work on interdomain routing is in its early stages. The discussion in this chapter was an attempt to capture the current state of the art. Interoperable interdomain (NNI) signaling and routing procedures with limited scope have been demonstrated under the auspices of the OIF. Experience gained from this would help toward understanding the problem better and focusing on immediate requirements.

THIRTEEN

Management Systems and the Control Plane

13.1 Overview of Transport Systems Management

The area of telecommunications management systems is quite deep and wide [Aidarous+94]. Our purpose here is to give an adequate review of these systems so that their role in relation to the control plane can be understood. We give examples of particular management system technologies and application scenarios to avoid the discussion becoming too abstract.

13.1.1 Functionality Provided by Management Systems

Prior to the movement toward a distributed control plane for optical transport networks, the answer to the question as to the functionality provided by management systems would have been fairly simple, that is, just about everything not done by hardware. As the control plane comes into existence, however, it is useful to understand the general taxonomy of management system functionality. This helps in understanding what management functions may be affected by the control plane, and, more important, the management system functionality that is *not* affected.

Different management plane standards have met with different degrees of success as discussed in later sections. But the general modeling of the telecommunications management process is extremely insightful. In the following, we attempt to describe these models, resorting to informal terminology where necessary (as compared with the descriptions in the related standards).

As described in ITU-T recommendation M.3400 [ITU-T00e], management system functionality can be characterized into five somewhat overlapping functional areas: fault management, configuration management, accounting, performance monitoring, and security management. An easy mnemonic to remember this list of functionality is FCAPS (Fault, Configuration, Accounting, Performance, and Security). We now give a quick overview of these areas, starting with their original definitions and then a description of their actual practice.

13.1.1.1 FAULT MANAGEMENT

A "fault" indicates a condition that prevents a communication system from delivering the service that was intended. Fault management includes fault detection, fault isolation, and, hopefully, the correction of the problem that caused the fault.

Management systems need mechanisms for detecting faults. Clearly, one of the worst ways to find out about a fault condition is via a phone call from the customer. Typically, alarms and other event notifications (section 13.2.3.1) are used for this purpose. Fault isolation can be based on standardized or vendor-specific mechanisms. For example, the alarm indication signals (AIS) and Remote Defect Indication (RDI) signals that are built into multiple layers of the SONET/SDH multiplex hierarchy facilitate the isolation of "broken" communications links (see Chapter 3). A software debugging log (section 13.2.3.3) could be a proprietary method using which a vendor isolates the cause of an intermittent control plane fault. Note that not all errors are considered faults. This is considered further under the heading of performance monitoring.

13.1.1.2 CONFIGURATION MANAGEMENT

As we have seen so far, there are a sizeable number of items that must be manually configured in an optical transport system. These include parameters associated with particular lines such as error reporting thresholds (e.g., above what BER threshold should a notification be sent); parameters associated with groups of lines such as protection groups (1 + 1, 1:N) and roles within a protection group (working/protect); and those associated with services such as setting up a cross-connect.

Of all the items that need to be configured in a transport network, the control plane is only concerned with the creation and deletion of cross-connects and their associated connection end points.

13.1.1.3 ACCOUNTING

In previous generations of transport systems, there was very little fine-grained accounting since connection hold times were long (e.g., months or years). Hence, management systems for transport networks typically did not have interactions with billing systems.

With the advent of the optical control plane, connections can be dynamically established, and thus interactions between management and accounting systems will be required. One approach to this is to let the management system keep records of the connection details, for example, source, destination, type of connection, duration, and so on. This information is appropriately referred to as a *Call Detail Record* (CDR). The content and formats of these CDRs have been standardized in the telephony world, and these formats have recently been applied to transport services in the form of CDR formats for the OIF UNI 1.0 [OIF01].

13.1.1.4 PERFORMANCE MONITORING

Due to the potentially large volume of traffic running over a single optical fiber, degradations in performance have traditionally been important to monitor in transport networks. In addition, by observing trends in performance data one can frequently replace "unscheduled downtime," that is, an outage, with a controlled maintenance activity that minimizes the impact on end users. SONET and SDH provide extensive support in their signal structure for performance monitoring at various layers of the multiplex hierarchy. From the management plane perspective, performance monitoring is focused on collecting, transferring, and trending these data. In addition, this information can be important in determining whether the terms of a particular Service Level Agreement (SLA) have been met.

13.1.1.5 SECURITY MANAGEMENT

Security is a rather broad topic. Of interest here are those aspects of security, which need to be supported by the management system. The descriptions below are based on the discussion in [ITU-T98b].

ACCOUNTABILITY • In a transport network, actions taken through the management or the control plane can have serious economic consequences. For example, consider taking a DWDM span and all the channels associated with it out of service. The volume of traffic affected in this case can be huge. Such actions should be performed for a good reason, following proper procedures. It is therefore important to designate those who can initiate such actions, verify their identify, and sometimes take measures to ensure that the parties responsible can not disavow taking a particular action.

Generally, the ability to take a particular type of action via the management system will be restricted to certain class of users. For example, most support personnel will need to know about current alarms and performance monitoring information. Only a small subset, however, will have the ability to set up and tear down connections. A still smaller subset will have the ability to actually set the privilege levels for other users. *Authentication* is the security aspect of verifying the identity of management system users or of communicating entities. A high degree of confidence about the identity of entities performing various actions is required for accountability. Accountability is particularly important if the person or entity performing an action can repudiate, that is, refuse to acknowledge, having performed the action.

The security aspect of *nonrepudiation* deals with two scenarios. Under the first scenario, the originator of an action (or message) denies having originated the action. For example, the originator may claim that his identity was forged. Under the second scenario, the receiver of a message denies the receipt of the message. Hence, he cannot be held accountable for the consequences of not performing the requested actions.

Availability • Availability pertains to both the management and the control plane, and it determines whether the underlying transport resources can be used. For example, a denial of service attack on the routing portion of the control plane may leave the management system without timely updates on the status of network resources. This may result in a higher probability of denied connection establishment requests.

Confidentiality • Confidentiality pertains to both stored information and transmitted information. With stored information, confidentiality becomes an issue of access control. With transmitted information, the network context as well as the sensitivity of the information becomes important in determining the appropriate techniques to be used.

Consider, for example, some of the information that a carrier might have concerning its customers, that is, line usage, service level subscribed to, and so on. A competitor may find this information very interesting. But this information may be transmitted unencrypted over internal carrier facilities. In this case, no special procedures are followed for ensuring the confidentiality of transmitted information, since interception by external entities is not a concern. The situation would be different if the information has to be transmitted on a network over which the carrier has no control.

Data Integrity • Upon receipt of a request to perform either a control plane or a management plane task, how does the recipient know that the request was not modified in transit, either accidentally or maliciously? Various error detection techniques such as cyclic redundancy checks are used to deal with accidental modification. To guard against malicious attacks, a cryptographic technique known as a *message digest* [Rivest92] can be used to detect if a message has been modified. Such capabilities have been incorporated into several Internet routing protocols [Stallings03, Moy98], and they can be turned on at the discretion of the operator.

Assessing Security • How does one generally assess the security of telecommunications control plane and management plane systems? The first step is to compile a list of threats that could be applied against such a system. For example, ITU-T recommendation M3016 [ITU-T98b] describes the following threats in detail: eavesdropping, spoofing, tampering with messages (including modification, delaying, deletion, insertion, replay, rerouting, misrouting, or reordering of messages), repudiation, forgery, and denial of service. Armed with such a list, a threat assessment can be made and put into the particular network context. Appropriate techniques for enhancing the security can then be applied.

13.1.2 Levels of System Management

Management capabilities tend to be distributed in a transport network for reasons of scalability, or more likely, due to vendor differences. Almost all nontrivial network elements contain some embedded management functionality. In particular, they support some type of management interface. A software system whose purpose is to manage a collection of individual network elements is called, appropriately, an *Element Management System* (EMS). A system that coordinates multiple EMSs (corresponding to different types of network elements) is called a *Network Management System* (NMS). These relationships are illustrated in Figure 13–1, which depicts a network consisting of DWDM equipment and SONET cross-connects.

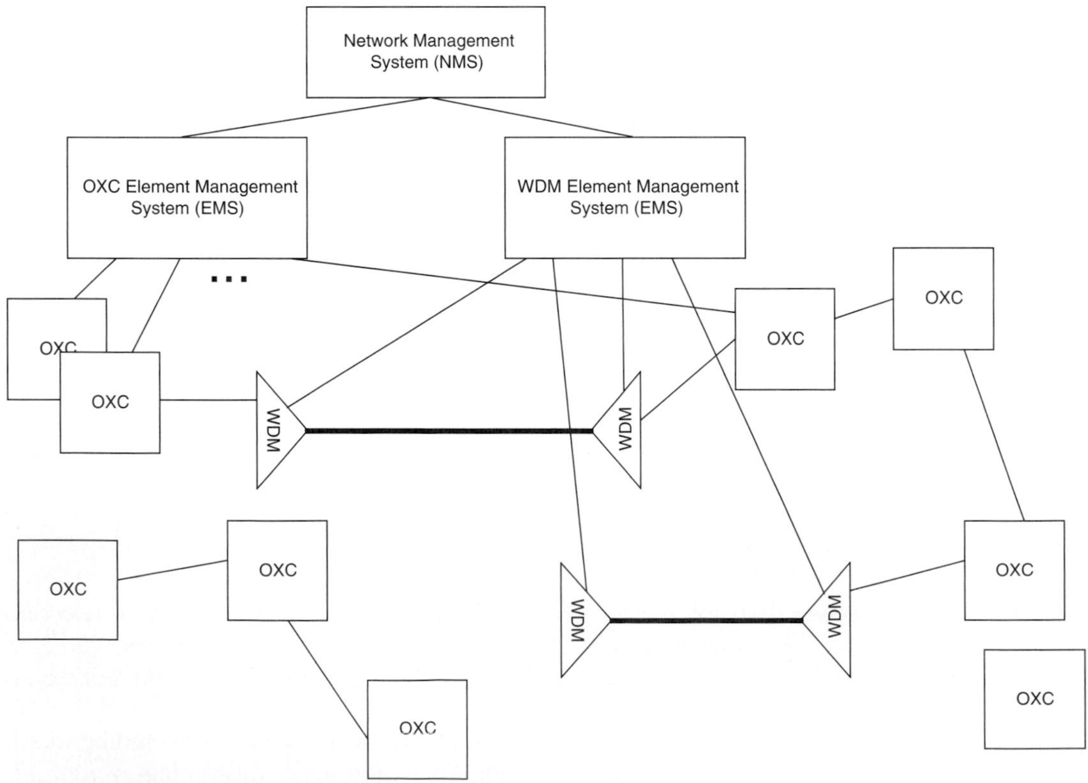

Figure 13–1 *A Network Consisting of OXCs, WDM Equipment, EMSs, and an NMS*

13.2 Information Models

It was stated earlier that telecommunications management is about configuring, monitoring, and trouble-shooting telecommunication services and equipment. Given that there is a plethora of different types of telecommunications equipment and services, any approach for standardizing the management process needs to start with a basic model of the equipment or the service to be managed. Such models are typically referred to as *information* models. These models in the past have been associated with specific management protocols. The trend in recent years has been to separate these models from particular management protocols and to describe them in a protocol-independent manner.

Almost all current approaches to describing these management information models are based on object-oriented terminology used in software design [Meyer97]. In addition, there is an abundance of formalism contained in the ITU-T recommendations [ITU-T92b]. In the following, we give an overview of these information modeling concepts and the key object models.

13.2.1 Managed Objects

A managed *object* is a representation of a real world entity that is being managed. More formally, telecommunications management information is structured in terms of managed objects, their attributes, the management operations performed upon them, and the notifications they emit [ITU-T92c]. The internal structure and operation of a managed object is hidden, and one cannot make assumptions about the implementation of the object. This is generally referred to as *encapsulation*.

As an example, consider an SDH regenerator section (SONET section) layer signal. As an object, its attributes include block error counts, background block error counts, and various other performance data (see Chapter 2). Besides the general administration of the signal (e.g., putting it in or out of service), management operations would include setting the section trace string and the expected section trace string. Notifications that may be emitted by this object include the Loss of Frame (LOF) alarm and a section trace mismatch notification. Figure 13–2 depicts a possible *Unified Modeling Language*[1] (UML) [Douglass98] diagram representing this section layer signal.

The data structure representing the set of all managed objects within a system or area of interest is referred to as a *Management Information Base* (MIB)

[1]UML is an object-oriented modeling language specified by the *Object Management Group* (OMG). Its specification can be obtained at www.omg.org.

EB: Error Block
BBE: Background Errored Block
ES: Errored Seconds
SES: Severely Errored Seconds
OFS: Out of Frame Seconds
RecJ0: received J0 string
ExJ0: expected J0 string
LOF: Loss Of Frame (notification)
notifyJ0mis: J0 mis-match (notification)

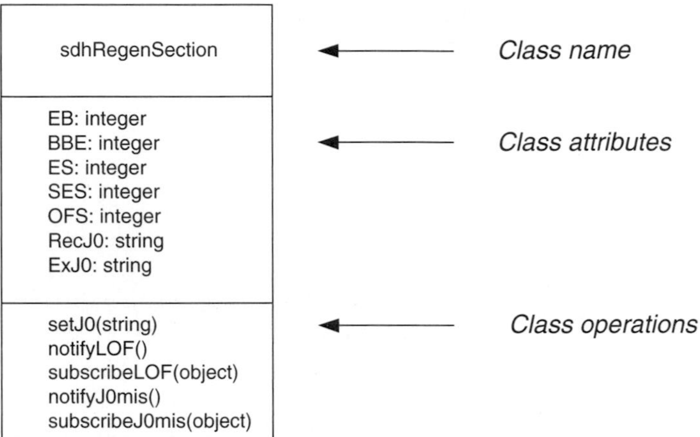

Figure 13–2 *UML Diagram for an SDH Regenerator Section Layer Object Class*

13.2.1.1 RELATIONSHIPS

Relationships between managed objects is defined in ITU-T recommendation X.732 [ITU-T92d] as follows:

> A relationship is defined by a set of rules that describe how the operation of one part of a system affects the operation of other parts of the system. A relationship is said to exist among managed objects when the operation of one managed object affects the operation of the other managed objects.

It is essential to understand the dependency, ownership, or other types of relationships among managed objects. For example a SDH VC3 (Trail Termination Point, TTP, see Chapter 5) has a relationship with a corresponding SDH AU3 (connection termination point, CTP). The AU-3 consists of the VC-3 plus an AU pointer, which indicates the phase alignment of the VC-3 with respect to the STM-N frame. A VC3 cross-connect terminates the AU3, extracts the VC3, and without modifying any of its contents, adapts it to a new AU-3 for transport in an outgoing STM-N frame. Hence, the VC3 (TTP) has a dependency relationship with both of these AU3 signals. In particular, if on reception of the AU3 a loss of pointer (LOP) is experienced, then this will have a deleterious effect on the VC3. The UML diagram shown in Figure 13–3 portrays this relationship.

13.2.1.2 CONTAINMENT

Containment is a strong form of dependency between managed objects. In this relationship, one managed object contains one or more other managed objects.

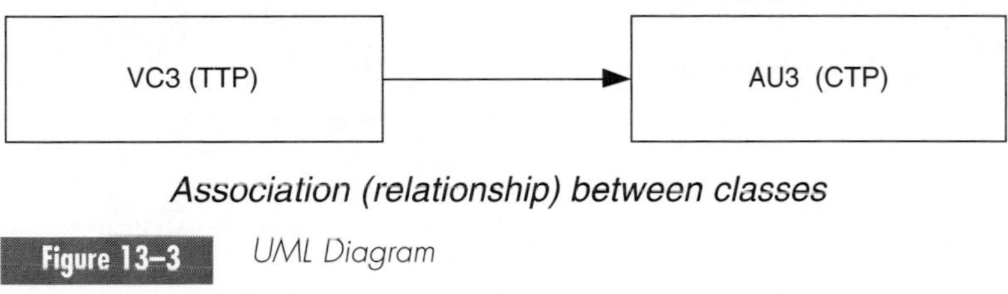

Figure 13–3 *UML Diagram*

A typical containment diagram is shown in Figure 13–4. Here, we see that a network consists of managed elements, which encompass various equipment, which in turn contains equipment holders (slots), circuit packs, and software [ITU-T95b].

Another important example of containment arises from the multiplex structures common in the optical world. For example, an SDH multiplex section (MS) layer signal (trail) transports a number (up to N) of AU-4 connections (the server layer for a VC-4 trail). Note that the fate of these AU-4s and their VC4 clients are intertwined with that of the SDH MS trail that contains them. This relationship is shown in Figure 13–5.

Containment relationships between managed objects are also used in their identification. In particular, managed objects are usually named relative to the objects that contain them. The general principles for *naming* are laid

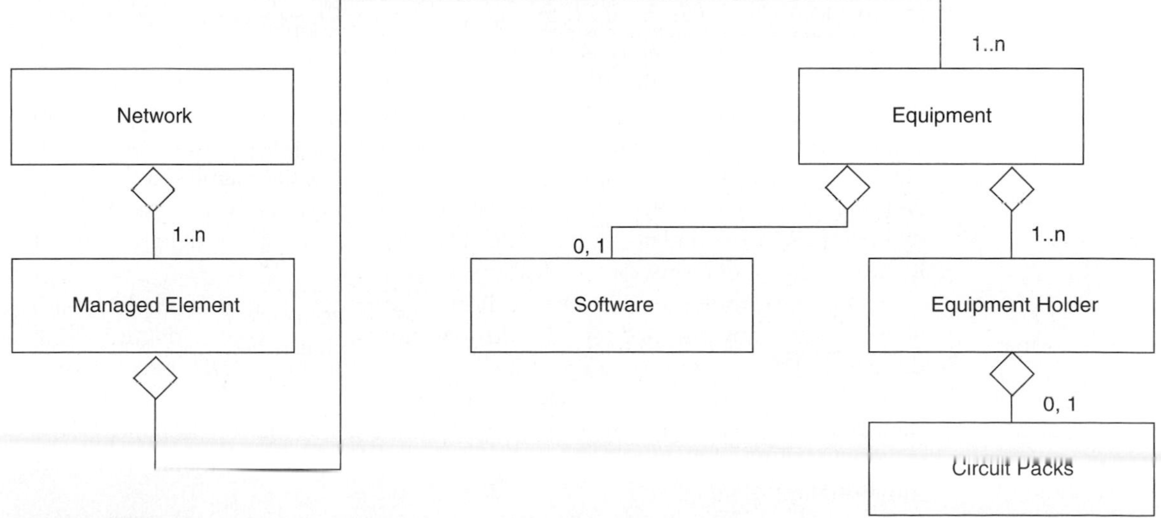

Figure 13–4 *UML Diagram Showing Containment Relationships*

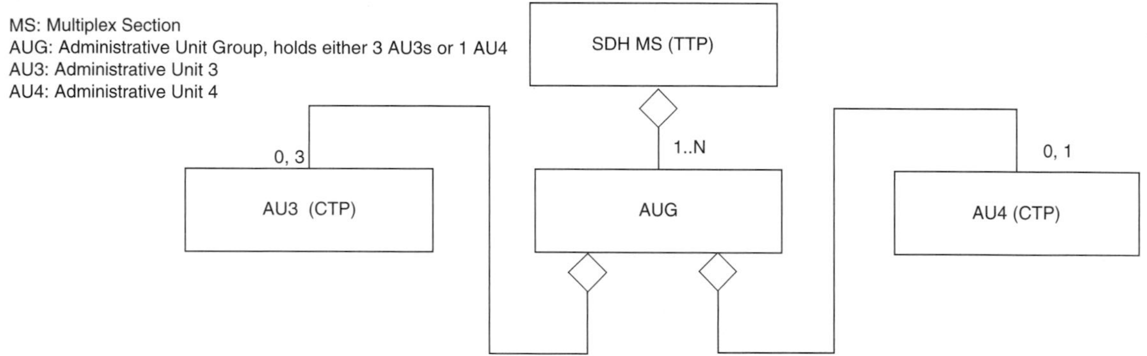

Figure 13–5 *UML Containment Relationship Diagram for an SDH STM-N Multiplex Section Signal*

out in reference [ITU-T92b] in which relative distinguished names (RDNs) are defined. Naming in general is rather straightforward. For instance, a specific AU-4 signal can be precisely identified in relation to an SDH MS signal, which in turn can be identified by the particular port, line card, shelf, and equipment that terminates the signal.

13.2.1.3 INHERITANCE

The broad type of a managed object is also referred to as its *class*. For example, a 4-port OC-48 (STM-16) line card can be considered as a class, many instances of which can be used in a given system. Classes are partitioned into related groups to form a hierarchy. The more general classes appear at the top of the hierarchy, and the more specific or specialized classes appear at the bottom. A class, which is related to another further up in the hierarchy, is said to have an *inheritance* relationship with the latter. In particular, a specialized class is derived from a more general class by defining extensions to the latter. Defining new operations, attributes, and/or notifications constitute such an extension. A general class, however, cannot be "extended" by deleting any of its attributes, operations, or notifications.

As an example, let us examine how inheritance is used in dealing with SONET/SDH *current data performance monitoring* objects. Figure 13–6 depicts a UML diagram representing certain interesting SDH performance monitoring classes. To understand the functionality of the classes at the bottom of this hierarchy, it is necessary to first understand the functionality of the classes at the upper levels of the hierarchy (as the former classes inherit this functionality).

At the very top of the inheritance hierarchy is the class *Top*. This class has two attributes: (a) ObjectClass, which gives the name of the class, and (b) NameBinding which gives the name of the object (of this class) and, if appro-

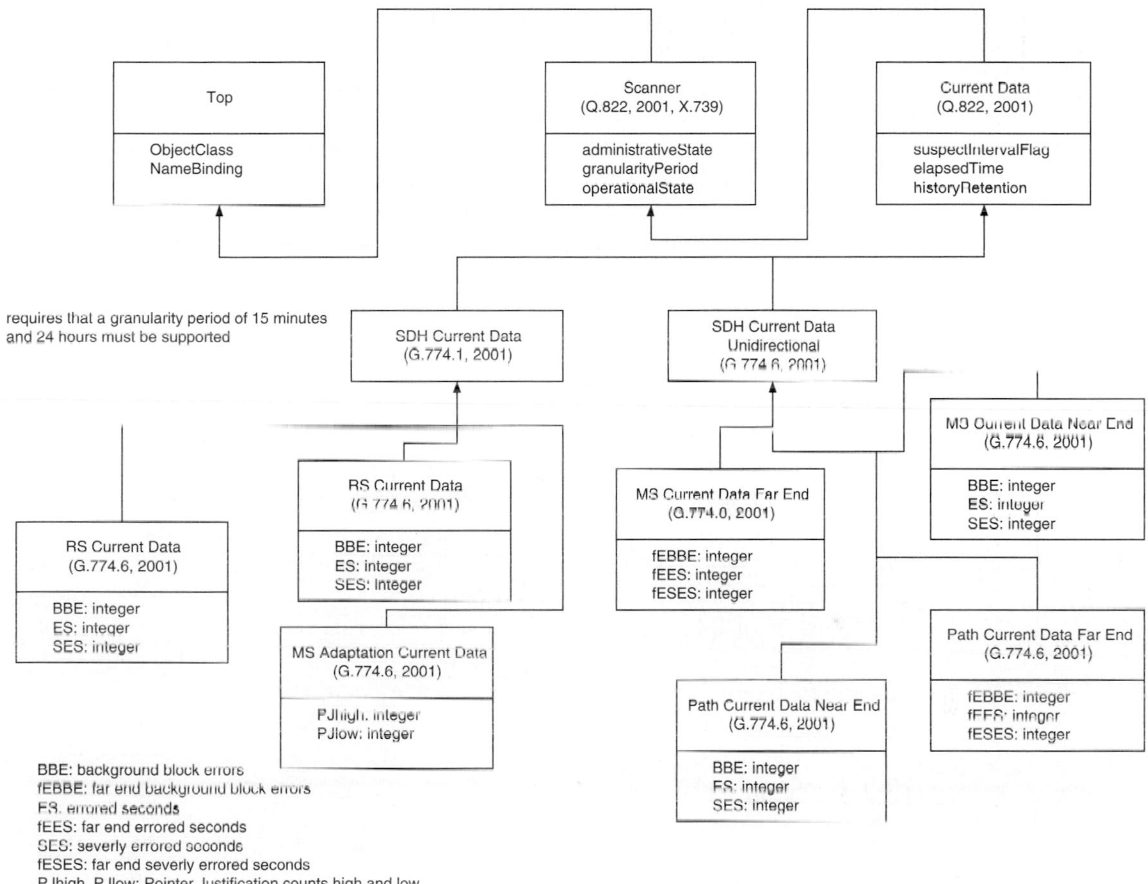

Figure 13–6 *UML Diagram of the Inheritance Hierarchy for Certain SDH Current Data Performance Monitoring Classes*

priate, the name of an object that may contain this object. This is somewhat similar to the functionality one finds in the Java programming language's *Object* class [Cornell+97], and it allows the determination of the type of object and its name. The *Scanner* class directly inherits the properties of the *Top* class [ITU-T94a]. The *Scanner* class represents data that are periodically collected, that is, scanned. The attribute, *granularityPeriod*, indicates the time interval between scans. Note that *Scanner* has both administrative and operations states, that is, the collection of data can be turned on and off and an indication as to whether data collection is working can be obtained. The next class down the hierarchy is the *CurrentData* class, which builds on the functionality of the *Scanner* class [ITU-T94a]. The *CurrentData* class adds the following attributes: *elapsedTime,* which indicates the time since the collection started; *historyRetention,* which indicates how many *CurrentData* objects should be kept as part of a history mechanism; and *suspectIntervalFlag,* which flags the potential corruption of data due to some unforeseen occurrence during the collection interval. Directly inheriting the *currentData* class are the *SDH CurrentData* [ITU-T01e] and *SDH Current Data Unidirectional* [ITU-T01f] classes. One important property of these classes is that they require a granularity period (from the *Scanner* class) to be able to take on the values of 15 minutes and 24 hours, respectively. Finally, layer-specific performance monitoring classes based on B1, B2, B3, M0/M1, and pointer events are derived from these classes. These are the *rsCurrentData, msCurrentDataNearEnd, pathCurrentDataNearEnd, msCurrentDataFarEnd,* and *msAdaptation CurrentData* classes.

Two points should be noted from this example. First, object-oriented information models utilizing hierarchy are quite general and extensible. Second, it can be a lot of work to decipher these models. In general, the deeper the inheritance hierarchy, the more work it takes to determine how the classes at the bottom behave. The designer of object-oriented software is usually advised not to create hierarchies that are too deep or wide [Meyer97, Booch96]. But the development of information models used in standards efforts is often distributed over time, and it becomes difficult to control the depth or breadth of the inheritance hierarchies. Actual software implementations of these models, however, tend to "optimize" by merging many levels of the hierarchy together.

13.2.2 State

The *state* of an object is given by the values assumed by all its attributes (both externally visible and internal). When dealing with certain types of managed objects, it is useful to refine this notion. In particular, reference [ITU-T92e] distinguishes between *operational, usage,* and *administrative* states, and defines attributes that describe these states.

The operational state attribute has two possible values, disabled and enabled. It describes whether the underlying resource is physically installed and working.

The usage state attribute has three possible values: idle, active, and busy. This describes whether the underlying resource is actively in use and, if so, whether there is spare capacity for additional users at a specific instant.

The administration of a managed object is independent of its operability and usage. The administrative state attribute has three values: locked, unlocked, and shutting down. The administrative state is used to permit or deny access to a resource. Note that the state of a managed object does not affect its ability to respond to management operations.

In addition to these attributes, there are also a number of *status* attributes that give further information on the state of an object [ITU-T92e]. These status attributes include alarm status, procedural status, availability status, control status, and standby status. The most important of these is the alarm status. This attribute can take on one or more of the following values: under repair, critical, major, minor, and/or alarm outstanding. The meaning of the levels of alarm severity is discussed in section 13.2.3.1.

13.2.3 Events and Notifications

A *notification* is information emitted by a managed object about an internal event. Important aspects of notifications include their targets and how they are controlled under different conditions. The notion of notification in telecommunications information models corresponds to object-oriented software interaction known as the *publish-subscribe* paradigm. Before delving into the control of notifications, it is instructive to examine one of the most important types of notifications in telecommunications management.

13.2.3.1 ALARMS

Alarms are specific types of notifications concerning faults or other abnormal conditions occurring within objects. Key ingredients of an alarm notification are the type of event that occurred, the perceived severity, and the probable cause. Other relevant information pertains to the time the event occurred and identification of the notification/alarm.

The following levels of alarm severity are defined in [ITU-T92f]:

- **Cleared:** Indicates the clearing of one or more previously reported alarms.
- **Indeterminate:** Indicates that the severity level cannot be determined.
- **Critical:** Indicates that a service-affecting condition has occurred and an immediate corrective action is required. This severity level may be reported when the underlying resource goes completely out of service and its capability must be restored.
- **Major:** Indicates that a service-affecting condition has developed and an urgent corrective action is required. This severity level may be reported when there is a severe degradation in the capability of the underlying resource and its full capability must be restored.
- **Minor:** Indicates the existence of a non-service-affecting fault condition and that corrective action should be taken in order to prevent a more serious (service-affecting) fault. This severity level may be reported when the detected alarm condition is not currently degrading the capabilities of the underlying resource.
- **Warning:** Indicates the detection of a potential or impending service-affecting fault before any significant effects have been felt. Action should be taken to further diagnose and correct the problem in order to prevent it from becoming more serious.

Table 13–1 *Alarm Notification Types*

Alarm Type	Definition
Communications	Concerned with the processes required to convey information from one point to another, e.g., loss of signal, loss of frame, etc.
Quality of service	Concerned with a degradation in the quality of a service, e.g., BER above a given threshold.
Processing error	Concerned with software related faults.
Equipment	Concerned with equipment faults, e.g., line card failure.
Environmental	Concerned with a condition relating to an enclosure in which the equipment resides, e.g., excessive heat, humidity, etc.

Table 13–1 lists the standardized alarm types [ITU-T92f].

A partial UML diagram corresponding to the formal alarm record object and its inheritance hierarchy is shown in Figure 13–7. A lengthy list of standardized probable cause values can be found in reference [ITU-T92f] and includes such items as loss of frame, fire detected, flood detected, and so on.

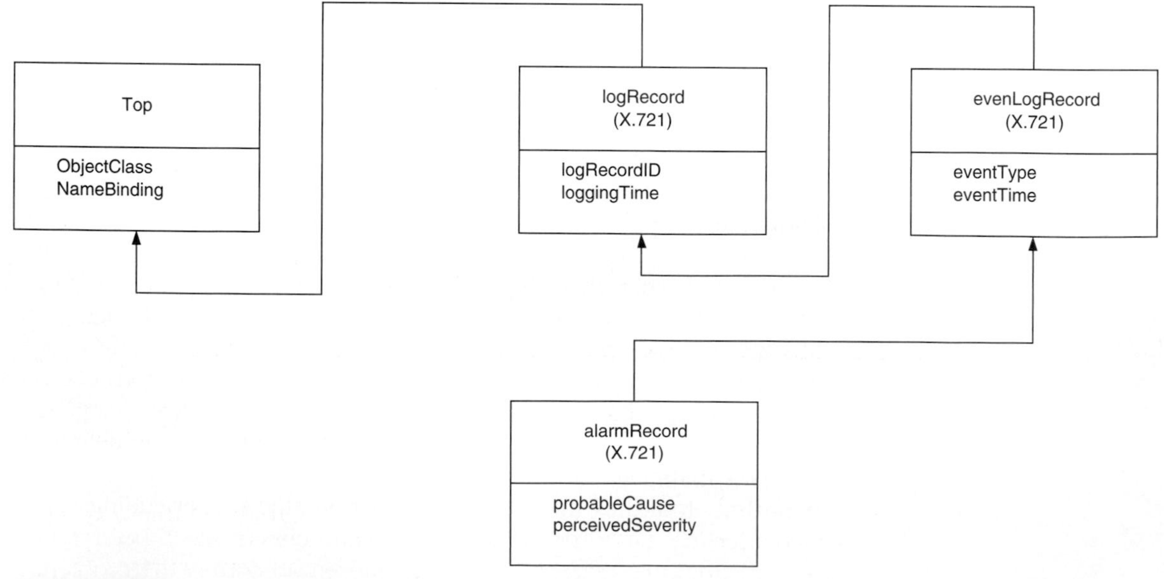

Figure 13–7 *UML Diagram (Partial) for the Alarm Record Class*

13.2.3.2 EVENT REPORTING CONTROL

In addition to alarms, there are a number of other notifications that can be sent. In particular, object creation, object deletion, and attribute change notifications would be more common than alarms if a control plane is used for provisioning. As an example, consider the creation of a cross-connect. If the cross-connect utilizes a previously idle connection termination point on a SONET line, a usage state change message (from idle to in-use) would be generated for the corresponding object.

When dealing with telecommunication managed objects, it is useful to go beyond a simple publish-subscribe paradigm under which a recipient must directly subscribe to receive notifications from the generator. Figure 13–8 shows a system containing a number of managed objects. External entities, shown as *notification subscribers,* register to receive notifications via an *event forwarding discriminator,* rather than directly "subscribing" to receive notifications from individual managed objects [ITU-T92g].

This approach has a number of advantages over the publish-subscribe method. First, it is not necessary to deal with a potentially feature-rich external interface when implementing a managed object. Second, this model allows subscribers to receive broad classes of events. For example, an event forwarding discriminator can allow a particular management system to receive all communication alarms of severity greater than minor from all SONET section and line layer objects within a given piece of equipment. Third, given the

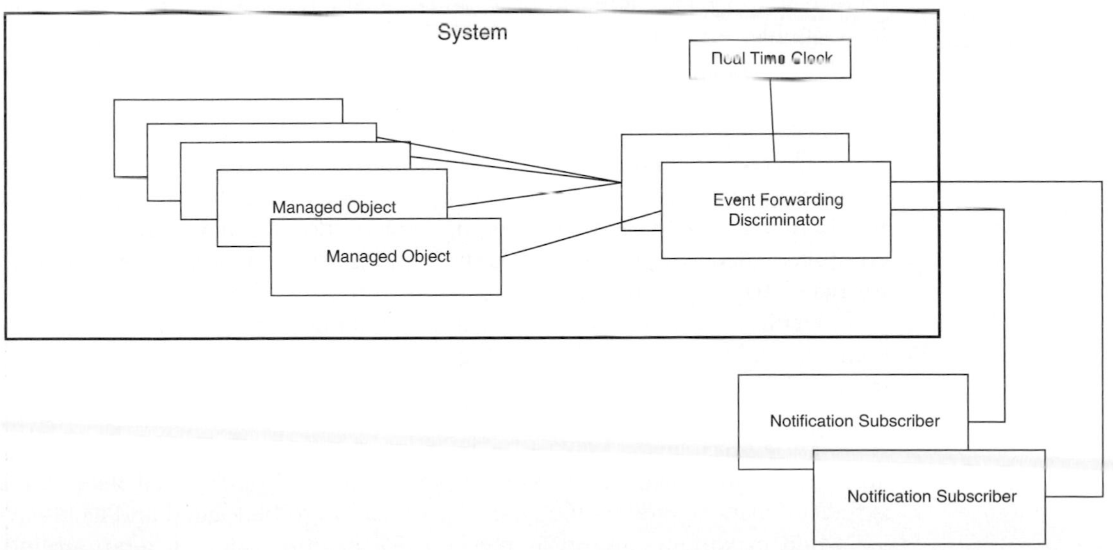

Figure 13–8 *UML Diagram Illustrating the Event Forwarding Discriminator Concept*

large number of possible notifications that may be generated and their differing importance, an event forwarding discriminator can be used to prioritize notifications, control their rate, and provide different services such as confirmed and unconfirmed delivery. This turns out to be an important function, because a single fault may result in multiple notifications with varying levels of importance. Such an event, if left uncontrolled, can cause "alarm storms" during which the control network is flooded with alarms. In this case, many ancillary alarms may cause a main alarm to be lost or delayed.

13.2.3.3 EVENT LOGS

Given the importance of alarms in telecommunications management, it is clear that any system that performs a significant communications function must support notifications. With more sophisticated equipment, it may be important to keep a log of events that aid in understanding system usage, failure modes, or other functions. It is possible to implement such a log when a system supports persistent storage such as a hard disk, flash memory, or battery-backed memory. These system logs can be the equivalent of a commercial jet's flight data recorder (black box) in that they allow the operator to piece together what may have caused an incident to happen.

What kind of information goes into a log? As per the information models in the ITU-T recommendations, the following *record* classes inherit from the generic *event log record* class [ITU-T92h]: alarm records [ITU-T92f], object creation, deletion, and attribute change records [ITU-T92i], security audit trail records [ITU-T92j], state change records [ITU-T92e], and security alarm report records [ITU-T92k]. There can be vendor specific records in addition to these, for example, software debugging records.

These records may be stored in many different logs rather than in a single event log. This allows some logs to have different access or modification privileges. This also eliminates the need to browse through a number of (irrelevant) records to find a specific type of information. For example, software debugging records would most likely be kept in a separate log since they would be meaningful only to the equipment vendor and not to the user of the equipment. Security audit trail records would most likely be kept in a log with restricted access privileges.

Figure 13–9 depicts a UML diagram illustrating *log* objects and their system context. Attributes of an individual log include the type of records held and the managed objects that these come from. This picture is similar to the one depicted in Figure 13–8 except that logs keep information entirely within the system.

A log is a managed object by itself [ITU-T92h]. It has a unique identifier, an administrative state (enabled or disabled), and an operational state. A log is further characterized by the type of information to be logged and its behavior when maximum capacity is reached, for example, does it wrap around, stop logging new info, emit a notification, and so on.

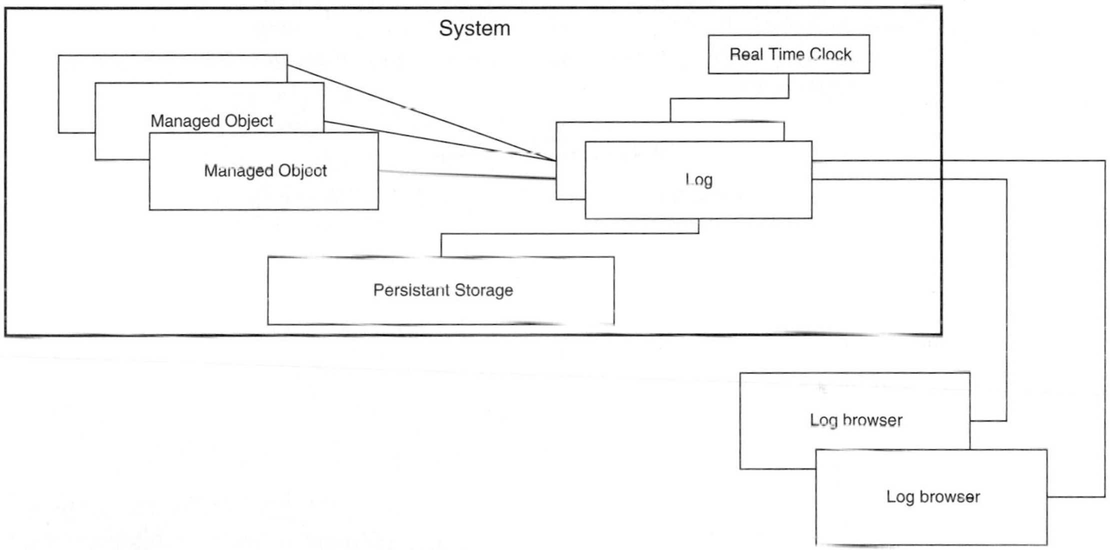

Figure 13–9 *UML Diagram Illustrating the Log Concept and Context*

13.3 Protocols for Systems Management

There are a number of standardized protocols for conveying telecommunications management information and performing management functions. These protocols have varying levels of penetration in the industry and have differing capabilities in implementing the information models outlined earlier. The following is a brief description of the most widely used protocols. The reader may consult the references for more in-depth information.

13.3.1 Transaction Language 1

Transaction language 1 (TL1) is a command string based protocol developed by BellCore (now Telcordia) in 1984. Since it is based on ASCII string commands, it can be used both for human-to-machine communication and for machine-to-machine communication. Although it is one of the older telecommunications management protocols, TL1 is still quite popular. One reason for this is that it is used as an interface between existing network equipment and existing operation support systems (OSS). A TL1-based management interface is usually *required* in equipment to be sold to U.S. Regional Bell Operating Companies (RBOCs).

TL1 supports the two basic modes of operations needed in a management protocol, that is, command/response interactions and the generation of autonomous events. Since TL1 messages are "human readable," it is also frequently used as a standard command line interface (CLI) for equipment management.

13.3.1.1 THE BASIC TL1 COMMAND MESSAGE FORMAT

The format of the TL1 command message is shown below:

```
command_code:staging_block::parameters_block;
```

Each of these fields is an ASCII string, subject to specific formatting rules. Command_code typically takes the form, "Verb-Modifier-Modifier", where the modifiers are optional. Due to TL1's historical lineage, the command codes tend to be cryptic. For example, common "verbs" are DLT (delete the object), ENT (enter or create the object), ED (Edit object properties), and RTRV (retrieve object info).

Staging_block has the form <TID>:<AID>:<CTAG>, where TID is the target identifier, that is, indicates the network element to receive this command, AID is the access identifier, that is, indicates the managed object within the network element to be acted upon, and CTAG is the "correlation tag" entered by the user. This tag is returned in the response by the system, so that a command and the response can be correlated.

Finally, as one might guess, the parameter block is where all the required or optional parameters of a command belong.

Example: Creating connection end points

Before a switch can set up a cross-connection, the end points of the connection have to be established. These are appropriately referred to as connection termination points (CTPs). One possible TL1 command for setting up an STS-3c CTP could be:

ENT-STS3C:MY-BOX1:A-7-3-1:REF137::NAME=CTP1;

Here, the TID field contains "MY-BOX1," the format of AID used by this manufacturer is <shelf>-<slot>-<subslot>-<timeslot> (A-7-3-1), "REF137" is the correlation tag, and the "NAME=CTP1" is the parameter that gives the CTP a name so that it may be used in other commands. Not shown are a host of optional parameters that may take on default values, for example, integration time on loss of pointer until an alarm is issued, and so on.

If another STS-3c CTP has to be created on a different line card, the following command can be issued:

ENT-STS3C:MY-BOX1:C-6-2-4:REF138::NAME=CTP2;

This command sets up an STS-3c end point in <shelf = C, slot = 6, sub-slot = 2, time slot = 4>.

The following command retrieves the parameters of CTP1:

```
RTRV-STS3C:MY-BOX1:CTP1::;
```

Example: Creating a cross connection

The following command can be used to create a cross-connection between the CTPs created above:

```
ENT-CRS-STS3C:MY-BOX1: CTP1, CTP2: REF139 ::NAME =CRS1,
FROMTYPE = CTP, TOTYPE = CTP;
```

13.3.2 The Simple Network Management Protocol

The simple network management protocol (SNMP) is very popular in data networks, but it is not used much in optical transport networks. SNMP is intended for machine-to-machine interaction, between an "agent" on a network element, say, and a management station. SNMP is currently in its third incarnation [Case+99], with the first version appearing around 1988 [Rose96]. The SNMP framework has four main aspects:

1. A data definition language used for specifying the management information. This language is directly machine-readable.
2. Management information bases (MIBs) that specify the management information for a particular application (using the data definition language).
3. A set of protocols for carrying out the management operations and conveying management information.
4. A security and administrative framework.

The fourth piece on security is new in SNMPv3 and has been a source of considerable debate in previous versions of SNMP. SNMP is based on a fairly simple "get-set" paradigm, that is, a GET command can be used to fetch information or a SET command can be used to set a variable to a particular value. In addition, a *sequence* of similar data entities can be easily traversed with a GET-NEXT operator. Finally, SNMP provides a mechanism for issuing autonomous events known as *traps*.

Since SNMP has not been used much in transport networks, there is a scarcity of standardized MIBs for managing optical networks. At the time of this writing, only one standards track RFC at the IETF was available concerning SONET/SDH interfaces [Tesink99]. Although this MIB is published by the

IETF, it is based on models and parameters defined in SONET/SDH standards. The existing MIB primarily covers performance monitoring. Because it is only concerned with SONET/SDH interfaces, it does not include items pertaining to switches as a whole, for example, creation/deletion of cross-connects.

13.3.3 The Common Management Information Protocol

ITU-T's Common Management Information Protocol (CMIP) followed SNMP in 1991. The overall framework for CMIP is similar in form to that of SNMP. CMIP, however, could probably be characterized as more "object-oriented." With CMIP, there was a set of standards that described the object management model, the syntax for defining these managed objects, and a protocol for performing operations on these managed objects and transporting the results [ITU-T92b, ITU-T92c, ITU-T92l, ITU-T92m]. CMIP, however, has not been a success. Among the reasons for this, the first is that vendors had to include a command line interface (also referred to as a *craft* interface) on the network element anyway. Due to the implementation complexity of the full object-oriented management service and the protocol, TL1 or a proprietary protocol was initially used rather than CMIP. CMIP was therefore relegated to serve as a protocol between the element and network management systems. Second, the data communications world had settled on SNMP and proprietary protocols. This left a small slice of the overall management pie to CMIP, making it hard for the protocol to reach a critical mass.

13.3.4 CORBA-Based Management

CORBA is an acronym for Common Object Request Broker Architecture. This denotes a standard[2] service and an associated protocol for making requests and receiving replies from objects on remote systems. CORBA originated in the distributed enterprise-computing context rather than in the telecommunications world. CORBA has found fairly wide acceptance within its scope of applicability, and a great deal has been written about its internals [Mowbray+97, Orfali+98]. CORBA is neutral to the hardware, the operating system, the network protocol, and the programming languages used, and therefore it can be used to glue together heterogeneous distributed systems.

CORBA, like SNMP and CMIP, contains a data definition language called the *Interface Definition Language* (IDL), which is used to specify the interface to the communicating objects. It should be noted that the implementation of objects is system dependent, but not the interface between them. Given an IDL description of the interface to a managed object, it is necessary to (a) bind it with the actual objects within a system and (b) enable these objects for distributed communications.

---

[2]CORBA is a product of the OMG. Its specification can be obtained at www.omg.org.

To bind the interface to actual objects, the IDL description is "compiled" to produce programs in one of different languages (C, C++, Java, COBOL, etc.) to interact with the internal objects in the system. It is the job of a piece of software known as the *ORB* (Object Request Broker) to enable these internal objects to communicate.

With a fairly well established CORBA infrastructure in place, the bulk of the challenge in using CORBA for telecommunications management is in refining the information models and in defining interfaces for specialized telecommunications management services. For example, a telecommunication management notification service tends to have some unique properties that may differentiate it from a notification service used in general enterprise computing [TMF00].

13.4 Relationship with the Control Plane

After a rather concise review of the management aspects in transport networks, we now examine the relationship between the control and the management planes in these networks. In this regard, it should be noted that the control plane is very focused on a select set of tasks. It is thus instructive to first look at the management plane functional areas and see where the control plane intersects them. Subsequently, we can examine how the control plane functionality complements those of the management plane.

13.4.1 FCAPS and the Control Plane

In this section, we examine how the control plane affects the management of fault, configuration, accounting, performance monitoring, and security.

13.4.1.1 FAULT MANAGEMENT AND THE CONTROL PLANE

The control plane generally has very little to do with fault management. There are, however, two specific areas in which it can help. First, a routing protocol can be used to distribute link status information between network elements. Note that this information would not be as complete as the standard state information, that is, operational, administrative, and usage states. Second, as discussed in Chapter 8, the control plane offers new options in restoration, that is, it gives us new methods and alternatives for fault correction. The bulk of fault management, however, is centered on notifications, alarms, alarm status, alarm logging, and alarm correlation, and is orthogonal to the control plane activities.

13.4.1.2 CONFIGURATION MANAGEMENT AND THE CONTROL PLANE

Management systems are used to configure the plethora of parameters that can be set in optical transport systems. The control plane only aids the establishment and removal of cross-connects or connection termination points. Due to this narrow focus, the control plane cannot replace the management plane for general configuration management. The control plane's restriction to the provisioning of connections, however, does make its use particularly suited to achieve interoperability between disparate systems.

13.4.1.3 ACCOUNTING, PERFORMANCE, SECURITY MANAGEMENT, AND THE CONTROL PLANE

Prior to the adoption of a control plane, there was little need for accounting management in transport networks. Thus, we can think of the control plane as actually driving the requirements for management plane functionality in this area. Similarly, one can see that the control plane does not assist in performance monitoring or security management but actually adds some new, if modest demands, in this area. For example, signaling and routing traffic statistics and packet error statistics are usually maintained to monitor the health of the control plane.

13.4.2 Discovery and Management

Before the advent of DWDM and the large increases in bandwidth capacities, there was little need for neighbor discovery. There just were not that many fibers to make the manual configuration all that error-prone or laborious. As the fibers in central offices and elsewhere have multiplied, this manual configuration of neighbor information into an element or network management system has become quite laborious and a source of errors. Some of these errors are more difficult to detect than others as discussed in Chapter 6.

Unlike other aspects of the control plane, there really is no management substitute for automatic neighbor discovery. The closest one gets is with the process of link verification, which has traditionally been done with SONET/SDH using the J0 (section layer) or J1 (path layer) trace strings.

Automated neighbor discovery combined with enhanced functionality on a management system (either element or network management) can provide complete network topology information. For this, a standardized or common network management interface to obtain neighbor discovery information is required. Figure 13–10 depicts the use of automated neighbor discovery interfaced to an EMS to discover the entire topology of the network. In this scenario, the EMS is provisioned with the address of the management interface of at least one node in a connected network. From this node, the EMS obtains the addresses of all the neighbors and the port mappings, as discovered by the node. The EMS can then continue checking these discovered nodes for nodes not already known to it until the entire network has been discovered.

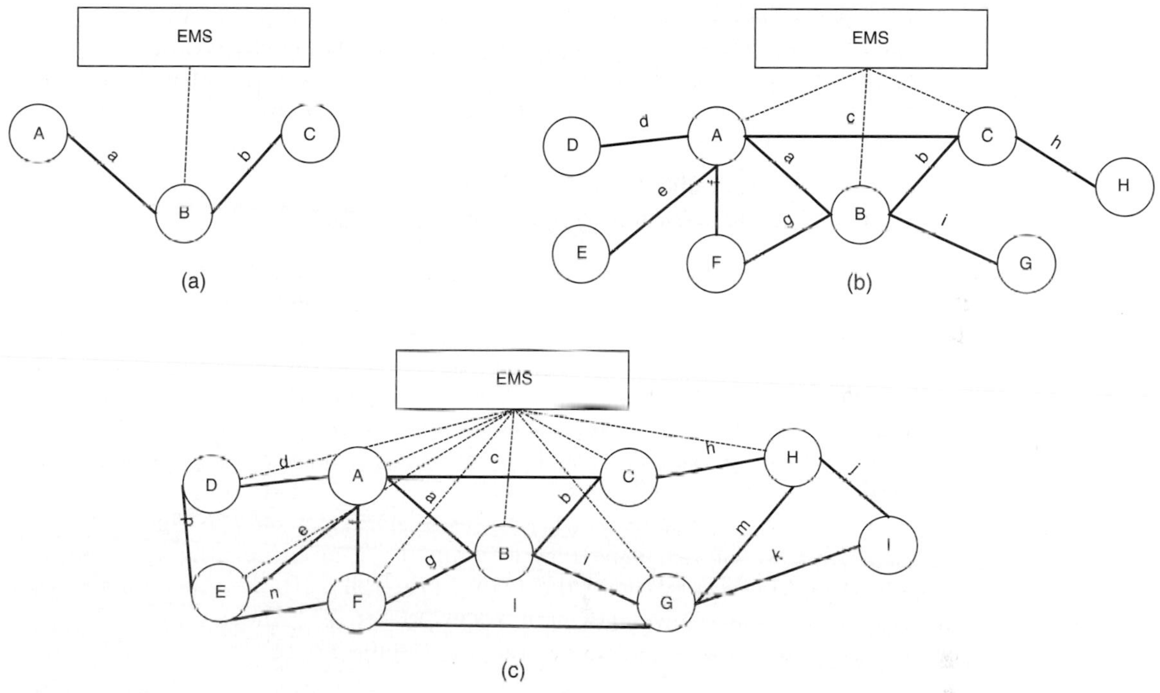

Figure 13–10 *Example of Network Topology Discovery via Automatic Neighbor Discovery and a Management Interface in the Network Element*

13.4.3 Routing and Management

We saw in the previous section that a management system combined with automated discovery can be used to determine the entire topology of the network. A distributed routing protocol can provide additional information to an EMS or NMS, with less complexity in the management system. By having a management interface to just one node participating in a distributed link state routing protocol, a management system can obtain the complete network topology, resource status information and other link properties discussed in Chapter 10. This information tends to be very timely, that is, most link state route protocols distribute update information quickly and efficiently. Because this information is also available from other nodes participating in the routing protocol, there is built in redundancy. In fact, if an outage is severe enough to partition the network into separate disjoint pieces, each piece will be able to provide updates (from any NE in that piece) to a management system. Hence, we see that routing protocols in optical transport networks can enhance the management system's view of the network without requiring any increase in the processing or other capabilities of the management system. They also allow for path selection/computation decisions to take place at multiple places simultaneously.

13.4.4 Signaling and Management

Signaling allows the establishment of individual cross-connects to be offloaded from the management system. Path computation can still be done by the management system, but it need not send messages to each NE in the path to establish the cross connections. Connection establishment is performed using distributed signaling, as described in Chapter 7.

Figure 13–11 illustrates connection provisioning using an EMS only, and Figure 13–12 shows the usage of an EMS and a signaling protocol for connection setup (the soft permanent connection (SPC) approach). It is assumed that the connection route has been computed by the EMS (Figure 13–11), or by the source NE (Figure 13–12). In the scenario depicted in Figure 13–11, the EMS must send a management command establishing the appropriate cross-connect to each NE in the connection route. Hence, the number of management plane messages sent is proportional to the number of hops (switches) in the route. In the second case (Figure 13–12), the EMS must only

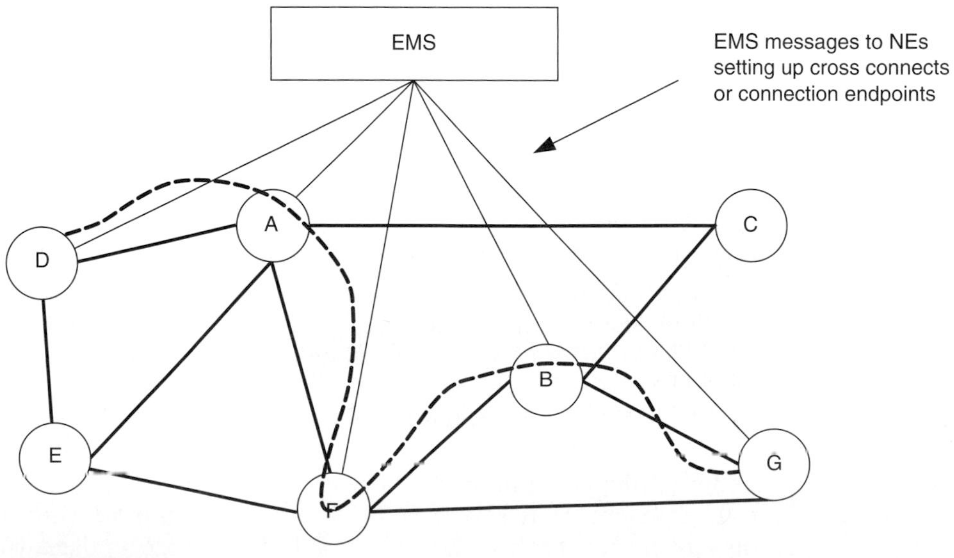

Figure 13–11 *EMS-Based Provisioning of a Connection from Node D to Node G*

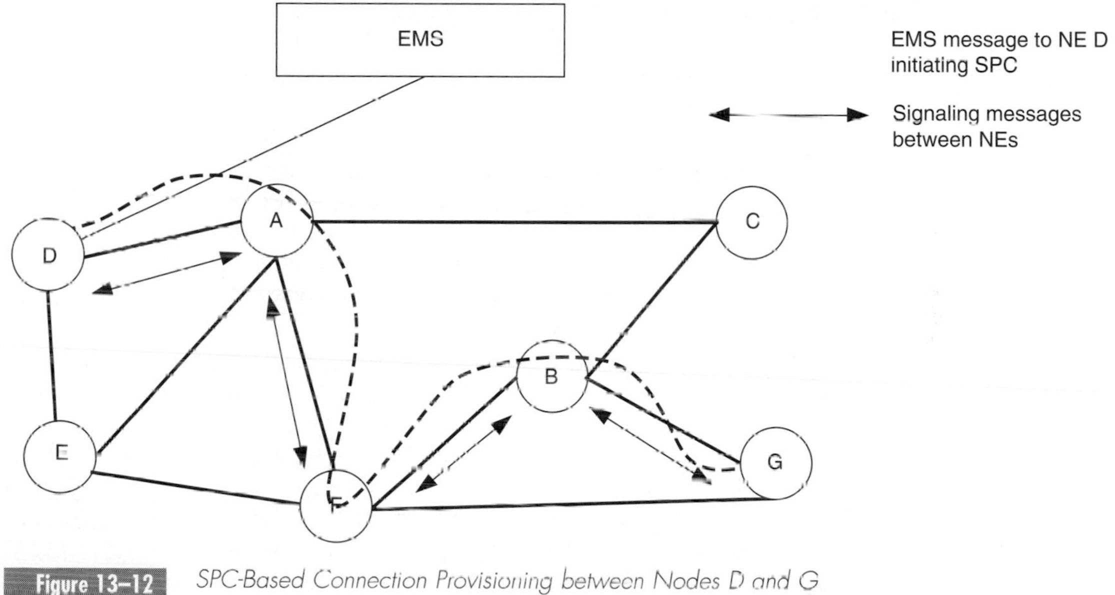

Figure 13–12 SPC-Based Connection Provisioning between Nodes D and G

send a management message to the source node. From then on, signaling between the nodes is used to establish the connection. This frees the EMS from the details of connection provisioning. Note that in some cases, such as with rings, signaling may not be all that useful. Hence, some implementations may just use neighbor discovery and routing, and leave connection establishment up to the EMS.

The advantages of signaling are more significant in the case of protection and restoration. Suppose that there is no signaling capability, and that a single EMS takes the responsibility for restoring all connections affected by a failure. To do this, the EMS must find an alternative route for each affected connection, and then set up the appropriate cross-connects in each NE. The number of messages sent by the EMS in this case is proportional to: (a) the number of connections impacted by the failure and (b) the average number of hops in each of the new routes. With signaling, the owner (the source NE) of a failed connection determines an alternative route and establishes the new connection (see Chapter 8). The work of determining new routes is distributed to many NEs, and there is no bottleneck (EMS) in the communication flow for setting up the new connections. Thus, signaling-based mesh restoration has better scaling properties and performance compared with a centralized method.

4.5 Interdomain Control and Management

As we have seen so far, a distributed control plane can aid a management system in some specific and useful ways. Due to the complexity of management systems and the plethora of standards and technologies used in their implementation, it is difficult to get management systems from different vendors to completely interoperate. From a provisioning point of view, it may only be desirable to have interoperability between control domains (see Chapter 12). In this case, an EMS may be used as the backend to a call controller and a routing controller as shown in Figure 13–13. Here, a distributed control plane spans all the domains, and interdomain routing and signaling are realized as described in earlier chapters. Within domain B, the connection segment is provisioned using the EMS. Clearly, an NMS that integrates the EMSs in different domains will be required for processing alarms, initiating end-to-end provisioning, and so forth, but the control plane here alleviates the NMS and the EMSs from the task of end-to-end path computation, interdomain signaling, and perhaps restoration.

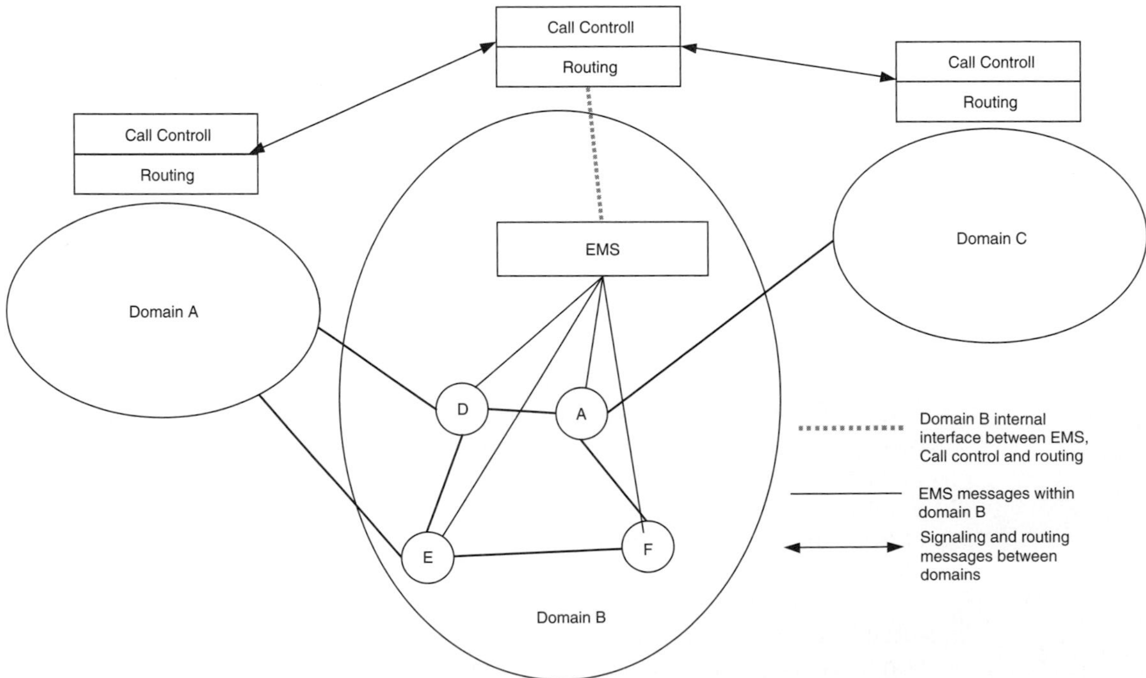

Figure 13–13 *EMS Serving as a "Back End" to Call Control and Routing in the Interdomain Control Plane*

13.5 Summary

The aim of this chapter was to give a brief overview of telecommunications management systems and to describe their importance in optical networks. The optical control plane is a recent development, and its functionality is limited in scope, that is, discovery, provisioning, and restoration. A lot more happens in the management plane, and some of the management plane mechanisms are fairly entrenched in carrier networks. The control plane, however, can aid the management plane in certain useful ways, as described in the latter part of this chapter. A good understanding of the management plane functions is essential to put the control plane developments in perspective and to gain an overall understanding of operational aspects of optical networks. A wealth of material is available on management systems and protocols, and the interested readers may start by looking into the references mentioned in this chapter.

F O U R T E E N

Optical Control Plane Internetworking

14.1 Introduction

We have so far examined different aspects of the optical control plane, including the architecture, the algorithms, and the protocols. In this chapter, we discuss the current status of standardization and deployment of the optical control plane in a multivendor, multitechnology network environment. Specifically, we describe the business drivers and inhibitors behind the optical control plane effort, the current state of the standards, the status of interoperable implementations, and the open issues that need to be resolved before wide-scale deployment of this new technology can begin.

14.2 Business Drivers and Inhibitors

In many ways, the optical control plane is a disruptive technology with the potential to revolutionize the transport infrastructure [Rajagopalan+00]. In today's business environment, however, there is very little appetite for new technology without a strong business driver. Hence, while there are differences of opinion regarding how standards should be defined and implemented, there is general agreement about why: It's all about making money! Service providers have a need to increase their margins by reducing opex, and increase their revenue streams by introducing new services. The need for a common optical control plane to automate signaling and routing is clearly present. The control plane introduces "agility" in optical networks and facilitates the quick introduction of revenue-producing services while reducing opex. The top drivers for a common optical control plane therefore are:

1. **New optical services:** The ability of disparate network elements to communicate over the control plane would enable new services and applications including bandwidth-on-demand, "time-of-day" bandwidth routing, optical VPNs, new levels of QoS, the ability to add or drop services, and the ability to respond to changing needs quickly.
2. **Operational cost savings:** A standard control plane can decrease operational overhead and cost. For example, standards-based protocols can reduce the testing and certification time (and expenses) when introducing new equipment into the network. They can also dramatically reduce the time to provision services. Benefits are quickly realized when the provisioning interval is reduced from forty-five to sixty business days to minutes, with human intervention only required at the ingress and egress nodes.

Although there are a number of business drivers, there are also a number of inhibitors. It takes time and money to develop standards, and the talent required for the effort is diminishing worldwide. Loosely defined standards tend to be implemented in different ways by the vendors. This causes more problems than the standards were intended to solve. Factors that inhibit the deployment of the optical control plane are:

- **Fragmentation of standards:** A single standards body is not capable of addressing all the aspects of the optical control plane. The IETF has taken the lead in defining the GMPLS suite of protocols for routing, signaling and link management. As GMPLS works its way into the ITU-T, there will be greater scrutiny, especially from the point of view of compatibility with existing transport network standards. Similarly, the ITU-T has little expertise in protocols that constitute GMPLS.

Critical issues such as billing, address management, restoration, and service-level agreements (SLAs) will have to be addressed before there is widespread adoption, and this level of expertise does not exist within a single standards forum.

- **Business issues:** An optical control plane can potentially reduce cost and increase revenues, but there are some issues. First, a significant initial investment is required to deploy this new infrastructure. Second, given the deep embedded base of legacy transport equipment, deployment can only be gradual, and it is not clear how quickly service providers can recoup their investment. Finally, the worsening telecom market environment has dampened the enthusiasm for rapidly deploying any new technology.
- **Clash of cultures:** Any change faces challenges from those used to the status quo. The IP-centric optical control plane technology is quite unfamiliar to the operators of transport networks, and its capabilities are unproven from their point of view. Concerns also arise as to how this cross-technology standard will affect organizational structures, specifically, the interplay between transport, switching, and IP organizations.

The good news is that despite these inhibitors the standardization process is moving forward. Also, many service providers have begun moving towards "next generation" transport networking with the objective of streamlining operations. The remaining hurdle is the convergence of various standards. This is the topic of discussion in the next section.

14.3 Different Standards: Competing or Complementary?

There are three main organizations developing optical control plane standards and implementation agreements: the Internet Engineering Task Force (IETF), the Optical Internetworking Forum (OIF), and the International Telecommunication Union Telecommunications Standardization Sector (ITU-T). Among these, the IETF and the ITU-T develop standards, while the OIF develops implementation agreements based on these standards. The main output of these bodies are: the GMPLS suite of protocols (IETF), Automatic Switched Optical Network (ASON)-related recommendations (ITU-T), and the Optical User-Network Interface (UNI) and Network-Network Interface (NNI) implementation agreements (OIF). It has been debated whether the different sets of standards and agreements produced by these bodies are competing or complementary. In the following, the activities of the various bodies are briefly reviewed along with the status of the standardization work in progress.

14.3.1 IETF

The notion of an IP-centric control plane for optical networks was first described formally in an IETF Internet draft in November 1999 [Awduche+01a]. Note that a number of vendors had already introduced proprietary control plane mechanisms before the draft was published. The architecture described in the draft was based on applying MPLS control concepts to optical networks. It was first called "Multi-Protocol Lambda Switching" or MPλS, but later it was recognized that the same concepts could be generalized to control any circuit-switched network, including TDM, optical and photonic networks. Thus, the term "Generalized MPLS" or GMPLS was adopted to describe the application of MPLS protocols for controlling other connection-oriented networks. The GMPLS-related work is being carried out under IETF's Common Control and Measurement Plane (CCAMP) working group.

Unlike MPLS, which has both a data plane and a control plane specification, GMPLS deals only with the control plane. The GMPLS architecture is described in an informational document, [Mannie03]. With regard to optical network control, the GMPLS suite of protocols addresses the following aspects:

- **Link management:** LMP [Lang+03a] is the IETF protocol specification for link connectivity verification, control channel management, link property correlation, and fault isolation (Chapter 6).
- **Topology discovery:** The link state IP routing protocols, OSPF and IS-IS for IP, have been extended with additional constructs to enable distributed topology discovery in optical networks [Kompella+02a, Kompella+02b] (Chapter 10). Work is ongoing on defining specific routing extensions for SONET/SDH networks [Mannie+03b].
- **Connection provisioning:** The two MPLS-TE signaling protocols, RSVP-TE and CR-LDP, have been generalized for connection provisioning in optical networks (Chapter 7). These are called the GMPLS RSVP-TE [Berger03b] and GMPLS CR-LDP [Ashwood-Smith+03], respectively. Specific extensions to these protocols for supporting SONET/SDH networks have been specified [Mannie+03a]. Other extensions are expected as new requirements are brought up.
- **Connection protection and restoration:** This is a relatively new area of work under the CCAMP working group. The aim of this work is to specify GMPLS RSVP-TE based protection and restoration signaling mechanisms. Presently, restoration related terminology, analysis, functional and signaling specification have been published as drafts [Mannie+03c, Papadimitriou+02, Lang+03b, Lang+03c].

The GMPLS signaling specification, and the RSVP-TE and CR-LDP extensions are currently proposed standard RFCs. GMPLS extensions for SONET/SDH as well as GMPLS OSPF and GMPLS IS-IS extensions are about to be published as proposed standard RFCs. LMP is in late stages of acceptance before being published as a proposed standard. The restoration related work is still in the Internet draft stage.

14.3.2 OIF

The OIF is a consortium of optical networking vendors and service providers (carriers) whose goal is to expeditiously develop interoperability implementation agreements. With regard to the control plane, the OIF has mostly followed the functional models developed by the ITU-T in identifying the control interfaces. As per these models, the OIF work has focused on the interface between the user (or client) and the optical networks (called the UNI), and the interface between control domains within a single carrier network (called the E- NNI, see Chapter 5).

- **Optical UNI:** The UNI is used by client devices to request optical network services, and the UNI implementation agreement was completed by the OIF in December, 2001 [OIF01]. This agreement is based on adapting the IETF GMPLS signaling specifications, notably, GMPLS RSVP-TE, CR-LDP, and LMP (with LMP used for neighbor and service discovery across the UNI), with certain customization for meeting specific carrier requirements. Work continues on version 2.0 of the O-UNI, with significant improvements in security, bandwidth modification, one-to-many call control, and several other features.
- **Optical NNI:** The OIF NNI implementation agreement is currently under development, and its publication is expected soon. This agreement is based on carrier requirements, which stipulate a highly scalable and reliable optical control plane. The OIF NNI work is addressing the signaling and routing aspects, and the solutions being developed are based on adapting the GMPLS signaling and routing protocol extensions, with additional customization.

The OIF work has led to the clarification of several issues with regard to the application of GMPLS protocols in public carrier networks. Interoperability trials based on the UNI and NNI specifications have taken place (see section 14.4), and these are expected to increase the confidence of large carriers about the deployment readiness of the optical control plane.

14.3.3 ITU-T

The ITU-T has been working on the architecture, functional models, and protocol specifics pertaining to ASON. The ASON architecture follows the client-server model with well-defined interfaces between the clients and an optical network, and between control domains within the optical network (see

Chapter 5). A series of recommendations have been published by ITU-T pertaining to control across these interfaces. The significant ones are:

- **G.8080:** The architecture of ASON [ITU-T01d].
- **G.7714:** Neighbor discovery [ITU-T02a].
- **G.7713:** Distributed connection management (DCM) [ITU-T03a]. DCM refers to signaling for connection provisioning, and G.7713 specifies the functional aspects. Specific protocol mechanisms aligned with the functional model are specified in G.7713.1 (based on P-NNI signaling), G.7713.2 (based on GMPLS RSVP-TE), and G.7713.3 (based on GMPLS CR-LDP).
- **G.7715:** Architecture and requirements for routing [ITU-T02b]. As with G.7713, it is expected that routing protocol specifics will be specified in companion recommendations, for instance, OSPF and IS-IS protocol extensions.
- **G.7712:** Architecture and specification of the Data communications network (DCN) [ITU-T01c]. The DCN is the communication infrastructure used for control communications between optical network elements.

Due to the involvement of major telecom carriers, the ITU-T work is generally taken to be the baseline for functional requirements. The IETF protocols are then adapted to meet these requirements, as seen from the work on DCM and routing above.

14.4 Interoperability Status

The existence of standards by itself does not guarantee interoperability. Consider, for example, SONET BLSR and SDH MSpring standards. Several years after being standardized, no interoperable implementations of BLSR/MSpring from different vendors can be found. The best way to ensure interoperability is to conduct trials involving multiple vendors to uncover problems in early specifications and promote multivendor interworking. In this regard, some significant optical control plane interoperability trials have occurred:

- **OIF UNI interoperability trial:** In the summer of 2001, the OIF sponsored an UNI interoperability trial involving twenty-five different vendors. The vendors underwent interoperability testing in the interoperability laboratory at the University of New Hampshire. Later, there was a public demonstration of interoperability at SUPERCOMM 2001 where the vendors successfully demonstrated UNI-N (network) and UNI-C (client) implementations to dynamically provision optical network services between clients. It is worth noting that the reference model used for this interoperability event was a subset of what later became UNI 1.0.

This interoperability event was a valuable experience for the equipment vendors, as well as the service providers. On the standards front, it helped in the refinement of OIF UNI 1.0 specification. It also helped in resolving certain issues related to the IETF GMPLS signaling specifications.

- **OIF NNI interoperability trial:** In the spring of 2003, the OIF conducted an NNI interoperability trial involving more than a dozen vendors. Both NNI routing and signaling were demonstrated. The NNI routing was based on extensions to OSPF-TE, and NNI signaling was based on GMPLS RSVP-TE. This trial demonstrated interdomain control, with multiple control domains represented by routing and signaling controllers (see Chapters 5 and 12).
- **IETF GMPLS interoperability survey:** A few multivendor GMPLS interoperability trials have been conducted. A number of vendors have also conducted private interoperability testing. As a part of the standardization process, the IETF conducted a GMPLS signaling implementation survey in which participants were asked to report the status of their implementation. A total of twenty-five participants, including equipment vendors, software vendors and service providers, responded [Berger+03]. From these responses it appears that GMPLS signaling implementation is making steady progress, although the recent telecom downturn may have slowed the pace a bit.

With regard to the ITU-T standards, multivendor interoperability trials are not a prerequisite for their progress. But given that the OIF implementation agreements are architecturally close to the ITU-T models, the OIF interoperability demonstrations serve as (limited) demonstrations of ITU-T standards.

14.5 Deployment Issues

The recent turmoil in the telecommunication industry has clearly altered the scope and the time frame of deployment of the optical control plane. In the early part of 2000, some predictions called for widespread deployment of intelligent optical networks containing hundreds or thousands or nodes, each with thousands of ports. This type of deployment, however, has not occurred so far. In fact, recent deployments of intelligent optical networks have consisted of smaller networks with perhaps tens of nodes. At the same time, some of the more sophisticated new applications that had been expected to be widely deployed are slowly entering the trial and testing phase. Several important issues listed below need to be resolved before wide scale deployment occurs.

- **Interoperability with legacy infrastructure:** Today's transport infrastructure consists of a huge base of legacy SONET/SDH based network elements. Any deployment of optical control plane has to coexist with this legacy infrastructure and gradually evolve with it. It requires careful planning, extensive testing, and a well-orchestrated evolution strategy to make sure that this transition is smooth and does not affect service.
- **Interoperability with management infrastructure:** Current transport networks are supported by legacy operations support systems (OSS) consisting of multiple layers of NMSs and EMSs. Any deployment of the optical control plane will require integration with the existing OSS and management systems.
- **Maturity of standards:** Standardization of the optical control plane is still far from over. Some components, such as provisioning, are more mature and have received closer attention than others, such as restoration. Certain other components, such as interdomain routing are still in early stages of development. The proposed standards must be tested more extensively and must undergo broad interoperability trials before final adoption and deployment.
- **Operational experience:** Most of the protocols that constitute the optical control plane have their roots in IP networks. The operational environment and requirements of transport networks are very different from those of IP networks. Transport network operators might want to develop some experience in using these protocols in limited settings before deploying them widely.

As a result of these conditions and the prevailing economic environment, the deployment of optical control plane is likely to be more evolutionary than revolutionary. Specifically, operators are likely to deploy components of the optical control plane that give them the biggest "bang for the buck." For instance, automatic neighbor discovery may first be integrated with the existing provisioning and inventory maintenance systems. Similarly, interoperable signaling for restoration (and perhaps provisioning) may be deployed before distributed routing is implemented.

In any case, deployment of the dynamic control plane in some shape or form seems almost inevitable. Its long term benefits outweigh the short term challenges. The architectural model based on control domains eases the gradual introduction of the optical control plane in carrier networks. As the standards mature, the operators are likely to get more exposure to this new technology and appreciate its benefits. Also, with time, data traffic will further increase, and the business case for a dynamic optical control plane will become stronger. So it is not a question of whether—but when—the optical control plane will be widely deployed.

Glossary

AAL ATM Adaptation Layer
ABN Area Border Node
ABR Area Border Router
ADM Add-Drop Multiplexer
AIS Alarm Indication Signal
AIS-L Alarm Indication Signal—Line
AIS-P Alarm Indication Signal—Path
AP Access Point
APD Avalanche Photo Diode
APS Automatic Protection Switching
AS Autonomous System
ASBR Autonomous System Border Router
ASE Amplifier Spontaneous Emission
ASON Automatic Switched Optical Network
ATM Asynchronous Transfer Mode
AU-n Administrative Unit—level n
AUG Administrative Unit Group
BER Bit Error Rate
BLSR Bidirectional Line Switched Ring
BGP Border Gateway Protocol
BIP Bit Interleaved Parity
BITS Building Integrated Timing Supply
CLNP Connectionless Network Protocol
CMIP Common Management Information Protocol
CO Central Office
CORBA Common Object Request Broker Architecture
CP Connection Point
CRC Cyclic Redundancy Check
CR-LDP Constraint Routed Label Distribution Protocol
DCN Data Communications Network
DFB Distributed Feed Back
DHCP Dynamic Host Configuration Protocol
DNHR Dynamic Non-Hierarchical Routing
DS-n Digital Signal—level n
DTL Designated Transit List
DWDM Dense Wavelength Division Multiplexing
EDFA Erbium Doped Fiber Amplifier
EGP Exterior Gateway Protocol
EMS Element Management System
E-NNI Exterior Network-Network Interface
E/O Electrical to Optical
EOS End of Sequence
ERO Explicit Route Object
ESF Extended Superframe
ES-IS End System to Intermediate System
FCS Frame Check Sequence
FEC Forwarding Equivalency Class
GbE Gigabit Ethernet
GFP Generic Framing Procedure
GMPLS Generalized Multi Protocol Label Switching
GPS Global Positioning System
HDLC High-level Data Link Control
HEC Header Error Check
HOVC Higher-Order Virtual Concatenation
IETF Internet Engineering Task Force
IGP Interior Gateway Protocol
I-NNI Interior Network-Network Interface
IP Internet Protocol
IS-IS Intermediate System to Intermediate System

ISO International Standards Organization
ISP Internet Service Provider
ITU-T International Telecommunication Union—Telecommunications standardization sector
LAN Local Area Network
LAP-D Link Access Procedure—D
LAPS Linear Automatic Protection Switching
LC Link Connection
LCP Link Control Protocol
LDP Label Distribution Protocol
LEC Local Exchange Carrier
LED Light Emitting Diode
LIH Logical Interface Handle
LMP Link Management Protocol
LOF Loss of Frame
LOP Loss of Pointer
LOS Loss of Signal
LOH Line Overhead
LOVC Lower-Order Virtual Concatenation
LSA Link State Advertisement
LSP Label Switched Path
LSR Label Switching Router
LTE Line Terminating Equipment
MEMS Micro-Electro-Mechanical Systems
MFI Multi-Frame Indicator
MIB Management Information Base
MPLS Multi Protocol Label Switching
MS Multiplex Section
MSOH Multiplex Section Overhead
MTBF Mean Time Between Failures
MTTR Mean Time To Repair
NCP Network Control Protocol
NE Network Element
NMS Network Management System
NNI Network-Network Interface
NUT Non-preemptible Unprotected Traffic
OA Optical Amplifier
OC-n Optical Carrier—level n
O/E Optical to Electrical
OEO Optical-Electrical-Optical
OIF Optical Interworking Forum
OOF Out Of Frame
OOO Optical-Optical-Optical
OOK On-Off Keying
OSI Open Systems Interconnection
OSPF Open Shortest Path First
OXC Optical Cross-connect
PDH Plesiochronous Digital Hierarchy
PDL Polarization-Dependent Loss
PDU Protocol Data Unit
PHY Physical (layer)
PIN Positive Intrinsic Negative
PLI Payload Length Indicator
PLR Physical Layer Regenerator
PMD Polarization Mode Dispersion
P-NNI Private Network-Network Interface
POH Path Overhead
POP Point of Presence
POS Packet over SONET/SDH
PPP Point-to-Point Protocol
PRS Primary Reference Source
PSTN Public Switched Telephone Network
PTE Path Terminating Equipment
PXC Photonic Cross-Connect
QOS Quality of Service
RCD Routing Control Domain
REI Remote Error Indicator
RDI Remote Defect Indicator
RIP Routing Information Protocol
ROW Right of Way
RRO Record Route Object
RS Regenerator Section
RSOH Regenerator Section Overhead
RSVP Resource Reservation Protocol
RSVP-TE RSVP with Traffic Engineering extensions
RTNR Real Time Network Routing
SAAL Signaling ATM Adaptation Layer
SCM Sub-Carrier Multiplexing
SDH Synchronous Digital Hierarchy
SLA Service Level Agreement
SNC Subnetwork Connection
SNMP Simple Network Management Protocol
SOH Section Overhead
SONET Synchronous Optical Network

SPE Synchronous Payload Envelope
SPF Shortest Path First
SRLG Shared Risk Link Group
SSCOP Service Specific Connection Oriented Protocol
STE Section Terminating Equipment
STM-n Synchronous Transport Module—level n
STS-n Synchronous Transport Signal—level n
TCM Tandem Connection Monitoring
TCP Termination Connection Point; Transmission Control Protocol
TCTE Tandem Connection Terminating Equipment
TDM Time Division Multiplexing
TE Traffic Engineering
TL1 Transaction Language 1
TTP Trail Termination Point
TU-n Tributary Unit—level n
TUG-n Tributary Unit Group—n
UDP User Datagram Protocol
UML Unified Modeling Language
UNI User-Network Interface
UPSR Unidirectional Path Switched Ring
VC Virtual Container; Virtual Concatenation
VCG Virtually Concatenated Group
VT-n Virtual Tributary—level n
VTG Virtual Tributary Group
WDM Wavelength Division Multiplexing

Bibliography

[Agrawal97] G. P. Agrawal, *Fiber Optic Communication Systems*, John Wiley & Sons, 1997.

[Aidarous+94] S. Aidarous and T. Plevyak (Eds), *Telecommunications Network Management into the 21st Century: Techniques, Standards, Technologies and Applications*, IEEE Press, 1994.

[Alexander+97] S. Alexander and R. Droms, "Dynamic Host Configuration Protocol," IETF RFC 2131, 1997.

[Andersson+01] L. Andersson, et al., "LDP Specification," IETF RFC 3036, 2001.

[ANSI94a] ANSI, "Synchronous Optical Network (SONET)—Tandem Connection Maintenance," T1.105.05–1994, 1994.

[ANSI95a] ANSI, "Synchronous Optical Network (SONET)—Basic Description including Multiplex Structure, Rates and Formats," T1.105–1995, 1995.

[ANSI95b] ANSI, "Digital Hierarchy—Formats Specifications," T1.107–1995, 1995.

[ANSI95c] ANSI, "Synchronous Opical Network (SONET) Automatic Protection Switching," T1.105.01 1995, 1995.

[ANSI96a] ANSI, "Synchronous Optical Network (SONET)—Sub-STS-1 Interface Rates and Formats Specification," T1.105.07–1996, 1996.

[ANSI96b] ANSI, "Synchronous Optical Network (SONET)—Network Element Timing and Synchronization," T1.105.09–1996, 1996.

[ANSI99a] ANSI, "Synchronization Interface Standard," T1.101–1999, 1999.

[Ash97] G. R. Ash, *Dynamic Routing in Telecommunications Networks*, McGraw Hill, November 1997.

[Ashwood-Smith+03] P. Ashwood-Smith and L. Berger, Eds., "GMPLS Signaling—CR-LDP Extensions," IETF RFC 3472, 2003.

[ATMF99] ATM Forum, "ATM Forum Addressing Reference Guide," AF RA-0106.000, 1999.

[ATMF02] ATM Forum, "Private Network-Network Interface Specification, Version 1.1," af-pnni 0055.002, April, 2002.

[Awduche+99] D. Awduche et al., "Requirements for Traffic Engineering over MPLS," IETF RFC 2702, 1999.

[Awduche+01a] D. Awduche and Y. Rekhter, "Multi-Protocol Lambda Switching: Combining MPLS Traffic Engineering Control With Optical Crossconnects," *IEEE Communications Magazine*, March 2001.

[Awduche+01b] D. Awduche, et al., "RSVP-TE: Extensions to RSVP for LSP Tunnels," IETF RFC 3209, 2001.

[Bellcore95] Bellcore, "Synchronous Optical Network (SONET) Transport Systems: Common Generic Criteria," GR-253-CORE, Issue 2, 1995.

[Bellman58] R. Bellman, "On a Routing Problem," Quarterly of Applied Mathematics, 16(1): 87–90, 1958.

[Benner01] Alan F. Benner, *Fiber Channel for SANs*, McGraw-Hill Professional, March 2001.

[Berger+01] L. Berger, et al., "RSVP Refresh Reduction Overhead," IETF RFC 2961.

[Berger03a] L. Berger, Ed., "Generalized MPLS Signaling—Functional Description," IETF RFC 3471, 2003.

[Berger03b] L.Berger, Ed., "Generalized MPLS Signaling—RSVP-TE Extensions," IETF RFC 3473, 2003.

[Berger+03] L. Berger and Y. Rekhter, Eds., "Generalized MPLS—Implementation Survey," IETF Internet Draft, 2003.

[Berstsekas98] D. P. Berstsekas, *Network Optimization: Continuous and Discrete Models*, Athena Scientific, 1998.

[Bhandari99] R. Bhandari, *Survivable Networks: Algorithms for Diverse Routing*, Kluwer Academic Publishers, 1999.

[Black00] Uyless D. Black, *IP Routing Protocols: RIP, OSPF, BGP, P-NNI and Cisco Routing Protocols*, Prentice Hall, February 2000.

[Bonenfant+02] P. Bonenfant, and A. Rodriguez-Moral, "Generic Framing Procedure (GFP): The Catalyst for Efficient Data over Transport," *IEEE Communications Magazine*, May 2002.

[Booch96] G. Booch, *Object Solutions: Managing the Object-Oriented Project*, Addison-Wesley, 1996.

[Bouillet+02a] E. Bouillet, et al., "Enhanced Algorithm Cost Model to Control Tradeoffs in Provisioning Shared Mesh Restored Lightpaths," in *Proc. OFC 2002*, March 2002.

[Bouillet+02b] E. Bouillet, et al., "Lightpath Re-optimization in Mesh Optical Networks," in *Proc. 7th European Conference on Networks & Optical Communications (NOC)*, June 2002.

[Bouillet+02c] E. Bouillet, et al., "Stochastic Approaches to Route Shared Mesh Restored Lightpaths in Optical Mesh Networks," *Proc. IEEE Infocom* 2002, June 2002.

[Braden+97] R. Braden, et al., "Resource Reservation Protocol (RSVP)," IETF RFC 2205, 1997.

[Briley83] B. Briley, *Introduction to Telephone Switching*, Addison-Wesley, July 1983.

[Cahn98] R. S. Cahn, *Wide Area Network Design, Concepts and Tools for Optimization,* Morgan Kaufmann Publishers, Inc., 1998.

[Callon90] R. Callon, "Use of OSI IS-IS for Routing in TCP/IP and Dual Environments," IETF RFC 1195, 1990.

[Case+99] J. Case, R. Mundy, D. Partain, B. Stewart, "Introduction to Version 3 of the Internet-Standard Network Management Framework," IETF RFC 2570, 1999.

[Cheng03] D. Cheng, "OSPF Extensions to Support Multi-Area Traffic Engineering," IETF Internet Draft, 2003.

[Chvátal83] V. Chvátal, *Linear Programming,* W. H. Freeman and Company, 1983.

[Coltun98] R. Coltun, "The OSPF Opaque LSA Option," IETF RFC 2370, 1998.

[Cornell+97] G. Cornell and C. S. Horstmann, *Core Java*, Second Edition, Prentice Hall, 1997.

[Dijkstra59] E. Dijkstra, "A Note on Two Problems in Connexion with Graphs," *Numerische Mathematik,* 1:269–271, 1959.

[Douglass98] B. P. Douglass, *Real-Time UML: Developing Efficient Objects for Embedded Systems*, Addison-Wesley, 1998.

[Dutton99] H. J. R. Dutton, *Understanding Optical Communications*, Prentice Hall, 1999.

[Ellinas+00] G. Ellinas, A. Gebreyesus Hailemariam, and T. E. Stern, "Protection Cycles in Mesh WDM Networks," *IEEE Journal on Selected Areas in Communications*, Vol. 18, No. 10, October 2000.

[Ellinas+02] G. Ellinas, et al, "Routing and Restoration Architectures in Mesh Optical Networks," *Optical Networks Magazine*, September/October 2002.

[Farrel+03] A. Farrel et al., "Crankback Routing Extensions for MPLS Signaling," IETF Internet Draft, 2003.

[Ford+62] L.R. Ford and D. R. Fulkerson, *Flows in Networks*, Princeton University Press, 1962.

[Fourer+93] R. Fourer, D. M. Gay and B. W. Kernighan, *AMPL: A Modeling Language for Mathematical Programming*, Boyd & Fraser Publishing Company, 1993.

[Gibbons85] A. Gibbons, *Algorithmic Graph Theory*, Cambridge University Press, 1985.

[Gorsche+02] S. S. Gorsche and T. Wilson, "Transparent Generic Framing Procedure (GFP): A Protocol for Efficient Transport of Block-Coded Data through SONET/SDH Network," *IEEE Communications Magazine*, May 2002.

[Green92] P. E. Green, *Fiber Optic Networks*, Prentice Hall, 1992.

[Grover+98] W. D. Grover and D. Stamatelakis, "Cycle-Oriented Distributed Preconfiguration: Ring-like Speed with Mesh-like Capacity for Self-planning Network Restoration," *Proceedings of IEEE ICC '98*, June, 1998.

[Halabi+00] S. Halabi and D. McPherson, *Internet Routing Architectures*, Cisco Press, January 2000.

[Hedrick88] C. Hedrick, "Routing Information Protocol (RIP)," IETF RFC 1058, June 1988.

[Hinton93] H. S. Hinton, *An Introduction to Photonic Switching Fabrics*, Plenum Press, 1993.

[Hjálmtýsson+00] Gísli Hjálmtýsson, et al., "Smart Routers—Simple Optics: An Architecture for the Optical Internet," *IEEE/OSA Journal of Lightwave Technology*, December 2000.

[Holmes82] Jack K. Holmes, *Coherent Spread Spectrum Systems*, John Wiley & Sons, Inc., 1982.

[ISO90] ISO, "Intermediate System to Intermediate System Intra-Domain Routing Exchange Protocol for use in Conjunction with the Protocol for Providing the Connectionless-mode Network Service (ISO 8473)," DP 10589, February 1990.

[ITU-T92a] ITU-T, "International Reference Alphabet (IRA)—Information Technology—7-bit Coded Character Set for Information Interchange," Recommendation T-50, 1992.

[ITU-T92b] ITU-T, "Information Technology—Open Systems Interconnection—Structure of Management Information: Management Information Model," Recommendation X.720, 1992.

[ITU-T92c] ITU-T, "Information Technology—Open Systems Interconnection—Structure of Management Information: Guidelines for the Definition of Managed Objects," Recommendation X.722, 1992.

[ITU-T92d] ITU-T, "Information Technology—Open Systems Interconnection—Systems Management: Attributes for Representing Relationships," Recommendation X.732, 1992.

[ITU-T92e] ITU-T, "Information Technology—Open Systems Interconnection—Systems Management: State Management Function," Recommendation X.731, 1992.

[ITU-T92f] ITU-T, "Information Technology—Open Systems Interconnection—Systems Management: Alarm Reporting Function," Recommendation X.733, 1992.

[ITU-T92g] ITU-T, "Information Technology—Open Systems Interconnection—Systems Management: Event Report Management Function," Recommendation X.734, 1992.

[ITU-T92h] ITU-T, "Information Technology—Open Systems Interconnection—Systems Management: Log Control Function," Recommendation X.735, 1992.

[ITU-T92i] ITU-T, "Information Technology—Open Systems Interconnection—Systems Management: Object Management Function," Recommendation X.730, 1992.

[ITU-T92j] ITU-T, "Information Technology—Open Systems Interconnection—Systems Management: Security Audit Trail Function," Recommendation X.740, 1992.

[ITU-T92k] ITU-T, "Information Technology—Open Systems Interconnection—Systems Management: Security Alarm Reporting Function," Recommendation X.736, 1992.

[ITU-T92l] ITU-T, "Management Framework for Open Systems Interconnection (OSI) for CCITT Applications," Recommendation X.700, 1992.

[ITU-T92m] ITU-T, "Information Technology—Open Systems Interconnection—Structure of Management Information: Definition of Management Information," Recommendation X.721, 1992.

[ITU-T94a] ITU-T, "Stage 1, Stage 2 and Stage 3 Description for the Q3 Interface—Performance Management," Recommendation Q.822, 1994.

[ITU-T95a] ITU-T, "Types and Characteristics of SDH Network Protection Architectures," Recommendation G.841, 1995.

[ITU-T95b] ITU-T, "Generic Network Information Model," Recommendation M.3100, 1995.

[ITU-T98a] ITU-T, "Synchronous Frame Structures Used at 1544, 6312, 2048, 8448 and 44 736 kbit/s Hierarchical Levels," Recommendation G.704, 1998.

[ITU-T98b] ITU-T, "TMN Security Overview," Recommendation M.3016, 1998.

[ITU-T98c] ITU-T, "Optical Interfaces for Multi-Channel Systems with Optical Amplifiers," Recommendation G.692, 1998.

[ITU-T99a] ITU-T, "Sub STM-0 Network Node Interface for the Synchronous Digital Hierarchy (SDH)," Recommendation G.708, 1999.

[ITU-T00a] ITU-T, "Network Node Interface for the Synchronous Digital Hierarchy (SDH)," Recommendation G.707, 2000.

[ITU-T00b] ITU-T, "Characteristics of Synchronous Digital Hierarchy (SDH) Equipment Functional Blocks," Recommendation G.783, 2000.

[ITU-T00c] ITU-T, "Characteristics of transport equipment—Description methodology and generic functionality," Recommendation G.806, 2000.

[ITU-T00d] ITU-T, "Generic Functional Architecture of Transport Networks," Recommendation G.805, 2000.

[ITU-T00e] ITU-T, "TMN Management Functions," Recommendation M.3400, 2000.

[ITU-T01a] ITU-T, "Link Capacity Adjustment Scheme (LCAS) for Virtual Concatenated Signal," Recommendation G.7042, 2001.

[ITU-T01b] ITU-T, "Generic Framing Procedure (GFP)," Recommendation G.7041, 2001.

[ITU-T01c] ITU-T, "Architecture and Specification of the Data Communication Network," Recommendation G.7712, 2001.

[ITU-T01d] ITU-T, "Architecture of the Automatic Switched Optical Network (ASON)," Recommendation G.8080, 2001.

[ITU-T01e] ITU-T, "Synchronous Digital Hierarchy (SDH)—Bi-Directional Performance Monitoring for the Network Element View," Recommendation G.774.1, 2001.

[ITU-T01f] ITU-T, "Synchronous Digital Hierarchy (SDH)—Unidirectional Performance Monitoring for the Network Element View," Recommendation G.774.6, 2001.

[ITU-T02a] ITU-T, "Generalized Automatic Discovery Techniques," Draft Recommendation G.7714, 2002.

[ITU-T02b] ITU-T, "Architecture and Requirements for Routing in the Automatically Switched Optical Network," Draft Recommendation G.7715, 2002.

[ITU-T03a] ITU-T, "Distributed Call and Connection Management," Recommendation G.7713, 2003.

[ITU-T03b] ITU-T, "Distributed Call and Connection Management based on P-NNI," Recommendation G.7713.1, 2003.

[ITU-T03c] ITU-T, "Distributed Call and Connection Management Mechanism Using GMPLS RSVP-TE," Recommendation G.7713.2, 2003.

[ITU-T03d] ITU-T, "Distributed Call and Connection Management Using GMPLS CR-LDP," Recommendation G.7713.3, 2003.

[Katz+02] D. Katz, D. Yeung, and K. Kompella, "Traffic Engineering Extensions to OSPF Version 2," IETF Internet Draft, 2002.

[Kodialam+00] M. Kodialam and T. V. Lakshman, "Dynamic Routing of Bandwidth Guaranteed Paths with Restoration," *Proc. IEEE Infocom 2000*, March, 2000.

[Kompella+02a] K. Kompella and Y. Rekhter, Eds., "OSPF Extensions in Support of Generalized MPLS," IETF Internet Draft, 2002.

[Kompella+02b] K. Kompella and Y. Rekhter, Eds., "ISIS Extensions in Support of Generalized MPLS," IETF Internet Draft, June 2002.

[Kompella+02c] K. Kompella, Y. Rekhter, J. P. Vasseur, T. W. Chung, "Multi-area MPLS Traffic Engineering," IETF Internet Draft, 2002.

[Labourdette+02] J. Labourdette, et al., "Routing Strategies for Capacity-Efficient and Fast-Restorable Mesh Optical Networks," *Photonic Network Communications*, vol. 4, no. 3, pp. 219–235, 2002.

[Lang+03a] J.P. Lang, et al., "Link Management Protocol," IETF Internet Draft, 2003.

[Lang+03b] J. P. Lang and B. Rajagopalan, Eds., "Generalized MPLS Recovery Functional Specification," IETF Internet Draft, 2003.

[Lang+03c] J.P. Lang and Y. Rekhter, Eds., "RSVP-TE Extensions in Support of End-to-End Recovery GMPLS-based Recovery," IETF Internet Draft, 2003.

[Lin+83] S. Lin and D. J. Costello, Jr., *Error Control Coding: Fundamentals and Applications,* Prentice Hall, 1983.

[Malis+99] A. Malis and W. Simpson, "PPP over SONET/SDH," IETF RFC 2615, 1999.

[Malkin98] G. Malkin, *RIP version 2*, RFC 2453, Internet Engineering Task Force, November 1998.

[Mannie+03] E. Mannie, et al., "Generalized Multi-Protocol Label Switching (GMPLS) Architecture," IETF Internet Draft.

[Mannie+03a] E. Mannie and D. Papadimitriou, Eds., "Generalized Multiprotocol Label Switching Extensions for SONET and SDH Control," IETF Internet Draft, 2003.

[Mannie+03b] E. Mannie and D. Papadimitriou, "GMPLS Extensions to OSPF and IS-IS for

SONET/SDH Control," IETF Internet Draft.

[Mannie+03c] E. Mannie, et al., "Recovery (Protection and Restoration) Terminology for GMPLS," IETF Internet Draft.

[Merlin+79] P. M. Merlin and A. Segall, "A Failsafe Distributed Routing Protocol," *IEEE Transaction on Communications*, vol. 27, pp. 1280–1287, September, 1979.

[Meyer97] B. Meyer, *Object-Oriented Software Contruction*, Second Edition, Prentice Hall, 1997.

[Mouftah+98] H. T. Mouftah and J. M. H. Elmirghani, *Photonic Switching Technology: Systems and Networks*, IEEE Press, 1998.

[Moy98] J. Moy, "OSPF Version 2," IETF RFC 2328, April 1998.

[Mowbray+97] T. J. Mowbray and W. A. Ruh, *Inside CORBA: Distributed Object Standards and Applications*, Addison-Wesley, 1997.

[Mukherjee97] B. Mukherjee, *Optical Communication Network*, McGraw-Hill, 1997.

[OIF01] Optical Interworking Forum, "UNI 1.0 Signaling Specification,"2001.

[Orfali+98] R. Orfali and D. Harkey, *Client/Server Programming with Java and CORBA*, 2nd Edition, John Wiley & Sons, Inc., 1998.

[Pan+03] P. Pan, et al., "Fast Reroute Extensions to RSVP-TE for LSP Tunnels," IETF Internet Draft, 2003.

[Papadimitriou+02] D. Papadimitriou, et al., "Analysis of Generalized MPLS-based Recovery Mechanisms," IETF Internet Draft, 2002.

[Perez+95] M. Perez, F. Liaw, A. Mankin, E. Hoffman, D. Grossman, A. Malis, "ATM Signaling Support for IP over ATM," IETF RFC 1755, 1995.

[Rajagopalan+91] B. Rajagopalan and M. Faiman, "A Responsive Distributed Algorithm for Shortest-Path Routing within Autonomous Systems," *Journal of Internetworking Research*, March, 1991.

[Rajagopalan+00] B. Rajagopalan, D. Pendarakis, D. Saha, R. Ramamurthy and K. Bala, "IP over Optical Networks. Architectural Aspects," *IEEE Communications Magazine, September 2000.*

[Ramaswamy+02] R. Ramaswamy and K. Sivarajan, *Optical Networks: A Practical Perspective*, 2nd Edition, Morgan Kaufmann, 2002.

[Rekhter+95] Y. Rekhter and T. Li, "A Border Gateway Protocol 4 (BGP-4)," IETF RFC 1771, 1995.

[Rivest92] R. Rivest, "The MD5 Message-Digest Algorithm," IETF RFC1321, 1992.

[Rose96] M. T. Rose, *The Simple Book: An Introduction to Networking Management,* Prentice Hall, 1996.

[Rosen+01] E. Rosen, A. Viswanathan and R. Callon, "MPLS Architecture," IETF RFC 3031, 2001.

[Saleh+91] B. E. A. Saleh and M. C. Teich, *Fundamentals of Photonics*, John Wiley & Sons, 1991.

[Sengupta+02] S. Sengupta, et al., "Analysis of Enhanced OSPF for Routing Connections in Optical Mesh Networks," *Proc. IEEE ICC*, 2002.

[Simpson94] W. Simpson, "PPP over SONET/SDH," IETF RFC 1619, 1994.

[Sklar88] B. Sklar, *Digital Communications: Fundamentals and Applications,* Prentice Hall, 1988.

[Sosnosky94] J. Sosnosky, "Service Applications for SONET DCS Distributed Restoration," *IEEE Journal on Selected Areas in Communications*, Vol. 12, No. 1, January 1994.

[Srisuresh+03] P. Srisuresh and P. Joseph, "OSPF-xTE: An Experimental Extension to OSPF for Traffic Engineering," IETF Internet Draft, 2003.

[Stallings03] W. Stallings, *Data and Computer Communications*, Prentice Hall, 2003.

[Stamatelakis+00] D. Stamatelakis and W. D. Grover, "IP Layer Restoration and Network Planning Based on Virtual Protection Cycles," *IEEE Journal on Selected Areas in Communications*, Vol. 18, No. 10, October 2000.

[Stern+99] T. Stern and K. Bala, *Multiwavelength Optical Networks: A Layered Approach,* Prentice Hall, 1999.

[Stewart99] John W. Stewart, *BGP4: Inter-Domain Routing in the Internet*, Addison-Wesley, 1999.

[Tanenbaum02] A. S. Tanenbaum, *Computer Networks*, Prentice Hall, 2002.

[Telcordia00] Telcordia Technologies, "Synchronous Optical Network (SONET) Transport Systems: Common Generic Criteria," GR-253-CORE Issue 3, 2000.

[Trivedi82] K. S. Trivedi, *Probability & Statistics with Reliability, Queueing, and Computer Science Applications*, Prentice Hall, 1982.

[Tesink99] K. Tesink, "Definitions of Managed Objects for the SONET/SDH Interface Type," IETF RFC 2558, 1999.

[TMF00] Tele Management Forum, "NML-EML Interface Business Agreement for Management of SONET/SDH Transport Networks, Version 1.5," TMF 509, 2000.

[Wroclawski97] J. Wroclawski, "The Use of RSVP with IETF Integrated Services," IETF RFC 2210, 1997.

Index